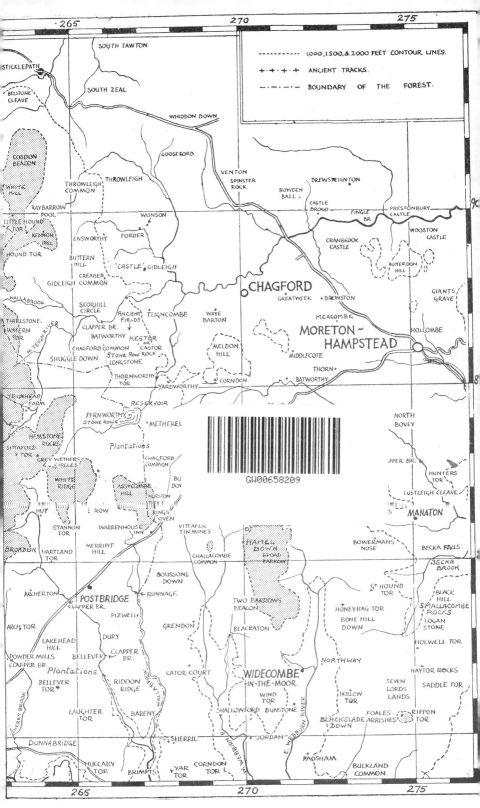

WORTH'S DARTMOOR

WORTH'S DARTMOOR

Compiled from the published works of the late

R. HANSFORD WORTH
M.Inst.C.E., F.G.S.

and edited by

G. M. SPOONER, M.B.E., M.A.
and
F. S. RUSSELL, F.R.S.

New edition with introduction by

G. M. SPOONER, M.B.E., M.A.

Fourth impression

DAVID & CHARLES
NEWTON ABBOT LONDON

First impression of this edition
published 1967
Second impression 1971
Third impression 1981
Fourth impression 1988

This book was first published by the executors of the will
of the late R. Hansford Worth in 1953 and was reprinted
shortly afterwards. This edition has been requested by many
Dartmoor lovers. The attention of readers is drawn to the
introduction of Mr. G. M. Spooner.

British Library Cataloguing in Publication Data

Worth, Richard Hansford
    Worth's Dartmoor.
    1. Dartmoor, Eng.
    I. Spooner, G. M.   II. Russell, F. S.
    942.3'53   DA670.D2

ISBN 0–7153–5148–6

Printed in Great Britain by
Redwood Burn Limited, Trowbridge, Wiltshire
for David & Charles Publishers plc
Brunel House, Newton Abbot, Devon

CONTENTS

I commend Dartmoor to the regard and the protection of all who desire to preserve unspoilt an ancient land, old when the hut-dwellers built their homes, now older but unchanged.

R. H. W.

INTRODUCTION TO THE 1967 EDITION

Few could have foreseen, in 1954, that the second impression of this book would be sold out in three years; still less that a need for a further printing would arise. Yet this is what has happened, and for very good reasons. It is now easier to appreciate the long-term value of this book amongst the informative literature on Dartmoor, if only because it contains so much basic factual matter. The demand for a reprinting has been impossible to ignore.

Warning, however, must be given that various advances in our knowledge of Dartmoor have been made since Hansford Worth was active. More especially, the archaeological picture has been much affected by the modern growth of this branch of study. New excavations with modern methods, and reassessment of the results of older work, are showing a more complex situation during the prehistoric period than Worth was prepared to admit. Anyone wishing to know more about the human occupation of Dartmoor in its appropriate context at different periods during the last two millenia B.C. should refer to Aileen Fox's recent well-illustrated book on the early history of the south-west (*South-West England* in the Ancient Peoples and Places series, Thames & Hudson, 1964)

Excavations apart, discoveries are still being made of hitherto undetected prehistoric structures, to reward observant explorers. The number of huts (p. 99) is now known to be well over 2,000, and at least three types of settlement can be recognized; there are five additional stone-rows (p. 202), one of which, discovered by Commander and Mrs. A. H. Woolner, across Harford and Ugborough Moors, is almost of megalithic dimensions; an overlooked stone-circle with a diameter of 124 ft can be added to the top of the list on p. 260. Of medieval and later structures finds can even more readily be made: for example, at least six additional blowing-houses (p. 289) have been detected, and the total number of warrener's vermin-traps (p. 157) of which remains have been traced now exceeds 50.[1]

The medieval settlement of Dartmoor is, indeed, attracting growing interest. Herdsman's quarters datable to the thirteenth century have been excavated by Lady Fox on Dean Moor, and there must be others elsewhere. Mrs. Minter's exciting work at Hound Tor has disclosed a stone-built hamlet abandoned about 1,250 A.D., with evidence of earlier wattle dwellings, renovated several times. Current excavations by the Ministry of Works are throwing new light on the history of Lydford as a Saxon burgh. There is still much to be learnt of the early history of Dartmoor farming and other activity in historic times,[2] provided the evidence is not obliterated by modern marginal-land reclamation projects.

As regards the physiography and geology of Dartmoor, much more is now known to specialists that can be gleaned from the Geological Memoir of 1912 and other pre-1960 writings (including Worth's), but the picture has still to be presented in a coherent form intelligible to the general reader.[3] The present revision-work on their maps by the Geological Survey is much to be welcomed. Some of Worth's ideas presented in the chapter on 'Physical Geography' will no doubt need modification: for example, it is possible for structures resembling tors to form below the ground surface.

Thanks primarily to the efforts of Dr. I. G. Simmons,[4] some pollen analyses of Dartmoor peat are now available, giving us the first real glimpse of the vegetational history of Dartmoor since the close of the Ice-Age.

Readers of the chapter on Wistmans Wood (one of the sites now in the care of the Nature Conservancy) may have difficulty in squaring some of Worth's observations, and older ones, with what can be seen today. This is because, as has only recently been appreciated, the wood has put on much new growth during this century. It has become more 'normal', and at the same time has lost some of its former richness in mosses and ferns, and also perhaps some of the impression of weirdness conveyed to visitors in former days.

In short, this volume must now be read or consulted in historical perspective.

As Worth himself advocated many years ago, Dartmoor is now administered as a National Park, with various areas, sites, or features given at least nominal protection of some degree. There is no doubt Dartmoor's special appeal and value to the nation in the future will depend much on the manner in which its destructible assets, with which much of this book is concerned, are respected and conserved. In this aim we cannot rely wholly on official measures, though these must increase: the co-operation of the public is vital. To the public, then, this reprint is dedicated.

G. M. SPOONER

5 September 1966

---

[1] R. M. L. Cook, *Transactions of the Devonshire Association*, Vol. 96, p. 190.

[2] See, for example, the studies by Mrs. C. D. Lineham and H. French in recent *Transactions of the Devonshire Association*.

[3] The need is partly met by *Dartmoor Essays* issued by the Devonshire Association in 1964.

[4] *Transactions of the Devonshire Association*, Vol. 94, p. 555: Vol. 95, p. 180.

THE publication of this volume fills me with pleasure and gratitude. Pleasure in the fulfilment of my dear husband's expressed wish that many of his papers and reports concerning Dartmoor should be reprinted and published in book form. Gratitude to those good friends of ours, who have made that publication possible.

First I would like to thank Mr. F. S. Russell and Mr. G. M. Spooner, who have been responsible for editing the book, making all the necessary arrangements for publication, and for seeing it through the press. The main burden of editing the text has fallen on Mr. Spooner, who has not only made the selection of matter for publication, but has also himself roamed over much of Dartmoor to check and verify many of the observations, thus ensuring as far as possible that the book should be accurate and up to date. His work is deeply appreciated.

My best thanks also are due to Mr. E. N. Masson Phillips for his great help, especially with reference to the geology of Dartmoor; and to Mr. H. E. Turner for so generously providing the facilities of a centre for the collection of subscriptions.

There are others, including Mr. H. P. R. Finberg, who have given help. To all I offer my most grateful thanks for their untiring efforts to make this Dartmoor book a success.

ANNIE E. WORTH

EDITORS' PREFACE

Richard Hansford Worth was born at Plymouth on 5 November 1868, the son of R. N. Worth, journalist, historian and geologist. He was educated at Plymouth High School for Boys (now Plymouth College), and became a civil engineer. His interests were many. He was a Member of the Institution of Civil Engineers, a Member of the Mineralogical Society, and a Fellow of the Geological Society of London; he was also a Member of the Newcomen Society. He was a Founder Member of the Marine Biological Association of the United Kingdom. He made many original contributions to knowledge, but will be best remembered for his painstaking studies of Dartmoor in all its aspects. He died in Plymouth on 11 November 1950. A full obituary is printed in the *Transactions of the Devonshire Association*, Vol. 83, pp. 17–21.

Hansford Worth's antiquarian work, following that of his father, was primarily devoted to recording observable features, eliminating the 'personal equation' as far as humanly possible, and avoiding speculation. His preoccupation with this approach—which made him reluctant not only to theorize but to interpret—can well be understood in view of the extravagances among past writings on Dartmoor antiquities, not excluding those of his senior contemporaries. (See, for instance, Appendix IV.) If archaeologists are ever able to give us a coherent picture of the kind of people who occupied the moor in prehistoric times, it will only be because a sound foundation has been laid of reliable field observations on surviving material evidence. Much is owed to Hansford Worth for this.

It had been his intention to assemble his published works on Dartmoor into book form, and indeed a number of his later papers in the *Transactions of the Devonshire Association* were written to form chapters in the projected book. He died before he could fulfil his hopes, but he left a sum of money for the publication of such a book, the proceeds of the sale of which were to go to the Devonshire Association.

That a need existed for a reliable source of information of this kind has long been felt, now more especially since the establishment of the Dartmoor National Park. Its appeal should be wide, since so much of the well illustrated archaeological matter refers to the numerous stone remains distributed over the moor, free to be viewed by any passer-by.

When Mrs. Worth gave us the opportunity to act as editors of this book we gladly undertook the task as a labour of love in memory of Mr. Worth, and as a duty towards the nation since it was evident that a complete work of this nature would stand as a permanent reference book for all those interested in Dartmoor. Indeed, the kind help which Mrs. Worth has given us has made this duty a pleasure.

Owing to present-day costs of printing final publication was only made possible by the many subscribers who willingly came forward in response to our appeal.

We are grateful to Mr. H. P. R. Finberg for examining the proofs and for advice, especially on typography; Mr. E. N. Masson Phillips for much valuable advice in all stages of preparation, his help with the geological and prehistoric sections being particularly appreciated; Lt.-Col. G. W. G. Hughes and Mr. A. G. Madan for their help in enabling us to sort required blocks and photographic negatives respectively; Mr. C. E. Birkett Dixon for reading the manuscript of the chapter on barrows; Mr. Bernard Hickey for drawing the endpiece maps; Mrs. D. B. Carlisle for compiling the subject index; and Dr. D. P. Wilson, who kindly also supplied two additional photographs, and Dr. J. S. Alexandrowicz for preparing fresh prints for illustrations requiring new blocks.

Acknowledgements are also due to the Councils of the Devonshire Association for the Advancement of Science, Literature and Art; the Plymouth Institution and Devon and Cornwall Natural History Society; and the Torquay Natural History Society; from whose publications this work has been compiled.

In conclusion we wish to record our thanks to the printers, Messrs. Latimer, Trend & Co. Ltd., for the care they have given to printing the book and their helpful advice in many matters which has proved so valuable in a private publication of this nature.

G. M. S.
F. S. R.

EDITOR'S NOTES

The task before us was to ensure that Hansford Worth's writings were so selected and arranged as to give the most complete and coherent account possible of Dartmoor, at least with respect to the many aspects that he had expressly studied. This aim was practicable because several summary articles had clearly been written with a view to incorporation as chapters of a Dartmoor book, and fell naturally into place.

Where no summary articles existed (e.g. for stone circles) extracts from available writings treating the subject have been combined with a minimum of manipulation of the text. In the same way when two articles partially covered the same subject, each contributing something lacking in the other (e.g. Dartmoor house), or when a supplementary had followed the main account (e.g. blowing-houses), the texts have been merged. The chapter on barrows, and this alone, has a more complex origin, as explained below.

As a policy, no alterations to the original text have been made other than those involving trimming of the punctuation, insertion of references, adoption of standard abbreviations, and other purely editorial treatment. Occasionally a word or phrase has been amended, when there are good grounds for believing that the author would himself have changed it; and obvious mistakes of transcription or overlooked printer's errors in the original have been corrected.

To the last-mentioned category belong several corrections to the raw data of position references, particularly to longitude and latitude bearings. These have been checked throughout the book, mainly in detail on 6-inch O.S. sheets, and have been amended when any difference greater than 1 second has been discovered.

Any other editorial intrusions into the text are clearly indicated as such. These include a few revised measurements or check observations, especially with regard to stone rows (pp. 202-47). Where, again, opinions opposing those of the author have been put forward with good claim, or where there is need to draw attention to more recent observations, an editorial footnote has usually been inserted. This has been done in justice not only to the reader seeking the most authoritative information, but also to the reputation of the author who has had no opportunity of qualifying opinions that are now being perpetuated in his name.

Illustrations. To reproduce some 160 photographs and 130 line text-figures would have been prohibitive had not most of the blocks been available. About 30 text-figures required new blocks, which have been made from printed reproductions of the originals. Some 25 half-tone blocks were required, of which only two had to be made from previous printed reproductions: several of the original negatives were found from which new photographs were printed and two illustrations were recovered from lantern-slides. One was re-taken in the field by Dr. D. P. Wilson. By these means all the illustrations in the original articles have been reproduceable. Several additional photographs have been included—a selection from the available store of Worth's blocks. Finally, to fill a gap, two extra photographs of hut-circles have been reproduced (Pl. 25B and 26A); as well as Dr. Wilson's view of Down Tor row and circle (Pl. 61).

The endpiece maps, which cover Dartmoor in four sections, were reproduced from amended drawings of Mr. B. Hickey, by permission of the Ordnance Survey.

Reference is frequently made to the 6-inch maps of the Ordnance Survey. The Numbers by which the separate maps are distinguished are clearly indicated in Fig. 12 on p. 101, and the plan there shown may serve as a key.

Place-names. No attempt has been made at uniformity in the spelling of Dartmoor place-names. As the author well realized, no uniformity is at present attainable, or even desirable. Many official spellings or forms adopted on current maps have no historical basis, and are not necessarily worthy standards. Care has been taken, in the Locality Index, to enter all the variants of one name used in the book, as well as to distinguish between different places with the same name (of which there are all too many examples).

Articles reprinted. A list of all articles reprinted in whole or in part is given at the end of these notes. Numbers in heavy type are assigned to these articles and are used throughout this explanation of the source of the contents of the book.

The Foreword is composed from the introductory paragraphs of 5, with an insertion on the Worth family taken from 31.

The Physical Geography chapter is the main subject matter of 5, comprising pp. 51 to 98 of the original (the remaining appendices being reproduced here as Appendix I, *q.v.*). Two insertions have been made (p. 18) from a later MS. (32), and a photograph of the Dewerstone Rock added (Pl. 4).

The account of the Dartmoor Granite is taken from an MS. article on Dartmoor geology (32), apparently intended for a book on Dartmoor. It deals strictly with the geological origins and structure of the rock, leaving later chapters to deal with the uses to which, as a stone, it is put by man. This is the most technical of all the articles printed here, but its interest and value have been pointed out by Mr. E. N. Masson Phillips, who has prepared the typescript for printing. Two figures, copied from rough sketches, have been reproduced (Figs. 9 and 10); but other intended sketches were not available. Some of these, however, had been published in earlier papers, and the reference has then been given. Many of the rock specimens referred to can now be seen in Torquay Museum.

A short survey of the Vegetation of Dartmoor is a reprint of 12, with the addition of Pl. 20. The systematic names of the flowering plants and ferns have been brought in line with the *Flora of Devon*, and that of the Reindeer Moss corrected. The ancient dwarfed oak woods were the subject of a joint paper by

Christy & Worth (36), of which Worth's contribution is here reproduced. See note on p. 98.

The next six chapters deal with the material that Dartmoor supplies for archaeological study and interpretation—remains of stone huts, pounds, graves, rows, circles, and menhirs. These, as generally accepted, are the legacy of an extensive colonization of the moor during the Bronze Age by a pastoral people simple in their habits but prone to expend energy in constructing monuments associated with burials. Their culture was essentially that of Early Bronze peoples, as Worth insisted, though possibly surviving into later periods of the Age in semi-isolation.

Though the Early Bronze Age provides the first evidence of habitation, Dartmoor prehistory starts much earlier. There is growing evidence, yet to be adequately collated, that palaeolithic, mesolithic, and neolithic hunters visited the moor. One of Worth's contributions to the evidence is given in Appendix III (p. 450, Pl. 90).

A good account of Hut-circles (to give the huts their usual name) is available (23). Three photographs showing remains of these dwellings (Pl. 25 A, B, Pl. 26), and a list of chief references to date, have been added here. The account of the prehistoric pounds is a reprint of 21.

The chapter on Barrows is an attempt at combining the summary articles written by Worth, in the 21st, 56th, and 69th Reports of the Barrow Committee (33, 34, 35), omitting matter not relevant to Dartmoor. Parts of the kistvaen section have been rewritten to bring statistics up to date, without, however, affecting previous conclusions. Fig. 58 has been revised and re-drawn. Some additional illustrations have been introduced: Fig. 51A from the 29th Barrow Report, Pl. 33A from the 53rd, and Pl. 33B from the 57th. Pl. 40A was published in 'Before written record' (15). Figs. 49 and 50, for which new blocks were required, were re-drawn. It is feared that this compilation necessarily falls short of any account Worth himself might have written with the same object in view. In bringing the survey up to date, for instance, he would no doubt have compared Dartmoor barrows and their contents with those of other parts of south-west England.

For the Stone Rows, 26 and 27 are combined. Several obvious printer's errors and errors of transcription have been corrected. Some revised measurements have been incorporated. A new photograph of the Down Tor row and circle has been added (Pl. 61). The matter in the editors' Addendum has not been included in the sections which summarize various attributes of stone rows.

To cover the Stone Circles, *sensu stricto*, the essential parts of 8, 16 and 20 have been fitted together. Figs. 80 and 81, which were originally published on a larger scale and printed on folders, have been reduced without loss of detail. The Menhir chapter is a reprint of 18.

Some account of the activities and customs of the Stannaries is derived from a long extract from 3, with a short section (on tin production) from 19. The field evidence to be obtained on Dartmoor from the remains of 'blowing-houses', or 'tinners' mills', is found in 19, expanded by its supplement 25. Some illustrations (Pl. 68 to 71) have been added from more detailed articles, to which a list of references is given on p. 328.

Established customs relating to tenure and Rights of Common are key topics in the next chapter, reprinted from **22**. There follows a description of various commodities that at one time were hewn from slabs of surface granite, or 'moorstone'—reprinted from **29** and **30**, with ten photographs added (Pl. 72 to 76).

Some observations on tracks and guide-stones are derived from **10** and **37**. One of the illustrations, that of the little clapper bridge in Snap Lane, Willsworthy, on the route of the Lichway, is here reproduced from the original in colour, and inserted as Frontispiece. It is a pleasant example of the author's water colour work, which, in his earlier years, provided a favourite pastime. 'Dorf' was his private *nom de plume*.

The chapter on the Dartmoor House is derived from **13**, to which certain sections of **11** have been grafted. The illustrations formerly appeared in either **11** or **13** or both, except Pl. 80 and 82 which have been added. The last chapter, on Place-Names, is a reprint of **4**.

Among the Appendices will be found a selection of articles or passages giving supplementary information bearing on the main subject-matter. They do not in any way exhaust the author's writings on Dartmoor.

Appendix I gives supplementary data on the subject, introduced on pp. 35–42, of the flow of Dartmoor rivers and their liability to flood. It contains Appendices II to VI of the 1930 Address (**5**), with some additions from **14**. Plate 88A is a substitute for the missing original.

Appendix II adds a little on Dartmoor granite, derived from **6**, with an addendum to the list of references on p. 63.

Appendix III, reprinted from **7** and **9**, combines the descriptions of two stone implements, examples of casual archaeological finds.

The extract reprinted as Appendix IV is from an address delivered as long ago as 1906 (**2**). It is included as an appendage to the stone-row chapter not only because, as a withering exposure of humbug, it provides entertaining reading, but also because it serves as a reminder of the influences which unprejudiced investigators have had to contend, even in this century. On Dartmoor the advance of knowledge has been arrested by the over-imaginative recorder, the over-enthusiastic restorer, and even (as here) by the scientist of repute who extravagantly exploited a pet theory. The necessary corrective to these tendencies was a strictly objective attitude which concentrates on exact observation and recording, keeping speculation to a minimum. This fact Hansford Worth, in his earlier years, realized more clearly than any of his contemporaries. It provided incentive to his researches and affected his outlook to the end.

Appendix V combines in condensed form the indices to references to barrows, etc., given as appendices to the 21st, 56th, and 69th Barrow Committee's Reports (**33, 34, 35**).

Appendix VI is a reprint of **24**. Appendix VII is extracted from **17**: in it, apart from special associations of Dunnabridge and Crockern Tor, will be found references to the medieval use of pounds.

Appendix VIII is a reprint of that part of **1** that concerns Dartmoor. In supplying answers to possible enquiries on derelict Dartmoor 'tramways', it re-introduces Worth's earliest published paper, written in 1888. A revealing passage (on p. 483) shows that even at this date Worth visualized Dartmoor as a potential National Park.

Finally Appendix IX, a reprint of **28**, gives Worth's deposition in 1947 at the Exeter Inquiry on the services' land requirements, an event long to be remembered by those present. His recommendations, it is fair to say, have not been wholly ignored; but his misgivings and main theme of dissent will hold force so long ever as parts of Dartmoor are used for battle-training.

G. M. S.

ARTICLES FROM
WHICH THIS BOOK IS COMPILED

(1) Worth, R. Hansford, 1888. Early western railroads. *P.I.*, Vol. 10, pp. 78–92

(2) — 1906. President's Address. *P.I.*, Vol. 14, pp. 187–220

(3) — 1910. The Stannaries. *P.I.*, Vol. 15, pp. 21–45

(4) — 1926. A note on Dartmoor place-names. *T.D.A.*, Vol. 58, pp. 359–72

(5) — 1930. Address of the President. *T.D.A.*, Vol. 62, pp. 49–124

(6) — 1930. Weathered granite. *P.I.*, Vol. 17, pp. 187–90

(7) — 1931. A flint implement of palaeolithic type from Dartmoor. *T.D.A.*, Vol. 63, pp. 359–60

(8) — 1932. The prehistoric monuments of Scorhill, Buttern Hill, and Shuggledown (Shoveldown). *T.D.A.*, Vol. 64, pp. 279–87

(9) — 1934. On a stone implement found near Wheal Jewell, Marytavy. *T.D.A.*, Vol. 66, pp. 315–16

(10) — 1934. Dartmoor tracks. *P.I.*, Vol. 17, pp. 350–6

(11) — 1935. The Dartmoor House. *Trans. Torquay Nat. Hist. Soc.*: 1934–5, pp. 23–30.

(12) — 1937. The vegetation of Dartmoor. *P.I.*, Vol. 17, pp. 285–96. [Lecture given in 1933, revised]

(13) — 1937. The Dartmoor House. *P.I.*, Vol. 18, pp. 34–47

(14) — 1938. The Dartmoor catchments. *British Waterworks Assn.: Rep. of General Meeting:* 1938, 27 pp.

(15) — 1938. Before written record. [Chapter in] *The Book of Plymouth*, pp. 137–164, British Medical Association, Plymouth

(16) — 1939. Two stone circles on Dartmoor, Swincombe Valley, and West Dart Valley, with a note on the 'Grey Wethers'. *T.D.A.*, Vol. 71, pp. 321–8

(17) — 1939. *In* account of meeting held on Dartmoor, on 25 August 1938. *Proc. Teign Naturalists' Field Club for year* 1938

(18) — 1940. The Dartmoor menhirs. *T.D.A.*, Vol. 72, pp. 191–9.

(19) — 1940. The Dartmoor blowing-house. *T.D.A.*, Vol. 72, pp. 209–50

(20) — 1942. A stone circle in the Plym Valley. *T.D.A.*, Vol. 74, pp. 207–10

(21) — 1943. The prehistoric pounds of Dartmoor. *T.D.A.*, Vol. 75, pp. 273–302

(22) — 1944. The tenants and commoners of Dartmoor. *T.D.A.*, Vol. 76, pp. 187–214

(23) — 1945. The Dartmoor hut-circles. *T.D.A.*, Vol. 77, pp. 225–56

(24) — 1946. Stray notes on the Teign Valley. *T.D.A.*, Vol. 78 pp. 161–170

(25) — 1946. Dartmoor blowing-houses (Supplement). *T.D.A.*, Vol. 78, pp. 281–4

(26) — 1946. The stone rows of Dartmoor. Part I. *T.D.A.*, Vol. 78, pp. 285–315

(27) — 1947. The stone rows of Dartmoor. Part II. *T.D.A.*, Vol. 79, pp. 175–86

(28) — 1947. Dartmoor and the Services Public Inquiry, 16 July 1947. *T.D.A.*, Vol. 79, pp. 211–25

(29) — 1949. The moorstone age, Part I. *T.D.A.*, Vol. 81, pp. 311–31

(30) — 1950. The moorstone age, Part II. *T.D.A.*, Vol. 82, pp. 329–48 [With Addendum by E. Masson Phillips, 1951, *T.D.A.*, Vol. 83, pp. 298–9]

(31) — MS. No. 1. 'By way of Preface'. [On the origins of the Worth family]

(32) — MS. No. 2. 'On the structure of Dartmoor'

(33) Barrow Committee of the Devonshire Association, 1902. Twenty-first Report. [Edited by R. Hansford Worth]. *T.D.A.*, Vol. 34, pp. 104–146

(34) — 1937. Fifty-sixth Report. [do.] *T.D.A.*, Vol. 69, pp. 75–110

(35) — 1950. Sixty-ninth Report. [do.] *T.D.A.*, Vol. 82, pp. 45–8

(36) Christy, Miller, & Worth, R. Hansford. 1922. The ancient dwarfed oak woods of Dartmoor. *T.D.A.*, Vol. 54, pp. 291–342

(37) Prowse, David C., & Worth, R. Hansford. 1934. On some guide-stones standing on the course of the old track from Tavistock to Ashburton. *T.D.A.*, Vol. 66, pp. 317–22

T.D.A. = Transactions of the Devonshire Association.
P.I. = Reports and Transactions of the Plymouth Institution.

FOREWORD

MY great-grandfather was born at Huckworthy Bridge, and for five previous generations, at least, his people had their homes in Sampford Spiney, Walkhampton, or one of the adjoining moorland parishes.

As to occupation the Worths of Walkhampton have been farmers for the more part, many have been agricultural labourers in their younger days, some throughout their lives. They have certainly been tinners, witness Francis who died in 1631 leaving his tinner's tools in his will, and John who was jurat for the Stannary of Plympton in 1553 and who probably came from Sheepstor. Many practised trades, were masons or stone-masons, or followed similar occupations. At times the near town of Plymouth drew some of them from their home, but the townward drift was never marked. To-day the wastage is probably much greater, but there are many descendants of the original stock around and near the old home parish.

If this illustrates the stability of our minor country families and their voluntary attachment to a limited homeland, it may also suggest that the motive of such attachment is a very real local patriotism, apt to remain active in such as become exiles and in their descendants.

As a Dartmoor man by descent, and, I hope, by adoption, I owe much to my father's country, not the least to my association with a group of investigators of whom I was the youngest, and am now the last.

Ormerod, Pengelly and Spence Bate, all of whom added to our knowledge of Dartmoor, I knew only as a boy may know his father's friends. I have since learnt the value of their work, as the introduction of a new method; the subsequent pursuit of which gave us what I have elsewhere called "the golden age of Dartmoor Archaeology".

In the years 1827 and 1828, Henry Woollcombe, Hamilton Smith, John Prideaux and Samuel Rowe conducted a survey, the results of which were presented by the last named in a paper read to the Plymouth Institution, on the 9 October 1828. Rowe continued the work, and in 1848 published the *Perambulation*, which is still of great value, an essential of the literature of Dartmoor.

Interest in the subject remained, as occasional papers in the *Trans-*

actions of the Devonshire Association evidenced, but it was many years before real advance was made. My father and I were steadily at work; we had conceived the idea that greater precision, more accurate and complete description were necessary if there were to be addition to our knowledge. To this end I engaged in a closer survey of our quarter of the moor, and especially in the preparation of plans and photographs.

No doubt this marked progress, but we were to have a colleague who became the first systematic excavator of prehistoric Dartmoor. The story of Robert Burnard's introduction to archaeology presents an unforeseeable chain of causes. His firm had waterside premises on the Cattewater, in the development of which considerable dredging operations became necessary. The material dredged interested him; and, partly as the result of an invitation to lecture at the Plymouth Institution, he inquired somewhat particularly as to its nature, deciding that, except for recent contribution by the clay-works, it was such as might be expected to be yielded by the debris and waste from the works of tin streamers. His paper on the dredging was followed by others on the stream works of Dartmoor; the first of which he read on the 22 March 1888. Always a lover of Dartmoor, his new interest quickly extended itself from the antiquities of historic time to those prehistoric.

Meanwhile, in 1889, I had published a descriptive account of the valley of the moorland Plym, with special reference to the prehistoric remains; this I had followed, in 1892, with a similar paper on "The Erme, Yealm and Torry". In the same year my father read his first paper on "The Stone Rows of Dartmoor".

Burnard was not content with the wide gap in our knowledge which must remain after the most careful survey, and in August and September 1893 he attacked the problem with the spade, selecting the groups of huts at Broadun and Broadun Ring for investigation. He associated with himself in this inquiry the Rev. Sabine Baring-Gould. The results which they obtained were so far unexpected that it became evident that further sites ought to be examined. In the following year, 1894, at the invitation of Mr. Burnard, the excavators were joined by Richard Nicholls Worth, Rev. W. A. Gordon Gray, Dr. Arthur B. Prowse and myself, and thus the first *"Dartmoor Exploration Committee"* was formed. In later years J. Brooking Rowe, John Duke Pode, Rev. George B. Berry, John Sparke Amery, Rev. Irvine K. Anderson and Basil H. Thomson were, at one time or another, members of the Committee during its active career. I, the survivor of the earlier members, would express the great indebtedness that we owe to Burnard and his colleagues, and my own sincere gratitude for the kindness and good-will which I received at their hands. Against those losses which are the penalty of age I set associations and memories of kindly friends, and full-filled Dartmoor days.

THE PHYSICAL GEOGRAPHY
OF DARTMOOR

BETWEEN the agricultural areas of North and South Devon lies the granite upland, known as Dartmoor. In old times the farms south of the moor were known as the 'South Hams', a term still in use, while the farms to the north formed a district called the 'North Hams'.

The intervening waste has long provided rough summer pasture, to which many a small border farmer still owes a modest success, while the rivers and streams of Dartmoor supply abundant water for the fertile lowlands. Camden describes it as '*Squalida montana Dertmore*', and Risdon apologizes for detaining his readers "on a place so wild, with so slender repast, where it is to be doubted you have taken the cold, or the cold hath caught you".

When Devon was disafforested in the reign of John, the Forest of Dartmoor was reserved as a royal hunting ground. Later it became an apanage of the Duchy of Cornwall, and it should now be more correctly described as a 'Chase'. Surrounding the Forest are further unenclosed lands, the Commons of Devon and certain other commons.

There is difficulty in defining the limits of Dartmoor. *Geographically*, it may be said to include the whole of the Forest, and of the surrounding unenclosed lands. This definition would, however, omit a considerable stretch of granite country which has been brought into cultivation, especially to the eastward. *Geologically*, it would be possible to confine it to the limits of the granite upland, extending to the boundary of the granite, irrespective of the state of the surface. It might then be queried whether the boundary should not be wide enough to embrace the halo of metamorphic rocks.

For our purposes we may adopt, as a compromise, the granite area with as much of the metamorphic halo as may be necessary or convenient.

The granite, with certain small outliers, covers an area of 248 sq. miles, extending $22\frac{1}{2}$ miles from north to south, and 18 miles from east to west. The greatest width from east to west occurs at about 5 miles south of the northern boundary of the granite; at 5 miles north of the

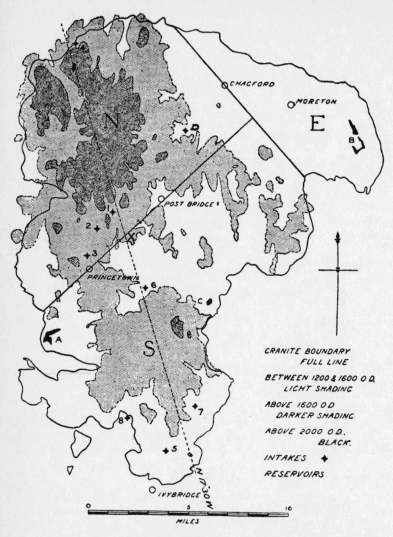

FIG. 1. Map of Granite area, with contours

Water-supply intakes: 1. West Dart, Devonport; 2. Cowsic, Devonport; 3. Black-abrook, Devonport; 4. Redaven, Okehampton; 5. Butter Brook, Ivybridge (with reservoir); 6. Swincombe, Paignton; 7. Bala Brook, Kingsbridge and Salcombe; 8. Yealm, Plympton.

Reservoirs: A. Burrator, Plymouth; B. Trenchford, etc., Torquay; C. Venford, Paignton; D. Fernworthy, Torquay.

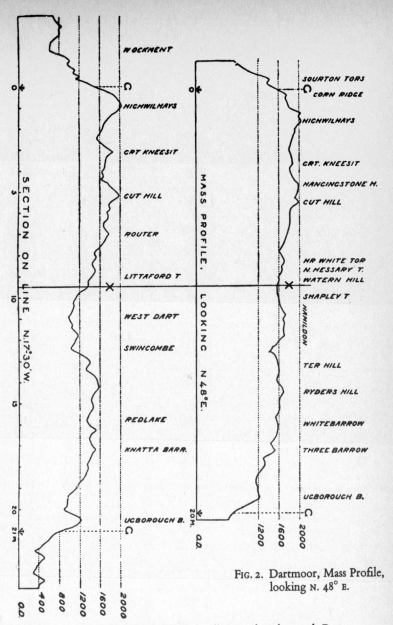

FIG. 2. Dartmoor, Mass Profile,
looking N. 48° E.

FIG. 3. Section on line through Highwilhays and Ugborough Beacon.

Vertical scales are to horizontal scales as 13·2 to 1.

'X' corresponds to same letter on Fig. 1, situate between Princetown and Postbridge at intersection of Section Line and Boundary between N. and S. districts. 'G', Granite boundary.

southern boundary the width is no more than 10½ miles. Not only is the northern part the wider, but it also attains a greater elevation, the highest ridge, from High Wilhays to Yes Tor (the 'roof of Devon'), reaches 2,039 ft above Ordnance Datum, and extends to within half a mile of the northern boundary. The greatest elevation within a similar distance of the southern boundary is 1,231 ft, at Ugborough Beacon (Fig. 1).

In the matter of height, the primary division of Dartmoor would be into two districts, northern and southern, the best formal common boundary being a straight line drawn through the railway station at Princetown and the Warren House Inn on the Princetown–Moreton-hampstead road. This line comes near coincidence with the road from Plymouth to Moretonhampstead; it passes a furlong north of Two Bridges, and an equal distance south of Postbridge; its direction is N. 48° E.

To the north of the suggested boundary the granite covers 105 sq. miles, and the principal heights range between 1,600 and 2,000 ft above mean sea level. South of the line the granite covers 143 square miles, and the summit levels of the principal hills range from 1,200 to 1,600 ft above sea level.

On reference to the map, section and mass profile (Figs. 1, 2 and 3), it will be seen that a little disturbance of these general statements arises from the heights of Hamildon and Ryders Hill in the southern district; yet these, with the summits of King Tor, Snowdon and Lee Moor, only account for a total of 1·19 sq. miles above the 1,600 ft contour; while in the northern district the area above that level is 26·34 sq. miles. It is, therefore, a fair approximation to take the 1,600 ft summit level as the division plane.

(In order to keep the differences in height clearly distinguishable the vertical scale of the section and of the mass profile has been much exaggerated with reference to the horizontal scale. Subject to this, the 'mass profile' is the skyline of Dartmoor as it would be seen from a great distance, a distance sufficient to eliminate all effect of perspective; it corresponds precisely to an architectural 'elevation'.)

There is good reason for adding a third division, the eastern district, derived in part from the southern and in part from the northern district above described, and severed from them by a straight line passing through the town of Chagford in a direction at right angles to the Princetown–Warren House boundary. It is characterized by summit levels ranging between 900 ft and a little less than 1,200 ft above sea level. The rainfall is materially less than that prevalent in the other districts, the surface granite is a little more thoroughly decomposed, and these features with its lower level have led to the extension of cultivation over large areas of granite subsoil.

The granite area would thus be subdivided into three districts:

(1) *The eastern.* Area 34 sq. miles. Summit levels between 900 ft and a little under 1,200 ft. No part above 1,200 ft.

(2) *The southern.* Area 120 sq. miles. Summit levels between 1,200 and 1,600 ft. Forty per cent, or 47½ sq. miles, above 1,200 ft. One per cent, or 1·2 sq. miles, above 1,600 ft.

(3) *The northern.* Area 94 sq. miles. Summit levels between 1,600 and 2,039 ft. Seventy-five per cent, or 71 sq. miles, above 1,200 ft. Twenty-eight per cent, or 26½ sq. miles, above 1,600 ft.

A glance at the map (Fig. 1) will show that there are two highlands, a northern and a southern, connected by but a narrow ridge, and elsewhere parted by the valleys of the Dart and its tributaries, and of the Plym and its sister the Meavy. The road from Plymouth to Moretonhampstead, which largely follows the line of an earlier track, slips through between the highlands. The old 'Abbot's Way', from Buckland to Buckfast, which crossed the centre of the southern highland, utilized a similar but less marked depression.

VEGETATION

Although the area of Dartmoor, taken as a whole, must be regarded as a plateau, it is much broken, and scored by valleys, deep or shallow. This variety of surface is combined with varied subsoil, with changing aspect and exposure, considerable differences in precipitation, differences in gradient and consequently in drainage, all features greatly influencing vegetation. In consequence there is no uniformity in the plant covering. Within a few miles of Princetown there are extensive areas of grass moor, of heather moor, of bracken, of moss and lichen moor, and of true bog-land with *Eriophorum vaginatum* and *angustifolium*; there is even original woodland (*Quercus pedunculata*) at Wistman's Wood.

The determinant of the nature of the vegetation is soil moisture, itself dependent on many contributory factors. Except on the outskirts of the moor, or where, as near Ditsworthy on the Plym, the altered rocks send overlying processes into the granite country; with these exceptions the ultimate subsoil is granite. This, however, does not imply uniformity. Beneath the surface soil the granite presents very varied resistance to disintegrating agencies; decomposed granite, except where kaolinized, gives rise to a substance locally known as 'growan'. The felspars disintegrate and part along their cleavages, without forming true clay, none the less suffering considerable chemical change. This is the disease of granite. It leaves a softened, but still coherent rock, far more porous than the parent stone. Its qualities are self-contradictory: it is soft, and easily excavated—but the moorland farmers have in past days excavated in this material caves for the storage of roots, and these caves required no lining or artificial support; it is porous, but it presents considerable resistance to the passage of water; it owes its origin to the decomposition of felspar, but the product is not clay. I shall refer to growan more than once; for the present the interest lies in the fact that granite presents a very varied opposition to change of this type. At the Sheepstor dam of the Burrator Reservoir the growan extended to a depth of at least 100 ft; in the valley of the Yealm I found sound rock under 6 ft of growan; there are many places where no such substance overlies the sound rock. Growan is not inconsistent with the presence of boulders, but except in valley bottoms it will not be found associated with stony ground, nor does it permit good subsoil drainage. An iron-pan will frequently be found at some little depth below the surface of the growan, showing that the upper part of the subsoil may be porous, but the level of constant saturation is soon reached. The principal deposits of peat on Dartmoor will be found over either clay or growan. Variation in the subsoil is therefore certain, and with it variation in the degree to which the soil is saturated.

The surface gradients range from gentle to very steep. The hill-tops are frequently rounded with relatively gentle slopes, from which it follows that Dartmoor has considerable resemblance to Ireland, in that, as Ortelianus wrote of that island: "*In summis et aerorum arduorumque montium verticibus stagna reperies et paludes.*" ("You find mires and bogs on the summits and crowns of the steep and breezy mountains.")

The fact is that, since the water cannot escape by surface flow, and cannot, except slowly, penetrate the peat and growan, steep and stony hillsides will usually, but not invariably, be found to be dry. The rainfall is by no means uniform, yet, except in the eastern district, it everywhere suffices to keep saturated for many months in the year any ground which is not naturally well drained.

The different plant associations thus find the conditions to which they are severally adapted. It should be noted that, while the soil of Dartmoor is everywhere peaty, true peat is by no means universally present.

Bracken (*Pteris aquilina*) is confined to relatively dry soils, and does not occur on true peat. Heather (*Calluna vulgaris*) prefers moderately dry soils, but will be found, although never dominant, associated with bog plants on the margins of bogs. The smaller and finer moor grasses accompany both bracken and heather in the drier lands. The coarser grasses grow on pure peat, under wet conditions, but not with constant saturation. *Eriophorum* is essentially a plant of the bogs, and with *Scirpus* spp. and *Carex* spp. has supplied most of the material from which the deeper peats have been formed.

Reindeer moss (*Cladonia sylvatica*), in its fullest development, is associated with true mosses and with whortleberry (*Vaccinium Myrtillus*). At Ditsworthy Warren it forms a dense carpet over many acres, some true mosses being associated with it, and the whortleberry more locally developed. The subsoil is largely altered slate, and the conditions vary from very wet to very dry, according to season and rainfall.

No doubt the surface covering of the moor has been affected by human interference. Swaling on wet ground will sometimes entirely remove *Calluna*, and I know instances in which the plant has not re-established itself in 30 years.

Erica cinerea, with its preference for drier ground, displaces *Calluna* on the steeper and stony slopes of the border hills; where the subsoil is metamorphic rock. It presents sheets of vivid colour on such hillsides as those of the Teign Gorge.

On the other hand *Erica tetralix*, which shows some slight preference for the metamorphic rocks, affects wet heaths with peaty soil, and is frequently associated with the coarser grass moors.

The *Sphagnaceae* are of localized habit, occurring in patches where springs issue, and beside slow running water. Without being rare they are unimportant in quantity as compared with true mosses such as *Hypnum*. The presence of *Sphagnum* usually indicates soft and some-what treacherous ground, not necessarily dangerous, but certainly in-convenient. The 'quaking bogs' are *Sphagnum*-covered.

In sheltered places within the moor, and in the border valleys, trees grow freely; but the actual area suited to afforestation above an eleva-tion of 800 ft O.D. is very small. It has been said that there is evidence, from tree remains found in the bogs, that trees at one time grew more freely upon Dartmoor. Wood has been found in the peat, according to the Geological Survey, south of Trowlesworthy Warren House in the Plym Valley, also at a point north-east of Torry Brook Head, at Cator Common, and in a valley between Cherry Brook Bridge and Post-bridge (presumably Gawler Bottom). For the more part this is described as birch. Moore, in Rowe's *Perambulation*, says that trunks of tolerably-sized trees have been occasionally found in the bogs. In the same work there is reference to the remains of trees in Taw Marsh. Brooking Rowe, in his edition of the same work, says: "at the head of the East Dart, below Great Hey Tor, in Stannon Bottom and elsewhere, branches of trees of considerable size have been found in the bogs. Near Princetown, in an enclosure made by the prison authorities, within a space of ten acres, upwards of twenty cartloads of wood, oak, willow and alder, were obtained without any trouble. One of the oaks measured 7 ft 6 in. in circumference near the roots."

It is doubtful whether the identification of "alder" as among the tree remains can be accepted, and it will be noted that these finds of bog-wood have, for the more part, been in relatively sheltered places, and are but few compared with the extent of the moor.

Certain it is that the only original woods now to be found on Dart-moor are in deep valleys, and within the protection of very rough, bouldery ground. The list is short, Wistman's Wood, Black Tor Beare, and Piles Wood, in the valleys of the West Dart, the West Ockment and the Erme, respectively.

The oak has three enemies on Dartmoor: the wind, grazing animals, and wet peat. The wind affects trees which have established themselves in otherwise possible situations, either pruning completely away all attempted growth to windward and any but very restricted growth in height; or, where the tree can find all-round shelter from boulders, reducing it to little more than a mat of contorted twigs. The highest placed tree in the North Wood at Wistman's is a good example of the pruning action of the wind where the oak cannot nestle between the boulders. The main trunk, which is exceedingly short, girths 69 in., two sister branches spring from the trunk, they girth 41 in. and 30 in. respectively. The height of the tree is 10 ft, its radial spread is 19 ft, all before the prevailing wind. This is at an elevation of 1,390 ft (Pl. 21A).[1] The south-easternmost tree of Black Tor Beare is the best example of matted growth. It grows in a patch of large boulders which provide a shallow shelter. "The tree has never accomplished a trunk, its three main branches crawl over the boulders, from which they but slightly lift themselves: their girths are 24, 28 and 37 in. respectively. From a tangle of secondary branches springs a matted confusion of twigs, to form (at a height of 7 ft) the canopy of the tree. In effect the canopy is a mere superficies, slightly domed in form, and 33 ft in diameter, almost a true circle in plan (Pl. 22B). This, at 1,530 ft above Ordnance Datum, is the highest situate oak in Devonshire." With these two examples before one it is impossible to imagine that the higher parts of Dartmoor can ever have borne oak-woods since the present climatic conditions have obtained. The grazing animals do not seriously interfere with well-established trees, but they destroy or cripple seedlings, and thus limit the spread of the woods and prevent rejuvenation. Against this danger the boulders, where sufficiently large and numerous, are a good defence. Acid peat soil is unsuited to the growth of oaks and its soft and yielding substance would afford no root-hold. Further, the frequent presence of an iron-pan precludes the growth of any deep-rooting tree. We may, I think, conclude that, with slight local variation, the vegetation of Dartmoor is to-day the same as it was in Neolithic times, and the Early Bronze Age. There are scars where agriculture, untaught by past failure, has exhausted its resources in the attempt to impose its yoke, but the unconquerable native flora heal the scars; and we may say of Dartmoor, as did the writer whom Rowe quoted with approval: "Perhaps it serves as it is the gracious purposes of Providence."

PEAT

When I said that, on Dartmoor, the determinant of the nature of the vegetation was soil moisture I had also in mind, as one of the consequences of excessive moisture, the formation of peat. In a temperate

---

[1] By 1952 this tree had a more flourishing aspect, much growth having occurred in the side branches. It had increased its height in the centre. (ED.)

climate, and with conditions of practically constant saturation, vegetable matter will undergo slow decomposition to ultimately become peat. This condition of saturation determines the areas which become peat bogs, as opposed to those which present mere peaty soil. There is much less peat on Dartmoor than is commonly thought; and it is only in exceptional circumstances that it attains any considerable depth. In the formation of eight miles of railway in the Erme valley no greater depth was found than 2 ft 6 in., until the head of the Redlake valley was reached. Here, at an elevation of 1,400 ft, the deposit varies between 6 and 11 ft in depth. In some other of the shallow and flat upland valleys, or pans, there is no doubt that twice this thickness of peat may be found, but only over small areas.

The dominant plant-remains in the peat are those of species still growing on the surface of the bogs: *Eriophorum* and its associates, to the practical exclusion of the *Sphagnaceae*. In all the deeper deposits there is clear distinction between surface peat and deep peat, usually with an intermediate layer of defined character. But there is no succession of varying botanical character; the most that may occasionally be found is a layer of birch wood, at depths of from 18 in. to 4 ft, and there is no evidence that this marks more than an incident in the history of the particular bog. Gentle slopes, such as those of hill-tops and shallow valleys, and elevations which lie above or near the mist level, characterize the sites of all the more important deposits, which are mostly found above the 1,200 ft contour. Not rainfall only, for this is at many places as great below this contour as above, but the frequency of rainfall and fog, and to some extent the reduction of temperature with height, are the favourable conditions.

The Geological Survey Memoir suggests that many valleys, formerly filled with peat, have been bared of that material by the operations of the tin-streamers. I find little evidence in support of this suggestion. Furthermore, it is to be remembered that the streamers were most interested in those valleys which were floored with gravels and small boulders, and such valleys would be relatively well drained and thus unsuited to the formation of peat. Where the subsoil is china clay, even though some material depth of peat may overlie it, the tinners frequently followed the course of the tin lodes in the kaolinized rock; never baring any extent of surface, but cutting gullies, such as those which existed at Redlake before the clay pit was opened, and are still to be found at Broadamarsh on the East Dart.

Redlake in the Erme watershed may be taken as presenting a typical Dartmoor bog. The top peat is fibrous, and shrinks but little on drying; when supersaturated it carries 83 % of water, and when dry it weighs 18 to 19 lb. to the cubic foot. Beneath this lies the middle peat, of a very dark brown colour; this, when saturated, but not supersaturated, contains 87·87% of water; when dry, it weighs 48¼ lb. the cu. ft.

The bottom peat is black; a sample taken at a depth of 6 ft may serve as typical of the best developed peats of Dartmoor. When saturated, but after draining until no more water will flow from it, it contains 86·50% of moisture, and weighs 64 lb. per cu. ft. A cubic foot thus consists of 55·36 lb. of water and 8·64 lb. of peat substance. The specific gravity of the latter is 1·247, so that, stated in volume, a cubic foot of peat consists of eight-ninths of a cu. ft of water, and one-ninth of a cu. ft of peat substance. If there were no pore space a cube of 12-in. side (or edge) would dry to a cube of 5·77 in. side; it does dry to a cube of 6·08 in. side; in other words the absolutely dry material occupies only one-eighth (approximately) of the space which it filled in the bog. Thus, in round numbers, it shrinks to 50% of its linear, and 12½% of its cubic, dimensions. In every cubic foot of this peat there is entangled water to the amount of 5·536 gallons. One hundred pounds of saturated peat yield 13½ lb. of dry substance.

Fuels are frequently analysed into 'volatile matter', 'fixed carbon', and 'ash'. So analysed this same sample yields (%):

	Volatile	Fixed carbon	Ash
Black Peat, Redlake	68·30	29·56	2·14
Plym Head	60·25	34·25	5·50

The results yielded by a sample from Plym Head are given by way of comparison.

All peat contains matter soluble in aqueous solutions of alkalis. This fact is utilized to determine the relative proportions of 'humic substance' and of 'fibre', but we cannot be said to have any very accurate knowledge of the composition of the soluble portion; we do, however, know that it is a colloid or a mixture of colloids. Ammonia is the most convenient alkali to use in this parting, since it can be removed from the solution by boiling. Examination of the same two samples gave the following percentages:

	Soluble	Insoluble	Ash
Black Peat, Redlake	21·00	76·86	2·14
Plym Head	22·50	72·00	5·50

The ammonia-peat solution is dark brown, somewhat red by transmitted light. It can easily be prepared of sufficient density to be used as a brown ink. If the ammonia be neutralized, or driven off by boiling, electrolytes precipitate the 'humic substance' in flocculent form, ultimately yielding a bulky jelly. Washing and drying give a brittle, black solid of pitchy lustre. This solid is very sparingly soluble in water, even on boiling; but alkaline solutions prove ready solvents.

Its sparing solubility in water accounts for the very slight discoloration which is found in the Dartmoor streams when in flood. On test it is rather surprising to find how comparatively little is the stain which ambers the flood waters.

There can be no doubt as to the colloidal nature of the soluble portion of the peat; the fibre varies in grain from recognizable fragments of vegetable matter to almost impalpable dust; together the two form a medium well adapted to entangle water and retain it. A very slight film of the finer particles of the fibre will entirely choke a filter paper. The water in saturated peat is, for practical purposes, as firmly held as in jelly. Of all the methods tried for freeing peat from its water of saturation none has been a commercial success, except the oldest and simplest, that of air drying. This requires for fair results a summer season with some approximation to the normal conception of summer weather, given which air-dried material is obtained containing about 25% of moisture. Summer does not always come to Dartmoor, and I have known seasons in which practically all the turf which had been cut for domestic use has been abandoned, as not worth carting in.

One result of the colloid content of peat is the formation of the very persistent foam that forms a feature of the Dartmoor streams when in flood.

Peat ashes are frequently red, from the presence of iron oxide: they are found also to contain a little lime. The deeper and more fully formed material is usually the redder, hence a red ash is regarded as an indication of good quality fuel. None the less, some of the best peat such as that from Plym Head, has a white ash. The colour depends wholly upon the character of the underlying rock.

The conversion of vegetable matter to peat involves chemical change, the production of the humus acids, and of carbonic acid. The escape of the latter, either in gas form or in solution, leads to a considerable loss of the original carbon. That carbon dioxide is produced has been evidenced by tragedy. A workman, whom I employed in sinking pits through the peat to a clay deposit, received instructions to test the air in the pits every morning before entering them. I had heard traditions of loss of life from foul air, but I had never known or received clear evidence of such a loss. For weeks the workman followed the instructions as to testing the air, and in no instance found evidence of any danger. Then, when the work had entered on the last few days, he omitted such test, and, on descending the pit, was within a few minutes overcome; another man, attempting his rescue, came near losing his life also.

The humus acids and the carbon dioxide alike attack the granite, but the carbonic acid appears to be the more powerful agent. The first effect is the leaching out of the iron contents of the rock. Much of the iron in the red granites and felsites is in the form of hematite, while a little is combined as silicates. If the hematite is removed the richest red rock retains at most a pale buff colour.

There is an indian-red felsite, which I have called 'felsite A', and which occurs at the surface of the granite on its western and southern borders, from the Plym to the Dart, and elsewhere sporadically (it is also found associated with the Cornish granites, as, for instance, at St. Dennis). This is a very compact rock, hard, and so uniform and fine in texture that it has a subconchoidal fracture. At and near Hen Tor in the Plym Valley it underlies a peat bog. Fragments are there found which have been bleached white, and have lost their flinty lustre. Many of the larger of these fragments, when broken, show a core of the red, unaltered felsite. The peat from this bog has a red ash. In the extreme, but rarely, the action does not cease with bleaching and loss of lustre, but extends to a complete softening of the rock to a porous condition; a softening sufficiently marked to have led to the rock being used for whitening hearths. The residue is never of a clayey nature.

Some part of the iron certainly combines with the humus acids, the remainder going into solution as ferrous bicarbonate. If there be any supposed difficulty in deriving a ferrous salt from hematite, it has to be remembered that hematite weathers to magnetite, so that magnetite may be invoked as an intermediary. When the ferrous bicarbonate solution escapes from the peat it rapidly loses the carbonic acid gas, and iron hydroxides are deposited. The result is seen in the coating of the rocks and pebbles in the beds of streams which rise in peat bogs, at such times as the flow of the streams is reduced in dry weather, and the iron solution concentrated. It is seen also in the iridescent film which occurs on small pools of peat water. This film, frequently stated to be oily matter, is none other than iron hydroxide; so that this alleged evidence of the presence of oil in peat bogs must be dismissed. Passing downward into the growan the same solution of ferrous bicarbonate arrives at the level of normal summer saturation, here the carbonic acid gas escapes, and the iron hydroxides deposit to form the 'iron pan'. Occasionally a granite stone of some size is found lying partly above and partly below the pan; if such a stone is broken an iron stain will be found extending completely across it in the plane of the adjacent iron pan, and continuous with it. The stone has shared with its surroundings the conditions as to saturation.

Peat is a convenient and pleasant fuel for domestic use. It can and has been used for steam raising, but its efficiency is relatively low, from 1·8 to 2 lb. of air-dried peat being the equivalent of 1 lb. of good ordinary coal. The high proportion of volatile matter, say 65 per cent as a mean, has enabled its use as a source of illuminating gas. The following passage is quoted from Ure's Dictionary of Arts, Manufactures and Mines, seventh edition, 1875. "On Dartmoor the peat is cut by the convicts, working in gangs; and, being dried, it is carefully stored in one of the old prisons. From this peat, by a most simple process, gas is made, with which the prisons at Princetown are lighted. The illuminating power of this gas is very high. The charcoal left after the separation of the gas is used in the same establishment for fuel and sanitary purposes, and the ashes eventually go to improve the cultivated lands of that bleak region.

Attempts were made here many years since to distil the peat for naphtha, paraffin, etc., but the experiments not proving successful, the establishment was abandoned."

The reference to the use of peat charcoal, in this instance a by-product, serves as a reminder that peat, when used for tin smelting, was first carbonized. This process certainly dates back to earlier than the year 1466, probably much earlier. In that year the tinners of Cornwall were granted a charter which included the right: "Quod ipsi et servientes sui infra forestam nostram de Dertemore in comitatu Devon ad libitum suum ingredi et intrare et turbas in eadem foresta in quocumque loco sibi placuerit fodere et succindere et carbones inde facere, et eos sic factos ab inde in comitatu Cornubie . . . abducere et asportare." "*To dig and cut turf and make coal therefrom,*" it being remembered that *coal* was at that time the phrase used where now we say *charcoal.* Peat charcoal has about the same calorific value as good English coal, and 100 lb. of air-dried peat yield about 36 lb. of charcoal. Not only, therefore, did the tinners obtain a much higher quality fuel, but the weight to be transported to Cornwall was greatly reduced.

That peat is still forming on Dartmoor cannot be doubted. The various stages in the process are traceable in many bogs, from the living vegetable to the most compact peat. At what rate the peat grows in depth cannot be ascertained. It suffers loss by solution, it represents far less than the original mass of vegetation from which it has developed, and there is some loss by surface wash. The rate of growth in depth may well be slow. Whether a condition of equilibrium, in which losses balance gains, ever arises may be a matter for doubt: probably a bog is always either growing or decaying.

Growth has certainly taken place since the Early Bronze Age. The long stone row in the Erme Valley, extending from the circle on Stall Moor to the barrow on Green Hill, presents gaps, real or apparent. The apparent gaps occur where the stones of the row have been buried by the growth of peat. On the west bank of the Erme, opposite Erme Pound, the row is lost for a space. Here the peat is sufficiently well developed to be worth cutting, and turf ties have been formed. The removal of the turf to the usual working depth has sufficed to uncover the stones of the row, still erect and firm set in the growan (Pl. 1A). The indication is that, since the stones were set in place, 2 ft in depth of peat have accumulated.

Decay is certainly taking place, especially in the hill-top bogs. It has been suggested that such decay sets in where the peat has slipped downhill and fissure partings have been formed. There is, however, no evidence of moving bogs on Dartmoor; and very little evidence of slips of any sort on the hillsides. One rather marked exception occurs in the valley of the West Ockment, above the Slipper Stones. Here there has been a considerable slide of ground on a steep hillside, where the underlying granite, as shown by the broad planes of bare rock, has an in-clination of from 1 in 1·66, to 1 in 2; but the slipped material is not peat. The bogs where disintegration is taking place are all situate either on the hill-tops or at the heads of valleys. It is probable that several causes con-tribute to the disintegration. In the first place the bogs which suffer are all dependent on rainfall only for their water supply, and are thus liable to become dry in long continued drought. This, in itself, would not waste the peat, but it would hasten the process in the presence of other con-tributory conditions. The other extreme, of excessive and unusual rainfall, might not only contribute to the loss when once begun, but might even be a first cause. The bogs absorb readily, but part with water slowly; a hill-top bog has low gradients and is badly drained, water standing on the surface in little puddles. Such water as does flow off follows no well defined channels, and the fibrous top peat resists erosion, but extreme rain might have sufficient erosive power to start a channel here and there, with local removal of the fibrous layer.

Once the compact peat, with broken fibre, is exposed, the decay of the bog has commenced. Drought dries the surface, and wind removes some of the dried material; renewed flow of water in the incipient channel removes yet more; and frost, the most powerful enemy of all, breaks down the cohesion of the peat and leaves it friable, the readier prey to drought and flood. A channel once formed drains the bog and hastens decay. At last a whole system of intersecting channels comes into being, and the remaining peat is reduced to hags, or detached mounds. On Dartmoor the slopes of Great Kneesit (Pl. 1B) and the ground around Cranmere Pool afford good examples of peat bogs in their final stages of decay. I believe, indeed, that Cranmere Pool itself is but an area of bog from which the last peat hag has perished, and that it was once in no way distinguishable from its surroundings. Burt, in his notes on Carrington's *Dartmoor*, writes of the bog around Cran-mere as being 40 to 50 ft in depth; whereas 4 to 5 ft is a much more accurate estimate. Bray thought that the water could not be more than 6 to 8 ft when the pool was full; it is very doubtful whether it ever held 2 ft of water. Rowe, in 1844, thought he traced evidence of the bank having been broken through on the northern side, and Crossing, with some diffidence, considers that there may be truth in the tale that the bank was cut by a miller, whose mill was on the Ockment, to obtain more water; a futile proceeding. If my view of its origin is right, Cran-mere has never had a continuous bank of appreciable height through-out, and has never held more than a few inches of water. This much is certain—in 1802, Bray found the pool dry, and dry it has been in every ordinary summer since.

Bogs fed from springs, or by the spreading of a stream, or constantly supplied by seepage from the adjacent ground are not liable to disinte-gration. Channels constantly carrying water may run through these with but local effect. In such bogs *Sphagnum* is the dominant plant; it will grow also in cotton-grass bogs where peat has been removed, and where water lies in shallow pools. Wherever the supply of, at most, slow-moving water is sufficient *Sphagnum* tends to heal and restore the damaged surface; but it cannot withstand the periodical droughts which occur in the flood-water channels cut through peat deriving its supply from rainfall only.

HILL AND VALLEY

Viewed as a whole Dartmoor is a table-land, elevated above the level of the 'in country'. Taken in detail it is found to present a very varied surface of hill and valley. In the ultimate this surface relief must be attributed to the work of denudation; but the denuding forces merely developed a pre-determined form. There is ample evidence that the present geography of Dartmoor presents contours which were those of the upper surface of the granite when it cooled in contact with the overlying sedimentary rocks. The hills represent points at which the granite rose higher into its overburden, the valleys are lines along which folds of slate or other rocks were pressed down into the granite surface. *At few points can the present surface be far below the original surface of the granite, when it cooled as a plutonic rock.*

The evidence for this statement is varied, falling chiefly under four heads:

(a) *The coincidence of the planes of the pseudo-bedding with the slopes of the hillsides.* The granite in cooling under the sedimentary cap contracted of necessity. Since the outer or upper layers of granite cooled first, the contraction led to cracks and planes of weakness, some of which were parallel to the surface of cooling. These as now exposed form the pseudo-bedding, simulating the strata of sedimentary rocks; others were approximately perpendicular to the surface of cooling, and now form the 'joints'. Pseudo-bedding and joints are thus of common origin, and their evidence is identical in effect, but that offered by the former is the more easily demonstrated.

The numerous exposures of granite afford ample opportunity for the study of the pseudo-bedding. The more resistant rock, which has defied the disintegrating effect of weather and of the peat-charged ground waters, forms tower-like masses on many hill-tops, and even on some hillsides. The rivers frequently flow over bare rock. From these exposures we learn that the pseudo-bedding may be very varied in character. It may so divide the rock that the deep layers with their cross joints resemble cyclopean masonry; or it may be so close set that the mass appears to have a lamellar structure, the vertical joints widely spaced. But, whichever form or whatever intermediate form it may assume, there is one general feature which is subject to few exceptions: it conforms to the slope of the ground.

On the hill-top the bedding is horizontal; in the bed of the valley the river runs over horizontal surfaces of granite; on the hillside the bedding and the surface slope are coincident. It is thus indicated that the cooling surface was at least parallel to the present surface of the land, and had a similar figure.

It has been suggested that the hills and valleys were first sculptured in solid rock, and the pseudo-bedding subsequently developed by the alternations of heat and cold, of day and night. Any such possible alterations would be wholly inadequate to have even a superficial effect, whereas the parting planes of the pseudo-bedding have been found at the greatest depths to which the granite has been worked.

A complete reply to the suggestion that the formation of these planes could have dated after the denudation of the moor is to be found in the occasional intrusions of later granitic matter, sill fashion, between the planes (as for instance at Belliver). These are not so common as intrusions between the more or less vertical joint planes, but are not rare, and the two forms of intrusion are associated. The pseudo-bedding planes were therefore in existence prior to the last stages of igneous activity.

Instances of the coincidence of the pseudo-bedding with the present contours are everywhere to be found. By way of illustration the following may be taken; the summit rocks of Littaford Tor, where the well-marked horizontal bedding, and equally marked joints leave blocks of the massive type (Pl. 2A); the hillside and summit rocks of Brae Tor, with horizontal bedding at the crest, and inclined bedding on the slopes of the hill; the structure being intermediate between massive and lamellar (Pl. 2B); the hillside rocks of Little Lynx Tor, showing inclined bedding parallel to the slope of the ground in a lamellar mass, in which, however, the lamellae are of moderate thickness (Pl. 3A); the verge of the hill-crest of Thurlestone, or Watern Tor, showing the first departure from the horizontal in a thoroughly lamellar mass (Pl. 3B); and the River Tavy, at Tavy Cleave, where the river flows over a horizontal bed of granite (Pl. 5A).

The inclined bedding on the sides of the valleys is, perhaps, best shown at the Slipper Stones on the West Ockment. One of these surfaces is shown in Pl. 5B. It is not the longest, but it extends full 60 ft up the hillside, and has a gradient of 1 in 1·8. Similar surfaces are to be found elsewhere on Dartmoor, as for instance on the west flank of Meldon (Chagford), where the rock slope is 45 ft in length, and has a gradient of one in 4½.

Nor is similar evidence wanting in the Plym Valley by the Dewerstone. It is true that in the Dewerstone Rock itself the vertical jointing is markedly predominant, but in the twin cliffs, which break from the hill above, the pseudo-bedding may be seen crossing the vertical joints at an angle so steep that it seems the mass must slide to the valley bed, yet through the centuries it has stood secure (Pl. 4).

(b) *Inclusions of altered rock in surface granite.* Two forms of inclusions are found in the granite of Dartmoor. Of the first form are fragments of a finer grained granite, usually with much black mica. These are very varied in size, the smaller being no more than a few inches in length, the larger certainly reach 30 ft in their greatest dimension, and probably, at places, exceed this magnitude. All the smaller inclusions, up to 3 or 4 ft in length, are ovoid, and have evidently been rounded by partial solution in the molten mass. All contain much secondary biotite. Some of the inclusions, always of considerable size, show cores of comparatively unaltered rock. One such occurs on Higher Whiten Tor: the centre is bright flesh-colour and very fresh; the margin is dark brown, and much more mica is there developed.

At the other extreme, the included rock has been so thoroughly re-melted that it has lost its form, and is now found involved with the normal granite in a complex flow-structure; such rock may be found at Lakehead Newtake, near Postbridge.

These inclusions, being of finer grain, resist the action of the weather better than does the normal rock, and stand raised above the general surface. Pl. 6A shows such an included mass in the granite of Kestor: its length is 4 ft 2 in., and its depth 1 ft 4 in. Kestor has a coarse granite cap, and a fine-grained pedestal: it is very probable that the greater part of the mass of this tor is one large included block.

Pl. 6B is a view of an inclusion in a boulder on the slopes of Beardown. It exhibits a feature which is frequent, that the junction of the fine and the coarse rocks weathers more freely than either of the masses. The diameter of this xenocryst is 25 in. The history of the granitic inclusions appears to be fairly certain. The intrusion of the Dartmoor granite must have been a relatively slow process, and it can hardly have proceeded at a constant rate. There were pauses, times of relative inactivity, and during such pauses, if marked, there was time for the granite to form a thin cooled crust at its contact with the sedimentary rocks. This crust, having been comparatively rapidly cooled, would have a fine grain. On the resumption of the intrusive movement it would be broken, and fragments would be taken up in the mass of the molten rock, there to be reheated, and again cooled, but at a less rapidity. The material of the crust would be likely to vary somewhat from the chemical composition of the normal granite, having acquired foreign constituents from the sedimentary rocks with which it had been in contact.

Inclusions of the second type are fragments of rocks foreign to the granite; sedimentary or igneous rocks with which the granite came in contact during its forward movement. None of this type that are known to me are more than 2 or 3 ft in greatest dimension; all are reduced by partial solution, and all are either ovoid or at the least subangular. Their material has been subjected to intense metamorphism.

Both types of inclusion may occur in the same rock-mass, as at Redlake, in the Erme Valley, where I found them, side by side, down to a depth of 120 ft below the present surface of the granite. Both types are obviously surface phenomena, originating at the contact of the granite and the overlying rocks; and neither is likely to occur at any great depth below the contact.

Inclusions of one type or the other are common over large areas of the moor. In the earlier days of geology the granitic type were regarded as 'basic segregations'; but one strong evidence against that identification is the fact that in the larger forms the original jointing has been preserved, which is rarely coincident with that of the surrounding rock.

(c) *Patches of sedimentary rock overlying the granite.* Residual patches of sedimentary rock, still overlying the granite, are by no means uncommon. There is one on Brown Heath, near Redlake in the Erme Valley; it is near the inclusions which have been mentioned as occurring at Redlake, and the two classes of evidence are mutually in support. This is 2½ miles within the granite boundary.

Altered sedimentary rocks are also found in Tor Royal Newtake, near Cholake Head, 2 miles east of Princetown, and 4 miles distant from the granite boundary. There are other similar inliers. Where these occur it is certain that the present surface and the original roof of the granite must be coincident.

(d) *The presence of the indian-red felsite, which I have called 'felsite A'* ('Petrography of Dartmoor and its Borders', *T.D.A.*, vols. 34, 35, 44, 49). Along the border of the granite, and at points within the border, there is to be found, from the Plym Valley to the Dart, a very compact and somewhat flint-like rock of a rich red colour. It is found as the surface form of the granite, a rock rapidly chilled by contact with the sedimentaries. It is found also where the granite is no longer covered by the sedimentary rocks, and is there evidence of the previous contact surface. Great quantities of this felsite are present in the beach material of Start Bay, and can only have been derived from Dartmoor, by way of the valley of the Dart. It is true that the beach material must be of considerable age; it cannot have travelled down the Dart since the time when the harbour of Dartmouth ceased to be a subaerial valley. But, on the other hand, no beach material, however resistant, can last for ever under the constant attrition to which it is subject; and geologically, its derivation from Dartmoor must have been recent.

From the quantity of this felsite on these and other beaches it is to be concluded that a considerable area of Dartmoor has not long been cleared of this superficies of the granite.

CHINA CLAY

Notwithstanding the evidence above cited, it must be allowed that, in parts, the granite has suffered material denudation. There is no reason why china clay should not have been as well and freely developed on Dartmoor as on the Cornish moors which lie at a lower level. We know that china clay, in mass, was formed only near the surface of the granite. It is still found on Dartmoor, but not in important deposits except near the edge of the granite, and only in patches of no commercial significance in the higher levels of the moor. Wherever it is present in good quantity there is ample evidence that the surface of the granite has not suffered any considerable denudation; that it has, in fact, been barely uncovered. The clay is not a material which, in the absence of some form of protection, can long resist denudation; and it may well be that Dartmoor, with its greater elevation, has been subjected to much more severe denudation than have the Cornish moors.

Thus we would expect that much clay-rock may have been removed by natural agencies. Fortunately, there is no need to depend on conjecture. Not only has the clay been removed, with its accompanying sand and gravel, but much of it has been redeposited where it can be seen and identified. The old lake-bed of the Bovey basin now yields 'Ball Clays', which are but the china clay of Dartmoor, removed by denudation and redeposited in association with the sands and gravels of the original clay-rock. The ball clays of Meeth and Peters Marland, in North Devon, had a similar origin.

China clay, or kaolin, is derived from the alteration of the felspar crystals in granite, *in situ*, and is always found, on Dartmoor, with the other constituents of the parent rock still in their normal position relative to the altered felspars. Kaolin is devoid of the alkalis of the original felspar, and has acquired water of hydration. The problem of determining the agencies which have removed the alkalis and supplied the added water has received many suggested solutions. It cannot be said that there is any general agreement among the authorities. I believe the chief agents in the alteration of the felspars to have been vapours, charged with fluoric and boric acids, and derived from the cooling granite. These would be powerless in the absence of a sufficient supply of water; the water I believe to have been meteoric,[1] and to have obtained access to the surface of the granite after penetrating the overlying sedimentary rocks. This explanation is in agreement with the superficial nature of the clay formation. The action would take effect at such points as presented the necessary combination of ascending vapours meeting descending waters. It is notable that the metamorphic rocks, where still at places overlying the clay, are all very highly tourmalinized, a feature consistent with the suggested explanation. The best example of metamorphic rock overlying clay is to be found at the Smallhanger Works in the parish of Plympton St. Mary.

[1] Derived from the atmosphere. (ED.)

THE TINNERS' INFLUENCE ON SCENERY

Strictly local kaolinization frequently accompanies the tin lodes; and on the other hand, narrow lodes of tin pierce the clay-rock. Such lodes occur at Redlake on the Erme, and at Broadamarsh on the East Dart. At each place they have been worked by the tinners to such depth as their appliances permitted. The presence of water, and the treacherous nature of the clay, which requires heavy timbering, limited their activities; but they furrowed the ground to an extent which is still marked. These tinners' furrows, or shallow gullies, are to be seen wherever a lode occurred in clay or growan; at places they cease to be shallow, and become prominent features in the landscape, as for instance in the neighbourhood of Fox Tor, where also clay may be found in small quantity. In the days of their later activities the tinners have executed bolder excavations, as at Chaw Gulley (Pl. 7A) and the other gullies connected with Vitifer and Birch Tor Mines, and at Erme Pits. Their works have influenced the scenery of the moor, not only in mere mining excavation, but also in efforts at drainage. Thus Ormerod describes the artificial deepening of the channel which served to lower the water level in the marsh above the junction of the Wallabrook and the North Teign; and a similar and even more clearly marked drainage channel has been formed by the deepening of the river bed between Sandy Hole and Broadamarsh on the East Dart, where the river has been confined between walls of dry masonry. Such cuts must have lowered the saturation level of the marshes by some feet, and rendered a greater depth of the tin lodes accessible.

In the *Memoir of the Geological Survey, Sheet 338*, on page 58 and following pages, is a discussion of the probable extent to which human agency has contributed to the present-day features of Dartmoor. It is there suggested that nearly all the upland valleys were formerly occupied by peat-bogs, and that these have disappeared in consequence of the operations of the tinners. But this suggestion I consider to be ill-founded. The valleys in which the tinners were interested were those with gravel beds overlying the rock or growan, and the bed of gravel would give such efficient under-drainage that the conditions of saturation necessary to the formation of peat would most probably never arise. The fact that a more peaty surface is sometimes found near the foot of the valleys, in the flats, is largely due to the absence of the gravel bed in some such places, and to the accumulation of the waste from the stream works. The tinners knew well enough that in attacking any deposit the lower parts should be worked first, and they would not work down from the upper levels to the flats. If they could work in Broadamarsh, as they very certainly did, there is no flat in any valley which they could not attack. And at Broadamarsh, it is not to be doubted, their improvement of the river channel, down to Sandy Hole, was, in part at least, with a view to assuring an efficient stream for the purpose of removing their waste, and preventing it cumbering their works.

Certainly, the law prohibited the conversion of the rivers into common carriers of tin wastes; but we know that the harbours of Devon and Cornwall suffered greatly from the waste brought down by the rivers; and the officers of the law may well have hesitated to interview the tinner in his working place at Broadamarsh. Even to-day the work of the tinner remains efficient, and the sand from the erodible banks of the river in this marsh is safely conducted through the narrow pass, and deposited, below the pass, at Sandy Hole, a circumstance from which that part of the valley takes its name.

The waste from the stream works is still discoverable at many places on Dartmoor. Mr. S. C. Chapman sent me a sample of very fine sand from the pipe line under Metherall, on the South Teign, which proved to be characteristic tin slimes; and I have found similar slimes in the Plym Valley and elsewhere.

The Surveyors also refer to the low cliff which frequently bounds the valley bed of the Dartmoor streams on either side, and suggest that this marks the limit to which the tinners worked toward the hill. The observation is probably just, although all such cliffs parallel to the stream, and bounding the alluvial flat, have not necessarily had this origin.

The tinners were very systematic in their methods, and when working in the deposits of small boulders and large pebbles, which frequently overlie the granite in the valley flats, they often proceeded by means of a series of parallel trenches. The larger blocks from each trench were used to build a rough wall on the verge of the trench, and the smaller stones, as each was examined and rejected as devoid of ore, were thrown out in mounds, behind and retained by the walls so formed. In this manner a series of parallel ridges would be formed, each of relatively small slope on the side far from the trench, each faced by a nearly vertical wall on the side toward it. These ridges are no unusual features in many valleys, they are perhaps as well preserved as anywhere in the Plym Valley at Drizzlecombe Burrows (Pl. 7B), and in the lower part of the Langcombe.

The tinners were also great hydraulicians, skilled in the construction of water-courses for the conveyance of the waters of the rivers and the streams to their works for the purpose of washing the ore; and to their blowing-houses, where the waters of the leats operated the water-wheels which provided power for the bellows of the furnace, for the crazing mills, and possibly for some rude form of stamps. Miles of these water-courses, or leats, are still traceable on the moor; and many are yet sufficiently marked to form features of the landscape. It was skilled work: little fall was wasted in the construction of the leats, and the points of intake were often very well chosen. It is significant that when, in 1559–60, the Corporation of Plymouth was seeking a supply of water other than the local sources then available, it employed a tinner, one "Mr. forsland of bovy", to survey and report.

TOR AND BOULDER

A hill may be called a 'tor' although it has no granite peak, but the instances are few. The modern use of the word, as indicating the granite mass capping a hill, is perhaps a restrictive use not wholly justified by tradition; but it is convenient, and does no real violence to ancient custom.

On the other hand, the use of the word 'cleave', as descriptive of a deep valley with abrupt slopes, is wholly wrong. A 'cleave' (very commonly pronounced 'clay') is a cliff; the valley bounded by cleaves is a 'gert'.

By geological usage the term 'boulder' has been restricted to apply only to transported blocks, moved by the agency of ice. I know no reason why we should consent to this limitation, and I propose to use the word as denoting any loose block detached from its parent rock by natural agencies. The equivalent in the language of Dartmoor is 'rock', and that might at times be ambiguous.

A 'clitter' or 'clatter', is a mass of boulders: it may be in the nature of a scree at the foot of the parent rock, or it may be more or less far removed from any rock exposure to which its origin can be directly attributed.

The tors crowning the hills owe their persistence to the resistance which their rock presents to weathering, and also to its horizontal pseudo-bedding. The first condition is essential, the second is subsidiary. There are masses with inclined pseudo-bedding which are yet stable, but it is a great source of weakness where the joint planes are open. The pseudo-bedding is either close set, dividing the rock into thin lamellae; or, at the other extreme, far spaced, producing layers of several feet in depth; every possible intermediate form is to be found. The views already given, of Littaford, Brae, Little Lynx and Thurlestone Tors (Plates 2 and 3) give examples varying from the structure which I designate 'massive' to that which I call 'lamellar'.

The cross-jointing, vertical or steeply inclined, is also variable. More usually two sets of vertical joints are present, in planes approximately perpendicular each to each. These, with the massive type of bedding, divide the rock into approximately rectangular masses, which simulate squared stones of cyclopean masonry. But vertical joints may occur which meet at acute angles. In the more lamellar masses the frequency of the planes of pseudo-bedding is accompanied by the rarity of vertical joints, and, in extreme cases, one set only of these may be developed. Chat Tor (Pl. 8) is fairly typical of the infrequent joints which accompany close-set bedding. Blackingstone Rock is coarsely lamellar, the lamellae are horizontal at the summit, and slope steeply with the hill-side to the north (Pl. 9A). Traces of an east and west set of joints will be seen in the near part of the mass figured: this view is taken looking N. 88° E. In the next view (Pl. 9B), looking N. 24°W., a set of well-marked vertical joints will be seen parting the apparently unbroken mass shown in the first photograph. This affords an instance of the development of one set of parallel joints to the almost complete exclusion of others. Blackingstone is perhaps the finest example of a dome-shaped tor.

At the other extreme we get such stacks as Bowerman's Nose (Pl. 10A), and the steeples of Staple Tor (Pl. 10B).

Both pseudo-bedding and joints are, in their origin, but planes of weakness. It is reserved for the weather to develop them. The parting may have been complete, but contact was not broken before the meteoric agencies took a hand in their development. Sometimes no more than a superficial groove marks the bedding or joint; sometimes the rock is worn back by the removal of the angles until a rectangular block has become a rounded mass, and in this way logan stones have been formed. Closely adjacent to the rock-basin on Mis Tor is a mass of rock which has been completely rounded in this manner (Pl. 11A); the height from the grass to the top of the block is 7 ft. Thornworthy Tor (Pl. 11B) is similar, but on a larger scale; the height from grass to the top of the block being 12 ft.

This suppression of angles naturally arises from the fact that at the angle the weather can work from two faces at once and, consequently, with greater effect. When the angle has been completely suppressed, the action becomes uniform over the whole surface, except that it is always more marked on the face exposed to the prevalent rain-bearing wind. Hard as granite may be, it yields to the beat of the weather; and on many a tor it would be possible to determine the approximate compass direction, on the darkest and most overcast night, merely by ascertaining the face of rock which was deepest graved by the weather, which would at once give the direction from which blows the south-west wind. In truly lamellar masses the contrast between lee side and weather side is best marked, as at Thurlestone Tor (Pl. 3B).

The tors sometimes show wide partings at vertical joints; partings which are not due to the loss of rock by weathering, but to movement in the rock mass. Slight partings might be supposed to have been caused by the action of frost, the blocks being wedged asunder by ice; but no frosts such as are now experienced could cause formerly contiguous blocks to move apart to the extent of several feet, and here we have a problem.

Two illustrations may be given, one from East Mill Tor (Pl. 12A) and another from Oke Tor (Pl. 12B). In the latter instance the matter is complicated by a slab of rock having been dragged after the moving block, and now bridging the gap. On Oke Tor some of the partings are as much as 4½ ft in width. Many explanations may be suggested. Mere slip under gravity is out of the question: the movement takes place on horizontal surfaces of rock, and the friction would itself retain the blocks in place on steep inclines. We may be dealing with earthquake effects, but that seems unlikely considering the precarious poise of many of the rock groupings which have survived. Lightning may have been the cause of movement, and, indeed, I have found fused surfaces coated with 'fulgurite' but not in connexion with these partings.

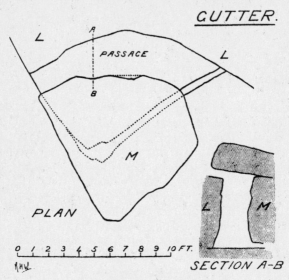

FIG. 4. Gutter, Plym Valley.
Parting in rocks of tor. Plan and section.

If, however, we may believe that a much colder climate once ruled Dartmoor, and shrouded it in a snow-field; then in the mass of ice and snow, we may see the wedges which drove apart the component blocks of the tors. Some examples of parting would still be left to be explained as due to other causes. For instance, there is a passage under a capping of rock on Gutter Tor, a plan and view of which form Fig. 4 and Pl. 13B respectively. It appears that the action of snow and ice is here precluded by the protection afforded by the complete covering. The parting is a breakage rather than the development of a joint or series of joints; and lightning may have been the agent. There is now no apparent continuing movement. I incised marks in the rock on either side of the gap, and in the past twenty-six years their distance has not varied.[1]

[1] If Dr. D. P. Wilson's photograph (Pl. 13B), taken in 1952, is compared with that originally published by the author, taken at least 23 years before, there is still no evidence of change. (ED.)

Some of the earlier writers speak of the spheroidal structure of granite, for which I know no evidence. Probably they were misled by the complete rounding of the edges of blocks, such as that shown in Pl. 11A, on Mis Tor. Not only subaerial weathering produces this effect. In all considerable areas of growan there are to be found masses of more resistant granite, frequently in boulder form; and where 'growanization' attacks more solid rock it proceeds along the joints and bedding, penetrating into the mass and dividing it into isolated blocks, the angles of which are rounded off in the same manner that weathering rounds the edges of surface exposures. A cutting into an old quarry at Inga Tor, near the Princetown railway, affords examples.

At places the removal of growan by denudation leaves these hard cores as surface boulders, and many of the large rounded masses found on the hillsides are such residuals. Pl. 13A shows two such masses near the Princetown railway, in Yes Tor Bottom.

In connexion with the supposed spheroidal structure of the Dartmoor granite it may be remarked that, did such structure exist, it must exercise a great influence on the work of the stone mason, who would have to count with it at every turn, as he now counts with the natural rectangular 'cleavage'. In fact, he finds that granite cleaves in true planes, always provided that he has regard to its 'grain'.

Surface blocks are also derived from the falling apart of the rock masses which crown the hills. Acres may be covered with the debris from one tor, so thickly piled that no soil has accumulated between the blocks, and no vegetation is seen. Such rock fields are known as 'clitters'. The blocks are frequently subangular, but may be well rounded. Clitters are not confined to the base of the granite masses, they frequently occur at some distance from any rock exposure. When so occurring they are at times demonstrably the last relics of a hillside tor that has wholly perished; but this explanation will not always serve. It is thus not the presence of single boulders that has to be explained, but the accumulation of a mass of boulders at one point. The colder climate of the ice-age, with its probable Dartmoor snow-field, affords an explanation which has been accepted by many; even an ice-field or snow-field, although not attaining the dignity of a glacier, may have its equivalent of glacial moraines; and its surface would certainly afford greater opportunity for block travel than does the present soil-covered moor.

The clitters whose principal axes lie along the hillsides, approximately on al evel contour, appear to have attracted most attention. There is, however, another form, in which from the principal confusion of blocks at the foot of the rocky tor there radiate, downhill, long, somewhat attenuated lines of blocks and boulders. So marked are these on Hen Tor, in the Plym Valley, that I formerly described them as rough banks formed by primitive man, who gathered the scattered boulders into rudely parallel lines, a theory which I now recognize as unsustainable. Hen Tor is a hillside tor, to the west the ground slopes from the tor to the Plym, on the east the ground slopes toward the tor from the higher land near Shavercombe Head. That gravity has much to do with the formation of clitters is shown by the fact that the amazing clitter of this hill lies wholly to the west of the rocks, and beyond the true clitter the lines to which I have referred extend yet farther downhill. Pl. 14B gives a view of the clitter of the tor, and Pl. 14A shows some indication of the linear arrangement of boulders. If we may assume that the supposed snow-field drifted with the gradient of the hill, westward, then it seems possible to identify the origin of each line of boulders with a point on the tor especially rich in its yield of broken rock; and this, I think, is the explanation. Mr. Gerhard Albers, of Hamburg, in an interesting paper on the clitters of Dartmoor, invokes the effect of deep frost penetrating the subsoil as an aid in explaining hill-creep and clitter formation, and cites the effect of this agent to-day in Spitzbergen (*T.D.A.*, Vol. 62, pp. 373–8).

A curious localized effect of weathering is the formation of rock-basins. These are basins or pans, of no great depth, hollowed in the surface of the granite. There is usually a regularity of form which simulates man's workmanship, and their artificial origin has been strenuously maintained. The Dartmoor Druid was a wholly artificial product, given to practices of lustration, of sprinkling holy water, and of human sacrifice accompanied by the disgusting habit of catching the blood of the victim. His originators seized with eagerness upon the rock-basins as the sacred receptacles by him formed and appointed for the various uses which his supposed practices suggested. The battle has been fought, and the geologists have won; these basins are now fully recognized as of natural formation. A weak felspar crystal is split along its cleavages by frost, its fragments are loosened, and later removed by the wind, and there is left a small hollow in which water may lodge. Further frosts attack the margin of the hollow, which extends in area and in depth. The process continues, lodgement of water, formation of ice, thaw leaving broken crystals, wind removing loose fragments. The final product is a rock-basin. With this origin there should be wide variation in size; and, indeed, I may note Gidleigh Tor, where there are several basins, of which the largest and best formed is oval in plan, measuring 32 in. by 22 in. and 5 in. in depth; while the smallest is 4½ in. by 4 in., and 1¼ in. deep.

That basins are still forming and growing seems most probable, but there are indications that the same colder conditions, to which reference has more than once been made, had a great part in the formation of all the larger examples, and that few have attained any real magnitude which do not date their origin to the days when the glacial period had but recently passed, or was yet passing.

If the Geological Survey memoir (sheet 338) were right, and on the whole question of rock-basins it is in frequent error, then most of the basins would be of very recent origin; for the statement is made that

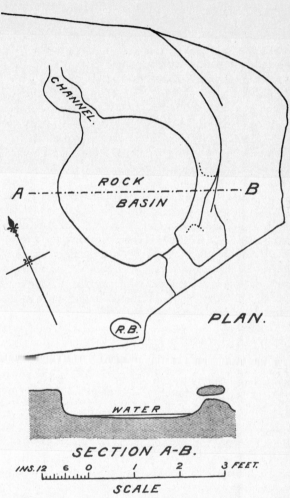

MISTOR PAN.

PLAN.

SECTION A-B.

SCALE

FIG. 5 Plan and section of rock-basin known as 'Mistor Pan'.

the shallower examples are probably deepening at the rate of a tenth of an inch in a year. My forty years' observation is wholly out of accord with this statement, and the matter can be carried far further than my memory permits.

We may take the well-conditioned example known as 'Mistor Pan'. A rock called by this name is given in the perambulation of 1609 as one of the bounds of the Forest; yet earlier, in 1291, the same name occurs in a charter of Isabella, Countess of Albemarle. There is thus written evidence from which we may gather that this was a well-marked object nearly six and a half centuries ago.[1]

In 1802, Bray describes it as 3 ft in diameter, and 6 in. in depth, the bottom flat and smooth, with a channel and lip to the north-east. In 1828, Rowe states the diameter as 3 ft, and the depth as 8 in. In 1858, Ormerod gives its diameter from N. to S. as 36 in. and from E. to W. 35 in.; the height of the sides 4 in. on the N., 5 in. on the S., and 6 in. on the E. and W. The centre half an inch below the level at the sides. Miss Sophia Dixon, writing in 1875, assigns to it a diameter of 3 ft, and a depth of 8 in. My measurements, taken in 1929, were 3 ft in diameter, and 7 in. in depth.

Allowing for slight divergence in the method of measuring the depth, it becomes obvious that there has been no appreciable change in this basin in the course of the last hundred and thirty years. It is such a well-known object, and so unique in its documentary record, that I have prepared a plan and section (Fig. 5), and have also given a view (Pl. 15A). It will be noted from the section that the basin, after piercing the first bed of granite, and excavating into the lower bed, has eaten its way through the side between the layers. It has also excavated along a joint and so formed a lip or channel.

As another instance of unchanging form I would cite the basin on Littaford Tor, described by Bray in 1802, as being in shape a rude oval, about 20 in. long, 18 in. wide, and 6 in. deep, and terminating in a point or lip. My measurements are 22 in. by 20 in. and 4 in. deep, and I agree as to the lip. Even if there has been a horizontal extension of this basin since Bray measured it, which is doubtful, it certainly has not deepened. This class of evidence could be multiplied; nowhere does it point to any appreciable increase in depth within the time of record.

If a basin has a lip or channel, by which it is partially drained, that channel is always developed along the trace of a vertical joint. If its sides are undercut, the undercutting is always connected with a bedding joint. The joint planes are lines of weakness in this as in other forms of weathering.

I give, as a good example of a rock-basin drained by a channel, a view and plan of the basin on Gutter, or Gut Tor, in the Plym Valley. The basin is about 34 in. long, it is difficult to define the point at which the basin ends and the channel begins; its extreme width is 22 in., and it is 10 in. in depth at the centre. The channel reaches the full depth of

---

[1] On O.S. maps the name is erroneously applied to part of the moor to the NE of the tor. (ED.)

the basin. There is a small companion, about 9 in. in diameter and 3 in. in depth, drained by a shallow channel (Pl. 17B and Fig. 6 in text).

The Geological Survey is mistaken in asserting that all the deeper basins are partially drained by channels. One of the deepest is situate on Kes Tor. It was discovered by Ormerod, and at the time of discovery was filled with peat and stone. Ormerod had it cleared of this deposit, and was told that it had been filled about a hundred years before, as presenting a small pool dangerous to sheep. Leaving it

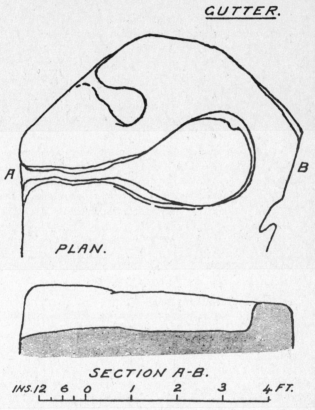

FIG. 6. Plan and section of rock-basin on Gutter, Plym Valley.

cleared, he had a railing erected around it. The modern tripper found it a convenient repository for his broken bottles, and, lest these should not fill the basin sufficiently quickly, he added stones and other rubbish. In 1930 I had it cleared once more. There is no channel draining this basin, which reaches a depth of 30 in. It passes through two layers of the pseudo-bedding, and has penetrated a third to the depth of 11 in. The water surface when the basin is full is 8 ft in length from N. to S., and 6 ft 8 in. wide from E. to W. Fig. 7 gives a plan and section of this basin, and Pl. 15B a bird's-eye view. The undercutting of the sides where each bedding joint is pierced will be clearly seen. The bottom of the basin is level. At the time that it was last cleared there was a gale of wind blowing, and snow was falling thickly; as a result, when the

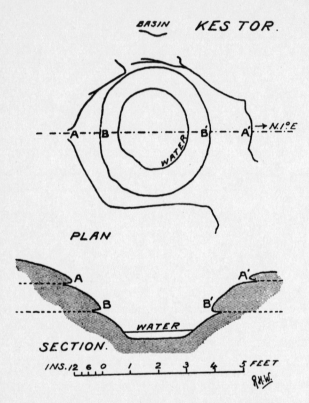

FIG. 7. Plan and section of large rock-basin on Kestor.

measurements were taken, two days later, about 3 in. of water stood in the bottom. Ormerod found that, from September 1856 to March 1858, it was never empty of water. Considering the depth of water which it can hold, and would hold in every winter, the defence which this would provide against frost, and the shelter which the floor enjoys as against the wind, it must be supposed that the origin of this basin and its growth to the present size, must be attributed to very different conditions of climate to those which now prevail; although after my experience of the 19th of April 1930, I will not deny the latter considerable severity.

All the rock-basins of Dartmoor are sunk in surfaces which are exposed to the full beat of the weather, and which were originally practically level; all are in comparatively coarsely porphyritic granite. Some have pierced the rocks in which they have formed; some have eaten their way through the parent block in a horizontal direction, as for instance at Rules Tor or Roose Tor in the Walkham Valley; some have grown until they have broken in upon adjacent basins. There are instances in which the slab which carries the basin has fallen from its original position, and is now inclined. Bray noted such a case at Over Tor, above Merivale. I might add another at Fox Tor, where there are two basins, partly coalescent, in a fallen block. An interesting example is afforded by a slab on Rundlestone Tor, the original 'Rundlestone', so-called from the roundels of two basins upon its surface. This rock has moved from a level to an inclined position, and the growth of one basin thereupon ceased, but the other could still hold some water, and continued its growth, with the notable feature that its floor is now level,

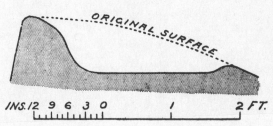

FIG. 8. Section of rock-basin in inclined slab at Rundlestone.

and no longer parallel to the surface of the slab; thus indicating that the level floor is not conditioned by the structure of the rock, but by the formative agents. Fig. 8 gives a cross-section.

Although the temptation is great to multiply examples, the above must serve as illustrating the principal features; and those interested may well consult Ormerod's paper in the *Transactions of the Geological Society*, vol. 15, p. 16 *et seq.* It is admittedly incomplete, but it is an example of how such work should be done.

I have spoken of the yield of granite to the disintegrating action of the weather. That is one side of the tale: if it is true that for many of the observed effects we must call in aid the climate of glacial and near-glacial times, then the resistance of the rock must also be recognized. Until within the last century and a half quarried granite was almost unknown. The masons used the best and hardest of the surface blocks and they have proved to afford a very reliable material, probably because they represent the survivors in a natural selection which eliminated those unfit to stand exposure.

All the blocks used in the construction of hut-circles and the rude stone monuments of the Early Bronze Age were surface stone, and there is no evidence that they have suffered from their long exposure. The variety of form available in these naturally quarried blocks, must have been a great assistance to the early builders; it arose from the varied nature of the jointing. To take the neighbourhood of Princetown— Lakehead Hill and Belliver Tor supply slabs of large area and relatively slight thickness, which were used for kistvaens and at a much later date for the 'posts' of Postbridge. (A recent suggestion that Postbridge is the bridge carrying the postman is charmingly mistaken: it is the bridge the spans of which are granite 'pawsts'.) From the one extreme of slabs we may turn to the other, where length is combined with small sectional area. Such stones were used for the menhirs. One of the summit blocks of Littaford Tor, still *in situ*, measures 16 ft 6 in. in length, 2ft 6 in. in width, and 10 in. in thickness. Every variety in shape is available in almost every locality; and sometimes the jointing is sufficiently regular to give the impression of blocks squared and dressed by the mason, such are to be seen in the Grey Wethers stone circles (p. 258).

Before leaving the question of the tors it is well to warn the unwary that estimates of height have frequently been published which have been grotesquely inaccurate. Take, for instance, Bowerman's Nose (Pl. 10A). This stack was described by Polwhele as attaining a height of 50 ft. Rowe corrects this and says that it barely stands 40 ft above the clitter, Page also says nearly 40 ft, Crossing agrees with Rowe and Page—the *actual height* is 21 ft 6 in. on the one side, and 26 ft on the other. The highest rock mass on Dartmoor is Vixen Tor, which stands 52 ft above the ground from which it rises on the north side, and 93 ft on the south side, where the ground is 40 ft lower.

THE BORDER HILLS

Many of the border hills are formed of altered slate, and these as a rule present much steeper slopes than do the granite heights. The material withstands the effects of weather, and is not liable to the alteration to growan, which softens the slopes of granite. There are exceptions, Tavy Cleave, the Dewerstone Valley and the slopes of Leather Tor for instance, where the granite hills compete with any on Dartmoor or its borders in gradient. But, in general, the gorges and the steep hillsides are in the altered sedimentary rocks. The contrast between granite and sedimentary contours is sometimes emphasized by immediate contact. Thus Great Nodden stands at the foot of the slope of Great Lynx Tor, springing from the riverside with almost startling abruptness, its form emphasized by sombre colour (Pl. 16A). The little river Lyd has been the agent which primarily brought this slope into being. The actual contour of the hill has been determined by denudation; and the substance lost in rounding the slopes is still to be seen, in part, in the screes whose ultimate destination is the stream, from the bed of which the stones are cleared by occasional floods. The Lyd still frets the foot of the hill, with what must now be but slight effect.

Other well known hills in metamorphic rocks bound the Meldon valleys north of Yes Tor, and form the gorge of the Teign at Fingle.

The bold peaks of Sourton Tors, which bound the in-country of North Devon, rise from three dykes of igneous rock on a base of altered slates and shales; while on the south of Dartmoor, Brent Hill is almost wholly igneous in origin; its namesake, Brent Tor, on the west, being igneous also; and both deriving name from their abrupt contour.

It is notable that, where granite and border rock meet on the same hill, the border rock more frequently reaches the greater absolute elevation. Thus, the calc-flintas of Peak Hill form a peak above the level of the granite of Sharp Tor and Leather Tor; while the slates of Round Hill, on Ringmoor, are higher than the granite of Gutter Tor. To some forms of denudation the granite is the less resistant. It will be seen later that this is not true of river action.

RIVERS AND STREAMS

Rivers and streams radiate in every direction from both the north and the south highlands. In the south the centre of radiation is a point approximately three-quarters of a mile north of the summit of Greenhill and nearly a mile south-east from Fox Tor, at an elevation of 1,580 ft. In the north it lies a little over a quarter of a mile east from Cranmere Pool, the elevation being approximately 1,825 ft. These points are thus the true centres of their respective highlands, physically but not geometrically.

By far the greater part of the rain which falls on Dartmoor finds its way to the English Channel; the Taw and the Ockment with their tributaries alone discharge their waters on the north coast. Of the whole granite area no more than 16·3 sq. miles lie within a watershed which drains to the Bristol Channel.

The rainfall is certainly sufficient to ensure a high mean yield of the streams; but much of the water comes off in floods, and the dry-weather flow is at the best no more than one-ninth of the mean flow, while in some streams it is less still. Floods, on the other hand, if ordinary, may attain a rate of flow 39 to 40 times that of the mean, or say 350 times the dry weather flow. These figures exclude from consideration either extreme droughts or those catastrophic floods which visit any locality once only in many centuries. Such a flood, from a relatively small watershed, say not more than one square mile, may, at its peak, attain a value 3,900 times the rate of flow in a dry, but not extremely dry, year. A flood of this extreme character occurred on the Redaven, a tributary of the West Ockment, on the 17 August 1917. A full account of this storm is given in *Trans. Devon. Assn.*, vol. 50, pp. 234–42. (See also Appendix I of this book, p. 438.)

In the matter of minimum flow, at times of the extremest drought, the majority of the Dartmoor streams are very favourably placed as compared with the general run of British rivers. Engineers have adopted a very convenient unit for stating the yield of a watershed, one cubic foot of water per second per thousand acres, hereinafter known as a 'cusec'. In round numbers a cubic foot per second equals 540,000 gallons a day. Now the principal streams of Dartmoor, the watersheds of which are neither very large nor very small, yield at extreme drought not less than 0·7 cusecs, or 378,000 gallons a day for each thousand acres of catchment. There are some which have never fallen so low; there are others which yield much less. Especially is the flow relatively small in the Eastern Division, from which Torquay obtains its supply. Here the Trenchford stream falls to 0·146 cusec, and the record of the Blackingstone stream stands somewhat higher, at 0·158 cusec, equivalent, respectively, to 78,840 and 85,320 gallons per day from each thousand acres. The variation is great, and, from the point of view of public water supply, of the utmost importance. It is not the Torquay watershed which is unusual in its characteristics, but the other more favoured Dartmoor areas which yield far above the average of British gathering grounds.

Another feature of importance, especially where storage is to be constructed, is the percentage of the actual rainfall which ultimately finds its way to the stream. This, in a normal year, may be as high as 92% on many Dartmoor rivers, but at Trenchford it is no more than 59·3%, and the Blackingstone stream, better in this as in minimum flow, secures 66% of the rainfall.

There can be no doubt that the actual intensity of the rainfall is a great feature in determining how much of the available rain shall find its way to the stream. Assuming in the first place that the loss by evaporation and vegetative transpiration were a constant of, say, 16 in. in the year, and that the surplus, after deducting this constant, fed the stream. Then a watershed with a rainfall of 70 in. would yield to the stream 54 in., or about 71½%, while where the rainfall did not exceed 40 in., the share received by the stream would be 24 in., or 60%. But this is not the whole explanation of the difference. The watershed with 70 in. of rain per annum permits at least 92% to find its way to the river, largely because the ground is never dried to any material depth, and at certain seasons, and those of heaviest rainfall, it is practically saturated for months at a time. From the saturated ground the rain comes near to running off as it falls. So that, while 16 in. is not far wrong as an assumed loss in catchments of smaller rainfall, the actual depth of rain lost on the upper watershed of the Yealm, in a year when the rainfall was 77·48 in., was no more than 6·16 in. The same condition of saturation, which leads to the rain flowing freely from the surface, conduces also to the formation of peat; the presence of which, in turn, conserves such rain as is absorbed by the ground, and enhances the dry weather flow of the streams. Thus, here as elsewhere, it is true that to those who have shall be given.

I have said that much of the total annual flow of the streams passes off as flood water. The floods rise with great rapidity, and fall but little less rapidly. I may take as an example the flood of midnight, 24 November 1929, from 800 acres catchment at the head of the Yealm. The rainfall which caused the peak of this flood cannot have been more than 2 in., but the ground was already fully saturated. Prior to the flood the river was falling, and had reached a flow at the rate of 5,682,000 gallons a day. In 2 hrs and 30 min. from the commencement of the flood the peak flow had been attained, and that was at the rate of 134,000,000 gallons a day. The last hour of the rise added 101,000,000 gallons a day to the rate of flow. The peak flow was maintained for a bare quarter of an hour, and then the fall began. In one hour the added flow due to the storm had fallen to 58% of its highest value, and in 2 hrs to 36%, shortly after which renewed rain checked the fall.

But from the other records we know that, in the absence of further rain, 5 hrs would have seen the reduction of the added flow to less than 10% of highest, 10 hrs to less than $2\frac{1}{2}$%, and 15 hrs to less than 1%.

It has often been said that there has, within living memory, been a change in the habit of the Dartmoor rivers. That the floods now rise more quickly, and fall with greater rapidity. I know no evidence in support of this assertion, and by 'evidence' I mean record, and not un-supported recollection. There has certainly been no physical change which could account for change in habit.

I have said that at times of saturation a large part of the rain passed direct to the river. This is true, and yet the proportion so passing may be less than the proportion estimated on the whole year, wet and dry. Taking a slightly wet year, the 800 acres on the Yealm yielded to the river 92% of the rain which they received. In November 1929, the wettest November on record, when the rainfall was 21·06 in., the river received no more than 85·37% of the rainfall, but the missing percentage was not lost to the stream in the ultimate: it went by way of deferred flow to swell the yield of the succeeding month.

November and December 1926 illustrate this point. That November was unduly wet, the rainfall being 14·31 in.; and the succeeding month was remarkably dry, the rainfall of December 1926 being but 1·22 in. The yield of the river in December was 28,976,563 gallons in excess of that which would account for the total rainfall of the month, the excess being equivalent to 76%. More than this, we can say that, starting as it did at a flow of 3,019,329 gallons a day, even if there had been an absolute drought throughout the month of December, the river would have yielded 39,830,000 gallons during the month. Thus, although flood waters are soon apparently exhausted, they leave a deferred flow, small in amount compared with their torrents, but of very real value and effect. (See Appendix I, p. 431.)

It is common ground that a large percentage of the available rain flows off in many Dartmoor streams, and that the dry weather flow in extreme droughts is unusually large. It has been sought to connect these ascertained facts directly with the storage capacity of the peat covering the moor. It is alleged that the peat becomes supersaturated in wet weather, and yields up the surplus water as a deferred flow. Experience and experiment both fail to support this suggestion.

The topmost layer of peat is usually fibrous, and of somewhat open texture; in this layer a certain temporary storage of water is possible. The pores are too large to retain all the water which is required to fill them, and this gradually drains away, and feeds the streams. The lower layers of the peat have the appearance of compact, homogeneous material. They contain about 76% of their dry weight of fine fibre, but this is set in a paste of humic substance, largely colloidal. When saturated the bottom peat contains 87% by weight of water, which may be described as 'tangled' in the colloids, and which may be dried out, but will not drain out.

When, therefore, it is stated that peat contains on the average $5\frac{1}{2}$ gallons of water per cubic foot, this is true, but the inference cannot be drawn that it is free to yield up a material part of this water by drainage, and again absorb a corresponding amount from the rainfall. To a slight extent supersaturation can occur, and a mass of peat is not wholly impermeable to water, but the frictional resistance to the passage of water is great.

From the moist surface of the peat the rain runs off readily to the streams. Water may be seen standing on peat lands after showers which would have been wholly absorbed by ordinary soil.

Beneath the peat lies the growan, and this affords the true storage of the Dartmoor catchments. Assuming the peat to become as far supersaturated as is possible, the surplus water can reach the river either by traversing the peat throughout, to do which it must pass through the whole breadth parallel to the surface and overcome a tremendous frictional resistance; or it can pass down through a few feet of peat and reach the growan, in which there is ample pore space for storage, and in which the frictional resistance to be overcome on the way to the river is much less.

It is not infrequently found that below the peat there are several feet of growan above an 'iron pan', this latter marking the level at which constant saturation occurs. The growan above this level is alternately saturated and drained, and it drains to the river. The water temporarily stored in the growan is preserved from evaporation by the wet blanket of peat above it. Were it not for this it would be constantly brought to the surface by capillarity, and there evaporated.

Peat, therefore, is a great agent in promoting the yield of the Dartmoor catchments, but it does not act as a reservoir in itself. When compact peat has once been thoroughly frozen, or when peat lands have been brought under cultivation, the relative impermeability of the substance is permanently lost, and its value as a watershed covering is lost also. Mere peaty soil has none of the peculiar characteristics of true bog peat.

The chief plants which grow on the bogs, as opposed to peaty soils, are xerophytes, and their transpiration makes no heavy call on the ground waters. In this respect the afforestation of the peat lands, could this be accomplished, would prove a source of loss; and, not only would the leaves of the trees rob the ground, but the lesser showers would be wholly expended in wetting the leaves, which would then part with the water by evaporation.

Where the rivers and streams leave the moor they pass from the granite to the altered sedimentary rocks; and the slopes of the valley sides usually become steeper; at times the river occupies a gorge with almost perpendicular cliffs. Gorges are not necessarily confined to the sedimentary rocks. The Avon between Shipley and Didworthy bridges flows in a channel deep cut in fine-grained granite, the repeated jointing of which divides it into small blocks, and aids erosion. The finest example of such a gorge, in sedimentary rock, is on the Lyd at Lydford. The mechanism of excavation is here very clearly seen: the gorge is a series of confluent pot-holes. The stream provided the power, the moor found the tools, which were pebbles and boulders of granite; and the local rock has been sufficiently hard and compact, while yielding to the river-granite drill, to retain the tool marks. The cliff side of the gorge presents arc after arc, parts of the original circumference of the pot-holes. On a smaller scale the process may be seen in operation at St. Nighton's Kieve, near Boscastle. There is also a gorge on the Yealm, in the woods at Hawns and Dendles, while the short but steep valley of the Shavercombe Brook, a tributary of the Plym, is of the same nature.

Small waterfalls are frequently formed at the junction of the granite and the sedimentary rocks. Here the smaller mass of the constituent blocks, marked out by the joints in the sedimentary rocks, plays its part, and affords the streams better facilities for excavation. The little fall on the Shavercombe is an example (Pl. 16B).

On their course through the sedimentary rocks in the vicinity of the granite the rivers occasionally meet granite veins across their track. These veins reinforce the neighbouring rock, and strengthen its resistence to erosion, and so, by creating ridges in the river bed, give rise to minor falls. So frequently does this occur that I have learnt to locate the granite veins by their effect on the contour of the bed of the streams.

If, off the granite, the valleys become more abrupt, within the bounds of the granite area they at places open out to broad flats. As the water-falls have origin in the strength of the granite, so the valley flats reveal its weakness. Kaolinization and alteration to growan are alike in one respect. Both greatly lessen the resistance of the rock to stream action; and, although both clay and growan frequently 'go to hill', yet here and there they occur on a river course, and the stream, wandering from side to side, creates for itself a broad valley. At Broadamarsh, the granite is in part kaolinized, in part changed to growan, and the name of that section of the valley of the East Dart is sufficiently descriptive of the form which it has taken. Very similar conditions probably obtain at Fox Tor Mire, there is known to be clay in the neighbourhood, and Whiteworks Mine bears a name which suggests that kaolinization was found to be somewhat marked. The flat above Cadover Bridge, on the Plym, is in kaolinized ground, but it is to be noted that the deposits of china clay which have proved commercially of value have been found, not in the valley flat, but where the clay has run to hill on the adjacent hillsides. In every instance some part of the flat is on growan, and not on clay.

Taw Marsh and the area known as Raybarrow Pool are further examples, the latter in a shallow valley very near a hill-top.

At Broadamarsh it appears probable that the whole course of the river through the marsh has been artificially lowered, in order that the tin-bearing gravels which overlay the softened rock could be more readily reached, and the strings of tin in the rock could be worked to a shallow depth.

Considerable deposits of small boulders and gravel are found under these marshes, and wherever a valley appreciably widens. But terrace gravels, stranded above the present levels of the river beds, are absent in the granite area. They occur along the courses of the streams after the sedimentary rocks have been reached; as for instance in the slopes of a railway cutting in front of Great Aish, at South Brent, where the gravels are about 50 ft above the present river bed; and on the other bank of the Avon by the roadside from the station to Lydia Bridge, near the Vicarage, at approximately the same height above the river.

The head of angular and subangular stones which usually overlies the kaolinized granite is not a river gravel, where found at any point except the floor of the valley. These stones are commonly called 'bluetts', sufficiently descriptive of their colour, they are quartz-schorl rocks derived from the denudation of the higher levels of the clay.

CLIMATE AND RAINFALL

We know too little of the climate of Dartmoor. By repute it is at times inclement, and Risdon apologizes for having detained his readers overlong on a place so wild, with so slender repast, where it is to be doubted they have taken the cold, or the cold hath caught them. From which it is clear that he had seen little of the moor, or he would have known that one may be 'properly shrammed with the cold' thereon, but catch a cold one can not.

The temperature is that which may be expected at the elevation. Thus, assuming a vertical temperature gradient of one degree Fahrenheit for every 300 ft, we may compare Princetown with Torquay. The mean temperature at Torquay, at an elevation of 12 ft O.D. is 51·1°, Princetown lies at 1,359 feet O.D., and the mean temperature should accordingly be four and a half degrees lower, or 46·6°. As given in the Meteorological Office's *Book of Normals* it is 46·2°, a close approximation.

The mean of the minima for the year is 45·6° at Torquay and 40·9° at Princetown, again a close approximation to the theoretical relation. The mean of maxima for the year is 56·6° at Torquay, and 51·4° at Princetown, showing that there is rather more difference in this respect than theory would suggest. If Sidmouth, instead of Torquay, had been taken as the standard the result would have been:

	Princetown as recorded	Princetown as calculated on basis of Sidmouth record
Maxima	51·4°	51·9°
Minima	40·9°	40·0°
Mean	46·2°	46·0°

In the matter of temperature, therefore, Dartmoor enjoys to the full the benefit of being a part, although admittedly a high part, of our favoured county.

The rainfall is certainly high, and the rainy days many. In 1929 there were 199 wet days at Princetown, as opposed to an average of 161 for the rest of Devon. It is perhaps hardly fair to take the conditions at Princetown as representative of the whole of Dartmoor, since it is nearly the wettest spot on the moor.

We have further to admit that, above the level of 1,200 ft, fog and mist are frequent. But the heavy rainfall is the price that we pay for the Dartmoor rivers; and, if an occasional wanderer is astray in the mist, without it our Dartmoor novelists would be lost indeed.

Relative to level the rainfall is heaviest on the south-west side of the moor, but heavy mean annual rainfall occurs at most stations along, and south of, a line drawn through the summits of Peak Hill in the west and Kestor in the east. North of this line, although the ground is higher, the rainfall lessens although remaining high.

The southern district and a narrow adjoining strip of the northern are the wettest, the eastern district is materially drier.

The heavier falls occur on the lee sides of the hills, and the heaviest on the lee of the first hills rising to 1,400 ft which meet the south-west wind. After this maximum the precipitation decreases although the ground may still be rising. The following table, showing a traverse from Plymouth to Devil's Tor will illustrate the point. Elevation is stated to the nearest foot, and rainfall to the nearest half-inch:

Station	Total Distance miles	Elevation feet	Rainfall inches
Plymouth, Drake's Place	0	149	38½
Plymouth, Hartley	1¼	321	44½
Roborough Reservoir	5¼	548	48
Burrator	9¼	755	62
Leedon Tor	12	1,165	64
Princetown	13¾	1,359	81
(Here is the valley of the Blackabrook)			
Cowsic Valley	16	1,352	74
Devil's Tor	17¾	1,785	53½

The distance in a straight line from Drake's Place to Devil's Tor is 17¼ miles. The stations are not rigidly in alignment.

Of these stations Princetown meets the condition of being in the lee of the first 1,400 ft ridge, Cowsic Valley is at approximately the same level, but in a valley rising facing the wind, and the rise continues unbroken to Devil's Tor. The line of traverse bears N. 24° E. It is unfortunate that little is known of the rainfall in the north quarter. With the growing utilization of the watersheds on the south for water supply we are now near a sufficient knowledge of the rainfall in that part.

We are fully informed as to the rainfall in the Eastern District, where the Torquay Corporation has long maintained gauges. The mean annual rainfall on the Torquay Watershed is approximately 34 in. This is less than half the fall enjoyed by the other Dartmoor catchments, which are used for water supply purposes, and the deficiency is obviously one of the elements making for the small minimum flow in drought, and the relatively small proportion of the rain which finds its way to the streams (0·19 cusecs as against 0·7 for the catchments with larger rainfall, and 62% of the available rain in the stream, as against 90 to 92%).

GEOLOGY

Many years ago I paused in the production of a series of papers on the petrography of Dartmoor, on the ground that the matter could not be adequately treated except with a detailed knowledge of the whole area. Here and now I have no intention of giving other than such slight sketch of the geology as may serve to illustrate or explain the preceding notes.

Many have been the workers on Dartmoor geology, and to all we owe some debt. For this reason I regret that I must, as a matter of duty, voice a complaint as to the methods recently adopted.

In sixty years investigators have secured from the moor all the specimens which were necessary to their work, without leaving an unsightly scar. In a tenth of that time, in recent years, methods have been adopted which have blazed a trail of unnecessary disfigurement across the whole face of the moor. Heavy hammers, used without need, have broken from the tors weathered prominences and angles, in blocks of absurd size, so that I find in my notebook such entries as: "Little Mis Tor, this tor has been abominably served by (geologists)." Nor has the mischief ended with the tors, there is evidence that the damage to the prehistoric circle known as the 'Nine Maidens', at Belstone, was also caused by geological hammers, and one of the stones in the Merivale Avenues has been damaged in a similar manner. The revival of interest in the geology of the district is to be welcomed, but it has brought us visitors whose methods can but be deplored.

Dartmoor geology presents many disputed problems, among them the primary question: "How came the granite in its present position in respect of the surrounding sedimentary rocks?"

The relation of the apple to its pastry environment is said to have puzzled a royal personage who came to Devon, and met with that local product, the apple dumpling. To him there was an easy reply, which we may hope was at once comprehensible and satisfying. But the question as to the granite and its surroundings has never yet been completely answered by any capable and conscientious geologist to his own entire satisfaction, much less to the satisfaction of other geologists, capable and conscientious or otherwise. As far as it is accessible to observation, the Dartmoor granite is dome-shaped on its upper surface, and it is quite safe to call it a 'boss'. But there are geologists who assert that it is a 'laccolite', thus claiming knowledge or evidence of its form at greater depths where observation is impossible.

No one would venture on the simple solution of its hidden form that 'it goes all the way down'. It must, therefore, have a lower boundary, and that boundary have some shape. To call the mass a laccolite is to say that it is somewhat like a mushroom, with a head expanding horizontally where the strata of the sedimentary rocks have been parted to give it place, and that this lenticular head has some sort of stalk or stem which fills the channel by which the igneous rock ascended to supply the mass of the mushroom head. Presumedly the stalk would have been connected with some lower reservoir of molten rock, the form of which has not been suggested.

But the Dartmoor granite is one of a series of bosses which form the backbone of Devon, Cornwall, and the Isles of Scilly, and there is good evidence that these bosses are connected beneath the surface. If each is a laccolite, and each has its stem, the whole would bear resemblance to an articulated caterpillar with many legs. A description which, although quaint, must be admitted to be incapable of performing the *reductio ad absurdum.*

The alternative is that there exists an elongated mass of granite, irregular in shape, isolated and self-sufficient, not fed by any lower reservoir through either necks or dykes, and that the upper protuberances of this mass now reach the surface and form the granite bosses of Devon and Cornwall. This alternative I prefer.

But the supporters of the laccolite theory assert that only by the horizontal parting of the strata, and the injection of the granite, can it be possible to explain the manner in which the granite is bordered, here by Devonian strata, and there by rocks of Carboniferous age. If the strata had been raised in a great arch by the granite dome, then, they allege, the older formation should everywhere have bordered the granite.

The difficulty does not appear serious. It is to be remembered that the intrusion of the granite was but part of a great mountain-building movement, and not in itself the cause of the upheaval, and that it very probably came only in the later stages of that movement. The compression to which the rocks had been subjected had already intricately folded them, and there were no horizontal strata to be parted by the granite.

The question as to whether the granite acted as a punch or as a wedge is fair, since punches and wedges are the agents for the application of force, and not, in themselves, sources of energy. Clearly it was an external force, applied to sedimentary rocks and to granite alike, which placed the latter in its present position. I believe the answer to be that the action was wholly that of a wedge, operating along the whole length of the axis of Devon and Cornwall, and as far west as the Scilly Isles. All the principal felsitic dykes in the necks, between the bosses, lie parallel to that axis, and occupy cleavages caused by the underlying wedge. As examples may be named, the Roborough Down elvan, the Bickleigh elvan, and the Cann Quarry elvan. To the north of Dartmoor the Meldon aplite ranges south-west for two miles, parallel to the granite boundary, and on the south a similar rock, in a much smaller dyke, shows in a quarry at Bittaford, and also conforms in direction to the boundary. The petrological similarity between these two rocks has not hitherto been recorded. Their precise relationship to the granite is undetermined.

To some slight extent the upward movement of the granite was aided by its own surface action. There was some stoping, some breaking away of the surrounding rocks, or more probably the invasion of shatter belts preformed by the processes of elevation. To a limited extent this is evidenced by the presence of sedimentary and other foreign rocks in the granite, but the relative infrequency of such inclusions, and their small mass and volume compared with the granite, indicate that stoping was not a serious factor.

No doubt there was absorption and solution of the surrounding rocks by the igneous magma. This also must have been relatively slight, since the effect on the chemical composition of the granite, although noticeable over wide areas, is inconsiderable. New minerals appear in the granite where such absorption has taken place; pink almandite garnets, pinite pseudomorphs after cordierite, and andalusite are the accessory minerals of granite which has absorbed some of the neighbouring sedimentary rocks, and thereby gained an excess of alumina. Where these minerals are found there is always other evidence that the granite is not far below the original surface of contact. In the valley of the Erme several square miles are occupied by pinitic granite, with occasional garnets. And garnets are found at Burrator, at Swell Tor, and elsewhere. The andalusite is mainly confined to granitic veins in sedimentary rocks. The best example is a vein in the slates of Great Nodden.

The purely surface action of the process of solution was well shown in a block quarried at Burrator on the slopes of Yannadon. That had happened of which examples are to be found near the margins of some felsite dykes; the molten rock, in contact with the sedimentary rock, which it was penetrating, had taken into solution at its outer layer some part of the contact rock. Hence the outer layer varied considerably from the mass in its composition. Before the granite at the contact had chilled, the continued forward movement swept from the contact face the material which had acquired the foreign matter, and this material became involved in the flow, without mingling and loss of individuality. In consequence, planes of darker rock, with much black mica, now represent the flow of the contact granite drawn out into the general movement of the normal rock; as a jet of coloured water might persist in a quiet stream, travelling perhaps for yards before becoming lost in the current. These planes, in the block at Burrator, appeared on the faces as narrow veins, varying from an inch to two inches in width. In these veins, but nowhere else in the rock, were garnets, some as much as five-eighths of an inch in diameter. The detailed description is more complex, and well illustrates the local variations which occur in granite. [See pp. 55–6 and Fig. 9 in the chapter which follows (ED.)]. On Pl. 17A a photograph of a part of this block is reproduced.

There is a marked feature of the Dartmoor granite, its great variability in colour, grain, presence or absence of porphyritic felspars of large size, and general appearance. Combined with this there is an equally marked uniformity of composition, if we omit the 'accidents', such as absorption of contact rock, subsequent alteration by the action of vapours during the last stages of the igneous activity, and weathering. The old idea of differentiated types of varied age appears to have been somewhat revived of late. I cannot accept this. I believe the intrusion of the granite took place in one operation: I do not say without pause. A sheet anchor of these who demand seperate intrusions of varied composition has been the darker material which occurs either as rounded inclusions of very varied size, or mingled in complex flow-structure with the normal rock, or again in very large irregular masses. All these are marked by a high content of alumina, and all are capable of explanation as being residuals of the contact rock affected by the adjacent sedimentary rocks, from which they have taken some part in solution. It is a feature which can only properly be interpreted with a much wider and more detailed knowledge than has usually been brought to the task. In earlier days, and even in recent years, these inclusions have been spoken of as basic segregations.

Nor do I believe that, since its consolidation, the Dartmoor granite has been faulted, or that any of its valleys are fault valleys. It has stood an island of unchangeableness amid the earth movements which have taken place since its formation. The very regularity with which the pseudo-bedding conforms to the contour of hill and valley is sufficient evidence. In the earlier stages of cooling the joints, already formed, opened here and there to admit felsitic flows, and some of these flows were later in date than the tourmalinization of the faces of other joints; but this is all the movement which can be proved. The attempt to make tectonic capital out of the direction of the joints appears to me to be mistaken. The joints are local in their origin, governed by the conditions prevailing from point to point when the granite cooled, and a statistical treatment of all the varied directions which have been observed shows their orientation to be equally shared between all points of the compass.

The age of the granite is a less complex question, and one on which there is some degree of agreement. Obviously it is younger than the Carboniferous rocks, since it sends into them veins and apophyses, and has subjected them to thermo-metamorphism. It is older than the New Red Sandstone, in the conglomerates of which fragments of Dartmoor granite are found. Doubtless it was originally deep covered by the sedimentary rocks: its plutonic form demands such covering. It has been disputed that it pierced its cover to spread lava flows over the surrounding country; but the evidence of detrital deposits is strongly in favour of the former existence of a Dartmoor volcano.

In the geological ages which succeeded its intrusion the granite has stood as an island out of varied seas. The waters of the Cretaceous sea lapped its flanks, in succession to the Liassic waves. Of their deposits on its submerged slopes there remain but pebbles in certain detrital deposits.

In these last few pages I have, I believe, dealt with as much of the geology of Dartmoor as is necessary to an understanding of its physical geography. My aim has been to correlate points on which, in other sections, I have touched. There may be, and must be, in a review such as this, some repetition. In this I have not hesitated where I thought it demanded.

THE GRANITE OF DARTMOOR

TO approach an understanding of the structure of any land it is
necessary to have recourse to geological history, and the extent
of our knowledge of such history will determine the measure of
success. In one respect the geologist is happy beyond other historians:
his evidence may be incomplete but it cannot be impugned on any
ground of uncertainty: that rests with the interpretation only.

The rocks of the Devonian period in Devon are all of marine origin,
but are not necessarily the deposits of a deep sea. Thus, the Devonian
limestones of South Devon, Plymouth, Yealmpton, Ashburton, Newton Abbot and Torquay, are fossil coral reefs, and there is no sound
reason for the supposition that the species of coral which built those
reefs were capable of living and growing at any greater depth below
the surface than can the species now living. At a generous estimate this
would give a depth of forty fathoms to the waters in which the reefs
originated.

No similar approximation can be given to the limit of depth at
which the rocks known as 'grits' have been formed, but sandstones of
any sort are not consistent with deep-sea beds. Accordingly the evidence of the series known as the Staddon Grits is also in favour of a
relatively shallow sea. More markedly the Wearde-Efford series of grits
in the Plymouth area is a deposit of shallow waters; indeed, since with
the Wearde-Efford series there are associated beds containing pebbles
up to at least 2 lb. in weight, the presence of a land surface in the immediate neighbourhood must be accepted (Worth, R. H., 1916, p. 246).

Nowhere in the Devonian series of Devon does there appear to be
any rock which must or can be regarded as a deep-sea deposit. While,
in South Devon at least, there is evidence that land cannot have been
far distant, possibly over the area now occupied by the English Channel.

In the Carboniferous Age Devon still lay below the waters of the
sea. The evidence as to the depth to which it was then submerged is
incomplete. It would certainly appear that at times deep-sea conditions
prevailed, otherwise it would be difficult to account for the radiolarian
chert beds; although it may well be that these beds were formed in less
than abyssal depths. On the other hand, speaking of the Carboniferous

47

system in general in this area, the frequent presence of grit beds and of plant remains must indicate relatively shallow waters. The series even develops sandstones and conglomerates, as for example at Ugbrooke Park, and these certainly indicate shallow water.

There must have been movements both of elevation and depression, which our evidence does not suffice to clearly indicate either as to periods or intensity. But it seems certain that during the Devonian and Carboniferous periods Devon formed a part of the bed of a sea, through which none but trivial areas rose to form dry land at any time; a sea which at the close of the Carboniferous Age had grown more shallow.

The crust of the earth never rests, and there are periods when it exhibits mobility far in excess of the mean, especially localized mobility. The evidence is to be found in the disturbance of strata which must in their origin have been approximately uniform and level. One such period of crust-crumpling followed, at what precise interval cannot be said, the last deposits in the Carboniferous sea. The compression was in two directions, east and west, and north and south respectively. Of these the north and south compression was the more significant, and ultimately resulted in the formation of a mountain chain, of which Devon and Cornwall are to-day the denuded remnant.

The rock strata formed during the Devonian and the Carboniferous ages were squeezed into far less than their original horizontal extent, and thus of necessity raised into a ridge the apex of which was far above their former level. Intense local folding of the strata was a necessary consequence; the folds ranging from microscopic to structural features causing inversion of strata. The confusion caused was such as all the generations of geologists have as yet but partially unravelled.

From north to south in Devon the minor waves of this great movement can be seen. Unlike the larger movements they can be recognized even by the unpractised eye, and need no toil in detection or interpretation. The eastern shore of Plymouth Sound exhibits the contortion of the Staddon Grits, in the Devonian series; the neighbourhood of Okehampton will supply an example in the Carboniferous of mid-Devon; and the coast carries the evidence to North Devon.

Thus the movement was distributed between major and minor folds, shear planes and faults, in accordance with the stresses caused by the general uplift. The whole movement must have covered a long period, developing at the then free surface of the earth, and extending to greater depths as the surface yielded. The last stage would be the upward squeeze of the molten rock which was later to form the granite of Dartmoor. This doubtless introduced a new feature in the dynamics of the movement, sustaining and yet further elevating the rocks above it. But there would be a partial relief of pressure on the north and south of the axis of the ridge which extended from Dartmoor to the Isles of Scilly, since the upward movement of the granite was accompanied by the partial depletion of the reservoir from which it derived. Similar relief may have been afforded at intervals along the length of the ridge, between the points at which the superincumbent strata most readily yielded. It may be from this cause that the granite now appears on the surface as a series of severed exposures. Thus came into being the mountain whose denuded stump is now Dartmoor.

Whether it was from the first an island, or whether it rose from surrounding land is not known; but never since its formation has it been wholly submerged.

THE DIFFERENT TYPES OF GRANITE

It has been suggested that the granite of Dartmoor belongs to three distinct types, the product of three separate movements. In a sense it may be said to present several hundred types, the product of strictly localized conditions, but throughout the mass there is a striking constancy of composition.

Two principal conditions have been the cause of such differences in chemical composition as have been detected:

(1) *Absorption of earlier rock material at contact surfaces.* The molten granite in contact with the sedimentary rocks through which it rose to its present levels exercised a limited solvent action, and superficially absorbed aluminous material. Only in such granite will be found the pinite pseudomorphs after cordierite, or the almandine garnets which are occasional constituents. The presence of cordierite demands the addition of magnesia, iron and alumina to the normal constituents in their normal quantity; and almandine equally demands the addition of manganese, iron and alumina.

In the extreme case of small veins of granite which have penetrated the slates the absorption of aluminous material has been sufficient to lead to a very free development of andalusite, a silicate of aluminium which contains 63% of alumina. Such veins are to be found at Great Nodden on the Lyd, near the Island of Rocks on the West Ockment, at Ford near Sticklepath, and elsewhere. In some of these veins the andalusite forms the bulk of the rock.

Associated with pinite and almandine, wherever these are found in the Dartmoor granite, there is always an unusual amount of dark mica, which more usually completely ensheaths the almandine crystals.

Wherever the garnet, the pinite and the excess of dark mica are found, there will also be other evidences that the present surface of the granite is not far below the original surface of contact with the slates. Thus, in the Erme Valley, there is pinite in the granite of the quarry on the eastern verge of Henlake Down; eastward from this, pinite is found at least as far as Cuckoo Ball, a distance of two miles, and northward to Lower Piles, a distance of two and a half miles.

At Henlake Down the actual contact of the granite and the slate may be traced; over the whole pinitic area occasional fragments of slate may be found; and at Brown Heath, five and a half miles north of Henlake Down, there is a considerable inlier of sedimentary rock.

Over the whole of this pinitic area occasional almandine crystals may be found.

(2) *The addition of constituents by subsequent penetration of the already consolidated granite by vapours and fluids as a last stage of igneous activity.* The principal constituents so supplied were fluorine and boron, and their effect has largely been to enter into combination with the pre-existing minerals of the normal granite, with the formation of new minerals, such as tourmaline and fluorspar, with topaz at times.

Their effect has not been purely additive, for some of the minerals of granite contain alkalis as essential constituents, and in the presence of fluoric or boric acid these alkalis may be removed from the mineral, by the formation of soluble compounds. In such manner the felspars may be reduced to kaolin, the alkalis being removed, water added, and an excess of silica set free—part to be possibly carried away and lost, part to be redeposited as veins elsewhere in the rock.

Thus, if we express the composition of orthoclase and of kaolin by the following formulae, without alleging that these represent the true constitutional formulae, we obtain:

$$\text{Orthoclase } (K_2O)\ (Al_2O_3)\ 6(SiO_2)$$
$$\text{Kaolin } 2(H_2O)\ (Al_2O_3)\ 3(SiO_2),$$

where kaolinization is seen to involve the loss of the potash of the original felspar, the addition of two molecules of water, and the loss of three molecules of silica.

This is but one example of the class of alteration which may be caused by percolating vapours and fluids of an acid character. It happens to be an important example quantitatively and commercially.

The fluorspar which occurs as an occasional constituent of the granite would seem to be derived as one of the products of attack by the same agents upon the relatively rare lime felspars of the rock. Calcium fluoride is nearly insoluble, whereas potassium fluoride is highly soluble, hence the preservation of the former in the rock, and the loss of the latter.

Geologically speaking, the formation of the borosilicate of the alkalis with iron and magnesium, which is known as *tourmaline*, and which also contains fluorine, is at least as important as the kaolinization of the felspars. There is no occurrence of kaolin on Dartmoor which is not associated with tourmaline, but tourmaline is frequently present where there are no indications of kaolinization.

It would appear that tourmaline is one of the original minerals of the granite, but in its principal development it is obviously the product of secondary action. It occurs in veins associated with quartz, and at times tin; it lines joint faces where its presence is frequently accompanied by a reddening of the adjacent rock; it completely permeates large masses of rock replacing original minerals, and especially felspars; it is said to replace mica, but this last change if it does occur in the granite is negligible in quantity.

The apparent vagaries of tourmalinization would no doubt be capable of systematization were we in possession of the necessary data. There are rocks in which the whole of the finer-grained ground-mass has been reduced to a mixture of tourmaline and quartz while the porphyritic felspars have remained unattacked; there are others of which the ground-mass has similarly suffered while the porphyritic felspars have been replaced by quartz alone; in yet other instances the ground-mass has remained unaltered but the larger felspars have all been replaced by quartz-tourmaline pseudomorphs. Nodules of tourmaline occur in porphyritic granites; and in fine-grained felsites there are at times to be found globular replacements of the rock by quartz-schorl material, some such globes may be six inches in diameter or over; they are entirely isolated, each with its own centre from which this form of alteration has spread, and they are not associated with veins of tourmaline.

The tourmaline linings of the joint faces are readily to be understood, since the joints would form the natural channels for the solfateric agents; but all the other forms of alteration involve the general penetration of the granite by the chemical agents and their selective action. No doubt there has been some physico-chemical cause for such selection, some reason why in places the smaller generation of felspars has been attacked while the larger crystals have escaped; or for the contrary effect; doubtless also some explanation for the origin of the tourmalinization of the fine-grained and seemingly homogeneous felsites at discrete centres, and its spread about those centres; but the determining influences are wholly unknown to us. This much is clear, wherever tourmaline is present in quantity it is of secondary origin, and subsequent to the consolidation of the granite mass.

There has been some variation in the attempted tripartite division of the Dartmoor granite. Godwin Austen claimed that there were three ages, those of the schorlaceous granite (the particular form of tourmaline most frequent on Dartmoor being known as 'schorl'), the porphyritic, and the elvan. At times the schorlaceous granite has been recognized as the product of secondary alteration, and in its place has been substituted dark fine-grained granite of a basic composition as the first of the supposed series.

Gradually the idea of granite of successive ages and distinct characters fell into disfavour. Years ago my father wrote (Worth, R. N., 1892, p. 127):

"What I have to suggest therefore is this: that instead of our granites and felsites being of three periods as Mr. Godwin-Austen held; or of two periods as we have been accustomed to hold of late; that they with the felspathic traps of Central and East Devon—are really one. I do not of course mean that they are absolutely contemporaneous, but that they are part of one and the same great series of igneous activities. That the elvans and felsites are later than the granites is clear, because they traverse them; but this may have happened at any period subsequent to consolidation, and need not infer any great range in time. What is equally to the purpose is the fact, hitherto too much overlooked, that porphyritic felsites traverse some of the felspathic traps, and must so far therefore be subsequent to them."

In their report on the petrography of the Dartmoor granite, Flett and Dewey (1912, pp. 38–42) give the following classification of types:

"I.   The normal granite, rather coarse-grained with large pheno-crysts of felspar.

"II.   Fine-grained granites that occur as veins in the normal granite. Many of these rocks are aplites. . . . They are later than the coarse granites but belong undoubtedly to the same magma.

"III.   Hornblende-oligoclase pegmatites with large crystals of quartz and felspar, also occurring as veins in the main mass though less commonly than the aplites. . . . A very remarkable pegmatite is found as a vein at Bittleford Down. It contains hornblende, an unusual mineral in granite pegmatites. . . . Nothing that is known about this rock would indicate that it has derived its hornblende from the digestion of a green-stone accidentally involved in the granite, for such inclusions occur in the Dartmoor granite, and have no resemblance to this pegmatite.

"IV.   Dark fine-grained biotite-granites, sometimes porphyritic and occurring as inclusions and basic segregations. . . . These occur in the form of spherical and spheroidal masses ranging in size from one inch in diameter to as much as six inches. . . . It is difficult to make certain whether they represent broken fragments of early basic masses of granite that were disrupted and partly dissolved by the later intrusions, but no large area of rocks of this type has ever been encountered, and hence the theory that they are segregations which crystallized as scattered lumps of small size, before the consolidation of the rest of the magma, is perhaps the most probable that can be advanced."

For my own part I would prefer a somewhat different classification. I would start with:

G.1. *A compact, almost flint-like, felsite.* This I have described under the name of 'felsite A' (Worth, R. H., 1902, p. 511; 1903; 1912; 1937). I have it traced from Legis Tor in the Plym Valley on the west, around the southern border of Dartmoor to Hayford in the Mardle Valley on the east. Wherever it occurs it forms the superficies of the granite and is obviously the chilled margin. Its gradual passage into the granite can be traced at places. Except for an occasional very fresh felspar, and for blebs of quartz, it has no porphyritic constituents. That large areas of this rock were exposed in quite recent geological times and have been removed by denudation is proved by its frequency as a constituent of the Start Bay beaches. It is obviously of the same age as the granite of which it forms the outer surface, and it presents one extreme of the very varied structure affected by the granite. In section it is cryptocrystalline.

Flow structure is not infrequently developed; often masked by the deep indian-red colouration, it shows well on some weathered and bleached surfaces, certain of the striae having resisted the weathering much more successfully than the general body of the rock, and thus retained their colour where their surroundings have bleached. Plate 18 (above) shows flow-structure in felsite A, as exposed by weathering, a specimen from the bed of the Ludbrook at the foot of Ugborough Beacon. Pl. 18 (below) shows a weathered surface of felsite A from Hole, near Chagford. The cryptocrystalline structure of the rock is indicated in the specimen I once figured from the Hen Tor area in the Plym Valley (Worth, R. H., 1902, Pl. III, Figs. 1 and 2).

G.2. *A very fine-grained rock, microcrystalline in most specimens.* This usually contains porphyritic felspar, and is frequently darkened by much small dark mica. The last, however, is by no means a constant feature.

This rock occurs as inclusions in the granite. All the 'basic inclusions' fall in this class; but it is by no means always basic in character.

Flett and Dewey (1912) appear to restrict the size of the inclusions formed by this rock to a range of 1 to 6 inches in diameter, having seen none larger. But these dimensions are greatly exceeded. I may instance an inclusion in a boulder at Beardown which is 25 in. in diameter (Pl. 6B) and another in the summit mass of Kestor which is 4 ft 2 in. in length (Pl. 6A); an example in the granite of Hey Tor Quarry measures 4 ft 6 in. by 3 ft 6 in.; while an inclusion in the summit rocks of Higher White Tor, West Dart Valley, is fully 10 ft in length

These dimensions by no means represent the limit: there are much larger masses of the same class of rock, occurring in a similar manner, but the complete boundaries of which cannot be traced in the field. One such occurs at Birch Tor, and another most probably at Kes Tor.

Rather frequently the more common form of this rock is referred to as 'blue granite', but the name cannot be universally applied since some forms are buff in colour, inclining to pink or brown at junctions with the including granite, and others are much darkened by biotite.

Since more normal granite is also at times called 'blue' where its shade justifies that term a certain ambiguity is occasioned. Thus Brammall and Harwood (1923) state that "in the normal 'blue granite' of the Haytor area, and in a somewhat similar type quarried at Prince-town, the content of garnet is almost negligible". On the other hand, Evans (1899), who first reported garnet from the Princetown area (Swell Tor) says "they [the garnets] are only found in what is technic-ally termed 'blue granite'." He was doubly right, for at Swell Tor not only are they found in what Brammal and Harwood call blue granite, but that rock itself occurs as patches of varied shape in the granite mass, and not continuously. It is coarser in grain than the usual inclusions.

Rather frequently, notably in Lakehead Newtake, near Postbridge, the inclusions occur in very irregular form. Partly the softening of the inclusions by the heat of the surrounding rock, partly their invasion by the solvent action of the same rock, have caused a marked departure from the normal ovate or spheroidal forms which the smaller included blocks affect elsewhere. There are embayments of the general mass in the inclusions and projecting tongues of the latter in the general mass. A broken surface shows common boundaries such as might be assumed by two highly viscous and immiscible fluids if slightly stirred together, but there are always abrupt and clear boundaries along which the rocks meet, and there is no mingling of substance.

G.2 is of frequent occurrence. I find that I have noted it in fifty-one localities, while I have entered twenty-two stations at which it was sought but not found. This is by no means a complete record, and the negative evidence has the common weakness of its class, that it may at any time be countered by a chance discovery.

G.3. *The general mass of the Dartmoor granite.* This may be either coarsely porphyritic or very fine in grain, with all intermediate forms. Granites of either coarse, medium or fine may each be found predom-inant over areas which are to be measured by miles. It is equally true that any two of the varieties may be found associated in quite small blocks of rock, even in hand specimens; while a single quarry may afford examples of all three. From Meldon Hill, Chagford, to Easdon will be found one area of coarse granite; Bonehill Rocks, Bell Tor and Chinkwell above Widecombe afford another area.

From the Princetown road near West View Cottages to Foggintor Quarry the rock is of intermediate type, and the surface blocks are sound workable stone. This may be taken as a typical exposure.

Perhaps the best continuous exposure of the really fine grain lies between Clazywell Pool and the Newelcombe brook, but the valley of the Avon above Brent Moor House is also notable. Here at Shipley Tor a coarse granite may be seen to meet really fine-grained material in the rock on the summit. Similar rock is to be seen to the south of Black Tor on the opposite bank of the river, and has been worked in the quarry above Brent Moor House. North of this the enclosure of Ryders Rings stands on an area of fine-grained felsite with schorl nodules. This, or similar felsite, can be traced at some parts of the moor as passing into felsite A. It also occurs as veins in the granite. One such vein, decomposed, will be found in the growan which forms the bank beside the Sheepstor Road near the Sheepstor Dam. Another occurs in the granite near Cumsdon Tor. In each instance the rock is red, although colour cannot be taken as diagnostic in a country where, as at Rutt Quarry near Ivybridge, eight or nine different colours occur in the same rock.

More important, perhaps, is the very general occurrence of globular schorl nodules in this felsite. At Ryders Rings the weathering of the rock has released the nodules and they occur in numbers in the surface soil, while at Cumsdon Tor they are still fast in the rock.

Where any of these grades, the coarse, the medium and the fine meet, the plane of contact may be wholly irregular, or it may follow the jointing or pseudo-bedding of the rock, or be regular but without reference to either jointing or pseudo-bedding. At one and the same exposure it may partly follow the joint and the bed, and in part depart from both.

At the quarry opened for the supply of stone to the Venford Dam of the Paignton Waterworks fine-grained material occurred interspersed with quite coarse, almost giant granite, both forming portions of the same blocks.

The passage from fine grain to markedly porphyritic is sometimes gradual, but confined to a very narrow width. This is especially apt to be found near junctions with the sedimentary rocks.

And either fine or coarse may be confined to a small area. An instance from the quarry opened on the flank of Yennadon Down close to the junction of the slate and granite may be cited. The quarry was worked for the purpose of supplying stone for the heightening of Burrator Dam. Certain of the blocks obtained were traversed by narrow veins or streams laden with biotite, and in these veins almandine garnets were found, up to five-eights of an inch in diameter. Biotite was also present throughout, but in much less quantity. To take one of the blocks for closer description. In this, as in all, the notes are necessarily limited to the extent of the block itself. From the edge, which is the limit of our observation, for a width of 3 or 4 in. the granite is fine in grain and without porphyritic felspar. This class of rock then meets, along an irregular boundary, a vein of very dark micaceous material, varying in width from ⅞ in. to not much more than ⅛ in. This dark vein meets on a very regular boundary a thin vein, about ¼ in. wide, of very light grey, on the far side of which the dark micaceous material again occurs to the same widths and with the same irregular junction with the granite. But the granite on this side of the composite micaceous-grey-micaceous vein is porphyritic, the felspars ranging up to 2 in. long and ¾ in. wide, and so lying as to indicate flow-structure parallel to the composite vein. The porphyritic granite forms a belt 3¼ in. wide, and then passes rather abruptly into granite of fine grain as at the edge of the block.

To those familiar with the contacts of felsitic dykes and their boundaries, interpretation is easy in part. The granite where it touched the adjacent slate took some part of the slate into solution and thus acquired additional alumina and iron, and some manganese. Before the material in contact with the slate had become solid there was a further movement of the invading granite which swept this contact material from the surface of the slate and caught it in the general advance, in which it was drawn out into veins of some persistence, as a thread of coloured water may maintain its individuality for some distance in a stream. On a larger scale the granite which had been near the slate, but not in actual contact, would have been rapidly cooled and its crystals would

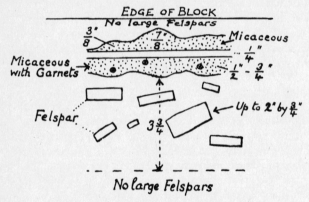

FIG. 9. Section of block from Yennadon.

be small; while but a few feet farther distant the cooling effect would have been much less and porphyritic crystals would have developed in the yet fluid mass. The general advance would mingle these two viscous fluids, and striae, large or small, would again result. It is to be noted that the porphyritic granite was still certainly fluid when the advance took place, since the felspars have arranged themselves in distinct flow structure.

Here within the space of a few feet I believe that we have the clue to the complexity of the structure of Dartmoor, as regards the relations of the various varieties of granite in the field. Fig. 9 is a drawing of part of the face of this block, and Pl. 17A provides a photograph. It would have been well to preserve the mass as a specimen, but this was impossible.

G.4. *Felsites and some pegmatites intrusive in the granite.* The grain of these felsites closely resembles that of the rock classed as G.2; and even the mineral composition is at times practically identical.

These felsites were intruded after the mass had developed both jointing and pseudo-bedding. They frequently occupy more or less vertical joints in the granite; less frequently they form sills and part the bedding; at times they may be seen to pass from the joints to the bedding and back again to occupy the joints; at times they break irregularly across from bed-joint to bed-joint, breaking through the intermediate bed. In the rock mass on the summit of Loughtor a vein of very hard and fine-grained granite forms a sill parting the horizontal pseudo-bedding, which it does not everywhere follow with precision, but at places crosses at a low angle.

Some few of these intrusive veins in the granite are exceptional in that topaz is freely developed. Veins presenting this peculiarity occur above Shipley Bridge on the Avon, immediately below the waterfall, and will be referred to later.

In another direction the pegmatites are also a departure from the normal, some would seem to be almost cotemporaneous with the mass of the granite, even as the pegmatite which occurs in the Meldon Aplite (see Worth, R. H., 1920) appears to be cotemporaneous with the aplite.

In this attempted classification I have purposely avoided undue stress on either mineral or chemical composition. I would be the last to ignore these features as aids to understanding, but the results obtained with the microscope and in the laboratory, useful as they are as aids to interpretation, must be subservient to field work. They may send you back again and again to the field, and may put many a promising theory to the test, but the final answer is not with them.

On all the evidence, and no item has been cited above which cannot be paralleled and supported, I conclude that the intrusion of the granite into the root of the Dartmoor mountain was a continuous process; it had its checks, and its periods of more rapid advance, but no breaks sufficient to constitute distinct stages in the process. I see no valid evidence of granites of differing ages and composition. One uniform magma rose slowly into its present position; its variations in grain have reference to the conditions of its cooling; its variations in chemical composition have reference to the class of rock with which it formed contact, and its opportunity for absorbing some part of such rock.

The forefront of the advancing granite at the start of the intrusion would meet cool sedimentary rock, and would be chilled sufficiently rapidly to form the rock which I have called felsite A. Rock so cooled would be solid long before its solvent action on the contact sedimentary rock could have any appreciable effect. The depth to which this rapid chill was effective is known to be but slight.

If no further material advance took place at any one point, there G.1 (felsite A) would remain in contact with the sedimentary rock. If a material advance took place both G.1 and the contact surface of the sedimentary rock would most probably be torn away and merged in the advancing material. The new surface of the granite would come into contact with rocks already heated, the chill would be slower, and none but a granular felsite might be expected to be found, perhaps a micro-granite. Later still, any forward movement would find the sedimentary rock yet higher in temperature and the granite would consolidate with an even coarser grain; finally, toward the end of the advance there might be no appreciable chill and the contact granite might attain so coarse a grain as to be properly described as 'giant'.

All the facts support this suggestion. Contact granite is to be found of every grain, from cryptocrystalline felsite to giant granite. With each upward stage of the advance the granite cap would be longer in solidifying and the possibility of its taking some part of the contact rock into solution would be enhanced.

It might well happen that in any one part of the granite surface a pause might suffice to enable the surface to take solid form to some depth; the next pulse might bring the molten magma which passed through and round the solid crust and between it and the sedimentary rock. Thus a coarser rock might both overlie and form veins of irregular shape and size in a finer and earlier consolidation.

At the same time it would be probable that fragments of the finer grain would be broken off and included in the coarser; thus G.2 would arise. All such fragments would probably, unless of exceptionally large dimensions, be well rounded by solution by the hot magma, even in some circumstances so thoroughly softened as to have new forms impressed by the flow. Larger inclusions would preserve their form, except for a rounding of any angles; and many would preserve the jointing and pseudo-bedding which they had assumed on cooling. All these features are in strict accord with that which has been found.

It may be noted that the presence of porphyritic felspars in both G.1 and G.2, if these are indeed the products of the first consolidation of the mass from point to point, fully accords with the view that orthoclase was the first of the minerals of the granite to crystallize out, possibly some of the quartz was of the same date, but that appears uncertain. Flett and Dewey, as well as other workers, have arrived at a similar conclusion on other grounds.

It is worth considering the points, that G.1 is confined to the southern half of the margin of Dartmoor, and that the southern half of the Dartmoor granite is at a distinctly lower elevation than the northern. It has been seen that the presence of G.1 demands that no advance should have been made after the first wave of intrusion. We thus seem to have some evidence that the upward movement of the granite continued in the northern part of the Dartmoor mass after it had ceased at the southern margin, and that the Yes Tor—High Wilhays ridge is not only

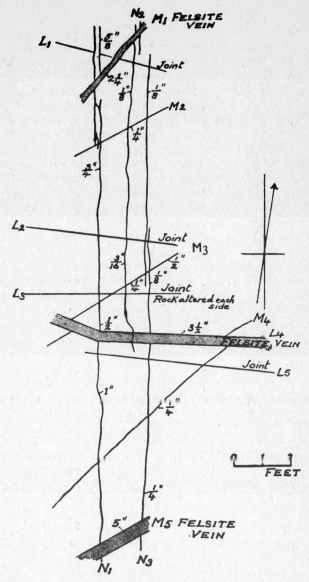

FIG. 10. Section of exposure below Shipley Waterfall, Avon.

the highest part of the mass, but is also the product of the last upward movement of which any trace survives *in situ*.

THE G.4 FELSITIC VEINS IN THE GRANITE

As regards any part of the granite mass the felsitic intrusions (G.4) are obviously the last effort of the intruding force; but it is quite possible that the intrusions in one area may be earlier in date than the surface of the general mass in another. All such veins and sills must be later than the consolidation of the rock in which they are found, since they follow partings which were only developed on cooling. Considering how narrow some of the veins are, their surroundings at the time of their injection must have been at a high temperature, although solid, for otherwise the material of the vein must have been cooled to the point of setting, and thus have barred its own advance.

The rock of some of the veins is abnormal, and appears to indicate the absorption of material from the sedimentary rock, masses of which may well be included in the depths of the granite.

Three such abnormal veins, each marked by a high content of topaz, are to be seen traversing the granite on a bare and water-worn surface below Shipley Waterfall on the Avon. The exposure is interesting. The joints disclosed may be collected into three groups, the members of each having the same general direction, but not attaining parallelism. On the measured drawing, Fig. 10, these groups have been distinguished as L, M, N, respectively. As to group L, the directions are as follows: L1, N. 85° w.; L2, N. 87° E.; L3, N. 81° E.; L4, N. 84° E.; L5, N. 87° E.

In group M the directions are: M1, N. 32° E.; M2, N. 54° E.; M3, N. 50° E.; M4, N. 39° E.; M5, N. 53° E. In group N the directions are: N1, N2, and N3, all N. 9° w., with slight irregularities.

The history of these groups after formation has been varied. Of group L, four joints are still very close, none are schorl-lined, but the rock on either side of L3 shows signs of slight alteration. L4 has opened to admit a vein of felsite $3\frac{1}{2}$ in. thick.

In group M three of the joints are schorl-lined, the other two, M1 and M5, have opened, M1 to admit a vein of felsite $2\frac{1}{4}$ in. thick, and M5 to admit a similar vein 5 in. thick. In group N all the joints are schorl-lined.

It will be noted that the veins of felsite dislocate the joints which they cross, and are not themselves traversed by such joints. From all the indications it is probable that the joints which are schorl-lined were in that condition before the felsite was intruded.

We may gather that after the granite had solidified and developed its joint-system there came a stress the consequent strain of which was relieved by the opening joints with an east and west trend, but which did not affect the north and south joints; and that this movement afforded the opportunity for the injection of the felsite. Except where joints are simultaneously opened by a general movement it would be impossible that felsite veins should thrust apart the large masses involved.

JOINTING IN THE GRANITE

The consideration of the Shipley exposure introduces the general question of the joints throughout the area of Dartmoor. Joints and pseudo-bedding are alike the result of the contraction of the rock on cooling. Their direction has been determined, everywhere, by the local conditions; and particularly by the form of the surface of the granite when it cooled. Thus, if the granite at any place formed a long ridge thrust up into the sedimentary rock, joints might be expected to be formed parallel to the axis of the ridge, and less regularly across the axis. Once formed, local or regional movements might influence the joints by opening out certain of them, and so emphasizing them, and by holding close yet others. But such movements would not bring into being a new set of joints, the strain being always met by the yield of existing parting planes.

Ormerod (1869) and others have claimed a certain predominance for joints bearing NNW. and E.-and-w. in the moulding of the tors. Ormerod cites de la Beche, who in turn had quoted Sedgwick and Enys, but the page references to de la Beche's report are inaccurate, p. 165 should be 164, and p. 171 should be 271. These authorities were writing of the granite of Devon and Cornwall as a whole. De la Beche, however, applies his remarks to the granite of Dartmoor, and includes in his statement that on a large number of observations it would be found that 80% differed by no more than 14 degrees from the (then) magnetic north, and another 15% differed from that direction by no more than between 14 and 20 degrees. Reduced to true north this would mean that 80% of all joint directions lay between N. 11° w. and N. 39° w. De la Beche was a wonderfully accurate observer and it might seem wholly unnecessary to check his observations. I have, notwithstanding, taken notes at 178 stations on Dartmoor, which include all but three of the tors which are rock-capped, and have measured the directions of 795 joints. These observations cover the whole extent of Dartmoor, ranging from Yes Tor on the north to Ugborough Beacon on the south; and from Feather Tor on the west to Hel Tor on the east. If there were any sort of real preponderance of NNW. and E.-and-w. joints it must show when these observations are statistically treated. I have plotted the results, compass fashion, taking firstly groups of five degrees (thus 45° would represent all angles between 42½° and 47½°), secondly, groups of 15°, and, thirdly, groups of 45°. The results show a slight preponderance of E.-and-w. joints, less than 2% of the whole number in excess of the mean. There is no sort of indication that NNW. is a favoured direction. Notwithstanding the relatively small number (795) of the observations which are possible, even when these have been made complete for each station, one is justified in concluding that no great directional regional force has been at work, but that the joints have been determined by purely local conditions. Had there been more joints to record, the uniformity of their distribution between all points of the compass would have been even more marked. Taking the compass constructed on the 15° groups, the east-and-west direction, which is the most favoured, represents but 10·7% of the whole, while with equal distribution its share would have been 8·33%; and this is the grouping which shows the greatest divergence from means.

If we take arcs of 28° to correspond with de la Beche's figures, we find that his favoured quarter contains 15·1% of the whole observations, whereas if the distribution had been uniform it would have contained 15·55%. It is therefore in deficiency. The supposed NNW. tendency may be dismissed: there is certainly no approach to his 80%.

Similar difficulties attend Ormerod's selected observations; thus he says that the main block of Watern Tor is divided into three by N.-and-S. joints. The actual direction of those joints is N. 39° W., thirty-nine degrees divergent from his statement. At Hey Tor Ormerod speaks of E.-and-W. joints, they are actually N. 74° E. and N. 60° W., representing errors of 16° and 30° respectively.

The difficulty of overtaking an error, especially when it has been supported by well known authorities, is admittedly great, and the labour involved considerable, hence the full treatment which has been given to this point.

It is quite safe to conclude from the evidence that the local conditions of cooling determined the direction of the joints, and also the matter of their being vertical or, in the alternative, inclined. Ormerod recognized that where the joints are inclined there is no rule as to the direction of such inclination; but he added that the east-and-west joints are inclined more than the north-and-south; possibly he means "are more often inclined".

Of inclined joints, that is to say joints which stand at 85° or less to the horizontal, I have noted 82. These are very irregularly distributed as to their compass bearings. If the matter is simplified by regarding all bearings from N. 45° W. round by north to N. 45° E. as north-and-south; and all bearings between N. 45° W. and west together with all between N. 45° E. and east as east-and-west, then there are 32 north-and-south inclined joints, and 50 east-and-west inclined joints, so that east-and-west are predominant. But the maxima of inclined joints occur around N. 60° E. and N. 60° W., respectively. As to inclination, the north-and-south joints deviate from the vertical by a mean of 20°, and the east-

and-west joints deviate from the vertical by a mean of 19·2°, a difference which is without significance.

Of all such joints, whatever the bearing, the number dipping with some southerly trend is to the number dipping with some northerly trend as 3 is to 2.

The same joint may dip both south and north, for instance there is at Vixen Tor a joint which strikes N. 60° W. and dips at different parts 51°, S. 30° W. and 64°, N. 30° E. There are many similar instances.

Where granite of fine grain occurs in the same tor as coarse-grained rock the jointing in the two rocks is rarely coincident. Thus at Lints Tor the joints in the coarse rock strike N. 2° E. and N. 82° E., while those in the fine rock strike N. 53° W., N. 16° W., N. 34° E. and N.83°W., here one of the joint-directions is common to both rocks. At Crowter, in the valley of the West Dart, the joints in the coarse rock lie N. 63° E., N. 30° W., and N. 7° W., while those in the fine rock lie N. 50° W. and N. 15° E. These divergences support the suggestion that the rocks consolidated at different dates.

A few marked coincidences within the area best known to an observer are very apt to lead him to hasty generalization, and of subsequent observations those which fall in with that generalization prove naturally the more impressive. In this manner it is possible to fall into ready error. With a wide area the statistical method affords the only safe way, but it is a time-devouring method, and time needs opportunity. As one to whom opportunity has been given I have been concerned to record the facts, and have of necessity indicated where my record diverged from previous statements. So far as that constitutes criticism of my predecessors, it is tempered with an indebtedness to them for the foundations of field geology. The work of the pioneers is to-day too little regarded.

REFERENCES

Brammall, A., & Harwood, H. F., 1923. The Dartmoor Granite. *Mineralogical Mag.*, Vol. 20, p. 51.

Evans, H. M., 1899. Garnets in Dartmoor Granite. *Trans. Devon. Assn.*, Vol. 31, p. 93

Flett, J. S., and Dewey, H., 1912. The Geology of Dartmoor. *Memoirs of the Geological Survey.*

Ormerod, G. W., 1869. *Quart. Journ. Geol. Soc.*, Vol. 25, pp. 273–80.

Worth, R. Hansford, 1902. The Petrography of Dartmoor and its Borders. Part I, *Trans. Devon. Assn.*, Vol. 34, pp. 496–527, 1903; Part II, Vol. 35, pp. 759–67, 1912; Part III, Vol. 44, pp. 677–80, 1937; Part IV, Vol. 49, pp. 343–4.

Worth, R. Hansford, 1916. The Dunstones of Plymouth and the Compton-Efford Grit. *Trans. Devon. Assn.*, Vol. 48, pp. 217–59.

Worth, R. Hansford, 1920. The geology of the Meldon valleys near Okehampton, on the northern verge of Dartmoor. *Quart. Jour. Geol. Soc.*, Vol. 75(2), pp. 77–118.

Worth, R. N., 1892. Devonian Granites and Felsites. *Trans. Devon. Assn.*, Vol. 24, p. 127.

THE VEGETATION OF DARTMOOR

FOR the more part the commoner plants and those which most
influence the scenery of the moor are herein referred to; and
necessarily this chapter must be concerned rather with ecology[1]
than with species botany.

One outstanding conclusion follows from the consideration of the
vegetation of this area—a dominant species is not necessarily dominant
where it finds the conditions best suited to its growth; if, that is to say,
we regard soil and climate only. It will be best suited to its surroundings,
but its surroundings may not be those which suit it best.

For every desirable habitat there are countless competitors and the
more vigorous and prolific species crowd out the lesser and weaker.
Of two plants, both suited to moderately dry ground, both capable of
growth in neutral soil, and both best served by these conditions, one
may be the more vigorous in dry and neutral soil but may be incapable
of enduring long continued soil saturation or acid soil; the other may be
by no means as well suited by wet as by dry ground, or by acid as by
neutral soil, and yet capable of making growth where the soil is both
wet and acid. Ousted by its vigorous competitor from the dry and
neutral ground it may well take refuge in a bog, where it may even
become the dominant plant. Endurance counts; a species which cannot
grow where there is lime in the soil has its opportunities restricted; a
species which neither needs lime nor is troubled by its presence has
larger opportunities; it may be driven to occupy a limestone area, not
because vegetatively it derives any advantage, but solely in escape from
overcrowding.

It thus follows that, while imitating the natural habitat is for garden
purposes a safe policy, it is not always the best. All plants in a well-kept
garden are allowed full room for development and are spared the
immediate competition of overcrowding. Soil conditions and climate
then become the determining factors and it may be found that the best
conditions are not those under which the plant is normally found.

In my own garden in Plymouth there appeared a species of *Carex*
which normally affects distinctively wet situations. It grew in a peat bed
side by side with *Calluna vulgaris*, a heath with a distinct preference for

[1] See also Harris (1938) and the relevant parts of Tansley (1939). (ED.)

64

moderation in the matter of moisture. Both species flourished, and the *Carex* became the finest specimen that I have ever seen. Again, that typical bog plant *Menyanthes trifoliata* (Buckbean) will grow and flower in loam in a pot, with no more care than that it shall be kept reasonably moist; although in nature it is found only where its feet are in running or constantly changing water.

Osmunda regalis (Royal Fern) is perhaps best suited by a constantly wet situation, and affects both peaty and sandy soils; it appears to love shade. But it will grow well in full sun. I have taken it from an old macadamized road. I have known it as a hedgerow plant, and it grows 4 to 5 ft fronds in my garden, where the ground is never more than reasonably moist.

As far as Dartmoor is concerned, excepting for the moment such of the commons as lie off the granite and on the metamorphic aureole, the presence or absence of any species is determined in the first place by the degree of moisture in the soil, and in the second place by competition. It is notable that where a true vacancy occurs, as where the turf has been lifted for 'vags' for fuel, the first immigrants to reoccupy the land are often ultimately ousted by other species. The race is always to the swift, but the battle ever to the strong.

Of trees, Dartmoor has, and has ever had, but few. There are three small areas of oak-wood, Wistman's Wood, Piles Copse and Black Tor Beare [these form the subject of the following chapter (ED.)]. The conditions at each of these woods reach the limit of severity which *Quercus pedunculata* can endure, yet, stunted and storm-tortured as they may be, the oaks not only fully occupy the sites, but maintain their woods with young trees. Each wood occupies a clitter of boulders, and the shelter afforded to the seedlings alike from storm and grazing animals has rendered possible their growth. Very certainly there are here no best conditions for growth, but there is opportunity, however limited, and the one plant of our native arboral which was fitted has seized that opportunity. There are a few associated mountain ashes, willows and hollies, but these are guests and dependants. Probably were these ancient woods destroyed they would be ultimately renewed. Miles from the nearest adult oak one often finds on the open moor a seedling, whose fate for lack of shelter and from the presence of grazing animals is but a short life.

Where, by some happy chance, the acorn falls in shelter, as at Shavercombe in the Plym Valley, an occasional tree is to be found. Probably with so heavy a seed as an acorn birds are the distributors. Winged seed such as that of the sycamore may be distributed by the wind: there have been two sycamores at Shavercombe. Hollies and mountain ash have their seed distributed by birds through whose intestines they pass unharmed, and similarly the hawthorn.

The highest placed Dartmoor oak grows on ground 1,530 ft above sea level at Black Tor, over the West Ockment. Hard by there is a mountain ash at an elevation of over 1,600 ft; while on the north slope of Yes Tor there grows, at an elevation of 1,420 ft, a hawthorn bush, the trunk of which girths 10 in., and the height of which is 9 ft: in some years it is covered with blossom.

In this survey it is impossible to discuss fully the other species of trees and shrubs on Dartmoor, the various willows, the birches, and in the lower valleys an occasional alder. The birch does appear to have been somewhat wider spread in past days, and the remains of dwarf birches are at times found in the peat bogs at some little distance below the surface.

The two species of Furze, *Ulex europaeus* and *Ulex gallii* are well represented to-day, although greatly restricted by man's interference. There is nothing easier or more tempting to burn, and the manner in which the unrestricted growth of either species will monopolize what might be useful dry pasture affords good excuse for the burning. At the same time, in the days when the Dartmoor pony was of value the preservation of a reasonable amount of furze was important. The younger growth is a good fodder, and is resorted to by the ponies in times of snow, nor do they confine themselves to the younger growth, but crushing the furze by beating it with their hooves they render much of the riper greenstuff edible. At one time the green furze, after being crushed, was used as fodder.

The furze has from prehistoric times been subject to restriction by its use as a fuel, giving the quick heat which its companion fuel the peat cannot.

Both species of furze affect the drier land, and fail where there is permanently moist soil. Although able to withstand the ordinary severities of a Dartmoor winter neither species is absolutely hardy, and exceptional frosts cause heavy mortality. Thus Briggs states that the frost of the severe winter of 1869 killed to the ground much of both *U. europaeus* and *U. gallii* on Roborough Down, and he cites Polwhele to the effect that the furze on all the commons of Devonshire suffered much by the severe winter of 1794–5, nearly three-fourths being killed.

U. europaeus is a plant of rapid growth, a bush grown from seed in a Plymouth garden, although lightly pruned, reached a height of 8 ft in ten years, and was of an equal diameter.

At places the remains of furze bushes will be found at some little depth below the surface of the peat bogs, for example near Ducky Pool in the Erme Valley, evidence that dry pasture has been replaced by peat. Such change in the soil conditions appears to have been rare and restricted.

Genista anglica, the Needle Furze, a dwarf ally of the last named species, is found only in wet situations and is rare. The one Dartmoor station which I personally know is Okehampton Park.[1]

[1] It is otherwise recorded from the parishes of Widecombe and Bovey Tracey (*Flora of Devon*). (ED.)

The heath family is represented by four species; of these the Heather, *Calluna vulgaris*, is most prominent, both from its luxuriant growth where undisturbed and from the area which it covers. It is a plant which prefers the drier soils, but can endure considerable constant moisture, and sends isolated skirmishers even over the margins of some bogs. None the less, a luxuriant growth of heather indicates dry lands. The colour of the flowers varies greatly, from an occasional rich crimson to a dull lilac, while white-flowered plants are not rare. These white sports would appear to seed true in many instances.

The largest patch of white heather which I have seen was growing on Brown Heath in the Erme Valley, and had an area of at least 7 sq. yds. The year after I found it it was destroyed by swaling.

Swaling, or burning, the heather is an operation which is practised to excess. The idea is to destroy the large bushes, which may grow to be knee deep, and to encourage young growth both of heather and of grass. The effect, especially where the ground is as moist as heather can well endure, is too frequently to create a waste of burnt twigs; and on some such wastes no effective growth of vegetation may establish itself even within as long a period as twenty years.

In swaling, the heather is lit to leeward and the flames work up the wind, it thus follows that even a slight breach in the continuity of the growth may put a stop to the further spread of the fire. The sparks are blown back over the area already burnt. Even a sheep track may suffice to check the spread of the flames. Pl. 19A shows a narrow track on Langstone Moor, Petertavy, with, on the left a burnt area, and on the right a relatively short growth of unburnt heather.

Exceptionally severe frosts are apt to destroy even well-grown heather bushes. Of the heaths *Erica tetralix*, the Cross-leaved Heath, is by far the most prominent; it grows only on wet or boggy ground, and invades the actual bogs. White-flowered plants are rather common. The flat hill-tops, where the water hangs but true peat bogs do not form, are its favourite ground.

Erica cinerea, the Fine-leaved Heath, prefers dry ground; it occurs sporadically, where conditions are suitable, over the whole area of Dartmoor, but its finest development is to be found off the granite on the steep hillsides of metamorphic rock, such as the slopes near Fingle Bridge. At times it is well developed on the stony 'burrows' left by the tinners, an area near Chalk Ford on the Mardle being especially notable. White-flowered plants are comparatively rare but very pure in colour when found.

Erica ciliaris (Dorset Heath) has not been found on the open moor,[1] but occurs in small quantity in its immediate vicinity. This is a plant

---

[1] A locality has long been known in the parish of Manaton "well out on Dartmoor at 1,250 ft elevation" (*Flora of Devon*). (ED.)

with a preference for moist ground, but quite capable of establishing itself under drier conditions.

It has been said, by those who should know better, that the wild Thyme, *Thymus serpyllum*, is not a Dartmoor plant. In fact there is scarce a border common on which it will not be found; at places in great profusion, as for instance along the track from Downtown Gate to the Lyd near its confluence with the Doetor Brook. It is not, however, confined to the borders, but is found here and there in the heart of the moor, its principle need, a thoroughly dry spot, being often secured by growth on the surface of a boulder.

The Whortleberry, *Vaccinium Myrtillus*, needs for its best development soil which is at all times moist, but not continuously wet. It can, however, withstand any degree of drought which is possible on Dartmoor, and it may be the dominant plant on areas where drought is at times extreme and prolonged. On the tongue of altered slate which stretches from Gutter Tor past Ditsworthy Warren to Shavercombe, the whortleberry and the Reindeer Moss, *Cladonia sylvatica*, form an association covering many acres, and defying alike the extremes of wet and drought. But for its best and most satisfying development the whortleberry needs protecting boulders, between which it often grows to a height of 3 ft, where the soil never dries completely, and the shelter is ample. At Dick Wheel (or Well) Pits, in the valley of the Doetor Brook there are such conditions; and the country folk come from far to pick the whortleberries, which are carried away by the gallon. An open woodland will sometimes afford almost as good a location, and a very prolonged season. In Buckland Woods, near Awsewell Rocks, on 5 December 1921, Mr. John Amery, my wife and myself found a fine crop of berries, of excellent size and perfectly ripe (Pl. 20).

The country folk always speak of 'Hurts', to the vast amusement of many whose speech has been polluted by literary English. But, as usual, when the schools seek to correct the countryman's speech, the schools are wrong. If ever there was an uninformed deviation from the path of verbal rectitude it is the word 'whortleberry', the Saxon form was *Heorotberie*, or *Heortberie*, Hart berry.

Eriophorum angustifolium and *E. vaginatum*, with associated mosses, but not with *Sphagnum*, are the dominant plants of the bog land, and the bulk of the peat is derived from their remains. These Cotton-grasses cover large areas which are rarely seen by the ordinary visitor to Dartmoor.

The cotton-grasses are at home at any elevation which Dartmoor reaches. See Pl. 19B for a view of the cotton-grass association on Snowdon, at an elevation of 1,600 ft. Constant saturation of the soil they endure perfectly; on the other hand the surface of some bogs becomes very dry in exceptional seasons; this drought the grasses endure also.

The cottony fibre attached to the seed of *Eriophorum* supplies a very

perfect means of dispersal, but there would seem a possibility that unequal dispersal should result from a prevailing wind direction. Since
the prevalent winds of Dartmoor are from the west the great majority
of the wind-borne seeds must pass eastward. There are no considerable
areas of cotton-grass to the west of the moor in the in-country, and
hence there should be a tendency toward the depletion of the cotton-
grass associations on the west, which can only receive seed during
periods of easterly weather, and a repletion on the east toward which
the drift is so much more frequent. There is some evidence to this
effect.

It must not be considered that bogs on which *Eriophorum* grows are
barren and useless from an agricultural standpoint. Certainly they bear
the one crop which is possible to them and cannot be made to yield
arable land, but with the exception of actual mires the surface is largely
capable of safely supporting the weight of grazing animals, and the
sheep, at least, have no objection to cotton-grass and its associates as a
green crop.

The bogs are directly dependent upon the rainfall for their moisture,
and Dartmoor rainfall is a very variable quantity. Thus in nine years'
records from the valley of the Upper Yealm there has been one February in which only 0·05 in. of rain fell in 29 days, and in one November 20·12 in. of rain fell in 30 days. The rainfall for the month of June
has varied between 2·09 and 7·43 in., and for the month of July between
1·12 and 8·48 in. On longer periods of years more extreme variations
have been recorded elsewhere.

The mires, on the other hand, are fed by springs or streams, and their
water supply is far more reliable. It is in the mires that *Sphagnum* may
be found in quantity. It is true that small patches of this moss will establish themselves at any place where standing or slow-moving water
exists, such as in the turf tyes[1] from which peat fuel has been taken;
these being below the general level of the bogs are to some extent fed
by seepage and are nearer permanent saturation than is the surface.

Thus it is that *Sphagnum* is a danger signal, indicating ground un-
safely soft to an unknown depth. None the less there are places where
the moss grows in very shallow water flowing slowly over relatively
hard and even sandy ground.

As far as Dartmoor is concerned the Buckbean, *Menyanthes trifoliata*,
is also confined to the mires, and to shallow pools which occupy depressions. It is sometimes associated with *Sphagnum*, growing up
through the moss, which it overtops. A mire where buckbean and
Sphagnum are associated lies a short distance south of Aune Head on
the right bank of the river, at an elevation of 1,450 ft.

The commoner species of Rush, *Juncus conglomeratus* and *J. effusus*,

---

[1] Channels or other depressions from which the turf has been removed:
originally a mining term. (ED.)

present some problems. Both will grow wherever the ground is permanently moist beyond the ordinary, although in merely moist patches of pasture *J. conglomeratus* will be the form far more frequently found. And both species will grow with their roots submerged. In really wet ground either may be the dominant species in any small area, while, a few yards off, the relative numbers may change. The conditions which favour the growth of one species rather than of the other have not been discovered, perhaps outside factors are not concerned, and it is merely a case of the first comer, of whichever species, having obtained a start in the race.

On the whole *J. conglomeratus* comes nearer being a true amphibian. Near the Wallabrook, on Huntingdon Warren, *J. conglomeratus* is to be found growing luxuriantly in a marsh, but more luxuriant yet is its growth on the summits of the rabbit buries, which are mounds of peat soil raised with intent to give dry conditions for the rabbit burrows. Similar instances occur elsewhere on the moor, so that it would appear that the opportunity afforded by light, well broken, peat soil, even when aerated by rabbit burrows, may outweigh the loss of moisture involved in such a roothold.

All the larger rushes have most substantial root systems, sufficient in any ground to uphold the heaviest man. Hence a mire can be safely crossed where the rushes grow sufficiently close, each to each, to be covered in the stride—so only you do not slip off the supporting root, the balance on which may prove to be precarious.

It is dangerous to generalize as to any family of plants, but it may perhaps be safe to assert that no British fern can live with its roots in stagnant water. Most, but not all, need constant moisture. The Bracken, *Pteris aquilina*, grows well in a dry ground, but secures its constant moisture by means of a deep root-system. The depth of its roots places it at a disadvantage as compared with surface-rooting plants when the level of constant saturation of the soil is shallow. Hence its specialization to meet dry surface conditions is fatal to it in wet ground. Wherever bracken grows upon the moor, there will be found dry, light soil. Even in the woods, where surface moisture is prevalent, the subsoil must be light and unsaturated if bracken is to grow.

It is interesting to note how even the most flourishing colony of this fern cuts out abruptly against anything approaching wet ground.

With full exposure on the open moor the bracken is usually relatively dwarf, not much exceeding 3 ft in height. There are exceptions. Some years ago I crossed the area of Berry Pound on the slopes of Hamildon, and, although the exposure is open, for some considerable part of the traverse I was unable to see over the ferns, which means, since my eyes are 5 ft 5½ in. above ground level, that the bracken was between 5 ft 6 in. and, probably, 6 ft in height.

In woods 6 ft in height is at times exceeded. There is a curious feature that those plants of bracken which have bifid or trifid terminations of their fronds are hardly ever found except in woods and their immediate neighbourhood.

Another fern which will grow well in open and fully exposed situations is the Male Fern, *Dryopteris Filix-mas*. This is certainly a common member of the woodland flora, but it also flourishes on the open moor, demanding only the presence of boulders for the protection of its roots against disturbance by the hooves of grazing animals. The fronds of the plants which grow in the open are of a yellower green than those from the woodland.

At one time the Royal Fern, *Osmunda regalis*, grew on the banks of our moorland streams, irrespective of any woodland shelter, but for the more part restricted to elevations not much exceeding 800 ft above sea level. All that has changed: it is now found only in woods, except for a rare straggler, and even then chiefly in woods which are difficult of access or from which the public is excluded.

The woodland specimens have ever been the finer: in old plants the caudex with its frond scars attains some height, and the fronds starting from this vantage point may reach 8 ft or more above ground level. I well remember one such plant, which grew in 'Stuggy Mash' (I purposely do not further identify the locality) and under the fronds of which my father, who was over 6 ft tall, could comfortable stand. As has been written earlier, such conditions are not essential to healthy and free growth, but actual drought is fatal. In western Ireland *Osmunda* is often grown as a fence; and in Cornwall it is still relatively common, but I will name no localities. The Royal Fern has three enemies: frost and drought which limit its range, and man who threatens its extermination. The plants which I myself grow have all been taken from situations where drought must ultimately have proved fatal.

At the other extreme of fern life stand the Filmy Ferns, *Hymenophyllum tunbridgense*, and *H. peltatum·(Wilsonii)*. The hand of man has been heavy against these also; but the eyes of man happily overlook many luxuriant growths. Their habitat is generally stated as—amongst moss in damp and shady places. This is accurate but not exhaustive; mossy rocks and mossy tree trunks are alike favoured, and rocks constantly wet with spray or seepage are most favoured. But I have also found the ferns in clefts in the summit rocks of tors, where shade was constant, but moisture failed at times. If these two alleged species are really distinct, then, from my own observation, there are hybrid forms.

The Wall Rue, *Asplenium Ruta-muraria*, and the Scaly Spleenwort, *Ceterach officinarum*, are both ferns which can endure drought, and are better without constant moisture. In my experience they are, on Dartmoor, found only on old walls. The Wall Rue occurs, for example, on the south face of Belliver Bridge; and the Scaly Spleenwort on the ruins of the old blowing-house at Eyelesboro. Now ruins, especially ruins of buildings the masonry of which has been set in lime mortar, are rare on the moor; and both these ferns have a preference for lime. It is, therefore, a tribute to the success of spores as a means of plant dispersal that these ferns should occupy many widely separated stations, with no intervening colonies of their kind.

Of the true mosses, whose name is legion, two only need be mentioned, the first because it is a marked feature of the ground covering, the second for its beauty and interest.

Polytrichum commune, the common Hair Moss, grows on the wet heaths, but more especially where the ground is wet but hard; associated with *Juncus conglomeratus* it forms the cover of many acres, and one might correctly speak of moss-and-rush moors as being at least as well defined as grass moors, heather, bracken, or cotton-grass moors. It is mainly a plant of the valleys, but not confined to them. The largest of our British mosses, it forms carpets of great depth; one author asserts that the depth of several feet is attained on Dartmoor, but I imagine that he did not carry a rule.

In comparison the Luminous Moss, *Schistostega osmundacea*, is very small, its frond-like growth rarely exceeds slightly over half an inch in height, and is delicate in the extreme. In place of growing boldly in the open it seeks some cave, a rabbit hole will serve, or the wall of an ill-lit stable, some place where none but feeble light can penetrate; but from this dark background it shines with a beautiful green luminosity. It has been said that it avoids cavities which have a south exposure, but this is incorrect, any cavity which is sufficiently deep to exclude all but feeble light serves it equally well, and one of the finest displays that I have seen was in an old potato cave at Yellowmead, Sheepstor, the entrance to which faced due south. Moisture is essential, so that buildings in which it is found must be not only dark but also damp. The luminous effect is due entirely to reflected light. The protonema of the moss develops cells with lenses which concentrate the feeble light upon the chlorophyll granules; these absorb such wave lengths as serve their purpose, reflecting back the remainder in the direction of its source. The little cells with their lenses can move to meet a varied direction of the light. I have grown the moss for several years, and have at times so moved it that the effect has been the same as that which would have been produced by moving the light source through an angle of 45°. The luminosity is then no longer apparent, but within twenty-four hours it is fully re-established.

There is a liverwort which, to a somewhat less degree, is also luminous. At first I thought that this plant was also lens-bearing, and, indeed, I photographed thread-like growths with globular expansions, much like threaded beads. But I have grown the liverwort for some years and have not succeeded in finding any further such growths associated with it; their nature is a problem for further inquiry.

I have, however, noticed that when the atmosphere is near saturation the tiny leaflets of the liverwort become closely bedewed with droplets of water. Visually these have much the same effect as the lenses of *Schistostega*, and the plant shines from its dark recess with a soft luminous radiance. There is good reason to believe that on merely passing notice it has often been wrongly identified as *Schistostega*. The droplets of water may very possibly play a part in the economy of the plant closely comparable to that of the lenses of the moss.

Two species of *Lycopodium* are to be found on Dartmoor. Of these *L. clavatum*, the Common Club-moss, is to be found on the dry moors, and is generally distributed, although with wide gaps in the distribution. Until recent years it has never been plentiful, but during this century it has increased considerably in one locality, but not generally.

L. Selago, the Fir Club-moss, is a plant of wet and boggy ground; its habit of growth contrasts with that of *L. clavatum* which is procumbent and trailing, whereas *L. Selago* is erect and branched, holding itself, as it were, above the moisture of the ground. *Selago* is very rare on Dartmoor, but fairly widely distributed.

I have heard it said that the Reed-mace was formerly plentiful at places, but I have seen no more than one small colony, and that has now disappeared. It grew near the Tavistock–Princetown road. Unfortunately, having found it, I thought it safe to leave to the next day its photographing; the next day came and so did some tripper who cut all the flowering stalks, and doubtless took them for the decoration of his, or her, sty. Thus it comes that I am not certain as to the species, but as far as I can recollect it was probably *Typha latifolia*..

I have placed this plant out of order, because I desired to close with the warning, which may have already been read between the above lines, that as regards any rare or unusual plant to disclose its locality is to secure its destruction.

Three garden plants are of interest, from their hardiness and from being occasionally found as 'escapes'. These are *Spiræa salicifolia*, the Willow-leaved Spiræa; *Aconitum Napellus*, Monkshood; and *Mimulus guttatus*, Monkey Musk. Both the Spiræa and the Monkshood are grown in gardens in and around Princetown, and are quite hardy at an elevation of 1,400 ft. *S. salicifolia* grows as a hedge plant at Rundlestone, and elsewhere. *Mimulus* is found in the streams and in miry places near streams; a few years ago it flourished in the Blackabrook, below Ockery, at an elevation of 1,200 ft.

THE ANCIENT DWARFED
OAK WOODS OF DARTMOOR

O NE does not usually associate the wild open wastes of Dartmoor
with woodlands of any kind. Yet the fact remains that two
of the most remarkable woods known to exist lie within its
bounds. These are Wistman's Wood, near the centre of the moor, and
Black Tor Beare (or Copse), near its northern boundary. Piles Wood,
in the southern part of the moor, is of somewhat similar type.

All these woods are so exceptional in their main characteristics as to
be unique, not only in Britain, but also probably in the whole world.
They are remarkable, not for luxuriant tree-growth or great extent, but
for their very diminutive trees and extremely limited areas; while the
excessive humidity of the region in which they exist and other extraordinary conditions amid which they grow add characteristics which
can only be described as weird.

Wistman's Wood, the smallest but most remarkable of the three,
has long been known, and not a few writers have given more or less
casual descriptions of it. The earliest is that by Tristram Risdon, of
Winscott, in North Devon, who wrote a description of his county
about 1620, just over three centuries ago, and this has been printed in
at least three editions. He describes the wood as one of the "three
remarkable things" to be seen on Dartmoor (1714 ed., p. 76, and
1811 ed., p. 223). The Rev. Samuel Rowe declared (1848, p. 175), a
trifle fulsomely, that: "The whole world cannot boast, probably, a
greater curiosity in sylvan archaeology than this solitary grove in the
Devonshire wilderness. . . . The ancient storm-stricken oaks of Wistman are without recorded parallel. . . . There is something almost
unearthly in their aspect." The late Canon Ellacombe described it as
"certainly the most weird and curious wood in England, if not in
Europe" (1896, p. 193). The latest and best general description of it is
that by Mr. William Crossing (1905, pp. 19–23). An excellent account
of it from the point of view of its plant ecology, by Mr. G. T. Harris
(1921), has appeared since most of the present article was written. Others
who have written on the wood are noticed hereafter.

Yet the fact remains that all descriptions of the wood hitherto published are either inadequate, misleading, or otherwise unsatisfactory.

Some of them are so pervaded by poetic fancies that they are ridiculous as serious accounts of the wood and its peculiarities. Such is the case, for instance, with N. T. Carrington's sketch of it (1826, pp. 55–6), which shows him to have been a very fully-licensed poet. It is still more the case with the remarks of Mrs. Bray (1879, pp. 85–102), the friend and correspondent of Southey. This lady's mind was obsessed by ideas of Druids, who (she imagined) dwelt in the wood, there offering up sacrifices and gathering mistletoe from the easily reachable branches of the dwarf oaks. She adds an ode "To Wistman's Wood"!

Black Tor Beare, though the larger of these two woods, is far less known and has received little more than passing mention from local guide-book writers and topographers. The same is true to an even greater extent of Piles Wood.

All three woods lie, curiously enough, in an almost straight line across the moor, and each about nine miles from its nearest neighbour. Only Wistman's Wood lies within the bounds of the ancient 'Royal Forest of Dartmoor'.

It may very well be that these woods are the last remaining examples of a limited number of similar groves which flourished formerly in some of the more sheltered combes on the moor and very likely were destroyed by the early 'tinners' in the course of their smelting operations, just as the ancient oak woods of Sussex were destroyed by the iron smelters in the sixteenth century. The members of the Geological Survey have expressed the opinion (1912, p. 60) that the tinners refrained from destroying Wistman's Wood chiefly because they realized that, even if they felled the trees, they possessed no means of transporting the logs across the surrounding 'clatter'. In any case, there is no reason to regard the woods as remnants of a primeval forest which once covered the whole of Dartmoor, as is commonly supposed locally (Burt, 1826, pp. 160–3); for there is no evidence that such a forest ever existed. Indeed, the conditions on the moor—especially as regards exposure to storm and exposure to grazing animals, and in a less degree as regards soil—would not favour it.

SOME COMPARATIVE DATA OF THE THREE WOODS

In past years much, mainly inaccurate, has been written as to Wistman's Wood; it is perhaps an advantage that it has also been contradictory. The other woods have none but a recent literature.

Although not neglected, the subject had found no adequate place in recent scientific publication, when Mr. Miller Christy, in a communication to the Linnean Society, challenged the silence of local botanists. The challenge was accepted by Mr. G. T. Harris, in the *Transactions of the Devonshire Association*, Vol. 53 (1921). At Mr. Miller Christy's invitation I have now joined in the present communication. If I may venture to add Mr. Harris as in effect an associated worker, then there are now available the observations and conclusions of three independent witnesses, who are mutually pledged to nothing, save an effort toward accurate statement of fact.

In all observations, and in the collection of all data, the personal equation of the observer is an hindrance to precision. Complete honesty of purpose will not, for instance, prevent a leaning toward selected trees of either a greater or a less height or girth than would make them fair representatives of the whole number. Against this the only safeguard is statistical evidence; which I have undertaken.

In each wood I have selected an area of 100 ft by 65 ft (6,500 sq. ft), and have counted the trees, measuring the girth and height of each. It remains that my selection may not have been fairly and fully representative. This others may judge; at Wistman's Wood I took the southeast corner of the South Wood, an area where the special characteristics of the oaks are well developed; at Piles Wood I took the north-east corner of the main wood, where the trees attain their best growth; and at Black Tor Copse I selected the north part, as containing the largest trees. Hereafter I shall refer to these areas as 'the selected areas'.

The statistics have been tabulated below. The following are the general results. The numbers of oaks in the selected areas are respectively: *Wistman's Wood*, 26; *Piles Wood*, 45; *Black Tor Copse*, 65; practically an arithmetic progression with a common difference of 20.

In Wistman's Wood the mean girth of these trees is 49 in., the least girth is 23 in. and the greatest 99 in. (It is to be noted that where a tree grows coppice fashion, with two or more trunks from one root, and no main trunk, then the girth of the largest of the sister trunks is taken as that of the tree.) Plotted as a curve, the girths as abscissae and the number of trees of each girth as ordinates, the curve for Wistman's Wood presents no true maximum, but about 84½% of the total number of trees have girths ranging between 23 in. and 64 in., and the distribution over that range is remarkably uniform. Outside the selected area the largest girth noted was 106 in.

The mean height of the trees in the selected area of Wistman's Wood is 14 ft 7 in.; the least being 9 ft and the greatest 20 ft. The curve shows a maximum at 16 ft and a lesser peak at 11 ft, but from 11 to 18 ft is the range within which 81% of the trees fall, and 42% are accounted for by the heights of 15 ft and 16 ft, taken together. Outside the selected area the greatest height noted was 26 ft 6 in.

In Piles Wood, in the selected area, the mean girth of the trees is 25 in., the least girth is 12 in. and the greatest 64 in. The curve of girths shows a marked maximum between 19 in. and 24 in., 42% of the total number falling within these limits. The greatest girth measured outside the selected area was 67 in., but larger trees probably occur. The mean height is 26 ft 1 in., the least being 16 ft, and the greatest 38 ft. The curve of heights shows a marked maximum at 24 ft, 23% of the whole

Table of girths and heights of every oak (except seedlings) within areas 100 ft by 65 ft in Wistman's Wood, Piles Wood, and Black Tor Copse, respectively

Girth	I	II	III		Height	I	II	III
	Number of Trees					Number of Trees		
Under 1' 0"	—	—	5		7' 0"	—	—	5
1' 0" to 1' 6"	—	12	8		Under 9' 0"	1	—	—
1' 7" to 2' 0"	3	19	14		10' 0"	2	—	—
2' 1" to 2' 6"	3	5	27		11' 0"	5	—	—
2' 7" to 3' 0"	3	2	5		12' 0"	—	—	—
3' 1" to 3' 6"	3	3	4		13' 0"	—	—	—
3' 7" to 4' 0"	2	2	2		14' 0"	1	—	—
4' 1" to 4' 6"	3	—	—		15' 0"	5	—	—
4' 7" to 5' 0"	3	1	—		16' 0"	6	1	—
5' 1" to 5 6"	2	1	—		17' 0"	—	—	—
5' 7" to 6' 0"	—	—	—		18' 0"	4	—	—
6' 1" to 6' 6"	1	—	—		19' 0"	1	1	1
6' 7" to 7' 0"	1	—	—		20' 0"	1	1	1
7' 1" to 7' 6"	1	—	—		21' 0"	—	2	—
7' 7" to 8' 0"	—	—	—		22' 0"	—	1	3
8' 1" to 8' 6"	1	—	—		23' 0"	—	4	5
					24' 0"	—	10	14
Average	49"	25"	27"		25' 0"	—	3	15
					26' 0"	—	5	3
					27' 0"	—	3	5
					28' 0"	—	2	1
					29' 0"	—	2	5
					30' 0"	—	1	4
					31' 0"	—	2	2
					32' 0"	—	2	1
					33' 0"	—	2	—
					34' 0"	—	—	—
					35' 0"	—	—	—
					36' 0"	—	—	—
					37' 0"	—	1	—
					38' 0"	—	1	—
					Average	14' 7"	26' 1"	25' 6"

I. Wistman's Wood, 26 trees, distance apart 13' 6".
II. Piles Wood, 45 trees, distance apart 10' 6".
III. Black Tor Copse, 65 trees, distance apart 8' 9".

number having this height. Outside the selected area the tallest trees stood 44 ft 6 in.

Within the selected area at Black Tor Copse the trees, excluding five seedlings or saplings, have a mean girth of 27 in., the greatest being 46 in. The curve shows a marked maximum between 25 in. and 30 in., 45% of the trees having girths between these limits. The greatest girth measured outside the selected area was 50 in., but there may be larger trees.

The mean height (again excluding the saplings) is 25 ft 6 in. The curve of heights shows a marked maximum at 24–25 ft, 48% of the total number of trees falling within these limits. No greater height than 32 ft, the maximum within the selected area, was anywhere found.

The 'distance apart' given above is a mean, arrived at in the following manner. Assume the ground divided into squares by two sets of equidistant parallel lines, chess-board fashion. Then if the trees were rearranged so that one tree stood in the centre of each square, the sides of such squares would have the following approximate lengths: at Wistman's Wood, 13 ft 6 in.; at Piles Wood, 10 ft 6 in.; and at Black Tor Copse, 8 ft 9 in.

The following notes may here be added. In each wood specific trees have been measured either by Mr. Harris, Mr. Miller Christy, or myself; in my own measurements I was guided by some special feature to the selection of the particular tree.

Wistman's Wood. Mr. Harris ascertained girths of 72, 75, 77, 78, 60, 93, 60, 72, 82, 72, 72, 77, 64, and 102 inches. Mr. Miller Christy obtained measurements chiefly between 40 and 60 in., with one of 78 in. Neither of these observers measured any trees for their height, except a few saplings.

The highest tree known to me in Wistman's Wood has a height of 26 ft 6 in., and a girth of 41 in. The tree, which I believe to have the stoutest trunk, girths 106 in , is 21 ft in height, and has a radial spread of 26 ft.

A good example of the deformed trees, I do not say the most deformed of all, for that would be difficult to determine, has a girth of 41 in., its height is 7 ft 3 in., and its radial spread, wholly before the wind, is 19 ft. On the other hand, the oak, quite certainly the most symmetrical, is young, its height is 14 ft and its girth 16 in.

Other measurements were: Girth, 69 in., height, 10 ft, radial spread, 19 ft. Girth, 58 in., height, 11 ft, radial spread, 21 ft. Girth, 20 in., height, 12 ft, radial spread, down the dominant wind, 10 ft, against the wind, 3 ft. Girth, 39 in., height, 13 ft.

Piles Wood. Here I have only my own measurements. The highest trees grow coppice fashion, many trunks from one root; they are situate in a little valley running up from near the river level; and, having the advantage of starting from lower ground than their neighbours, while reaching the same general level of the upper surface of the canopy of the wood, are necessarily taller than less favoured trees. I found one such tree having five trunks (possibly seven). The girths are 31, 25, 24, 21, and 24 in.; the height is 44 ft 6 in.

An isolated tree, at the north-east corner of the wood, is of a type that might grow anywhere under normal conditions; its girth is 49 in., and its height 28 ft, its trunk is somewhat over 7 ft to the first branch. Hard by is another type, the girth 67 in., but the trunk rises little more than a foot from the ground and then branches into four, the largest branch having a girth of 36 in. The height is 29 ft and the radial spread 20 ft 4 in. A young oak, near the river, well grown and symmetrical, measures, girth 19 in., height 17 ft 6 in.

The procumbent type, so frequent in Wistman's Wood, is very rare in Piles Wood except in the outliers to the east of the main wood. Here an excellent specimen of the single trunk procumbent has a girth of 34 in., a height of 12 ft 6 in., and a radial spread of 19 ft 6 in. The many-trunked type, with no visible main trunk, is also represented: one tree has three trunks, 34 in., 21½ in., and 22½ in. in girth respectively; its height is 11 ft 6 in. Some young isolated trees show the procumbent trunk in its origin, one such girths 8½ in, is 4 ft 8 in. in height, and trails away down wind for a length considerably greater than its height.

At Piles Wood a new feature appears, shrub oaks covering continuous areas and reaching no greater height than 8 ft. Isolated, or in twos and threes, such oaks occur at Wistman's Wood, but here they form little thickets on the high ground above and eastward from the main wood. The girths are always small, and the plants are rather shrubs than trees.

Black Tor Beare or Copse. Mr. Harris gives the following details: girths 26, 21, 21, 35, 26, 40, 20, 19, 29, 33, 21 inches. Another tree is mentioned having a girth of 26 in. Twenty-five feet is given as the probable height of some trees, and 7 ft as the height of a tree at the eastern end of the copse, which has decumbent branches. Small scrub oaks of 18 in. in height are also mentioned.

My own notes include the following: a tree having a girth of 49 in. with a comparatively long straight trunk, the height of which I have not yet measured; another tree having a trunk of only some 2 to 3 ft in height, the girth 44 in. and the height 16 ft 6 in; yet another, having but little over a foot of trunk, its girth 50 in., and its height 21 ft 6 in. These three are in the north part of the wood, where also is a sapling of girth 4 in., and height 4 ft 5 in. By the river are some detached oaks, one, free standing, girths 12 in. and is 5 ft high. Others hug boulders as creepers might, as tightly pressed to the rock surface as ivy; one such girths 16 in., climbs a rock 4 ft 6 in. in height, sprawls over its upper surface, and rises 4 ft 6 in. above it.

In the south parts of the wood, as to which I shall write later, I measured two straight-stemmed trees, 17 in. girth by 15 ft 6 in. height;

and 18 in. girth by 16 ft height; also shrubs from 10 ft to 8 ft in height, and 14 in. to 3½ in. in girth; I noted scrub oaks of about 18 in. in height.

An isolate tree at the south (or eastern) end of the wood is probably that referred to by Mr. Harris. It has no true trunk, but three main branches spring from one root, and girth 24, 28, and 37 in. respectively, the height is 7 ft 4 in., and the greatest radial spread is 20 ft. The actual diameter of the canopy is, however, less than double this, being 33 ft, and, on plan, the canopy covers a wellnigh perfect circle.

I have placed these comparative data here because I believe it important to present them to a single view, rather than scattered over many pages. Since they include details of importance to the further discussion of the features of these woods, I shall not hesitate to repeat them when occasion needs.

WISTMAN'S WOOD

In common with Mr. Harris, I have been much impressed by the importance of certain features of trees in the north wood. One oak, which is at the south-east corner of the north wood, is situate on the highest ground of all, at an elevation of 1,390 ft above Ordnance Datum. It has three sister branches (I do not call them 'trunks' for reasons which will appear later). All three branches are, in their lower parts, at least one half stripped of bark. Two have slight vitality left, yet one of these has thrown out a branch which, in 1921, made shoots 2¼ in. in length. Two of the branches to which I refer unite in a 'trunk' before joining the root; this 'trunk' girths 69 in., and the branches 41 in. and 30 in. respectively. The height is 10 ft, and the radial spread is 19 ft, all before the prevailing wind (Pl. 21A).[1]

A little distance down the hill is situate a more remarkable oak, which springs erect from the ground to a height of a little over a foot, then leans toward the wind, but before it has reached 5 ft in height has turned away from the wind and becomes horizontal; at this point it divided into two branches, which dip at an angle of 34° with the horizontal, then slightly recover, but the secondary branches from which rest upon the ground. The girth, near the ground is 41 in., and on either side of the trunk the wood is bare of bark for 6 in. in width, and is decaying. Yet from a branch on this deformed and decaying tree there springs a secondary, of vigorous growth. In 1920 this bore shoots

---

[1] By 1952 this tree had come to resemble others in the wood, much growth from side-branching having taken place. The tree now presented a continuous canopy, which in the centre reached a height conforming to that of the outermost branches (these had perhaps gained a few inches on the condition shown in the photograph on Pl. 21A). The biggest side branch which had grown up since 1922 was 11 in. in circumference. The terminal part of the low horizontal trunk (reaching towards the left margin of the photo) had been lost. There was also evidence of good subsidiary growth in other parts of the North Wood. (ED.)

of 5½ in. in length, and in 1921 it made shoots 8¾ in. in length. The same tree shows in some parts very restricted growth, say ¾ in. in the year. The radial spread of this oak is 19 ft, all away from the wind, the height of its topmost twig is 7 ft 3 in. above the base of the trunk (Pl. 22A).

Both the oaks above described bore acorns in 1921, and this year also (1922), and both belong to the species *Quercus pedunculata*.

As indicators of the direction of the most crippling wind the oaks in this north wood are almost unanimous in their evidence, differing only 12 degrees as to its direction, the mean trend pointing to the WNW. as the most destructive quarter.

The older trees present evidence of frustrated effort to send out branches against the wind, the younger trees accomplish some temporary success. Thus one which I measured girths 20 in., its trunk rises 2 ft 6 in. to the first branch, the total height of the tree is 12 ft, its radial spread before the wind is 10 ft, and against the wind it is 3 ft. From my observations it is only a question of time until the growth against the wind will be suppressed; the height materially reduced; and the branch, which springs at a height of 2 ft 6 in. may, if it survives, take on the duty of the trunk. I give the qualification as to its survival, since a branch, the girth of which is 9 in. has been split in halves, both halves being as yet living.

On this evidence I most cordially agree with Mr. Harris as to the effective wind pruning to which these oaks are liable. But I would also point to the extraordinary recuperative power shown by aged and decayed trees.

As to decay, this is rather marked throughout the whole of Wistman's Wood; in my selected area eleven oaks out of twenty-six showed clear signs of its ravages.

Turning to the other end of the scale, it has been suggested that the soil conditions, and the difficulty as to the supply of water, whether arising from drought, undue transpiration, or sourness of the soil, in themselves prevent normal growth and partly induce the unusual habit of the trees. I think the recuperative power of the old trunks negatives this suggestion, but we have further evidence against it. In contrast with the abnormalities which I have described, there must be set instances of normal and well-proportioned growth. Probably the most striking of these is a young oak in the Middle Wood (Pl. 21B). This has a girth of 16 in. and a height of 14 ft. So straight is the trunk that from the topmost twig a line drawn to the centre of the base for two-thirds of the height lies within the thickness of the trunk, and nowhere falls more than 2 in. outside the trunk. The tree is in no way especially favoured as to soil; some of the most contorted oaks are its immediate neighbours; it is on the lee side of these and thus had some shelter in its youth; it now overtops them. Merely it is not old enough to have gathered full experience of the trials which await it; granted time and I have little doubt the wind will work its will with this tree also. Such an example proves that there is nothing in the stock, no inherited tendency, nor anything in the soil or climate (if we except the devastating wind and occasional unusually severe frost) which produces abnormal forms of growths.

At first I had written that I had *no doubt* as to the future effect of the wind upon this young oak. I have since substituted the words *little doubt*, and this in view of the next example, also to be found in the Middle Wood, a tree having a girth of 41 in., and a height of 26 ft 6 in. The trunk springs straight and erect for the first 10 ft.; then it parts into branches which all have a strong upward tendency. It is true that the trunk has some branches at a lower level also (the lowest at 3 ft from the ground), but so has the young oak, and in each these rise in a normal manner. There is a curious feature in this tree; side by side with the upright trunk, and apparently from the same root, is a smaller trunk, the girth of which is 33 in., and this is procumbent.

Here then is the tallest tree observed in the wood, preserving in respectable age the qualities which mark the vigorous youth of its neighbour. A companion selected for comparison, has two trunks or branches from one root, both so badly decayed that little more than half the circumference of either is left, the present girths being 39 in. and 31 in. They rise but a short distance from the ground, and then branch away almost horizontally: the total height to the topmost twig is 13 ft. Another tree forms a bow, rising from the ground and again entering it like a pegged-down rose shoot and, like it, having a close growth of twigs and shoots from its upper surface.

The north part of Wistman's Wood presents a very good example of a phenomenon which I have named 'the boulder break'. A place where the boulders are of such a size, and so deeply piled the one upon the other, that never through the ages has sufficient humus gathered to fill the interstices and present a surface upon which vegetation could seize. There is growth of whortleberry and wood rush on the larger boulders, but between them cavities only. Such spaces are necessarily breaks in the wood, devoid of trees. Throughout the wood these conditions occur sporadically, and they account for the greater distance apart of the trees in Wistman's Wood as compared with Piles Wood or Black Tor Copse. Trees farther apart receive less mutual shelter, and hence there are more deformed trees in Wistman's Wood; but deformity is not absent from either of the other woods, in which there are similar and even larger boulder breaks, but where the condition is not so uniformly present.

I would add that I nave seen no oak of the sessile variety (*Quercus sessiliflora*) in Wistman's Wood,[1] and that the climbing Corydalis

---

[1] Mr. G. T. Harris (1938), however, "after a long and painstaking examination" established the presence of *Quercus sessiliflora* in both Wistman's Wood and Black Tor Beare, with a sprinkling of hybrids. (ED.)

(*Corydalis claviculata*) is plentiful in places and should be added to the flora given by Mr. Harris. Kingston and Jones name this locality. I found a few small hollies, one in the selected area, where also were three mountain ash trees. The 'Coral Moss' (*Cladonia coccifera* Willd.) grows upon some of the oaks.

PILES WOOD

Piles Wood lies on the Erme, in enclosed land, a mile and a half above Harford Bridge. Situate on the east bank of the river, on a slope facing west, it has sheltering it the steep slope of Sharp Tor, rising 300 ft above the highest ground of the main wood. Facing it, on the west, is the even steeper Staldon, of similar height.

From north to south the wood is some 530 yds in length; its width varies between 150 yds and 83 yds. At its north end it extends almost to the river bank, elsewhere a strip of rough pasture or meadow, from 30 to 70 yds in width, lies between the wood and the river; on the bank of which there are, however, a number of trees. This meadow is very gently sloping ground, but the hillside in the wood itself has, for the most part, a gradient of about 1 in 2½.

The ground within the copse is thickly strewn with boulders; there is certainly more granite than soil on the surface. At places boulder breaks occur; one of these deeply indents the western margin of the wood, the others are relatively small and the canopy of the trees is almost continuous above them.

The area of the wood, as shown upon the Ordnance Survey, is 13½ acres. There are outliers on the higher ground to the east, which the Ordnance Survey does not indicate. The highest ground in the main wood is 1,040 ft above Ordnance Datum, the lowest point is at an elevation of 860 ft or thereabout. The highest outlier stands at about 1,080 ft.

A notable feature of the wood is the very regular surface of the canopy as a whole, unbroken by any of the trees, the upper surface of which is indeed more regular than that of the ground in which they grow. The existence of one little valley in thus hidden; the trees within it rise to the same general level as their neighbours, and the valley becomes the nursery of the tallest trees, which attain a height of 44 ft 6 in.

Taken as a whole the growth is much nearer the normal than in Wistman's Wood. As against a mean height in the latter of 14 ft 7 in., there is here 26 ft 1 in.; and compared with a greatest height at Wistman's Wood of 26 ft 6 in., at Piles Wood some trees reach 44 ft 6 in. But to some extent this arises from the fact that in the main wood at Piles the trees spend their energy largely in upward growth, at Wistman's Wood largely in horizontal, or even decumbent, spread. A tree at Wistman's Wood may have a total height of 7 ft 3 in., but what serves it as trunk and the topmost twigs of that trunk may rise, perhaps, 4 ft in an approximation to the vertical and extend 18 or 19 ft horizontally. Straighten the tree out and place it erect and it would stand some 22 or 23 ft. I have checked this by an actual example, and it somewhat understates the facts.

At Piles the trees are closer set than at Wistman's Wood, in the proportion of 110 sq. ft to each tree in the former to 182 sq. ft in the latter; in my note on Wistman's Wood I have suggested the relative distributions of soil and boulders as the reason. This is in accord with my observation of the local variations in this respect within Piles Wood itself.

In patches of very rough, bouldery ground to the east of the main wood there are outliers; here the growth is strictly comparable with that prevalent at Wistman's Wood, the same restricted vertical and dominant horizontal extension prevail, the same relatively large area is allotted to each tree.

Between these outliers and the main wood are patches of oak shrubs, close set, tangled, and no more than 8 ft in height; boulders standing much above the surface are rare in these shrubberies.

At about the same level there are certain small trees in the open, which obviously live a very hard life. These are of great interest as exhibiting the nature of the education which has trained the procumbent trees in their life habit. The plants are small. Two which I measured were 8 in. and 8½ in. in girth, and 5 ft and 4 ft 8 in. in height respectively. Each had a radial spread greater than its height. That the trees are young is undoubted, but that tree, the girth of which was 8½ in. and the height 4 ft 8 in., was crowded with flowers this spring. I judge this to involve that its least age is twenty-four years, since at or about that age Mr. J. S. Amery's seedling from Wistman's Wood first flowered (in, it must be noted, a much more favourable situation).[1] If my surmise as to its minimum age is correct, then the stem of this tree (trunk is too great a name) would show about eighteen annual rings to the inch. Much more important, because demonstrable, is the manner in which these trees have attained their present procumbent form; this has not been by any bending of the trunk. At a very early stage the leading, upward, shoot was suppressed, its place was taken by a side shoot, still upward in direction. This, at less than 18 in. from the ground, was also suppressed, its place also being taken by a side shoot of upward direction. At less than 2 ft 6 in. from the ground the last-named shoot suffered the same fate; this time none but an approximately horizontal growth was allowed to retain life. The history of subsequent mutilations has been the same, growth upward is inhibited, growth against the wind may not survive, only horizontal or decumbent growth before the wind is possible.

[1] This was grown in private grounds at Ashburton, and was 27 years old in 1922. It was raised from an acorn potted by Mr. J. Brooking Rowe. The tree was felled in 1929. (ED.)

In older tree all trace of the suppressed efforts toward upward extension is of necessity lost, except in rare instances; but, in fact, the apparent trunks of these procumbent trees are really branches, borne by a trunk which rarely rises more than a very few feet from the ground.

Wistman's Wood is a specialist in deformity, except for a few striking instances of strictly normal growth. Piles Wood, with its more varied conditions, is far more informative. Piles Wood has its own examples of normal growth. There is the young tree near the river, girth 19 in., height 17 ft 6 in., whose trunk from the topmost twig to the centre of the base does not deviate from the straight line by more than six inches. There is the much older tree at the NE. angle of the main wood, whose girth is 49 in. and height 28 ft, while others can easily be found. It has its procumbent trees in the outliers; one, for instance, with girth 34 in., height 12 ft 6 in., and radial spread 19 ft 6 in.; and the two small plants described above. It has its shrubby oaks, and all these can be studied and compared in the surroundings which have imposed upon them their peculiar form.

Decay is not as marked at Piles Wood as at Wistman's Wood. In both selected areas there are the same number, 11, of decayed trees, but in the former this 24% of the total, and in the latter it is 42%.

In the selected area at Piles Wood there are, in addition, 8 oaks which are quite dead. A dead trunk here has some chance of standing awhile.

In Piles Wood I saw no oak of the sessile-flowered species, all which I noted belonged to *Quercus pedunculata*.

I feel certain, although I can produce no proof, that Piles Wood has been felled, in part, at least. It is situate where the trees could be removed (not easily it is true!) and probably it has been resorted to for timber and firewood, but this must have been very many years ago.

BLACK TOR BEARE

I have adopted the old name, which was in use at least as late as the early part of the seventeenth century. 'Beare', as meaning a wood or copse, is frequent in place names around Dartmoor. (It may even be ventured that 'Beardown', opposite Wistman's Wood, takes its name from the proximity of the latter.)

This wood is situate on the left bank of the West Ockment, on a slope which faces the south-west. It occupies the lower part of the hillside and trespasses upon the relatively level ground by the river. The lowest point of the wood is 1,200 ft above Ordnance Datum, the highest part is at an elevation of 1,530 ft, and the ridge of the Black Tors, as far as it is an effective shelter, rises to about 1,650 ft at its highest. The other side of the valley is formed by the slope on which are the 'Slipper Stones'. These are bare, smooth surfaces of granite, coincident in their dip and strike with the general slope of the hillside. Some of these surfaces extend at least 60 ft up the hill, the average dip is about 30°, or approximately 1 in 1·7. Smooth and regular, and standing at so steep an angle, it is no wonder that these rock faces should have been called 'slipper', as the true Devonshire equivalent for 'slippery'. It is rather surprising that Crossing should, by implication, suggest the name to have been derived from a block wearing "the form of a huge slipper". Be this as it may, the hill of which they form a part is steep and high and affords shelter to the wood opposite to it.

The length of the wood from NW. to SE. is about 1,000 yds, its width varies from under 50 yds to over 100 yds. The Ordance Survey shows it as a long, irregular strip, touching the river at two points, but elewhere at a varying distance from the bank, averaging about 50 yds; its area 14½ acres. This last is too large, the south-eastern part, in place of being continuous woodland, as shown in the Survey, is much interrupted by boulder breaks; 10 to 11 acres would probably be nearer the truth.

According to Crossing (1909, p. 196) there is documentary evidence that Black Tor Beare once occupied a larger area. He says that "it probably extended from the Island of Rocks into the forest" of Dartmoor. There is no evidence, known to myself, which points to any former extension toward the I·land of Rocks, but at a Court of Survey, holden at Okehampton on 15 August 1608, the jurors made the following presentment (*Dartmoor Pres. Assn.*, 1890, p. 55):

"Item further also they do present that William Chastie (by his owne confessyon) kild a stagge with a pece or gun nere a month since about Blacktorrebeare (which is part in the forest of Dartmoor and part in venvill) and that he did it for Sir Thomas Wys . . . and delivered the same to the said Sir Thomas at his house at Sidnham, at which tyme he told him that he had kild the same dere in the fforest."

The statement, if made, that "Blacktorrebeare" lay part in the forest would involve, if accurate, a former considerable south-easterly extension, the present forest boundary being more than half a mile distant, at Sandy Ford; and the same jury had found (p. 54) the boundary to run "unto Steinegtor and from thence linyallie to Langaford, alias Sandyford, and so from thence linyallie to the ford which lyeth in the east syde of the chapple of Halstoche", essentially the line now recognized as the limit of the forest. Notwithstanding which, saving the possibility of an occasional tree on the river bank, I find it impossible to believe that there was any material extension beyond the present south-eastern limit of the wood, the exposure is prohibitive. On the other hand, the name of Black Tor Beare may have attached to an area larger than the copse itself; the phrase used is "*about Black Torrebeare*", and "*about*" the copse may well·be a description which would extend to cover land as far as the forest.

This is not the only reference to Black Tor Beare being within the forest. At the manor and forest court of Lydford north, held 21st September 1587, the jury upon their oaths presented (p. 139) that a certain William Bowden had cut certain oaks in "Blacktors Beare infra Forest pd", and it was ordered that he be summoned to answer at the next court. He duly obeyed the summons and was fined three pence. But one must be careful not to accept the literal rendering of 'Forest' in these presentments. The word was loosely used, as such instances as the following will show. It was presented that a certain wall between the lands of Richard Ellacot, called Sowtherley, and the Forest of Dartmoor, and a certain gate called Sowtherley gate were ruinous and fallen; and, at another court, that a hedge of John Ryetche between a tenement of the said John called Sowtherley and the lands of Dartmoor of our Lady the Queen was ruinous. Now no part of Southerly adjoins the forest, and it is evident that in the first instance the words "*Forest of Dartmoor*" are loosely used, where "*solū Dñe Rñe de Dartmore*" was correctly written in the latter; and, even more correctly, at times the term was "*solū Dñe R^{ne} iuxta Forest*". We need not accept the entry as evidence of any larger copse than that at present existing.

But it is evidence that, notwithstanding the great difficulty of removing timber, trees were cut, probably for firewood, and equally probably the wood was removed by pack-horses. In addition to unauthorized wood-cutters there were those who acquired their timber in a more regular fashion. There is in existence a document, without date, but early seventeenth century, entitled "Review of Woods", which contains the following entry (p. 59): "Forest of Dartmoor and of 44[l] for the price of 2[a] of wood growing within the Chase of Dartmoor so sold to Bartholomew Gidley. And of 40[s] for 8[a] underwood growing within the Forest of Dartmoor, in a certain place there called Black Tores Beare." The two acres sold at £44 must evidently have comprised well-grown timber, and were certainly not within the boundary of the true forest; they would probably have been either in the parish of Gidleigh, or of Chagford. The relative value of 8 acres at Black Tor, 5s. an acre as compared with £22, gives a very fair indication that, then as now, little real timber grew there. It seems probable that 8 acres was the computed total area of the copse at Black Tor at that time, if so it was certainly no larger than at present. It will be noted that it is described as underwood.

This gives us a date, at or about 1618–20, when the copse was probably cut, and hence few of the present trees could be more than 300 years old.

There follows a long gap in the available written record; then, on 27 May 1830 we find Miss Dixon viewing the wood. This lady, the authoress of certain poems entitled 'Castalian Hours', was active in body as in mind; the opening words of her Journal (1830, p. 3) are "Wednesday, May 19th, 1830, left Princetown at half-past four o'clock—a pleasant mild morning; the larks soaring up and singing at every step." It may be added that at nine o'clock she breakfasted at Tavistock. She concludes the day's notes: "Our direction was now taken through several pleasant fields and shady lanes towards Horsa Bridge, over the Tamar, about three miles distant, where we terminated the day's excursion, having travelled from the time of our leaving the Prisons twenty-five or thirty miles, and continued walking, with slight interruption, during a period of fifteen hours."

On Thursday, 27 May, she visited Black Tor. She had no adventures, apart from the fact that "the clouds suddenly collapsed" (a rather frequent incident on and about Yes Tor). Her description of the copse and its neighbourhood is worth quoting. She writes (pp. 29–30): "The ground from Eastor [Yestor] to Blackator is a peat bog, whence most probably the name of this latter hill. The descent of the river is very steep, and entirely covered with blocks of stone, similar to those which strew the sides of Eastor. Among these stones, and growing in their very crevices, are many mountain ashes or rowan trees, some old and moss grown. All along the side of the hill overlooking the course of the West Ockment, is a growth of dwarf oak, mostly quite young, and now appearing in the red leaf common to such bushes. This place, which is known by the name of Blackator Copse, bears the strongest resemblance to Wistman's Wood, near Twobridges, in every particular, except that the trees are of much more recent date than those in the valley of the Dart, the antiquity of which gives rise to so many varying conjectures. Blackator Copse is certainly a remarkable place, and well deserving a visit from the explorers of the moorland districts, both on account of the singular disposition of the bushes and trees, which extend over a space of, perhaps, upwards of ten acres; and also for the sake of several grand views on the West Ockment, especially where it contracts its course between the descent of two craggy hills, and rushes among the stones below with great violence."

Miss Dixon's estimate of the area is interesting. We now have (a) my own estimate, in 1922, of 10 to 11 acres; (b) Miss Dixon's figure, ninety-two years before, of 10 acres; (c) the sale, in or about 1620, over 300 years ago, the area being set at 8 acres. The probability is that, for the past three centuries, the area has been practically constant. In connexion with this constancy it is curious how clearly defined is the boundary of the wood, more especially along its higher side.

It is strange that the Rev. Samuel Rowe, in his *Perambulation of Dartmoor*, omits all reference to Black Tor Copse. He writes (p. 242): "The scenery on the West Ockment, in the deep glen at the foot of Black Tor, is grand and impressive, but will not long detain us from tracing the course of the river onwards."

The lowest and best-sheltered ground in Black Tor Beare lies at the north-west end. Here, in my selected area, are trees up to 32 ft in height and 46 in. in girth. Here, if anywhere, the wood was cut in or about 1620; the ground is very bouldery, but is the easiest of access in the whole copse. If we take this largest tree as being 300 years old, its diameter is very nearly 15 in., its radius 7½ in., and there should be 40 annual rings to the inch. Buller's tree at Wistman's Wood had a radius of trunk of 4½ in., and there were 163 annual rings, which gives 36 rings to the inch. Remembering that the earlier rings are frequently obscured, this is further evidence in favour of the possibility of 40 years to each inch of radius of trunk.

On the average, each tree occupies an area of 76¼ sq. ft. Even at this north-western end, as the growth climbs the hillside, its form changes, and the oaks degenerate to mere bushes of 7 or 8 ft in height. Such bushes form the higher margin of the copse throughout its length. Toward the south-eastern end they form the greater part of the whole growth, standing but 4 or 5 ft apart, and having girths up to about 15 in. None the less, where the wood is at its widest, and also on some of the lower slopes, larger trees occur, even in the south-eastern part. These are from 7 to 8 ft apart, some are as high as 16 ft and girth 18 in.; such trees are frequently of symmetrical growth.

Near the south-eastern extreme the mountain ash becomes a prominent member of the tree community. I believe that, even at the centre of length of the wood, a mountain ash there growing is one of the largest trees in the wood, but I have not yet measured it. This species is much hardier than the oak, and outlying specimens are to be found at least 1,590 ft above Ordnance Datum. As to the oaks, their relative size clearly depends upon the exposure, until we take the next downward step from the bushes 8 ft in height to scrub oaks 18 in. high. Above the main wood at the south-east is a belt of such scrub oaks, extending about 20 ft from the wood, the little plants being from 4 to 5 ft apart. They are actually sheltered by the adjacent copse, and hence no question of exposure can be entertained; the nearest to the main wood are on ground but a foot or two above it, so that elevation is not the cause of their dwarf growth. I have assured myself that they are kept down by grazing animals. If this be so, the question at once arises how the main wood itself has ever reached this point. I think the answer is clear: there is here an abrupt change in both the surface of the soil and the fall of the ground. Within the wood boulders are very numerous and form much of the surface; without the wood boulders are either absent or more widely apart. Within the wood the ground slopes 10 ft down in 17 ft horizontal; without the wood it slopes at a little more than half this angle. The change in this latter respect is not quite so marked at all points; indeed, where the scrub oaks are best developed the change in gradient is not great. I conclude that, although the cattle sometimes enter the wood for shelter, there was nothing to tempt them there before the trees grew. This steep and bouldery hillside was not everywhere and as a whole impassable to animals, it was merely devoid of grazing and hence free from their attentions. Where the change to soil without boulders (or with less boulders) coincides with the change to a flatter gradient, there sheep and cattle constantly feed, and even the scrub oaks get little chance. Where the change takes place without a marked alteration of gradient, there, on the steep slope, the animals feed less frequently and the scrub oaks can just maintain themselves. It must also be remembered that the leaf-mould from the trees has levelled up the ground between the boulders, so that it is now much less rough within the wood than when the trees first established themselves. The scrub oaks are also hampered by the entry of disease into the plants, through the surfaces broken by the animals.

Alone of all the trees in the wood the little oaks, so suppressed, produce abnormally small leaves. An occasional shoot is normal in leaf area, but the general matted growth is very different; although it may be matched in much-trimmed hedgerows in lower ground, the trimming at Black Tor being done by grazing animals.

I take two twigs as fair examples; on the one the first six leaves from the apex aggregated 57·0 sq. cm. in area, the largest leaf having an area of 13·1 sq. cm.; on the other the first six leaves from the apex aggregated 60·2 sq. cm., the largest leaf being 16·4 sq. cm. I compare with them a shoot from a bush oak at Black Tor, having the least leaf area which I measured in any of the 'bushes', the combined area of six leaves was 126·75 sq. cm., the largest leaf was 38·0 sq. cm. The length of the internodes of the scrub oak was not as markedly deficient, the length above the seventh leaf on one twig was 30 mm., and on the other 22 mm.; on the bush oak the corresponding length was 44 mm. (See also scrub oak from hedgerow in Bickleigh Vale, the first entry in table on p. 92.)

Before further pursuing the question of leaf area and internode length, I add a note on the extreme south-eastern tree of Black Tor, already referred to as being on the highest ground, at 1,530 ft above Ordnance Datum (Pl. 22B). This isolated tree grows in a patch of large boulders, a slight hollow in which affords its lower growth some shelter. When or how it found the soil necessary to its seedling life would appear an insoluble problem, were there not at the present a last-year's seedling growing under its shelter on the moss and other vegetation which covers a part of the surface of a boulder. The tree has never accomplished a trunk, its three main branches crawl over the boulders, from which they but slightly lift themselves; their girths are 24, 28 and 37 in. respectively. From a tangle of secondary branches springs a matted confusion of twigs, to form the canopy of the tree. In effect the canopy is a mere superficies, slightly domed in form, and 33 ft in diameter, almost a true circle on plan. This, the highest situate oak in Devonshire, is vigorous and healthy, neither the soil nor the exposure has affected its vegetative power. Pruned remorselessly by the wind, restricted to a canopy wholly out of proportion to its root and branch system, rising no more than 7 ft 4 in. from the boulders around its base, it makes good each year its loss of leaf-bearing twig, with generous shoots bearing leaves of more than average area. This year, 1922, on the 17th of June, it had already put forth new twigs, many of which were 9 in. (229 mm.) in length, and bore 18 leaves apiece; a larger number were 6 in. (152 mm.) in length and bore 12 leaves apiece. Taking the top six leaves of a representative shoot, their area totalled 213·3 sq. cm., the largest of the six leaves had an area of 54·6 sq. cm.; the length of the twig from the apex to the insertion of the seventh leaf was 69 mm.; the conjugate diameters of the twig below the sixth leaf, measured in millimetres and multiplied together, gave a product, 11·58 (hereinafter called the relative area of stem). All these are above the mean of measurements from fifteen selected Devonshire trees. I compare this tree with a fine oak growing at Shaugh Bridge, whose girth is 152 in., and the corresponding data for which are: total area of first six leaves 215·1 sq. cm., area of largest leaf of the six 54·6 sq. cm., length to insertion of seventh leaf 46 mm., product of conjugate diameters of stem (in mm.) 11·02. Another, and larger, oak at Shaugh Bridge has a girth of 156 in. and a height of 58 ft; its data are: total area of first six leaves 375·9 sq. cm., largest leaf 67·3 sq. cm., length to insertion of seventh leaf 32 mm., relative area of stem 11·88. The Black Tor oak may be the most amazing tangle which ever had the name of tree, but its vegetative capacity equals that of very fine and shapely examples. The Shaugh Bridge oaks were measured later in the year and the terminal leaves had more fully acquired their final growth; allowance being made for this, the Black Tor tree compares even more favourably.

I shorten the discussion of this question of leaf area and internode length by inserting a table, in which representative twigs are entered in order of the total area of their first six leaves. [Reference letters refer to particular trees, some of which are represented more than once.] It will be seen that, if we except the scrub oaks, the Black Tor trees take place quite regularly among examples from the most favourable localities for growth. The relative areas of stem vary with so many circumstances which it is impossible to insert here that no general comparisons can safely be made. The meaning of the term 'relative area of stem' is explained above, the approximate actual area in square millimetres can be obtained by multiplying the tabular numbers by 0·7854, treating the section as an ellipse. I may note that in Black Tor Beare all the trees which I have examined have been of the *pedunculata* species, but the two trees examined near the Island of Rocks were both *sessiliflora*, the only specimens of this species which I have seen in the course of the inquiry.

Some comparative leaf sizes are illustrated in Fig. 11.

In the selected area in Black Tor Beare twelve trees out of sixty-three living oaks are in part decayed; this is a proportion of 19%, as compared

TABLE OF TWIGS CARRYING SIX LEAVES

	Total leaf area sq. cm.	Largest leaf sq. cm.	Length to 7th leaf mm.	Relative area of stem
Scrub oak, hedgerow, Bickleigh Vale	34·0	7·5	56	1·82
Black Tor, Scrub oak	57·0	13·1	30	2·09
Black Tor, Scrub oak	60·2	16·4	22	2·31
A Wistman's (Middle) Wood	99·2	26·0	28	5·50
Postbridge, 1040, O.D.	112·4	25·2	37	10·22
B Wistman's (North) Wood	112·6	27·5	59	9·13
Island of Rocks	114·5	28·2	61	4·25
M Shaugh Bridge	124·5	31·7	18	5·02
X Black Tor (bush oak)	126·8	38·0	44	8·28
Postbridge, 1160, O.D.	146·3	33·3	44	13·90
X Black Tor (bush oak)	150·3	31·6	74	7·27
Okehampton Park	157·6	34·5	49	6·84
Farleigh (South Hams)	169·1	39·8	58	13·76
Thornhill, Plymouth	193·2	42·9	17	11·66
Postbridge, 1050, O.D.	193·4	40·0	25	5·78
A Wistman's (Middle) Wood	202·5	40·6	74	8·33
L Tavistock, long shoot	211·5	49·8	65	7·51
Y Black Tor, SE. tree	213·3	54·6	69	11·58
M Shaugh Bridge	215·1	54·6	46	11·02
B Wistman's (North) Wood, long shoot	219·7	40·7	94	22·41
L Tavistock ,short shoot	225·7	53·7	16	11·83
Wistman's (Middle) Wood	255·9	47·1	32	17·64
Island of Rocks	258·2	54·6	82	13·87
C Wistman's (Middle) Wood	268·9	74·3	36	17·65
L Tavistock, short shoot	270·6	58·2	16	10·84
Wistman's (South) Wood	289·4	67·1	31	6·17
Shaugh Bridge, 13 ft girth	375·9	67·3	32	11·88
Wistman's (Middle) Wood[1]	def.	97·8	18	25·77
L Tavistock, long shoot	411·5	104·7	96	10·49
E Wotter (very exceptional)[2]	608·6	156·5	37	26·31
Mean (29)	208·6	50·3	45	11·01
Mean, excluding scrub oak and 'E' (26)	204·7	49·0	47	11·10
Mean, excluding Wistman's, Black Tor and 'E' (15)	212·0	47·9	44	9·92
Mean of Wistman's Wood (8)	206·9	52·6	46·5	14·07
Mean of Black Tor, excluding scrub (3)	163·5	41·4	62	9·04
D 'Druid' Seedling (Wistman's Wood stock)	332·7	85·9	33	18·62

[1] Seventh leaf 118·0 sq. cm.; some leaves defective.
[2] Excluded from all means.

with 24% at Piles Wood, and 42% at Wistman's Wood. There are also fourteen oaks which are dead. Two small saplings are to be seen springing from the roots of trees, otherwise apparently dead, and on one root the three main branches are quite dead, but a shoot 4 in. in girth and 4 ft in height is growing healthily.

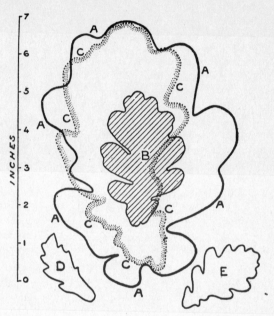

FIG. 11. Comparison of largest leaves from shoots bearing six leaves each.

A (*Full line*), from tree at Wotter, Lee Moor, area of leaf 156·5 sq. cm.
D (*Hatched*), from tree at Shaugh Bridge, girth of tree 152 in., area of leaf 31·7 sq. cm.
C (*Dotted*), from deformed tree in Wistman's (Middle) Wood, area of leaf 97·8 sq. cm.
D, from hedgerow near Bickleigh Bridge, scrub oak, owing its characteristic scrubby growth to hedge-pruning, area of leaf 7·5 sq. cm.
E, Black Tor Beare, scrub oak, grazed down by animals, area of leaf 13·1 sq. cm.

Note. The above reference letters do not correspond to those given in printed table.

I noted two mountain ash trees in the selected area, both small, from 5 to 6 in. in girth and 8 ft in height; but just outside that area is a mountain ash of 44 in. girth and 28 ft in height. Ivy is frequent, and at places is growing strongly. *Corydalis claviculata* grows in quantity on the boulders around the isolated tree at the south-eastern end, at an elevation of 1,530 ft O.D. Ferns are plentiful, the following list of species is

incomplete: *Polypodium vulgare, Dryopteris dilatata, D. Filix-mas, Blech-
num Spicant, Pteris aquilina.*

SUMMARY AND CONCLUSIONS

The three woods have much in common. As regards site, each stands
on a steep slope of westerly aspect in a deep valley. It is obvious that
east winds are good for neither man, beast, nor oaks. Notwithstanding
the extraordinary effect that winds from the wnw. have had upon the
oaks at Wistman's Wood, and upon some of the highest-situate oaks
at Piles Wood and Black Tor, we may be in some danger of over-
estimating the inclemency of the climate. At Wistman's Wood there
are many hut-circles along the side of the hill above the Middle and
North Woods and above the ground between them; at Piles Wood
there are hut-circles on the hillside well beyond the trees; and our predecessors of the early Bronze Age had a very good idea of desirable sites
for their habitations; especially they liked dry ground with a warm
exposure. I yield Black Tor to the pessimistic critic; there no early man
had the hardihood to build his dwelling.

Each of the three woods springs from soil which chiefly consists of
boulders; in fact, the association of boulder and tree is so marked that
evidently the presence of the former is necessary to the origin of the
wood. Several reasons suggest themselves. It has been held, by Mr.
Harris among others, that the shelter of the boulders was essential to
the first seedlings as protection from the storms. It has been held, by
Mr. Miller Christy among others, that the boulders protected the seedlings from grazing cattle: certainly at parts of each wood no cattle could
penetrate in consequence of the roughness of the ground. I myself have
above suggested that the cattle, where not of necessity excluded, found
nothing to tempt them into the area, in consequence of the absence of
herbage among the boulders; and this although I have seen a Kerry
cow walk a quarter of a mile over its native hills to crop a square yard
of greenstuff: our Dartmoor cattle are not as hard pressed. These argu-
ments do not exhaust the benefits which the trees derive from the boulders. I believe there is truth, partial at least, in all the above. But there is
another advantage which must be allowed considerable weight. In
shallow and yielding soil no oak, exposed as on these hillsides, could
find an abiding place for its roots; once beyond the sapling stage it
must become a windfall. But, wedged in the crevices between the
granite blocks, and wandering far in search of the sparse soil, the roots
find such anchorage as must be necessary to sustain the eccentric load of
procumbent trees; as a foundation therefore the boulders are an essential.
And I would repeat that you must not too closely judge the past by the
present, the ground was rougher in all these woods when the trees first
colonized them; in the course of ages the accumulation of leaf-mould
has smoothed away many of the irregularities which formerly existed.

It was long ago noted by de la Beche (1839, p. 476) that oaks grew well on 'growan' soil, growan being the decomposed granite surface which forms the subsoil of so many acres of Dartmoor (see p. 7). I have given instances of the recuperative power and vegetative capacity shown by certain trees; in so doing I may not have specifically stated that in each of the three woods which we are considering there is ample evidence that each season's growth is healthy and normal, being fully up to the standard of lowland oaks. The difference is that in these woods such growth is not additive in successive seasons, being largely expended in making good the losses which are brought by most winters. There may perhaps be a little disadvantage caused by the shorter growing season enjoyed by the trees on the Dartmoor highlands, but this is certainly not very marked.

Among the boulders the oaks have wide-spreading root systems; the soil is merely a filling of the interstices of the 'clatter' of rock, and a considerable length of root is necessary to place the tree in contact with a sufficiency of humus. It is notable that, in each of the woods, even the older trees show a strong tendency to the continued formation of adventitious roots, which spring from the base of such trunk as the tree may possess. It is, I think, from these more recent and shallow-seated roots that suckers arise at some distance from the parent tree. The root system not infrequently retains its vitality after the subaerial growth has been destroyed, and fresh saplings then spring to replace the lost tree. There seems to be an opinion among foresters that the regenerative capacity of the oak largely fails at the age of ninety years or there-abouts, and trees coppiced after that age will doubtfully make fresh growth. This certainly is not true of the ancient woods of Dartmoor. I think that it would be difficult to fix an age limit at which the roots, deprived of their trunk and branches, cannot replace them; there may well be root systems in full life at Wistman's Wood which are older than any of the trees. The circumstances are in part like those of plants which propagate by runners or by other vegetative processes: one cannot say that the plant ever dies until it has been extirpated as a species from a given area of ground. But, more than that, there is here the great vitality exhibited by the original root, apart from its adventitious extensions.

If, then, the growth and vitality of the trees is such as I claim for them, how are we to account, first for their small absolute size, and secondly for their small size relative to their age? The answer is that the trunk and branch system of any tree, until decay sets in, is directly pro-portioned to the leaf area which it has borne and the period of time over which it has borne it. If each winter, or most winters, a proportion of the leaf-bearing twig is killed off, if even whole branches suffer break-age, then the tree as a whole can never attain the full canopy which the vigorous growth during the successive summers of its existence

would represent, could such growth be preserved. Trunk area for trunk
area, these stunted trees carry certainly less than one-quarter, in some
instances less than one-sixth of the leaf area which trees having similar
girths would carry in sheltered situations. I am sorry that I have not
found time to make exact comparisons. It follows that the increase in
diameter of the trunk will each year be only from one-fourth to one-
sixth (or such other proportion as precise measurement may disclose)
of the increase of a lowland oak. After a time the canopy of leaf becomes practically a constant, destruction and reconstruction balancing,
but the trunk and branches continue their slow increase in diameter.
We can make one, approximate, comparison if we ignore the possibility
of the small procumbent tree at Piles Wood being older than the Wistman's Wood seedling now growing, at the age of twenty-six years, in
Mr. J. S. Amery's grounds at Druid. The little oak at Piles Wood has
a girth of 8½ in., Mr. Amery's oak, at the same height above the ground,
girths over 15 in., and this latter tree spent the first seven years of its
existence in a pot. In diameter of trunk the more favourably situated
tree has come near a ratio of 2 to 1 as against the exposed plant, and this
in a little over a quarter of a century. The Piles Wood oak is 4 ft 8 in.
in height, the Druid tree reaches 14 ft, a ratio of 1 to 3. The Piles Wood
oak branches away from the wind and in that direction only; the Druid
tree branches toward all quarters of the horizon; the leaf area borne
by the Druid tree must be at least eight times that of the tree at
Piles Wood. So great a divergence, attained at such an early age, is
excellent evidence of the possibility of extreme divergences in later
years.

I have already pointed out that the young procumbent oak at Piles
Wood must have 18 annual rings to the radial inch, more probably 20;
the Druid oak has 11 rings only in the same distance.

Laslett counted the number of annual rings in 21 different specimens
of English oak; his first ten trees were of relatively slow growth; at 9 in.
diameter they gave a mean of 28 annual rings, or just over three to the
inch; at 6 in. diameter they gave 3⅔ rings to the inch. The Druid oak
has three times this number, but its early life in the pot probably
cramped it somewhat, and it must also be remembered that Druid is
practically 600 ft above sea level. Comparing Laslett's figure of 28
years age for 9 in. diameter with Buller's oak from Wistman's Wood,
showing an age of 163 years for the same diameter, we have actual
figures for the difference between normally grown timber and that of
our Dartmoor woods. Had I taken Laslett's second ten trees, which
gave a mean of 16 years age at 9 in. diameter (admittedly magnificent
specimens) the comparison would have been more striking. Now all
Laslett's trees were such as yielded marketable timber, and the length
of trunk has also to be considered; on the other hand, the Dartmoor
oaks must be credited with the immense amount of wasted effort which

they have had to put forth in the shape of growth destroyed soon after its formation. I have no doubt that the leaf area borne by the trees measured by Laslett was greater than the leaf area of the Wistman's Wood oaks of similar girth, in at least the inverse ratio of their respective ages. This would give from six to ten times, as the proportion of the leaf canopy of the well-grown oaks to that of the dwarfed trees, figures which certainly are not unreasonable.

There is a small collection of trees of varied species at Shavercombe, in the Plym Valley. Here the little Shavercombe brook, passing, in its course, from the granite to the altered sedimentaries, has carved out, for a short distance, a steep-sided valley; the head of the depression being formed by a waterfall (Pl. 16B). From the moorland above, the existence of this gully cannot be detected until one is almost upon its verge. Here, in the shelter of the steep sides of the depression, grow fifteen trees, comprising nine mountain ashes, two sycamores, two willows, one hawthorn, and one oak. Not one of these trees shows a twig above the crest of the valley side. The oak is of the pedunculate species, its girth is 34 in., and its height 24 ft; it twists its trunk so as almost to hug the cliff from which it springs; its next neighbour of the same species is two miles distant, which raises the question of how the acorn reached this remote spot, and by what chance it fell in this one sheltered valley of such small area, rather than upon the unfriendly moor. From time to time I have found the remains of acorns upon the open moorland at least a mile to two miles or more from the nearest oak trees. Another problem is the arrival of the seed of the first of the two sycamores, the nearest possible parent being also two miles distant, but I do not doubt the capacity of a high wind to effect the transport of a sycamore seed over this distance.

Isolated thorn and mountain ash trees occur in various parts of the moor, their distribution is not hard to explain, and in hardiness these species far surpass the oak. On the slope of Yes Tor, at an elevation of 1,420 ft, is a hawthorn tree, wholly unsheltered from any quarter. It girths 10 in. and stands 9 ft high, and this year (1922) it has been covered with blossom.

Four hundred yards north-east from Black Tor, at an elevation of 1,570 ft, are two mountain ash trees, which as seedlings had shelter from boulders, but have now outgrown it. Both stand 12 ft 10 in. in height, the girth of one is 17 in. and of the other 11 in.; and both are strong and healthy. Another, somewhat unhappy-looking, mountain ash occupies an even more elevated position in another cluster of boulders not far distant. It is a peculiarity of the mountain ash that, unlike the oak, it bends before the blast, the trunk and branches taking a permanent set; even so, it never assumes the procumbent form which is forced upon the oak by successive amputations.

This, however, is trespassing beyond the subject, and long as this

chapter may be it leaves sufficient of interest untouched to make un-
pardonable its expansion with foreign matter.

EDITOR'S NOTE

The above chapter comprised Worth's contribution to a 'symposium'
(as he preferred to call it) on the Dartmoor Oak Woods, published
under joint authorship with Miller Christy, F.L.S. (Christy and Worth,
1922, *Trans. Devon. Assn.*, Vol. 54, pp. 291–342). Christy contributed
an account of the botany of Wistman's Wood, which is amply summarized in Tansley's *The British Isles and their Vegetation*. The latter
work gives a prominent place to this wood among the descriptions of
British oak woods, devoting to it four pages and twelve excellent
original photographs. An outstanding feature of Wistman's Wood is
the abundance of ferns and mosses growing as epiphytes on the trees.

The uniqueness of the Dartmoor oak woods has often been stressed,
and doubt exists whether any counterparts exist elsewhere in the world.
In discussions on this topic, however, it appears to have been overlooked that stunted oak woods remarkably similar to those on Dartmoor occur on the wind-swept cliff slopes of North Cornwall, between
Millook and Crackington. A detailed comparison should prove interesting.

There have been several attempts to derive the name of Wistman's
Wood. It has been regarded as a corruption of the Celtic *uisg-mœn-cœd*
or 'rocky wood by the water' (S. P. Oliver), or as a corruption of
'Welshman's' Wood (Crossing). But Risdon in 1620 used the present-
day spelling; and the first syllable is presumably 'wisht' of Devon dia-
lect, meaning 'spookish' or 'uncanny'. The 'wisht'-man is regarded
either as an ancient medicine-man or hermit (Warden Page) or as the
Devil (*Place-Names of Devon*, p. 198). May not, however, the most
direct rendering, namely, 'spookish being' or '*bogey-man*', give a satisfactory derivation of the name ?

G.M.S.

REFERENCES
(See also General References, p. 497)

Dixon, Miss, 1830. *A Journal of Ten Days' Excursion on the Western and Northern
    Borders of Dartmoor.*
Ellacombe, H. N., 1896. *Plant Lore and Garden Craft of Shakespeare.*
Harris, G. T., 1921. Ecological notes on Wistman's Wood and Black Tor Copse,
    Dartmoor *Trans. Devon. Assn.*, Vol. 70, pp. 37–55.

THE DARTMOOR HUT-CIRCLES

HUT-CIRCLES are the walls, or ruins of the walls, of pre-historic buildings, constructed for use as dwellings, possibly in some instances as stores, while it has been suggested that others were cattle-sheds.

There are at least 1,500 hut-circles on Dartmoor. Of these 200 have been examined by excavation since Mr. Robert Burnard led the way in August and September 1893, at Broadun and Broadun Ring. The excavations have been conducted by the Dartmoor Exploration Committee, appointed by the Devonshire Association. In respect of 120 of the huts the work of excavation may be regarded as satisfactory; the remaining 80 received treatment which was neither thorough nor well ordered.

That there has been great divergence of method may be judged by the following comparison. At one site it was found necessary to employ labour to the extent of 106 man-days in the excavation of five huts, or at the rate of 21·2 man-days per hut; at another site fifteen huts were excavated with a labour expenditure of but 32 man-days, or at the rate of 2·133 man-days per hut, and even so the committee-man in charge complained that exceptional circumstances caused an undue expenditure of labour. Thus the time given to the excavation of a hut at the first site was to the time given at the second site as 10 to 1. A dual disability attaches to hasty work; in the first place such objects as may be found are but imperfect evidence since the conditions of their finding are not properly ascertained or noted, in the second place no valid conclusion can be derived from the apparent absence of any particular object or class of objects. The obligation to weigh and assess evidence attaches to all forms of research, not least to archaeology.

DISTRIBUTION OF THE HUTS

No formal census of the Dartmoor hut-circles has ever been taken. and some writers have been inclined to exaggerate the number. A reasonable approximation is possible; the Ordnance Survey shows most of the known huts, but certainly not all. Other workers and my-self have noted and planned huts which do not appear on the Ordnance Survey, and, taken together, these sources indicate a total of 1,330.

There remain others not accounted for in this enumeration, and I estimate that there may be 1,500 in all.

Taking the 1,330 which are fully ascertained it is possible to indicate their distribution. For this purpose I have worked by areas; no plan on a reasonable scale could give precise individual locations. The unit of area adopted has been the quarter sheet of the six-inch survey, each quarter sheet covering six square miles, three miles from east to west, and two miles from north to south.

The greatest density of distribution is found in the area of sheet CXIX, NW., where there are 161 huts or at the rate of 27 to the square mile. This sheet covers the valley of the Yealm at and above Hawns and Dendles, extending to and including some part of the boggy land toward the source of the river, land on which there are no huts. The unit of area next in density of occupation is covered by sheet CXII, SE., Trowlesworthy and Ditsworthy Warrens in the Plym Valley: here there are 136 hut-circles, or at the rate of 23 to the square mile. Taking the whole of the 42 quarter sheets which are included in the census, the mean number of huts per quarter sheet is 32, with the extremes of 161 and 0; and the mean number of huts per square mile is a little over 5. In the map (Fig. 12) no attempt is made to locate the individual huts, but the total for each quarter sheet is uniformly distributed over its surface.

Certainly there have been losses, huts which have disappeared, leaving no trace. Areas once open moorland have long since been enclosed to form the 'ancient tenements'; from such areas the foundations of the hut-circles have been removed as hindrances to agriculture, or in other instances to provide stone for the fences. On the more recent newtakes, which are still largely moorland, the loss has been less complete, since the chief cause has been the use of the stone for fences, and there being little arable land, clearance for agriculture has been slight.

Always, since formal roads have existed, there has been robbery and destruction for the purposes of the highways; this may have been checked somewhat, but it has been active in quite recent years. On Shapley Common near Cullacombe Head there were two prehistoric pounds, of which one contained seven huts and the other contained three, while there was one hut outside the pounds (See *Second Report of the Dartmoor Exploration Committee*, 1895). In the years 1924, 1925, a contractor removed the pound walls completely, and all the huts except No. 1, Western Pound, the stones of which were much too large for his purpose. He did not waste labour on breaking them, but took the smaller and left the larger standing.

The stone was used as bottom ballast over trenches formed in the road for telephone cables. In another part of the moor a hut was destroyed to provide material for a rock garden. These are not by any means unaccompanied examples of destruction.

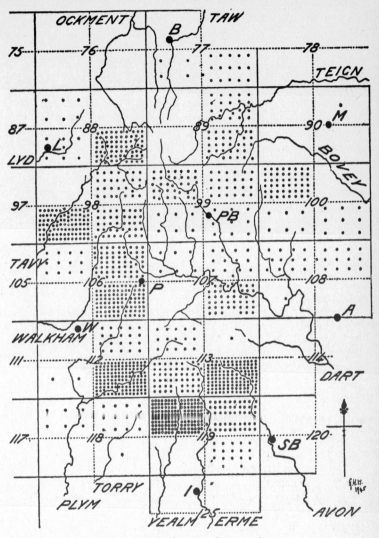

FIG. 12. Distribution of Hut-circles.

A, Ashburton; B, Belstone; I, Ivybridge; L, Lydford; M, Moretonhampstead;
P, Princetown; PB, Postbridge; SB, South Brent; W, Walkhampton.
Numbers refer to the Ordnance Survey six-inch sheets.

But, when all these sources of attrition have been considered, it remains that in the enumeration which has been made there are included areas which have been unaffected by robbery and are as fully occupied as we can conceive any area to have been; and yet others from which the total absence of huts cannot possibly be attributed to any cause but the unsuitability of the ground. All things considered the estimate of 1,500 surviving hut-circles is not in any way likely to be markedly deficient. And yet Baring-Gould has written (*Book of Dartmoor*, p. 48): "With regard to the numbers of people who lived on Dartmoor in prehistoric times, it is simply amazing to reflect upon. Tens of thousands of their habitations have been destroyed; their largest and most populous settlements, where are now the 'ancient tenements', have been obliterated, yet tens of thousands remain." He places a population of 2,000 persons in a circular space a mile in diameter (0·795 mile) at Postbridge. (The population of the whole parish of Lydford, some 80 sq. miles in area, is at present about 2,300.) He claims that the camp on Whittor served 2,500 people, and he ascribes 21,000 persons as residents in the Erme Valley.

When it is said that tens of thousands of huts have been lost the only possible reply is that such loss is improbable; when, on the other hand, it is asserted that tens of thousands still remain a positive denial can be given. And, further, on Baring-Gould's own estimate, even one unit of ten thousand would involve a population numbering 60,000 men, women and children of a race largely dependent on hunting, possessed of but a rudimentary agriculture but to some extent pastoral. Dartmoor, even the Dartmoor of those days, would be wholly inadequate to their maintenance.

Test Baring-Gould's accuracy by his reference to the Erme Valley. he says (op. cit., p. 48): "Take the Erme Valley, high up where difficult of access; the number of huts there crowded on the hill slopes is incredible." One may assume that 'incredible' is to be taken as involving *beyond all reasonable expectation or experience*. The fact is that 'high up' the number of huts is very small; there are few or none. But, taking the whole moorland valley of the Erme, which will include the lower and intermediate slopes where huts are more frequent, there are by count 136 hut-circles, to ensure full measure and meet any possible omissions 12½% may be added, giving a corrected total of 153. The area involved is 9·9 sq. miles, say 10. There would thus be at the most 15·3 hut-circles to a square mile. The Yealm Valley, without the added 12½%, gives 27 hut-circles to the square mile over one area of 6 miles, and the Plym 23 hut-circles per square mile over a similar area. Now 15 huts to the square mile would hardly appear incredible even if this density were not exceeded in adjacent valleys, nor would such a number give rise to crowded hill slopes.

Views of typical hut-circles, as they survive to-day, are given in Pl. 25.

DETAILS OF CONSTRUCTION

Of 137 huts which have been accurately measured the mean internal diameter, to the nearest foot, was found to be 17 ft. The median value occurs at 15½ ft: that is to say, as many huts have diameters in excess of 15½ ft as present less diameters (Fig. 13).

On excavation the floor of a hut is rarely found at a less depth than eighteen inches below the level of the surrounding country, two steps down being provided at the entrance. These steps are formed in un-hewn granite. The actual depth at which the floor lies was determined by the amount of topsoil which it was necessary to remove to arrive at the surface of the gravelly subsoil of decomposed granite, or 'growan'. Once reached the growan is firm to the tread and in no wise clayey; but it is soft enough to be readily smoothed and freed from any in-equalities by the use of even the most primitive scraping or excavating tools. The wall of the hut is most usually founded on or in a surface

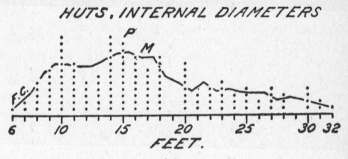

FIG. 13. Internal diameters of huts.

similarly freed of all topsoil. It would appear that the first step toward the construction of a hut was the removal of turf and topsoil over the whole area to be occupied by floor and wall.

It may be noted that many of the small burial mounds, where these are cairns, are found to have been heaped upon areas cleared in this same manner.

When the hut lies on a hillside, as do by far the greater number, the surface of the subsoil follows the slope of the hill. Some little addi-tional excavation is common on the uphill side, to partly correct the level of the floor, but a cross fall nearly always remains, involving gradients in the floor at least 1 in 10 in many instances.

As a general rule, in well-preserved huts and those which have not been the subject of secondary occupation in later times, it is a feature of the walls that the inner faces are lined with slabs, thus presenting as regular a surface as the material would permit, with a minimum of joints. These liners, for so we may name the slabs, were as truly a surface finish as is the plaster on the walls of a modern room. But they were also at times structural features. When of sufficient area and thickness they formed, firm set in the growan or 'calm', the whole inner wall of the hut except for the gaps left between them in consequence of their irregularity of form; or above those which did not rise to the same general height as the others. These gaps were filled with dry stone masonry. At times, however, the available liners were too thin, and consequently too light; or the slope of the ground called for a more substantial retaining wall on the higher side. In such instances the liners were backed with dry stone masonry, which in itself bore the pressure of the bank or hillside. A good example of this composite type of wall occurred at Metherel, Hut 1, in the valley of the South Teign (Fig. 14).

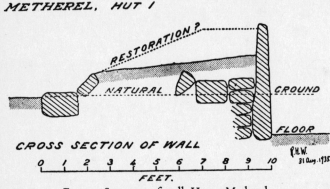

FIG. 14. Structure of wall, Hut 1, Metherel.

This also exhibits one type of circle construction, in which the inner wall of dry stone masonry and liner was backed by an earth bank, in that instance 8 ft 6 in. wide at the base, including the stone work, and with stones disposed to support the toe. Less frequent is the wall, narrower in construction, with a stone face on either side (thick slabs being most frequently used) and the space between the faces filled with soil and small stone. An example, dissected by fence builders for the sake of the smaller stone, may be seen near Moorlands opposite Prince Hall (Fig. 15). The interior diameter of this hut is 28 ft, the thickness of the wall 6 ft. In this type of structure a proportion of the stones will usually be found to be post-like rather than slab-like, but always a flat face, even though narrow, is presented to the interior of the hut.

The size of the slabs forming the inner lining depended on the material available. A really large stone, otherwise suitable, was a temptation to the builders, although the labour of its transport and erection may have been great. In Hut 2 at Metherel there are large slabs; the largest forms a rough triangle set on its base. The base measures 12 ft 6 in., the height of the apex above the floor is 6 ft 10 in., and the mean

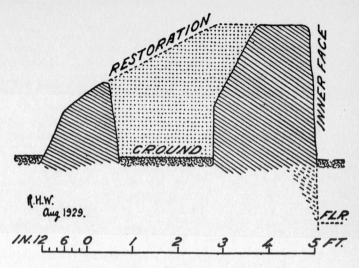

RESTORATION

INNER FACE

GROUND

R.H.W.
Aug 1929.

FLR.

IN. 12 6 0   1   2   3   4   5 FT.

FIG. 15. Structure of wall, hut at Moorlands.

METHEREL
HUT 2.

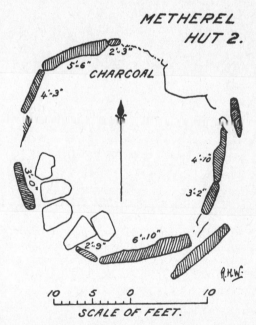

2'-3"

5'-6"

CHARCOAL

4'-3"

4'-10"

3'-0"

3'-2"

2'-9"

6'-10"

R.H.W.

10   5   0   10

SCALE OF FEET.

FIG. 16. Plan of Hut 2, Metherel.

thickness may be taken as 1 ft 4 in. This involves a weight of at least 3½ tons, assuming the variations in thickness to have led to an over-estimate in that dimension. Somewhat similar dimensions are attained in a hut on Shapley Common, in the Western Enclosure, where the largest slab measures 7 ft 3 in. in length at floor level, stands 4 ft 9 in. above the floor, and has an average thickness of 1 ft 1 in.: its least weight would be 1½ tons. This circle proved too much for the road contractor who swept all else from the common, huts and pound walls alike; it was too substantial to be converted to ballast at a profit. See Fig. 16 for a plan of Hut 2, Metherel, and Pl. 24 A and B for views of this circle. On all plans the figures written against the several stones indicate their greatest height above floor level.

The irregular form of the slabs, and the fact that no sort of trimming was attempted, left interspaces, especially near the top of the walls, which were filled in with dry stone walling. There are sites, such as Shavercombe and Riders Rings, where slabs are not to be found in the immediate neighbourhood: in such places the whole wall of the hut was constructed in dry walling. This form of structure has nowhere proved as permanent, and the walls are now more usually mere mounds of rubble.

In those hut-circles which have been the subject of secondary occu-pation, of which few have been exhaustively examined, the walls, where they required reconditioning or rebuilding, have always been restored in dry masonry. In one probable instance of secondary occu-pation, on Brown Heath above Hook Lake in the Erme Valley, the outer face of the bank forming the wall of the hut-circle has been faced with dry masonry, to an extent not known elsewhere.

The entrances are invariably placed facing south to south-west, the builders being evidently of the opinion that even the rains and gales from that quarter were preferable to the storms from the north and nor'-nor'-west which, on Dartmoor, are the greatest enemies of all living things. With walls no more than 4 ft 6 in. in height above floor level, and the floor usually sunk 1 ft 6 in. below ground level, the entrance is of necessity low, 3 ft in height being rather exceptional. At Hut 2, Legis Tor, the clear height is 2 ft 9 in., and the clear width 1 ft 4 in., while two steps lead to the floor of the hut, eighteen inches below the threshold. Other examples are: Metherel Hut 1, entrance 2 ft 9 in. high by 2 ft 2 in. in width; Grimspound Hut 4, 2 ft 5 in. high by 2 ft 1 in. wide; Hut 7, 2 ft 6 in. high by 2 ft 1 in. wide; Hut 12, 3 ft high by 2 ft 9 in. wide. The means of these five examples are, height 2 ft 8 in., width 2 ft 1 in.

At Grimspound, close by some of the entrances, stones were found lying in the turf. From their shape and length they were reasonably identifiable as the lintels of the entrances. Drawings were given in the first report of the Dartmoor Exploration Committee in which these supposed lintels were shown replaced on the jambs; and it was in each instance made clear in the text that the stone when found was displaced and lying on the ground. But Prof. V. Gordon Childe (*The Bronze Age*, p. 160) has written: "In some later Huts (Late Bronze Age) on Dartmoor the megalithic jambs and the stone lintel above them are still in position." And he cites the Dartmoor Exploration Committee as authority. The period to which he assigns the huts will be the subject of later remark. The alleged miracle by which these small stones have been sustained precariously balanced on the door jambs must be at once dismissed.

For illustrations see Fig. 17, plan and section of entrance to Hut 1, Metherel, and Fig. 21, elevation of entrance to Hut 4, Grimspound, with lintel restored to its original position. Pl. 26A gives a view of a hut-circle on Ger Tor, Tavy Cleave, showing the jambs of the entrance.

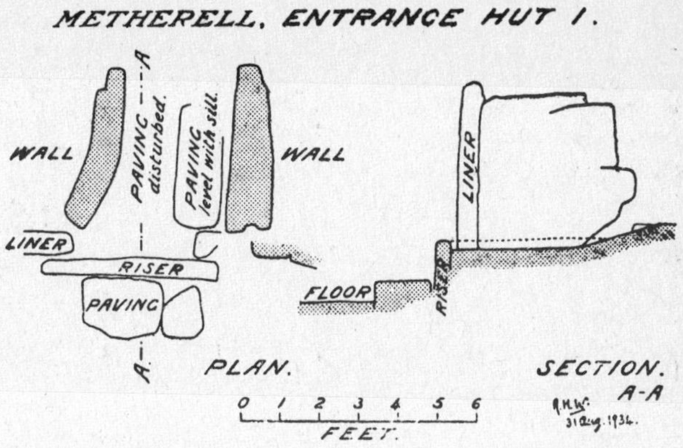

FIG. 17. Plan and section of entrance, Hut 1, Metherel.

In T.D.A. 77, Pl. 8, is a view of a robbed circle on Bagtor Down, the entrance being rather unusually high, one stone measuring 4 ft 5 in. in height, and 4 ft 6 in. in width. Pl. 26B is a view of entrance to Hut 2, Legis Tor, looking into the hut.

The structure of the roof is a matter for conjecture. The fact that the interior of the hut-circle is always unencumbered by stone, except such as has fallen from the wall, is sufficient proof that the roof was not a stone structure of the beehive type. The probable inference is that its framework consisted of poles set as rafters, radiating from the apex and resting on the centre of the wall, thus forming a cone. The lower end of the rafters would thus be farther apart than would be convenient for any form of thatching, and it is probable that some form of interlaced or wattle work would there be used; unless, which is unlikely, short lengths of pole were set horizontally across the rafters, as purlins, and secured by lashing. It has been thought that flat stones set in the centre of the floor may have formed bases for vertical poles, supporting the rafters at the centre; some few hut-circles have been found with stones so placed. In one instance a hole was found sunk in the calm at the centre of the floor; this hole was 8 in. deep, 4 in. in diameter, and had a 'gob' of charcoal at the bottom (Shapley Common, Hut 1). On Langstone Moor, in Hut 10, a hole, similarly placed, was 8 in. in depth and 3 in. in diameter. These holes have been supposed to have been formed for the reception of the feet of centre poles. But so few are the central flat stones, and the holes, that it seems unwise to draw any general conclusion; especially when it is remembered how frequently the hearth occupies the centre of the floor, to the obvious exclusion of the idea that centre poles were in use in those huts.

The nature of the ultimate cover of the roof, however framed, is also a matter for speculation. Skins stretched over the frame have been suggested, but skins were probably too much in demand for other purposes, and in any event would not have been well suited to permanent buildings, such as these huts certainly were. The alternative would seem to be thatch of some sort, turves, heather or rushes, all readily available and all well suited to provide a weatherproof roof. Amid all the uncertainties this much may be accepted as assured—the huts were not roofed with stone in the manner of the beehive huts of the Early Iron Age. The walls are not suited to such form of structure, and the large amount of stone necessary to roof even a small hut-circle must, on the collapse of the roof, have left the floor heavily cumbered with rubble. With the larger circles of, say, 30 ft in diameter, this consideration becomes even more obvious. No such rubble is found.

A coned roof, discharging the rain which it received on to the earth and stone centre of the wall, may seem an improbable and objectionable expedient; but it may be recalled that the 'black houses' of Lewis discharged the rainfall from their roofs on the peat-filled centre of a wall faced with rubble masonry within and without; and what would seem the necessarily damp conditions were endured well into the days of living memory by a race more advanced in civilization than the Dartmoor people of the Early Bronze Age. Baring-Gould in his *Book of Dartmoor*, 1900, writes: "Occasionally round stones, flat on one side and convex on the other, have been disinterred in the huts. They served to protect the apex of the roof, where the poles were drawn together, from the action of the rain, which would rot them, as well as to prevent the rain from entering at this point. An example of a stone of the same character may be seen in actual use on the thatched circular pounding house on Berry Down, near Throwleigh" (p. 70). This passage is an instance of too facile interpretation, comparable with Major Hamilton Smith's identification of an unfinished edge runner for an apple mill as the circular capstone of a fallen cromlech, at Merrivale. It is the more surprising in view of the fact that no form of dressed or shaped stone has yet been found as part of the structure of any hut.

These circular stones are also referred to in the third report of the Dartmoor Exploration Committee (*T. D. A.*, Vol. 28, p. 180, 1896), wherein it is stated that four have been found, at Whitten Ridge (2), Kings Oven (1) and Buttern Down (1). Three of these stones have diameters of 24 in., 19 in. and 17 in., respectively, and are from 2 to 3 in. thick; the fourth, found at Buttern Down, is 3 ft 6 in. in diameter, and 6 in. thick. I may add that there are other such circular stones lying about on the moors wholly apart from hut-circles, and in especial there are several lying singly and together on Belstone Common. The smaller are the capstones of rick staddles, the larger are millstones, in various stages of manufacture. It is not surprising that they are at times found in hut-circles, which were regularly used as quarries by the stone-masons. The idea of a circular stone, whether of 2 ft or 3 ft 6 in. diameter, and whether 3 or 6 in. in thickness, poised insecurely on the apex of the cone formed by the light and irregular branches which made the structure of the roof, and closing the aperture which must have been left for the escape of the smoke from wood and peat fires suggests conditions of anxiety and discomfort in which the danger attaching to this prehistoric substitute for the sword of Damocles was aggravated by the certainty of ultimate asphyxiation.

The Early Iron Age buildings of west Cornwall are found to have been provided with drains which took away from their floors such water as seeped through the ground or found access through defective walls and roofs. No such provision was made on Dartmoor, nor, apparently, was it necessary. The substantial bank, at least 6 ft to 8 ft in width, which formed the walls, and the growan or calm of the floors could not exclude the possibility of damp, but were efficient against the access of as much water as would form pools upon the floor or need a drain for its removal. The only water I have ever seen in a hut after or during excavation has been such as has arisen from heavy rain falling directly on the surface of the newly bared floor.

The entrances were sometimes provided with shelter walls forming a manner of porch. This feature is local and by no means common; it is found in some huts at Grimspound, Shapley Common and Whitten Ridge. The shelter wall is always on the right-hand side of the entrance, looking out from the hut; and hence is so placed as to afford partial protection from the north-west wind. The best developed of such walls is to be found at Hut 3, Grimspound (Fig. 18). Here the wall curves round and completely shelters the entrance from the south-west. On the other hand, Hut 12, in the same pound, has a shelter wall which extends radially in a straight line (Fig. 19).

At Foales Arrishes[1] there is a large hut-circle (of 30 ft inside diameter)

[1] See footnote on p. 126.

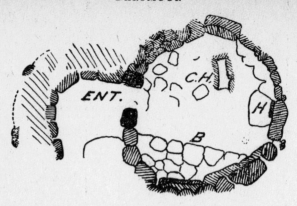

FIG. 18. Hut 3, Grimspound.

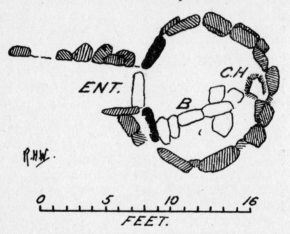

R.H.W.

0   5   10   16
FEET.

FIG. 19. Hut 12, Grimspound.

which is now involved in a number of rectangular fields of later date; parallel to the outer face of the wall, and 4 ft 3 in. from it, is a wall which partly encloses a space 13 ft in length by 4 ft 3 in. in width, open at the east end and closed at the west. This has all the appearance of a shelter wall such as has been described; but, although it closely adjoins the entrance it does not shelter it or extend across it. The space so marked out is in part paved, and may formerly have been wholly paved. The intent of this adjunct to the circle is unknown. Baring-Gould, on faith of the charcoal found on the floor, says that it was a kitchen. He also says the hut "had a seat carried round part at least of the interior, made of branches that were held from spreading by sharp stones planted upright in the floor" (op. cit., p. 178). There are but three stones which can be called in evidence as being possibly planted in the

PLATE I

A. Stones of a prehistoric row disclosed by turf-tye. Long stone row, Erme.

B. Denuding peat. Slopes of Great Kneesit.

PLATE 2

A. Bedding and jointing of massive type. Littaford Tor, view looking N. 70° W.; height 10 ft.

B. Bedding intermediate between massive and lamellar, sloping with hillside. Brae Tor.

PLATE 3

A. Lamellae of moderate thickness, sloping with hillside. Little Lynx Tor.

B. Fine lamellar bedding, showing first deviation from horizontal, near hill top. Thurlestone, Watern Tor, looking E.

PLATE 4

Pseudo-bedding at a steep angle: Dewerstone, cliffs on south-east side, viewed from south west.

PLATE 5

A. Horizontal bedding of rock in valley, River Tavy, under Tavy Cleave.

B. Slipper Stones, West Ockment. Length of sloping rock face over 60 ft, gradient 1 in 1·8. View looking S. 10° E.

PLATE 6

A. Inclusion, Kestor. Length, 4 ft 2 in., height, 1 ft 4 in.,
the block with the square-topped notch in it.

B. Inclusion, Beardown. Diameter 25 in.

PLATE 7

A. Tin-work near Birch Tor: Chaw Gulley.

B. Tinner's burrows: Drizzlecombe, Plym Valley.

PLATE 8

Lamellar bedding with rare, but well-marked joints. Chat Tor,
Rattlebrook Hill; view looking s. 61° e. Height 9 ft 6 in.

PLATE 9

A. Blackingstone. View looking N. 88° E.

B. Blackingstone, showing vertical joints in domed, lamellar tor.
View looking N. 24° W. Height about 35 ft.

PLATE 10

A. Bowerman's Nose. View looking N. 8° W. Height 21 ft 6 in.

B. The 'Colossi', Staple Tor. View looking N. 70° W. Height 24 ft.

PLATE 11

A. Rounded block. Great Mis Tor. View looking
N. 50° W. Height to top from grass, 7 ft.

B. Rounded block. Thornworthy Tor. View looking N. 43° E. Height to top
from grass, 12 ft.

PLATE 12

A. Parted blocks. East Mill Tor. View looking N. 38°–30′ E.

B. Parted blocks forming natural gateway. Oke Tor. Clear
height of gateway, 7 ft 5 in. View looking N. 18° E.

PLATE 13

A. Residual boulders. Yes Tor Bottom, near King Tor.

Photo: *D. P. Wilson*, 1952.

B. Parting in rocks. Gutter, Rigmoor Down, Plym Valley.

PLATE 14

A. Linear arrangement of boulders forming part of clitter. Hen Tor.

B. Clitter, Hen Tor, Plym Valley.

PLATE 15

A. Mistor Pan, and view of perforation through side.

B. Rock-basin, Kestor.

PLATE 16

A. Great Nodden, Lyd Valley.

B. Shavercombe Waterfall, Plym Valley.

PLATE 17

A. Quarried block from Burrator, showing vein of contact granite drawn into general mass. 'A—A': light vein in centre of vein of contact material; above this—fine-grained granite; and below—porphyritic granite with flow structure.

B. Rock-basin, Gutter.

PLATE 18

Felsite A. Weathered Surface.

Above: Ludbrook, Ugborough.   Below: Hole, Chagford.

PLATE 19

A. Swaling checked by track. Langstone Moor.

B. Cotton-grass Moor. Snowdon, 1,600 ft. O.D.

PLATE 20

Whortleberry in fruit, photographed 5 December 1921.
Awsewell Rocks, near Ashburton.

PLATE 21

A. South-east tree, Wistman's (North) Wood.

B. Young tree, Wistman's (Middle) Wood.

PLATE 22

A. Procumbent oak, Wistman's (North) Wood.

B. South-east tree, Black Tor Beare.

PLATE 23

A. Wistman's (South) Wood, interior

B. Wistman's (South) Wood, interior.

PLATE 24

A

B

View of Hut 2, Metherel, (A) looking N.; (B) looking SE. (Wall from
inside hut.)

PLATE 25

A. Hut-circle, Legis Tor.

Photo: *G. M. Spooner*

B. One of the larger hut-circles, Merrivale, with others in middle distance. Middle Staple Tor, Staple Tor and Roos Tor in background.

PLATE 26

Photo: *G. M. Spooner*

A. Hut-circle on Ger Tor, Tavy Cleave, with prominent door-posts.

B. Entrance of Hut 2, Legis Tor, showing door-posts.

PLATE 27

HUT 2 RIDERS RINGS.

0   1   2   3 INS.

HUT 2 METHERELL.

0   1   2   3   4 INS.

R.H.M.

B. Whetstones from Riders Rings and Metherel.

A. Flints from hut-circles.
a and *b*: worked flint flake, Hut 2, Metherel.
c and *d*: flake with edge ground and polished (the upper edge shown in figure), Hut 4, Legis Tor.

PLATE 28

Vermin Traps. (1) Legis Tor, side (top) view. (2) Legis Tor, end view.
(3) Gutter, side (top) view.

PLATE 29

Slate shutters of vermin traps. (1) Legis Tor Pound.
(2) Near Shadyback Tor.

PLATE 30

Cairns. 1 and 2, Corndon Tor summit. 3, Corndon Tor, 550 yds
northward of summit.

PLATE 31

Cairns. 1, Near Corndon Tor. 2 and 3, Drizzlecombe.

PLATE 32

A. Three Barrows, central cairn.

B. Kistvaen, Thornworthy, looking N. 60° W.

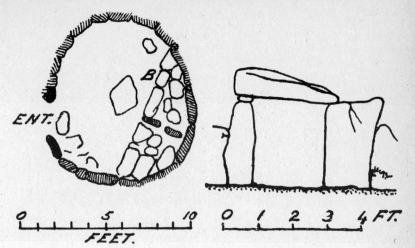

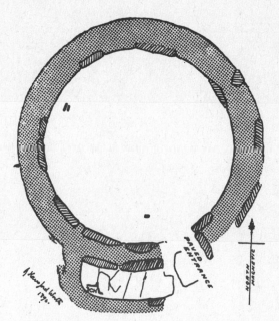

FIG. 20. Hut 16, Grimspound.   Fig. 21. Entrance, Hut 4, Grimspound.

FIG. 22. Hut 1, Foales Arrishes.

floor. One is near the entrance and measures 9 in. by 3 in. on plan. The other two form a pair, placed 22 ft away from the single stone as measured parallel to the circumference. One of this pair is 9 in. by about 3 in. on plan, the other 15 in. by about 4 in. The first stone stands 4 ft away from the inner circumference of the hut, the centre line between the pair is 2 ft 5 in. from the inner circumference. Kitchen and seat are alike guesswork.

Fig. 22 affords a plan of the hut known as No. 1, Foales. Arrishes, the wall of which is narrower than is usual, being from 5 ft to 4 ft in thickness.

FITTINGS

The hearth is commonly held to be the first essential of a British home, and on Dartmoor the accepted view can certainly be approved. The formal hearth of the Dartmoor hut-circle was a slab of fine-grained granite, set in the floor with its surface slightly above floor level. Somewhat rarely the slab is set below the general level of the floor and edged with stones pitched to form a surround at the floor level. The position of the hearth is varied; in about half the examples it is at or near the centre of the hut, but in others it is found against the wall, either opposite the entrance or not far within the entrance, on either the right or left side. No complete records have been kept, but in some groups the left side seems to have been preferred. A formal hearth is by no means a necessity, and there are many huts which show ample evidence of human occupation, and yield charcoal in considerable quantity, but have no hearth-stones; the bare floor served. At Legis Tor, of ten huts excavated, two returned no charcoal, and the remaining eight all showed charcoal, cooking holes and cooking stones (see below). But only in two of the eight were there stone hearths. Hearth-stones vary in size, for example: 53 × 33 in.; 36 × 24 in.; 32 × 24 in.; 25 × 22 in. and 24 × 17 in. They vary in condition with material and length of service. There are few which are not fire-cracked, and more than a few that appear to need immediate renewal. Although granite was used for the hearth of Bronze Age man and the furnace of the Elizabethan tinner it is not really effective as a refractory.

With the hearth was associated the cooking hole: man desired not only personal warmth, but also a hot meal. The cooking holes have been interpreted by reference to the known methods employed in cooking by later, but still primitive, races. Essentially the cooking hole is a small pit sunk in the floor of the hut, and at times bordered with stone set level with the floor. In size and shape it varies. In Hut 2, Legis Tor, it is kidney-shaped, about 2 ft in length and 10 in. in breadth, and 7 to 8 in. in depth. In Hut 7 in the same enclosure the dimensions are 14 in. in length, 7 in. in width and 8 in. in depth. In Hut 8, Rifle Range, Princetown, 1 ft long, 9 in. wide and 10 in. deep. Some of the holes are circular, as at Hut 1, Rifle Range, Princetown, 16 in. in diameter and 12 in. deep, and Hut 4 in the same group where a hole 18 in. in diameter and 12 in. in depth was found. Hut 12 in this group had a cooking hole entirely lined with stone. After the stone lining had been removed the hole measured 3 ft 6 in. in diameter and 1 ft 2 in. in depth. Allowance being made for the stone lining, this hole must originally have been a little less than 2 ft 6 in. in diameter, and 11 in. in depth. It contained about a wheelbarrow load and a half of charcoal. Other huts have yielded cooking holes lined with stone, for instance, Hut 8, Legis Tor, where the hole was completely stone-lined.

It does not appear that the cooking holes were in general of sufficient size to take any but small joints.

The above data may serve for the description of one form of cooking hole; there was another type, markedly different in construction and almost certainly different in use; this may properly be described as the 'cooking-pot hole'. It may be briefly but fully described as a cooking-pot of rough earthenware set in the floor of the hut in such manner that none but a small height of the rim stood above floor level. It is curious that this has not been formally recognized as a separate type. There are indications that it was in common use, and two very perfect examples have been recorded.

In May 1896, in Hut 7, Legis Tor, I found a cooking-pot hole, the first which had been observed in approximately perfect condition. "On the western side of the hut, a crock, or cooking pot, of unornamented pottery, was found set in the 'calm', below the level of the floor. The pot was badly cracked, but was temporarily held together by the contained earth and ashes. Its outer surface was in actual contact with the calm and no ash whatever was found outside it. This crock was successfully lifted and examined, before the cohesion of its contents failed, and left fragments only, which cannot, unfortunately, be properly restored. In diameter it measured, at its widest point, 10 in. Its total depth, including the rim, which was found inside it when it fell to pieces, was a little over 12 in. Two cooking stones were found in it. Curiously enough, the bottom of this pot which had been cracked while in use, had been mended *in situ* with white china clay, a mass of clay having been pressed into the bottom, to fill up cracks and cement together the broken fragments. This crock had a hemispherical bottom, and could not have been stood on a plane surface." From my log I may add that there was no fillet at the base of the neck.

This was the contribution to our knowledge yielded by the Plym Valley. Mr. Robert Burnard was at the same time excavating in the adjoining valley of the Meavy, at Raddick, and within less than twenty-four hours he happened upon a parallel find, in Hut 5 of that settlement, "nearly opposite the supposed entrance was the hearth, slightly raised, against a large stone in the wall. To the right of this, the cooking hole, under a large slab that had fallen forward out of the wall. This slab, in falling, had protected from destruction a fine vessel of rude hand-made pottery, occupying the cooking hole, and fairly intact. It had (except for the rounded base) the peculiar shape of the Cornish urns used for burials in the time of incineration, with a rib running as a hoop round it, $2\frac{1}{2}$ in. from the lip, and the portion above this was ornamented by zigzags. The bottom of the bowl was rounded.[1] This was distinctly seen when it was *in situ*; but when taken out, the bottom, which was very broken, went to pieces. In order to extract the vessel, it was necessary to destroy the cooking hole. The vessel measures $10\frac{1}{2}$ in. in height, and is 10 in. in diameter at the top. The rib is 1 in. thick." The quoted

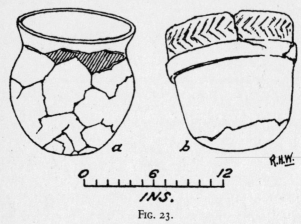

FIG. 23.

a. Cooking pot, Legis Tor, Hut 7.
b. Cooking pot, Raddick, Hut 5.

descriptions are from the Third Report of the Dartmoor Exploration Committee, 1896, and were written while all the circumstances were fresh in the minds of the excavators. Fig. 23 *a* and *b* are from drawings of these two pots.

Comparing the descriptions it will be seen that both had a greatest diameter of 10 in., that the depth of one was a little over 12 in., and of the other the depth was $10\frac{1}{2}$ in. The recovery of each involved the destruction of the cooking hole, so tightly were they set in the calm. The base of each was spherical, and that base much cracked.

The material from which each had been formed was thick, coarse and hand-made; but in finish they varied. No ornament of any kind was found on the Legis Tor pot, nor any strengthening fillet; the Rad-

[1] Fortunately this pot has survived and still exists in Plymouth City Museum. It appears to have a flat, not rounded, base and somewhat resembles the late Bronze Age 'bucket urns' of the Deverel-Rimbury series. (See Fox, 1951, plate X.) (ED.)

dick pot had a strengthening fillet at the base of the neck, and the neck bore chevron ornament.

Judging from the manner of their setting, these pots were probably never intended to be lifted. They may have held water which was heated by the simple expedient of dropping in heated cooking stones. The material of the pots was certainly not fireproof, and water could not have been boiled in them over the fire. But set in the calm and closely packed around, if cracked they would still be held together, and would be approximately leakproof. Cracked they would be, by heat, and by the fall of the cooking stones on to the bottom of the pot. It will be noted that two cooking stones were found in the pot at Legis Tor.

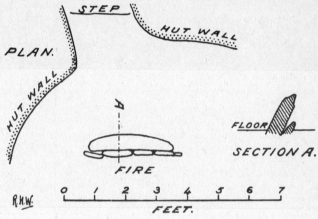

FIG. 24. Fireplace, Hut 2, Riders Rings.

The suggested interpretation reasonably fits the evidence, but necessarily admits neither proof nor disproof. If it is correct, then the cooking holes without pots may be taken to have provided the baking facilities for the hut dwellers, while the cooking holes with pots served as the saucepans. Roasting over the open fire would probably be practised also, the meat being held on a wooden skewer, or with larger joints impaled on a wooden spit. Fires were needed, not for cooking only, but also for heating the huts. Certainly the same hearth or fireplace might serve both purposes. A fire could be lit with safety anywhere on the levelled subsoil which formed the floor of the hut, although unpaved; and, indeed, many of the huts, even where quantities of charcoal were found, appear to be devoid of stone hearths. The probability is that where stone hearths were found the fire, for all purposes, was confined to them. There is one example of a fireplace which seems to indicate the work of an original mind. This was found in Hut 2, Riders Rings, in the Avon Valley (Fig. 24). The fire was placed some 4 ft within the entrance of the hut, and in the direct line of the entrance. There was no stone hearth, but the fire was shielded from the draught of the entrance by a flat stone set in the floor, 2 ft 9 in. wide at floor level, and standing 13 in. above the floor, leaning slightly away from the entrance. On the inner side toward which it leant the stone was trigged or wedged with a number of small, thin stones, to resist the tendency to fall which might follow its leaning position. At the inner foot of this stone was a shallow pit in the floor, filled with charcoal and ashes. In position and construction this fireplace would seem to have been unusually well designed.

A feature in many huts is the 'dais', a paved area adjoining the wall and raised somewhat above floor level. The edge forms a chord of the inner circle of the walls, and the area of the dais is thus a segment of a circle. At times the line of the circumference is slightly deformed to give the dais greater depth and area.

The term 'dais' was rather an unfortunate selection. It implies a place of especial honour, a division of society into the aristocratic sheep and the plebeian goats. We know nothing of the social distinctions which may have afflicted society in the Bronze Age, we are not even entitled to assume their existence; but the obvious purpose of the so-called dais was that of a seat or reclining place by day, and a bed by night. It would be much better to call it a bench. The bench is always, so far as it has yet been found, in one of two positions, either on the right hand on entry, that is to say on the east side; or facing the entrance and somewhat inclined to the east. Rarely, if ever, is the bench more than from 6 to 8 in. above the floor.

Fig. 18 is a plan showing a right-hand bench in Hut 3, Grimspound, and Fig. 20 a plan of Hut 16, Grimspound, with a bench facing the entrance. This latter bench is parted in two by stones set on edge, with their top edges 1 ft 7 in. above floor level. No similar partition has as yet been found elsewhere.

These benches are one of the features which suggest that there were local methods and fashions. They are found at Grimspound and Shapley Common, and there are some doubtful indications of benches at Broadun and Broadun Ring, while their presence has been suspected elsewhere, on very slight grounds. There is no present evidence that raised paved benches ever existed outside the neighbourhood of Grimspound, but further excavations may possibly give cause to vary this statement. In the third Report of the Dartmoor Exploration Committee, 1896, it is said: "It has been observed that in the huts as yet explored, near the borders of the moor, these paved platforms are not found; that, however, in their places, except at Legis Tor, are found stones, planted in the floor at intervals, standing some 9 in. above it in line; and it is thought probable that in such cases, wood being easily procurable the bed-seats were made of logs, and that these peg-like stones were used to hold the logs in place." I have seen nothing which I could so interpret. The hut at Foales Arrishes has already been referred to, see page 112, and Fig. 22.

It seems probable that some bed place, with or without a stone bench as a foundation, was practically universal. The stones can hardly have been acceptable as a couch without some covering of heather or other padding. It is possible that in some instances, as at Legis Tor, the area used as a bench was paved, not with raised paving, but at floor level. It is not probable, hardly possible, that at Legis Tor it should have been the unpaved area of the hut on which the seat or bench was placed. This use was suggested in the Third Report of the Dartmoor Exploration Committee, 1896, but, on the one hand, it places the bench on the left of the entrance in place of on the right, and on the other it would inextricably mix up the bench or bed and the cooking hole and fireplace, an improbable and certainly inconvenient combination.

Of paving in general it may be said that probably in all huts there were at least a stone threshold and steps down into the hut. Sometimes there was a small paved area outside the entrance. Where there was a bench, certain stones were selected and set to make the boundary between the bench and the floor a fair approximation to a straight line. And where there was a bench the greater part of the floor has always been found to be unpaved. No floor has been found completely paved, but many have been found completely unpaved. The paving stones are always thin natural slabs, random in shape and size, unwrought and unshapen.

The extent of the paving would appear to have been largely influenced by the presence or absence in the immediate neighbourhood of a supply of suitable stone; perhaps also by the quality of the subsoil, whether more or less resistant to damp. The builders were not so bound by custom as to fail in special methods where special needs had to be met. Hut 4, Legis Tor, affords an instance. The entrance is well defined, and paved. Elsewhere the whole of the meat[1] earth had been removed, and the subsoil exposed as usual. But subsequently the floor against the entrance had been raised by filling the excavation with loose rubble stone, almost to the level of the outer ground; and the work completed by paving over this loose rubble, the thickness of the paving completing the raising of the floor to the outside level; so that here there was the almost unique feature that there were no steps down into the hut. There can be no certainty, but the probable explanation is that the floor near the entrance, where it would be at its lowest, proved leaky, and water was liable to lodge there; on the discovery of which the floor was deliberately raised to a drier level, on porous filling. The whole of the southern or lower part of this hut, where it is lowest, was paved.

---

[1] The humus layer or top-soil. (ED.)

Very possibly the intent of benches in general was, in part at least, to raise the seat or bed higher above possible damp.

It is not known how the difficulty was met which must have arisen where the fire was placed against the wall of the hut. It must have been dangerously near the thatch, or other roof covering.

Possibly the under side, or ceiling, of the roof was coated with clay daub over and near the fire. This would have been an efficient protection. Wattle and daub chimneys were in use many centuries later, in the early English houses. The Bronze Age may, however, have had other methods, which we have no means of tracing.

OBJECTS AND MATERIALS FOUND IN HUT-CIRCLES

Charcoal and *ashes* should perhaps take first place among the products of excavation. They are clear evidence of human occupation. At times ashes and charcoal are found distributed over the whole area of the hut; more usually they are chiefly concentrated around the hearth or fireplace and in the cooking holes. The wood burnt was small, little more than twigs, nothing which could not be gathered by hand, without the need of tools to cut or chop. Nowhere has anything in the nature of even a small log been found. The Dartmoor Exploration Committee's Reports state that: "The charcoal from the interior of the moor shows that the wood was oak and alder, and that it was small. But at the confines of the moor large pieces of charred wood have been found." (Third Report, 1896.) It would, perhaps, have been better to have written '*larger* pieces of charred wood'. As to the identification of oak and alder, it must be admitted that alder is not likely to have formed any considerable part of the fuel, except on the borders of the moor, and that the various willows and the furze bushes probably contributed not a little to the fuel. The charcoal requires more detailed examination. It is certain that peat was also burned in considerable quantity, large quantities of peat ashes having been found in some huts.

Cooking stones are found in distinctly varying number; some at least occur in the great majority of huts. As a rule no attempt has been made to make a precise count, and in some huts it is to be feared that they were missed by, or in consequence of, the undue haste of the excavators. At Legis Tor, Hut 2 yielded 30 cooking stones, and in Hut 7 between 30 and 40 were found; on the other hand, at the Rifle Range, Princetown, 5 cooking stones were found in Hut 3, and 6 in Hut 6.

The cooking stones, or pot boilers, are rounded pebbles from the rivers, or from river gravels. Since they have been water-worn they represent the harder and finer-grained varieties of the granite and elvans, and include some pebbles of quartz-schorl rock from the veins in the granite. As to size, about 5 in. × 3½ in., and 1 to 1½ in. in thickness would be an approximate average. Very many are fire-cracked; some of the coarse-grained pebbles have been rendered very friable; and, on the whole, the need for renewal must have been frequent.

It is believed that the cooking holes, with or without pots, and the cooking stones, were the kitchen utensils of their day; and this belief has the sanction of the recorded habits of later primitive races, and of the circumstances and conditions in which both holes and stones have been found on Dartmoor. Baking could be accomplished by placing a number of well-heated cooking stones in the bottom of a cooking hole, putting the meat on these stones, packing other heated stones around and over the meat, and possibly drawing and spreading over the whole hot embers from the hearth. This method would foreshadow the baking on the hearth which many of us have seen, and of which I myself have often heartily enjoyed the product. In such baking a circular iron plate was first heated and bedded on the hearth in ashes, the dough was placed on the plate, an iron crock inverted over the dough, and ashes and embers heaped over and around the crock. As a finishing touch, to brown the crust, a small bundle of furze was placed over and around the crock, in place of the ashes, and lit.

And the small ovens in the chimney corner, as well as the much larger ovens of the baker in later years, shared one feature with the cooking hole. The direct heat of a fire did not accomplish the baking; but first the oven was heated until its structure of stone, earthenware or brick had taken up and become a store of the heat; the matter to be cooked was then placed in the oven and the entrance closed. By the borrowed heat of the oven-lining the cooking was accomplished (and still is in some places). The cooking stones were merely an earlier device for heat storage.

In the matter of boiling the transfer of the heat of the fire to the water was, we believe, accomplished in a similar manner by the intermediary of cooking stones. The coarse earthenware of the day was certainly not fireproof, and could not with safety be placed over a fire. The pot, partly filled with water, was accordingly placed in a hole formed in the floor of the hut; and then hot stones were rolled or lifted into it from the hearth. The speed and efficiency of this method of heating water would be governed by the specific heats of the stone and the water respectively. The strain on the first of the stones to be dropped into the cold water must have been considerable; and it is small wonder that they are so often cracked and fretted, while the soup must have partaken of the nature of stone broth, with sand and gravel as solid constituents. The teeth of prehistoric man are often found much worn on the crowns; it has been supposed that grinding or crushing cereals with stone made his bread gritty, but his soup may have had its part in the wear.

Seeking a recent parallel for this method of transferring heat to a liquid, I recall that I have seen ale warmed in a village inn by the agency of a poker heated in the fire and then plunged in the glass or pot, a method which could at one time be regarded as standard.

Domestic pottery found in the huts, while varying somewhat in material and finish, may all be fairly described as coarse, thick and underburnt. None which has as yet been found has been thrown on the wheel. The body of the ware usually consists of from 40 to 45% of sand, and 60 to 55% of clay substance. The clay contains sufficient iron to burn to a distinct red superficially, even with the light firing which the ware has received. This at once suggests that the clay used was not derived from the granite area. China clay with 1·50% of ferric oxide burns to no more than a deep ivory shade, while blue ball clay from the Bovey Beds, containing 3·30% Fe_2O_3, is used in white and cream pottery. Clay from the hut-circle pottery contains from 5 to 12% of ferric oxide (the last figure is unusually high).

China clays from the granite area, which on casual observation appear to have more than the usual content of iron, have yielded no greater than 2·36 to 3·10% of ferric oxide, and cannot have supplied the material used by the Bronze Age potter. It appears, therefore, that the source was not strictly local. But it need not have been distant: there are patches of clay, not far outside the border of the granite, which would make up into such ware as is found in the huts. Physical considerations support the chemical evidence. China clay lacks the necessary plasticity and cohesion for the manufacture of objects as large as the cooking pots, of such a thickness, and painfully made by hand moulding. It would neither dry nor fire without deformation and heavy losses by cracking. The far more plastic clays from the metamorphic and sedimentary areas would certainly demand skill in handling by primitive methods, but would so far respond to that skill as to prove practicable material.

The proportion of sand found in the ware is little, if any, greater than that naturally occurring in the clays as raised from the pit. It obviously affords another possible line of inquiry. Its nature varies with the locality from which the shards are taken, which indicates variety of origin for the clay. Comparatively rarely some sand would appear to have been added, the addition being such as could have been derived from the beds of streams in the granite area. In what is believed to be the natural sand of the clay the recognizable rock fragments include quartz-schorl rock, altered slate which may have come from the metamorphic aureole of Dartmoor, and, in a few instances, fragments of hornblendic rock, probably from epidiorites such as are found on Cox Tor, Whittor, Horndon, and at other points on the Dartmoor border.

The pottery was probably made on Dartmoor, certainly in the immediate neighbourhood, and the clay derived from the nearest known deposits of sufficiently plastic material.

It has been said that some of the ware is washed with clay-slip, to afford a better surface finish. This must be doubted: the mere moulding of the pot by hand would bring to the surface some part of the water used in tempering the clay, and the potters' hands would also be kept moist to avoid adhesion by the clay; from these two causes there would be sufficient superficial water to produce a surface of true clay substance, thus giving the appearance of a slip wash. I have seen nothing for which this explanation would not suffice.

The thickness of the normal cooking pottery of the hut-circles ranges approximately between seven and twelve millimetres; but at times fragments of other vessels are found of from 4 mm. to 7 mm. in thickness, which, in this respect as well as in the quality of the ware, closely resemble the pottery found in the kistvaens; the resemblance may, in fact, be reasonably interpreted as identity[1]. With this thinner ware a finer clay was used, containing much less sand, but apparently derived from the same sources. No change was made in the workmanship or the type of ornament. The word *beaker* has sometimes been used as descriptive of these vessels; but, if the ordinary acceptance of the word is regarded, it is an unfortunate selection. To most, it may be presumed, a beaker is a drinking vessel: the particular objects here referred to have capacities of approximately 5 to 6 pints apiece, when filled to within $\frac{1}{4}$ in. of the rim, which seems excessive in a drinking vessel.

One feature is common to all the pottery. The outside surfaces are red (rarely brown), the inside is black, excepting in some few examples where it is slightly reddened near the rim. The thickness of the ware is also black after the first 2 mm. from the outside, sometimes after the first millimetre.

These conditions arise from the method of firing. The ware was not fired in an oven or kiln, but in the open. The pot was stood, either on its base or mouth down, and a fire maintained around it. The mouth-down position would be the more efficient, and must have been adopted for those pots which had approximately hemispherical bases. We may believe that the advantages of the inverted position were soon discovered. Fired in this manner the exterior of the pot received the greater heat, in an oxidizing atmosphere; and the inside attained a less tempera-

---

[1] A recent view is that the pottery from the kistvaens consists of beakers, characteristic (as are certain associated finds) of the Beaker Folk of the Early Bronze Age; whilst that from the hut-circles, such as it is, belongs to vessels of other types, of which the earliest appears to be of Middle Bronze origin. The hut-circles have also yielded pottery attributed to the Late Bronze Age (e.g. Raddick Hill, Legis Tor, and Smallacombe Rocks) and to the Early Iron Age (e.g. Foales Arrishes and Kes Tor). (See Radford, 1947, 1949; Fox, 1951.) Some of the other recoveries from barrows suggest Middle Bronze. For these and other reasons the dating of the various remains on Dartmoor appears to present a more complex problem than originally seemed likely. (ED.)

ture in an atmosphere deficient in oxygen. The result of these conditions would be just the distribution of colour which is found in the ware.

It has been suggested that the black inner surface, and the dark, frequently black, shade in the thickness of the ware have arisen from carbonized foodstuff. But these colour conditions affect all the pottery, except a few of the thinnest pieces. They are present in cooking pots and food vessels alike; and, rather remarkably, the cooking stones have not been found stained, although they shared contact with food during its preparation. It is true that from one specimen of pottery it was found possible to recover a trace of grease, the last remnant of a prehistoric stew. It is obvious that recoverable grease cannot have been carbonized, and cannot have contributed to the black shade of the pottery.

There is one known exception to the statement that china clay was not in use. The cooking pot which was found in the cooking hole of Hut 7, Legis Tor, had been mended *in situ* with china clay, by the simple expedient of taking a kneaded mass of that material and pressing it into the bottom of the pot as it stood in the hole. The broken bottom was supported by the ground in which the pot had been sunk, and thus the leaks could be staunched by this internal application of puddle. The mend was made with raw clay, and there was nothing in the operation which partook of the nature of pottery manufacture. It is interesting as showing that the hut-dwellers were acquainted with china clay, and their failure to use it in the manufacture of pottery was thus a matter of deliberate choice.

As to the shape and size of the vessels our knowledge is necessarily limited by the fragmentary condition of much which has been found, the decay of the broken edges of the fragments, consequent on the rough nature of the ware, and its incomplete firing. By good luck two of the cooking pots were found under such conditions that their dimensions and form could be observed at the time of their discovery (see Fig. 23). The Legis Tor example had a greatest diamater of 10 in. and a height of 12 in.; that from Raddick Hill was equal in diameter, but 10½ in. in height. As far as can be judged from fragments found in other huts these were fair examples of the usual size. On the other hand, although both pots had rounded bases, they differed in other respects. The body of the pot from Legis Tor was approximately globular, the neck somewhat constricted, with an outward flare to the rim. The Raddick vessel was bucket-shaped, banded at about 2½ in. from the rim, and with no constriction at the neck. At Legis Tor the pot was wholly without ornament; in the other instance the space between the band and the rim was covered with a chevron pattern. It was a coincidence that both these pots had rounded bases: from what has been found elsewhere on Dartmoor it is a fair conclusion that some, at least, of the cooking pots had flat bases.[1]

[1] See footnote on p. 114.

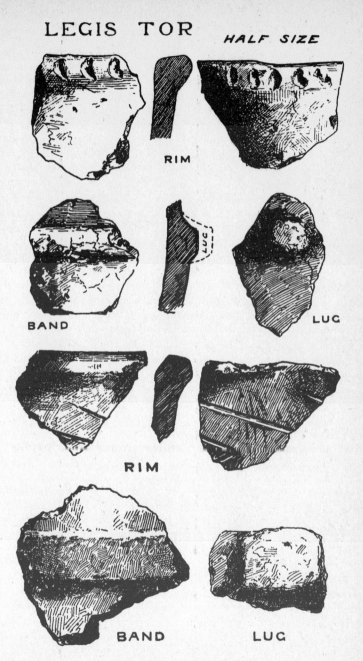

LEGIS TOR

HALF SIZE

RIM

BAND

LUG

RIM

BAND

LUG

Fig. 25. Pottery from Legis Tor.

Pottery actually found in the cooking holes may safely be identified as cooking pots, but most huts yield from the floor surface fragments of a similar type of ware, and these may be classed as the remains of storage vessels. There are local variations in the details of such vessels, both as to structure and ornament; and these variations are strongly suggestive of local manufacture, tastes and prejudices. We have already seen that the provision of shelter walls at the entrance to the hut was a habit rather narrowly localized. To come to much later days, I was surprised some years ago to learn, at an edge-tool mill on the Teign, that it was still necessary to keep separate templates for the manufacture of hedge-hooks and suchlike tools, to meet the tastes and needs of the different small districts supplied, each of which has its own traditional curve and balance of the blade, and will content itself with none other. In face of this modern instance one may readily accept that parochialism as a mental habit long preceded and will probably outlast the parish as a unit; parochialism is and has been a partial antidote to over-centralized standardization.

At Legis Tor, in the Plym Valley, nine out of ten of the huts in and near the pound yielded fragments of pottery of the 'storage' pot type. These were fully illustrated in the third report of the Dartmoor Exploration Committee (*Trans. Devon. Assn.*, Vol. 28, pp. 10–13). Two features were apparently constant, a thickened band or belt encircling the greatest diameter of the pot, and lifting lugs arising on either side of the belt. In the matter of ornament, this was found below the rims, between the rims and the belt. There was considerable variety. Indentations made with the thumb or finger-nail were in frequent use, the simplest form being a series of such indents on the outer circumference of the rim. In one instance the nail marks are set below the rim, which itself bears crossed, incised lines. The nail mark is also found associated with dotted line, the dots being impressions of a square, hollow point, possibly a bird's bone. This same type of dot is also used in chevrons, associated with incised horizontal lines. And chevrons in continuous incised lines are also found. See Fig. 25 for some types of ornament.

Bands, as being thicker and stronger than the body of the ware, and lugs, which are solid lumps measuring on the average 1¾ in. along the length of the band, 1¼ in. in depth across the band, and 1 in. in total thickness, are both, like the rims of the pots, apt to survive where the rest of the ware has perished. It should, therefore, be of some significance that, except at Legis Tor, bands are relatively rare, and lugs almost unknown on Dartmoor. It may be that an undue importance attached to mere ornament has led some at least of the excavators to neglect the significance of structural details; but, none the less, this is an instance in which negative evidence has a higher value than usual.

A comparison may be made with the pottery found in the huts near Smallacombe Rocks, in the Leighon (Beckabrook) Valley, 1,300 yds

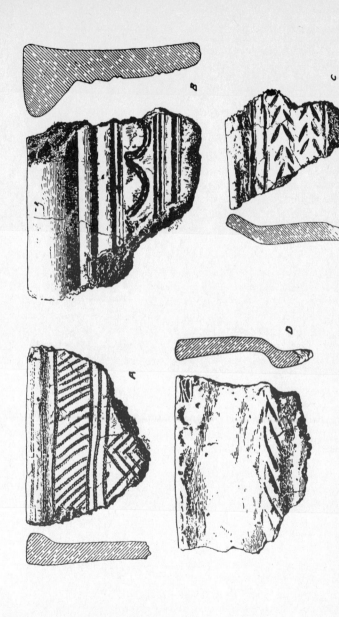

FIG. 26.

A, from Hut 4, Smallacombe Rocks × ⅓.
D, from Hut 2, Foales Arrishes × ⅓.

B, from Hut 1, Smallacombe Rocks × ⅔.
C, from Hut 8, Foales Arrishes × ⅓.

north (approximately) from Hey Tor. In this ware the line constituting the pattern was produced by pressing a twisted cord or thong into the wet clay, thus obtaining a sunken cable-pattern. Fig. 26A reproduces the pattern impressed on the rim of a pot from this site. The ornament consists solely of straight lines, and, in type if not in detail, agrees well with much which has been found in Devon and Cornwall. The fragments of a pot from another hut at Smallacombe Rocks are, on the other hand, unusual in form and decoration, but not in material. The body of the pot is usually thick, but it is the rim in which this thickness is carried to an extreme. This rim forms a heavy cornice, below which are shallow mouldings. The principal feature of the decoration is a band of festoons encircling the pot below the rim, and formed by the impression of a twisted cord. Up to the present this design has not been met elsewhere on Dartmoor (Fig. 26B).

The enclosures known as Foales Arrishes lie 330 yds east of Pil Tor, at the head of the Blackslade Water. The enclosures are relatively recent, but in and around them are hut-circles. From this site, which is distant from Smallacombe Rocks some 1¾ miles, came a fragment of pottery which may be cited as a further example of the types prevalent on the eastern side of the moor. This specimen has the use of the finger nail as a link with the pottery from Legis Tor, while, in common with the pottery from Smallacombe Rocks, it shows lines formed by the impress of a twisted cord. But, while it shared these features of technique, the pattern of the ornament is in no way related to the other cited examples; unless, indeed, the arrangement of the nail marks may be supposed to be influenced by the chevron motif, as might be claimed. On the other hand it might well be argued that the nail marks are an early example of design founded on natural forms, and their arrangement suggested by the growth of leaves on a trailing stem. Argument would be unprofitable, and it is sufficient to recognize that the pattern was held to be a pleasing expedient for breaking the monotony of a surface. It remains that in southern Dartmoor nothing in the style of Smallacombe B or Foales Arrishes C has been found.[1] (See Fig. 26 C and D for a drawing of the pottery from Foales Arrishes.)

Pottery without ornament occurs in all districts, and it may be mere chance that the excavations at Metherel on the South Teign yielded none but undecorated pottery. As one now sees, it would have been well had greater attention been given in general to the question of ornament, and more complete evidence collected. But it does seem clear that differences in taste and method were not merely individual, but also local. I can find no evidence to justify an assumption that these divergencies were associated with difference in period or date.

[1] The Foales Arrishes sherds have been ascribed to Iron Age A (Radford, 1947, p. 17). That the huts there were of this later period is now plausible in the light of the recent discoveries at Kestor. (ED.)

FIG. 27. Bottom of crock from Hut 2, Yes Tor Bottom.

Flat-bottomed vessels, when of large diameter, presented a problem. The strength of the pottery was not suited to this form of construction. Hut 2 at Yes Tor Bottom, Walkham Valley, yielded the remains of a pot which was 11 in. in diameter at the base. This had been strengthened by the formation of a cross in relief on the inner side of the base (see Fig. 27). The method adopted in reinforcing the relatively large plane surface has been noted elsewhere, but this is the one example so far discovered on Dartmoor.

Stone Implements. Flint chips have been found in most huts which have been excavated with reasonable care. It is probable that many chips which have no secondary working were of real use in practice, and, indeed, may show signs of wear, and obviously have been in use.

There are also implements which Evans very discreetly suggests may be called 'worked flakes'. These show secondary chipping and were obviously shaped for defined purposes; but what those purposes may have been can only be conjectured. Such implements have been found in a number of huts. A good example came from Hut 2, Metherel, and is illustrated on Plate 27A, figs *a* and *b*. A similar implement was found in the open, near Yar Tor. Another worked flake, from Hut 4, Smallacombe, is described and illustrated in the fifth report of the Dartmoor Exploration Committee (Pl. II, fig. 3, in the report). It is there described as a knife, but could equally well, or better, be called a duck-bill scraper; one is grateful for the noncommittal phrase *worked flake*.

Undoubted scrapers are not infrequently found in the huts; these are chiefly of the horseshoe type, as at Hut 1, Whittor; while in Hut 7, Foales Arrishes, there was found a hollow scraper, with two hollows.

Arrow-heads are very rare in the huts; one only has been recorded, from West Dart Head. It was barbed and tanged, with one barb lost by breakage. It is possible that one worked triangular flake from Hut 5, Legis Tor, had found use as an arrow-head.

On the floor of Hut 4, at Legis Tor, I found a flake of flint which had been struck by one blow from a pebble, and had received no secondary chipping. An unusual feature is that a straight edge has been sharpened by grinding and polishing. The grinding is confined to one face, and gives a cutting edge with much the angle of a chisel. (Pl. 27A, figs. *c* and *d*.) Such a tool may with certainty be identified as a knife. I have called it "unusual": an understatement since, in my experience and, as

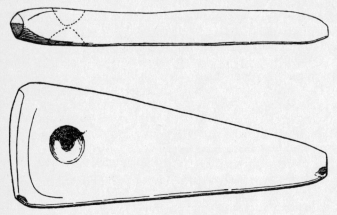

FIG. 28. Whetstone from Legis Tor.

far as I know, in the experience of others, it is unique on Dartmoor; but Evans (op. cit., p. 290), describing British flakes with ground edges as by no means common, mentions, but does not illustrate, a number of examples, some of which may in many respects resemble the Legis Tor implement.

Whetstones have been rather frequently found in such excavations as I, personally, have conducted. The material is most usually a micaceous grit, often red-brown in colour, sometimes grey. Some of these stones have evidently been shapen. I will mention two good examples. A whetstone from Hut 2, Riders Rings, in the Avon Valley, is 3¾ in. in length, 1½ in. in width at one end, and 1¼ in. at the other end; its average thickness is ⅜ in. (Pl. 27B). Its surface bears full evidence of use. The second example referred to came from Hut 8, Legis Tor, in the Plym Valley (Fig. 28). Interest attaches to it in that more work had been expended on its shaping, and that work had never been completed. It lay upon a slab of stone upon which it had evidently been ground to shape; and it had been intended to perforate it for suspension, but the drilling, for which a sand-drill was used, had never been completed. The hole, started from each side, had fallen short of meeting in the centre, by a bare film of stone, at the time that the worker laid down his task, to which he never returned; one wonders why. The length is $5\frac{1}{4}$ in.; the width at the end toward the perforation is just under 2 in.; at the other end, or rather a little away from it, the width is $\frac{5}{8}$ in. The mean thickness is nine-sixteenths of an inch. Most of these stones, however, have had little work expended in shaping them; for instance, a broken, flat pebble, from Hut 2, Metherel, in the valley of the South Teign (Pl. 27B). The shaping of this stone had been confined to grinding the broken edge to remove its asperities. Its dimensions are $5\frac{1}{8}$ in. × $3\frac{3}{4}$ in., with a greatest thickness of $1\frac{1}{4}$ in. The natural edges of the pebble have been battered, and there are slight striae on one face adjacent to the battered edge, and two close-set grooves on the other. Both faces have been smoothed by friction, but one face more markedly. Similar grooves are not infrequent on these stones, and may have been caused by their use for bringing to a point such objects as bone or bronze needles. The face which is shewn in the plate is that which bears the grooves referred to.

Mullers have been found in some of the huts, their material in most instances being the same class of grits as was used for the hones. These mullers may have been used for crushing grain, and possibly roots, among which may have been the roots of bracken. Evans remarks that fern roots are still in use as articles of diet by some races. A muller found in Hut 11, Legis Tor, is illustrated on Plate IX, Third Report of the Dartmoor Exploration Committee, *T.D.A.*, Vol. 28, 1896. It is $6\frac{1}{2}$ in. in present length, oval in section with a greatest diameter of $2\frac{3}{4}$ in.; broken at one end, and at the other worn to plane facets. Except for these mullers no form of grinding implement has been found, not even a saddle-quern.

Slick-stones were the early equivalent of the flat-iron, and lingered in use long after prehistoric days. They have been found in fair number and, for the more part, consist of suitable pieces of altered slate from the metamorphic aureole of the granite. This material, while hard enough to be efficient in such matters as rubbing down seams in sewn skins or coarse fabrics, is soft enough to carry light scores as the result of friction on the material dealt with, and on the thread used in the stitching.

If it is correct to assume that some at least of the pottery which has been found was once in use as storage vessels, then it might be expected that some form of cover was once in use for the protection of the contents. In several huts pieces of slate of a rudely circular form have been

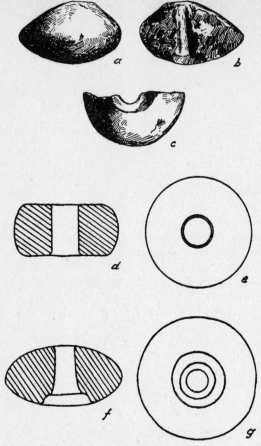

FIG. 29.

a, b, c. Spindle Whorl? from Legis Tor.
d, e. Spindle Whorl from Lyd Valley.
f, g. Spindle Whorl? from Hartland.

found. In one, Hut 12, Raddick, "on the left of the entrance was found a rudely circular, thin slab of micaceous slate, unhappily broken by the pick, measuring 9 in. in diameter and ¾ in. thick; and under it were the fragments of a crushed shallow vessel of pottery; part of the lip was found; the mouth would be 7 in. to 8 in. in diameter".

With one possible exception no spindle-whorl has been found. That possible exception is a small broken object from a joint between the paving stones of Hut 2, Legis Tor; see Fig. 29, *a, b, c.* This I described as a spindle-whorl, without the expression of doubt, and without quali-fication. It had features in which it varied from any spindle-whorl known to me, but I had never seen one made in earthenware, and was willing to accept some deviation in type in the unusual material. In 1943, however, I had submitted to me a similar object in stone, found by Mr. Egerton Godwin at Clovelly, North Devon. The normal type of spindle-whorl is a short drum, perforated along the axis of the cylinder with a hole which has practically equal diameter throughout its length. There may be a very slight constriction at the centre of the length, the hole having been drilled from either end, and subsequently broached: see Fig. 29 d and e, drawn from an example found in the Lyd Valley by the late Mr. John Cowling.

The Clovelly specimen is illustrated in Fig. 29, f and g. It will be seen that neither this nor the object from Legis Tor are cylindrical, but in each the vertical section is an oval. In each the perforation lessens in diameter from end to end, and in each the perforation expands into a countersink beyond its greatest diameter.

The oval cross-section makes for inefficiency in an object which has to function as a flywheel, and, while prehistoric man did not think in terms of moments of inertia, there is ample evidence that he readily learnt by experience the most favourable disposition of material in his implements. It was not without reason that the common pattern of spindle-whorl was a cylinder. When one finds this type of object which we are considering, in practically identical form at places so far removed as South Dartmoor and the north coast of Devon, we may reasonably assume that the type was devised to meet a defined need, and that a common need. Probably its purpose was that of a weight or plummet, and the countersink was formed to house the knot which held the weight on its suspending cord.

Baring-Gould (1900, p. 47) writes: "That the occupants of the moor loved to play at games is shown by the numbers of little round pebbles, carefully selected, some for their bright colours, that have been found on the floors of the huts. That they used divination by the crystal is shown by clear quartz prisms having been discovered tolerably fre-frequently." This in error; the number of 'little round pebbles' which have been found is quite insignificant, and the proportion of those found which were 'brightly coloured' is trivial, possibly three such coloured pebbles have been found. As to quartz crystals, no more have occurred than can be fully accounted for by those naturally present in the Dartmoor soil.

In some huts ruddle (red iron oxide) has occurred, and it may have been brought to them for use as a pigment; but there are places, Metherel for example, where ruddle is native to the soil.

One small quartz crystal was found, the pyramid end of which bore evidence of considerable wear. It would appear to have been used as a drill.

Bronze. No bronze has as yet been found in any Dartmoor hut, which may be evidence that few, if any, of the huts were hastily abandoned. The only suggestion of hasty departure was at Hut 11, Legis Tor, where it might appear to be implied by the abandonment of the part-worked whetstone at a stage so near completion. Bronze was too valuable for its loss to be held lightly, and even in the matter of flint arrow-heads it is notable that one only has been found in a Dartmoor hut.

DATE OR PERIOD

The hut-circles and their associated pounds may be safely assigned to the Early Bronze Age.[1] It can hardly be that the greater number of the huts were ever in occupation at one time, as the land could not have supported the population. On the other hand it is not possible to know the causes which, from time to time, led to the abandonment of certain of the huts, and the construction of others. It is curious that what may be called the intensive occupation of Dartmoor appears to have been confined wholly to one stage of culture.

REFERENCES

Burnard, Robert, 1894. Exploration of the hut circles in Broadun Ring and Broadun. *Trans. Devon. Assn.*, Vol. 26, pp. 185–96.

Dartmoor Exploration Committee Reports. I (1894). Exploration of Grimspound. *Trans. Devon. Assn.*, Vol. 26, pp. 101–21. II (1895) [Shapley Common], Vol. 27, pp. 81–92. III (1896) [Whiten Ridge, Legis Tor, Rifle Range, Raddick Hill], Vol. 28, pp. 174–99. IV (1897) [Tunhill Rocks Foales Arrishes, Smallacombe Rocks], Vol. 29, pp. 145–65. V (1898) [Huccaby, Yes Tor Bottom, W. Dart Head], Vol. 30, pp. 97–115. VI (1899) [Whittor, Lade Hill Bottom], Vol. 31, pp. 146–55. VII (1900) [Langstone Moor plan], Vol. 32, p. 138. VIII (1902) [Standon Down], Vol. 34, pp., 160–5. X (1905) [Wedlake], Vol. 37, pp. 141–5. XI (1906) [Watern Oke], Vol. 38, pp. 101–13. XII (1935) [Riders Rings, Metherel], Vol. 67, pp. 115–30. XIII (1936) [Metherel], Vol. 69, pp. 143–50.

Fox, Lady Aileen, 1951. Early settlements on Dartmoor and in North Wales. *Archaeologia Cambrensis*, 1951, pp. 167–8.

Radford, C. A. Ralegh, 1947. Address of the President: The Dumnonii. *Trans. Devon. Assn.*, Vol. 79, pp. 15–30.

Radford, C. A. Ralegh, 1949. *In* Report of Conference of Prehistoric Society, Devonshire Association, and Devon Archaeological, Exploration Society Exeter, 1949. *Archaeological News Letter*, Vol. 2, No. 7, pp. 110–15.

[1] See footnote on p. 121 (ED.).

THE PREHISTORIC POUNDS
OF DARTMOOR

THE prehistoric pounds of Dartmoor have received little notice, and of that little an undue proportion has been devoted to Grimspound. Grimspound is not a good point of approach to the subject, and is not sufficiently representative, the less since the unfortunate reconstruction of a considerable length of its wall.

There are many pounds on Dartmoor, especially in the south, and notably in the valleys of the Walkham, Plym, Yealm, Erme and Avon.

Classification is useful for descriptive purposes, as long, and only as long, as it is divorced from all suggestion of difference in date, origin and, largely, of purpose. The primary and only classification which I suggest is into *simple* and *compound*. The *simple* pound is a close of land wholly surrounded by open moor, from which it is separated by a stone fence; it has no subdivisions. It may have no hut-circle within its fence, or there may be one or more hut-circles. The *compound* pound is an agglomeration of two or more simple pounds, adjacent and contiguous. It would appear that this class is almost always formed by additions to an originally simple pound. The enclosure became insufficient in area for a growing need and a second enclosure was added, to be followed in some cases by a third, and even a fourth. Very rarely indeed is there any sign of an enclosure, once formed, having been subdivided by an internal fence. As far as my observation extends there is always at least one hut-circle in some part of every compound pound.

There are one of two exceptional instances of simple pounds with the appearance of having been sub-divided by internal fences; for instance Round Pound, near Batworthy, Chagford, and an unnamed example near Bovey Combe Head, North Bovey; both mentioned and figured by Ormerod (*Rude Stone Remains*, privately printed, p. 11). It is not certain that these were not the subjects of late interference or addition.

The prevalent idea that pounds are normally circular or oval in plan is mistaken. The angles are certainly rounded, with rare exception; and the more part of the walls curved in plan; but considerable lengths of approximately straight wall are frequent; and any fair approach to a true circle is very rarely seen. In the absence of actual survey it is easy to be in error.

The following examples have been selected for description.

SIMPLE POUNDS

(1) *Shavercombe*, Plym Valley. Six inch to the mile O.S., cxiii, sw., lat. 50°-28'-44", lon. 3°-58'-57". (Fig. 30.)

Diameter N. and S. 154 ft, greatest diameter E. and W. 154 ft. Not circular, but with an approach to a symmetrical outline. Area within

SHAVERCOMBE.

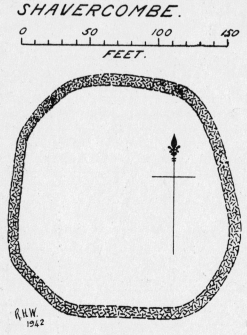

FIG. 30.

walls 0·458 acres. No hut-circle. Mean elevation of ground approximately 1,150 ft O.D. Ground slopes northwards.

This pound, on the flank of Shavercombe Tor, in the Plym watershed, lies near the border of the granite. The fence or wall had an original thickness of 4 ft 6 in. It is built in granite, with large stones in the bottom course. There are many long stones, rather like broad gateposts: these are laid lengthwise along both faces of the wall, and filled between in the centre with small stone. The upper part was probably similarly faced, but with smaller blocks. Although there is no hut in the pound, there are two or three rather large hut-circles higher on the hill, off the granite area, and these are mounded up, rather than built, in quite small stone, mainly of altered slate, with none of the usual slabs lining the inner faces of the walls. A curious instance of indisposition to fetch building material from even a short distance.

(2) *Hingston Hill*, Meavy Valley. Six inch O.S., cxii, NE., lat. 50°-30'-26½", lon. 3°-59'-13". (Fig. 31.)

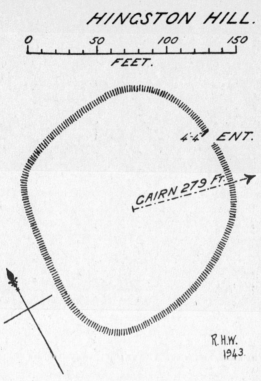

FIG. 31.

Approximately E. of Down Tor and NNE. of Combeshead Tor. Diameter N. and S. 143 ft, E. and W. 140 ft. Not circular but rather pear-shaped. Area within walls 0·410 acres. Mean elevation of ground approximately 1,220 ft O.D. Ground slopes slightly westward. Thickness of wall is 4 ft 6 in. The entrance is marked by a slab-like stone which extends through the thickness of the wall, and stands 4 ft 4 in. high. It is doubtful if the wall was of much greater height. Two hundred and seventy-nine feet from the centre of the pound, in a direction 15° S. of E., lies the centre of a cairn of 54 ft diameter at the base, and 36 ft diameter at the top. The Down Tor stone-row points to this cairn.

There is no hut-circle in this pound, nor any in the immediate neighbourhood.

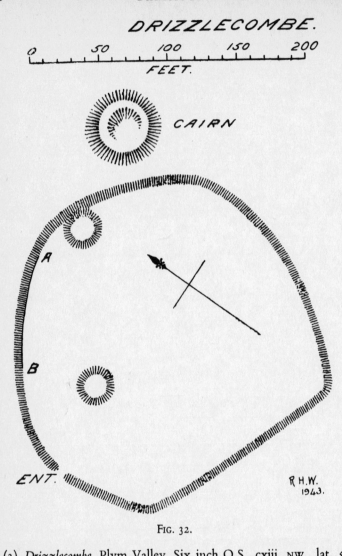

DRIZZLECOMBE.

CAIRN

A

B

ENT.

R H.W.
1943.

FIG. 32.

(3) *Drizzlecombe*, Plym Valley. Six inch O.S., cxiii, NW., lat. 50°-29′-11½″, lon. 3°-58′-59″. (Fig. 32.)

Diameter N. and S. 210 ft, E. and W. 220 ft. Not circular, as, on the S.W. there is a considerable length of straight wall. The fence or wall had an original thickness of between 4 ft 6 in. and 5 ft; it is much ruined in parts, but to the NW. there is a length, A to B on Fig. 32, where an inner lining of slabs can be clearly traced.

Area within walls 0·823 acres, mean elevation of ground 1,200 ft

O.D. Ground slopes to the sw. with a mean gradient of 1 in 7. This pound may be said to be entangled with the megalithic remains at Drizzlecombe, the cairn which forms the north-east extreme of which lies but a few yards outside the pound wall. There are two hut-circles within the enclosure. The entrance is in the western wall. There are other pounds in the immediate neighbourhood.

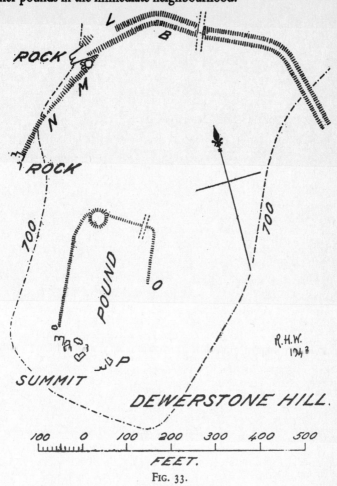

FIG. 33.

(4) *Dewerstone Hill*, Plym and Meavy valleys. Six inch O.S., cxviii, NW., lat. 50°-27'-22½", lon. 4°-3'-35". (Fig. 33.)

This is unusual in that it lies within an area severed on one side from the surrounding land by an outer, double, wall. The site constitutes the south extreme of the summit of the ridge which parts the valleys of the Plym and Meavy at their junction.

The wall of the pound is now incomplete, having probably been robbed to build the enclosure wall of an oak copse. To the south the pound wall ties in on the west side with the rock exposure of the summit. On the east side it probably ran from o to P on Fig. 33, and tied in similarly. In shape it is approximately rectangular with rounded angles.

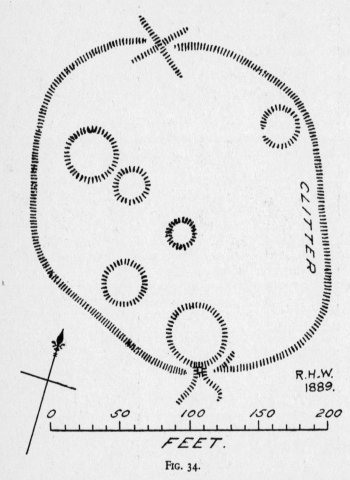

FIG. 34.

The area within the walls was probably 1·14 acres, the length of the pound 280 ft, and its breadth for the more part 175 ft. Mean elevation of the ground approximately 710 ft O.D., sloping slightly east and west from the centre of its breadth. There is one hut-circle, which is involved in the pound wall. The thickness of the pound wall is about 4 ft.

One hundred and fifty yards to the north of the pound the neck of the ridge is crossed by two parallel walls. These are ruined, but there is a clear space between the ruins of the outer and inner walls, averaging 9 ft in width. The walls were apparently about 5 ft in thickness, and if reconstructed on the centres of their present ruins would stand with a clear space between them of from 12 to 13 ft. Their plan is convex to the north, and they bend round on the east and west to tie in with natural rock exposures on the steep slopes of the hill which lie below the 700 ft contour. In Fig. 33, it is to be noted that at and near B there are confused ruins of some buildings within the walls. At L the outer wall dies out, a steep slope and natural rock replacing it. From M to N there is now no wall, but the steep hillside has been scarped, the only trace of earthwork. The general slope of the hill below the 700 ft contour, east, south and west is about 1 in 2½ with local precipices.

There is nothing on Dartmoor comparable with this, except on the summit of Whittor, Petertavy, where there is a double-walled enclosure, the space between the ruins of the two walls varying from 10 to 40 ft. There, also, there is no earthwork.

(5) *Trowlesworthy*, Plym Valley. Six inch O.S., cxii, SE., lat. 50°-27'-42½", lon. 4°-0'-29". (Fig. 34.)

On the slope of Little Trowlesworthy Tor, from which it bears SW. 800 ft, diameter N. and S. 220 ft, E. and W. 210 ft. Not circular, but approximately pear-shaped. The fence or wall 4 ft to 4 ft 6 in. in thickness. The eastern wall is built for some part of its length on a clitter of rock. Area within enclosure 0·873 acres. There are six hut-circles of very varied diameters within the pound.

The curious arrangements of walls at the seeming entrances are the wing-walls of vermin traps, as to which see later (p. 157).

Mean elevation of ground 1,000 ft. O.D., slopes to the west, mean gradient 1 in 6.

(6) *Merrivale*, on north of main road, south of Over Tor, Walkham Valley. Six inch O.S., cvi, SE., lat. 50°-33'-23½", lon. 4°-2'-16". (Fig. 35.)

Approximately triangular with one curved side. Original thickness of wall may have been 4 ft. Area within walls 0·484 acres. Mean elevation of ground 1,160 ft O.D., slopes to west with a mean gradient of 1 in 13. One hut-circle involved in wall, three others outside wall.

This pound has been the subject of recent addition and slight alterations. There is now an abandoned garden contiguous with the west wall and the foundations of a cottage lie to the north of the garden.

We know something of the history of these recent structures; Bray, in 1802, found a man building the foundations of the cottage, under lease, as he said, from Mr. Lopez (Mrs. Bray, *Borders of the Tamar and the Tavy*, 1st ed., Vol. I, p. 247). The man apparently intended taking in a few acres of ground, and possibly proposed the area of the pound as the first of his fields. But there is no evidence that he did more than build the cottage and fence the garden. Much more recently the obliging readiness of a local inhabitant has added to the ruin the charm of tradition. At the point marked with a cross in the cottage ruins (Fig. 35) there stands a squared, roughly worked slab, 3 ft 4 in. in height, 2 ft 5½ in. broad, and 10 in. thick. It formed the face of the chimney

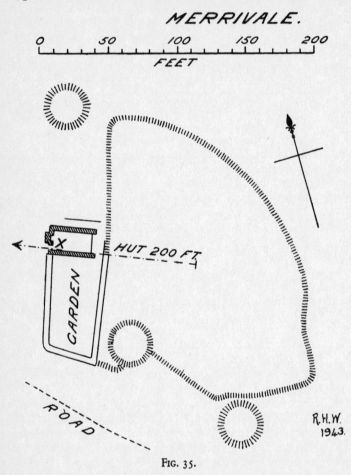

Fig. 35.

breast. This stone attracted the attention of a passer-by, and he asked a roadman who was working near whether he knew anything of it. To which the roadman at once replied that it was *Moses Bawden's grave*. He received an acknowledgement for his help, and the stranger made a note. Somewhere this potential tradition awaits publication. It may be well to record that my friend, the late Mr. Moses Bawden, well known in the mining world, and sometime member of the Devonshire Association, does not lie buried by the roadside at or near Merrivale.

The simple pounds vary greatly in area, two extreme instances may be cited.

(7) *Shapley Tor*, Valley of the East Webburn. Six inch O.S., c, NW., lat. 50°-37'-14½", lon. 3°-50'-11". (Fig. 36.)

This pound lies a thousand yards north of Grimspound, almost touching and to the north of the track from West Coombe to Bennetts Cross. Its greatest diameter is 87 ft, and its least 70 ft. It is very irregular in shape, and contains a hut-circle 31 ft in diameter, the area enclosed by the wall of the pound is 0·12 acres. Approximate elevation 1,475 ft O.D.

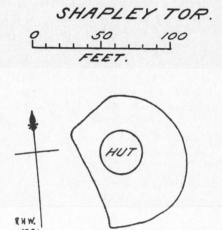

FIG. 36.

(8) *Broadun*, East Dart Valley. Six inch O.S., xcix, NW. and SW., lat. 50°-36'-9", lon. 3°-55'-41". (Fig. 48.)

This pound was first recognized by the late Col. Arthur B. Prowse, and described in his paper on 'The Ancient Metropolis of Dartmoor', *T.D.A.*, Vol. 23, p. 311. The wall has in part been incorporated in a newtake wall, in part it is much ruined; but the outline can be clearly traced. The two longest diameters which can·be drawn at right angles measure respectively 333 yds and 290 yds. The area of the enclosure is approximately 14½ acres, and there are within it 39 or 40 hut-circles. The mean approximate elevation is 1,350 ft O.D., and the slope of the ground lies SSE.

I have not made a detailed survey, but there is certainly no significant error in the above description. From a comparison of the details of (7) and (8) it will be seen that the ratio of 100 to 1 as between the areas of the largest structures and the smallest is certainly exceeded. It must, however, be conceded that Broadun has few if any equals.

(9) *Routrundle*, north, Walkham Valley. Six inch O.S., cvi, SE., lat. 50°-31'-41", lon. 4°-2'-26".

(10) *Routrundle*, south, 600 ft to the sw. of (9).

For details of (9) and (10) see later, under heading 'Pounds involved in later enclosures' (p. 153).

(11) *Grimspound*. Six inch O.S., c, NW., lat. 50°-36'-46", lon. 3°-50'-12". (Fig. 37.)

Diameter N. and S. 490 ft, E. and W. 413 ft. An irregular quadrilateral with curved sides and rounded angles. Area within walls 3·943 acres. Twenty-four hut-circles within the pound, none in the vicinity outside. Mean elevation of ground approximately 1,530 ft O.D., mean gradient 1 in 8½, sloping north-west.

One must not take Polwhele too seriously when he is writing as to dimensions, but his statement as to the wall of Grimspound is that "in several places where it is entire it is about six feet in height, and of the same thickness" (*History of Devon*, Vol. 1, p. 140). Spence Bate says: "The average height of the rampart is still about six feet, but the width of the base is fully twenty feet." (*T.D.A.*, Vol. 4, p. 497). Ormerod takes the view that "the height was about six feet, and the width from six to ten" (*Rude Stone Remains*, p. 14, privately printed). Burnard records: "The facing stones are many of them of large size and dry laid—the total thickness of the wall in the most perfect portion facing the south-west, being from eight to ten feet thick." (*Pictorial Dartmoor*, Vol. ii, p. 26.) The Dartmoor Exploration Committee has not been quite consistent in its description of the wall. In its first report (*T.D.A.*, Vol. 26, p. 113) the following passage occurs: "Twenty-five yards north of the western exit of the track which runs through the pound, the wall has both faces perfect. The width is here 9 ft from face to face. The outer face is still 4½ ft high, the inner 1½ ft. A little further on the wall is 10 ft thick. The wall by hut vii is 9½ ft. The inner face is there 4 ft 4 in. high." With these figures I agree. In the second report, however, the figures are varied considerably, on a general review of the wall, and it is there stated (*T.D.A.*, Vol. 27, p. 82): "At the base the heap of ruins that forms the wall measures, where two faces remain undisturbed, about 12 feet."

My own view is that the original width of the wall varied from 8 ft to 9 ft 6 in., with a prevalent width of 9 ft. This estimate might perhaps be a little too generous, in view of the possible spread of the foundations blocks under pressure of the not inconsiderable weight which they bore.

I have always held that it was a mistake to rebuild the structure to accord with the Committee's views of what it ought to be, especially as no single section through the ruins at any point where the rebuilding was contemplated was made and published. And so I ventured to dissent from the conclusions of my colleagues; a task a little difficult for the youngest member. The matter will be found discussed later, under the heading of 'Structure of the Walls' (p. 150).

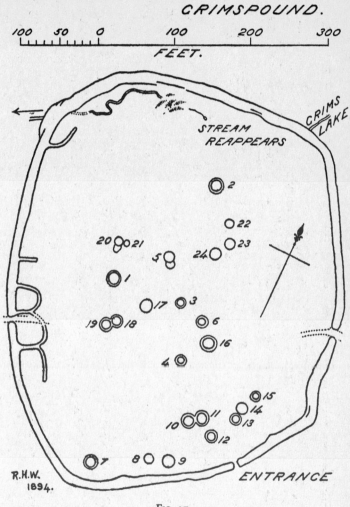

FIG. 37.

There is no doubt as to the entrance. It lay on the south, toward the eastern end of the south wall. The opening is from 6 ft 6 in. to 7 ft in width, walled on either side, and the way paved and stepped. The side walls do not exceed 5 ft 6 in. in height, and I see no reason to suppose that the pound wall was more than, at the most, a few inches higher. The entrance squarely faces the slope of Hameldon, which here rises 150 ft in 200 yds; a curious location were the intent of the pound military or protective. At the opening itself the gradient is 1 in 5. The necessity for paving is apparent to anyone who is familiar with the condition to which cattle reduce the land at field gates. But something more than paving there must have been. The Dartmoor Exploration Committee speaks of the water from Hameldon trickling through the opening. It does much more than trickle; it rushes in miniature waterfalls down the steps, and in a storm blows up in one's face. It would seem that a catch-water gutter was necessary when the pound was occupied, and there is some evidence still traceable that there was such a gutter to the south of the entrance.

As to the other two entrances, in the west and east walls respectively, these are mere gaps, with no side walls, and that on the west opens into a small court built against the pound wall, the wall of which court has also been breached to permit the modern track to be formed. The alleged paving of these entrances is no more than the foundation of the wall. These openings are recent.

As to the water supply, Grims Lake runs under the wall at the north-east angle, disappears in bouldery ground, emerges to surface some forty yards farther on, pursues a rather devious course, generally parallel to the north wall, and passes out under the wall at the north-west angle. This is apparently the natural course of the stream, and the pound was built so as to enclose a part of that course. Grims Lake dries in seasons of drought and cannot have been an entirely dependable source of supply.

COMPOUND POUNDS

(12) *Legis Tor*, Plym Valley. Six inch O.S., cxii, SE., lat. 50°-28'-8", lon. 4°-0'-55".

Forty-seven years ago, in reporting on my excavations at Legis Tor, I referred to a plan as accompanying the report ('Third Report of the Dartmoor Exploration Committee', *T.D.A.*, Vol. 28, p. 184). That plan was never issued; I now supply the omission (Fig. 38).

The pound comprises four enclosures. Their order of construction can readily be determined. A on plan is the only close the outline of which is in no way affected by its neighbours; one hut-circle is involved in the wall. The perimeter of B is affected by the intrusion of a part of A: there is no hut-circle in this close, but there is one immediately outside the wall and coupled with it by an arc of walling. The outline of C is modified by both A and B; there are nine huts within its area, and it may be said to share with A one hut, except that the entrance is from A. From C has been severed the space marked C', one-half the wall of which has been borrowed from C. Two of the hut-circles already

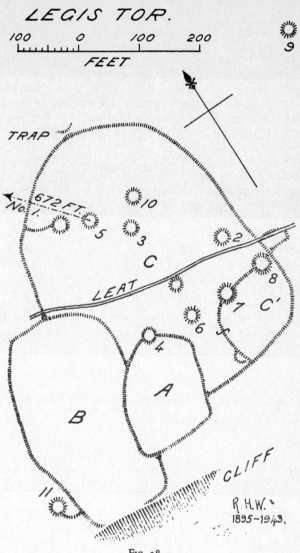

LEGIS TOR.

100   0   100   200

FEET

9

TRAP

672 FT.
No. 1.

10

5   3   2

C

LEAT   8

1   C'

6   f

4

A

B

CLIFF

11

R. H. W.
1895-1943.

FIG. 38.

attributed to c were involved in the wall of c′, and from the position of their entrances may be regarded as having been taken over by the latter. There is also something which looks much like a half hut.

The areas are: A, 0·429 acres; B, 1·200 acres; c + c′, 2·631 acres; c′, 0·266 acres. Total area, excluding walls, 4·260 acres, somewhat larger than Grimspound.

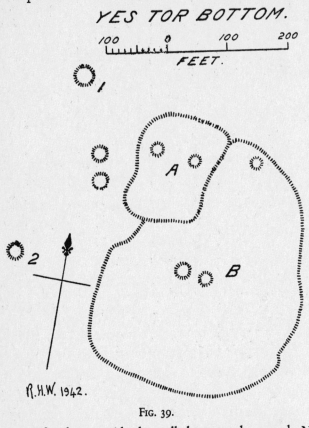

FIG. 39.

There are few huts outside the walls but near the pound; No. 11 already referred to; No. 9 shown on plan; and, considerably farther away, No. 1, the position of which is indicated by an arrow.

A low cliff parallel to the river has encroached on B, a portion of the south-west wall of which has thus been lost.

A modern leat, for the supply of water to Yeoland Consols in the Meavy Valley, made within my recollection but now disused, passes through close c.

The mean elevation of the ground is 960 ft O.D., the slope is to the south, and the mean gradient is 1 in 8·6.

The original thickness of the walls was between 4 ft and 4 ft 6 in. Sections are given later. At the point marked 'Trap' on the plan the wall has been adopted as part of a vermin trap formerly used in connexion with Legis Tor, or New, Warren: compare Trowlesworthy (5).

(13) *Yes Tor Bottom*, valley of the Walkham. Six inch O.S., cvi, SE., lat. 50°-32'-15", lon. 4°-1'-18". (Fig. 39.)

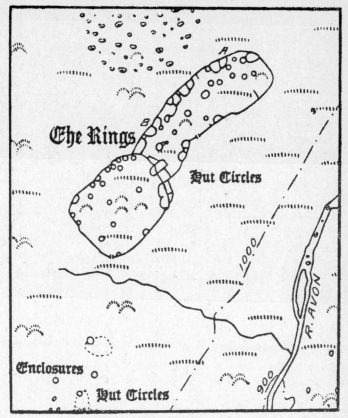

FIG. 40. Riders Rings. Scale 12 inches to 1 mile.

The hut-circles of this small settlement were excavated by Mr. R. Burnard and the Rev. S. Baring-Gould ('Fifth Report of the Dartmoor Exploration Committee', *T.D.A.*, Vol. 30, pp. 99–104).

There are two closes of which A on plan has an area of 0·450 acre. This was obviously the earlier of the two. To it was subsequently added B, having an area of 2·144 acres. There are in A two hut-circles, in B three huts, and adjacent to the pound are four more huts, with one other not far distant: a total of ten which may fairly be said to be associated.

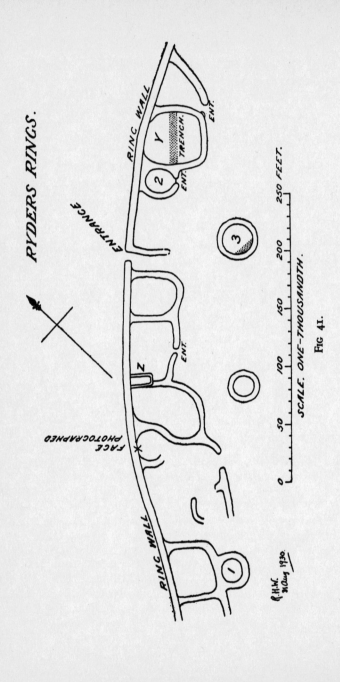

RYDERS RINGS.

RING WALL

Y
ENT. TRENCH.
2
ENT.

ENTRANCE

3

RING WALL

ENT.

Z

FACE PHOTOGRAPHED

RING WALL

1

R.H.W.
26 Aug. 1930.

0   50   100   150   200   250 FEET.

SCALE. ONE-THOUSANDTH.

FIG 41.

The walls had an original thickness of 4 ft 6 in. Sections are given later. The mean elevation of the ground is 1,200 ft O.D. The slope is to the south, with a mean gradient of 1 in 9, but locally the gradient varies from 1 in 4 to 1 in 18.

Hut 1 (see plan) was found to have been the subject of secondary occupation by tinners in the historic period.

(14) *Riders Rings*, or *The Rings*, Avon Valley. Six inch O.S., cxiii, SE., lat. 50°-27'-50", lon. 3°-51'-42". (Figs. 40–2.)

Two hut-circles in this pound were excavated by myself in August 1930, and the pound wall examined. I had hoped to prepare a complete survey during the past year, but conditions have not permitted. I accordingly use, by consent, a map which has previously appeared and which is adapted from the Ordnance Survey. The pound has two compartments, of which the southern was the first built. The area of this

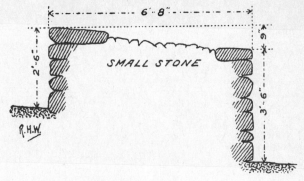

FIG. 42. Riders Rings: section of the wall of the north pound.

southern section is approximately 3·24 acres, that of the northern is approximately 3·73, making a total of 6·97 acres. Each section contains at least 17 huts. Both have courts built against the walls; these courts are few in the southern compartment, but in the northern they attain a development unmatched elsewhere on Dartmoor.

Fig. 41 gives a survey which I made of a length of the wall of the north pound, that length which lies between A and B on Fig. 40. The mean elevation of the site is 1,100 ft O.D., the mean gradient is approximately 1 in 5, and the ground slopes south-east.

The wall is built with two faces of relatively small stones, and a filling of yet smaller stones. Its thickness is 6 ft 8 in., both faces still stand over considerable lengths; in places it is 4 ft 3 in. in height, and it was probably originally somewhat over 5 ft high; see Fig. 42, and 'Twelfth Report Dartmoor Exploration Committee', *T.D.A.*, Vol. 67, pp. 116–19.

STRUCTURE OF THE WALLS

Some at least of the larger stones used in the megalithic monuments appear to have been brought to their site from a distance, but the material for the walls of the pounds is nowhere traceable to other than the immediate locality. This involves that pounds were not erected where building material was not locally available; but it does not follow that such material should be uniform in nature from site to site.

Thus Grimspound (11) comes near the higher extreme in size of blocks in the construction of the wall, and the material is porphyritic granite; while Riders Rings (14) affords an instance of the other extreme and the use of the smallest efficient blocks of stone, in that case fine-grained red felsite. And yet, judged by any other standard, Riders Rings is a more important structure than Grimspound.

It is true also that the builders not only took the material nearest to hand, but they took it as it came. Nowhere can any trace be found of trimmed or broken stone. As nature yielded it, so it was used. And this might well be expected: the modern waller with his steel tools can split or trim as he will, while the pound-builder of the Early Bronze Age had but stone hammers, and pebbles used as hammer-stones. The painfully wrought stone hammer was a work of art which would not have survived half a dozen attempts to trim a granite block, and the cruder pebble mounted in a handle or wielded in the hand would have met no greater success. The alternative was skill in making the best use of that which was available, and of that skill there was no lack.

The pound-builder picked a site where an immediate supply of building material was available, provided it was otherwise desirable. Naturally he avoided enclosing areas too greatly encumbered with surface stone. Thus a visit to Legis Tor (12) will show that the linear clitters which descend the face of the hill were carefully evaded. But an otherwise desirable site not infrequently presented an excess of surface granite: if it were to be cleared a place of deposit for the surplus had to be found, and that place was the wall, which could be thickened to the necessary extent.

Similar problems in different ages often find similar solutions, and there are modern fences on Dartmoor the unusual height and thickness of which are made up of excess of surface stone. Good examples may be seen near Wapsworthy in Petertavy parish.

Two conditions made for unusual thickness of wall: large blocks which in the absence of facilities for trimming could not be reduced to reasonable size, and surplus stone for which a place of deposit was required. Both conditions were operative at Grimspound (11).

Many large stones are slab-like or have at least one plane face of considerable area: such were not laid in the wall on their flat but were set upright on the inner face, exposing their greatest surface. There are

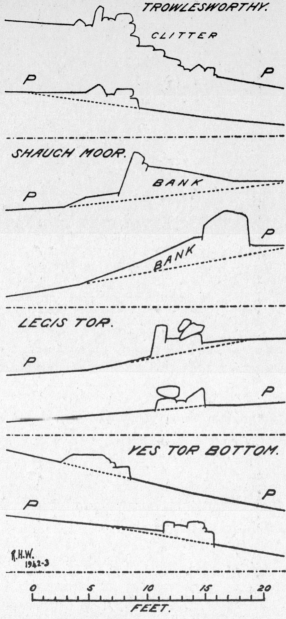

TROWLESWORTHY.

CLITTER

P   P

SHAUCH MOOR.

BANK

P

BANK

P

LEGIS TOR.

P

P

YES TOR BOTTOM.

P

P

R.H.W.
1942-3

0   5   10   15   20

FEET.

FIG. 43. Sections of pound walls.

walls where practically the whole of the inner face is so formed, with a minimum of ordinary walling, as, for example, Hurston Pound (Six inch O.S., lxxxix, SE., lat. 50°-38′-5″, lon. 3°-51′-47″) mentioned by Crossing; and Shaugh Moor (Six inch O.S., cxviii, NE., lat. 50°-26′-49″, lon. 4°-2′-18″). This method has also been used in the historic period: a marked instance can be seen in the northern hedge of the road near Shaugh Prior as one approaches the village from Shaugh Bridge.

Sometimes, as on Shaugh Moor, the fence is lined on the inner side with slabs, and banked up on the outer side with stone and earth; an arrangement very effective in confining cattle within the enclosure, but of no value in the exclusion of any person or animal from the pound.

Where the fence consists of normal walling the pound wall is built with two faces, unconnected by any throughers or ties, and with smaller stones set in the centre. The most marked example is at Riders Rings. This absence of throughers is largely due to the fact that the stones could not be cut or trimmed, and only a few would present themselves of the required length, neither so long as to project beyond the face of the wall, nor so short as not to reach, at least nearly, from face to face.

Finally it may be noted that to-day the normal height of a Devonshire hedge is from 4 ft 6 in. to 5 ft, while the top bar of a field gate stands some 4½ ft above ground level.

See Fig. 43 for sections of pound walls.

The wall of Grimspound needs individual consideration. The Dartmoor Exploration Committee decided that the wall really consisted of two independent walls, with a space between. The Committee did not stop there. It reconstructed a length to show that the material could be so disposed; but this was no evidence, since the material could be disposed in many ways. It was held, and correctly, that if the wall were solid it could not have been more than 5 ft high. This, incidentally, is the full ordinary height of a pound wall. But it was also held to be "absurd that a wall of huge stones, ten feet thick, should be only five feet high". My own view is that the wall was formed of huge stones because large blocks were all that were available. I think that 9 ft in thickness is a fairer measurement than 10 ft; and consider that the necessity for clearing the area of the pound, to some extent at least, caused the use of more stones than would normally have been the case. If a 9 ft wall, 5 ft high, were an absurdity, we may consider what was substituted for it; this was an arrangement of two parallel walls with a space of approximately 3 ft 6 in. in width between them. Even so the Committee had to conclude that: "the walls were apparently not high enough to serve as a defence against an enemy, and the hollow between the walls would, it is supposed, make the defence of them difficult". Certainly the two walls could more easily be thrown down than could the same material disposed in one structure. The defenders would less readily be able to bestir themselves in defence of the wall; and any

defender who found himself in the space between the walls might as
well have his hands tied behind his back. On the other hand, for a
cattle enclosure, 5 ft is ample height of wall, and we have the fact that
the side walls of the entrance are but 5 ft 6 in. in height.

There are double walls on Dartmoor, on the Dewerstone Hill (4)
with a space between the walls or from 12 to 13 ft, and at Whittor,
where that space varied between 10 and 40 ft; room enough in either
for a fighting man to give a good account of himself. Both on the
Dewerstone Hill and at Whittor the sites offer good defensive possi-
bilities; at Grimspound there are none.

I know no physical evidence which supports the Committee's
conclusion.

POUNDS INVOLVED IN LATER ENCLOSURES

The pound builders selected the most favourable sites, but often at
an elevation unsuited to modern agriculture. None the less they sometimes occupied land which has since found favour with later enclosers.
Thus pounds and hut-circles alike are to be found on modern farm-
land, and the pounds themselves have sometimes preserved their individuality in the new role of fields. Roundy Farm, in the Meavy Valley
(six inch O.S., cxii, NE., lat. 50°-30'-48", lon. 4°-0'-22"), most probably
owes its name to the fact that many of its little fields are still readily
recognizable as prehistoric pounds, in which are fair sprinklings of hut-
circles. The doorway of the old farmhouse, now removed to Burrator,
bears the date 1668, and there is reason to believe that in or about that
year the land was taken in. In the same valley, at Stanlake (six inch
O.S., cvi, SE., lat. 50°-31'-20", lon. 4°-1'-0"), at least one compound
and one simple pound, with a number of hut-circles, preserve their
identity among the farm enclosures.

The instances could be multiplied almost indefinitely, and from all
the moorland border; but we may take No. (9) and (10) already
referred to, Routrundle in the Walkham Valley. Here there are two
simple pounds, each of which functions as a field (Fig. 44).

The northern pound contains 0·601 acre and there is a hut-circle,
not quite centrally placed. The southern pound has an area of 0·734
acre, there is no hut-circle. The distance between the walls of the two
is 400 ft. From the plan it will be seen that the pounds stand out distinctively even in this group of irregular fields. Routrundle is at least
a reasonably old tenement; the first mention of which I have knowledge is in a survey of Walkhampton manor, 1585, where Richard
Worth appears as tenant of Rowtrendall, under lease of 1556. The
present pronunciation of the name is Rutrundle. It may be ventured
that the roundels or pounds had part in determining the name.

While some pounds have in prehistoric days been utilized as fields in
farms where most of the closes are later, others have been used without

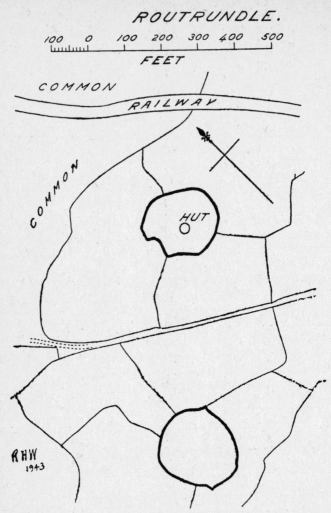

FIG. 44. Routrundle. Pounds surrounded by later enclosures.

any addition save that of a court and square-built house. One such transfer to more modern uses has already been mentioned, Merrivale (6). Others are: Willings Walls, in the Plym Valley (six inch O.S., cxii, SE., lat. 50°-28'-26", lon. 4°-0'-10"), and Brockhill Foot, in the valley of the Avon (six inch O.S., cxiii, SE., lat. 50°-28'-22", lon. 3°-51'-58"), as good an instance as any. The list might easily be enlarged. In effect these pounds have been appropriated as small, ready-made, newtakes.

LYNCHETS

Lynchets are ridges or terraces formed where the plough has been used on hillside enclosures and arise from the furrow being turned downhill. Dr. E. C. Curwen claims to have found them in the Dartmoor pounds, and cites Trowlesworthy (*Antiquity*, Vol. i, pp. 281–4). Mr. E. H. Rogers (*Torquay Natural History Society, Transactions*, Vol. viii, pp. 177–8) quotes Curwen, accepts that the pounds on Trowlesworthy are lynchetted, and adds that the pound on Legis Tor (12) is well lynchetted. But he doubts whether the accumulation of soil against the foot walls of the pounds can be fairly attributed to cultivation. Very certainly there are other means by which such a result might come to being through the ages; there has been for instance a growth of soil of from 18 in. to 2 ft over the floors of the hut-circles since they were abandoned, even over the floors of huts which were reoccupied in the sixteenth century by the tinners. Nor do I think that we may credit man in the Early Bronze Age with the possession of ploughs; more probably his best tool for breaking the soil was a digging stick.

Statements of this nature send one into the field once more: it is not enough that one has no note of lynchets, nor ever suspected their existence. I have revisited Trowlesworthy and Legis Tor, and the sections of the walls of these pounds (Fig. 43), will show that at Legis Tor (12) there is nothing whatever in the nature of accumulated soil against the inside of the lower wall of the pound, while at Trowlesworthy (5) the greatest depth of soil so accumulated is 9 in., and this dies away to nothing in a width of 6 ft. At Yes Tor Bottom (13) the greatest accumulated depth is 5 in., which dies away to nothing in a width of 7 ft. 6 in. Lynchets may be removed from the picture.

POUNDS AND HUT-CIRCLES

As I have said, simple pounds may have no hut-circle within the enclosure; they may or may not be in the immediate vicinity of huts. Thus there are huts quite near the pound at Shavercombe (1), while there are no huts within a quarter of a mile of Hingston Hill (2).

Where there are huts obviously associated with a pound, whether simple or compound, they may all lie within the enclosure, as with the 24 huts at Grimspound (11), or some may be within and some without the wall, as at Yes Tor Bottom (13).

A pound is not a necessary adjunct of a cluster of hut-circles; at Whittenknowles Rocks, Plym Valley (six inch O.S., cxii, SE., lat. 50°-29'-8", lon. 3°-59'-39") there is a cluster of 23 huts, but no pound; 600 yds south, on Eastern Tor, is a pound enclosing one hut. At Watern Oke, on the Tavy (six inch O.S., lxxxviii, SE., lat. 50°-37'-58", lon. 4°-1'-49"), there is a group of 60 huts, with only some slight connecting walls, but no certain pound, and there is another group of 18 huts devoid of connecting walls; while Riders Rings (14) enclose at least 34 huts, although there are none outside.

'CELTIC FIELDS'

On or near the borders of cultivation attempts have been made at enclosure from time to time. The small fields then formed are marked most usually by their rectilinear fences and sharp angles; in complete contrast, not only with the work of the pound builders, but also with that of the earlier agriculturists of the historic period. A great part of these enclosures have gone back to the moor; many of them were formed on lands where hut-circles existed. There has been a tendency to couple the enclosures and the circles, and term the closes 'Celtic Fields'. Ormerod (*Rude Stone Remains*, p. 10 and map) describes and figures a group of such enclosures near Teigncombe; these are so modern in type that they are even provided with accommodation roads. But Omerod held that the hut-circles were "the dwellings of the old workers and washers of tin" and is prepared to accept that they would have been in use during the first ten centuries of the Christian era, and as the streaming for tin in the district near Chagford appears to have in a great measure ceased by the time of Queen Elizabeth, the time between those periods may, he held, probably be taken as that when the huts were abandoned. In justice it has to be remembered that he wrote before the spade had done its work.

Another group of such fields that has been cited is at Foales Arrishes, on Pil Tor (six inch O.S., cviii, NW., lat. 50°-34′-6″, lon. 3°-46′-55″), where the mere fact of the enclosures retaining the name of their tenant should have warned off all celtophiles.[1]

CONCLUSIONS

The pound walls were normally from four to five feet in thickness, and five feet in height. Very rarely, and under exceptional conditions, the walls were from six feet to nine feet in thickness, and some, perhaps, were six feet in height. One form of structure, where the wall was banked-up on the outside and stone-faced within, was efficient in enclosing, and wholly inefficient in excluding. There is no trace of strategic method in the selection of site. Sir Gardner Wilkinson held that Grimspound was "well placed to command the passage over the hills". It commanded nothing, and could be by-passed on either side, over ground presenting no difficulty.

King, Ormerod and Shortt all held that Grimspound was a fold for cattle. Ormerod extends that view to other pounds. It seems that such was their one effective use. It is quite true that a wolf or a human enemy could pass the wall; but with either the true danger was that they might

---

[1] See footnote on p. 121 (ED.).

stampede or drive away the animals. Against this, a substantial fence was complete protection, as long as the gateway was held, or any breach in the wall. In the Early Bronze Age, and much later in early feudal times, raids and shock tactics were the order of the day, theft the principal inducement. Such tactics must either succeed of first intention, or fail. The delaying effect of the pound wall was effective in precluding immediate success.

And, if we consider uses in times of peace, the storms of Dartmoor would drive flocks and herds far from their intended lairs, wolves might scatter them, and even well-mannered animals are apt to stray on their own initiative. Pastoral peoples might well sleep sounder at night in the knowledge that their wealth was safely disposed within a fence.

It remains to be considered whether the pounds were not only folds but also fields in which crops were raised. The presence of the animals does not appear consistent with growing crops, and the manner in which the huts are scattered over the pound is often such as would leave little ground without a right of way across it to someone or other. But crops there may have been, if the possibility of wooden fences is conceded.

As to the courts which line the inner face of the walls of some pounds, it seems probable that they were cattle and sheep pens; if so the animals might have been confined therein, leaving space available for crops. But nowhere, except in the northern half of Riders Rings, are such courts in any way a marked feature.

It is to be noted that the builders were content to rely upon the presence of neighbouring streams for their water supply, and took rather a generous view of the word 'neighbouring'. For them it meant some source, not too far off, to which the cattle could be driven for watering, and from which water could be fetched for human needs, while it is not to be thought that those needs were exacting. There are exceptions: in some few pounds the wall is an arc, the chord of which is the bank of a stream; such an instance will be found at Raddick, in the Meavy Valley (six inch O.S., cvi, SE., lat. 50°-31'-30", lon. 4°-0'-31").

VERMIN TRAPS

This subject is admittedly a by-lane in archaeology, but it chances to lead direct to the subject of pounds. Spence Bate, writing in 1871 (*T.D.A.*, Vol. 4, pp. 501–2), mentions the pound on Trowlesworthy (5) and its 'entrances', of which he says: "I think that these two kinds of works at the gateways or entrances to the camp are evidence of the military character of the enclosure, since they were evidently designed to prevent a rush of many men, it being impossible for more than one person to pass at a time. . . . The whole plan, I think, is an interesting specimen of ancient military engineering." In 1889, when preparing my paper on 'The Moorland Plym' (*P.I.*, Vol. 10, pp. 299–300), I accepted the views which Spence Bate had expressed and with the enthusiasm of youth soon added to the list of these works of fortification. Another pound adjacent to (5) was found to have entrances similar to the northern entrance of (5). There were openings in the warren walls provided with similar approach wings, and there were even clitters of tors in the same sort 'defended'. This embarrassment of riches should have warned me, especially when I found the structure on Legis

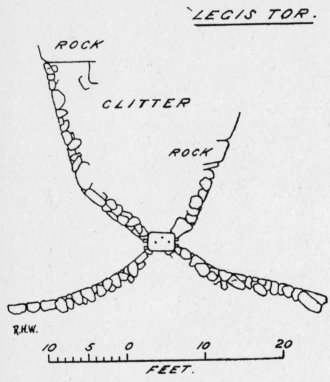

FIG. 45. Vermin Trap. Legis Tor.

Tor, presently to be described. None the less I published my finds as military works, and contented myself with treating the Legis Tor example as an unsolved mystery.

Such a contented frame of mind could not well continue, and I had the happy thought of approaching my friend, Mr. Richard Lavers, the warrener at Trowlesworthy. He could tell me that he had heard that the structures were vermin traps, for the elimination of stoats, weasels and other small animals of prey; but he did not know how the traps were set. Richard Lavers died on 15 March 1914, at the age of 94.

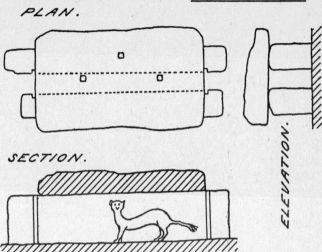

FIG. 46. Vermin trap at Legis Tor.

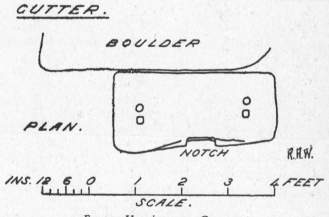

FIG. 47. Vermin trap at Gutter.

The traps in their complete form—most are now somewhat ruined
—consisted of short tunnels, usually 3 ft 6 in. in length, about 4 in.
wide and 11 in. high in the clear. The bottom paved with granite,
and the sides built in the same stone, covered in with a slab of granite
3 ft 6 in. in length and from 1 ft 6 in. to 2 ft in breadth. At each end
of the tunnel the sides were vertically grooved so that shutters might fall
in the grooves and close the ends of the traps. Three or four holes, sunk
in the top of the coverstone, were obviously used in connexion with
the tripping apparatus which let down the shutters and sprang the traps.
Leading up to either end of the tunnels were wing walls. Any stoat,
passing that way, would find it easier to run through the tunnel than to
climb the low wing walls. The animals were permitted to use the passage unmolested, until one day the trap was set, tripped by the animal
on his way through the tunnel, and the beast confined. Figs. 45 and 46
give details of the trap on Legis Tor, and Fig. 47 is a plan of the cover-
stone of a trap on Gutter.

These two traps are at the foot of the summit rocks of their respective tors, and both Legis Tor and Gutter will be found within the area
of six inch O.S., cxii, SE. But the traps are not marked on the survey.

See Pl. 28, figs. 1 and 2, for views of Legis Tor trap; fig. 3 for the
trap coverstone from Gutter.

I have been puzzled as to the material from which the shutters of
these traps may have been made; recently when revising the plan of
Legis Tor pound (12) I noticed that the north wall had been used to
form two of the approach wings (Fig. 38, p. 145) to a tunnel which had
itself been ruined, and, by chance, I found, tucked away in a crevice in
the pound wall, two roofing slates cut to the correct shape for shutters,
each perforated for suspension, and each worn by use. Since which I
have been able to confirm the use of roofing slate in other instances
(see Pl. 29). Nothing better than slate could have been adopted, in-
destructible by weather and unpierceable by the teeth of rodents or
carnivores.

We cannot fix a date as that of the first construction of the traps.
The only hint afforded is by the coverstone at Gutter; this has been split
to reduce it to an appropriate size, and the split has been made by the
old 'slot' method which was in universal use up to the end of the nineteenth century, and was later displaced by the 'drill'. Nor do we know
when they fell into disuse. Moore (Rowe's *Perambulation of Dartmoor*,
1st ed., Appendix v, p. 236) has a note: "These animals [rabbits] are
preserved in warrens, at Ditsworthy and Trowlsworthy on the moor,
surrounded by enclosures to prevent them from straying. Traps are
set in the walls, whence most of the wild animals of the preceding list
have been obtained." These words were written in 1847–8, but do not
necessarily involve that the traps were still operated. From the fact that
Lavers was not fully informed as to the method of their use it would

appear that they must have fallen into disuse some years before 1847.

This method of trapping was not confined to the warrens of Ditsworthy and Trowlesworthy; I have seen cross walls on the summit of Sheepstor, obviously the remains of traps. These were in better order and condition when, in 1802, Bray visited the tor (*Borders of the Tamar and the Tavy*, 1st ed., Vol. 1, p. 234). He noted: "We discovered near the top of the tor two stone ridges, almost covered with turf, that intersected each other at nearly right angles, and formed a cross. In the middle was a flat horizontal stone. Measuring from this central point, the ridge to the east was twelve paces, west six, north seven, and south eleven. We afterwards discovered a larger one below, at the south side of the tor. At first we conjectured they were sepulchral monuments; and afterwards thought they might have been folds for sheep. . . . But after all, these conjectures are entitled to little attention."

BROADUN RING.
WALL.

R.H.W.
1894.

0   1   2   3   4   5   6
FEET

FIG. 48. A section of wall of Broadun Ring,
a good example of one type.

My late friend, Mr. C. W. Dymond, could tell me that similar structures at Worlebury had puzzled him, but that he had been told that those also were traps and connected with a warren.

In conclusion it may be permissible to anticipate another difficulty which may arise in connexion with the pounds, the presence of shallow granite troughs in the walls of two of them. These will be found on Shaugh Moor (six inch O.S., cxviii, NE., lat. 50°-27'-9½", lon. 4°-1'-45") and on the southern slope of Butterdon Hill, above Addicombe, Erme Valley (six inch O.S., cxix, SE., lat. 50°-24'-29", lon. 3°-53'-54"). The explanation in either instance is the same: the stone-masons have never hesitated to use prehistoric walls as quarries and have selected from them such stone as suited their needs; their habit in the past was to work the stone on the open moor where found and to bring home the finished article. It results that part-finished work lies here and there upon the moor. These troughs are only part-finished, and lie in the pound walls because, in those walls, stone was found suited to conversion. Archaeologically they must be described as recent.

PERIOD

Of the localities mentioned above, huts have been excavated at Broadun (8), Foales Arrishes, Grimspound (11), Legis Tor (12), Merrivale (6), Riders Rings (14), Watern Oke, Whittor, and Yes Tor Bottom (13), with results everywhere consistent with the period being that of Early Bronze.[1]

The word 'recent' has been used in this chapter as synonymous with the phrase 'within the historic period'.

[1] See footnote on p. 121.

DARTMOOR BARROWS AND KISTVAENS

FORM AND STRUCTURE OF BARROWS

A BARROW is essentially an artificial mound raised on the site of one or more interments. Varying with the period and with the race erecting the barrow, it may in plan be either round, long (i.e. elliptical or ovoid), or may assume a more complex form, such for instance as that of a ship.

All known Devonshire barrows are of the round type. The diameter at the base of the Devonshire barrows varies from 9 or 10 to 120 ft and over. The present height above the surrounding ground varies from a barely perceptible mound to a heap 12 ft high, and possibly more.

Although very small barrows frequently prove disappointing on excavation, it must not be thought that the probable yield of any can be estimated *pro rata* to the size.

The mounds are made in various ways and of varying materials. Where stone of convenient size was readily obtainable the barrow usually became a cairn formed of stone only; where stone was practically absent earth and soil were used; where stone was sparingly obtainable the centre of the barrow is frequently a small cairn, and this is covered with soil to a greater or less depth.

CAIRNS

These are more usually found in the Dartmoor area, although by no means infrequent elsewhere. Off Dartmoor barrows constructed wholly of stone are usually of small size.

A complete list of the known cairns would be much too long for insertion here. On Dartmoor, Drizzlecombe, Pen Beacon, and Three Barrows Tor yield excellent examples of the larger size; while small examples are found at Cosdon, Raddick Hill, Shaugh Lake, and elsewhere. Instances occur, as at Fernworthy, where topsoil or 'meat earth' was removed over the area to be occupied by the cairn, and the stones rest on the subsoil or 'calm'.

Cairns are peculiarly liable to disturbance and robbery: they are ready-made collections of loose stones more or less suitable for many purposes. On Wigford Down one was removed as road-metal; on Birch Tor a similar robbery was partly accomplished; Western Whittaburrow was partly remodelled to form a house for the workmen at Redlake peat works; visitors from Torquay and other towns have been known to spend many hours, week-end after week-end, remodelling the cairns to suit their tastes; the cairn known as 'Heap of Sinners' on Huntingdon Warren has been built up to a grotesque cone; treasure seekers through the ages have dug into the cairns and scattered the stones; ferreting parties have dug out ferrets which had lain up; merely climbing about on the cairns, by both men and animals, must have much disturbed their contours; there is probably no one example of which it would be safe to state the original form and dimensions. Even the Ordnance Survey, and more recently the Army practising surveying on Dartmoor, have contributed to the deformation of these relics.

A common error attributes too great a proportion of the cairns to the hill-tops, especially on Dartmoor. Large cairns are possibly more frequent on the summits, but large cairns are found where the necessary loose rock is most easily obtained. They are by no means unknown in the valleys—as for instance the cairns on the western slope of Pen Beacon, which lie 300 ft below the summit level; or Giant's Basin and its companion at Drizzlecombe, which are merely on a hillside; or the cairn west of Ditsworthy Warren House, which is well down in the valley. Again, if it is true that there is a summit cairn at Shavercombe Head, it has a companion in the same valley, 270 ft lower in position.

A curious feature of some of the summit cairns is that they are constructed around and over natural exposures of rock, and thus have the summit rocks of the tor, or a part of them, as a core. This certainly adds to the apparent size of the stone heap and gives it greater prominence; but it has not as yet been discovered how, under such circumstances, the interment was placed. The remains of such a cairn are to be found on the summit of Yar Tor, and, a little away from the summit of Corndon Tor, a considerable cairn may be seen to have been founded on a rock outcrop. Other localities might be named, as, for instance, Lynch Tor in the Tavy Valley.

A view of the cairn near the summit of Corndon Tor is given in Pl. 30 (1). Its present height is 10 ft 6 in. It is founded on a natural exposure of rock, as is shown in Pl. 30 (2). The diameter is *c*. 84 ft. Five hundred and fifty yards a little west of north of it lies another cairn, its height 12 ft 6 in., which has been much disturbed. The approximate diameter is 120 ft (Pl. 30 (3)). This cairn has a companion about 120 yds away to the ENE., standing on sloping ground, its height 6 ft 6 in. on the uphill, and 12 ft 6 in. on the downhill side, and its diameter approximately 66 ft (Pl. 31 (1)). Pl. 32A gives a view of the summit barrow on Three Barrows, Erme Valley, its height 8 ft 6 in., and its diameter 139 ft.

The group of remains at Drizzlecombe terminates to the north-east in a cairn of 56 ft diameter and 7 ft in height (Pl. 31 (2)). Associated with the same group is the mound known as 'Giant's Basin', 71 ft across and 10 ft high, deriving its name from a central unnatural depression which is 6 ft 6 in. deep (Pl. 31 (3)).

EARTH BARROWS WITH CENTRAL CAIRNS OR WITH DOMED LAYER OF STONES

In Devon as a whole, both earth barrows and composite barrows, partly of earth and partly of stone, the materials separate, are numerous. Earth, however, appears to have been considered a less desirable material than stone for the construction of a barrow; and where stone was not present in sufficient quantity to provide a considerable mound, the core of the barrow immediately over the interment was frequently formed of this material and earth heaped on outside and over to increase the size of the erection.

Hameldon (Hamel Down) provides a Dartmoor example of a small central cairn in an earth barrow, and in this instance the margin of the barrow is built in stone also. On White Hill, Lydford, a rude domed kist covers a pit in the calm.

PAVING

A rudely paved area is frequently found under barrows and cairns. The pavement usually consists of selected flat stones, or stones as flat as the neighbourhood will provide.

It may be sometimes this paving has served purpose as a hearth; but at other times, as at Two Barrows, Hameldon, the paving is connected with, and an apparent extension of, the cover-stone over an interment (see p. 166).

Paved circles adjoining kistvaens, and giving evidence of having served as hearths for considerable fires, have been found at Deadman's Bottom, Langcombe, no barrows having been erected over the circles.

One of the Red Barrows on Soussons Common (Barrow No. 2) was found to have a paved area adjoining an interment pit, the area of paving stones being very similar to that found in a barrow near Halwill, North Devon.

RING CAIRNS

Rings formed of stones of the size usually used in the construction of cairns are sometimes found. The stones are thrown together with no attempt at walling, and excavation has proved that we are not dealing with rough hut-circles. These 'ring cairns' are puzzling. The history of one, situate at the higher point of Wigford Down, is known. Here the ring is the margin of a large cairn which has otherwise been completely removed for road-mending and hedging, having for years been utilized as a convenient quarry. The same explanation may apply to some other instances, but very doubtfully to all.

THE INTERMENT

Some barrows, especially among the smaller examples, appear to have been erected immediately over the site of the cremation without any effort having been made to localize the interment.

In others the ashes, or a portion of them, were gathered into a small pit sunk in the subsoil and sometimes covered with a selected stone; or the ashes were placed in a vessel which again had the protection of a kistvaen or built chamber of some sort.

INTERMENT PITS IN SUBSOIL

Interment pits containing ashes are rarely of any considerable size. A cairn explored by Mr. Burnard, situate in Stannon Bottom, yielded an urn-shaped pit, 18 in. wide at the mouth, swelling to 20 in. at the broadest part, and 15 in. deep. The illustrations (Fig. 49) show the shape of this pit and its relation to the cairn.

A cairn near Hemstone Rocks, opened by the Dartmoor Exploration Committee, also yielded an urn-shaped pit 12 in. in diameter at the mouth, 17 in. at the widest part, and 22 in. in depth (Fig. 50). This pit had a cover-stone.

In a barrow on White Hill, Lydford, the pit was paved, and in another barrow on the same down the pit was covered with a rude domed 'kistvaen'.

These pits are also to be found sunk beneath the floors of genuine kistvaens, as at Great Gnat's Head and Deadman's Bottom, Plym Valley.

In Lar Tor Newtake three out of eight small cairns were opened, and under each was found an interment pit in the subsoil, containing much charcoal. Two of these pits measured 24 in. × 15 in. × 16 in. deep, and 16 in. diameter × 24 in. deep, respectively, all three pits being covered with flat stones, set leaning inward, with a flat stone immediately over the pit.

The following is a list of the chief localities on Dartmoor from which pits sunk in the subsoil under barrows and cairns have been reported. Dimensions can be given for some of the pits.

> Archerton Newtake, between Row Tor Marsh Brook and Cherry Brook: two cairns.
>
> Archerton Tennis Ground: kistvaen, cavity lined with small stones.
>
> Chagford Common: four small cairns.
>
> Drizzlecombe: cavity 36 in. × 20 in. × 18 in. deep, no cover-stone.
>
> Great Gnat's Head, Plym Valley: kistvaen.

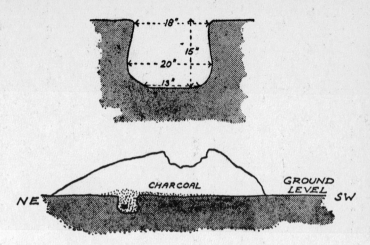

Fig. 49. Cairn at Stannon Bottom: (*above*) pit in 'calm', (*below*) section.

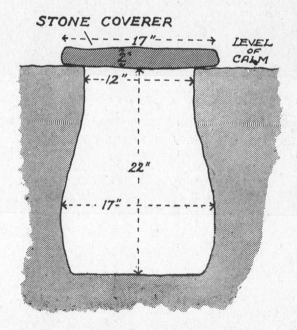

Fig. 50. Pit under cairn near Hemstone Rocks.

LANGCOMBE *NEAR PLYM*

VIEW, *LOOKING N APPROXLY.*

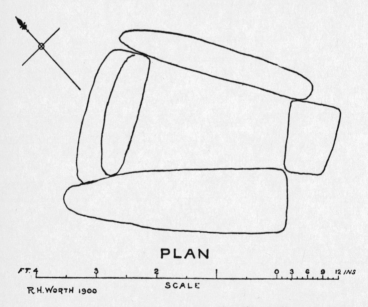

PLAN

SCALE

R.H.WORTH 1900

FIG. 51. Kistvaen, Langcombe, Plym Valley.

VIEW   *LOOKING S. 22° W.*

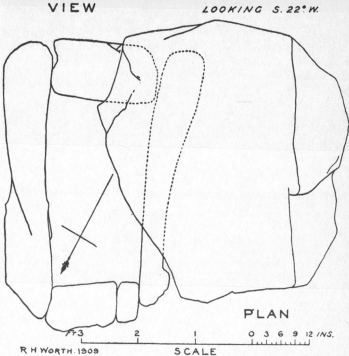

PLAN

3   2   1   0 3 6 9 12 *INS.*

R H WORTH. 1909   SCALE

Fig. 51A. Kistvaen, Ringmoor Down, near Legis Lake.

Great Whiten Tor, Postbridge: pit covered by flat stone.

Grey Wethers, near: two small barrows.

Hare Tor, near Tavy Cleave: 18 in. to 24 in. deep.

Horns Cross, near: 15 in. diameter, 17 in. deep.

Hurston Ridge.

Hemstone Rock, north of: three cairns, cover-stone to one pit.

Lakehead Hill, kist near Bellaford Newtake Gate, 15 in. diameter, 11 in. deep.

Langcombe, Deadman's Bottom: kistvaen.

Langstone Moor.

Metherel, circle No. 6, 36 in. × 30 in. × 12 in. deep, large cover-stone.

Pen Beacon: "cover-stone with hollow space under".

Riddon Ridge.

Ringmoor, near Brisworthy Circle: 24 in. diameter, 7 to 8 in. deep.

Soussons Common, Red Barrows, No. 1 and 2.

Stannon Bottom: pit, urn-shaped.

White Hill, Lydford: three barrows, in one of which the pit was paved, and in another it was covered over with a rude domed kist of large stones.

Wedlake Combe and Walkham Valley, between.

Whittor, east of, near Langstone Menhir, 8.

KISTVAENS

There is sufficient evidence that Devonshire kistvaens, with certain rare exceptions, were originally covered by barrows, although some now stand practically free on the surface.

A kistvaen as a means of localizing the interment is a more elaborate device than a mere pit in the subsoil, with which, however, it may be found associated.

The term has been and is used somewhat loosely, being applied to the stone chest of the well-known Dartmoor type, consisting of four slabs of stone on edge, and forming the sides, with a fifth slab as the cover-stone; and also used in connexion with small domed chambers built of many stones, or oblong chambers in which the sides are walls of dry rubble.

In the Dartmoor type the sides and cover-stone are slabs of granite. As a typical example of a Dartmoor kistvaen, an illustration is given of one in Langcombe, near Plym Steps (Fig. 51), another on Ringmoor Down, near Legis Lake (Fig. 51A), and photographs of two others on Plate 33. These and the Thornworthy Kist (Pl. 32B) are among the more perfect specimens to be found on the moor.

On the summit of Great Nodden, near the source of the River Lyd, is a small grave, first reported by Mr. F. Brent. The local stone is slate, and this has been utilized to build a small walled kist, "wedge-shaped in form, the broad end semi-circular, and the sides somewhat elliptical, fining off into almost a point". "The sides are built of pieces of slaty stone, so arranged that the cleavage sides of the stone form a fair perpendicular wall all around, no slabs or large stones being used."

A paved floor was present in a small kist on Langstone Moor (see p. 174). On Legis Tor is a kist set on an earth-fast boulder, which supplies a floor. It is usual, however, that the floor of a kistvaen should be the bare subsoil, the side and end stones being slightly set in this, the topsoil or 'meat earth' surrounding the sides on the outside, the cover stone above the original surface of the ground, and over all a barrow or cairn.

Langstone Moor kist when opened was found to have been refilled after construction with subsoil material containing small pieces of wood charcoal and a little bone ash. On Watern Down, Chagford Common,

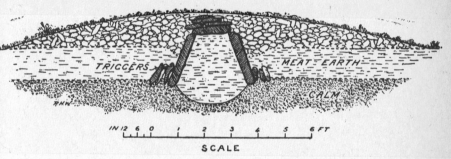

FIG. 52. Section of cairn and kistvaen, Raddick Hill.

a kistvaen was found similarly filled with subsoil material, in which was embedded a beaker; on Raddick Hill Mr. Burnard found another in-filled kist; and at Thornworthy a kist was found filled, or almost so, with black soil. All these were previously undisturbed examples, and it would appear obvious that some kistvaens at least were filled in immediately after the interment, and before the cover-stone was put on or the barrow raised. Every undisturbed example hitherto found on Dartmoor agrees in this particular, but four instances are not sufficient for a generalization.

The Raddick Hill kistvaen is in some sense a connecting link between the domed form (well illustrated from Broad Down, East Devon) and the perpendicular-sided form, for here the sides were sloped toward each other and small stones used to replace the usual covering slabs (Fig. 52).

Double kistvaens are not unknown, as for example on Cosdon Beacon, where the foot-stone of one kist is the head-stone of another.

The following list of kistvaens, long as it is, is unlikely to be complete. No kists, it is believed, are included which are not of the typical Dartmoor form. The great majority have been individually described, with photograph (or sketch) and plan, in the Reports of the Barrow Committee (from the nineteenth onwards). The locations are grouped in areas which approximate to watersheds.

Avon
Brentmoor House
Brockhill Ford

Erme
Butterdon Hill
Lower Piles
Brown Heath, nr Erme Pound
Redlake Foot
Staldon Moor (Stall Down)
Burford Down

Yealm
Dendles Waste
Harrowthorn Plantation, N. of
Ranny Brook, two
   (second *teste* Falcon)
Ranny Brook, N. of

Plym
Lee Moor, E. of Trowlesworthy
Lee Moor, Willing Walls Warren, two
HentorWarren and Shavercombe, five
Langcombe, nr Plym Steps
Langcombe, Deadman's Bottom, five
Langcombe, 'Grimsgrave'
Langcombe, opposite 'Grimsgrave'
Langcombe, sw. of 'Grimsgrave'
Calveslake
Great Gnat's Head
Drizzlecombe, three
Leeden, NW. of Drizzlecombe
Gutter, summit
Gutter, N slope

Legis Tor, two
Legis Lake, Ringmoor
Wigford Down

Meavy
Outcombe, Deancombe
Down Tor
Raddick Hill, two
Old Rifle Range, Hessary
   (*teste* Rowe)
Stanlake
Lether Tor

Walkham
Ingra Tor
Merrivale
Langstone Moor, nr circle (small, with paved bottom)
Vixen Tor

Tavy
Langstone Moor, E. of Whittor (made of local greenstone)

Lyd
Doe Tor

East Ockment
Winter Tor (*teste* Prowse)

Taw
Cosdon, end of triple row, two in one barrow
Cosdon, N. side of summit, two

Teign
Watern Tor, towards Hound Tor
Shuggledown (Barrow F)

Shuggledown, nr Thornworthy Corner

Thornworthy, two in one barrow

Fernworthy (Barrow No. 2)

Hemstone Rocks, N. side

Meacombe

Bovey

Watern Down, Hurston Ridge (previously undisturbed)

King's Oven, Watern Down, nr

Hound Tor, nr Manaton

Webburn

Blackslade Down

Hameldon (Hamel Down), SE. slope

Grimslake, source

Soussons Common, Ephraim's Pinch

Dart

Yar Tor

Stannon Newtake, Postbridge

Roundy Park, Postbridge

Chittleford Down, N. of Archerton House

Archerton Tennis Ground

Cherrybrook and Router Brook, between

Stennen Hill, Powder Mills, two

Lakehead Hill and Newtake, six

Bellever Newtake

Black Newtake, nr Cherrybrook, three

Dunnabridge Common

Dunnabridge Pound Farm

Muddy Lakes Newtake

Crow Tor

Beardown House, NE. of (*teste* Bray)

Round Hill, nr Two Bridges, three

Blackabrook, foot of Round Hill, three

Blackabrook, near Blackey Tor

Royal Hill, nr Blackabrook, 'Crock of Gold'

Royal Hill, SE. side, three

Nun's Cross Farm

Fox Tor Mire, near, two

Childe's Tomb

Fox Tor Newtake, two

Joan Ford's Newtake, Swincombe

Hensroost, Skir Hill

A typical kistvaen, then, is a small chest with sides and ends of stone slabs, resting on natural subsoil, and over all a stone cover. A 'dolmen' (p. 180) may differ from a kistvaen only by its greater dimensions, although most dolmens comprise in their construction more than the essential five slabs which go to form the typical kist. But the term kistvaen has at times been loosely used, and applied to any small burial chamber constructed in stone. If accompanied by adequate description, however, this usage is convenient and free from objection.

Since size enters into the definition, it is convenient to deal with this statistically. It is not every kistvaen which is sufficiently well preserved to enable accurate measurements to be taken, but seventy-three measurable Dartmoor examples give the following results. The average internal length is 3 ft $1\frac{1}{2}$ in. (median, or positional mean, 3 ft 0 in.) the average internal width is 1 ft 11 in. (median, 1 ft 10 in.). The depth, measured from the underside of the cover-stone to the bottom edge of the side stones, can frequently only be obtained by excavation; it is known as regards 28 of the above 73 kistvaens, and the average (and median) depth is 2 ft 7½ in.

Two kists were originally reported with lengths of 7 ft and 6 ft 6 in. These are at Merrivale, and Roundy Park, Postbridge. With another on the summit of Lakehead Hill they had once been 'restored'—much too generously, as is now certain. The longest kist, when these are excluded, is 4 ft 9 in. The largest of the selected group is 4 ft 6 in. long, 2 ft 10 in. wide, and of unknown depth. This kistvaen is on Willings Walls Warren, in the Plym Valley, and was first reported by T. A. Falcon (*T.D.A.*, Vol. 37, p. 458). It was illustrated in B.R. 51 (*T.D.A.*, Vol. 44, p. 115). Another, in Black Newtake, has a length of 4 ft 9 in., width of 2 ft 3 in., and depth of 2 ft 7 in. (*T.D.A.*, Vol. 57, p. 62).

The greatest ascertainable depths are: 3 ft 3 in., which has twice been found, and one which varied from 3 ft 2 in. to 3 ft 5½ in. (Redlake Foot).

The kistvaen smallest in its every dimension is 1 ft 9 in. in internal length, 1 ft 1 in. in width, and 1 ft 2 in. in depth. It once lay on Langstone Moor, Petertavy: now it is housed in the Plymouth City Museum. This little chest had a paved floor (p. 171).

There is no evidence that any of the side, end or cover-stones were artificially shaped to their purpose in any of the Dartmoor kistvaens, or anywhere in Devon. As regarding the plan of the structures the normal method of construction, in which the end stones are set between the side stones, renders any regulation of the length of the side stones quite unnecessary; while the end stones need only be so selected that there is no excessive inequality. In the matter of the depth of the stones a ready adjustment to bring the upper edges to one level was found in setting at a greater or less depth in the subsoil. The cover-stone had merely to be large enough; irregularity of outline was held to be permissible. Even the desirable feature that all the stones should be slab-like was by no means universally observed. The one essential was that the surfaces actually lining the chamber should be reasonable approximations to flat planes. It is none the less a fair general description of these structures that they are built of slabs of rock. These the natural jointing of the granite on Dartmoor, and of the sedimentary rocks elsewhere, provided reasonably ready to hand.

In a kistvaen of somewhat more recent date on Samson in the Isles of Scilly the side stones are grooved to receive the end stones. Nothing similar has been found in Devon. The absence of this grooving in Devon cannot be accounted for by superior hardness of the stone, since the Samson kist, like those on Dartmoor, is built of granite.

The kistvaen known as the 'Crock of Gold', in Tor Royal Newtake, may be taken as a type of normal construction (Fig. 53). The side stones are held apart by the end stones, and one of these being somewhat the longer the width at that end is greater.

CROCK OF GOLD.

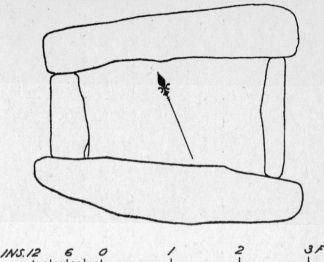

FIG. 53. Kistvaen in Tor Royal Newtake, 'Crock of Gold'.

JOAN FORD'S NEWTAKE.

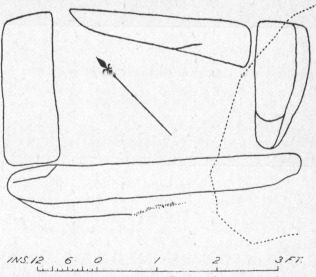

FIG. 54. Kistvaen in Joan Ford's Newtake, Swincombe.

The builders were, however, willing to make the best of the material readily available, even at the expense of departure from the normal plan. Accordingly we find at Joan Ford's Newtake a kistvaen in which one of the side stones occupies the normal position relative to the end stones, but the other side, being too short to be so placed, has been set between the ends (Fig. 54).

At Belliver, where one end has been lost, the other end is wholly outside the sides, reversing the usual position (Fig. 55). On Blackslade Down a very perfect kistvaen shows both ends set outside the sides (Fig. 56; Pl. 33A). Such deviations from the normal as are above illustrated are rare.

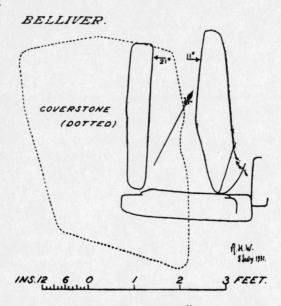

FIG. 55. Kistvaen at Belliver.

The manner in which sides of very unequal length may be worked in to quite a regular structure may be seen at Shavercombe 'C' (Fig. 57). It is extremely rare to find two stones used to form one side of a kist, but an undoubted example occurs near Fox Tor Mire Newtake.

The most massive structure of which I have knowledge is to be found at Meacombe (Pl. 42A), where not only are the sides very thick, but the cover, although but 4 ft 7 in. × 4 ft, weighs over 2 tons.

DIRECTION AND LENGTH OF KISTVAENS

Of the known Dartmoor kists there are three in which the true direction of length cannot be determined with certainty, although in each at least two stones are still in their original position. Two of these

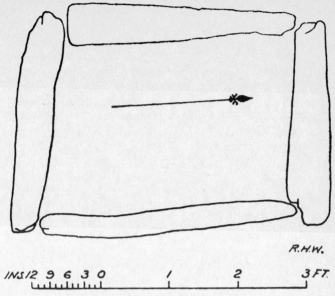

R.H.W.

INS 12 9 6 3 0   1   2   3 FT.

FIG. 56. Kistvaen at Blackslade Down.

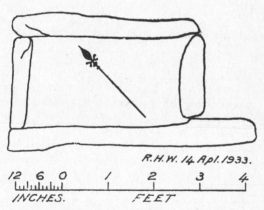

R.H.W. 14 Apl. 1933.

12 6 0   1   2   3   4

INCHES.   FEET

FIG. 57. Kistvaen 'C' at Shavercombe, Plym.

are practically equilateral squares, hence either of two directions at
right angles may be the direction; and the third was also in all probability a square.

Apart from these three, and a small number which have been 'restored', there are eighty-three Dartmoor kistvaens for which the direction of length has been accurately ascertained. With very few exceptions values lie between north and west (or between south and east).

With north used as reference point, the mean bearing is N. 42°-24′ W.,
if the arithmetic mean is taken. The median bearing lies at N. 44° W.

What may be called a 'spectrum' of these bearings has been drawn,
a line to each kistvaen. Where two directions coincide two lines are
shown, displaced sufficiently to be distinguishable. It will be seen from
this spectrum (Fig. 58) that, if we except the two extreme records not
included—one N. 20° E. and one E-W.—, the remainder, eight-one out
eighty-three, fall within the range N. 2° E. and N. 82° W., an arc of 84°.

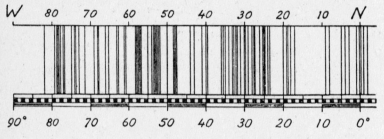

FIG. 58. Distribution of directions of kistvaens.

There are, indeed, only three records in the NE. quadrant, and two
of these have a deviation from N. of 2° or less. By contrast seventy-
seven lie in the NW. quadrant, being fairly dispersed over it as far as
about 80° W. (Two others are due N.)

The odds are too great for this bias of 77 to 3 to be a chance effect.
It is natural to assume some underlying idea. Alignment on the setting
sun has been suggested although, since for 'NW.' we might easily read
'SE.', the rising sun would have its claim. But, indeed, neither rising nor
setting sun would serve to explain the alignment. For in the latitude of
Dartmoor the bearing of the setting sun lies between the limits of 38°
south of west and the same angle north of west; and this total range
of 76° merely overlaps the arc of the kistvaen range by 30°. On the one
hand none of the kistvaens that point north of N. 52° W. can possibly
have been aligned on the setting sun; and on the other hand no kistvaens were aligned on the winter sunset, since (with one exception)
none point between S. 52° W. and N. 82° W. As far as our present knowledge extends no direct astronomical explanation appears possible.
Fig. 59 shows graphically the details given above and is possibly a
clearer statement than any which can be written.

There are localities which are especially rich in kistvaens, and there is some interest in inquiring whether there is any trace of uniformity in the direction of length of the kists within the area of each group.

There are five kists in and about Deadman's Bottom in the Plym watershed; their respective alignments are 57°, 54°, 66°, 30°, and 20°, all west of north.

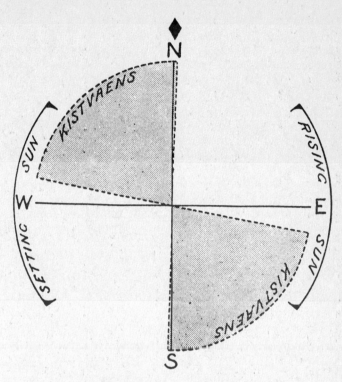

FIG. 59. Orientation of kistvaens: 81 out of 83 measured are orientated within the range indicated.

Five kists are to be found in the Hentor-Shavercombe area in the same valley: the alignments are 63°, 53°, 44°, 43°, and 26°, all west of north.

Three kists lie in a stretch of 590 yds in Langcombe, also in the Plym watershed: their alignments are N. 1° E., N. 82° W. and N. 52° W. respectively.

Of three on Round Hill, near Princetown, the alignments are 74°, 71°-30′, and 67°-45′, all west of north.

Four on Royal Hill, near Princetown, align 79°-15′, 76°-40′, 65°-10′, and 57°-30′ respectively, all west of north.

Three on Lakehead Hill align respectively N. 73° W., N. 52° W., and N. 33° W.

Thus it would appear that proximity does not by any means involve uniformity: indeed, at Thornworthy, two kistvaens lying in one and the same barrow diverged 30° in the direction of their lengths.[1]

DOLMENS OR CROMLECHS

As has been said, the essential characteristic of the dolmen distinguishing it from the kistvaen is its greater size. Thus Chun or Chywoone dolmen, in Cornwall, is in its structure essentially a kistvaen. Its internal dimensions are approximately 5 ft × 5 ft, and it might quite logically be classed as a kistvaen. Zennor Quoit is somewhat larger, and the structure at Trethevy in its perfect condition must have measured at least 6 ft × 5 ft internally.

All these are approximately rectangular, four-sided, chambers with cover-stones. In some it takes more than one stone to form a side, but we have seen that this feature may be found in the kistvaen also. At Lanyon Quoit it can no longer be determined that the enclosure of the space under the cover-stone was ever complete, but stones may well have been removed.

There are three structures in Devon which may reasonably be described as dolmens: the well-known Spinsters Rock at Drewsteignton, the grave on Brent Fore Hill near Corringdon Ball Gate, and the grave on Cuckoo Ball in the parish of Ugborough. Other alleged dolmens or cromlechs have from time to time been reported, but these are either undiscoverable, or when found are obvious errors of identification.

The Spinsters Rock now consists of a cover-stone standing on three supporters. It is quite impossible to describe the space under the cover-stone as being enclosed. Probably many of the stones which formerly constituted the walls of the chamber have been removed long years ago. As it now stands this dolmen is a restoration, having fallen on the last day of January 1862, and having been restored in the same year. Ormerod (*J. Roy. Archaeolog. Inst.*, Vol. 29, 1872) makes it clear that the supporters are not now in their original position. Unfortunately he had made no plan of the structure before its fall. He had, however, made sketches with the *camera lucida*, and these, as given in the paper referred to, are here inserted (Fig. 60).

The remains at Brent Fore Hill (Pl. 34) and at Cuckoo Ball (Pl. 35) are so far wrecked and incomplete that there is little to be said of them except that the former existence of genuine chambers is clearly indicated.

---

[1] One of these is shown on Pl. 32B. The other is on view in Torquay Museum (ED.)

N.º 1

N.º 2

N.º 3

From North

Fig. 60. Drewsteignton Cromlech—'Spinster's Rock'. After Ormerod.

RETAINING CIRCLES

The retaining circle is sometimes unnecessarily spoken of as a 'peristalith'. It is a circle of stone surrounding an interment, sometimes lying within the margin of the barrow, as in the cairn on Birch Tor, to which further reference will be made. Sometimes it would appear that the circle must always have been wholly outside the margin of the barrow or cairn, as for instance the circle on Soussons Common, where the diameter is, however, no more than 28 ft and it is certain that a mound covering the kistvaen has been removed. The Stalldon Moor circle, with a diameter of 45 ft, and with the remains of a barrow within the circle, is an example of a clear-standing circle which does not appear to admit of doubt: it lies where there is no probability that the barrow would ever have been robbed. The majority of the circles around Dartmoor barrows where there are kistvaens are between the limits of 9 ft and 20 ft in diameter: very few exceed 20 ft. It is difficult to be certain whether all circles around kistvaens were originally within the barrows, but it is probable that the majority were covered by the mounds.

As to structure, the retaining circles are of two main classes: the *Open*, in which the stones are set at intervals in the circumference, a clear space separating each from its neighbour; and the *Closed*, in which the stones form a closed circle, each making contact with its neighbour on either side. Of *Open Retaining Circles*, Soussons Common, already referred to, affords a good example (see Pl. 36A and Fig. 61). A circle in Lakehead Newtake may also be cited (Fig. 62 and Pl. 36B). The diameters are 27 ft 8 in., and 19 ft respectively. Figures set against the stones on the plans indicate their height in inches, and all diameters are internal. In these two circles the stones are of no considerable size, but fairly represent average conditions. They are also, as will be seen, set vertically.

There are retaining circles in which the stones are taller and more pillar-like. One such lies at the south end of a stone row near Spurrells Cross, in the Erme Valley (see p. 206). Here two of the stones, now fallen, measure 4 ft 9 in. × 1 ft 3 in., and 3 ft 7 in. × 1 ft 2 in. respectively. But these pillar-like stones are less frequently found.

In a distinct variety of the open type the stones in the circle are few and are slab-like: they are set leaning out from the barrow. Such a circle is to be found around the central of the three adjacent barrows in the Drizzlecombe group (Fig. 73, p. 211). The structure is even more marked in that, in this instance, the slabs have been trigged by smaller stones on the outside, to ensure that although leaning they shall not fall (see Pl. 37A).

The circle around the kistvaen commonly called 'Grims Grave', in Langcombe, Plym Valley, is also constructed with outward-leaning slabs, nine of which still stand. The diameter of the circle is 18 ft.

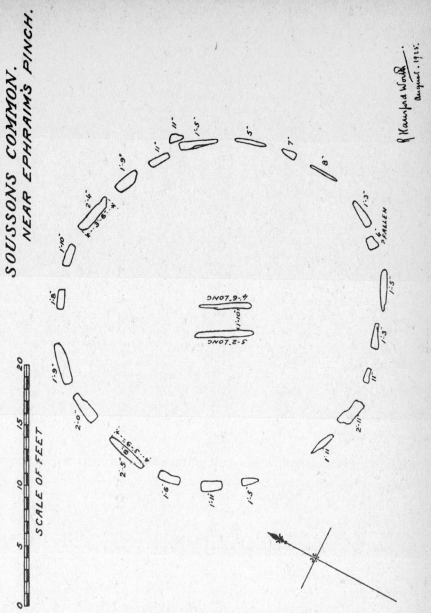

FIG. 61. Soussons Common, circle near Ephraim's Pinch.

In the year 1925 a certain road contractor, not content with wholly destroying groups of hut-circles on Shapley Common, together with their pound walls, attacked a cairn on the summit of Birch Tor. He removed large quantities of stone and came upon the tops of the stones of the retaining circle, which was well within the margin of the cairn.

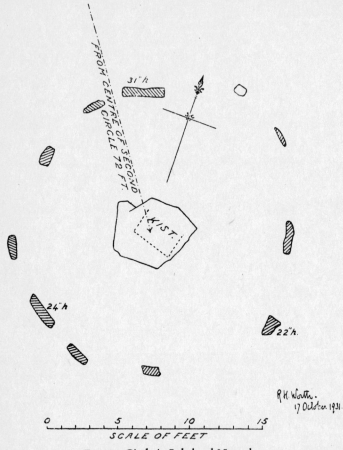

FIG. 62. Circle in Lakehead Newtake.

These stones were large slabs, set so as to lean inward at an angle of about 30 degrees to the vertical. Certainly the contractor made clear the construction of the cairn, but one owes him no measure of gratitude for that, the less since, having met with these stones of the retaining circle, and finding them at once earth-set and too large for his purposes, he set to to break them down with the hammer, carting the rubble to the roads. At this stage the writer intervened.

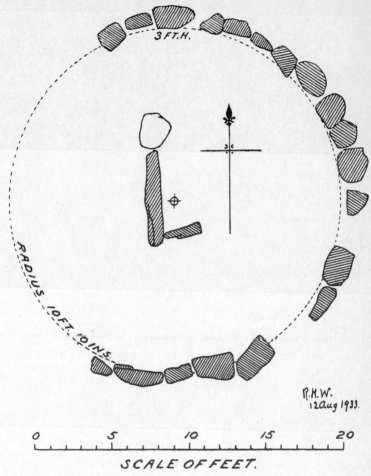

FIG. 63. Hound Tor: kistvaen and retaining circle.

Of *Closed Retaining Circles* there are two varieties clearly marked. There is some difficulty in finding descriptive nomenclature, but I have called them the '*random*' and the '*kerb*'. In both there is an attempt at regularity in the level of the upper edges of the stones forming the circle. But in the *random closed retaining circle* the stones are irregular in

METHEREL 6.

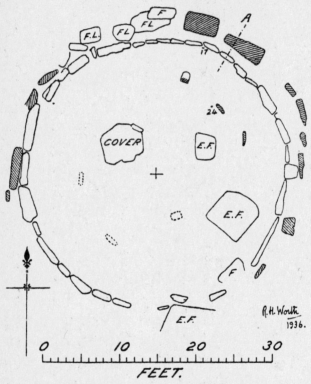

FIG. 64. Circle 6 at Metherel.

shape, and somewhat irregular in setting. An excellent example is the circle around the Hound Tor kistvaen (see plan in Fig. 63 and view on Pl. 37B).

The *Kerb Circles* are much more precise in construction. They are built wholly of stones selected as having one long edge straight, which edge is set uppermost; and almost wholly of stones which are thin parallel slabs. The upper edge of the circle maintains an unbroken line. These kerbs rarely reach to more than a few inches above the level of the ground surface, but extend down to the subsoil, in which they are firmly set. In no known instance is there evidence of any considerable mound within the kerbs: indeed, it would appear likely that they were the enclosing circles of platform cairns in most, if not in all, instances. The topsoil within the kerbs was removed, the subsoil bared, and a layer of stone deposited, of such a depth as to rise somewhat above the level of the original surface.

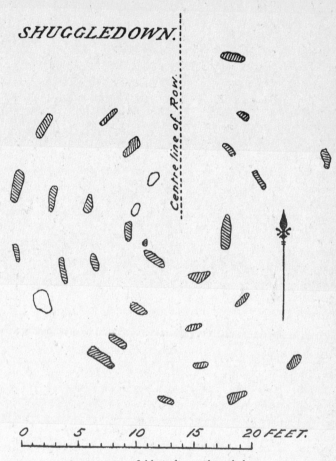

FIG. 65. Fourfold circle on Shuggledown.

Drizzlecombe, Plym Valley, affords a typical example (Pl. 38A). The depth from the top of the kerb to the level of the subsoil varies between 15 and 20 in. The diameter of the circle is 11 ft.

At Metherel, Circle No. 6 also shows a kerb, the diameter being 33 ft 6 in. and the top of the kerb standing 17 in. above the surface of the subsoil. This brings us to the further feature that there may be more than one cincture to an interment. When this is so the circles are approximately concentric, but are not necessarily all of the same class. At this circle, which is threefold, there are clear traces of an inner *open* circle of approximately 22 ft diameter, outside which lies the *kerb* of 33 ft 6 in. diameter, and surrounding the whole is a second *open* circle of stones, which vary considerably in size, the diameter of this outer circle being approximately 37 ft (see Fig. 64, Pl. 39B). The view shows three stones of the inner circle, a length of the kerb, and the largest stones of the outer circle. Plate 39A gives a view of Lowton Circle.

It may be noted that at Drizzlecombe there was no kistvaen within the kerb, but only an interment pit. At Metherel there was no kistvaen, but a large cover-stone, under which was found an interment pit.

A kistvaen on Yar Tor lies immediately within a *random closed* circle, having a diameter of about 10 ft 6 in. There is an outer *open* circle of *c.* 34 ft diameter.

Of fourfold circles two may be cited. The first lies at the head of one of the stone rows on Shuggledown, Teign Valley (see p. 220). Here it would seem that all the circles have been of the *open* type. The inmost has a diameter of 8 ft, and the outermost of 27 ft 6 in. (Fig. 65).

A much larger fourfold retaining circle lies on Yellowmead Down, Sheepstor. This has been restored, practically all the stones having fallen. The inmost circle has much the character of a kerb, in that the stones are set very closely, although not in actual contact; but they stand higher above the original ground level than do kerb stones. The second circle consists of relatively small stones, somewhat larger are used in the third, while the largest stones are to be found in the fourth or outermost. The diameter of the inmost circle is 20 ft, of the outermost *c.* 65 ft (internal measurements) (see Fig. 66; Plate 38B and Pl. 48).

It thus appears that an interment on Dartmoor may lie in a barrow without a retaining circle, or there may be one, two, three or four retaining circles; and, where there are more than one, they need not all be of the same class.

It has been suggested that the retaining circles were the 'houses' of the dead, intended to be analogous to the hut-circles, but against this stands the fact that none can be claimed to reproduce in any way the structural features of the huts; while manifold circles are inconsistent with the idea.

There is yet a third class of retaining circle possibly to be found on Dartmoor, one that is familiar in the Isles of Scilly and certainly occurs on Exmoor. This is an enclosing wall of dry masonry. Very possibly the ring of loose stone found by Spence Bate around the margin of a barrow on Hameldon was the ruin of such a wall.

The following is a representative list of barrows with retaining circles, the internal diameter of the circle given in brackets.

YELLOWMEAD DOWN.

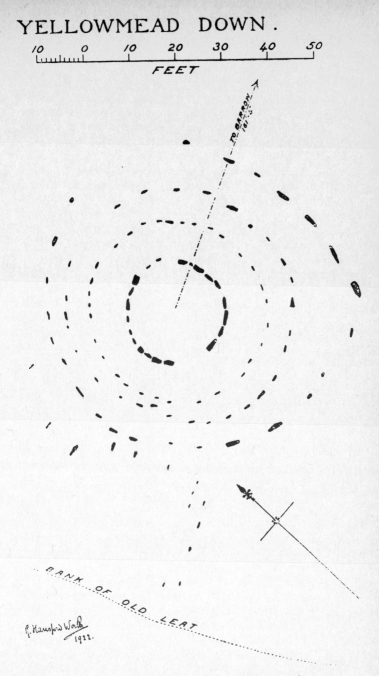

FEET

FIG. 66. Fourfold circle on Yellowmead Down, Sheepstor.

Archerton Tennis Court (7 ft)
Belliver Newtake (15 ft)
Black Newtake (1) (24 ft 3 in.)
Black Newtake (3) (24 ft 6 in.)
Brockhill Ford, Avon (26 ft)
Burford Down, Erme (16 to 17 ft.)
Butterdon Hill, Erme (40 ft approx.)
Chittleford Down, between Router and Cherry Brooks (9 ft
Collard Tor (26 ft 6 in.)   10 in., plus wall)
Croft, The, Petertavy (?)
Drizzlecombe (kerb, 11 ft mean)
Dendles Waste (11 ft mean)
Dunnabridge Common (12 ft)
Hare Tor, near Tavy Cleave
Hensroost (9 ft mean)
Hound Tor Down (21 ft 8 in.)
Lakehead Newtake (19 ft)
Lakehead Newtake (double circle, over 50)
Lakehead Newtake (22 ft)
Lakehead Newtake (18 ft)
Lakehead Newtake (19 ft)
Langcombe (16 to 18 ft).
Leeden, NW of Drizzlecombe (20 ft).
Lee Moor (8 ft 6 in.)
Lee Moor, Willings Walls (10 ft)
Legis Tor (12 ft)
Lether Tor (16 ft 6 in.)
Lower Piles (14 to 15 ft)
Merrivale
Nine Stones, Belstone (23 ft mean)
Pen Beacon, slopes of
Ringmoor Down (11 ft 2 in.)
Royal Hill, southernmost (15 ft mean)
Royal Hill, middle (17 ft mean)
Royal Hill, by track, 'Crock of Gold' (10 ft mean)
Shaugh Moor (?) (50 ft)
Shuggledown (fourfold, inmost 7 ft 9 in. mean, outermost
    28 ft 3 in. mean)
Soussons Common
Soussons Common (27 ft 8 in. mean)
Soussons Common, Red Barrows (part of circumference only)
Spurrells Cross (45 ft mean)
Stanlake, Meavy Valley (18 ft)
Stannon Newtake (11 ft 9 in. approx.)
Stennon Hill, near Powder Mills

Top Tor, Widdecombe
Wigford Down (20 ft 6 in.)
Yar Tor (double circle, 10 ft 6 in. and 34 ft)
Yellowmead Down (fourfold, inner circle 20 ft, outermost
    circle 61 ft mean)

BARROWS AND STONE ROWS

It may be broadly stated that while many barrows, in fact the
majority, are devoid of associated rows, no reasonably perfect stone
row can be pointed to that has not its associated barrows, cairns, or
kistvaens.

At places the barrow with its enclosing circles forms the head of the
row, as for example two instances at Drizzlecombe and another at
Cosdon. At places the barrow interrupts the row, usually occupying
a position with its circle at or near the centre of its length, as at Merrivale; or a barrow may merely be adjacent to the row, as with the long
row starting on Stalldon Moor, Erme Valley. Again, these varied
forms of association may be present together.

For examples the chapter dealing with stone rows should be consulted.

FORMS OF BURIAL: CARNAL INTERMENT AND CREMATION

Carnal interment is unknown on Dartmoor, and practically unknown in Devon.

The evidence as to presumed inhumations in certain Dartmoor kists
rests entirely on the occasional discovery of human hair in them. Two
such instances (one at Whiten Tor, above Powder Mills) were reported
to Mrs. Bray. The genuineness of this testimony was problematical
until a similar discovery was made during excavations on Soussons
Common. A fine kistvaen was unearthed in the centre of a sepulchral
circle (Fig. 61 and Pl. 36A) and in a cavity in its north end were found
two large coils of human hair. There is little doubt that this represents
an act of attempted witchcraft in comparatively recent times and has
no prehistoric significance (see *T.D.A.*, Vol. 35, p. 142).

While no traces of carnal interment have been found in any Devonshire mound-covered kistvaen, there is nothing in the form of dimensions of many kists to render inhumation impossible. A chest, 2 ft 6 in.
to 3 ft in length, by 2 ft in width and depth, is normally ample for a
contracted interment.

That cremation was widely practised by the Devonshire barrow
builders is very certain. The strongest and only reliable evidence of
cremation is burnt bone: burnt human bone is the one certain evidence.

On Dartmoor burnt bone has been found at the following sites:

Archerton Newtake, between Row Tor Marsh Brook and
    Cherry Brook: in pit under cairn

Chagford Common: in pit under small cairn
Fernworthy: kistvaen (in barrow 2 at end of stone row)
Great Whiten Tor, Postbridge (bone ash): in pit under flat stone
Hamel Down, 'Two Barrows': under flat stone covered by
  barrow
Hamel Down, 'Single Barrow'
Hemstone Rocks, N. of: in pit under cairn
Langstone Moor: kistvaen
Moor Barton, near Moreton: in rude kist under cairn
Soussons Common, Red Barrows, Nos. 1 and 2 (human)
Stannon Bottom: in pit under cairn

Burnt bone was either mixed with the lower layers of soil in the barrow, partially gathered into a pit in the subsoil, or placed in an urn. In either of the latter alternatives it is frequently found that no adequate attempt has been made to gather the whole of the ashes, or else perhaps the cremations may sometimes have been so thorough that few or no recognizable fragments of bone remained to be collected. Bone, whether burnt or unburnt, is in some soils peculiarly liable to perish, and in this manner evidence may have been lost.

The cremation appears frequently to have taken place on the actual spot over which the barrow was subsequently raised; in evidence of which charcoal is often found, even in barrows which yield no bone or recognizable bone ash; and where the soil is a stiff clay it has frequently been baked in a manner involving the previous existence of a considerable fire. At Langcombe and elsewhere it would appear possible that paved circles were constructed as crematoria and the ashes removed to adjacent kistvaens; while some of the so-called 'sacred circles', as at Fernworthy, have also been the sites of fires, perhaps in connexion with cremation, but whether or not cannot be determined.

Charcoal remains have been recorded from a number of excavated barrows. In the past charcoal has probably often been overlooked, or, if found, not recorded.

OBJECTS OF MAN'S HANDIWORK FOUND IN DARTMOOR BARROWS

Pottery

There is no conclusive evidence that any Devonshire barrow has yielded wheel-thrown pottery. Or rather, if definitions present difficulties, it might be safer to state only that no pottery has been found which might not have been hand-made.

In size the vessels discovered have varied widely. Among the comparatively few obtained from Dartmoor, an inverted urn unearthed at Hurston Ridge had a diameter of about 17 in. This one approached the largest of its class. The more ordinary sizes may be instanced from Watern Down—height, 10 in.; diameter at mouth, 7 in.; diameter at

neck, 5½ in.; greatest diameter of body, 7 in.; thickness of material
⅜ in. (Fig. 69); and from Langcombe: height probably 7⅛ in.; diameter
at mouth, 4¾ in.; greatest diameter, 6 in.; diameter at base, 4⅞ in.; and
thickness of material, ¼ in. (Fig. 67). These were both beakers, the
latter possibly degenerate.

The clay from which the pottery was made is sometimes rough in
the extreme, containing much sand and gravel, and the material is frequently very imperfectly baked. On the other hand there are instances
in which selected clay appears to have been used and the firing process
to have been thorough.

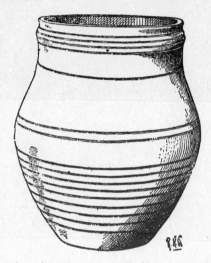

FIG. 67. Beaker from kistvaen in Langcombe, near Deadman's Bottom.
× ⅛ (Restored).

A small fragment from a ruined kist at Drizzlecombe is barely
one-fifth of an inch in thickness, of a rather fine clay, well burnt and
hard, and the outside bright red in colour; the inside is, however,
brown. This feature of a red outer and brown inner surface is common.
It does not, usually at least, arise from any difference in the clay, but
originates in the fact that the outer portions have been more thoroughly
fired (see p. 121).

The outsides of the vessels are almost constantly much smoother and
better finished than the inner portions, the difference being sometimes
very strongly marked.

Much of the pottery bears incised ornament of parallel lines and of
chevrons, including the variety of the latter known as 'herring-bone'.
As an illustration of parallel line work a sketch is here inserted of the
beaker found in Langcombe, near Deadman's Bottom (Fig. 67). The

FIG. 68. Beaker from Fernworthy, showing chevron, parallel, and hatched
work combined in the ornament.   × ⅔

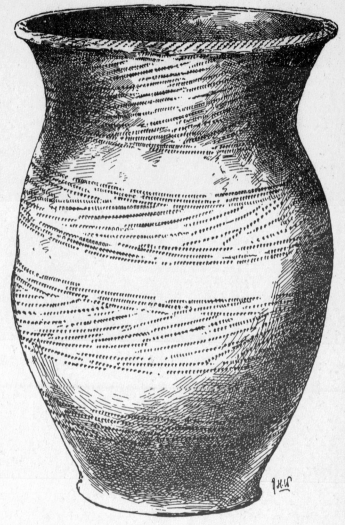

FIG. 69. Beaker from Watern Down, showing interrupted (dotted) line
work. × ½

beaker from Fernworthy (Fig. 68) shows chevron, parallel, and hatched work combined; and that from Watern Down (Fig. 69) shows inter-rupted, or dotted, line work—the line being formed in a series of dots indented by a pointed instrument.

Contrary to what has been suggested for other localities, there is little difference, if any, in the character of the domestic pottery found in the Dartmoor hut-circles and the pottery from the Dartmoor bar-rows. Ornamentation equally elaborate has been found on either, and work as careful, in material equally good, comes from the hut-circles as from the barrows.

It may be that the pottery from the barrows is on the whole slightly thinner, and smoother on the outer surface, perhaps more thoroughly ornamented; but its best is no better than many hut-circles have yielded. Similar in form, material and ornament, there is a strong suggestion of identity in date.

How far the vessels found have been cinerary, and how far some may have contained food interred with the dead, it is difficult to decide; many were certainly the former, some may have been the latter. The earlier reported researches have to be read with care.

Finally, the barrow pottery is of the type which in the present state of our knowledge we associate with the Bronze Age.

The following list summarizes the finds of pottery in Dartmoor barrows:

Chagford, Thornworthy: in kistvaen
Croft, The, Petertavy: a vessel, in rough earthenware, contain-ing a cooking stone, within a circle of stones doubtfully a retaining circle of a barrow or a small hut
Drizzlecombe, Plym Valley: fragments in kistvaen (Fig. 71)
Fernworthy: beaker, in pit under cairn (1) (Fig. 68)
Hurston Ridge: large urn inverted, in pit under cairn
Lakehead Hill, Postbridge: remains of a large and a small vessel in a kistvaen
Langcombe, Deadman's Bottom: broken beaker in kistvaen (Fig. 67)
Moretonhampstead, Mardon: fragments
Pen Beacon
Riddon Ridge: fragments
Soussons Common, Red Barrow No. 1
Stannon Hill: 'pot of money'
Tunhill Rocks, Blackslade Down, SE. of: thin pottery
Watern Down: a beaker in kistvaen (Fig. 69)
Wigford Down, Plym Valley: fragments of a beaker in kistvaen (Fig. 71)

Flint

Flint flakes and implements have been found in barrows in all parts of Devon, including Dartmoor; but these objects cannot always be connected with certainty with the interment. Some flints are of the simplest manufacture; others are worked scrapers, knives, and arrow-heads of careful make.

Three knives and three scrapers of excellent workmanship were taken by Mr. Burnard from a kistvaen at Lakehead Hill, near Postbridge (Fig. 70). Three barbed and tanged arrow-heads of the Bronze Age were taken from a kistvaen in Langcombe, Deadman's Bottom, and another arrow-head from the kistvaen on Calveslake Tor (Fig. 71). Other flint finds have been as follows:

> Archerton Newtake, kistvaen: worked flint flakes
> Calveslake: 3 flakes with above-mentioned arrow-head
> Crow Tor, kistvaen: flint scraper
> Chagford, Thornworthy, kistvaen: 4 flint tools
> Croft, The, Petertavy
> Drizzlecombe, barrow with kerb circle: large horse-shoe scraper (Pl. 40B), and 3 chips
> Fernworthy, cairn: knife
> Hemstone Rocks, north of: flake in kist and flakes in cairn
> King's Oven: scraper
> Merrivale Bridge: scraper and flake
> Metherel, No. 6: chips (not in interment pit)
> Redlake Foot, Erme, kistvaen: 2 worked flint flakes (*T.D.A.*, Vol. 82, p. 45)
> Riddon Ridge: flake
> 'Single Barrow', Hamel Down: square implement
> Soussons Common, Red Barrows, an arrow-head
> Whittor: flint flakes, but no trace of sepulchre
> Whittor, east of, near Langstone Menhir: several barrows

All worked flints as yet found have been of Neolithic or Bronze Age types. At Fernworthy flint has been found associated with bronze, also with horn.

Bronze

The records of bronze from barrows in Devonshire are not numerous, although that material cannot be described as scarce or exceptional. Within the Dartmoor area, however, whatever may have been true when the barrows were constructed, bronze is now decidedly rare. Possibly some of the rifled kistvaens originally contained implements of that metal, but if so no record remains.

During the thirty-five years prior to 1937 there was only one new occurrence. Total finds are as follows:

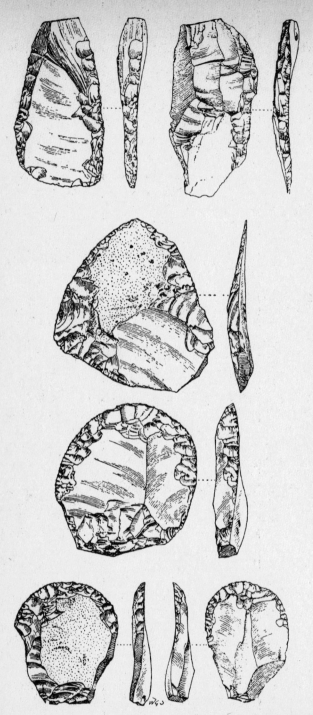

Fig. 70. Flint knives and scrapers, from a kistvaen on Lakehead Hill.

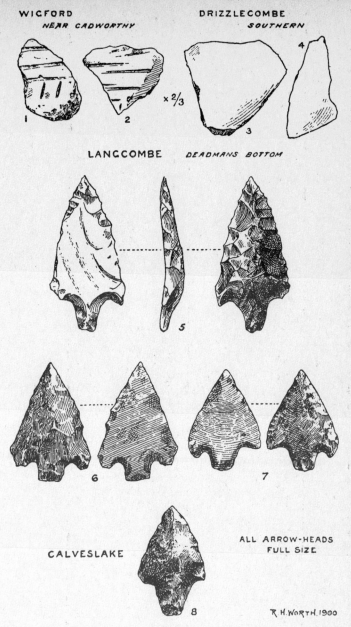

WICFORD
NEAR CADWORTHY

DRIZZLECOMBE
SOUTHERN

x 2/3

LANGCOMBE   *DEADMANS BOTTOM*

CALVESLAKE

ALL ARROW-HEADS
FULL SIZE

R. H. WORTH. 1900

FIG. 71. Pottery fragments and flint arrow-heads from Dartmoor kistvaens,

Bridford and Christow: several celts found in some cairns (Lysons)

Fernworthy: fragment from cairn

Hamel Down, 'Two Barrows': dagger (Pl. 41)

Moor Barton, near Moretonhampstead: spear-head (? copper)

Raddick Hill: small piece from kistvaen

Soussons Common, Red Barrows, No. 1:·2 fragments

Lower Lowton Down: in two cairns

Ilsington: a 'well-finished celt' reported found in 1790

Stone Implements other than Flint

An archer's wrist-guard or bracer of the Beaker period (Bronze Age) was taken from a kistvaen at Archerton Newtake. It had been "fashioned from a fine, gritty stone, and rubbed down perfectly smooth. It is perforated at each corner; two of the holes on the reverse side are countersunk to accommodate the knots of the thongs which bound the guard to the wrist. The obverse is slightly convex and the reverse concave."

An oval implement of yellowish-white soft slate is recorded from a cairn on Pen Beacon, and a similar but larger implement, spatula-shaped, and perforate at one end, from Whittor (east of), near Langstone Menhir.

A 'polishing stone', from Merrivale, and a possible sling stone, from Shaugh Lake, complete this scanty list.

Other Objects

The bronze dagger found by Spence Bate at Hameldon[1] had, associated with it, an amber pommel ornamented with gold pins. This had probably been attached to the hilt. Photographs of these important recoveries are given in Pl. 41. They were originally illustrated in colour in *T.D.A.*, Vol. 5, Pl. II, facing p. 554.

A horn dress fastener or button was found at Fernworthy.

In a barrow at Moor Barton, near Moretonhampstead, was found, in addition to a spear-head, a glass bead and an 'amulet of soft stone'.

CONCLUSION

Much information to be found in the original reports has of necessity been glanced over. These sources should be consulted, and it is the main purpose of this summary to provide a guide or key to them. (See Appendix V for Index.)

It must be recognized that there is yet much to be learnt in the matter of our Devonshire barrows. The mere description of all known Dart-

[1] The Hameldon barrows have been recognized as westerly outliers of the Wessex culture of late Early to early Middle Bronze Age. The account of Devon barrows of this period given by Lady Aileen Fox (The Broad Down (Farway) Necropolis and the Wessex Culture in Devon, *Proc. Devon Arch. Explor. Soc.*, Vol. 4, pp. 1-19, 1948) shall be consulted. (ED.)

moor kistvaens has not yet been completed, and there are certainly kistvaens as yet unknown. In the matter of discovery I would especially acknowledge with gratitude the assistance which I have received from a band of Dartmoor enthusiasts, Mr. L. Button, Mr. R. C. E. Carpenter, Mr. J. H. Dobson, and Mr. Morcom, all of Plymouth; and more latterly from Mr. C. E. Birkett Dixon, who has taken up accurate surveying. I have been indebted to others also, whose assistance will be found acknowledged in the various reports.

In the matter of excavation more work is certainly needed, but it should not be hastily undertaken, nor impatiently conducted—after fifty years' experience I am fully convinced that any class of intensive inquiry is undesirable. Leisurely work is the best, even if it limits the possible output of a lifetime. Only in general record do I feel the need for haste: the forces of attrition which threaten our ancient monuments become more rather than less active with the passing years.

If possible any monument which is known to be threatened with destruction should certainly be fully investigated by excavation. Otherwise a very conservative attitude is best. Advance in knowledge by no means keeps pace with feverish activity in digging.

THE STONE ROWS OF
DARTMOOR

THERE are on Dartmoor certain rows of stones, each stone wholly unwrought, each set upright in the ground and standing free above the surface at a greater or less distance from its neighbours on either side. These rows are approximately straight, but curvature and even abrupt changes through a small angle often occur. There is nothing to suggest that such departures from the right line are in any instance purposeful; they may be attributed to faulty workmanship or difficulties of alignment on undulating ground. The rows may be either *single* consisting of but one line of stones, *double* where two approximately parallel lines have been constructed with an intervening space of no more than a few feet, or *treble* consisting of three parallel lines similarly arranged. At one time I would have written, and I think I have written, that there was a *sevenfold* row on Dartmoor, but a recent precise survey has shown that this is divisible into one *single* and two *treble* rows.

In the matter of nomenclature these rows have presented a problem; they have been variously named 'alignments', 'avenues', 'parallellitha' and 'cursi', no one of which terms meets the need for generality, as absolute in nomenclature as in mathematics; most imply a knowledge of the use and intent of the rows which is certainly mistaken. I have, accordingly, adopted my father's expedient and used the accurate and noncommittal phrase *Stone Rows*. His discussion of this matter will be found in his first paper on the subject on page 387 of Vol. 24 of the *Trans. Devon. Assn.* (R. N. Worth, 1892).

It may be thought that the above description of the stone rows admits some confusion with lines of boundary stones, and of granite posts marking tracks across the moor. But boundary stones and guide posts are spaced far apart. Thus, the boundary between Harford and Ugborough Moors is defined by stones set at least 100 yds apart, and the guide posts on the Tavistock-Ashburton track on Long Ash Common (Fig. 116) are set at intervals of 200 yards. In addition to this, these are stones which have been cleft. Only in one instance do I know any ambiguity, and that is easily resolved. The boundary between Ugborough

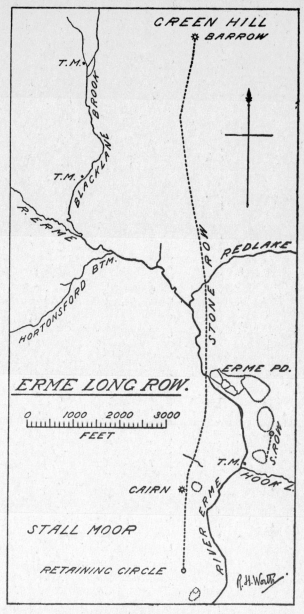

FIG. 72. Plan, Stall Moor—Green Hill (1).
Scale 1 inch to 30 chains (1,980 feet). "T.M.", Tin Mill (Historic Period).

and Harford Moors is in part defined by a prehistoric stone row; and when, in 1803, this boundary was agreed between disputants, and marks were set up, certain stones were added to the stone row to tender it more prominent. But these added stones can at once be detected, since they bear the drill marks incidental to their cleavage.

The number of stone rows known to exist on Dartmoor is large, and even of late years there have been additions made to the list. When my father wrote his first paper on the subject, in 1892, he mentioned 28 rows as fully ascertained; this number I now reduce by classing six single rows, then mentioned, as two triple rows, giving a net of 24. In the synopsis which follows I mention 62, and I have no reason to doubt that more remain to be discovered. Some rows which have been reported I have excluded from the list, being satisfied that they are mistaken attributions.

I arrange the list topographically, proceeding by watersheds. Where a tributary does not join the main river until after it has left the moor I treat it as having an independent watershed.

ERME

In the matter of stone rows the valley of the Erme claims pre-eminence. The Stall Moor–Green Hill row is not only the longest on Dartmoor, but also, as far as is at present known, the longest in the world, and the Butterdon–Sharp Tor row, while not its equal, is a fitting companion.

1. *Stall Moor–Green Hill*

Devon, 6 inch O.S., cxiii, sw., lon. 3°-55'-23¾″, lat. 50°-27'-47¾″, position of retaining circle at south end of row. (Fig. 72; Pl. 1A, 43, 44.)

Single row. At the south end, on Stall Moor, is a barrow with retaining circle and a trench outside the circle. The internal diameter of the retaining circle is 50 ft 8 in. The length of the row is 11,150 ft, at the north end it terminates in a barrow on Green Hill, to which there is no retaining circle. The azimuth of this row varies between N. 23° E. and N. 12° W., its direction of length from end to end is N. 0°-30' E. It passes from Stall Moor on the right bank of the Erme, across the Erme, to the left bank by Erme Pound and, continuing its course, crosses the Redlake and ascends Green Hill. Consequent on the difficulties of alignment caused by the undulations of the ground it has many changes in direction. At a little over half a mile from the southern end the row becomes imperfect for a space. But wherever its course is crossed by a turf-tye it becomes distinctly visible, and all the stones are found in place. The apparent gaps have not been caused either by the sinkage nor removal of the stones, but by the growth in depth of the peat, which has covered them. Indeed, the whole monument has suffered little from robbery, the circle on Stall Moor being unusually perfect

(Pl. 43). The stones of the row vary in size from point to point, according to the local supplies which were available. There are no really large stones. The largest is perhaps to be found in the Stall Moor circle; it measures 1 ft 8 in. × 1 ft 9 in. × 5 ft 5 in. in height. For a photograph of Stall Moor Circle and a part of the row, see Pl. 43. Pl. 44 herewith gives a view of another part of the length of the row, and Pl. 1A (p. 8) shows the row as disclosed by a turf-tye. See also Fig. 72 for a plan of the row.

Not only is the length of this row 2·112 miles, but the elevation of the ground at its northern end is 333 ft above that at its southern termination. In both respects it surpasses any other known row. Elevation at Green Hill 1,553 ft O.D.

2. Butterdon Row

High above the left bank of the Erme, and near the water-parting between the valleys of that river and of the West Glaze, lies Butterdon Row. Full knowledge of its former extension was not available prior to the discovery of a map, made in 1799–1800 by John Andrews of Modbury, and his notes relative to the map.

The south end of the row lies close to the summit of Butterdon Hill, starting with a barrow with a retaining circle 35 ft in diameter. The positional reference is, Devon, 6 inch O.S., cxix, SE., lon. 3°-53'-27½", lat. 50°-24'-48¾", at an elevation of 1,180 ft. Single row, length 6,280 ft, terminating at the north end in a fallen menhir at an elevation of 1,250 ft. Direction of length from end to end N. 9° W. The row is convex toward the east to the extent of 160 ft.

At a distance of 5,390 ft north of the barrow on Butterdon there stands a stone with a cross incised upon it, once known as Hobajons Cross. The row formerly extended to and beyond this stone, but this extension was swept away in the year 1803, for what purpose I do not know. On Piles Hill, 890 ft to the north of the cross lies a fallen menhir, known as the Longstone, the former terminal of the row (p. 269).

Certain stones standing in the row between its southern end and Hobajons Cross will be found to have been split and formed by the drill and tare and feather method. These were added when the row was accepted by the disputing parties as the boundary between Harford and Langford Lester Moors. In the same year, 1803, a modern boundary stone was erected beside the Longstone. For a view of Hobajons Cross see Pl. 93B; for discussion see Worth, R. H., 1941a.

3. Burford Down

Starts at a retaining circle at the south end, the circle 33 ft in diameter, at an elevation of 850 ft. Position, Devon, 6 inch O.S., cxix, SW., lon. 3°-55'-9", lat. 50°-25'-30".

Single row, length c. 1,200 ft, direction of length N. 1° W., dying out at a newtake wall [but see p. 247 (ED)]. This row has been robbed of many of its stones, but is still a good example. Two hundred and eighty feet eastward of the retaining circle at the south end of the row lies another retaining circle of 18 ft diameter, within which is a kistvaen.

4. *Brown Heath, Erme Pound*

At the north end is a cairn, which within my recollection once contained a kistvaen. There is a retaining circle of 31 ft internal diameter. Position, Devon, 6 inch O.S., cxiii, SE., lon. 3°-54'-55", lat 50°-28'-17". Elevation *c.* 1,300 ft.

Double row, length *c.* 540 ft, direction of length N. 10° E. At a point 90 ft from the centre of the cairn the row touches what may be a hut-circle. Four hundred and fifty feet farther south it touches and is partly lost in the wall of a pound which lies to the west. It is possible that this is the true end of the row, and that, before the pound wall fell in ruin, the row and the wall were not in actual contact.

5. *Near Spurrells Cross*

At the south end is a cairn, 50 ft in diameter, with but two remaining stones of the retaining circle. Position, Devon, 6 inch O.S., cxix, SE., lon. 3°-53'-19½", lat. 50°-25'-21½". Elevation, *c.* 1,170 ft.

The row has apparently been double, but since only seven stones still stand and, with six sunken stones, form the fixed points now determinable, it is difficult to ascertain the original spacing. The distance apart of the lines may probably have been about 3 ft 6 in., and the spacing along the lines about 3 ft. The length of the row is 370 ft as measured from the centre of the cairn, and the direction of length is N. 20° W. The largest standing stone is but 2 ft in height.

6. *Glasscombe Ball*

At the north-east end is a barrow or cairn, now deformed, but probably originally of 14 ft diameter. Position, Devon, 6 inch O.S., cxix, SE., lon. 3°-53'-24", lat. 50°-25'-40½". Elevation, *c.* 1,170 ft. Probably a single row, length from centre of barrow at NE. 276 ft, direction of length N. 42°-29' E. All stones fallen, the largest being 3 ft 7 in. long by 11 in. broad.

There is a second cairn, 13 ft in diameter, and distant 37 ft centre of cairn to line of row, near the south-west end.

YEALM

7. *Staldon* (Pl. 45)

This row begins and ends without formal terminals, there is neither barrow nor menhir. By far the greater part of its length lies in the Yealm Valley, but at its northern extremity it just enters the Erme watershed. The position of the south end is, Devon, 6 inch O.S., cxix, NW., lon. 3°-55'-35½", lat. 50°-26'-31". Elevation, south end 1,200 ft, north end 1,320 ft.

Single row; length 1,643 ft, direction of length, end to end, N. 4°-45′ W. The southern length of 783 ft lies due N., the northern length of 858 ft lies N. 9°-45′ W. This divergence gives a convexity of 72 ft to the east.

At 1,193 ft from the south end the retaining circle of a barrow touches the row on the east side of the row; its internal diameter is 13 ft. After restoration, and no plan was prepared previous to restoration, those stones to the north of and nearest to the circle were left in line pointing to the circle's centre. That line should point to the western circumference of the circle, making with the southern part one continuous row, tangential to the circle. There are two cairns abreast the line north of the retaining circle, one with its centre 135 ft away from the row to the east, and the other with its centre 92 ft to the west.

South of the retaining circle the stones in the row, where closest set, are from 9 to 10 ft apart centre to centre. North of the retaining circle, where closest set, the stones are from 8 to 10 ft apart, but the large stones toward the north end are from 30 to 50 ft apart (Pl. 45). Since these large members range to over 8 ft in height such wide spacing is not inappropriate, but it is the extreme which is met on Dartmoor. There may have been some robbery, and some stones may be missing, but this unusual spacing is evidently to a large extent original.

No other row on Dartmoor is as prominent in the landscape; standing on the crest of the ridge between the Yealm and the Erme the large stones are seen on the skyline from many points in the Erme Valley; they have the appearance of a line of mounted men advancing toward the observer. Size and position both contribute to their effect.

8. Penn Beacon

If the Yealm shares with the Erme the fine row just described, it must share with the Tory Brook this rather trivial relic, which lies on the western border of its watershed.

The row is single, and but 66 ft in length; the direction of the length is N. 82°-38′ W. There are no terminals, whether barrows, menhirs or other. The position of the eastern end is, Devon, 6 inch O.S., cxix, NW., lon. 3°-58′-22½″, lat. 50°-26′-43¾″. The largest stone standing is but 14 in. × 15 in. × 31 in. high. This row is obviously no more than a remnant. Elevation of ground, 1,230 ft.

TORY BROOK

9. Penn Beacon, lower slopes

Four hundred and sixty-six yards W. by s. from the last mentioned row lies a fair-sized cairn. In a direction s. 30°-10′ W. from this runs a very short double row. There are but two pairs of stones, the length of the row as measured from the margin of the cairn is 24 ft, and the rows are 1 ft 10 in. apart, inside measurement. The direction of length of the row, referred to the north point, is N. 30°-10′ E. The position of the cairn is, Devon, 6 inch O.S., cxix, NW., lon. 3°-58'-44", lat. 50°-26'-41½". Elevation of ground, *c.* 1,100 ft.

10. *Cholwich Town Waste*

There is a retaining circle of approximately 18 ft internal diameter, with six stones still standing, at the north end of this row. Position, Devon, 6 inch O.S., cxviii, NE., lon. 3°-59'-37", lat. 50°-26'-32½". Elevation, *c.* 810 ft.

The row is single, its length *c.* 700 ft, the direction of length N. 22¼° E. Although imperfect in places, it is a well-marked row, and some of the stones are larger than ordinary.

11. *Collard Tor, western member*

The first example of a group of rows in this synopsis, and in this instance the simplest possible example, the group consisting of but two members. There are two cairns lying in a line which ranges N. 83°-50' W., at a distance of 47 ft centre to centre. The western cairn has no retaining circle. The position of this cairn is, Devon, 6 inch O.S., cxviii, NE., lon. 4°-1'-50½", lat. 50°-26'-24½". Southward from this cairn runs a single row, which I call No. 11. The length of this row is 216 ft, and the direction of length N. 2°-10' E. The row has been much disturbed, and has probably lost in length.

12. *Collard Tor, eastern member*

The eastern cairn has a retaining circle, 26 ft 6 in. in diameter, with five stones standing, and another approximately in place. Southward from this cairn runs a single row, No. 12, the second of the group. It is 275 ft in length, and the direction of length is N. 3°-20' W. The rows thus diverge somewhat as they extend from the cairns. The condition of this row is much as that of No. 11. The elevation of the ground at the cairns is *c.* 850 ft.

PLYM

13. *Shaugh Moor*

At the south-west end is a retaining circle, 50 ft in diameter. Position, Devon, 6 inch O.S., cxviii, NE., lon. 4°-2'-13", lat. 50°-27'-7½" at centre. Single row, length 587 ft, measuring from the centre of the circle. Direction of length N. 20°-40' E.

The spacing of the stones in the row varies between 3 ft 3 in. and 5 ft centre to centre. There is a hut-circle within 10 ft of the retaining circle, and to the south. A barrow lies 360 ft W. a little S. from the retaining circle. This row can readily be found, the south end being approximately 200 yds east from the Cadover road, in the line of the south fence of Shaden Plantation. Elevation of ground *c.* 820 ft.

Trowlesworthy Group

This group has but two members. It lies north-east of the head of the Blackabrook, by the Lee Moor Leat.

14. *Trowlesworthy Group, eastern member*

At the north end is a retaining circle, 22 ft in internal diameter, and consisting of eight stones. Position, Devon, 6 inch O.S., cxii, s.e., lon. 4°-0'-20½", lat. 50°-27'-27¾". The row is double, the stones spaced at *c*. 6 ft centres in the rows, and 4 ft to 5 ft across the rows. Length 426 ft, direction of length N. 11°-50' E. The row is slightly convex eastward. This row was disturbed by workmen in the year 1859, but they were checked before much mischief had been done.

15. *Trowlesworthy Group, western member*

The east end of this row lies *c*. 350 ft west of the centre of the circle which heads No. 14. Row 15 points approximately to the circle at the head of Row 14.

A single row, 254 ft in length; direction of length is N. 82°-30' E. At the west end is a small menhir 4 ft in height, and at the east end there are possible indications of a retaining circle of about 20 ft diameter. The stones of the row are spaced at approximately 5 ft centres. It will be noted that the two members of this group differ widely (by 70°-40') in direction. The mean elevation of the ground is *c*. 920 ft.

16. *Ringmoor*

A single row for the main part at present, but double at places, possibly once double throughout. There is a retaining circle at the south end, of 40 ft 6 in. diameter. Position, Devon, 6 inch O.S., cxii, se., lon. 4°-1'-36", lat. 50°-28'-33½".

The row is 1,740 ft in length, the direction of the length is N. 12°-10' E. It terminates to the north in a fallen stone, 4 ft in length and measuring 2 ft 6 in. × 1 ft 6 in. at the base.

Five of the stones of the retaining circle were imported in an effort at restoration; the original condition of this circle may be seen on the plan given on page 234 of *T.D.A.*, Vol. 73. On that same page it is stated in error by myself that the row is 400 yds in length. Instead of looking up my records I accepted the Ordnance Survey, which is in error. Mean elevation of ground, *c*. 970 ft.

Drizzlecombe Group (Fig. 73)

This is the most neatly arranged group on Dartmoor, and, with the possible exception of Merrivale, the sole example which shows what by our modern standards would be regarded as planning. As it stands it would permit additions which would leave an entirely symmetrical arrangement, and there is at least one indication that such additions may have been contemplated.

The rows are best described by reference to the plan (Fig. 73), and the general position determined by that of Giants Basin shown on the plan, which is, Devon, 6 inch O.S., cxii, se., lon. 3°-59'-6", lat. 50°-29'-5". It may be noted that the contour of the pound which lies just south-west of the large cairn at the north-east extreme of the group, and has two hut-circles within it is shown a little too regular; its correct contour can be seen in Fig. 32, p. 136. For present purposes the matter is unimportant. [See also the note appended to the legend. (ED.)]

It will be seen that abreast of A on the plan is a standing stone. If a line be drawn from this stone to the north-westernmost of the three barrows below the pound, one then has a completely symmetrical collection of rows, and this may have been contemplated.

In this group we have three rows, each terminating at its north-east end in a barrow, and at its south-west end in a menhir; rows perfect and strictly defined; with the aid of the plan it will not be necessary to do more than give their respective detail.

17. Drizzlecombe Group (A)

A barrow, uncircled, 18 ft in diameter, at the north-east end; at the south-west end a menhir, 12 ft 6 in. in length as fallen, 10 ft 6 in. high as erected (Pl. 59A). Length of row 488 ft, direction of length N. 47°-30′ E. The row is in part double, in part single, and it is doubtful whether it was ever wholly double.

18. Drizzlecombe Group (B)

A circled barrow, 29 ft in diameter at the north-east end; and a menhir 9 ft 5 in. in length as fallen, 7 ft 9 in. in height as erected, at the south-west end (Pl. 59B). Length of row 491 ft, direction of length N. 50°-30′ E. The row is single throughout, except for one pair of stones next the menhir.

19. Drizzlecombe Group (C)

A circled barrow, 34 ft in diameter, at the north-east end; and at the south-west a menhir, 17 ft 10 in. in length as fallen, 14 ft in height as erected (Pl. 57B, 58, 59B). The row is single throughout, and the stones are more widely spaced than in either of the other rows. Length of row 276 ft, direction of length N. 44° E.

It will be noticed that row B points to the cairn at the top of the plan; and that there is another alignment in this group, not a row, marked

---

[1] In this plan the menhirs are shown as they lay fallen. They were reerected in their correct positions (as proved by the socket-holes) at the ends of the rows (Pl. 57B, 58, 59).

The Kerb Circle (Pl. 38A) is incorrectly placed. It should be transferred to a point 280 ft ssw. of the adjacent kistvaen.

A ruined barrow with retaining circle is situated a little s of E of the point where the kerb circle is drawn, being in alignment with the centres of Giants Basin and the westernmost of the three central barrows.

Between the ruined circle and the pounds are two heather-grown circles (huts?), one of which aligns with menhirs A and B.

Row C is 20 ft shorter than shown, the length originally recorded by Worth himself proving correct. Row B is somewhat concave to the SE. (ED.)

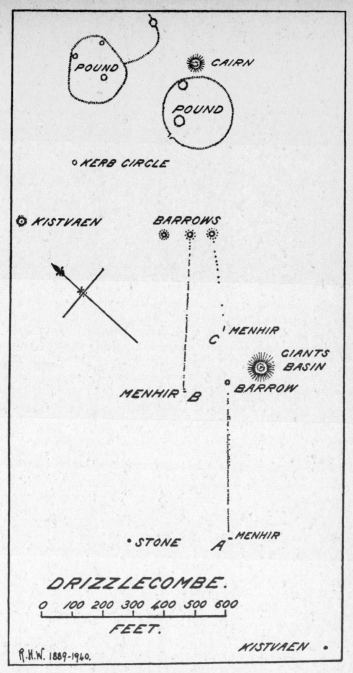

FIG. 73. The Drizzlecombe group.[1]

out by three graves, namely the kistvaen in the bottom right-hand corner, the cairn known as Giants Basin, and the cairn at the top of the plan.

There are shown on this plan, two large cairns, four barrows, two kistvaens, and a kerb retaining circle around an interment pit. There are also two pounds and six hut-circles. It would not appear that the living were anxious to remove their dead to a distance, as has so often been suggested, or perhaps I should say asserted.

The elevation of the ground at Giants Basin is approximately 1,100 ft; and its gradient, falling from north-east to south-west is approximately 1 in 22. This is one of the few groups in which all parts can be seen from all parts, and perhaps this has had an influence on its symmetry.

MEAVY

20. Down Tor (Pl. 61)

Although this row is commonly named after Down Tor, it lies, not on the slopes of that tor, but on Hingston Hill, and is in fact nearer Combshead Tor. At the west end of the row is a barrow with retaining circle, the circle 37 ft in internal diameter. Position, Devon, 6 inch O.S., cxii, NE., lon. 3°-59'-35", lat. 50°-30'-19½". Near the circle the stones of the row are exceptionally large, that nearest the circle having been measured when fallen by Burnard and found to be 12 ft 10 in. in length (Pl. 61); as re-erected it now stands 9 ft 6 in. high. In the matter of record this row has been unfortunate; it is called after a Tor on whose slopes it does not stand; it is shown on the first edition of the Ordnance Survey as pointing towards a pound, to which it does not point; Spence Bate appears to have intended this row when he wrote of one in this locality as being 800 yds in length; Burnard by an obvious slip attributed to it a length of nearly 600 yds. Its actual length as measured from the centre of the circle is 1145 ft[1]. The direction of length from end to end is N. 71° E.; it is somewhat convex toward the north. Its apparent eastern termination is in a small menhir, which measured, as fallen, 7 ft 6 in. in length and 3 ft in breadth. In the line of the row but 620 ft[1] from the terminal menhir is a cairn 57 ft[1] in diameter at the base, and 36 ft diameter at the top.

Accepting the result of Burnard's careful examination, that the total number of stones in this single row was 174, it results that the average spacing of the stones, centre to centre, is 6·48 ft[1]. The mean elevation of ground is c. 1,210 ft; the row lies along the water-parting between Deancombe and Newleycombe brooks.

21. Black Tor, Stanlake

A double row, the northern member of which is almost wholly

---

[1] New measurements. (ED.)

merged in an enclosure wall. The best fixed point from which to locate it is the blocking stone at the north-east end, the position of which is, Devon, 6 inch O.S., cvi, SE., lon. 4°-0'-53", lat. 50°-31'-32½". The wall or fence is the western boundary of Stanlake farm against the moor.

This double row is so near a fence that the needs of the wall builders have led to the robbery of even that line which is clear of and parallel to the hedge; but, in a length of 950 ft in all there are left 66 stones. The stones are of medium size, for example, 1 ft 1 in. × 1 ft × 2 ft 3 in. high, 2 ft 7 in. × 10 in. × 2 ft 3 in. high, 1 ft 7 in. × 1 ft 7 in. × 2 ft 6 in. high, and the blocking stone 9 in. × 3 ft 5 in. × 2 ft 6 in. high. (The first measurement is always that of the stone along the row, the second is the thickness of the stone at right angles to the row, and the third is the height above ground.)

The direction of the length of the row is N. 50° E. There are remains of at least 14 hut-circles and some small pounds 800 ft south of the south-west end of the row. The mean elevation of the ground is 1,127 ft.

The *Harter Group*, in the angle between the Meavy and the Harter Brook, near their confluence, contains two rows.

22. Harter Group, the northern row

Double row. At the eastern end is a barrow with a retaining circle of 29 ft 4 in. internal diameter, of which seven stones still stand, two lean, and five are fallen. Position, Devon, 6 inch O.S., cvi, SE., lon. 4°-0'-27", lat. 50°-31'-38". The length of the row is at least 450 ft; it extends to very near the bank of the Meavy. The direction of length of the row is N. 76°-30' E. The spacing of the stones is rather irregular, from 6 to 7 ft centre to centre along the row, and, as a mean about 5 ft apart centre to centre across the row. Some of the stones are of a fair height, from 4 to 5 ft.

23. Harter Group, the southern row

This row starts from a barrow at the eastern end. This barrow has no retaining circle; its centre is *c*. 36 ft from the centre of the circled barrow, centre to centre. The row is single, length *c*. 165 ft, direction of length N. 58°-30' E., there are gaps in this row, and the stones are comparatively few; it has probably been robbed. Mean elevation of ground 1,125 ft. The divergence between the directions of length of the two rows constituting this group is 18°.

24. Sharpitor, northern flank

A double row which lies partly in the valley of the Meavy, and partly in that of the Walkham, its length crossing the water divide at the crest of Peek Hill, a little south of the Princetown Road.

At the west the row starts from a cairn, but recently discovered as the result of a chance disturbance of the surface; at the east it ends in a blocking-stone. The length from the centre of the cairn to the block-ing-stone is 366 ft; and since the spacing along the row has been fairly regularly 5 ft from centre to centre, before the row was so extensively robbed there should have been 138 stones at least. There are now 41, of which 11 are fallen. None of the stones left are other than small, the largest being the two last at the east end, one of which measures 23 in. × 7 in. × 19 in. high, and the other 22 in. × 9 in. × 42 in. high. The space from centre to centre across the rows averages 6 ft, but it varies considerably, between 3 ft 10 in. and 7 ft 10 in.; it tends to widen to-ward the eastern end. The direction of length is N. 64° E. The row is easily found as it lies but a few feet south of the wayside pool at the top of Peek Hill. The position of the cairn is, Devon, 6 inch O.S., cvi, SE., lon. 4°-2′-10″, lat. 50°-31′-1″.

On the eastern slope, 255 ft from the blocking-stone, and in the prolongation of the line of the row, is a cairn with a retaining circle of 11 ft 6 in. internal diameter. The position of this cairn relative to the row is the parallel of that which exists at Down Tor (20). The row certainly points to the barrow, but terminates far short of it. The eleva-tion of the ground is 1,212 ft O.D.

25. Sharpitor

Eight or nine feet south from the last stones of row 24 is a small set stone. Two other stones, obviously set, make a line with the first, and certainly seem to be the commencement of a row which trends more to the north than does 24, and would cross the produced line of 24 between the blocking-stone and the isolated cairn. The difficulty is to find any certain continuation of the line marked out by the three stones; there are too many surface stones which confuse the issue. Direction of length N. 48° E.

26. *Sharpitor, foot of eastern slope*

At the foot of Goatstone Hill, 100 yds from the junction of the track to Routrundle with the road to Princetown is a short but interesting row. It is double, short, consists of but few pairs of stones; but those pairs are more closely set, and the row is therefore narrower, than in any other known example. For instance there is one pair of stones 12 in. × 8 in. × 14 in. high, and 9 in. × 8 in. × 16 in. high respectively, the space between which is 6 in., or, stated as distance between centres, the setting is 14 in. Six inches is a restricted width for either a racecourse or a processional path, uses to which some would have us believe the stone rows were placed.

When I found this row it seemed to me that possibly it was a set of stones used for the roller bearings of a flat-rod, a mining device, but no sort of bearing was to be found on any stone; also the row starts with a ruined cairn at the west end, and cairns are not usual adjuncts of flat-rods.

The length of the row is 120 ft; its direction N. 88° E.; the elevation of the ground is 1,130 ft O.D.

The position of the ruined cairn at the west end is Devon, 6 inch O.S., cvi, SE., lon. 4°-1'-46½", lat. 50°-31'-7¼".

WALKHAM

Merrivale Group. Longash Common (Fig. 74, 116)

This group consists of two double rows and one single; and not far removed is a stone circle, with two menhirs near it (Pl. 60B). It has been suggested that the remains of stone rows can be traced in connexion with these menhirs, but this must be regarded as doubtful.

To simplify description a plan of these rows has been prepared, necessarily to a small scale, which does not permit the plotting of individual stones, and demands some exaggeration of the width of double rows, and the diameters of small circles. [A full plan was published with the Second Report of the Dartmoor Exploration Committee.]

27. *Merrivale Group (A). The northern double row*

No cairn or barrow is directly connected with the row, but at its eastern end it is closed by a blocking-stone. The length of the row is 596 ft, and its direction N. 83°-30' E. I have referred to my original survey notes as to the width between the rows, which, as is perhaps usual, is irregular. On the average of 17 pairs of stones I find the mean distance between the rows is 3 ft 6 in. with extremes of 4 ft 6 in. and 2 ft 8 in.; while the mean distance from centre to centre of the stones across the row is 4 ft. The distance from centre to centre along the rows, where complete, gives a mean for twenty pairs of 5 ft 6 in., with extremes of 7 ft 9 in. and 4 ft 7½ in.

28. *Merrivale Group (B). The southern double row*

This row overlaps row A at both ends, and is not quite parallel to it. From the east end of row A to row B, centre to centre, the least distance is 80 ft 6 in., the corresponding measurement at the west end is 106 ft. Row B is closed at the east end by a blocking-stone; at the west end there is neither barrow, menhir nor any other formal termination. At a distance of 427 ft[1] from the east end of the row, and 438 ft[1] from the west end, lies the centre of a retaining circle of 12 ft internal diameter which interrupts the row; within this circle is a small barrow. This feature, which is unique on Dartmoor, is placed so near the true centre of length that, if the row builders had any respect to symmetry, one may well argue that it is improbable that the row ever extended to the west to any material distance beyond its present termination.

I have taken this circle and barrow as the fixed point for defining the

---

[1] Corrected from the full plan. (ED.)

position of the group; the data are: Devon, 6 inch O.S., cvi, NE., lon. 4°-2′-27½″, lat. 50°-33′-15″.

The length of row B is 865 ft,[1] and the direction of length is N. 81° E. The mean of 17 pairs of stones gives an internal width of 2 ft 10 in. between the lines of stone, with extremes of 1 ft 9 in. and 3 ft 9 in.; while the mean distance from centre to centre of the stones across the row is 3 ft 4 in. The distance from centre to centre along the rows, where complete, gives a mean of 7 ft 1 in. with extremes of 9 ft 10 in. and 5 ft 3 in., for twenty pairs.

29. Merrivale Group (C)

Measuring 142 ft westward from the centre of the barrow which breaks the line of row B, and 15 ft southward from the centre of the row one reaches the centre of a barrow of 9 ft diameter, from which starts row C. This is a single row, 138 ft 8 in. long as measured from the centre of the barrow, the direction of length being N. 24°-15′ E. The spacing of the stones in this row appears to have been 3 ft centre to centre, when the row was perfect. Row C has all the appearance of being an afterthought.

Regarding the group as a whole, row A has no directly associated sepulchral remains; a cairn stands in the centre of row B; and C starts from a cairn or barrow at its northern end. South of B, and near it, there are also a large kistvaen, and the ruins of a fair-sized cairn. And, near this collection of graves, there are, it should be added, a number of hut-circles; here, again, the living did not avoid the graves of their people (Pl. 25B).

In one of these huts lies a worked stone, the circular runner of a cider mill. Col. Hamilton Smith had no difficulty in seeing it as a fallen cromlech (Pl. 75B).

The mean elevation of the ground is c. 1,150 ft.

30. Langstone Moor, Petertavy

Single row, length c. 330 ft, probably somewhat longer when complete, direction of length N. 2° E. There are now but eighteen stones, the largest of which stands no more than eighteen inches above ground. The original spacing may have been about 5 ft.

At the north end are the remains of a barrow, now reduced to little more than a rubble ring. At the south end is the menhir known as the Longstone, from which the moor probably takes name. This menhir and the stones of the row are of local stone, epidiorite, there being no granite in the immediate vicinity. Between 100 and 300 yds west of the Longstone lie four cairns and a kistvaen. The Longstone was re-erected in 1893. (See p. 270 and Pl. 60A.)

It is to be regretted that, during the late military occupation of Dart-

---

[1] Corrected from plan. (ED.)

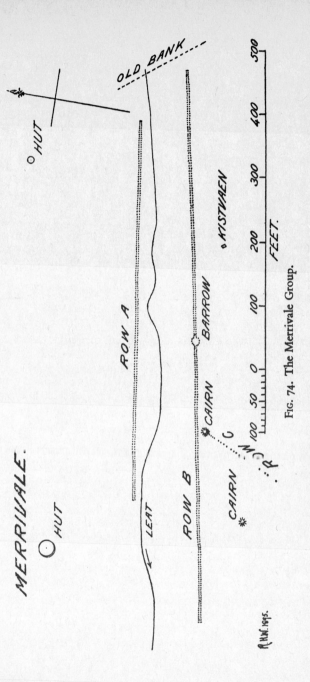

Fig. 74. The Merrivale Group.

moor this menhir has been used as a target, while the fine stone circle
above Clay Tor has been wrecked. This can only be described as
wanton mischief; it was no accident.

The position of the Longstone is, Devon, 6 inch O.S., xcviii, SE.,
lon. 4°-2′-54½″, lat. 50°-35′-22½″. Mean elevation *c.* 1,420 ft. Ground
practically level.

TAVY

31. *Cocks Tor*

On the summit of Cocks Tor there are traces which may indicate
the former existence of one or more stone rows. With this possible
exception there are no known rows in the valley.

LYD, WEST OCKMENT, AND TAW

No stone rows are known in these valleys.

EAST OCKMENT

32. *Oke Tor*

In 1894 my father reported the existence of a much ruined row on the
west slope of Oke Tor. His report will be found on page 300 of Vol. 26
of the *T.D.A.*. He never visited the spot again, nor was I able to visit
it during his lifetime. But he was not of a speculative habit, and a
survey would probably confirm his report.

With this probable exception stone rows are unknown in the valley
of the East Ockment.

NORTH TEIGN, BLACKATON BROOK

33. *Cosdon*

The first of the triple rows which is met in this general survey. It
lies near the summit of Cosdon, east of the water-parting between the
Taw and North Teign valleys, and the Taw comes near to claiming a
share in the row. The length, measured from the centre of a circled
cairn which stands at the west end, is 447 ft, the direction of length is
N. 85° w. The position of the cairn is, Devon, 6 inch O.S., lxxvii, sw.,
lon. 3°-55′-19″, lat 50°-42′-27″. Its diameter is 26 ft, and it contains the
remains of two kistvaens; the retaining circle is very irregular. There
is no formal feature to mark the termination of the rows at their eastern
end. The stones, where the rows are perfect, are spaced at a mean distance centre to centre along the rows of 4 ft 4 in., with extremes of 5 ft
10 in. and 3 ft 4 in. At 225 ft from the west end there is a slight change
in direction and the rows turn somewhat northward; they are thus convex to the south to the extent of some 4 to 5 ft. This change of direction
may be said to divide the row into a western and an eastern section,
between which some differences exist. Thus the spacing, centre to
centre, across the rows is:

Western part, N. row 4 ft 7 in., centre row 4 ft 3 in., S. row total 8 ft 10 in.

Eastern part, N. row 5 ft, centre row 5 ft 8 in., S. row, total 10 ft 8 in. These are the means of as many measurements as can be accurately taken. The total width in the first perfect set of three at the west end is 7 ft 6 in., and for the last perfect set at the east end it is 10 ft 3 in. The largest stone standing, before restoration, was 42 in. × 12 in. × 45 in. high.

The mean elevation of the ground is *c.* 1,430 ft.

A detailed plan was published with the Third Report of the Dartmoor Exploration Committee, *T.D.A.*, Vol. 28. I accept full responsibility for a draughtsman's error, whereby true north was indicated on the compass drawn on that plan 36° to the west of its correct position. Those who have copies should make the correction.

NORTH TEIGN AND SOUTH TEIGN

Shuggledown Group (Fig. 75; Pl. 46A and B)

This is an elongated and very irregular group, lying in part in the valley of the North Teign, in part in the valley of the South Teign, between Batworthy and Thornworthy Corners. A suitable reference point is the fourfold retaining circle which lies at the head of row A; the position of this is, Devon, 6 inch O.S., lxxxix, SE., lon. 3°-53′-48″, lat. 50°-39′-27¾″. The contour of the ground is important, but it can only be approximately given. At the north end of the group the level is *c.* 1,320 ft above O.D. Twelve hundred feet south it has risen to *c.* 1,360 ft O.D. and at the Three Boys, 1,100 ft farther south, it has fallen to *c.* 1,310 ft O.D. It follows that, except near the summit level, there are no points from which the half of the group can be seen at the same time as parts of the other half. The group was never intended to be seen as a whole, which is not surprising since there are many individual rows the whole length of which cannot be seen at one time; except, in these days, from the air.

See Fig. 75 for a plan of this group, without reference to which it may be difficult to follow the description. Greater detail is given in *T.D.A.*, Vol. 64, pp. 283–7.

34. *Shuggledown (A)*

The eastern row of the group is double. Its length is 596 ft, and the direction of length is N. 1°-40′ W. The mean inside measurement between the lines is 3 ft 6 in. (in the group the distance between the lines is throughout the internal distance).

Standing so near the Batworthy enclosure, the row has been much robbed; in its whole length there are now but twelve pairs of stones and fifteen single. The spacing of the stones along the rows is a little over 6 ft, centre to centre.

At the north end there is no special feature; at the south the row ends in a fourfold retaining circle; the internal diameter of the outermost circle is 29 ft. Two fallen stones next to the circle are much the largest in the row; one is 11 ft 6 in. in length, and the other 7 ft 4 in. (Pl. 46A). The larger has been adopted as a boundary stone of Chagford parish. Southward from the circle, approximately in the line of the row, and 65 ft from the circle, centre to centre, is a small barrow.

35. *Shuggledown (E)*

To the west of row A lies row E, 220 ft distant from it at the north end, and 60 ft distant at the south. This is a double row, 476 ft in length; the direction of length being N. 21°-15′ W. The mean interval between the lines is a little over 4 ft, but it varies considerably. No special feature marks either end, neither menhir, blocking-stone nor barrow.

This row has been much robbed, so that for the greater part of its length it is now single.

36. *Shuggledown (C)*

Due south of the southern end of row E is the northern end of row C at a distance of 60 ft. This is approximately due west of the fourfold circle, and 65 ft 6 in. from its centre.

Row C is double, the lines being 5 ft apart, inside measurement. Its length is 386 ft to the centre of the barrow, 13 ft in diameter, which forms its terminal point to the south. The direction of length is N. 28°-30′ W. This row has not been badly robbed and most of the pairs of stones are complete.

37. *Shuggledown (G)*

Three hundred and twenty-five feet *c*. S. 25° E. from the cairn which forms the south extreme of row C is the north end of another double row, 485 ft in length, direction of length N. 3° W. This terminates to the south in a fine menhir (10 ft 5 in. in height) known as the Longstone (Pl. 46B). The Longstone now forms a boundary of the parishes of Lydford, Chagford and Gidleigh, also of the Forest of Dartmoor. It provides an excellent example of a boundary determined, at least as long ago as A.D. 1240, by the convenient presence of a landmark, rather than a bondstone erected to mark a boundary.

The distance between the lines of stones is 3 ft 3 in., inside measurement. The row is fairly complete at its northern end, but becomes very ragged as it approaches the Longstone, having evidently lost many of its stones by theft.

38. *Shuggledown, from the Longstone southward*

Due south of the Longstone, at a distance of 555 ft. is an isolated stone, erect but leaning, of which 4 ft 6 in. in length is above the ground. This is the last of three stones, formerly known as 'Three Boys', its companions having gone to form gateposts to a neighbouring enclo-

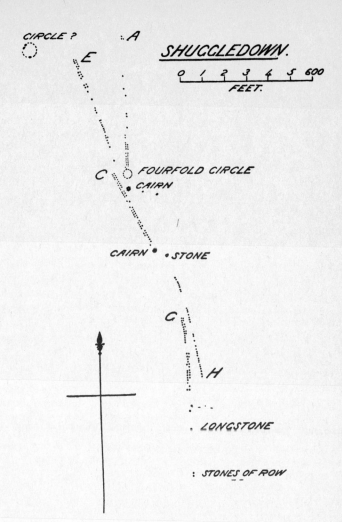

FIG. 75. The Shuggledown group.

sure. Between the Longstone and Three Boys, there remain a few set stones, the remnants of a double row.

Ormerod states that, in 1858, the pits left by the removal of the other stones from this double row could still be seen in the turf. The length of this row was thus 555 ft, and the direction of length due N. As to the Three Boys, it has been suggested that they were the supporters of a dolmen; but the remaining stone would certainly not be suited to this use, and probably they were merely stones larger than the general run, such as are frequently found near the termination of a row.

It cannot be determined whether the Longstone originally stood in a row 1,040 ft long; or whether row G at first terminated in the Longstone; and the southward extension was an afterthought. The slight deviation in direction which occurs at the Longstone is certainly insufficient to determine the question.

39. Shuggledown (H)

Returning to row G, abreast of this, and overlapping it to the north, is a single row on the east, at a mean distance of c. 40 ft. This appears to end in a blocking-stone not far from the cairn which forms the southern terminal of row C.

The southern 295 ft of its length bears N. 11° W., but to the north the row extends a further 260 ft (making a total length of 555 ft) to the supposed blocking-stone, bearing somewhat west of the direction above given.

SOUTH TEIGN

Fernworthy Group (Fig. 76)

The Fernworthy Group consists of two fairly well preserved double rows, and the remnant of another. It is unusual in that a stone circle (as opposed to a retaining circle) is more closely associated with the rows than in any other group. A plan is needed to supplement the written description (see Fig. 76).

40. Fernworthy (A), southern row

A stone in the face of a stone wall is probably taken from the row, of which, for present purposes, it has been taken as the end. The row is double, and measured from this assumed end to the centre of a cairn 25 ft in diameter which forms its northern terminal; it is 210 ft in length. The direction of length is N. 4°-30′ E.[1] The internal width is 3 ft 6 in, equivalent to 4 ft 1 in., centre to centre, of the stones, and the spacing of the stones along the length of the row is 3 ft, centre to centre.

Seventy-two feet north from the centre of the cairn is the centre of a stone circle 64 ft 6 in. internal diameter. This circle is very nearly complete, with twenty-six stones standing and only four missing. In

---

[1] Corrected figure. (ED.)

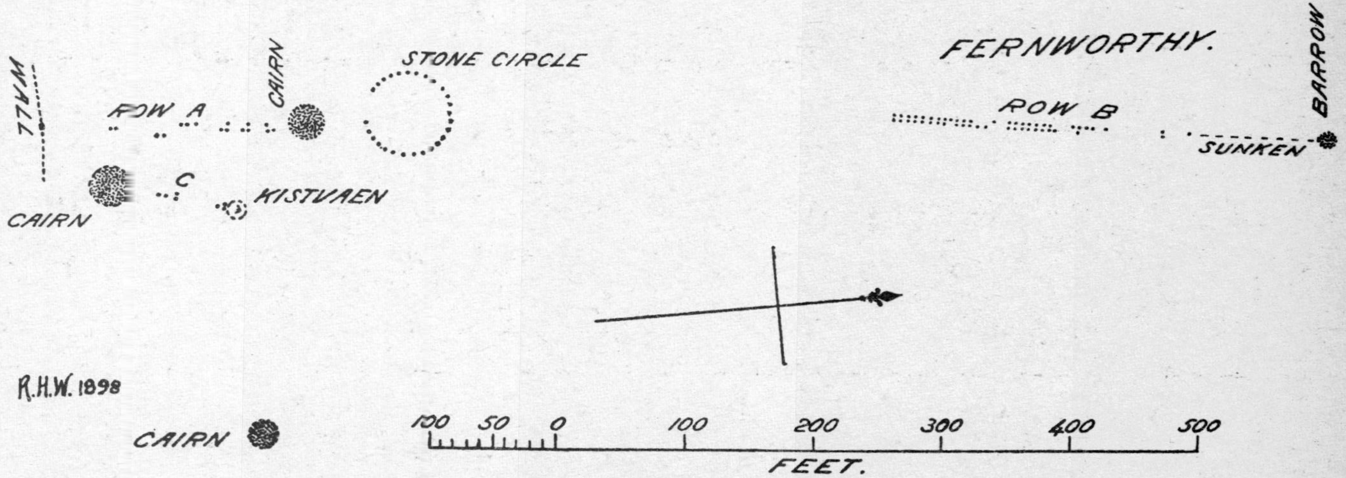

FIG. 76. The Fernworthy group.

1898 the circle was examined, nothing being found except charcoal lying on the surface of the calm or growan; there was no trace of any burial.

The position of the stone circle is, Devon, 6 inch O.S., lxxxix, SE., lon. 3°-54'-9", lat. 50°-38'-26½".

41. Fernworthy (B), northern row

Three hundred and fifty feet N. 6° E. from the centre of the stone circle lie the first stones of row B. This is a double row, reasonably perfect at the south end, but to the north most of the stones are either lost or buried. It terminates in a small mound or barrow at the north end. Its length is 340 ft as measured to the centre of the mound. The direction of length is N. 10° E. The lines average 3 ft 3 in. apart, inside measurement, equivalent to 3 ft 10 in. centre to centre; the stones stand at intervals of 5 ft 7 in. centre to centre along the row. B has been said to point to the stone circle, but its line is tangential to the west circumference.

42. Fernworthy (C)

Abreast of row A, at a distance of 44 ft to the east, lies the centre of a cairn; and at a distance of 72 ft from the row a kistvaen in a barrow. From the centre of the cairn to the kist is a distance of 104 ft; between the two are clear evidences of a ruined double row, which is thus 104 ft in length. The direction of length is N. 24° E.[1]

From the graves associated with this group has come the best evidence which we have as to the probable period to which the rows must be attributed; a food vessel of beaker ware, and a horn button or dress fastener. It will be remembered that beaker ware was found in a kistvaen associated with the Drizzlecombe rows. The elevation of the ground at the stone circle is 1,350 ft O.D., falling somewhat north and south from this point.

43. Assacombe (Pl. 62)

A double row, the stones small for the most part, barely 18 in. in height; but with three which are larger next to the cairn (20 ft in diameter) which forms the terminal at the north-east. These stones are c. 7 ft 6 in., 4 ft 6 in. and 4 ft 6 in. high respectively. The row is nearly perfect, but markedly irregular; the width across the lines varies from 5 ft 6 in. to 6 ft 6 in., centre to centre of stones. To the south of the row, and about 10 ft away from it near the south-west end is a circle, probably a hut-circle.

The row is c. 430 ft in length; the direction of length is N. 57°-30' E. The position, as determined by the centre of the cairn is, Devon, 6 inch O.S., xcix, NE., lon. 3°-53'-40", lat. 50°-37'-39". The ground level

---

[1] Corrected figure. (ED.)

varies from about 1,400 to 1,460 ft O.D., the cairn being at the highest point.

44. *Watern Hill, Chagford Common*

A double row, and one of the best examples on Dartmoor. Should properly be shared between the South Teign and the Bovey, since its whole length lies along the water-parting between the valleys of those streams. At the south, which is the higher end, is a cairn 22 ft in diameter. In the eastern line the first stone measures 4 ft 10 in. at the base and stands 5 ft 10 in. in height; its width at the top is 11 in. This is the largest stone in the row. Its companion, in the western line, is of not much beyond the average dimensions. At the north end is a blocking-stone, 8 in. by 24 in. at base, and 3 ft 10 in. in height.

Throughout the lines there is considerable variation in the size of the stones, of which there are fifty pairs, none being missing. Two pairs of originally small stones have sunk somewhat and now stand but a few inches above the surface.

Measured from the centre of the cairn the row is 473 ft in length; the direction of length is N. 21°-30′ E. The distance between the lines is wider than usual; the mean width measured internally is 5 ft 10 in., with a minimum of 4 ft 4 in. and a maximum of 8 ft 2 in. From the centre to centre of the stones the mean width is 6 ft 5 in. But the spacing is more regular than the extremes suggest; between the limits of 5 ft and 6 ft 6 in. are included 97% of the internal measurements.

Measured along the rows the pairs are spaced at a mean interval of 9 ft 1 in., with extremes of 6 ft and 11 ft 7 in., but here again a large part of the measurements falls within a much less range of variation; 80% of the number lie between the extremes of 8 ft 3 in. and 10 ft.

An obviously intentional feature is the widening of the space between the lines as the cairn is approached. The pair next to the cairn are 8 ft 2 in. apart, the interval is reduced to 7 ft 6 in. in the next pair to the north, then follow intervals of 6 ft 3 in. and 6 ft respectively. In a length of 31 ft 6 in. there is an addition of 2 ft 2 in. to the width.

There are three hut-circles abreast of the row, the most distant being 300 yds from it.

The position of the centre of the cairn is, Devon, 6 inch O.S., xcix, NE., lon. 3°-52′-37″, lat. 50°-37′-36″. The ground stands at 1,400 ft O.D. at the centre of the row, and the gradient is 1 in 10, falling to the north.

45. *Stannon, south slope of White Ridge*

Starts with a cairn at the north or uphill end. The row is double, fairly well preserved for a short distance from the cairn, but dilapidated to an increasing degree as the newtake wall is approached to the south. The length is at least 620 ft, as measured from the centre of the cairn; and the direction of length is N. 1° E.

Position of cairn, Devon, 6 inch O.S., xcix, NE., lon. 3°-54'-10", lat. 50°-37'-6½"; elevation of ground at cairn *c.* 1,475 ft O.D.; gradient *c.* 1 in 24, falling south.

This row might well be in part attributed to the East Dart Valley, since it lies on the water-parting.

EAST AND WEST WEBBURN STREAMS

46. *Challacombe, by Chaw Gully* (Pl. 47)

Triple row, which lies on the water-parting between the watersheds of the East and West Webburn rivers, on the north slope of Challacombe Hill. The row terminates to the south in a blocking-stone of unusual size, which, in Pl. 47 (2) will be seen breaking the skyline, and in the foreground of (1), of the same plate. The northern end of the row was destroyed by the excavation of Chaw Gully, and we cannot say what was there; but if it were a barrow, then that barrow lay at the lower end of the row. The three lines are well marked, and little damage was done to them when the row suffered restoration, except that a stone in the middle row was turned to form a blocking-stone across that one row. This stone will be seen in the foreground of Pl. 47 (2).

More than this there were loose stones scattered to the west of the north end of the row; an attempt was made to re-erect these in the places in which 'they should have been'. Nothing coherent came of that attempt, but it has been translated as presenting a stone circle, and some additional rows, very short and very imperfect. The probability is that the stones were drawn back here when the topsoil was removed prior to the excavation of the east end of Chaw Gully, and as they fell from the cart or sled, so they lay. It is not safe to see in this monument any more than a good example of a triple row, with some respectable stones used in its construction. The lines are farther apart at the north than at the south end, where they gather in somewhat to meet the blocking-stone. The present length is 528 ft, but how much has been lost at the north end cannot be determined. The direction of length is N. 23°-30' W. The position of the blocking-stone to the south is, Devon, 6 inch O.S., xcix, NE., lon. 3°-51'-5", lat. 50°-36'-39½". The elevation of the ground is *c.* 1,460 ft O.D. at the blocking-stone, and it falls north at a gradient of *c.* 1 in 11.

DART

47. *Sherril Down, Sherberton Common*

The history of this row is one of misfortune. It was discovered by the brothers Amery in the year 1894, visited by them and my father in 1895, and by 1897 had disappeared. It lay beside a road, a very dangerous situation. The approximate position was, Devon, 6 inch O.S., cviii, SW., lon. 3°-50'-48", lat. 50°-32'-57". The row was double, with rather an unusual width between the lines, which were 8 to 9 ft apart in the clear. On the other hand the spacing of the stones along the rows was unusually close, and there appeared to have been some inserted at a later date, which brought the spacing closer yet. At the north end were traces of a barrow, possibly with a retaining circle. The length was c. 225 ft, and the direction of length c. N. 4° W. Some of the fallen stones were nearly 5 ft in length, so that it was by no means a trivial structure.

The elevation of the ground is approximately 1,125 ft O.D.

BECKY BROOK

48. *Trendlebere Down, north-east slope of Black Hill, Manaton*

Close to the road from Haytor to Manaton, 100 ft to the north of that road, about 600 yds north of Yarner Wells.

Probably a double row, much robbed, and many of the stones fallen; but there is still one undoubted pair of set stones which stand 3 ft 1 in. apart, face to face as measured across the row.

Starts at the south end with a ruined cairn, some 50 ft in diameter, but now reduced to a mere ring cairn. Terminates to the north in another ruined cairn, also reduced to a ring. At this end there is a mound which looks like an independent cairn, its centre 50 ft to the west of the line of the row. But this is more probably a remnant of the row cairn, turned back by the roadmen, who have despoiled both terminal cairns. The distance between the centres of the terminal cairns is 412 ft. The direction of length of the row is N. 4° E., the level of the ground at the south end is 1,086 O.D., and the gradient falls northward at 1 in 12.

There now (1946) remain sixteen stones in all, seven set and nine fallen. Although the site is on slate, outside the boundary of the granite, all the stones are granite. Among the fallen stones the following lengths were observed: 4 ft 6 in., 3 ft 9 in , 3 ft 7 in., 3 ft 6 in., 3 ft 4 in.; the stones still set stand 2 ft 4 in., 2 ft 2 in., 1 ft, 1 ft 10 in., 10 in., 9 in. and 6 in. respectively. The position, as determined by the centre of the southern cairn, is Devon, 6 inch O.S., c, SE., lon. 3°-44'-37", lat. 50°-35'-57¼".

EAST DART

49. *Yar Tor* (Fig. 77)

A triple row, which has lost much at the hands of the road-makers but as to which some record remains to supplement the information still obtainable on the site. The original length of this row must have been at least 1,500 ft.

The southern part was noted in 1894 by the brothers Amery and my father; it ran very near the road to Sherril and Babeny from Ollsbrim; 54 ft in length were traceable. The space between the outer rows was, in width, 7 ft 6 in., say 8 ft 3 in., centre to centre of the stones. The direction of length, as ascertained with a pocket compass was NW. magnetic, a sufficient approximation to the direction of the remnant still to be seen to indicate that the row pointed toward the Yar Tor kistvaen. That remnant is very slight, one stone, now 23 in. in height but of which the top has been deliberately removed. It stands 156 ft 6 in. to the south of the kist. The kistvaen is set in a barrow, and has two retaining circles, an inner random kerb, 11 ft 6 in. outside diameter, and an outer open circle of 36 ft outside diameter.

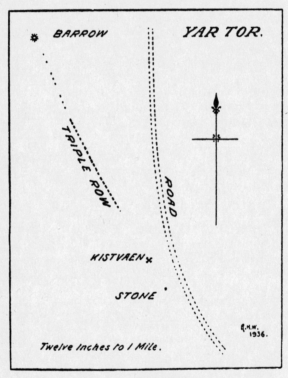

FIG. 77. Yar Tor, triple row.

For a distance of 262 ft north of the kistvaen no stones of the row are traceable. In the intervening space are many old enclosure banks. For a further distance of 500 ft the row is comparatively perfect; then it becomes ragged, with many blanks, until, at a distance of 1,173 ft from the kist it apparently dies out, abreast of a barrow that lies a little to the west of the line. The whole row thus described is convex to the west, and its azimuth varies from N. 32° W. at the kistvaen to N. 24° W. near the north end.

The distances between the rows vary somewhat, from

w.—5 ft 8 in.—central.—4 ft 8 in.—E. Total 10 ft 4 in.

to   w.—6 ft 6 in.—central.—6 ft 8 in.—E. Total 13 ft 4 in.

and   w.—5 ft 3 in.—central.—6 ft 3 in.—E. Total 11 ft 6 in.

The stones are spaced at about 4 ft to 4 ft 6 in. centres along the row. The stones are small, 12 in. × 4 in. × 8 in. high is a fair example, and 18 in. × 19 in. × 32 in. high is perhaps the largest still standing. They are somewhat larger at the north end than farther south.

The elevation of the ground is *c*. 1,200 ft O.D. at the north end of the row, and 1,283 ft O.D. at the kistvaen, with a falling gradient of *c*. 1 in 15 toward the north.

The position of the kistvaen is, Devon, 6 inch O.S., cviii, sw., lon. 3°-51′-39″, lat. 50°-32′-56½″.

The Ordnance Survey revision of 1904 shows a stone row running practically due north from the kistvaen for a distance of 480 ft, and ending in a hut-circle. This is wholly wrong.

When complete this row crossed the water-parting of the East Dart and Dart valleys at or near the kistvaen.

50. *Laughter*

A double row, present length *c*. 657 ft, but has been much robbed, probably for the building of newtake walls, one of which lies athwart the row. Direction of length N. 67° W.

At the north-west end stands a fine menhir; when fallen this was measured as 12 ft in length; it has been re-erected to stand 8 ft 8 in. in height (Pl. 56B). Twenty-three stones remain in the length of 657 ft. The width across the row, centre to centre of the stones, is 4 ft at the north-west end, but widens to over 6 ft to the south-east. Most of the stones are between 1 and 2 ft in height; but at the south-east end there are two which are larger, one being 3 ft 4 in. × 8 in. × 4 ft 6 in. high. These larger stones suggest that there may have been a barrow at this end; if so, we have an instance of a row with a menhir at its higher end and a barrow at the lower.

Position of menhir, Devon, 6 inch O.S., cvii, NE., lon. 3°-54′-13″, lat. 50°-33′-43″. Elevation of ground at menhir *c*. 1,300 ft O.D., gradient, falling SE. *c*. 1 in 22.

51. *Lakehead Hill, near summit*

Prior to the year 1895 there was, near the summit of Lakehead Hill, a moss-covered heap of stones; whatever had been there was then a total constructive loss. This was investigated and restored to its supposed original condition. There emerged from the process a large kistvaen, with coverstone complete; and it is fairly certain that this feature could be relied on, except that the kistvaen is outsize for the stones comprised. The restorers state that the kist "was originally surrounded by a circle". Of the circle, six stones alone remain. One curious feature is that a stone row starts from within the circle, extends east for 44 ft, and consists of 11 stones, and the socket holes of two more have been discovered. How much farther the row went is not known. Instead of running in a straight line, it describes a curve, the direction of the chord of which is N. 87°-30′ E.

There may well have been a retaining circle, but in the absence of a plan of the ruin as it was before rebuilding it is no more than a probability. Since, however, the restored 'row' presents two features unknown elsewhere on Dartmoor, in that it starts from within the retaining circle, and follows a markedly curved course, the direction of length from end to end is N. 86°-30′ E., the least that can be said is that this part of the effort at restoration is unfortunate. It certainly carries no conviction. The group is prominent, and has the appearance of importance. It has been figured by later antiquaries as a type, but no valid argument can be founded on its present features.

Position, Devon, 6 inch O.S., xcix, SE., lon. 3°-54′-51″, lat. 50°-34′-55″.

WEST DART

Lakehead Hill, west slope

A number of stone rows have been reported as on Lakehead Hill, most of them as admittedly doubtful. I am unable to find more than two which appear to have good credentials. Even these have no formal terminals.

52. *Lakehead Hill*

A single row, no more than 60 ft in length. Direction of length N. 74° W. Four hundred feet to the east lies a kistvaen in the line of this row, which may originally have extended as far. Position of row, Devon, 6 inch O.S., xcix, SE., lon. 3°-54′-58″, lat. 50°-34′-56″.

53. *Lakehead Hill*

A single row, 400 ft in length. Direction of length N. 22° W. Is at present to all appearances isolated, there being no cairn or barrow in the line of its direction. Position of row, south end, Devon, 6 inch O.S., xcix, SE., lon. 3°-55′-2″, lat. 50°-34′-44″. Approximate elevation of ground at south end 1,300 ft O.D., falling slightly toward the north.

54. *Tor Royal Newtake, Moorlands*

Now first reported. A single row which crosses the path from Moorlands to Princetown at a point 90 yds west of the gate to Moorlands. Length 98 ft, with a very doubtful southerly extension of a further 210 ft. Direction of length N. 28° W. Elevation of ground *c.* 1,150 ft O.D. No cairn or barrow now existing. Position, Devon, 6 inch O.S., cvii, SW., lon. 3°-56′-35″, lat. 50°-32′-38″.

55. *Conies Down*

In the Cowsic Valley, which I treat as tributary to the West Dart. Found by Burnard, whose description I have in part used. A double row, 588 ft long, direction of length N. 3° E. Less than a dozen stones still stand; there are others, fallen or buried.

No distinct traces of a cairn or barrow; but at the north end a fallen stone which may be a blocking-stone; if so this is a parallel to Challacombe (46), where there is a blocking-stone at the higher end. The south end of the row comes very near to the Lichway. The ground elevation at the north end is 1,660 ft O.D., and the ground falls south at a gradient of 1 in 10.

Position of the north end, Devon, 6 inch O.S., xcviii, SE., lon. 3°-59′-54½″, lat. 50°-35′-37″.

AVON

Until within the past few years no stone row was known in the valley of the Avon but, in 1932, I chanced upon an example near Black Tor.

56. *Black Tor, Avon Valley*

I had hoped to survey this row in 1946, but have been unable. The row lies on the plateau to the west of Black Tor. It is interesting as being one of the few rows with terminal barrows at both ends.

GLAZEBROOK

Glazebrook Group, Corringdon Ball (Fig. 78)

This group is trivial in the matter of construction, but extremely interesting in its arrangement. It was usual to describe this as a seven or eightfold row; but my father, in 1892, pointed out that the northernmost line was certainly an independent structure with its own eastern terminal; whereas the remaining rows all had a common terminal to the east, in a retaining circle. He made the total number of lines to be eight. Crossing, in 1909, adopted this view. I myself had always spoken of the row as sevenfold. When in doubt there is but one course to follow, make a survey. In 1946 I made a survey; with the result that I find one single, and two treble rows; with two stones clear of all the rows but pointing direct to the centre of the retaining circle which heads the two treble rows.

57. *Corringdon Ball* (A)

A single row, starting on the east with a cairn, 22 ft in diameter and 2 ft in height. At some time this cairn has been opened. The first stone of the row lies 58 ft west of the centre of the cairn; there is a modern stone fence very near, and robbery has been considerable. The row clearly extends for 507 ft from the centre of the cairn, but with long intervals between the last few stones.

The stones are small; the mean dimensions of fifteen stones which still stand are, along the row 15 in., at right angles to the row 8 in., and height 14 in., the highest standing 25 in. Stones which just break the surface of the ground, standing only 3 in. or less above it, are excluded from the mean. It would appear that the original spacing, centre to centre, along the row, may have been 3 ft 6 in. The direction of length is N. 48°-30′ E.

58. Corringdon Ball (B)

Forty-one feet to the south-east of the centre of the cairn lies the centre of a retaining circle of 37 ft internal diameter. This forms the terminal of two triple rows. Seven stones of the circle still stand, and there is one fallen. The largest stone measures 11 in. × 10 in. × 24 in. high, and the smallest is 15 in. × 6 in. × 13 in. high.

Row B is triple, its northern line is parallel to row A, and its length from abreast the centre of the circle is 260 feet. Taking the northern line, the mean dimensions of the stones still standing are 14 in. × 5 in. × 9 in. high, and the tallest stone is but 12 in. above ground. In the middle line the mean dimensions of standing stones are 12 in. × 7 in. × 10 in. high, and the tallest stone stands 21 in. For the width centre to centre across the lines the figures are:

East end, N. line—3 ft—central line—4 ft—s. line.
West end, N. line—4 ft—central line—5 ft—s. line.
Thus the total width is 2 ft greater at the west end.

The distance, centre to centre, between the south line of row B and the north line of row C is, at the east end, 18 ft 6 in., and at the west end 10 ft, so that the triple rows converge as they leave the circle.

59. Corringdon Ball (C)

A triple row 219 ft long as measured from abreast the centre of the circle. This row overlaps the retaining circle; since the direction of the southern line points 6 ft clear of the circumference, and the middle row is just tangential to the south of the circle. The stones are all small, the dimensions of the one still standing in the northern line are 15 in. × 9 in. × 6 in. high; none of the other stones in this line reach more than 3 to 4 in. above the surface. In the middle line there are two stones of 13 in. × 6 in. × 6 in. high and 9 in. × 6 in. × 7 in. respectively; the others are sunk to nearly ground level; and in the southern line there are two stones of 18 in. × 8 in. × 13 in. high, and 7 in. × 7 in. × 11 in. high respectively, the others being sunk to nearly ground level.

The widths, centre to centre, across the rows are:

East end, N. line—7 ft 6 in.—central line—5 ft 6 in.—s. line.
West end, N. line—4 ft 6 in.—central line—3 ft 6 in.—s. line.
Thus the total width is 5 ft 6 in. less at the west end.

The three rows A, B and C are, as a group, convergent to the west, if we take the central lines of rows B and C as the directions of those

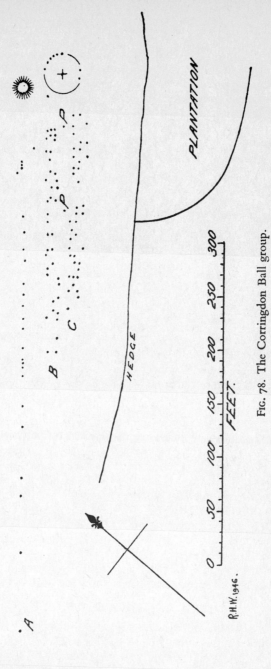

CORRINGDON BALL.

PLANTATION

HEDGE

FEET.

0 50 100 150 200 250 300

R.H.W. 1946.

Fig. 78. The Corringdon Ball group.

rows. We then get the following directions of length: A, N. 48°-30′ E.; B, N. 50°-30′ E.; C, N. 53°-30′ E.

In the interval between B and C there are two stones 78 ft apart, each marked P on the plan. A line through these stones, if produced to the east, passes with precision through the centre of the circle; and if produced west passes clear of both rows A and B. No other stones can be found on this alignment, and it cannot be called a row. Possibly the apparent arrangement is but chance.

Position of circle, Devon, 6 inch O.S., cxix, NE., lon. 3°-52′-39″, lat. 50°-26′-5½″. Elevation of ground at circle 1,000 ft O.D. Ground practically level along length of rows.

60. *Brent Fore Hill*

Devon, 6 inch O.S., cxix, SE., lon. 3°-52′-31″, lat. 50°-26′-10″, the position given being that of the centre of the cairn at the east end. A double row. Very near the Corringdon Group, and lying to the north-east of that group, with the stream of the East Glaze intervening.

This row was found in 1945 by Mrs. Z. W. E. Watkin, and independently in 1947, on the occasion of a visit by the Plymouth Branch of the Devonshire Association to the neighbourhood. It happened that the evening light was peculiarly favourable, and Mr. Masson Phillips detected on the hillside some four or five stones which appeared to be set in a row. Inspection proved that these stones were indeed set and the row was traced up the hill to its termination in a cairn.

The length of the row from its present western end to the centre of the cairn is 410 ft. The direction of the western half of the row is N. 53° E., while the eastern half lies N. 57° E., a small deviation. From its position, and the practical identity of its direction, it is possible that this row is part of the Corringdon group.

At 194 ft from its western end the row is crossed by the course of a disused leat, and 131 ft farther on the present Corringdon leat crosses the row. These have created considerable disturbance, with the result that the last set stone occurs at 255 ft.

Forty-two stones in all are undoubted members of the row; of these twenty-seven are set and standing, and fifteen have fallen. None are large, the tallest standing stone is 2 ft 3 in. high, one fallen stone is 2 ft 9 in. in length, two still standing measure respectively 1 ft 10 in. × 11 in. × 1 ft 9 in. high, and 1 ft 11 in. × 1 ft 3 in. × 1 ft 8 in. high.

Five pairs of set stones still stand, the distance apart of the stones in the pairs, measured between the inner faces are respectively: 3 ft 2 in., 2 ft 11 in., 2 ft 6 in., 2 ft. 2 in. and 1 ft 10 in.; giving a mean of 2 ft 6 in.

Along the length of the row the distance apart of the stones is ascertainable with certainty in twelve places; these distances, from centre of stone to centre of stone are respectively as follows: 6 ft, 6 ft, 5 ft, 5 ft, 5 ft, 5 ft, 5 ft, 4 ft 6 in., 4 ft 6 in., 3 ft 9 in., 3 ft 6 in., and 3 ft, giving a mean of 4 ft 8 in. It will be seen that there is considerable irregularity in this respect; but nine measurements lie within the limits of 6 ft and 4 ft 6 in, and only three are outside this range.

Elevation of ground at cairn 1,030 O.D.; gradient 1 in 12, falling south-west.

61. *Glasscombe Ball, north-east slope*

A row of exceptional interest, which lies 300 yds s. 41° w. from Glasscombe Corner, in the valley of the West Glaze.

The southern 368 ft in length is a double row, and the northern 212 ft 6 in. is a single row; it is perfectly clear that the northern part has lost no stones which would have constituted its second line had it been originally double. The change from double to single is abrupt, and complete.

At the south-west end of the row are the remnants of a cairn, much reduced, but traceable, and at the north-east end is a retaining circle of which many of the stones have fallen; three of the fallen stones measure 4 ft 6 in., 3 ft 6 in. and 2 ft 7 in. long respectively. It would thus appear that at either end was a grave.

In the double portion the lines are at a mean distance of 5 ft 5 in., centre to centre, with extremes of 6 ft and 4 ft 6 in. The stones are spaced along the lines at 7 ft 5 in. mean distance, centre to centre, with extremes of 9 ft 6 in. and 5 ft 6 in.

In the single portion the stones are spaced along the lines at 10 ft 1 in. mean distance, centre to centre, with extremes of 11 ft and 7 ft 8 in. It is the western line of the double row which is continued as a single row. It will be noted that the spacing along the row is markedly more open in the single portion. The largest stone occurs in the single row, 24 in. × 13 in. × 41 in. high.

The total length, from centre of cairn to centre of circle, is 635 ft. The position of the circle at the north-east end is, Devon, 6 inch O.S., cxix, NE., lon. 3°-53'-5", lat. 50°-25'-51". The elevation of the ground at the sw. end is c. 1,110 ft O.D., with the ground falling north-east at a gradient of 1 in 12. Direction of length N. 36° E.

LUDBROOK

62. *Cantrell, near moor gate, Ugborough Moor*

A double row, with a cairn of mean diameter of 22 ft at the north-east end. Length from centre of cairn 153 ft, direction of length N. 44°-20' E. The lines are from 7 ft to 12 ft apart, centre to centre, the spacing in the lines is about 5 ft 6 in., centre to centre. The largest standing stone is 27 in. × 9 in. × 29 in. high. The position of the cairn is Devon, 6 inch O.S., cxxv, NE., lon. 3°-53'-23", lat. 50°-23'-54¾".

Elevation of ground at cairn c. 750 ft O.D., falling to the south-west along the row at a gradient of 1 in 12.

SINGLE, DOUBLE AND TREBLE ROWS

We thus have details of 62 rows, as a basis for statistical analysis, and may first take the simplest classification.

On Dartmoor there are 25 single rows, 28 double, and 5 treble. There is also one row which is clearly double as to one end, and single as to the other; and the difference between the ends is certainly original, and not the result of any later interference (61). Another example is in part double, in part single, and there is no evidence to suggest that it was ever wholly double (17).

Where rows are associated to form a group, the members of the group are rarely all of one class. Thus, at Trowlesworthy (14-15) one row is double, the other is single. At Drizzlecombe (17-18-19), of three rows two are single, one is in part double. The Harter Group (22-23) consists of one double and one single row; while at Corringdon Ball, Glazebrook (57-58-59-60) two treble rows are associated with one single and one double.

SIZE OF INDIVIDUAL STONES, OMITTING TERMINAL MENHIRS

In every row there is much variation in the size of the stones. In practically every row some of the stones are insignificant in size, while still significant as part of the alignment. There are stones which have never stood more than 6 to 9 in. above the surface. On the other hand, omitting terminal menhirs, and those occasional large stones which are to be found standing next to the graves, we may cite the entirely exceptional series at the north end of Staldon (7) some of which stand over 8 ft in height.

Even in such a considerable example as the triple row on Yar Tor (49) a fair average for the size of the stones is 12 in. × 4 in. × 8 in. high, while the largest is but 18 in. × 19 in. × 32 in. high. The largest upright at Glasscombe Ball (61) measures 24 in. × 13 in. × 41 in. high.

In general it may be said that of the stones many are less than 18 in., few are more than 3 ft in height; this remark is applicable to rows which have suffered little or no interference since their construction. The case of those which lie near newtake walls is one of greater poverty. Robbery for walling purposes has reduced some to insignificance. An extreme instance is to be found at Shuggledown, from the Longstone southward (38); there, of a double row originally 555 ft in length, there now remain but two small stones, and one larger (which formerly had two somewhat longer companions). The ordinary stones of the row went to make the newtake wall of Thornworthy; the two larger stones were taken for gateposts, and their companion was left as being too large for the wall, too small for a post.

Another example is the group at Corringdon Ball (57-58-59) which was robbed for the purpose of the Corringdon Newtake wall. The largest stone now standing is but 25 in. in height, three others are 21, 20 and 18 in. high respectively, and with a very few exceptions none of the others exceed 10 in. in height, and many stand less than 5 in.

The larger stones which are sometimes placed next to the terminal barrow are, perhaps, best mentioned here; a few examples will suffice. At Down Tor (20) the stone next the retaining circle of the barrow is 9 ft 6 in. in height; it is followed by a short series of stones in descending order of height, but all well above the average in the row (see p. 212, and Pl. 61).

At Assacombe (43) the three stones nearest the barrow are respectively 7 ft 6 in., 4 ft 6 in., and 4 ft 6 in. in height; this is a double row (Pl. 62). A double row at Shuggledown (34) starts, at a fourfold retaining circle, with two stones, both fallen, the one 11 ft 6 in. and the other 7 ft 4 in. in length (Pl. 46A); and on Watern Hill (44) another double row starts at a barrow with a stone 5 ft 10 in. in height in the east alignment, while its companion in the west alignment is but a little larger than the average of the row. These are notable examples; but it may be said that, in general, the stones nearest the grave give evidence of selection, being for the most part larger than the average; and no comparatively small or insignificant stones are used in that position.

With the exception of such as have been selected for special positions, the factor which governs the size of the stones is the material available within a reasonable distance; the importance of a row, as determined by its length, is not necessarily reflected by the size of its individual members.

THE SPACING OF THE STONES IN THE ROWS

In this section all obvious gaps left by loss or robbery have been excluded from consideration.

No row is a strictly regular structure, and the spacing of stones in any row may vary considerably, especially the spacing along the length of the row. Thus, at Merrivale A (27) the mean longitudinal spacing, centre to centre, is 5 ft 6 in., with extremes of 4 ft 7 in. and 7 ft 9 in.; Merrivale B (28) has a mean distance of 7 ft 1 in., with extremes of 5 ft 3 in. and 9 ft 10 in. At Watern Hill (44) the mean longitudinal spacing is 9 ft 1 in., while the extremes are 6 ft and 11 ft 7 in.; but in this instance there is greater regularity than the extreme figures suggest, since 80% of the measurements fall within the limits of 8 ft 3 in. and 10 ft.

Subject to the qualification as to irregularity it remains that the mean of the measurements in any row has a real descriptive value, and I have selected twenty-six rows the condition of which is sufficiently perfect to give validity to the measurements. I have accordingly ascertained the mean longitudinal distance, centre to centre, between the stones in each of the twenty-six rows, the highest figure which I obtained being 10 ft 1 in. and the lowest 3 ft; while the mean of all the means is 5 ft 7 in. In this calculation I have rejected the north end of the Staldon Row (7) where the entirely exceptional spacing of from 30 ft to 50 ft is to be found. That spacing has been accurately ascertained, but it is in a class to itself.

Of the rows which I have used in this calculation, some are single, some double and some treble. For the seven single rows the mean of means is 5 ft 7 in., the same dimension as for the whole group; while the four treble rows give a mean of 4 ft 10 in. As far as a figure based on so few examples has any validity, it would appear that the tendency was to space the stones along the length of treble rows at less distance than in either the single or double.

The width across, at right angles to the length, I have measured between the stones, from face to face, and not from centre to centre, in other words the width of the track between the stones; but in using the word 'track' I have no intention of suggesting a processional path. Fourteen double rows are included in the measurements, and the results are: the highest figure obtained is 9 ft 6 in. and the lowest is 1 ft 10 in., while the mean of means is 4 ft 2 in.

The figures for the treble rows are, highest 6 ft 5 in., lowest 3 ft, mean of means 5 ft. It would appear that the stones were spaced wider apart in the treble rows than in the double; but here again, the data are insufficient to show a deliberate intent.

In considering the width across the rows I have purposely left out of account the double row on Sharpitor at the base of the eastern slope (26), where the space between the stones is but 6 to 7 in.: this row is in a class to itself.

Even as there was a strong tendency to place the best and largest stones next to the barrow, so there is clear indication that the rows were at places purposely widened as they neared the grave. A good example is afforded at Watern Hill (44), where the width between the two stones next to the barrow is 8 ft 2 in., and 36 ft farther from the barrow the width is reduced to 6 ft.

TERMINALS

In their original form it is probable that all rows had formal terminals at either end. These terminals, where still in being, take one of three forms: (1) a barrow or cairn, with or without a retaining circle; (2) a menhir, being a stone larger, especially in the matter of height, than the ordinary stones of the row; (3) a blocking-stone, standing across the space between double rows, or the spaces between treble rows. Such blocking-stones are set with their greatest width at right angles to the lengths of the row, while the normal stones of the row always stand with their greatest width parallel to the length.

PLATE 33

A. Kistvaen, Blackslade Down. View looking s. 7° E.

B. Kistvaen, Stennen Hill, No. 1. View looking s. 14° E.

PLATE 34

Brent Fore Hill, near Corringdon Ball Gate.

PLATE 35

Cuckoo Ball, looking N. 55° E.

PLATE 36

A. Retaining circle, Soussons Common.

B. Retaining circle with central Kistvaen, Lakehead Newtake, looking w.

PLATE 37

A. Stone in retaining circle, Drizzlecombe.

B. Retaining circle with central kistvaen, Hound Tor.

PLATE 38

A. Kerb circle, Drizzlecombe.

B. Yellowmead circle, near Sheepstor, from centre.

PLATE 39

LOWTON.

METHEREL

Retaining circles at Lowton and Metherel.

PLATE 40

A. Flint arrow-heads from northern Dartmoor.

B. Flint scraper from Drizzlecombe.

PLATE 41

Bronze dagger and amber pommel from Hameldon.

PLATE 42

A. Meacombe kistvaen, looking s. 53° e.

B. Lakehead Newtake, retaining circle (near circle illustrated in plate 36), looking west.

PLATE 43

Stall Moor circle and row, looking south.

PLATE 44

Stall Moor—Green Hill Row (No. 1) looking north. The row extends to the horizon.

PLATE 45

North end of Staldon Row (No. 7), looking north.

PLATE 46

A. Shuggledown, looking from the fourfold circle to Batworthy Corner.

B. The Longstone, Shuggledown. (Kestor in distance.)

PLATE 47

Challacombe Row (No. 46)
(1) Looking N. 20°–30′ W. (2) Looking S. 24° E.

PLATE 48

Yellowmead Circle, near Sheepstor, looking N. 35° W.

PLATE 49

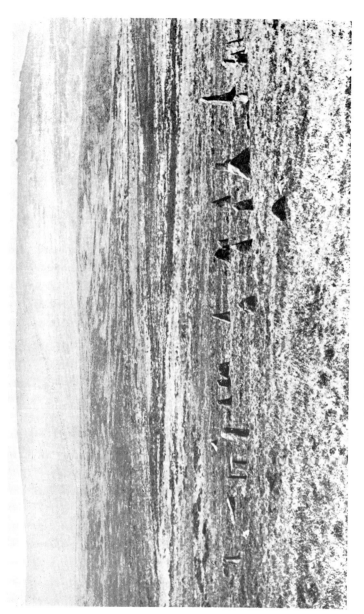

Scorhill Circle, Gidleigh, looking WSW.

PLATE 50

A. Tallest stone in Scorhill Circle.

B. Stones stolen from Scorhill Circle used in bank of leat.

PLATE 51

A. Sherberton Circle, general view.

B. Down Ridge Circle, largest stone.

PLATE 52

Willing Walls stone circle, groups A and B.

PLATE 53

Willings Walls stone circle, groups B, C, and D.

PLATE 54

Beardown Man.

PLATE 55

A. Beardown Man, from s. 58° w.

B. Harbourne Head Menhir, from s. 56° e.

C. Harbourne Head Menhir, from n. 39° e.

PLATE 56

B. Laughtor Newtake Menhir.

A. White Moor Stone.

PLATE 57

A. Hanging Stone, Lee Moor.

B. Drizzlecombe C, fallen.

PLATE 58

A

B

Drizzlecombe C, after erection: (A). looking westward, (B). looking eastward.

PLATE 59

A. Drizzlecombe A.

B. Drizzlecombe B (C in distance).

PLATE 60

B. Merrivale Menhirs.

A. Menhir on Langstone Moor.

PLATE 61

Photo: *D. P. Wilson*

Down Tor, Retaining Circle and Row. Note the exceptionally large stone in the row adjacent to the circle.

PLATE 62

Assacombe, large stones at end of row adjacent to retaining circle.

PLATE 63

A. Probable feeding chute, Brisworthy Burrows.

B. Feeding chute, Longstone, Sheepstor, for comparison with the above.

PLATE 64

A. Mortars, Brisworthy Hamlet.

B. Mortars. Mill Corner, Plym.

Thirty-eight rows have barrows at one end (1-3-4-5-6-9-10-**11**-**12**-13-14-**15**?-**16**-**17**-18-19-20-22-**23**-**24**-**26**-**29**-**30**-33-34-**36**-**40**-**41**-43-**44**-**45**-**47**?-**51**-**57**-**58**-**59**-**60**-**62**.)

Of these barrows twenty are without retaining circles, and their reference numbers are printed in heavy type.

Four rows have barrows at both ends (1-42-48-61); of these 1, 48 and 61 each have one circled barrow, and one barrow without a circle, while neither barrow at 42 is circled.

Two rows have each a barrow interrupting the length of the row (28-49), and in each instance the barrow is circled.

There are thus forty-four instances in which a barrow or barrows form a definite part of the row.

Ten menhirs appears as terminals (2-14-16-17-18-19-30-37-38-50). A menhir at one end and a barrow at the other occur in seven instances (2-14-16-17-18-19-30). Menhirs are especially liable to removal to serve as gateposts and for other utilitarian purposes, while cairns and barrows are convenient sources of precollected stone. It is a matter for congratulation that so many have been left in association.

Only eight blocking-stones are known, seven certain and one doubtful (21-24-27-28-39?-44-46-55). Two rows (24-44) have at one end barrows, at the other blocking-stones. One (28) has a barrow in the centre, and a blocking-stone at one end; at the other end no terminal remains. Rows 21-27-46-55 have no terminals at the ends remote from the blocking-stones.

The largest and most prominent blocking-stone is that which closes the south end of the Challacombe row (46) (Pl. 47). This is about 5 ft in width at the base and over 6 ft in height. It is well to repeat that a stone set athwart the middle row of this row somewhat in the manner of a blocking-stone is, in its present position, no more than the product of a modern restoration.

A recent writer, Brailsford (1938), has stated that the end of a Dartmoor 'alignment' is almost invariably marked by a transverse blocking-stone. This is certainly incorrect even if menhirs are to be accepted as 'blocking-stones', without regard to the question whether they be transverse or not. He also says that sometimes the first as well as the last stone is placed transversely, and cites Assacombe and Cosdon, both of which are restorations, and two instances at Trowlesworthy Warren, where he may have mistaken stones in the retaining circles of the barrows. But even that explanation will not suffice; the one perfect circle at Trowlesworthy has the stone next to the row turned with its broad face pointing along the row, which is most unusual, and effectively counters his statement.

THE LENGTH OF THE ROWS

No row is complete, nor can its original length be ascertained with certainty, unless it has a formal terminal at either end. It is not safe to relax this rule, although it seriously restricts the number of measurements available.

This requirement limits the number of ascertained lengths to fourteen (1-2-14-16-17-18-19-24-30-38-42-44-48-61), but the list certainly includes both the longest and the shortest Dartmoor rows. There are none longer whether perfect or imperfect, and all which are shorter have obviously been the victims of extensive spoliation.

The greatest length is 11,150 ft (1), and the least is 104 ft (42). I give the whole list: 11,150 ft; 6,280 ft; 1,740 ft; 634 ft; 555 ft; 491 ft; 488 ft; 473 ft; 437 ft; 426 ft; 366 ft; 330 ft; 296 ft; 104 ft. The mean of which is 1,698 ft, but this figure is obviously unduly influenced by the exceptional lengths of the first three.

Provided we keep in mind the fact that every incomplete row must, to some extent, be of less than its original length, it may be useful to take a view of the figures excluded above as lacking in precision; arranging them in groups, with 50 ft intervals. The results are: 0 to 50 ft in length, one row; 50 to 100 ft, three rows; 100 to 150 ft, two; 150 to 200 ft, two; 200 to 250 ft, four; 250 to 300 ft, four; 300 to 350 ft, one; 350 to 400 ft, two; 400 to 450 ft, four; 450 to 500 ft, three; 500 to 550 ft, three; 550 to 600 ft, five; 600 to 650 ft, one; 650 to 700 ft, one; 700 to 750 ft, one. Followed by individual lengths of 865 ft, 950 ft, 1,038 ft, 1,200 ft, 1,500 ft, 1,643 ft. The whole giving a mean of 509 ft in length.

I conclude that no row in its original condition was less than 100 ft or more than 11,150 ft in length; that the majority lay between the limits of 220 and 620 ft; and that six rows had lengths ranging between 880 ft, and 1,740 ft, while the two outstanding examples were 6,280 ft and 11,150 ft in length respectively.

SELECTION OF SITE

Elevation above sea level appears to have had little direct influence on the choice of sites. Stated in feet above Ordnance Datum the distribution of the rows is as follows:

750 to 1,000 ft	16%	1,400 to 1,600 ft	12%
1,000 to 1,200 ft	37%	above 1,600 ft	2%
1,200 to 1,400 ft	33%		

The lowest site is at 750 ft, and the highest at 1,660 ft.

But, indirectly, elevation makes for deeper deposits of peat; and where any but a slight depth of peat is to be found the setting of stones in firm and stable manner is not possible. Above 1,300 ft O.D. this precluded the use of all but a small area.

At a level of about 1,250 ft on the Stall Moor-Green Hill row (1) it appears at first sight that the builders miscalculated in this matter, since the stones seem to have sunk; but, in truth, it is not the stones which have sunk; they are firm set, but the peat, originally shallow, has grown in depth to the extent of about 2 ft. In most places, whether the site be on ordinary soil or on shallow peat, some growth in depth has taken place, and the stones are less prominent accordingly.

Although the elevation of the ground does not appear to have exercised much influence over the choice made, there is another matter of level which I believe to have been regarded as a matter of extreme importance, the gradient. The gradients along the length of the rows are distributed in the following proportion:

1 in 6	2·5%	1 in 22	12·5%
1 in 10	15·0%	1 in 36	2·5%
1 in 11	5·0%	1 in 40	2·5%
1 in 12	12·5%	Slight to level	45·0%
1 in 15	2·5%		

Now these are gradients which, among the hills of Dartmoor have to be sought for, if the flats by the riversides are to be avoided; and even the riversides are often steep and irregular.

It has followed that many of the rows are located on the ridges between the watersheds, for there the longest lines of easy gradients are to be found. Take as an example the row at Challacombe (46) where the gradient ranges from 1 in 11 to level, and is concave, so that the whole row can be seen from either end. If that row had been directed east toward the course of the East Webburn, it would have run into a gradient of 1 in 4, or if to the west toward the course of the West Webburn, the gradient would have been 1 in 10, and in either instance the ground would have been convex; so that but a short distance of the row would have been visible from any point. I do not suggest that there are not many rows in which the one end is hidden from the other by the convexity of the ground; but from the barrow it is always possible to view a considerable length of the row.

An even better example is the Down Tor row (20) which lies along the water-parting between the Deancombe and Newleycombe brooks. From the barrow the ground gently inclines, then for a short space becomes level, and subsequently gently rises. The site of the row is thus concave, and its whole length can be seen from either end.

Of the shorter rows some, such as Langstone Moor (30), were kept on approximately level ground by being set parallel to the contours on relatively flat-topped hills.

The steepest site is at Assacombe (43) where the gradient is 1 in 6 (not steep for a Dartmoor hill) and the row literally charges down the hill; but the row is short, and the ground, although inclined, is nearly a true plane.

It was not until I gathered into a narrow compass the available data that I realized the extent to which this question of suitable gradients dominated the direction of the various rows. I believe it to be the determining feature, and that we need seek no further clue to their orientation.

How far this principle of site selection was justly followed may be judged from the fact that Drizzlecombe (17-18-19), on what by these criteria is the most perfect site, presents to the modern eye the most perfect of the groups; and Merrivale (27-28-29), on a site but little less in accord with the same criteria, would be classed second in order by modern standards.

But evidence is not lacking that the search for the ideal was not always successful, not always perhaps pursued with due diligence; while the Stall Moor-Green Hill row (1) demonstrates that Dartmoor had no room for a monument on such a scale as a row $2\frac{1}{8}$ miles in length, except at the sacrifice of perfection.

The vagaries of that row have broken the hearts of the astronomers. At its south end it leaves the retaining circle on Stall Moor and takes a direction N. $1\frac{1}{2}°$ E.; meeting a little cross valley it diverges to N. $20\frac{1}{2}°$ E. in order to cross it approximately at right angles; then for a short space it points N. $14\frac{1}{2}°$ E., and following this swings back to a trifle W. of true N. to make a crossing of the River Erme at a point where that stream can be intersected at right angles, since otherwise the river and the row would be involved in a struggle for the same site; from the crossing the row proceeds in much the same direction, to cross the Redlake, also at right angles; it then continues its course up the slopes of Green Hill for 770 ft, its direction being N. 10° W. At this point its line was far out of that necessary to close on the summit of Green Hill, and another diversion had to be made to N. 11° E., which completed the course. The direction of the row from end to end is N. 2° W.

In making this statement I have purposely omitted some minor deviations in direction, in the interest of simplicity; had I introduced them the irregularities would have been greater. Add to the divergences in alignment the variations in gradient which arise from the various hills and ridges crossed or climbed, and one may judge why really long rows must be rare on Dartmoor.

ORIENTATION

I once thought that the general trend of the rows lay in the north-east quadrant, differing in this from the orientation of the kistvaens which lies toward the north-west quadrant.

As regards the rows this was an error, such as may well arise when one writes too soon, and on incomplete knowledge. It may be an error to write too soon, but delay may mean that one does not write at all. I do not know that this is a sufficient excuse.

Now that the evidence is fairly complete the question of orientation seems to have taken a purely geographical significance. Perhaps one should have guessed as much from the frequent minor irregularities in

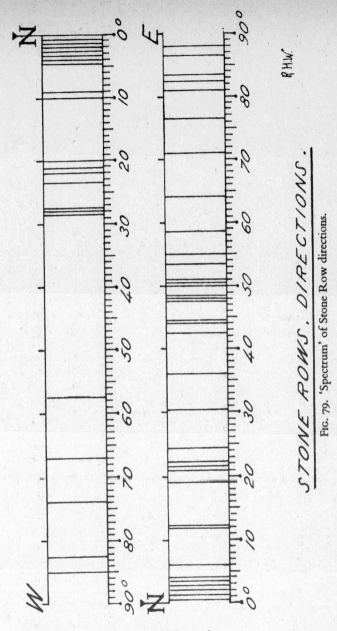

FIG. 79. 'Spectrum' of Stone Row directions.

The following corrections should be made:
The line for $57\frac{1}{2}°$ w. (above) should be transferred to $57\frac{1}{2}°$ E. (below)
,, ,, ,, $10°$ w. (above) ,, ,, ,, $10°$ E. (below)
,, ,, ,, 6 E. (below) ,, ,, ,, $10°$ E. (below)
,, ,, ,, $0\frac{1}{2}$ w. (above) ,, ,, ,, $4\frac{1}{2}°$ E. (below)
A line for $11°$ w. should be added (above).   (ED.)

individual rows, culminating in the divergencies of the Stall Moor-
Green Hill example.

None the less there are those who will rightly wish to know full
details as to the direction taken by the rows. To shorten the statement
I have prepared a diagram on which the several directions are marked
(Fig. 79). This shows that within the limits N. 4° E. and N. 4°-45′ W.
lie the directions of fourteen rows, these I call the north group, none
being 5° distant from that direction. Thirty-three rows point farther
to the east, and thirteen point farther to the west. Brailsford (1938,
p. 446) states that the rows tend to run approximately east and west,
which is an obvious error; but adds: "In other cases the direction
seems to be governed by the form of the ground," with which, in
greater detail, I agree. Neither of us is, it would seem, prepared to
attribute any ritual significance to direction.

The fact that sites were dictated by geographical conditions does not
necessitate that all the members of a group should have the same direction of length. The Shuggledown rows (34-35-36-37-38-39) are a
definite group, although on opposite slopes of a hill; their directions of
length are N. 1°-40′ W., N. 21°-15′ W., N. 28°-30′ W., N. 3° W., N., and
N. 11° W., divergence which still leaves north as the nearest cardinal
point. But at Merrivale (27-28-29), in consequence of the greater
breadth of the approximately level ground, a greater divergence was
possible, the bearings being: N. 83°-30′ E., N. 81° E., and N. 24°-15′ E.

THE ASSOCIATION OF BARROWS AND ROWS

Forty-four of the Dartmoor rows include barrows as integral parts
of their construction.

The rule is that the barrow is placed at the higher end of the row;
this rule is subject to occasional exceptions, which will be dealt with
later. No question of compass bearing is involved; the higher end, be
it north, south, east or west, receives the barrow. Thus, in the Shuggledown group, rows 34 and 36 lie on the north side of the summit of the
hill, and their barrows are at the south ends. Row 37 lies on the south
slope of the hill; it has a menhir at the south end, so that the barrow,
which by analogy we may assume it to have had, must have been at
the north end. Taking all the Dartmoor rows which have each one
barrow, in thirty-one instances it is at the higher end; in four cases the
ground is so far level that it is difficult to say which is the higher end,
except by the use of a level. In one instance (1) the ground falls from
either end of the row to a central dip, and there is a barrow at either
end. There are three examples of barrows at either end, where the
result is a barrow at the higher and another at the lower end. Of these
cases one is especially interesting, Glasscombe Ball (61): here there is a
barrow at the higher end, from which runs a double row; this row is
abruptly replaced by a single row in the same direction and that, at

the lower end of the composite row, terminates in another barrow. Thus we have a barrow which is the starting point of a double row which runs some distance and abruptly changes character, becoming a single row, which continuing the same direction, ends in a barrow. There is no doubt that the double part of the alignment was always double, and the single part was always single. The spacing along the row is also different. In' the double part the average distance centre to centre of the stones is 5 ft 5 in., and in the single part it is 7 ft 5 in. The arrangement certainly suggests an original row with a barrow at the higher end, the row being double; to which at a later date was added a length of single row, terminating in a barrow at the lower end.

It may be that in all the rows with barrows at each end the second barrow is a later addition.

There are other exceptions to the rule, Shuggledown (38), Challacombe (46), Laughter (50). In the first and last of these the higher end of the row is terminated by a large menhir, so that, if there were a barrow it must have been at the lower end, where there is now no terminal. In each instance there is some evidence in favour of the view that there was formerly a barrow at the lower end, the stones of the row, near that end, being distinctly above average in size, a feature common as the barrow is approached. If this is so, then Shuggledown may be another example of later addition; row G having been first constructed, terminating in the Longstone, and a further row added south of the Longstone and terminating to the south in a barrow. Rows 38 and 50 have both been badly robbed by newtake wall builders.

Challacombe (46) is more like Laughter (50). The row terminates at its highest point in a large blocking-stone, this is to the south; to the north the end of the row has been wholly removed in the formation of a gully-working for tin. Yet it must have been here, at the lower end, that the barrow, if any, stood. Whatever the explanation, these are three undoubted exceptions to the rule; unless we are to believe that no barrows were ever associated with either of the three rows.

There are two instances of barrows interrupting the course of a row, Merrivale (28) and Yar Tor (49).

CONCLUSIONS

Barrows occur in such number as integral parts of rows as to leave no doubt the rows are sepulchral monuments.

The orientation of rows is so varied, and so intimately connected with physical conditions that it can have no ritual significance.

The intended length of a row largely determined the selection of the site. But the Long Row on the Erme (1) is sufficient evidence that the builders were prepared to sacrifice perfection to length when they had reason to desire the latter; some details of other of the longer rows support this.

Rows as we now find them were not always completed in one operation; where there are two terminal barrows one is probably a later addition. And where either a barrow or a menhir breaks the length of a row it was probably once a terminal (I exclude the Merrivale example, where the row distinctly widens out to embrace the barrow).

While the rows are undoubtedly sepulchral monuments, the underlying idea which gave them value in the minds of their builders remains unknown; no study of detail has afforded a clue.

Addendum (ED.)

WEST DART (CHERRYBROOK)

54A. *Great Whiten Tor*

A ruined double row, originally recorded by the D.E.C. (*T.D.A.*, Vol. 30, pp. 98–9), and doubtless omitted above by an oversight. Reexamined by G. M. S. in 1952. O.S., xcix, sw., position of upper end lon. 3°-57'-3", lat. 50°-35'-19". Altitude 1,645-1,607 O.D. Direction of length N. 13½° E., the main part pointing direct towards the peak of Great Whiten Tor, i.e. to the present summit cairn (in the opposite direction it is in line with Littaford Tor summit). The slope of the ground is 1 in 8·6.

This is a genuine row and conforms with the author's criteria, although the original positions of both ends are now uncertain and there is no trace of associated barrow. Its precise orientation towards the summit of the tor on whose slope it stands looks significant. The long axes of those stones which still stand are notably orientated in the direction of the row.

The minimum certain length, taken from a pair of prominent erect stones, which appear at first sight to mark the southern (lower) end, to the most northerly surviving pair, was measured as 264½ ft; but the row may well have extended another 15 ft uphill, and about 50 ft downhill a pair of stones sunk in damp ground is in true alignment. The length of 330 ft recorded originally is thus accounted for. Loss of stones at the lower end to newtake walls is suspected, and the original length may well have been greater.

Fallen stones are not readily distinguished from natural surface stones which become frequent near the north end, and which lie at various angles, but the total count in 1952—15 stones on the west side and 10 on the east—agrees with the original count. The spacing is irregular.

The row tends to deviate to eastward of its main alignment near its upper end. It is marked on the O.S., but placed over 200 ft NW. of its true position.

This is the second highest row on Dartmoor, exceeded only by its distant neighbour on Conies Down (55). It is also the second steepest, its gradient being surpassed only by that of the Assacombe row (43).

ERME *(cont.)*

3. *Burford Down (cont.)*

Mr. Hamlyn Parsons has recently found that this row continues on the level beyond the newtake wall, as far as a robust prostrate stone, partly embedded, which appears to have been a terminal menhir. At some time this stone has been split with a drill, and is now in two pieces. Entire it was between 9 and 10 ft long. The length of the row to the setting of this stone has been measured as 1647 ft.

REFERENCES

Brailsford, J. W., 1938. Bronze Age stone monuments of Dartmoor. *Antiquity* Vol. 12, pp. 444–63.

Worth, R. Hansford, 1903–18. The stone rows of Dartmoor, Part VI. *Trans. Devon. Assn.*, Vol. 35 (1903), pp. 426–9; Part VII, Vol. 38 (1906), pp. 535–7; Part VIII, Vol. 40 (1908), pp. 281–2; Part IX, Vol. 43 (1911), pp. 348–9; Part X, Vol. 50 (1918), pp. 402–4.

Worth, R. Hansford, 1932. The prehistoric monuments of Scorhill, Buttern Hill, and Shuggledown (Shoveldown). *Trans. Devon. Assn.*, Vol. 64, pp. 279–87.

Worth, R. Hansford, 1941a. Dartmoor: 1788–1808. *Trans. Devon. Assn.*, Vol. 73, pp. 203–25.

Worth, R. Hansford, 1941b. Retaining-circles associated with stone rows, Dartmoor. *Trans. Devon. Assn.*, Vol. 73, pp. 227–38.

Worth, R. N., 1892–96. The stone rows of Dartmoor. *Trans. Devon. Assn.*, Vol. 24 (1892), pp. 387–417; Part II, Vol. 25 (1893), pp. 541–6; Part III, Vol. 26 (1894), pp. 296–307; Part IV, Vol. 27 (1895), pp. 437–42; Part V, Vol. 28 (1896), pp. 712–13.

THE DARTMOOR STONE CIRCLES

A STONE CIRCLE, in western archaeology, is to be distinguished from the hut-circle, which is the foundation of a dwelling, and the retaining circle, which is an adjunct of the grave, associated with the cairn or barrow (see pp. 182–191).

The purpose of the hut-circle is fully understood, and the associations of the retaining circle are known, but not its ritual intent, if any. The stone circle, according to our terminology, is larger than either the hut or any but a few of the retaining circles, unfitted by structure for use as a habitation, unassociated, as far as can be ascertained, with graves. There is some evidence that large fires were lit within the stone circles, but no evidence as to the purpose of those fires. To avoid all suggestion of knowledge which is not ours, we have taken the trivial name 'stone circle', and applied it as a specific name to those circles of stone which are neither huts, retaining circles, nor pounds.

Characteristic examples are the circles at Brisworthy (*T.D.A.*, Vol. 35, p. 99), Buttern Hill, Scorhill, and Sherberton, and the 'Grey Wethers'. Others survive at Whitemoor, Fernworthy, Down Ridge, Merrivale, and Langstone Moor.

SCORHILL CIRCLE

Scorhill circle has long been known, and often described, but, as often happens, the descriptions have gathered more each from the other than has always accorded with accuracy, and where they have not borrowed they are inconsistent. As far as I know the circle has never been carefully planned and the plan published, an omission the more surprising in that it has been fully recognized as one of our principal Dartmoor monuments, indeed, most writers have agreed with Rowe in the importance which they have attributed to it. ("This is by far the finest example of the rude but venerable shrines of Druidical worship in Devonshire.") It is certainly a fine circle, well placed on ground which slopes to the south and west, and commanding an extensive view of the valleys of the North Teign and Wallabrook. It has suffered much spoliation, but has been spared from the hand of the restorer.

Rowe, in the *Perambulation*, says that but twenty stones were standing, several having fallen. Croker, writing in 1851 three years later, says that twenty-seven stones formed the circle, of which several were prostrate. Ormerod states that in 1858, twenty-nine stones were erect, and two prostrate. Murray's Handbook, 1865, sets the tale at twenty-six standing stones, and six fallen, and it is to be noted that Murray gives the accurate diameter of the circle, 88 ft. Chudleigh (first edition ?1891) reports twenty-three stones as then standing, but does not say how many lay fallen; his sketch appears to show seven. Brooking Rowe, as editor of the third edition of his uncle's work, states that, in 1896, twenty-four stones were standing, and eight had fallen.

It is very difficult to account for these discrepancies, one can not even say that the record shows a progressive loss of standing stones, either by robbery or collapse. Nor is there at the present any difficulty in discriminating between the standing and the fallen. The matter is further complicated if we refer to the one descriptive reference which appears in the *T.D.A.*: Spence Bate, Vol. 4, 1871, p. 514. There we find the entry: "There are thirty-one stones, all of which are in position excepting two which have fallen. *Rowe says that there are thirty-seven, two of which have fallen.*" The italics are mine. Pursuing this statement, I find that, in the first volume of the *P.I.*, Rowe, as the result of investigations made in 1827–8, stated that the stones were "thirty-seven in number, *ten* of which are fallen". It is traditional of certain groups elsewhere in Britain that no two counts can be made agree, a tradition which may be better founded than I had heretofore credited.

I have gathered in the following table, all the data which I can find on my shelves; the list is certainly not complete.

Date	Authority	Stones erect	Stones fallen	Diameter feet	Probable number of stones when complete
1827–8	S. Rowe	27	10	90	—
1848	S. Rowe	20	—	100	—
1851	Croker	Erect and fallen 27		—	—
1858	Ormerod	29	2	90	51
1865	Murray	26	6	88	55
1876	Spence Bate	29	2	—	—
1878	R. N. Worth	—	—	90	—
1879	Lukis and Andrews	24	8	—	—
1889	Page	25	several	85	—
1891	Chudleigh	23	?7	72	—
1896	Brooking Rowe	24	8	90	52
1900	Baring Gould	24	8	92	—
1909	Crossing	24	8	90	—
1931	The Author	23	7	88	65 to 70

I conclude that twenty-four stones were standing in 1879, and that for many years that had probably been the number.

A stone next to and east of the cart track on the southern circumference of the circle, is shown by Lukis and Andrews as standing, but "leaning in": this has since fallen and is easily identified. It would appear to have fallen before Chudleigh visited the circle, so that from 1891, at least, there have been but twenty-three standing stones. This leaning stone added to the stones shown by Lukis and Andrews as fallen should bring the total of fallen stones to nine certain, and one queried; but I cannot accept some of the stones which they plan as being other than casuals, never involved in the circle.

Their survey also shows that the outlying stone to the south of the circle, which I mark as having the end cut off, had already in 1879 been so mutilated. Upon their survey the north point has been reversed, and indicates the south.

I believe that Brooking Rowe took his information in 1896 from Messrs. Lukis and Andrews, and that Baring-Gould and Crossing copied him.

I am indebted to the Society of Antiquaries for the opportunity of quoting from the survey made by the Rev. W. C. Lukis and Col. Andrews, the Society having very kindly supplied me with a tracing of his plan.

We may call yet another witness, Williams, the artist who illustrated the first edition of Rowe's *Perambulation*. Williams was rather artistic than accurate, in such matters as scenery, or the precise form of a stone, but he is likely to have shown just as many stones as he could see. He shows twenty-one stones standing: it is conceivable that one or two were obscured by those drawn, but hardly probable that six were so hidden.

Rowe makes the assertion that the two tallest stones yet erect stood at nearly opposite points of the circle, and that statement has constantly been repeated. The stones in question are easily identified, and are still erect; but they are not diametrically placed. The angle which they subtend at the centre of the circle is 146°-30'-0" and not 180°. None the less, I have quite recently been told that the opposition of these two stones must have some hidden meaning. And, while there is some ground for supposing that the present tallest stone has always occupied that prominence, it is by no means certain that among the fallen stones and those removed there have not been successful rivals to that which is now the second in height.

The dimensions of the stones now standing are as follows, starting with the tallest and proceeding clockwise. The dimensions are given in the following order: height above ground, width tangential to the circle, thickness radial to the circle.

8 ft 2 in., 2 ft 2 in., 3 ft; at 2 ft 6 in. above ground 2 ft 3½ in., 1 ft 7 in./

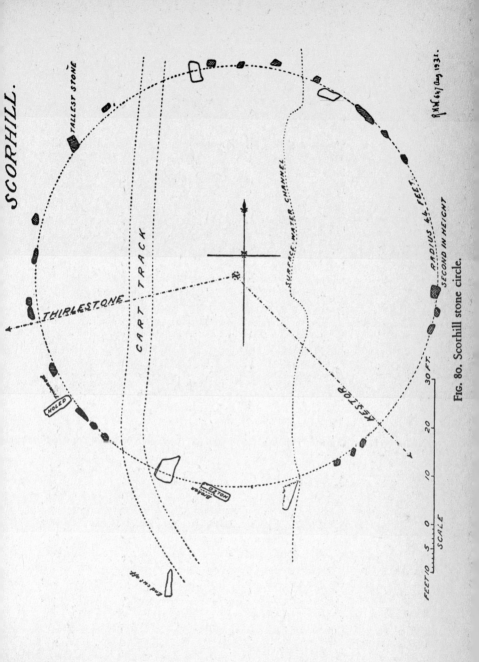

SCORHILL.

TALLEST STONE

SECOND IN HEIGHT

RADIUS 44 FEET.

A.M.W. 6¼ Aug. 1931.

THIRLESTONE

CART TRACK

SURFACE WATER CHANNEL.

HOLED

PROCKEN

HOLED

BROKEN

KESTOR

End cut off

FEET 10 5   0   10   20   30 FT.

SCALE

Fig. 80. Scorhill stone circle.

3 ft 7 in., 3 ft., 11 in., / 4 ft, 2 ft, 1 ft 3 in. / 3 ft 3 in., 1 ft 7 in., 1 ft 2 in. /
2 ft 7 in., 2 ft 3 in., 1 ft 1 in. / 2 ft 10 in., 1 ft 2 in., 1 ft 1 in. / 4 ft 2 in.,
5 ft, 1 ft / 3 ft 11 in., 2 ft 2½ in., 1 ft 4 in. / 3 ft 7 in., 2 ft 6 in., 9 in. /
5 ft 7 in., 2 ft 7 in., 1 ft 7 in., the second highest / 3 ft 6 in., 2 ft 3 in.,
9 in. / 3 ft 7 in., 1 ft 11 in., 10 in. / 2 ft 8 in., 1 ft 6 in., 9 in. / 2 ft 11 in.,
1 ft 4 in., 8 in. / 3 ft 4 in., 1 ft 9 in., 11 in. / 3 ft 8 in., 1 ft 8 in., 10 in. /
3 ft, 1 ft 9 in., 10 in. / 2 ft 10 in., 3 ft 6 in., 7 in. / 4 ft 11 in., 2 ft 6 in.,
1 ft / 4 ft 2 in., 2 ft 10 in., 8 in. / 3 ft 2 in., 1 ft 7 in., 10 in. / 4 ft 7 in.,
3 ft 2 in., 10 in. / 4 ft 8 in., 3 ft 2 in., 10 in.

The nearest formal circle which will approximate to the actual
setting of the stones has a diameter of 88 ft, and the deviations from
this ideal are but slight, in fact the circle is unusually near geometrical
truth.

In addition to the fallen stones, but little displaced, and one which
has been somewhat removed from the circle, it is locally recognized
that other original members of the monument have found utilitarian
use not far away. There is a pot-water leat to Scorhill and other farms
which contours the hillside to the west and south of the circle, and at its
nearest is less than 60 yds distant. Here it crosses a mire, and it has been
found difficult to maintain its lower bank, with the result that the circle
has at some time been raided to provide stones to retain the water.
The stones are all columnar, and beyond doubt the local view that they
came from the circle is correct. The following are measurements of
the more important of these: 4 ft 9 in, 1 ft 6 in. / 7 ft 10 in., 1 ft 8 in.,
1 ft 1 in., has been split off from a larger block of the same length/
5 ft 5 in., 1 ft 2 in., 1 ft 2 in., also appears to have been split off a larger
piece / 6 ft, 2 ft 7 in., 1 ft? / 4 ft 9 in., 1 ft 11 in., 1 ft / and several smaller
broken pieces.

In addition to this direct robbery, three of the fallen stones yet remaining at the circle have been attacked; one lying outside has been
shortened, by how much cannot be said, but its original length must
have exceeded 6 ft; two have been holed for splitting longitudinally,
off one a piece has been taken, and the other has also been trimmed.
The perpetrator of these last outrages was caught in the act, his desire
was for gate-posts, but he had to obtain them elsewhere.

A rough cart track crosses the circle, leading to the fords on the
Wallabrook and the North Teign. This track now passes through the
western half of the area; roughly parallel to it, but in the eastern half, is
a surface-water channel, which represents a former track. Why a route
should be taken through the circle is difficult to conceive. The one point
of interest is that the water channel has cut well below the surface and
eveals nothing but the natural subsoil.

The illustrations which I submit are: a plan of the circle, surveyed
on the 6 and 7 August 1931 (Fig. 80); Pl. 49, a view of the circle, looking westward; Pl. 50A, a view of the tallest stone; and Pl. 50B, the stolen

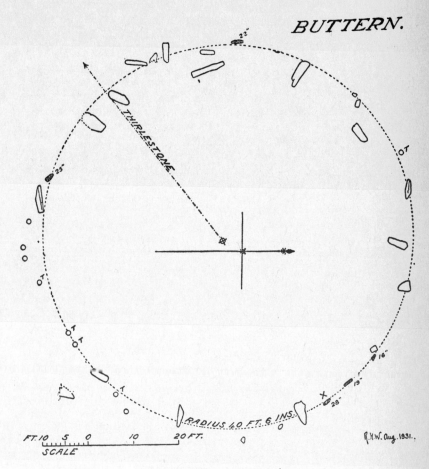

BUTTERN.

THIRLESTONE

22"

25"

T

16"

19"

X 28"

RADIUS 40 FT. 6 INS.

FT.10 5 0 10 20 FT.

SCALE

R.H.W. Aug. 1931.

FIG. 81. Buttern stone circle.

stones in the side of the leat. In the plan those stones which are still erect have been indicated by hatching.

BUTTERN HILL CIRCLE

At the foot of the western slope of Buttern Hill lies another circle, slightly smaller than that on Scorhill. Here five stones are still erect, nineteen have fallen, triggers give clear indication of the position formerly occupied by five stones now lost, and there are some doubtful, and small, stones. The tallest member now standing is but 28 in. above ground, and of a curious shape, which seems to be purely natural in origin. The gatepost merchant has been here also, and some of the fallen stones owe their present shape to his interference, being now more columnar than before his attack. The nearest equivalent true circle would have a diameter of 81 ft.

In 1931 a great part of the turf within the circle was skimmed off for fuel, in accordance with an unfortunate habit which prevails in the Chagford district, where little true peat-cutting is now done. Although this habit disfigures the moor, and destroys pasture, it has one slight advantage. It reveals the worked flints that so often lie immediately under the turf; and this, and not the greater prevalence of implements, has probably led to the marked predominance in our museums of flints from the north and east of Dartmoor. So far nothing has been found as the result of this operation within Buttern Circle.

A Plan of Buttern Hill Circle is given in Fig. 81.

SHERBERTON CIRCLE

Sherberton Circle occupies a commanding position on the crest of a ridge at an elevation of about 1,100 ft above mean sea level (Pl. 51A).

There are nine stones still erect and in place, one stone erect but probably slightly displaced, and two fallen stones.

The stones which are still erect and in place are distributed over about one-half of the circumference, from somewhat west of north, around by the east to somewhat east of south. Taking all the stones into account about two-thirds of the circumference are occupied.

The stones in place are small, two reach a height of 2 ft 3 in., two are only 1 ft 4 in. in height; the average of the largest dimensions on plan is approximately 2 ft.

It is obvious that there are many gaps in the circle; and the needs of the builders of the closely adjoining stone-fences suffice to explain these. Indeed one stone-fence, of early date, cuts off a segment of the circle to the west, and beyond this fence the original circumference is unmarked by any remaining member of the circle. But at A, Fig. 82, the largest stone still standing, which reaches 4 ft 10 in. in height, and is about 4 ft 6 in. in width, would appear to be a member of the

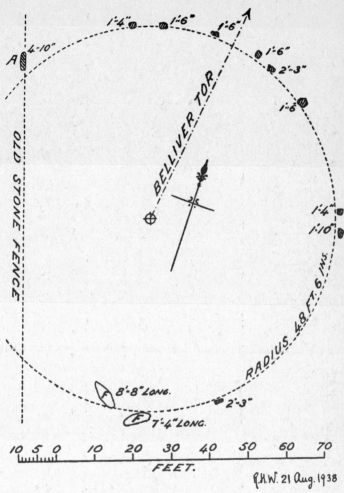

FIG. 82. Sherberton stone circle.

circle which has been slightly displaced to accord with the alignment of the old stone-fence of which it now forms a part.

The two fallen stones are 8 ft 8 in. and 7 ft 4 in. in length respectively.

The diameter of the true circle which most nearly accords to the intiernal circumference is 97 ft. There is no trace of any barrow or carn, and it appears to be a wholly isolated monument.

This circle has long been known and is shown on the first edition of the 6 inch O.S., cvii, sw., Devon; lon. 3°-55′-13½″, lat. 50°-32′-31″

DOWN RIDGE CIRCLE

Down Ridge Circle lies on a north slope at an elevation of about 1,225 ft above mean sea level. There are but four stones still erect and in place. There are three fallen stones on the circumference; and there is one stone which is neither earth-fast nor fallen, but which rests against two of the erect members of the circle, this seems certainly the result of interference in years long subsequent to erection. The whole group, erect and fallen, occupies but a quadrant. Here, as at Sherberton, there has been much loss by robbery, and here too the walls of the adjacent enclosures supply sufficient explanation of the theft.

The stones are relatively large, slab-like and not columnar. The four erect stones stand respectively 3 ft 2 in., 3 ft 9 in., 3 ft 6 in., and 5 ft 9 in. in height. The largest measures 9 ft 9 in. in width, 10 in. in thickness, and 5 ft 9 in. in height (Pl. 51B). On the plan, Fig. 83, the stone which leans against its neighbours is marked B.

The diameter of the true circle which most nearly accords to the internal circumference is 81 ft 2 in.; there is no trace of any barrow or cairn, and it appears to be a wholly isolated monument.

This circle was first noted by Burnard, and is one of the many additions which he made to our knowledge of Dartmoor. It is not shown on the first edition of the 6 inch O.S., but appears in later editions. The sheet is cvii, sw., Devon, and the location lon. 3°-53′-52″, lat. 50°-31′-56½″.

In general, stone circles have the component stones placed some little distance apart, each from each. The spacing may be irregular, and the irregularity does not always appear to be due to subsequent disturbance; but it is unusual that any stone should touch its neighbour. There are two which come near contact, on the west part of the circumference of Scorhill Circle.

At Down Ridge there are four stones, two standing and two fallen, which must originally have made a continuous length of circumference amounting to at least 24 ft at and near the letter B on the plan (Fig. 83). This portion is so unlike what is usually found that it raises the question whether this is not really a retaining circle around a grave. The matter could possible be settled by excavation; there is certainly no superficial evidence of a grave.

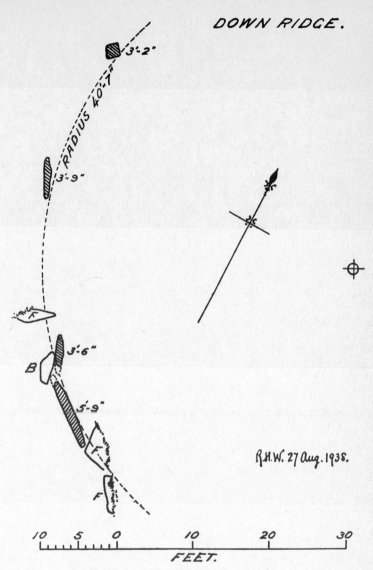

DOWN RIDGE.

RADIUS 40'·7"

3'·2"

3'·9"

B

3'·6"

5'·9"

F.

F.

R.H.W. 27 Aug. 1938.

10   5   0   10   20   30
╷╷╷╷╷┤╷╷╷╷┤   │   │   │
              FEET.

FIG. 83. Down Ridge stone circle (remains).

The effect of robbery from the circles is to remove the stones of most useful size, leaving on the one hand the smaller as being unworthy of removal, and the largest as being difficult. Thus, where there has been much theft, the remaining stones may be a very misleading sample. In this connexion it might be recorded that when the huts and enclosures on Shapley Common were swept away to the roads, almost the sole survivor of the group was a hut-circle, the stones of which were most unusually large.

THE GREY WETHERS

These two circles, situated on the crest of a ridge eastward of Sitta-ford Tor, are probably among the more familiar of the Dartmoor stone monuments. They have been subjected to 'restoration'. An account of the original condition was given by Burnard in 1891.

When preparing the table on p. 260, I found the following choice of figures for the diameters of the north and south circles of the Grey Wethers:

Authority		North Circle ft	South Circle ft
Burnard	..	100	105
Chudleigh	..	81 abt.	81 abt.
Crossing	..	100	105 abt.
Falcon ..	..	100 abt.	over 100
Murray	..	120 abt.	120 abt.
Rowe	..	120 abt.	120 abt.

It is true that the statements were mostly qualified as being approxi-mate, and that Chudleigh's '27 yards' may have been a misprint for '37 yards', although it occurs in both editions of his book; none the less there was no authentic figure to be derived from the collection.

Personally I was hampered by the fact that I had made no survey of these circles before their 'restoration', but, happily, the Rev. W. C. Lukis, F.S.A., had, in 1879, made such a survey, and the Society of Antiquaries of London has very kindly supplied me with a copy, with permission for its use. It is only by complete survey that the diameters of these circles can be accurately determined. I have checked Lukis's plotting, and find that the true circles which most nearly accord to the circumferences have the following diameters—for the North Circle 103½ ft, and for the South Circle 116½ ft. The distance between the centres of the circles is 130 ft, less a few inches. See Fig. 84.

In 1879 the North Circle consisted of nine standing, and six fallen stones, and three holes were traceable; from which stones had been removed. Burnard, in 1891, gives nine standing, seven fallen, and one almost wholly buried.

The South Circle, in 1879, consisted of seven standing, and twenty fallen, of which two were nearly buried. Burnard, in 1891, gives seven

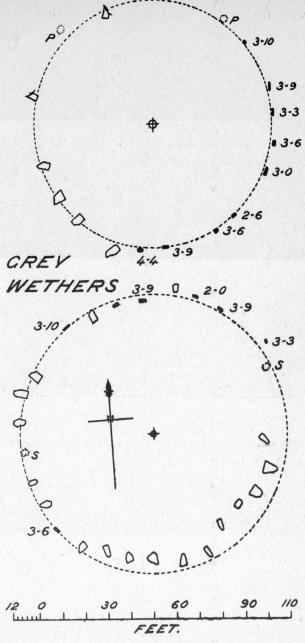

FIG. 84. The Grey Wethers.

standing stones, and twenty fallen, of which three were almost wholly buried. Stones have certainly been removed from both circles, but it would appear that in the north the original spacing was 11 ft centre to centre, and approximately the same in the south; this would give twenty-nine as the full original number in the north, and thirty-three in the south. If these were the numbers the precise mean distances from centre to centre would have been, North Circle 11·17 ft, South Circle 11·06 ft, respectively.

The tallest erect stone in the North Circle was 4 ft 4 in. in length above ground, 2 ft 9 in. in width, and from 1 ft to 1 ft 6 in. in thickness at base; the shortest erect stone was 2 ft 6 in. in height. Both these stones as they show above ground are approximately rectangular, with level tops.

In the South Circle the tallest erect stone was 3 ft 10 in. in height and 2 ft 7 in. × 1 ft at the base; the shortest stone stood no more than 2 ft in 1879, and Burnard says 2 ft 7 in. in 1891, which is possible.

There were no fallen stones in either circle of which it could be said that they probably stood higher than 4 ft 8 in.

It has been sought to argue that some of the stones are rectangular by reason of having been hand-dressed. For this there is no evidence, and the shape is merely an incident of the natural jointing of the granite. Similar stones are to be found on the slopes of Sittaford Tor, among the clitter.

COMPARATIVE SIZES OF CIRCLES

It may be useful to collect a statement of the diameters of the Stone Circles of Dartmoor. In the following list those figures which are starred have not the same precision as the majority, by reason in some instances of the circles having been 'restored', without any adequate survey having been first made. It is certain, however, that no error of consequence occurs in the list.

Grey Wethers, South Circle	..		116½	ft
	North Circle	..	103½	ft
Sherberton	..	..	96	ft
Scorhill	..	..	88	ft
Buttern Hill	..	..	81	ft
Down Ridge	..	..	81	ft
Brisworthy	..	..	79	ft
Cosdon, Whitemoor[1]	..		66*	ft
Fernworthy[2]	..	..	64½	ft
Merrivale[3]	..	..	62	ft
Langstone Moor..	..	..	67*	ft

All the unstarred figures represent internal diameters.

[1] See p. 266.   [2] See p. 222.   [3] Fig. 116.

The great number of retaining circles are much smaller than any stone circles, but the largest retaining circle, the outer member of the fourfold group on Yellowmead (Pl. 48), is larger than the smaller stone circles, being 65 ft in internal diameter.

AN UNUSUAL TYPE OF STONE CIRCLE IN THE PLYM VALLEY

Shortly after the publication of my paper on the Moorland Plym (*P.I.*, 1890, Vol. 10) I found on Willings Walls Warren a stone circle which is unlike any other circle known on Dartmoor. I showed the circle to the Rev. H. H. Breton, who published a somewhat inaccurate description in Part I of his booklet on *Beautiful Dartmoor*, p. 48 of the first edition, and p. 54 of the second. In especial he says that there are six clusters of stone, whereas there are but four certain clusters, with doubtful indications of a fifth, although the fifth did most probably exist at one time.

A reeve,[1] or stone bank, crosses the Hentor Brook at a point 400 yds above the Lee Moor Leat, its general direction approximately NE. by N.; north of Hentor Brook it forms the hedge of the old Hentor Farm; south of the Brook it is an isolated bank. At approximately 500 yds from the Brook, to the SE. by S., it is touched on the north side by the circumference of the circle referred to.

Turning back along the course of the reeve toward Hentor Brook, at a distance of 330 ft from the circle, one passes a kistvaen which lies 170 ft away from the reeve to the right (Fifty-first Barrow Report, *T.D.A.*, Vol. 64, p. 115, where the circle is also briefly mentioned). At 200 ft farther along the reeve, and at a distance from it of about 50 ft to the left, lies another kistvaen (Nineteenth Barrow Report, *T.D.A.*, Vol. 32, p. 49, as Lee Moor). We may describe the circle and the kistvaens as the Lee Moor - Willings Walls Warren group, and thus emphasize the tendency to grouping of sepulchral remains which is found, not only in the Plym Valley, but also on Dartmoor in general.

The circle is not shown on any edition of the Ordnance Survey; it should be found on 6 inch, Devon, cxii, SE., in lon. 3°-59'-57", lat. 50°-28'-7½".

Fig. 85 in the text supplies a plan of the circle, the four undoubted groups of stones being marked respectively A, B, C and D; while the words 'Large Stone' indicate a stone in the reeve which may be a displaced remnant of the fifth. It will be seen that, for a distance of 60 ft the reeve interferes with the circumference of the circle; and somewhere in this length the fifth group is most probably merged. The nearest true circle approximating to the actual internal circumference has a diameter of 137 ft 6 in.

---

[1] See Crossing (1909), p. 32, for discussion on Dartmoor 'reaves', which were old boundaries of one sort or another. (ED.)

WILLINGS WALLS.

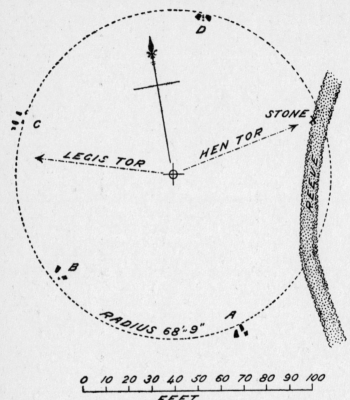

FIG. 85. Plan of Willings Walls Circle.

There is no trace of a barrow within the circle, nor is there any trench around it.

Plans of the individual groups of stone are given in Fig. 86 in the text, as A, B, C and D. There is nothing in these plans to suggest that the groups were ever kistvaens, nor does examination on the ground afford any suggestion to that effect. The groups have one feature in common; in each two stones are clearly outstanding and exceed the other members of the group in size. In each these two stones have their longer axes set approximately radially to the circle. It is perhaps desirable to qualify this general statement by noting that in group A the third member, although distinctly smaller than the other two, is not so markedly less as are the minor stones in the other groups; and that

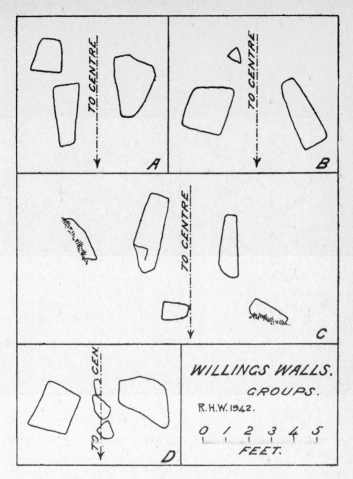

FIG. 86. Details of Groups, Willings Walls Circle.

in group D one of the larger stones does not now point distinctly radially to the centre of the circle, but this is a fallen stone and has been subject to disturbance. Plates 51 and 52, A, A'; B, B', C and D give views of the stone groups. Of these A is taken looking out from the centre of the circle, A' is a view of the same looking a little west of north; B is a view of group B taken looking out from the centre of the circle, B' is a view of the same looking approximately north; C and D are views of the groups indicated by those letters, in either case taken looking out from the centre of the circle.

These views and the plans should serve to convey as much information as would an examination of the circle on the ground. I confess that, after my long knowledge of the monument, and my recent survey, I have no suggestion to make as to its nature or intent, beyond the purely negative conclusion that the stone groups have never been kistvaens. Its association with the two kistvaens which are not far distant may have significance; in the same way that the association of stone rows with graves must be felt to contain some part of the explanation of their intent.

It may be noted that if the full number of clusters was originally five, and they had been disposed at the points of a regular pentagon, their distance from centre to centre would have been, in round numbers, 80 ft. The actual distances are: A to B 80 ft, B to C 67 ft, C to D 89 ft (mean of B–C and C–D 78 ft). There remains sufficient space for: D to lost member 81 ft, and lost member to A 81 ft. It seems probable that the figure was originally five-sided.

THE DARTMOOR MENHIRS

THERE are on Dartmoor certain standing stones, unwrought, undoubtedly erected by man, and from their position in association with lines or circles of lesser standing stones, or in isolation, presumedly of significance at the time of their erection.

Such stones have been variously called 'Menhirs', 'Longstones', 'Standing Stones' and 'Rock Pillars'. They are by no means peculiar either to Dartmoor or to Devon.

It seems desirable to discriminate between such standing stones, which are marked by their relative dimensions and special position, and those which form the mass of such remains as Stone Rows and Stone Circles. And this although the usage of some authors is to speak of every member of a row or circle as a menhir, whatever its actual size. In practice such discrimination involves no difficulty on Dartmoor, nor any niceties of artificial classification.

Of the various terms available, *Menhir* has the sanction of long usage, and the advantage that we can share it with the French antiquaries, although in France the tendency is to a less restricted use, and a stone row may be described as consisting wholly of menhirs, especially where the size of the stones is such that each may fairly be described as a 'longstone'.

The Dartmoor menhirs may be classified under two headings: (1) the isolated and 'self-sufficient', and (2) those associated with stone rows.

ISOLATED MENHIRS

There are few isolated menhirs on Dartmoor; two certain examples still stand, and two as to which some doubt is possible.

Beardown Man. The words 'Beardown Man' will be found on the 6 inch O.S., sheet xcix, sw., near Devils Tor, but the precise position is not marked; the menhir lies a little to the west of the Tor, at, approximately, lat. 50°-35'-55½", lon. 3°-59'-3".

This is a fine stone, remotely placed in wild surroundings, but its isolation is tempered by the presence of a cairn some 270 yds to the south, a further evidence of the former presence of prehistoric man. I cannot find that this cairn has ever previously been mentioned.

The menhir is 11 ft 4 in. in height, and its breadth being three times its thickness, its appearance varies much with the point of view. It may seem, as in Pl. 54, a mere needle of stone; or present itself with all the apparent massiveness due to its width, as in Pl. 55A.

The actual dimensions at ground level are N. 3 ft, W. 1 ft 6 in., S. 2ft 11 in., E. 11½ in. Its greatest width above ground level is 3 ft 3 in., and its greatest thickness above ground level is 1 ft 1½ in. on the one side, and 10½ in. on the other, giving a mean of 1 ft.

Harbourne Head. This menhir is situate about 500 ft west of the head of the Harbourne stream. It is not indicated on the first edition of the 6 inch O.S., sheet cxiv, SW. But a bench-mark is given (1123·7) which is in fact cut on the stone. Lat. 50°-28′-14″, lon. 3°-50′-12″.

In contrast to the Beardown Man, which tapers but slightly toward the top, the profile of this stone is triangular.

The length of the stone above ground is 8 ft 1 in., its width at ground level 3 ft 7 in., and its thickness 13 in. on the one side and 10 in. on the other. Its greatest width a little above ground level is 3 ft 3 in., and its greatest thickness 11 in. The stone leans considerably to the west. Two views are given, Pl. 55 B and C.

The *White Moor Stone* will be found marked on the 6 inch O.S., sheet lxxxix, NW., in lat. 50°-41′-17½″, lon. 3°-56′-5″.

This stone forms the boundary of the parishes of Lydford, South Tawton and Throwleigh, which raises the unfortunate question whether, in its present position, it has not always been a bound-stone; if so it may possibly have been stolen from the stone circle which lies 520 ft. away to the NNW. On the other hand the presence of that circle is favourable to the contrary view, that the stone is in its origin prehistoric, and has been adopted as a boundary by a later race.

I cannot find that I ever noted the measurements of this menhir; Crossing gives the approximate dimensions as 5 ft 6 in. in height, 3 ft in width and somewhat less than 6 in. thick. The largest stone in the circle I measured as 4 ft 7 in. high, 3 ft 4 in. wide and 7 in. thick; so that the dimensions are of the same order. My photograph, in itself far from successful, suggests that Crossing has underestimated the thickness of the White Moor Stone (Pl. 56A).

Lee Moor, the *Hanging Stone* or *Leaning Rock*. Not shown on the O.S., it lies within the area included in sheet cxviii, NE., location lat. 50°-27′-21½″, lon. 3°-59′-44″. Seven feet nine inches in length ofthis menhir stand above ground, but the vertical height does not exceed 6 ft 9 in. consequent on the stone being 38° out of the vertical, whence its alternative names.

The stone measures 3 ft 7 in. by 1 ft 10 in. at the base; incised on one face are the letters 'C B', from which it would appear to have been used as a bound, but I have been unable to ascertain what property it bounds. I believe this to be a genuine menhir of prehistoric date, but doubt has been cast upon this by its use as a bound-stone. It has to be remembered in this connexion that there are undoubted ancient menhirs which have similarly been adopted as boundary marks; for instance the 'Longstone' on Shuggle Down. Crossing curiously overlooks the pronounced lean of the rock and suggests that the name 'Hanging Stone' may imply the former existence of a dolmen. See Pl. 57A.

The *Hanging Stone* stands in an area where there are many remains of prehistoric times; 440 yds from it, to the south-east, is a chambered cairn; and 847 yds a little north of west, lies a stone row; these are the nearest members of a considerable group.

Elsewhere there are other stones, now fallen, which may have been 'isolated menhirs'. Any columnar stone of considerable length, exceeding, say, 9 ft, may be so claimed by the enthusiast; especially where it lies in ground otherwise free from surface stone. But such claims are too speculative for serious consideration.

I will mention perhaps the most hopeful of these doubtful cases. The boundary between the parishes of Harford and Ugborough, in the Erme Valley, is marked by a series of modern boundary stones; alongside one of these, on Piles Hill, lies what appeared to be a fallen menhir. We now have documentary evidence that this is so (see pp. 205 and 269).

Two other possible menhirs are to be found in the same watershed, on Beacon Plain, 500 yds east from Hangershell Rock. The more easterly of these stones is 18 ft 4 in. long, measures 19 in. by something over 26 in. at the base, and 27 in. by something over 19 in. at the centre of its length, while the other end is 15 in. by 11 in. in section. Fifty-seven yards away, on a bearing 6° south of west, lies another stone, 18 ft in length, 5 ft 6 in. wide at one end, and tapering to a blunt point. The stones are entirely isolated on a grass moor, where there are very few surface stones, and those relatively small. They have none of the appearance of surface boulders. And they are such as might have been brought from the clitter of Hangershell Rock. If they were menhirs, then they were the largest known on Dartmoor. The location of the eastern stone is O.S., cxix. SE., lat. 50°-25'-4¾", lon. 3°-53'-14".

MENHIRS DIRECTLY ASSOCIATED WITH OTHER REMAINS

On Dartmoor the only remains with which menhirs are found associated are the stone rows. In Cornwall central menhirs are found in some of the stone circles, but some doubt may be felt as to whether they formed part of the original monument. There is no trace of a central menhir in any Dartmoor stone circle.

Drizzlecombe, otherwise *Thrushelcombe*

At Drizzlecombe, in the valley of the Plym, is the most complete of all the groups of stone rows and barrows which are to be found on Dartmoor. There are three stone rows, not strictly parallel in direction, but having a general trend very near indeed to NE.–SW. At the north-east end of each row is a barrow; and at the south-west end of each a menhir. In the year 1889, when I surveyed this group, all the menhirs lay fallen. In July 1893 they were placed erect as they now stand.

On the plan of this group of remains the menhirs have been marked 'A', 'B' and 'C' respectively, starting from south-west and proceeding north-east. See Fig. 73 (p. 211).

Menhir A was measured as it lay in 1889; its length was 12 ft 6 in., it was 5 ft wide at the wider end, and 1 ft 5 in. wide at the narrower, its thickness approximately 1 ft 6 in. As erected, it stands 10 ft 6 in. in height, and measures at the base 5 ft 10 in. by 1 ft 3 in. It will be noted that at 2 ft from the end the stone is wider than at the end.

Menhir B, measured in 1889, was 9 ft 5 in. in length by 2 ft 9 in. in width. As erected it stands 7 ft 9 in. in height, and measures 2 ft 9 in. by 1 ft 2 in. at ground level.

Menhir C, measured in 1889, was 17 ft 10 in. long, 4 ft wide about 3 ft 6 in. from the wider end, but tapering to that end, and 2 ft 7 in. wide at the narrower end, its thickness about 1 ft 2 in. It now stands 14 ft in height and measures 4 ft 2 in. by 1 ft 2 in. at ground level. At the head of the menhir there is a curious excrescence on one side; this is purely natural, the effect of the jointing of the granite. This is the tallest menhir on Dartmoor.

It will be seen from the plan that A and B fell with their lengths at right angles to the rows with which they were associated, whereas the length of C lay practically in the direction of its row. This, in itself, would indicate that A and B originally stood with their broad sides lying in the direction of the rows, and C with its broad side across the direction of the row. Excavation proved that this had been the fact, the pits formerly occupied by the bases of the stones were clearly defined, and little if at all deformed. No reason can be assigned for this difference of position.

A view of menhir C, as it lay in 1889, is given on Pl. 57B. Pl. 58 A and B afford two aspects of the same menhir after its erection.

Pl. 59A is from a photograph of menhir A, and Pl. 59B presents menhir B. In either instance a part of the associated row is included.

The Drizzlecombe group finds place on sheets cxiii, NW. and SW. of the 6 inch O.S. of Devon, and the adjacent sheet cxii SE. The first edition gives a very incomplete survey, no stone rows or menhirs being shown. But Giant's Basin (Pl. 31), which may be regarded as the principal member of the group, is indicated on all editions of the survey, sheet cxii, SE., lat. 50°-29'-5", lon. 3°-59'-6".

Shuggledown, the *Longstone*

Second in importance may be placed the group of stone rows and barrows on Shuggledown, in the parishes of Chagford, Gidleigh and Lydford (pp. 219-222 and Fig. 75).

The Longstone is not far from the centre of a double stone row, 485 ft lying north of the Longstone, and 555 ft south thereof. It is conceivable that it was once the terminal stone of a row[1], which was subsequently extended beyond it, but there is no proof of this. It marks the boundary of the three parishes above mentioned, and is referred to as the 'Langstone' in the 1240 Perambulation of the Forest of Dartmoor. The menhir stands 10 ft 5 in., and measures at the ground level, N. 35½ in., E. 24 in., S. 33 in. and W. 21 in.

6 inch O.S., lxxxix, SE., lat. 50°-39'-17", lon. 3°-53'-44". See Pl. 46B, for view of the Longstone.

Piles Hill, the *Longstone*

This is the northern terminal of the Butterdon row. It is fallen. It is 8 ft 5 in. long, and measures 2 ft 3 in. × 1 ft 6 in. at one foot from the base, and 11 in. × 5 in. at the other end. Situated on Piles Hill at an elevation of 1,250 ft (see p. 205).

Merrivale, Long Ash Common, Walkhampton Parish

The well-known group of stone rows (p. 215), cairns, kistvaen, stone circle and menhir or menhirs at Merrivale (Figs. 74, 116) may be given third rank among the Dartmoor groups. But it is to be remembered that this ranking is from our modern viewpoint, and from that alone.

The principal menhir stands not far from the stone circle; there is a smaller menhir near it, and between the two lie the remains of a barrow. There are also a few scattered set stones, the intent of which cannot be ascertained.

The large menhir stands 10 ft 4 in. in height; at the base it measures S. 2 ft 6½ in., W. 1 ft 4 in., N. 2 ft 8 in., E. 1 ft 8 in. It tapers to S. 8 in., W. 11 in. at the top. The south face lies in a plane bearing N. 63° E.

The smaller menhir is distant 35 ft from the larger. Within memory it had never stood erect, prior to its re-erection in 1895; it has since again fallen, which is the less to be regretted where it must be admitted that much about its restoration was problematic. The greatest section of the stone measures 1 ft 3 in. by 9 in., and its length as it lies on the ground is 7 ft 1 in.

The larger stone will be found marked on 6 inch O.S., sheet cvi, NE., lat. 50°-33'-9", lon. 4°-2'-31½". See Pl. 60B.

Laughtor, Laughtor Newtake, Lydford Parish

Six inch O.S., cvii, NE., lat. 50°-33'-43", lon. 3°-54'-13". Not shown on first edition.

---

[1] And is treated as such in the previous chapter. (ED.)

This menhir stands at the north end of a stone row (p. 229); after long lying fallen it was erected in 1893. The stone was over 12 ft in length, it now stands 8 ft 8 in. above ground, and measures at the base 2 ft 5 in. by 1 ft 3 in. For view see Pl. 56B.

Langstone Moor, Petertavy Parish

This menhir stands at the south end of a stone row, at the north end of which there would appear to have been a barrow. There can be little doubt that the adjacent moorland took its name from this stone. The ordinary modern pronunciation of that name is *Lanson*, but the Ordnance Survey prefers to mark it as *Launceston*. It is to be noted that the original spelling of longstone, everywhere on Dartmoor, was 'langestone'.

Prior to the year 1893 the stone had long lain on the ground; its length is 11 ft 8 in. and its greatest width 2 ft 1 in., its greatest thickness 1 ft 7 in. As re-erected it stands 9 ft 2 in. in height. It differs from all other Dartmoor menhirs in that the stone is not granite, but a block of the igneous rock which occurs on and around Whittor, and which may be described as an epidiorite.

The location is 6 inch O.S., xcviii, SE., lat. 50°-35'-22¾", lon. 4°-2'-54½". The stone is not shown on the first edition of the survey.

For a view see Pl. 60A.

EXCEPTIONALLY LARGE STONES IN STONE ROWS

Although I would not extend the definition of 'menhir' to include them, I think it well to refer to the fact that the stones next to the barrows, which frequently occur at one end of the stone rows, are often obviously selected of far greater than the ordinary length of the general assemblage of stones forming the rows. Especially does this appear to be the case where the barrow has a retaining circle. But many rows do not show this feature. Three instances may be cited where such unusually large stones occur.

Assacombe, Lydford Parish

A barrow with a retaining circle lies at the east end of the stone row (p. 224). The stones near to the retaining circle are much larger than the general run of stones in the row, and the largest is next to the circle; it stands 6 ft 2 in. and measures 2 ft 2 in. by 11 in. at the base (Pl. 62). The stone has been re-erected.

Location, 6 inch O.S., xcix, NE., lat. 50°-37'-39", lon. 3°-53'-35½". The row is not shown on the first edition of the survey.

Shuggledown, Chagford and Gidleigh Parishes

The fourfold circle lies at the south end of a stone row (p. 220), the two stones in the row next the circle are both fallen and both are unusually large. One measures 11 ft 6 in. in length, and the other 7 ft 4 in. (see Pl. 46A and Fig. 65).

Location, 6 inch O.S., lxxxix, SE., lat. 50°-39'-28", lon. 3°-53'-47½".

Walkhampton Common, between *Down Tor* and *Coombeshead Tor*

A barrow within a retaining circle lies at the west end of the row (p, 212); the stones for some distance from the barrow are far larger than the general run, decreasing in size with distance from the barrow. The stone next to the retaining circle stands 9 ft 6 in. See Pl. 61.

Location, 6 inch O.S., cxii, NE., lat. 50°-30'-19½", lon. 3°-59'-34½".

UNCLASSIFIED

Quintins Man, Lydford Parish

Six inch O.S., lxxxix, sw., lat. 50°-38'-15", lon. 3°-57'-1".

This place-name would appear to indicate the former existence of a menhir, but the object to which it is now applied is a cairn. We have no Dartmoor example of a menhir standing on a cairn, and it is not within living memory that any menhir stood either on or near this particular cairn.

Longstone

The word 'Longstone' or 'Langstone' occurs as a place-name on Dartmoor, where no menhirs either now exist or are known to have been. It is sometimes assumed that the name may be taken as good evidence of the former presence of a menhir, but this not a safe assumption. *Lang*, as a surname, is not unknown on Dartmoor, where it is at least as old as the days of Elizabeth; and, with the precedents of 'Proutytown', 'Cudliptown' and 'Cholwichtown' it would be unsafe to deny the possibility of derivation from a personal name. The word certainly suggests inquiry where it occurs.

THE STANNARIES

ANTIQUITY OF CUSTOMS AND PRIVILEGES

THE origin of the tin works in the West of England is hidden in prehistoric obscurity. The Bronze Age knew our western tinners, and geological changes as important as the shift of the relative levels of land and sea divide us from the days when the industry originated.

More than this we cannot say; the industry grew, it became an oversea commerce, as which we find it of importance in Roman times, and the tinners ultimately developed into an organized body enjoying privileges secured it by customary law.

Of the growth of this mass of custom we have no trace. It must probably have been far developed when as yet the social order characteristic of feudalism was only foreshadowed. The ore did not attach to the ownership of the soil; it was never in the right of the landlord, although he might be entitled to toll of the tin raised. Over against the growing restrictions of private ownership in land was set one apparently anomalous right, the survival of an earlier order. The tinner might freely and without restriction, except as to certain special injuries which might result therefrom, search for tin wherever its presence was suspected and work it regardless of the consent of the owner of the soil. He could secure to himself by proper procedure the mineral right in lands which he had bounded, subject to tolls determined by custom. Such a right must have had an effect on the divisions of society which we may not now realize unless on special consideration. The full burthen of villeinage can never have fallen on the Stannary districts of Cornwall and Devon. As Lewis, in his book on the Stannaries of the South-West, says: "Where bounding prevailed it was open to the poorest villein to become his own master simply by laying out a claim and registering its boundaries in the proper court." Amid much that was inchoate certain clear privileges such as this of bounding were well established and unquestioned long before written evidence is available. The first document which clearly indicates the conditions obtaining in the Stannaries is dated 1198, and is a return made by the Sheriff of Devon and Cornwall and William de Wrotham and others to Hubert, Archbishop of Canterbury, the Lord G. FitzPeter, and to the Barons of the Exchequer, in pursuance of two writs or precepts issued to the Sheriff by the Archbishop. The first of these gave the Stannaries in charge of the said de Wrotham, not as the first incumbent of the office of warden, as Lewis incorrectly states, but in succession to the said Geoffry Fitz-Peter. The tinners were to have the same freedom which they had and enjoyed formerly, and none to remove tin by land or sea without de Wrotham's licence. The second letter orders an inquiry into the weights of the first smelting and the weights of the second smelting. Thirdly, Geoffry FitzPeter writes confirming.

The result is that de Wrotham and those who were to be associated with him present a report the terms of which bear clear witness to the antiquity of much that first finds record in their return.

They speak of the just weight of tin in Devonshire in the following words: "The just and ancient weight of the city of Exeter, by which anciently now and at all times the second smelting of the tin was wont to be made," and similarly for Cornwall. And in their report they propose certain ordinances for the collection of revenue and the government of the Stannaries, which include the following:

"All the diggers and buyers of black tin and the first smelters of tin, and the traders in tin of the first smelting, shall have the just and ancient customs and liberties, established in Devon and Cornwall."

No language more precise could have been used to indicate that already in 1198 there was an organized trade enjoying customary laws and liberties of origin ancient even at that date. No charter or grant, royal or otherwise, is cited. The Crown, it is true, claimed farm of tin, and the tin was the property of the Crown, but I cannot agree with Sir George Harrison that there had ever been any formal lease from the Crown to the tinners. That either the local territorial magnates or the Crown itself should ultimately take toll of the tin was unavoidable. But the Crown taxed the industry without the formality of leasing the Stannaries to the tinners. As a result of the very inquiry which we have been considering a new toll was imposed, which raised additional revenue. But the tinners were neither consulted nor is there any evidence that they were consenting parties, nor did they derive any advantage or fresh liberties compensatory. There is no evidence of any lease even at this date.

The Commissioners, if so we may term the Sheriff of Devon, de Wrotham and others who took part in the inquiry, were at care to ascertain the accustomed weights and to report the dues to the King given by ancient custom. They know that for every thousandweight of tin there were given to the Lord the King by ancient custom thirty pence for the farm of the Stannaries in Devon, and for the cost of carriage to the market towns; and in Cornwall the King received five shillings. This they set forth with precision; they can afford to pass in the most general terms the privileges of the tinners, and so we lose evidence that might have been of value.

But the object in hand was to ensure and increase the King's revenue, and the method simple.

"We also inform you that the Lord the King, from the time after William de Wrotham took the Stannary, shall have of new annual rent from every thousand weight, weighed by the weight of the second smelting, one mark of silver, which weights of the second smelting in Devonshire and Cornwall are admeasured by equal weight and established by equal quantity."

There follow provisions for collecting the new rent and the old farm, but no corresponding new grants to the tinners. There are provisions also against smuggling, which must obviously have offered a profitable field for enterprise. Of these fiscal regulations few need be quoted.

In each town where there should be a second smelting (not within the walls of Exeter or Bodmin) there was to be one house at the hiring of the King appointed for the second smelting, weighing, and stamping, and no one should presume to conduct their operations elsewhere as he valued himself and his goods.

In Exeter and Bodmin the accustomed places might be used, but the presence of the King's representatives was to be essential.

Here we have a clue to the 'Furnum Regis', or King's Oven, near Postbridge, a place appointed for the second smelting "at the hiring of the King". No man or woman, Christian or Jew should presume to do any of the following things:

To buy or sell any tin of the first smelting, nor to give or remove any from the Stannary until it be weighed and stamped.

To have in their possession any tin of the first smelting beyond a fortnight, unless it be weighed or stamped.

In market towns and boroughs, on sea or on land, to keep beyond thirteen weeks tin of the first smelting weighed and stamped, unless it be put into the second smelting and the mark discharged.

To remove tin either by sea or land from out the counties of Devon and Cornwall without the licence of the Chief Warden.

Also good and lawful men are established in the ports around Devonshire and Cornwall, to take the oaths of all steersmen and mariners there landing that they will not remove, nor allow to be removed, in their ships, any tin unless it be weighed and stamped by the royal customs, and unless they have a writ from the Chief Warden.

The result of this new rent must have been eminently satisfactory to the King, who received from it in 1199 the sum of £600 19s. 5d. His farm of tin, as previously collected, and which he still retained, had in 1197 been £166 16s. only. Thus at one stroke he had multiplied his revenue more than fourfold.

In 1201 John issued the first charter of the Stannaries. The document is short; it accomplishes much in few words. Privileges confirmed as expressedly of ancient custom are "digging tin and turfs for smelting it at all times, freely and peaceably, and without hindrance from any man, everywhere in the moors and in the fees of bishops, abbots and counts, and of buying faggots to smelt the tin and of diverting streams for their work in the Stannaries", and apparently as of ancient right also that they should not leave their work at the summons of any man unless he be the Chief Warden of the Stannaries or his bailiff.

The charter then proceeds to declare that the tinners are of one farm and always in Royal demesne. This declaration carries with it of necessity freedom from pleas of serfs. A special judiciary is set up for them in the Chief Warden and his bailiffs.

Now this last feature of the charter was a blow to the manorial system, at that time fully developed. Whatever in the past may have been the struggle between the tinners and the manorial lords, here was a refuge not only for free men from absorption in the manor, but for the acknowledged serf. The latter could change masters at will; if he became a tinner, he became also the King's villein and serf no longer. Since this encouraged the multiplication of workers in the Stannaries, and hence the increase of their output, it followed that the King, with an eye to revenue, acted wisely.

But John was not strong enough to maintain the position which he had assumed, and in 1215 he promises the manorial lords that they shall not lose by reason of the Stannaries aught of the services or customs which they are accustomed to have from their men and serfs. None the less their men, whoever will, may go for tin, their serfs may not.

Lewis appears to think that the Stannary courts, of peculiar jurisdiction, take origin in the charter of John. But I agree with Sir George Harrison, who places the jurisdiction of the Warden on the surer basis of ancient custom, and who goes so far as to say that omissions in Royal Charters would be of no import, and grants therein are merely confirmatory in this matter. We shall presently see that the charter of 1305, 33 Ed. I, is plainly expressed on this matter.

Lord Coke says the Stannary Jurisdiction "is guided by special laws, by customs, and by prescription time out of mind".

Thus as I view it the struggle is not between the tinners seeking greater freedom and the manorial lords desirous of maintaining their existent rights, but between the lords as representing a new order of things and the tinners fighting for their ancient privileges. It was essential that the power of the Crown should be invoked, and the predisposition of the Crown toward the tinners' side of the contest was ensured by an enlightened self-interest.

John's concession to the manors was never fully enforced; there were restrictions of the tinners' ancient rights, such restrictions as the relative strength of the parties rendered possible, and in the fifth year of Henry III we find instructions given for the emancipation of the Devon Stannary from these encroachments. But the battle must always have been maintained in some sort. In 1252, 36 Henry III, that monarch confirms the charter of John (1201), and thus formally sets the seal to his policy of supporting the tinners.

The Bailiff of Blackmore,[1] giving an historical account of his Stannary in 1586, ignores entirely the charters of John and Henry. We are at liberty to presume his reason to have been that he regarded them as merely confirmatory of rights pre-existent. To him the charter is that of 1305. On the other hand, it might be argued that he was ignorant of the previous charters; but that can scarcely be, for he gives the story of the purchase of the 1305 grant, the application for which made reference to Henry's confirmation of John's charter.

As to the times before 1305, the Bailiff writes:

"Now forasmuch as I have somewhat said touchinge the searching for Tynn before the yeare 1291 (the year of the expulsion of the Jews) & from thence forth of the purchasing of the charter by the Tynner[s] of Blackmore wth the Courts & particular charges thereof issueinge out yearely to the prince there arresteth now somewhat to write by ancient Records partely found of the Customes w[ch] the Tynner[s] had before the charter (of 1305) to them graunted I say that they alwaies used to work and seeke for Tynn in wastrell ground & alsoe in the princes soveragn waies to carry & recarry theire tynn to places convenient and necessary to be dressed clensed and purified. In like manner or wise to Convey the Courses of waters to theire seuerall workes for the purifieinge of their tynn haueinge liberty likewise to digg mine search make shafts pitch bounds & for tynn to worke in places for their most advantages. Exceptinge and Reserueinge only all Sanctuary grounds Church yards mills bakehouses and gardens payeinge and yeeldinge only to the Prince or Lord of the Soyle the 15th ffote or Boll for the Toll of their Tynn to farme. Provided alwaies that if it chanced the said Tinners in their mininge to subvert or worke up anie mans Howse or else anie Highway whereby it might Cause the Howse to fall or one that Travells should be troubled in the Journies then in this Cause the Tinner or Tinners subuertinge the premisses should to theire own expenses make or cause to bee made the said Howse or Highfairinge way so subverted and undermined soe Lawfull & sufficient as they weere before the tyme of theire workinge & undermineinge."

And in confirmation of this he quotes a plea framed up against Richard Davy, of Camborne, husbandman and tinner, by John Jenkin, for that the said Richard Davy did by force and arms enter upon six acres of land at Chivendu, the property of the said John Jenkin, and dug and subverted the said six acres, for the which he, the said John, claimed £10 by way of damages. To this plea, framed in the 31st Henry VIII, Richard Davy pleads in defence ancient custom and pre-

[1] The name of the Stannary which included the Hensbarrow and St. Austell district. (ED.)

scriptive right substantially as above set forth. It is worthy of note that he cites no charter, not even that of 1305.

THE STANDARD WEIGHTS

There is a matter in connexion with the customary weights in the Stannaries which has been at times misunderstood.

In the days when the extraction of tin from the ore was a matter of two operations, the first and second melting, one of the duties imposed upon William de Wrotham was an inquiry concerning the admeasurement of the 'weights of the first and second meltings'.

On the 19th day of January, in the ninth year of the reign of King Richard, 1198, he inquired upon oath, in full county court at Exeter from 26 wise and discreet jurors, concerning the just weights of tin in Devonshire, and they found that the just and ancient weight of the city of Exeter, by which anciently, and now and at all times the second melting of tin was wont to be made, is, and always ought to be, of such quantity that to the just and ancient weight of the first melting of tin, anciently, now, and at all times, was, and is, as eight to nine, which it ought to be by the weight of the city of Exeter, of the second melting, and for this reason, viz. because for every thousand-weight by the greater weight there are given to the Lord the King, by ancient custom, thirty pence for the farm of the stannaries in Devonshire, and for the cost of the carriage to the market-towns, and because the tin wastes in the second melting.

Which finding was sufficiently clear to the men of that day, but other days other ways, and it has deceived even so shrewd a commentator as Burnard (P.I. x, p. 102), who paraphrases it: "In other words for every nine pounds of crude tin of the first stamping presented to the Stannary refiner, eight pounds of pure tin capable of taking the second stamp must be returned to the owner." This is wholly mistaken. The first thing to note is that there was the Exeter standard for weighing the tin of the second melting, and there was the 'greater weight' for weighing the tin of the first melting, and these were in the proportion of 8 to 9; in other words the pound used in weighing the tin of the first melting was to weigh 18 Exeter ounces.

The tin of the first melting contained valueless foreign matter, and, in equal quantity, was of less value than the refined tin from the second melting. Also it was liable to a tax of 30 pence per thousand-weight, and was of less value by the amount of that tax. Also the first melting took place near the tin-work, but the second melting could only be made at an authorized market town, and it cost something to carry from the tin-work to the market town, by the amount of which necessary cost it was of less value. From each and all of these three last causes the price of tin of the first melting should be lower than that of the second melting. The buyer, therefore, had to say "I cannot pay as high

a price", and that is what we should say to-day. But this involved calculation; if second melting tin were worth £3 per thousand-weight,
what would be eight-ninths of £3, the true value of first melting tin—
as a matter of fact the answer would be £2 13s. 4d., quite an under-
standable figure in those days—but the result would often involve
awkward fractions of the penny, and in any event it needed arithmetic.
The habit of the time was to say "I must get more for my money", not
"I must pay a lower price". Hence the simple expedient of using a
heavier standard pound for the tin of the first melting. The scales themselves adjusted the price, and made the calculation.

In Cornwall the ratio was higher, 7 to 8, so that the greater pound
for weighing tin of the first melting was in fact the equivalent of $18\frac{2}{7}$
Exeter ounces. This because the tax on tin of the first melting was twice
as much as in Devon.

Rather than smile at these entirely logical methods, let us remember
our fiction known as 'Summer Time', which would have shocked the
twelfth century.

THE CHARTER OF EDWARD I

The charter of Edward I, 1305, to which reference has been made,
was granted on the petition of the Cornish miners—the Bailiff says on
the petition of the miners of Blackmore alone. Cornwall and Devon
are treated individually[1] and a charter granted to each. On this charter
the Stannaries thereafter rested.

I reproduce, from the Harleian MS., a translation of the charter of
Edward. You will note the precise manner in which many of its provisions are declared to be confirmatory of ancient rights:

"A true Copie of the Charter or grant made by King Edward the
first Englished verbatim.

"Edward by the grace of god king of England Lord of Ireland and
Duke of Aquitaine to all Archbisshops and Bisshops Abbots Priors
Errles Barons Justices Sheriffs provostes ministers and to all bayliffes &
other his faithfull subjects greeting. Know ye yt we for the amendment
of our Stannaries in the County of Cornwall and for the quiet of yt of
our tinners of the same have granted for us and our heires that all tinners aforesaid working in the Stannaries wch are our demesnes so long
as they work in the same stannaryes be free and quite from all pleas of
villanies & from all pleas and plaints of our Court and of our heires &
in what manour soever touching so yt they shal not answeare before any
oure Justices or ministers or of our heires for any plea or plaint growing
within our Stannaries aforesaid for the tyme being (pleas of land liffe
or lym excepted) nor yt they depart from their works by soⅿons of
any of the officers of us or our Heires but by the sⅿons of our said

[1] Not for the first time. Separate juries were empanelled, and separate enquiries held, for Devon and Cornwall in 1198. (ED.)

warden. And yt they be quite from all tallages Tolles Stallages Ayds &
other Customs whatsoever for theire oune proper goods in the tounes
portes and faires & markets wthn the County aforesaid. We have
graunted also to the same tynners yt they may dig tyn & turves for
melting of tyn everywhere in our lands moores and wastes & of all
other persons whatsoever in ye County aforesaid. And the waters &
water courses for the works of the Stannaryes aforesaid to turn where
& as often as need shall be & to buy bushement for the melting of tyn
as of old tyme hath bin accustomed to be done w^tout let of us or our
heires Bishops Abbots Priors Errles Barons or other persons whatsoever.
And y^t our warden aforsaid or his leiftenant hold al pleas growing
betwene the tyners aforsaid also betwene them and other foreners of
all trespasses plaints & contracts made in places wherein tyn works
wthin ye stannaries aforesaid likewise arising. And yt the same warden
have free powre to Justifie the tynners aforsd & other foreyners in such
places & to do iustice to the pties as right requireth & as heretofore in
the sd Stannayes hath bin accustomed. And if any of the sd tynners in
any thing shall offend whereby they ought to be imprisoned yt they be
arrested by the warden & in our prison of Lostwithiall & not els where
be kept & detayned untill they be delivered according to the law &
custom of our Realme. And if any the tinners aforsaid upon any fact
wthn the County aforesaid not touching the foresaid stannaries shall put
himself upon the enquiry of the Contey one halfe of the Jurors of the
enquest shall be of the tynners aforsaid and thother half of forenors.
And of fact altogether touching the stannarys aforesaid the enquests be
made as heretofore they have bin accustomed. And if any of the same
tynners be fugitive or outlawed or commit any offence for wch he
ought to loose his cattes yt the same cattes be apprised by the warden
aforsaid and our Coroner of the said Cowntie & by them to the next
villages delivered to answere thereof to us and our heires before the
Justices of Oyer in the Cownty aforesaid.

"Furthermore we Will and straightly Com̄ad that all Tyn as well
white as black wheresoever it shal be bestowed and wrought in the
countie aforsaid be wayghed at Lostwithiall Truro & Helston by our
wayghers thereto ordayned & marked under the forfeture of all the
Tyn aforsaid. And yt all that tyn be coyned in the same touns yerely
before our said warden before the day of St Michaell in September
under the forfeyture aforesaid. We haue granted also for us & our
heires yt all our tynners aforsaid all y^is tyn so wayed lawfully may sel
to whom they will in the townes aforsaid doing thereof to us and our
heires the tonnage and other the customs due and used Except we or
our heires will buy the said tyn our selves Wherefore we will and for
us and our heires straightly com̄aund that our tyñers aforsaid haue all
liberties free Customs and quitanncs above writen and that the same
w^thout let or impechement of us or our heires Justices Exchetors

Sheriffes or other our bayliffes or ministers whatsoever they reasonably enioy use in forme aforsaid. Thes being witnesses &c."

Whether the tinners presumed upon their rights or whether the "foreigners" infringed them is not clear, but the Stannaries and the people without the Stannaries continued the struggle, of which we have seen previous evidence. In 1309 the Sheriff of Cornwall endeavoured to levy on the chattels of the Blackmore tinners, and was mobbed in consequence. The Commonalty fought hard, and certainly brought sufficiently serious accusations against the Stannaries.

At times the tinners responded with complaints of wrong suffered by themselves. Doubtless the tinners presumed on their privileges, and even made them the means of extortion, equally undoubtedly the hundred and manor court made constant effort to oust the peculiar jurisdiction of the Stannaries.

The people of Devon complain that the tinners were digging into and destroying their tilled fields, woods and gardens; the tinners assert that the manorial lords are impleading them for pleas of serfs.

In 1318 we see an effort to limit the area covered by the Stannaries and set to it bounds and limits, whereas in fact it extended wherever tin might be found. The recital of the ill deeds of the tinners is lengthy and serious, and it is Devon which complains.

The Stannary men commit trespasses and assault men of the county in divers hundreds outside the bounds and limits of the Stannary, nor permit themselves to be brought to justice according to the law and custom of the realm, and when the hue and cry is raised against them, they take and beat the King's bailiffs and the bailiffs of others holding liberties there, and, leading them into the Stannary, imprison them in the Stannary gaol until ransom is paid. They commit many acts of extortion, dig for tin where it has not been the custom to do so, and extort money for the privilege of being left undisturbed; they seize the King's bailiffs sent to those parts to levy his debts, and put them in prison for a ransom; they appropriate the tenth part of the refined mineral which ought to be paid to the lord of the soil. The Stannary bailiffs are persons of desperate character; they prevent people attending the hundred courts, they distrain the very tithing men that they do not attend and make their presentments as they should. The warden takes money to extend tinners' privileges to persons not entitled to them. Our hundreds and those of others are impoverished.

I think the plaint unduly forced; the result is not known. If we believe their opponents, the tinners continued their career of varied crime; if we believe the tinners, acts of violence were committed against themselves, their works broken down, their tin taken.

Bearing in mind that the tinners were men working in complex partnerships where honesty and fair dealing between party and party were essential, that they were bound by very rigid laws and practically enjoyed unlimited self-government, I am prepared to believe that their independence was at times a temptation to them, but I realize that they can hardly have been a pirate crew. No doubt the seignorial lords regarded them as masterless men; no doubt they disturbed an ideal of government centred in feudalism. I incline to think the attacks upon their liberties were more persistent than their interference with the foreigners. Such attacks they resented to the full of their power. Be all this as it may, the Stannaries won and brought all classes of men to plead in their courts.

A very pretty dispute was constantly kept alive as to who were tinners and thus entitled to Stannary privileges. The Stannary Parliaments, Committees of Judges, the Privy Council Chief Justices Fleming and Coke, and Parliament itself, all had a hand in defining the extension of the term tinner; again the result was with the Stannaries, although the fortune of war was varied, and not until the Stannary Act of 1837 did it become assured that all adventurers, agents, labourers—in short, all in any way connected with mines either in supplying materials or otherwise, were to be held as miners and free to sue and be sued in the Stannaries. Yet for centuries of dispute that in effect was the interpretation which had force.

The Bailiff of Blackmore, in the document mentioned, is not very clear as to who are the tinners, and his definition is very inconclusive. He is sarcastic as to "Some beeinge dealers for tynne so bent to theire oune effection that when occasion of trouble cometh only uppon Tynners, either touchinge theire princes service or else the paymt of money or otherwise then they say that they are noe Tynners. On the other parte the same men goeinge about to receive theire debts att the hands of theire Creditors & barred thereof by meanes of a forrayners plea sett with the Courte ag^t them then confesse they them selves to bee Tynners and will not sticke to plead the same in Courte for recovery of their debts by the Stannary Courts." He instances also "The merchant that buyeth white Tynne as merchants of our County the Londoners and likewise all other merchants w^{t}soever, these undoubtedly when fortune ronneth against the poore Tynners will stoutly affirme themselves to bee noe Tynners, and yett I can not see by anie Reason but that they should bee the most principall Tinners of all others for when they implead fforraigners to Recover theire debts they will be Tynners & Craue the priuilidge thereof, likewise if the question fall out about the burninge of the white Tynne att the Conages then to seccure theire tourne they clayme the benifitt of the Charter of Tynners."

Not only these but lesser persons could endeavour to suit their purposes by claiming as tinners when that course liked them, and disclaiming when that in turn became profitable. The Bailiff had "often tymes heard one question. A Tynner haueinge a right in a TynneWorke for a year or two a spaliard workeinge for a day or two, the Tynner setteth away the right of his Tynworke, the worker & spalliard give over workinge, all these I say castinge of theire occasioned exercises will alleage & say they weere Tynners indeede but now they are none as whoe sayth the Smyth the Tayler the ffuller or the Weaver the Carpenter giueinge over theire occupaçõns are noe longer Smyths & Taylers Weauers ffullers or Carpenters whereas in very deede as I suppose a man beeinge once knowne for an Artificer is alwaies accounted for an Artificer, once a Tinner and ever a Tynner."

STANNARY JURISDICTION

The Stannary Parliament was traditionally held as a joint meeting for Cornwall and Devon on Hingston Hill until 1305; after that date, for Devon on Crockern Tor and for Cornwall at various towns. Very little is known of the early Parliaments; probably their office was always "to consult, enquire, and take deliberation to resolve upon such orders as in their judgments shall be thought expedient for the redressing and amending of any inconveniences or abuses within the Stannaries, and to reduce things in question and doubtful (touching liberties and customs) to a certainty."

Under the Pardon and Charter, 1507, Henry VII, the Cornish Convocation consisted of twenty-four stannators, six nominated by the mayor and council of each of the following towns: Lostwithiel, Truro, Launceston, and Helston. This Convocation had a wide power of veto in ordinances, etc., even when Royal, which touched the rights of tinners. The Devon Parliament was more democratic: Chagford, Tavistock, Ashburton, and Plympton Stannary districts, each at a special court to which all tinners in the most inclusive use of that term were given entrance, selected twenty-four stannators, making ninety-six in all.

Whether or no a 'Great Court' held at Tavistock for the Stannaries of Cornwall might be considered a Parliament I am not prepared at the present to decide. But from the nature of the representation the presumption is in the affirmative. At this Court or Parliament was passed an Act—27th August, 13 Eliz.—the intent of which was better to enforce the provisions of two previous Acts of the Parliament of England for the better preservation of the havens of Plymouth, Falmouth and Fowey from the ill effects brought about by the discharge of streamworks waste into the rivers falling into those havens. The Bailiff of Blackmore gives the text of this Ordinance of the Tinners' Court, which sets limits of distance from the streams within which works may not be prosecuted, demands proper precaution for the interception of sand, gravel and other waste, and imposes heavy penalties for breaches of its provision.

The holding of a Court for Cornwall at Tavistock was in itself sufficiently unusual, and probably the whole procedure was, strictly speaking, an informality, although effective.

The Bailiff of Blackmore recites in full the charge of the Stannary Courts, and as this serves well as an epitome of the Stannary laws and customs, I now present it:

THE CHARGE OF THE STANNARY COURTE

Good men you shall understand that wee are assembled this day for a good and Godly purpose That is to minnister Justice (That is to say That I with you and you with mee may endeavour with al our powers to put doune vice and to extoll virtue) all which to bee breife is comprehended in brief in this word Justice, which is thus defined Justitia est virtus tributurus q^d suum est signifying as much as to restore every man to his proper right. Now iff itt be as Cicero and the Learned remaines with diverse others haveinge noe hope of Salvation had such a remorse unto Justice that they greatly extolled and wrote very largely in praise thereof what should wee then Christians doe needes must we earenestly imbrace Justice according to the saying of our Blessed Saviour & Master Christ "q^d Cesaris est date" let every have his right. And for that cause this Courte is called the Leete Courte, as much as to say dies Leta wherein wee may bee joyed when vices are soe suppressed and virtue soe regarded That every man may quietly enjoy that thing that is his. Now the refformacōns of enormityes & offences must needes bee brought to passe by matters of record whereuppon you uppon your oathes, doe you endeavor therefore, ffirst you good men that are sworne shall inquire of all comon bakers amonngst you that make wholesome bread for mans body keepe us the Assise of them, you shall doe (us to witt) Alsoe all brewers and Tapsters that brew and keepe not the Assize and sells by cupps Ditches bolls & by measures unsealed you shall doe (us to witt) And also for your ffoote ffares quartes & measures wether anie Tinner use anie double measures that is to say a greate measure to buy with and a small measure to sell with or useing deceite among the Queenes Leige people

Alsoe of all such persons as have measures to meete Tynn with all which have not brought them hither of this Lawe courte To bee assured of such you shall require & doe us to witt.

Alsoe if there bee any lanes or wayes stop or returned out of right course into a wrong course to the annoyance of the Queenes Leige people by the occacōn of Mines Pitts Shafts Hatches & Tynnworks & by the maker thereof not repaired and if such offend us you shall inquire and doe &c

Alsoe you shall inquire If anie Tynners have stollen anie Tynn & theire receivers so that my Lord Wardens officer may seise the same Tynn soe stollen to ye use of the Queenes Majesty.

Alsoe all Strayers coming within the right Tything of this Stannary Courte of Blackmore of Horses Sheepe Swine or anie other beasts which have beene there the space of a yeare & not challenged & the Q: Majesty not answered thereof yee shall inquire &c

Alsoe if there bee any among you that have kept black Tyn unblowne after the ffeast of St. Michaell Tharchangell where the Tyn is How much itt is and whoe is the ouner thereof ye shall inquire and do us &c

Allsoe you shall inquire & doe us &c of all corrupt Tayle & Tyn and the makers and blowers thereof which have made the Tyn and not yett the accustomed marke or lr̄e oppon the same, That is to say Hard Tyn not having this lr̄e H Sinder Tyn not haveinge this lr̄e S: pillion Tyn this lr̄e P: And Retillion Tynne this lr̄e R by deceit whereof the merchant Travelers beyond the seas have often tymes stoode in greate danger besides the greate Losse they have susteyned thereby

Moreover yee shall inquire as such as blowers of white Tynne and are not here att this Lawe day to take theire oathes according to theire antient Custome ffor the true & just execucōn of theire ffunction in that behalfe the names of them that make default you shall ffinde out et supra &c

Allsoe yee shall inquire of the officers of the Coynage or else of the Courtes as the Bayliffes Tything men Tollers or any other officers whatsoever wither they omitt or slacke in any thinge to doe theire dutyes and beeing ffound out they shall likewise present.

Allsoe yee shall inquire & true present make of all Colliers that carry coale to blowing houses in packs which are not ffilled with 3 bushells after 20 gallons to the bushell in measure ffor soe much they bee by antient Custome.

And allsoe yee shall inquire wither the Keeper of the Goale his under keeper duty or deputyes or anie of them so omitt to doe anie one of theire dutyes in negligent keeping of the prisoners as willingly suffering them to escape. The partye pīt not beeing satissfyed of his debt or otherwise If the keeper under keeper or his deputy take excessive ffees above the ffees in that behalfe of the prisoners (That is to say) all the prisoners comeing into the Goale 6^d & every day beeing in the Goale att the keepers ffinding 4^d & every day beeing att large att the keepers ffinding 5^d Butt if hee be in the Goale & list to bee att his oune ffinding then ought they to pay nothing unto the keeper ontill such tyme as hee list to bee at the keepers ffinding and then to pay according to the rate.

Allsoe you shall inquire & doe us to witt of all such as doe Implead any Tynner in anie fforreigne Courte out of the Liberty of the Stannary for matters determinable in this Courte.

Likewise if any Tynner impleads another in anie fforeigne Courte ffor causes there to bee tryed beetweene them.

Allsoe if the worker of anie Tynworke bee kept or strayted of the course of his water to serve the comodity of working theire Tynne wheres theire custome hath beene to ffetch theire water by a certeyne order as to them prescribed in anie place or in anie ground without deniall of anie person the offenders herein yee &c

Allsoe yee shall inquire & doe us &c if anie Tynner or Spalliard ffetceth a warr^t or supersedeas of the peace agt anie Tynner or Spalliard except itt bee ffrom the Warden or his deputy

Allsoe yee shall inquire of the said offenders (That is to say) if any person or persons enter into a Tynworke with fforce or violence to take any Tynne out of anie Tynworke

Allsoe yee shall inquire if any person or persons give or promise any Tynworke or any parte of any Tynworke that is variance between partye & partye to anie gēnt Juror or to any other to the intent to beere him out in the Tryall of the Tytle thereof of these yee shall inquire & make us to witt accordingly.

Allsoe yee shall inquire and do us to witt of the names of all those Tynners or Spalliards which doe or will refuse to pay any reasonable sum̄s as shall bee assessed uppon them to bee paid towards our princes service the confirmation of the Charter or towards anie other necessary cause ffor the comon wealth of the Stannaryes.

Allsoe if any person or persons have disceiyed or brought out of possiōn any Tynner of any Tynneworke or of any parte of any Tynnwoorks which he had the possion of by the space of a yeare & a day peaceably (except itt bee only by order of Lawe) of the offenders hereof yee shall inquire.

Allsoe yee shall inquire of anie such person or persons that sell & deliver any white Tyn beffore the tyme that is coyned whereby the Q: Majesty hath lost her coynage & duty to her grace apperteyneinge.

Now to speake of the Appellacons to be used by severall degrees that is the order that hath beene decreed by the moste Honorable Councell. That if any Tynner bee wronged, ffirst hee ought to complayne to the Steward of the Courte And if hee bee ffound ptiall and doe him noe Justice then lett him the Vice warden And if hee doe noe Justice lett him complayne to the Under Warden And if hee cannot then obteine Justice lett him complayne to the Q: Councell. If you have knowne any to breake this Godly decree you shall of such offenders doe &c

Allsoe you shall doe &c If any Steward Bayliffe Major or anie other officer Take any Tollage in anie Marketts or ffaires of anie Tynner or Tynners in Townes Portes ffaires or Marketts of theire owne proper goods.

Allsoe If the Bayliffe under Bayliffe or any Speciall Bayliffe beeing authorised by the Courte to arrest any by virtue of his writt or warr^t to him directed take more than 6^d for his arrest of such offenders shall inquire & doe &c

And whereas diverse Tynners in working of theire streame works with fflouds have conveyed & carryed theire rubble gravell from the said worke to the greate Rivers and from thence to the Streame disuing them to the Havens of Plymouth, Tynmouth, ffalmouth & ffoy to the greate Hinderance & decay of the Havens &c

CATEGORIES OF TINNERS

I must now refer to a manuscript notebook, lent to me by my friend Dr. Brushfield, which provided details not previously obtainable. It proved to be the account book of a master tinner in 1586 and a few preceding and following years.

Its utility and interest lie in the full manner in which it fills a gap in the economic history of the Stannaries by giving us details as to wages, where formerly we had none but very general statements. It shows the relations existing between the capitalist adventurer of Elizabethan days and his workmen.

I have given an account of these relations founded on my somewhat arduous wrestle with a system of bookkeeping which states balances but leaves to the reader the calculation of the method by which they were reached.

Reviewing the evidence I obtained[1], we can divide the labour contracts as follows:

[1] Set out in detail in the original article. (ED.)

Spalliards—Men working by the day, journeymen, and receiving 2s. per week, casual labourers taken on at the wash and other times.

Labourers—(a) Men having yearly contracts in fixed wage, but no interest in the results, receiving not more than £4 10s. the year.

(b) Dole-workers, who were given a part share in the mine for the year or half-year and took part of their masters' profits, but also worked a part share for his benefit, and for that were paid a reduced wage, usually 20 shillings a year.

An intermediate class between Tinners and Labourers.—Such men took half tin, half wage. It is really another form of dole work, but the terms used are mostly different. The tinner "bargains" with a dole worker; he "sets his right" to this class. The wage was usually half of £4 10s. or thereabouts (£2 5s.). This class became for the year actual partners in the works.

Tinners—(a) Who took over at a rent a share in the work. The rent usually stated as a percentage of the tin raised, the fifth dish or such like.

(b) The man who owns a share in a work and himself performs the labour.

Master Tinners—Who own shares in works, but either employ labourers or sett their rights, taking no personal part in the labour

THE GROWTH AND DECAY OF TIN PRODUCTION ON DARTMOOR

It is not only interesting, but for present purposes useful, to consider the statistics of the production of Dartmoor tin. There are varied sources of information available, and all these have the merit of being of the best class of evidence, namely—bookkeeping. The interests of the Crown and of the Duchy of Cornwall in the revenue to be derived from the Stannaries have ensured that the accounts shall be very completely kept; and, although there are gaps in the evidence, it is surprising how. adequate are the data. It is necessary to remember in interpreting records that the Stannary thousandweight (m) was the long thousand of 1,200 lb., and the hundredweight (c) contained 120 lb.

George Randall Lewis (*The Stannaries*, Appendix J, p. 252) has abstracted the yearly returns wherever recoverable. He had no special interest in the Dartmoor tinner except as part of a system, but his figures are very informative when dissected for our present purpose.

In the thirteenth century the data are incomplete, but at the close of that period, in the years 1290 to 1299, inclusive, the average annual production of Devonshire tin was 75,244 lb., or 33·6 tons[1]. (These and

[1] A century earlier the output from the Dartmoor stream-works had been far greater, probably because this area was being adequately exploited for the first time. It has been estimated that between the years 1171 and 1189 the average annual output was about 640 thousandweight (343 tons), which not only exceeded the production of the whole of Cornwall at the time, but was nearly

all the following figures have reference to 'white tin', the metal.)
Between the years 1300 and 1400, with the exception of the years of
the Black Death, the annual production varied irregularly between
the extremes of 43,600 lb. or 19·5 tons, and 164,400 lb. or 73·4 tons.

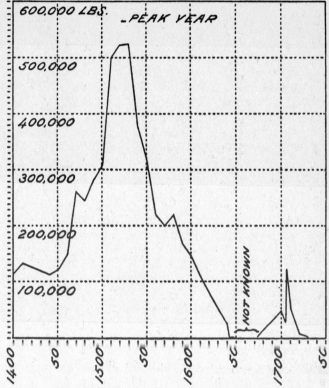

FIG. 87. Growth and decay of Dartmoor tin production.

Throughout the fifteenth, sixteenth and seventeenth centuries the
evidence is sufficiently complete, except for the Commonwealth
period, when Devon and Cornwall are merged. The graph, Fig. 87 in
the text, shows the growth and decay of the industry. The peak decade
was centred on the year 1530, and the peak year was 1524, when
564,288 lb. were produced, or about 252 tons.

From these peaks there was a rapid descent, and in the decade whose
central point was 1640, production had already fallen to 23,384 lb. per
year, when the Civil War brought the Dartmoor Tinners' business to

50 per cent higher than the later peak of production in Devon reached around
1520. By 1243, when Cornwall again took the lead, the annual return had
fallen to 74 mwt. (c. 40 tons). (See Finberg, 1949.) (ED.)

an end temporarily, no tin being coined in either of the years 1643 to 1646, inclusive. Although production was ultimately resumed, it was relatively trivial, except for one single year, 1706, when there occurred a peak of 123,636 lb.

In the graph, Fig. 87, averages of ten-year periods have been used, except in the eighteenth century, when the annual fluctuations have in part been followed.

The figures used are for Devon as a whole, but in the matter of tin production Devon is Dartmoor, other sources being negligible, especially during the period concerned.

The following attempt to arrive at the total production of white tin on Dartmoor, between 1400 and 1650, is sufficiently well based to be within a possibility of error of one-half of 1% either way.

	Tons	Tons per year
1400–1450	2,704	54
1450–1500	5,196	104
1500–1550	9,944	199
1550–1600	4,655	93
1600–1650	1,250	25

The fifty years, 1500–1550, were, therefore, the golden age of the Dartmoor tinworks, and, with an almost perfect symmetry, the most successful year was 1524, with 252 tons.

It has to be remembered that the figures used are those of the metal which paid dues; it is known that smuggling successfully evaded the dues to a variable extent, and at times the smugglers must have met with considerable success, if we may judge by the effort made by the authorities to check them by regulations and ordinances. But we have no sufficient knowledge to apply any correction to the above figures, to meet this source of error. It is probably quite safe to assume that the relative magnitude of the trade is at all times fairly and accurately reflected in the official figures.

In and around the year of greatest production, 1524, the price of tin stood at about fourpence per pound, so that the greatest annual gross value realized by the trade was practically £9,405, a very substantial sum at the then value of money.

REFERENCES

Finberg, H. P. R., 1949. The Stannary of Tavistock. *Trans. Devon. Assn.*, Vol. 71, pp. 155–84.

Lewis, George Randall, 1908. *The Stannaries. A Study of the English Tin Miner.* London. 2nd ed., 1924.

Harleian MS. 6380. [An account of the Stannary of Blackmore, by its bailiff, 1586.]

An MS. account book of a master tinner including year 1586 ('Brushfield MS.')

THE DARTMOOR BLOWING-HOUSE

WHEN William de Wrotham was appointed to inquire into matters concerning the Stannaries, and all that appertained thereto was committed to him, one, and not the least intent was that he should increase the king's revenue from that source. De Wrotham showed neither subtlety nor imagination, but with direct simplicity added to the existing tax of thirty pence per thousand-weight of tin of the first melting, an additional imposition of thirteen shillings and fourpence on each thousandweight of tin of the second melting.

This effectively enhanced the royal revenue, since tin of the first and second meltings were one and the same, save for their stage of manufacture.

The present interest lies in the evidence that, in the year 1198, the process of recovery of the metal from the ore was operated in two stages, the first a comparatively rough reduction, the second a refining process. The first melting was carried out at or near the mine or stream-work. It seems to have involved no more elaborate plant than a hole in the ground with a fire built over it, and the ore built in to the body of the fire, where a comparatively low temperature would serve to reduce the metal.

Such a smelting place would leave little evidence, and on Dartmoor none has yet been found. In Cornwall it seems clear that tin of the first smelting has been found at times in the pit into which it settled through the fire. Borlase (*Natural History of Cornwall*, p. 163) writes that, in the stream works in St. Stephen's Branel, there were found now and again some small lumps of melted tin, 2 in. square and under: what he had seen cut with difficulty, and was more harsh and gritty than the common melted tin. His description may well refer to tin of the first melting.

With the improved methods of the blowing-house one melting sufficed. In the blowing-house a formal furnace was constructed and the fire was urged by a bellows, actuated by a small water-wheel. Precisely when this improvement was effected is not known, but Randall Lewis (*The Stannaries*) points out that it must have been made sufficiently early to have been in common use by the middle of the fourteenth century, since the Black Prince shared in the profits of several at Lostwithiel in 1359. Very early in the fourteenth century the separate tax on tin of the first smelting was abandoned, and coinage dues charged on the finished tin. It seems probable that this may have resulted, in part at least, from the substitution of the single process in the blowing-houses. Accordingly one may say that on the available evidence it is not safe to date the earliest blowing-house before 1300, or, on the other hand, to place its possible date more than a few years later.

For at least four centuries the blowing-house remained the sole device for smelting tin ore. It saw some changes and improvements; thus Carew, writing in 1602, refers to enlarged and improved 'chimneys' for catching the flue dust with its content of tin. But not until the years 1705 or 1706 did the reverberatory furnace threaten its predominance, and even then the charcoal-fuelled blowing-house put up a long and stiff fight against its coal-fed rival. Pryce (*Mineralogia Cornubiensis*, p. 136), writing in the year 1778, or thereabout, describes a blowing-house, and gives figures as to the consumption of charcoal. Used with stream tin he says that it gives a superior quality, fetching ten or twelve shillings a hundred more than mine tin; "because it is smelted from a pure mineral by a charcoal fire; whereas mine tin is usually corrupted with some portion of mundick,[1] and other minerals, and is always smelted with a bituminous fire, which communicates a harsh sulphureous injurious quality to metal".

It would appear that a blowing-house might, therefore, be of a date very near the end of the eighteenth century. So that for five hundred years this method of smelting was in use, for the more part in sole use.

Throughout this period tin was continuously produced on Dartmoor, excepting during some of the years of the Black Death; thus in 1355 no tin was returned from Devon. From 1643 to 1646, inclusive, the Civil War had a similar effect; then, in the process of natural decay, the years 1734 to 1740 inclusive were also barren; and, with the exception of 1741, 1742, 1743 and 1744, the remainder of the eighteenth century showed nothing but negligible production.

The last years of the industry are hardly likely to have seen the construction of blowing-houses, and none on Dartmoor are likely to be of later date than 1740. We may except the smelting-house at Eyelesborough Mine (p. 303), which may not in fact be technically a blowing-house.

Since the first consideration in the selection of a site was readily available water-power, and since the best sites would always retain their predominance in this respect, and the leat once constructed would always be a useful work, needing no more than clearing, it is improbable that any structure which we now find should be the first to occupy the site; and there can be little hope that any really early work remains.

---

[1] Iron pyrites. (ED.)

Not Time's destroying hand, but the continued requirements of the industry must have obliterated the traces of early work. Nor had the buildings the simple strength of the hut-circles. On the other hand, nothing is more permanent than earthwork, and the leat should survive wherever a blowing-house has been, unless obliterated by the subsequent working of the area for stream tin.

In a letter to Mrs. Bray, under date 5th October 1835, Mr. Edmund Pearce of Tavistock writes: "In and about the old stream-works there are now to be seen several remains of the Phoenician smelting-houses, called by the miners Jews' Houses: from one of these, near the confluence of the East and West Dart, about three years since, there was taken tin ore, which was redressed and smelted at Crowndale, by the present Tavistock Smelting Company; and not far from this place there was found a block of Jews' tin, supposed to be the most ancient in existence, and now in the possession of a gentleman of this town. The surface of this block betrays marks of great antiquity, being much corroded by the influence of those external agents to which it has been exposed." (Bray's *Tamar and Tavy*, 1836, Vol. 3, p. 254.)

The blowing-house referred to was most probably that at Week Ford on the West Dart, three-quarters of a mile above Dartmeet (p. 294); none other is known which would answer to the description. It has been impossible to trace the ingot, inquiry at Tavistock eliciting no response; and the 'ore' which was redressed and smelted at Crowndale may be safely assumed to have been slag, which was often discarded while still containing an appreciable percentage of tin.

Other than this the first detailed account which recognized the probability of any of the rectangular buildings on Dartmoor having been smelting places appeared in the first volume of the *T.D.A.*, Part V, p. 46, where John Kelly describes the lower blowing-house on the Yealm. In a footnote he adds that Spence Bate had found another rectangular building in which there was, in addition to mould-stones, a furnace (August 1866).

In the same *T.D.A.*, Vol. 4, pp. 136–7 (1878), P. F. S. Amery published a description of the crazing mill[1] and mould and mortar-stones at Gobbet. But no systematic record was attempted before the publication of Burnard's *On the Track of the Old Men, Dartmoor*, in the tenth volume of the *P.I.*, this paper, read in March 1888, was followed by a second, under the same title, in March 1889. And in the eleventh volume of the same *Journal* appeared a third paper by the same author, entitled *The Antiquity of Mining on Dartmoor*, and read in February 1891. The present writer made his first 'find' in 1890, and published some data in March 1892, in the *P.I.*, Vol. 11. Since that date evidence has been constantly accumulating, and has from time to time been

---

[1] A mill for crushing the tin ore, see p. 318. (ED.)

published in the *T.D.A.* It is impossible to suppose that it is complete, but the writer was not prepared to find that it referred to forty-three sites in all, and feels that after fifty years' work, it would be gambling with the span of life to defer a general review of our knowledge.

The occasion seemed appropriate for the first meeting of the Devonshire Association at Chagford, that ancient stannary town, where even the churchwardens invested their funds in tinwork ventures (G. W. Ormerod, *On the Traces of Tin Streaming in the Vicinity of Chagford*, *T.D.A.*, Vol. I, Part V, pp. 110–15).

SYNOPSIS OF FIELD EVIDENCE

The following is a list of all those blowing-houses of which there are known remains on Dartmoor. The arrangement is under river valleys, proceeding from east to west, and upstream. Houses on the banks of the main rivers are first given, and followed by those on the tributary streams.

The notes on each house are arranged in the following order: (a) References to previously published descriptions, in which '*P.I.*' refers to the *Journal of the Plymouth Institution*, '*T.D.A.*' to the *Transactions of the Devonshire Association*, and '*C.*' to Crossing's *Guide to Dartmoor*. (b) The number of the quarter sheet of the 6-inch Ordnance Survey of Devon, within which the site lies, and the latitude and longitude positioning the site. (c) Brief notes on each site.

In this list each house bears a number, to facilitate future reference.

SOUTH TEIGN

1. *Outer Down*, T.D.A. lix, 343; O.S. lxxxix, NE., lat. 50°-39'-48½", lon. 3°-51'-54". Internal dimensions of building 38 ft by 17 ft, divided into two compartments. Walls 2 ft 7 in. to 2 ft 9 in in thickness. Well marked leat, which still carries water to another site. Wheel may have been 10 ft in diameter and 1 ft 4 in. breast. A broken mould-stone, the cavity measuring 12 in. by 9 in. at the bottom. Another mould from this house has been removed to the grounds of Outer Down; it measures 16 in. by 13½ in. at the top, and 13 in. by 10 in. at the bottom, and is 8 in. deep (Pl. 69A). It would contain 367 lb. of tin when filled. (Dimensions of mould-stones refer to the cavity of the mould.) There is also a mortar, 11 in. in diameter and 7½ in. deep, this, also, has been removed to the grounds of Outer Down (Pl. 69B).

2. *Opposite Thornworthy*, on the right bank. T.D.A. lxi, 403. C. 259. O.S. lxxxix, SE., lat. 50°-38'-38", lon. 3°-52'-41". Internal dimensions of building 33 ft 6 in. by 13 ft 6 in. There was formerly a mould-stone on this site, but this has been lost, very possibly when the trench for the Torquay water-main was cut. This trench disclosed much slag, and also sand and slimes from tin-dressing.

3. *Metherel Hut-Circles*. T.D.A. lxvii, 119, and lxix, 143. O.S. lxxxix,

SE., lat. 50°-38'-27", lon. 3°-52'-53", and lat. 50°-38'-24", lon. 3°-53'-1". Two hut-circles, known as No. 3 and No. 4 respectively. Neither had been a smelting place, but both had been used by tinners as stores, and possibly shelters or dwellings. There was ample evidence that the circles had been occupied in the early Bronze Age, and that the tinners' occupation was a secondary matter; its date approximately fixed by a silver York penny of Henry VII, found with stream tin and slag in Hut No. 3. Both huts yielded slag, and pottery consistent with the date of the coin.

3a. *Yes Tor Bottom Hut-Circle*. T.D.A. xxx, 99. O.S. cvi, SE., lat. 50°-32'-17", lon. 4°-1'-21". In the valley of the Walkham, inserted here out of geographical order as parallel and confirmatory to the last. In this hut the Dartmoor Exploration Committee found tin slag and fragments of glazed pottery, while a lower stratum yielded flint chips and typical Bronze Age pottery. Experts at the British Museum assigned the tinners' pottery to the fourteenth or early fifteenth centuries. But the finds at Metherell indicate that such pottery might well have been at any date within the fifteenth century, perhaps a little later. Both here and at Metherell there is evidence of the partial reconstruction of the walls of the huts.

BOVEY

4. *Ridge Ley*. T.D.A. lxx, 453. O.S. lxxxix, SE., lat. 50°-38'-15", lon. 3°-51'-54". Two small troughs near the ruins of Ridge Ley farm-house. These are very possibly mould-stones diverted to agriculture; but the identification lacks certainty. The moulds measure respectively 20 in. by 13 in. and 5¼ in. deep—possible weight of ingot 366 lb.; and 13 in. by 11 in., depth 5¼ in., possible weight of ingot 201 lb.

On the ground of uncertainty these weights have been omitted from the table (p. 315), with which, however, they would not be inconsistent.

DART

5. *Venford Brook*. T.D.A. lxxii, 201. O.S. cvii, SE., lat. 50°-31'-20", lon. 3°-51'-26". The site now lies below the waters of the Paignton Reservoir. A mortar-stone, with three mortars in a line, was removed from the site, and now lies by the drive near the caretaker's house.

It may be well to refer to a smelting place near Ashburton, which Burnard mentions in *P.I.* xi, on page 98. This furnace lies on the left bank of the Dart, in *Awsewell Woods*, about half a mile above Holne Bridge. There are large heaps of slag, but these are evidently iron-slag and not the product of tin-smelting operations. An iron lode has been worked close by, and in a map of date 1605 the building is marked as 'Iron Mill'. See John Amery's Presidential Address, *T.D.A.* lvi, page 95, for full details.

EAST DART

6. *Barracks, Postbridge.* T.D.A. lxx, 452. O.S. xcix, SE., lat. 50°-35′-33½″, lon. 3°-54′-35″. Ruined buildings, one of which can be identified as a pig-stye, but none as a blowing-house; there has been much interference with this site. Two moulds, each measuring 23½ in. by 14 in. at the top, 16¼ in. by 8½ in. at the base, and 8 in. in depth. Possible weight of ingot 487 lb. As these are duplicates, only one entry in their respect has been made in subsequent tables.

7. *Wallabrook: Soussons and Runnage.* T.D.A. lxx, 453. O.S. xcix, SE., lat. 50°-36′-0″, lon. 3°-52′-34″. The ruins of the blowing-house lie on the right bank, and its leat is clearly traceable. On the left bank, built into the enclosure wall, is a mortar-stone, having three mortars on the one side, and four on the other (Pl. 71B). Largest mortar is 8 in. diameter by 3 in. deep, the smallest is 7 in. by 2½ in.

8. *Stannon Brook: Hartiland Moor.* T.D.A. lxx, 452. O.S. xcix, SE., lat. 50°-38′-58¼″, lon. 3°-54′-35″. Remains of blowing-house, much ruined and disturbed. Mould-stone in adjacent stone fence. Mould 14½ in. by 11½ in. at top, 11½ in. by 8½ in. at bottom and 4 in. deep. Possible weight of ingot 210 lb.

WEST DART

9. *Week Ford*, or *Beara House.* P.I. x, 104, 226. O.S. cvii, SE., lat. 50°-32′-6″, lon. 3°-53′-18″. Blowing-house, internal dimensions, 20ft. 6 in. long on one side, 18 ft 6 in. long on the other, 13 ft in width. Furnace 4 ft in width. Leat, raised foundation for launder to wheel, and wheel-pit. The wheel may have been 10 ft in diameter, by under 2 ft breast. Several mortar-stones, one with three mortars linearly arranged. A stone with two bearings much polished by iron axles 1⅝ in. diameter. This building is sometimes known as 'the Mill'.

9a. *Week Ford*, No. 2. Thirty-six feet downhill from the building last described lies another blowing-house. The water, having passed over the wheel of the upper house, was conducted to the wheel of the lower, the steep hillside permitting this double use. The wheel-pit of No. 2 is no longer clearly marked, but the bank which confined the water is distinct.

The internal dimensions of the building are 33 ft by 16 ft; the thickness of the walls varies slightly, but averages 2 ft 9 in. There is a small chamber (6 ft 9 in. by 4 ft 9 in.) built at one corner. The doorway of the house is well marked, with a stone sill, and a jamb grooved for the wood frame. The upper house has similar stone jambs. There are two window openings.

Two possible furnaces are indicated, one a recess in the wall, measuring 3 ft 2 in. by 3 ft 2 in., the other in the centre of the width of the building, but nearer to one end. This much resembles a similar furnace, in more perfect condition, at Merrivale (40).

There is a mould-stone, the mould measuring 15¾ in. by 12 in. at the top, and 12½ in. by 9 in. at the bottom, and between 5½ in. and 5 in. in depth. The possible weight of the ingot would be 192 lb. There are many mortar-stones, of which two or three show three mortars in a row. The mortars are large, some being 10 in. in diameter by 9 in. in depth.

These two blowing-houses at Week Ford have been resurveyed, and plans will be found in *T.D.A.* lxxii, 201.

10. *Gobbet, Swincombe. T.D.A.* iv, 136; lxxii, 201. *P.I.* x, 107. O.S. cvii, SE., lat. 50°-32'-19", lon. 3°-54'-44". Much ruined blowing-house, internal dimensions about 30 ft by 16 ft, leat clearly traceable. Two mould-stones; one mould 15¾ in. by 11½ in. at the top, 12 in. by 9 in. at the bottom, and 5 in. deep. Possible weight of ingot 191 lb. Burnard notes the similarity between this mould and that at Week Ford. A second mould is much eroded by use; its probable original dimensions were 17 in. by 15 to 10 in. at the top, 9 in. by 8 in. at the bottom, and 5 in. deep. Possible weight of ingot 183 lb.

There are several mortar-stones; the largest mortar is elliptical on plan, the conjugate diameters being 12 in. and 7½ in., the depth is 5 in.

This is the only Dartmoor blowing-house at which both the upper and the lower stones of a crazing mill have as yet been found. The grinding faces of these stones are 3 ft in diameter (Fig. 96).

Not only is this the first house recorded in this synopsis at which the crazing mill is found, but it is also the first to be mentioned at which smaller cavities, known as sample moulds, are present in the mould-stone. The first stone referred to above has two such cavities, these are 3 in. by 2½ in., and 3 in. by 2 in. respectively, and both are ¾ in. deep. (Burnard says "two inches deep", which is an error.) Such sample moulds would contain a little more than one pound of tin apiece.

There are considerable grass-grown heaps of broken slag, in gravel form.

11. *Deep Swincombe. P.I.* x, 111. *T.D.A.* lxxii, 205, and Baring-Gould, *A Book of Dartmoor*, 114. O.S. cvii, SE., lat. 50°-31'-50", lon. 3°-54'-56½". The walls of the building still stand to the height of 3 ft; its internal dimensions are 21 ft 6 in. by 8 ft 6 in. At one end of the building there is a covered chamber, probably a 'cache', and very possibly a late addition or alteration. Outside the building, to the south, lies an earthfast boulder, in which a shallow trough has been worked, 26½ in. along the long sides, 16 in. wide at one end and 12 in. wide at the other; its effective depth is from 3 in. to 1¼ in., but owing to the sloping surface of the stone the hollow is 5 in. deep at one end. (Baring-Gould gives the depth as 5 in., which might mislead.) An ingot would therefore be a slab, 3 in. thick at one end, and 1¼ in. thick at the other, and would weigh 166 lb. The identification of this trough as a tin mould is open to great doubt. In shape and size it is unlike any known mould.

This objection might be met by the assumption that the house is the earliest known example, and belongs to an age with different custom in the matter of moulds, but there is no evidence for such an assumption. The position of the supposed mould is a greater difficulty. It lies outside the house, on the opposite side to the door. The place for a mould is within the house, close to the furnace, and for obvious reasons. In the present instance the molten metal would have to be carried through the door, around the end of the house, some little distance along the side, and some little way from the side, a total distance of 104 ft. It may be said that disused or broken moulds were not infrequently removed from the blowing-houses, but this is an earthfast boulder, and not a block which can be carried about, and it certainly is neither broken nor worn.

The building lacks the first essential of a blowing-house, and that is water-power. There is no trace of either a leat or a wheel-pit. There is no other essential of a smelting place, unless it be the supposed 'mould'. Baring-Gould mentions and describes a 'furnace base', but this I have never seen, nor is it mentioned by Burnard.

A tinner's hut or store it may well have been, but certainly not a blowing-house.

AVON

12. *Below Henglake*. T.D.A. lxv, 316. O.S. cxiii, SE., lat. 50°-29'-9½″, lon. 3°-53'-50″. The blowing-house measures 17 ft 6 in. by 12 ft 3 in. internal, and the walls are 2 ft 6 in. in thickness. The furnace recess is 4 ft in width by 2 ft 9 in. in depth. There is a bank to bring the leat to the wheel, and the wheel may have been 9 ft in diameter, and 1 ft 2 in. breast. The leat is clearly traceable. There are two mortar-stones, the one with two mortars on either face (four in all), these vary between 7½ in. and 6 in. in diameter, and from 2⅜ in. to 2 in. in depth. A second stone has but one mortar, oval in plan, with co-ordinate diameters of 11 in. and 9 in., and a depth of 4¼ in.

The house, of which a general view is given in Pl. 68A, is on the left bank of the Avon.

13. *Fishlake*. T.D.A. lxv, 318. O.S. cxiii, NE., lat. 50°-29'-46″, lon. 3°-54'-34″. A doubtful building, with some features consistent with its possible status as a blowing-house, but no confirmatory evidence. Internal dimensions 19 ft 6 in. by 7 ft 6 in., which is small for a blowing-house.

GLAZEBROOK

14. *Near Glaze Meet*. T.D.A. lxiv, 275; lxxii, 205. O.S. cxix, SE., lat. 50°-25'-37″, lon. 3°-52'-29″. Internal measurement 20 ft 6 in. by 13 ft 6 in. at one end, and 12 ft at the other. The thickness of the walls is varied, from 1 ft 8 in. to 2 ft 8 in. There is a well-preserved wheel-pit; the wheel may have been 8 ft in diameter by 1 ft 4 in. breast. There is

a raised bank for the leat; and a chamber which may have been intended to collect flue-dust. One mortar-stone with four mortars, two on each of two adjacent faces (Fig, 99).

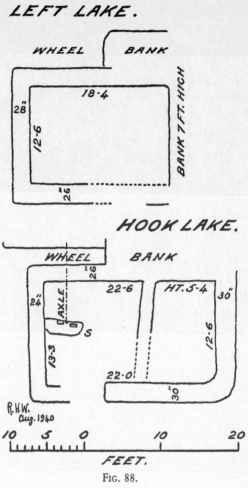

Fig. 88.

(*Above*) Dry Lake (Left Lake).   (*Below*) Hook Lake.

The furnace would appear to have been in the corner adjoining the wheel-pit, where there is a flue leading into the chamber already referred to, but there are no distinguishable remains. The type of furnace was probably late, since there is a stone in the woods on the left bank of the stream, not far away, to which my attention was directed by Mrs. Eckett Fielden, to whom it had been indicated by Miss Cole, of

Brent. This proved to be a float, or furnace base, in part formed. The length of the stone is 4 ft 4 in., its breadth 1 ft 7 in., and its average depth 13 in. On the surface is a channel, 1 ft in width, 3 ft in length, and 1 in. in depth at one end, running out to nothing at the other. The workmanship shows that the stone had as yet been no more than roughed to shape.

ERME

15. *Woods above Ivybridge, right bank. T.D.A.* lxx, 453. O.S. xcix, sw., lat. 50°-24'-5", lon. 3°-55'-11".

No remains of any buildings are discoverable, and the only evidence is a stone with one large and well-formed mortar, measuring 10⅞ in. in diameter by 4¾ in. deep.

16. *Below lower Dry Lake. T.D.A.* lxxii, 205. *P.I.* xi, 183, O.S. cxix, NE., lat. 50°-26'-53½", lon. 3°-54'-51". A stone lying under the left bank of the Erme, and having two mortars, 9½ in. in diameter and 7 in. in depth.

16a. *Dry Lake.* O.S. cxix, NW., lat. 50°-27'-13½", lon. 3°-54'-58". On the right bank of the *Dry Lake*, a small stream which lies a little north of *Left Lake*, and about 100 ft from the bank of the Erme. Here is a building which has been either a blowing-house or a knacking-mill. Its internal dimensions are 18 ft 4 in. by 12 ft 6 in., the walls are between 2 ft 2 in. and 2 ft 4 in. in thickness, and there is a raised bank to conduct the water to the wheel. No mortar-stones or mould-stones have been found, but the floor is much encumbered with debris, and an exhaustive search would need excavation. The leat comes from the Erme, and is about 1,100 ft in length; it is somewhat higher in level than is needed to feed the wheel, and the water could pass over the wheel, or in the alternative direct to the Dry Lake, through a walled outlet. Probably the water was used from this outlet for washing the pulverized ore.

This may well be the building from which was derived the mortar-stone found in the bed of the Erme (16). See Fig. 88 for plan.

17. *Hook Lake.*[1] *P.I.* x, 235; xi, 101. C. 399. O.S. cxiii, sw., lat. 50°-28'-9", lon. 3°-55'-4". The building measures internally 22 ft 3 in. long, by 12 ft 6 in. wide at one end and 13 ft 3 in. wide at the other. It is divided into two compartments by a cross wall, which appears to be of later date than the main walls. The walls vary in thickness from 2 ft 6 in. to 2 ft. There is a raised bank to conduct the water to the wheel; the wheel-pit is well preserved and the wheel may have been 8 ft 6 in. in diameter and 1 ft 6 in. breast.

There is a stone formerly described as a mould-stone, which has been broken, or more probably purposely split. It contains four cavities: a

---

[1] Re-examined in 1940, when measurements were revised and the stone bearings identified.

supposed 'mould', broken, of which the part that remains is 11 in. long and 3 in. deep, increased over some of the area to 7 in. deep, apparently by breakage; two circular depressions, of about 2 in. diameter; and a slot 12 in. long, 3¼ in. wide, and 3¼ in. deep (it measures 11 in. by 2 in. at the bottom).

The two ,roughly circular depressions (originally thought to be sample moulds) prove to be bearings for an iron axle. One of the bearings is only roughed out, the other has been polished by use. The slot mentioned last may have taken the plummer-block of the water-wheel, but, in view of the other bearing adjacent, it probably had another use. From the plan, Fig. 88, it will be seen that the stone is so placed that the axle of the water-wheel may well have taken a bearing in the polished groove. If this were a knacking-mill, then the axle would

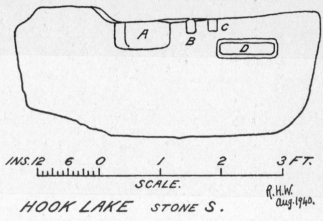

FIG. 89.

have borne a cylinder with projecting pegs which engaged with and lifted the stamps; the stamps would require a framed support, and that support might have had one leg set in the 12-in. slot. The positions of the bearing and the slot are just what would be expected were this so. Fig. 89 gives a drawing of the stone, on which 'A' indicates the broken 'mould', 'B' the polished bearing which has had use, 'C' the bearing which has not had use, and 'D' the slot in which I suggest that the frame of the stamps was set. Pl. 66B is from a photograph of the stone.

That this building may have been a blowing-house would appear from the presence of what is possibly a broken mould. That it was subsequently a knacking-mill is probable. In this connexion it is to be noted that immediately opposite Hook Lake is the valley of a small stream which joins the Erme on the other bank. This valley is known as *Knackersmill Gulf*. There is an enclosed space, and in it two square buildings, neither of which have the characteristics of mills; there are no wheel-pits, and no leats. Any leat must have come from the Erme as the stream in the Gulf is trivial. It looks like a little settlement for the workers at Hook Lake, and from its proximity to Hook Lake, and the fact that the Gulf looks out on the building there, it may well be that it took its name from the Hook Lake knacking-mill; there was certainly nothing of the sort in the Gulf itself.

18. *Left bank of Butterbrook*, north-east of *Tor Rocks*. *T.D.A.* lxv, 319. O.S. cxix, SE., lat. 50°-24'-59", lon. 3°-54'-42".

The building measures 34 ft by 16 ft internally. The leat is clearly traceable from above a small waterfall, some 70 yds upstream. A part of a broken mould lies within the house, the depth of the mould was 3 in. Outside the house lies a stone in which a mould has been partly formed; the present dimensions are 13½ in. by 11½ in. and 1½ in. deep. There are two broken mortar-stones, each now with one mortar. The mortars measure 8 in. diameter by 3 in. deep, and 7½ in. diameter by 3 in. deep, respectively.

Within the house are two stones in each of which is a round hole, 1⅛ in. diameter, the inner surfaces worn smooth and polished with use, evidently sockets for the axle of some machinery.

19. *Knackersmill Gulf*, a shallow valley with a small stream, on the right bank of the Erme, immediately opposite Hook Lake foot. There is no blowing-house here. But there are the remains of two small square buildings, and the name clearly indicates the former existence of a stamping-mill in the immediate neighbourhood (see above). O.S. cxiii, sw., lat. 50°-28'-9½", lon. 3°-55'-17".

20. *Blacklane Brook* (A). *T.D.A.* lxv, 316. C. foot of 374. O.S. cxiii, sw., lat. 50°-29'-7½", lon. 3°-55'-57". The building measures 17 ft by 8 ft internally. Crossing says that there are the remains of a watercourse leading to it, and identifies it with the *Wallack Mill* mentioned in 1538 as being let to Richard Coole and Thomas Hele (both Cornwood men). But it is small for a blowing-house, and I cannot trace any leat or watercourse.

21. *Blacklane Brook* (B). *T.D.A.* lxv, 316. O.S. cxiii, NW., lat. 50°-29'-31", lon. 3°-55'-57". The building measures 11 ft 6 in. by over 18 ft, inside measurement, and lies on the right bank of the little tributary which flows from *Ducky Pool*. The leat is clearly traceable, and there is the usual raised bank to take the launder which fed the wheel. No moulds or mortars are to be seen, but there is a stone with a bearing well worn and polished. This building may well have been ' *Wallack Mill* '.

YEALM

22. *Lower Blowing-House*. *T.D.A.* i (5), 46; *P.I.* x, 109; xi, 178. O.S. cxix, NW., lat. 50°-27'-16½", lon. 3°-56'-50". Internal dimensions of building 28 ft by 19 ft and second compartment 17 ft by 18 ft. The

walls 2 ft 4 in. in thickness. Dimensions of wheel-pit not ascertainable. No mortar-stones to be seen. Two mould-stones, each with two moulds. In one stone the first mould measures 15 in. by 9 in. at the top 12 in. by 6½ in. at the bottom, and 4 in. in depth. There is a notch in the edge at the centre of one end, which held the core forming the hole in the ingot by which it could be suspended. If cast without this hole the ingot would weigh 113 lb. as a maximum.

The second mould in this stone measures 17½ in. by 11 in. at the top and 14½ in. by 7 in. at the bottom, and is 6 in. deep. The largest possible ingot would weigh 185 lb. There is in this stone a sample mould, measuring 4 in. by 2½ in. by ¾ in. deep.

Connecting the two moulds is a channel, which extends to the bottom of one of the moulds. It has been thought that this channel was purposely made, but no satisfactory statement of the purpose has been suggested. It seems certain that it owes its origin to the failure of the granite under the heat of the molten tin, and the consequent spalling of the stone.

The second stone contains two moulds, one of which is broken; the complete mould measures 17 in. by 10 in. at the top, 12 in. by 6½ in. at the bottom, and 6 in. in depth; it would hold 195 lb. of tin. The broken mould measures 16 in. by 9½ in. at the top, 12½ in. by 6½ in. at the bottom, and 5½ in. in depth; it would hold 169 lb. of tin.

This house is on the left bank of the river, below the abrupt fall in the course of the Yealm, which is so marked a feature.

23. *Upper Blowing-House. P.I.* x, 111; xi, 179. *T.D.A.* xlvi, 284. O.S. cxix, NW., lat. 50°-27'-27½", lon. 3°-56'-53½". Internal dimensions of house 29 ft by 10 ft, walls 2 ft 7 in. in thickness. Two mould-stones, one within the house, the other outside. The mould within the walls measures 16 in. by from 12¾ in. at one end to 11½ in. at the other end on the top, and 12½ in. by 9¼ in. at the bottom, and is 4¼ in. deep. It would contain 174 lb. of tin.

The mould outside the building measures 18 in. by 12½ in. at the top, 12½ in. by 6½ in. at the bottom, and is 4½ in. deep. It would contain 193 lb. of tin.

No mortar-stones have been found.

This house is on the right bank of the Yealm, a little above the sudden fall above referred to.

PLYM

24. *Brisworthy Burrows (Mill Park). T.D.A.* xlvi, 285; lxi, 401. O.S. cxii, SE., lat. 50°-27'-49½", lon. 4°-1'-46". The internal measurement of the house is 32 ft by 13 ft. One wall, which is built against the adjacent ground is still over 6 ft in height. The house suffered considerably when a small cottage was built close to it in recent years.

No mould-stone has been found. Formerly there were mortar-stones within the house; these have disappeared, but one remains outside and has two mortars, each 6½ in. in diameter and 3 in. deep.

There was a stone at this house, which was lost years ago, but which I described in detail in *T.D.A.* xlvi. I then considered it to be the furnace base. I have since seen many of the granite chutes which were used to convey pigs'-meat from the outside of the styes to the trough within. None of these precisely resemble the stone in question, but none very closely agree each with each. I think it very probable that this stone was a feeding chute, the work of forming which was not complete. Nothing like it has been found at other blowing-houses. One can be certain of one matter; the Mill Park blowing-house was never in use

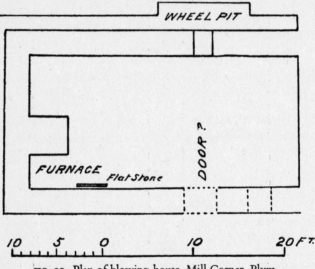

FIG. 90. Plan of blowing-house, Mill Corner, Plym.

as a sty. See Pl. 63A for a view of the stone found at Mill Park, and Pl. 63B, for a view of a feeding chute from the old homestead of Long-stone, Sheepstor.

25. *Brisworthy Hamlet. T.D.A.* xlvi, 286. O.S. cxii, SE., lat. 50°-28'-5", lon. 4°-1'-46". The remains of the house are trivial; the leat which supplied the wheel still exists and has been extended to serve a modern clay-works. The remains are involved in more recent hedges, and have, doubtless, been much robbed. But there remains one stone which is unlike anything found elsewhere. The mortars are usually formed in selected, fine-grained, granite or elvan, occasionally in quartz-schorl rock; but here an attempt has been made to utilize a boulder of ordinary granite, which has since been used to form one side of a gateway. The attempt met with no success; although sufficient perseverance was shown. There are on the face of this stone the beginnings of no less than

fifteen mortars, the largest 4 in. in diameter and the smallest $2\frac{1}{2}$ in.; none has been carried to a greater depth than $1\frac{1}{8}$ in. See Pl. 64A.

26. *Mill Corner.* *P.I.* xi, 174; *T.D.A.* lxi, 402. O.S. cxiii, sw., lat. 50°-28′-59″, lon. 3°-58′-57½″. Inside dimensions of the building 23 ft 8 in. by 13 ft 9 in. Walls 2 ft 7 in. thick. Mouth of furnace 3 ft 7 in. wide, depth 4 ft 4 in (Fig. 90). Well-marked wheel-pit, 10 ft long by nearly 3 ft in width; the wheel may have been 9 ft in diameter, with 2 ft breast. No mould-stone has been found, but there are five mortar-stones. The largest mortar is 8 in. in diameter, the others do not exceed 6 in. The depth of the mortars varies between $2\frac{1}{2}$ in. and $3\frac{1}{2}$ in.

In *T.D.A.* lxi I stated that the mortars had been lost to view. I am glad to say that they have since been uncovered once more. See Pl. 64B for a view of these mortars. One has been split and a part removed since the photograph was taken.

27. *Left bank of Plym, above Langcombe.* *T.D.A.* xlvi, 286. O.S. cxiii, NW., lat. 50°-29′-15½″, lon. 3°-58′-8½″. The building is much ruined, but its internal dimensions can be ascertained to have been 20 ft by 9 ft 6 in. There is one mortar-stone, with two large mortars, the one oval in plan, conjugate diameters 13 in. and $10\frac{1}{2}$ in., and depth $5\frac{1}{2}$ in., and the other $10\frac{1}{2}$ in. in diameter and $4\frac{1}{2}$ in. deep.

28. *Right bank of Plym, above Langcombe.* No previous reference. O.S. cxiii, NW., lat. 50°-29′-22″, lon. 3°-58′- $2\frac{1}{2}$″. Internal dimensions of building 17 ft by 10 ft. Thickness of walls, 2 ft 9 in. Leat still traceable. Definitely identified as a blowing-house by the broken remains of a mortar.

29. *Drizzlecombe: Eyelesborough Mine Blowing-House.* *P.I.* x, 235. O.S. cxiii, NE., lat. 50°-29′-28″, lon. 3°-59′-8″. Although much remains of this structure, it has been so far ruined that the details of its arrangement can only be guessed at. The house was at work in the early years of the last century, and it is not surprising that the leat is clearly traceable. The internal dimensions of the building are 60 ft by 20 ft, and the walls are 2 ft in thickness. There is a well-marked wheel-pit, and the wheel was probably 16 ft in diameter, and of about 2 ft breast, perhaps a little less.

This was the last tin-smelting place at work on Dartmoor, and cannot claim undoubted status as a blowing-house, since the furnace was possibly of the reverberatory type. Loss of tin in flue dust was evidently recognized, and a flue, over 70 ft in length, was constructed. The cross-section of the flue is 2 ft 3 in. in width, by 2 ft in height; there is a side opening for access. See Fig. 91.

Eyelesborough Mine was still at work in 1826, in which year Burt wrote: "At present in work are Vittifer in North Bovey, and Ailsborough in Sheepstor, which has a smelting house, where 100 blocks were coined for Michaelmas quarter, 1824." (Preface to Carrington's *Dartmoor*, p. lxi, 1826.)

It may be noted that the slag from the Eyelesborough furnace differs in type from any found at the blowing-houses, in consequence of the use of lime as a flux; and, although the mass is still glassy, it contains many crystallites.

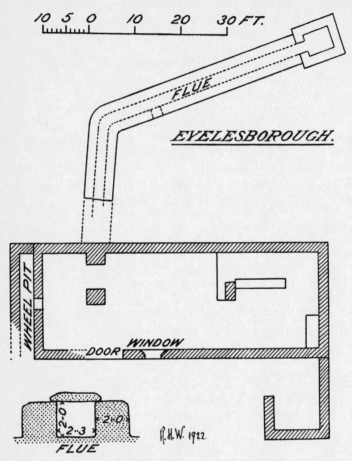

FIG. 91. Eyelesborough Mine blowing-house.

MEAVY

30. *Yeo Farm. T.D.A.* xlvi, 285. O.S. cxii, SE., lat. 50°-29'-2", lon. 4°-2'-34". No building known, but a mortar-stone has been built into the wall of an outhouse of the farm, and two others lie in the yard; in each of these an iron ring has been inserted. The main door of the farm-house bears the date 1610. This was the home of the Woolcombes, and in 1639 John Woolcombe of Shitteslowe was interested in tin works at Crosbeame and Pocock Hill, in the parish of Walkhampton. The

initials on the porch are 'I.W.', so that the builder of the farm may have been this same John Woolcombe. 'Shitteslowe' is a variant of 'Sheepstor'.

Under this same heading it may be well to refer to a mould-stone which formerly stood in the woods near Marchants Bridge, but seems to have been removed. The cavity is not rectangular, the ends measure 12 in. and 10 in. respectively, and the sides 19 in. and 17 in. The depth ranges from 3 in. to 2⅝ in. If the stone was in fact a finished mould, then it would have held 152 lb. of tin, but probably it was incomplete and intended to be deeper, and to hold about 200 lb. *T.D.A.* xlvi, 284. O.S. cxii, SE., lat. 50°-29'-2", lon. 4°-2'-58".

31. *Longstone*. *T.D.A.* lxi, 402; lxx. 451. O.S. cxii, NE., lat. 50°-30'-3", lon. 4°-1'-46". The site is now flooded by Burrator Reservoir. Two mould-stones, both now removed to the west side of the reservoir, near the *Lawn*. One stone bears a complete and also a broken mould; the complete mould measures 20 in. by 15¼ in. at the top, 17½ in. by 13 in. at the bottom, and is 8 in. in depth; it would hold 569 lb. weight of tin. There is a sample mould measuring 4½ in. by 2½ in. and 1¼ in. in depth. In the same stone are the remains of a smaller mould, of which it can only be said that its width at the top was 9½ in. The complete mould is the largest known on Dartmoor. On the other hand the single mould is one of the smallest; it measures 11½ in. by 7½ in. at the top, 9½ in. by 5¾ in. at the bottom, and would contain tin to the weight of 56 lb. (Pl. 71A). There is also a mortar-stone with two mortars, the rock being quartz-schorl; this lies at the foot of one of the reconstructed doorways in the rockery on the west bank of the reservoir. Before the reservoir was constructed the leat which formerly supplied the blowing-house was clearly traceable.

32. *Nosworthy*. *T.D.A.* lxi, 402; lxv, 311. O.S. cxii, NE., lat. 50°-30'-29", lon. 4°-1'-12½". On the left bank of the Meavy, between Nosworthy and Leather Tor bridges. The internal dimensions of the house are between 16 and 15 ft in length, and 13 ft 4 in. in width. The leat can still be traced. No mould-stones have been found, but there are at least eleven mortar-stones, one of which has four mortars, two on each of two adjacent faces. The largest mortars are 9 in. in diameter, by 3½ in. deep.

Some of the mortar-stones have been diverted to use as bearings for small iron axles, probably in connexion with the bellows (Pl. 70B).

There are two slotted stones, the slot in either case 21½ in. in length, by 4½ in. and 3¾ in. in width, respectively. Neither stone is a finished product; neither is at all likely to have been connected with the tin trade. They are such stones as took the ends of the beam bearing the footstep of the upper mill-stone in old flour and grist mills, and were probably intended for such use when there was a thought of converting this building into a grist-mill.

33. *Riddipit. P.I.* x, 229. *T.D.A.* lxv, 314. O.S. cxii, NE., lat. 50°-30'-47½", lon. 4°-1'-0½", 267 yds above Leather Tor bridge, on the left bank of the Meavy. One wall of what was probably the blowing-house still stands. There are four mortar-stones, three of which have been used for paving a track, at a wet spot. One of these pavings has four mortars, in confluent pairs. The largest mortar on the site is 9 in. in diameter and 3 in. in depth.

34. *Black Tor Falls, left bank. P.I.* x, 106 (as *Har Tor*). *T.D.A.* lxv, 314. O.S. cvi, SE., lat. 50°-31'-35½", lon. 4°-0'-39½". The ruins of the house are unusually well preserved; the main door with its lintel and a portion of the wall above it are preserved. The lintel bears the inscription 'XIII', in letters from 2¼ in. to 2½ in. high, obviously Roman numerals. This may have some connexion with the registration of the blowing-houses.

The house measures 17 ft 6 in. by 14 ft 9 in. internal, the furnace is 4 ft wide by 6 ft deep. There is a second compartment built on to the house, and some of the stone used is unusually large and well dressed. This compartment measures 14 ft 6 in. by 10 ft 10 in. It has been supposed to include the wheel-pit, but this is doubtful. The leat can still be traced. No mould or mortar-stones have been found.

Recently Mr. P. H. G. Richardson, R.N., of Dousland, found the stone bearing of the water-wheel lying on the top of the wall of the wheel-pit. He has very kindly given me facilities for examining it. The material is quartz-schorl rock, which has taken a good polish in the bearing. The stone has a somewhat irregular outline; its extreme length is a trifle over 6 in., its height a little under 5½ in., and it is 3 in. thick. The upper edge, Fig. 100, shows a much-worn bearing which extends completely across the thickness of the stone. A dotted arc in the figure indicates the position of a second bearing, which has seen little wear, and occupies a part only of the depth of the stone (on the right-hand lower corner as drawn).

Notwithstanding the dimensions of the larger bearing, it may be doubted whether the diamater of the iron axle much exceeded one inch; it was certainly not more than one and a half inch.

35. *Black Tor Falls, right bank. P.I.* x, 106 (as *Har Tor*). *T.D.A.* lxv, 314. O.S. cvi, SE., lat. 50°-31'-36", lon. 4°-0'-40".

The house measures 17 ft 8 in. by 11 ft 6 in. internally. The furnace is 4 ft in width by 4 ft 4 in. in depth. The clavel or lintel over the furnace mouth still remains, and in 1893 there remained nearly 3 ft in height of the chimney above the clavel (Pl. 65A). A little later a colt fell into the chimney and the stonework was taken down to release the animal. The leat can be clearly traced, and the probable site of the wheel-pit identified. No mould-stone has been found. There are three mortar-stones, each with mortars back to back on opposite faces. One of these with two mortars on each opposite face, is shown in Pl. 65B.

Another of these stones has been used as a bearing for a small iron axle. In 1933 Mr. T. Davey found, close to this house, a granite ball, of

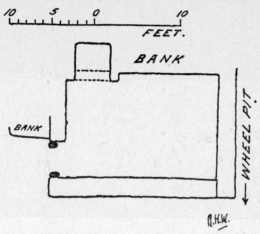

Fig. 92. Blowing-house, Black Tor Falls. Revised plan.

which the least diameter is $3\frac{3}{4}$ in. and the greatest is $4\frac{5}{16}$ in. It is obviously artificially formed, and suggests the possibility that it may have been used as a pounder or pestle in conjunction with the mortars. Nothing similar has been found elsewhere, but few of the houses have been cleared of debris or their contents examined.

During the winter of 1940–1, either in consequence of natural decay or, as I fear, following the robbery of stones from the building, the furnace collapsed and the clavel or lintel has disappeared. This same disturbance, from whatever arising, extended also to the south-east angle of the building, where it has had the effect of disclosing the position and detail of the entrance doorway, a matter not before apparent. I am accordingly able to give a revised plan, see Fig. 92.

Two further mortar-stones were found during the year 1941, both lying to the south of this house, one of them in the bank of the stream, where it had been uncovered by a flood, and the other, found by my wife, but a few yards from the house.

36. *Sheepstor Brook: Colleytown, right bank.* T.D.A. lxiv, 273; lxx, 451. O.S. cxii, NE., lat. 50°-29'-20½", lon. 4°-1'-15½". Considerable remains of the blowing-house, but dimensions not clearly recoverable. Course of leat very well marked. There is a mould-stone, which has been moved to a cart-shed by Colleytown Farm, and built into a wall (Pl. 66A and Fig. 94). The mould measures 16¼ in. by 12½ in. to 11 in. at the top; 12½ in. by 8½ in. at the bottom; its original depth was 6½ in., but at the centre it is now 7½ in. deep, having been deepened by use. There is a groove at the centre of the edge at one end; and there is a

sample mould measuring 3½ in. by 2¼ in. by 1¼ in. deep. The mould would hold 277 lb. of tin, and the sample mould would yield an ingot weighing 2½ lb.

There are two mortar-stones each with eight mortars, four on the front, four on the back, set quadrilateral-wise. The mortars are from 6 to 6½ in. in diameter and from 1¾ to 2¾ in. deep.

Considerable quantities of sand and tin slimes are to be found close to the house, the waste from washing the crushed ore.

37. *Sheepstor Brook: Yellowmead.* T.D.A. xlvi, 288; lxv, 307. O.S. cxii, NE., lat. 50°-29'-23½", lon. 4°-0'-36½". There are ample remains of the blowing-house, but the structure has been used as a quarry and much disturbed in parts; the original dimensions cannot be ascertained. One side of the wheel-pit is in good order, with a well-worked stone having a recess for the plummer-block of the wheel axle. The float from the base of the furnace has been built into a hedge not far away (Pl.70A), and a mortar-stone stands on another hedge. There is a stone with a bearing for a small iron axle, and also a small broken mould, very neatly cut in Roborough Down elvan. The width of the mould at the top is 7¼ in. and at the bottom it is 4½ in., the depth is but 2½ in. Taking a normal proportion of width and length, this mould would give an ingot of no more than 36 lb. in weight, the smallest from Dartmoor.

At Yellowmead Farm is one of the stones of a crazing mill, 28 in. in diameter. This probably came from the blowing-house; and, at the head of a stroll wholly occupied by tinners' burrows, at the foot of which stands the house, there is a part-made mould-stone, the mould measuring 20 in. by 16 in. and having been cut to a depth of 2¼ in. A large piece of slag was found near this house, and contained prills of tin.

38. *Deancombe Brook: Outcombe.* T.D.A. lxv, 308. O.S. cxii, NE., lat. 50°-29'-58", lon. 4°-0'-9". All details of the structure of the house are preserved, save only the roof. The building is not rectangular, but is planned to fit the natural features. Its mean internal dimensions may be taken to be about 15 ft by 14 ft. There is a well-marked wheel-pit, with a tail-race, and a raised bank to conduct the water to the wheel. The wheel may have been 9 ft 6 in. in diameter and of 2 ft breast.

The mouth of the furnace is 4 ft in width, and the clavel over the mouth is still in place.

No mould-stone has been found, but there are at least a score of mortar-stones within and without the building; one mortar outside the building is 7½ in. in diameter by 2¾ in. in depth.

The upper stone of a crazing mill lies within the house; its diameter is 1 ft 11 in., and its greatest thickness is 5 in. (Pl. 67B and Fig. 97).

One of the stones coping the wheel-pit has a bearing such as has been described as occurring at other houses; it is improbable, but not impossible, that it served for the axle of the water-wheel.

Sand from crushing, and tin slimes, occur in quantity.

WALKHAM

39. *Little Horrabridge.* T.D.A. lxxii, 205. O.S. cxii, NW., lat. 50°-30'-25", lon. 4°-5'-40½". No structure which can be identified as a blowing-house. Three mortar-stones built in at the base of the quoins of relatively modern sheds. One stone is 2 ft 7 in. in length and has four mortars in a line (the greatest number known to be so arranged) (Fig. 98). The mortars are 6 in. in diameter and from 2½ to 3 in. in depth. The other two stones have two mortars each. There is a fourth stone set as the foundation of a wooden shed; this has six mortars, one discrete, three confluent, and two confluent. There is also a stone with a bearing for a small iron axle.

40. *Above Merrivale Bridge, left bank.* P.I. xi, 102. T.D.A. lxiii, 361. O.S. cvi, NE., lat. 50°-33'-33½", lon. 4°-2'-37½".

The building measures 32 ft by 15 ft 6 in. internally, and the walls are 2 ft 9 in. in thickness. The furnace is still preserved; it measures 2 ft by 1 ft 8 in. internally, and the sides are still standing to the height of 4 ft 6 in. (Pl. 68B and Fig. 93). The worked float still forms the bottom of the furnace, but slightly displaced as to level. No mortar-stones have been seen.

The mould-stone lies close to the furnace, and hard by the door. The mould measures 17¼ in. by 12 in. at the top, 12¼ in. by 7½ in. at the bottom, and is 6½ in. in depth. There is a notch in the upper margin at one end, but not centrally placed. The mould would hold 254 lb. of tin. There is also a sample mould 3½ in. by 2 in. by 1¼ in. deep, which would hold about 2¼ lb. of tin.

The wheel-pit was probably within the house, at one end.

41. *Above Merrivale Bridge, left bank,* higher blowing-house. P.I. xi, 103. T.D.A. lxiii, 364. O.S. cvi, NE., lat. 50°-34'-2½", lon. 4°-2'-38". The inside measurement of the house is 32 ft 6 in. by 15 ft. The walls are from 2 ft 4 in. to 2 ft 6 in. thick.

The wheel-pit is well defined, and the wheel may have been 10 ft in diameter and 1 ft 2 in. breast.

A mould-stone lies close to the door. The mould measures 15¼ in. by 11 in. at the top, 12 in. by 8 in. at the bottom, and is 6 in. deep; it would hold 193 lb. of tin. There is a sample mould, 3¼ in. by 2¾ in. by 2 in. in depth, which could hold about 4½ lb. of tin. No mortar-stones have been seen.

42. *Above Merrivale Bridge, right bank.* T.D.A., lxiii, 365. O.S. cvi, NE., lat. 50°-34'-15", lon. 4°-2'-42". The blowing-house, which is less well preserved than the two preceding examples, is not rectangular. One long side measures 38 ft 9 in., and the other measures 33 ft; one end is 14 ft and the other is 12 ft 6 in. in length, all being internal measures. The wheel-pit is well defined, and the wheel may have been 8 ft 6 in. in diameter, by 1 ft 6 in. breast.

No complete mould-stone has been found, but there is a broken mould, 8 in. wide at the top, length not ascertainable, depth not less than 3 in. It appears to be of an older type than the moulds in the houses on the left bank.

No mortar-stones have been found in the house, but in the bed of the river, where the newtake wall meets it, there is a stone with a hollow which may be a mortar. The position is lat. 50°-34′-22½″, lon. 4°-2′-40″.

TAVY

43. *Will.* T.D.A. xlvi, 286. O.S. xcviii, NW., lat. 50°-36′-50″, lon. 4°-4′-26½″. The site of the blowing-house is not known, and the remains consist of a mould-stone only. The mould measures 15½ in. by 11½ in. at the top, 12½ in. by 9¼ in. at the bottom, and 5½ in. in depth. It would hold 215 lb. of tin. There is a sample mould which measures 3½ in. by 2½ in. and 1¼ in. in depth, and would hold approximately 2¾ lb. of tin.

Addendum

E. WEBBURN

44. *Widecombe, North Hall.* (*Devon and Cornwall Notes & Queries,* xviii, pt. 5, par. 136; 1935.) O.S., c. SW., lat. 50°-34′-36″, lon. 3°-48′37″. Mortar-stone built into wall of linhay adjoining North Hall. It has three basin-shaped hollows on each side, these shallower on one side. The author agreed in conversation that this was a mortar-stone, and mentioned another very similar in the adjacent garden of the Post Office, near the road. (ED.)

TECHNICAL DETAILS

LEATS

The leats were, for the more part, short, sites having been selected where the gradient of the stream or river afforded a fall of some twelve feet in a short distance. But the tinners went long distances for water for the stream works, and sometimes for water for the blowing-house. The leat at Outer Down (1) is nearly half a mile in length, and at Brisworthy Hamlet (25) is 1,100 yards long. But there are no more than 70 yards between the intake and the wheel at the Butterbrook (18).

From inspection of their present channels, and from a knowledge of those few leats which are still in use for other purposes, it would appear that few can ever have had a greater capacity than 60 cu. ft of water a minute (540,000 gallons a day). And in many instances the streams from which they are taken would not yield this supply except after recent rain.

WATER-WHEELS

Water-wheels were all of the overshot type, with launders taking the water on to the whele. On the average the wheels were 9 ft 3 in. in diameter, the largest 10 ft, the smallest 8 ft. On the average the breast was 1 ft 6 in. with extremes of 2 ft and 1 ft. Three of the wheels may have had 2 ft breast; these were exceptional and may have driven crazing mills as well as bellows. For the rest 9 ft by 1 ft 3 in. is a fair average, and the depth of shrouding was probably about 6 in. Such a wheel, if well built, could take 130 cu. ft of water a minute, and develop 1·33 h.p., but the speed would be too great for such slow-moving machinery as the bellows, and the leats were not designed for such a flow; with 60 cu. ft a minute the wheel would develop 0·66 h.p., and that was probably the extreme capacity of all but a few of the wheels. The largest may have yielded approximately 2 h.p.

BELLOWS

As to the bellows there is, naturally, no physical evidence of their form; wood and leather could not be expected to have survived. They were probably always much like the contemporary smith's bellows.

In the last days of the blowing-house in Cornwall Pryce describes them as being "two large bellows, worked by a water wheel, the same as in the iron forges. They are about eight feet long, and two and a half wide at the broadest part". He was describing a blowing-house larger than any of which remains are to be found on Dartmoor.

In some of the houses (9, 18, 21, 32, 35, 37, 38, 39) there have been found granite bearings much worn by small iron axles; in many houses these have probably been overlooked. In most instances the bearings are open, and would not retain any axle subject to a lifting action. It is probable that they took the fulcrums of some form of rocking beam or rollers of a flat-rod, and that these may have worked the bellows. But as to this there is no certainty.

FURNACES

In many of the houses the position formerly occupied by the furnace is clearly indicated. But what now remains would appear to be rather the frame within which the furnace was built, and from which the furnace, which was in nature a temporary structure needing frequent renewal, has been lost. What remains are areas surrounded by walls on three sides, and open to the house on the fourth. These have much the appearance of unusually narrow hearth-fires. Of eight such examples, in five the opening from the house is 4 ft in width, one is 3 ft 7 in. and one 3 ft. If we describe them as recesses we may note that they are formed in two different ways. They may stand within the area of the four walls of the house, partitioned from the rest of the floor by a stout wing-wall—as at Mill Corner on the Plym (26). See Fig. 90.

Or the recesses may jut out from the building, being partly formed in the thickness of the wall. As an example Black Tor, Meavy (35), may be taken: here the structure is unusually complete. The granite clavel or lintel still bridges the opening and supports the remnant of the chimney breast, while, in 1893, a portion of the chimney yet remained. See Fig. 92 for a plan of this house and Pl. 65A for a view of the recess as it stood in 1893; this is an enlargement from a negative taken from the far side of the river; Pl. 65B is a view of one of the mortar-stones.

The following recesses are known. First those which may be described as 'Inner': Yealm, Higher (23), recess 3 ft wide by 6 ft 4 in. deep. Mill Corner, Plym (26), recess 3 ft 7 in. wide by 4 ft 4 in. deep. And the recess at Merrivale, Walkham, lower (40), was also within the house, but its dimensions cannot be fixed. As to 'Outer' recesses the following are known: Week Ford, W. Dart (9), 4 ft wide by 4 ft deep. Below Henglake, Avon (12), 4 ft wide by 2 ft 9 in. deep. Black Tor, Meavy, left bank (34), 4 ft wide by 6 ft deep. Black Tor, Meavy, right bank (35), 4 ft wide by 4 ft 4 in. deep. Outcombe, Deancombe (38), 4 ft wide, depth uncertain. At both of the last two houses the clavel still stands.

There are two sources of information as to the form of the actual furnace, a description by Pryce of the 'castle' in use in 1778 (*Mineralogia Cornubiensis*, p. 136), and the remains of a furnace in the Merrivale blowing-house (40).

Pryce is describing something larger than we may expect on Dartmoor; he writes: "The fire-place or castle is about six feet perpendicular, two feet wide in the top part each way, and about fourteen inches in the bottom, all made of moorstone and clay, well cemented and cramped together. The pipe or nose of each bellows is fixed ten inches high from the bottom of the castle, in a large piece of wrought Iron, called the Hearth Eye. The Tin and charcoal are laid in the castle, stratum super stratum, in such quantities as are thought proper. . . . Those bellows . . . throw in a steady and powerful air into the castle; which, at the same time that it smelts the Tin, forces it out also through a hole in the bottom of the castle, about four inches high, and one inch and a half wide, into a moorstone trough six feet and a half high [probably a misprint for 'long'] and one foot wide, called a Float; whence it is ladled into lesser troughs or moulds, each of which contains about three hundred of Metal."

The feature of this description is the small sectional area of the furnace compared to its height, a feature necessary to a successful blast-furnace, and retained even to modern times in the blowing-houses of Saxony. We may be sure that the Dartmoor furnace had something of this proportion on a smaller scale.

At the first blowing-house above Merrivale Bridge on the left bank of the Walkham (40) there still stands a furnace of a type which shows that, here at least, the proportions above suggested were adopted. Pl. 68B and Fig. 93 show the details of this furnace.

This furnace is 1 ft 10 in. wide by 2 ft deep at the base, and is 4 ft 10 in. in height. Its floor consists of a stone which just fits within the sides of the furnace and came somewhat beyond it to the front. In this stone is

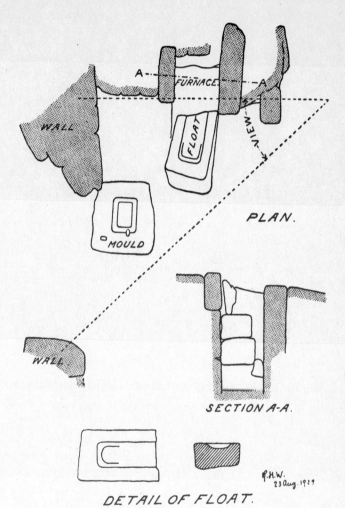

PLAN.

SECTION A-A.

DETAIL OF FLOAT.

R.H.W.
23 Aug. 1929

FIG. 93. Detail of furnace, Merrivale.

cut a channel 13 in. in width, shallow, but deepening somewhat toward the front. I have called this the 'float', although its use does not appear to correspond strictly with that which Pryce calls by the name. It brought the tin outside the furnace to a point at which it could be ladled out.

Such a furnace, closed at the front with a flat stone, or with temporary walling, would in effect be strictly analogous with Pryce's 'castle'. Over it might have been built the chimney, in this case within the house, and it is significant that the wall has been buttressed, as though against the weight of some such structure.

Although no such complete furnace has been found elsewhere, a precisely similar float exists at Yellowmead (37) (Pl. 70A), and another, partly made, at Glazebrook (14), and others may well have been buried and overlooked. It is certain that the ore, fuel and blast must have been confined, and that there was no open hearth process. The earlier method of confinement appears to have been the construction of a circular furnace, tapering somewhat at the bottom; R. N. Worth mentions such a furnace at Lower Hill House, Warleggan, in Cornwall; it was built of granite, reddened and broken by the heat (*Journal of the Royal Institution of Cornwall*, No. 13, p. 76). A similar furnace is to be seen at the old 'Iron Mill' on the bank of the Dart, under Hepstock and Awsewell Rocks. This is not strictly comparable since it was used for iron-smelting; still, it was a blast furnace, in use in the year 1605. A part of its interest lies in the fact that the furnace is constructed between two masses of masonry, the permanent abutments of the perishable furnace, and the foundation of its chimney (44). The blowing-house at Outer Down (1) shows a similar arrangement of masonry with a gap in which the furnace was probably constructed.

MOULDS (Pl. 66A, 69A, 71A)

All known Dartmoor mould-stones are of granite, saving one, at Yellowmead (37), which has been formed in Roborough Down elvan. The moulds are approximately rectangular, with bevelled sides, and, when new, are flat in the bottom. With constant use the stone surface disintegrates, especially at the bottom, which deepens in the centre and becomes concave. Finally the heat splits the stone, and a new mould becomes necessary.

There are instances of two moulds cut in one stone, not always of the same size; and small sample moulds are frequent.

Colleytown (36), provides a typical mould; a view is given on Pl. 66A, and a measured drawing as Fig. 94. The section shows the deepening at the centre of the mould by heat erosion; on the plan the sample mould will be noted on the top right hand, and in the centre of the outer margin of the mould at the top will be seen the notch, a stick rested in which, and against the opposite bottom angle of the cavity, left a continuous hole running diagonally through the ingot. This and the sample are not constant features.

INGOTS (Pl. 67A)

The following is a tabular statement of the weights of the ingots which could be cast in the respective known moulds from Dartmoor, assuming the moulds to be in new condition, and filled to the brim.

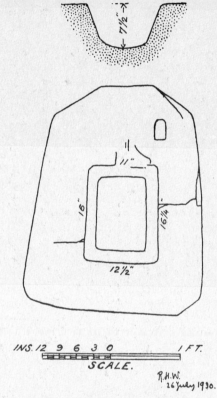

FIG. 94. Colleytown Mouldstone.

The arrangement is in ascending order of weight, and no deduction has been made in respect of the perforations which are known to have been moulded in some of the blocks:

Possible weight of ingots (lb.)
Mean of 18: 224 lb.
36? 56 113 169 174 183 185 191 192 193 193 195 215 254 277 367
487 569
Mean of 13: 195 lb.
113 169 174 183 185 191 192 193 193 195 215 254 277

The first three weights, and the last two, are obviously of a different order from the thirteen which form the body of the table, and, accordingly, we should expect to find that the actual ingots produced when the moulds were in use would average about 195 lb. in weight, or probably somewhat less. This can be tested by reference to the record of the coinage at Michaelmas, 1595, Devon. There were presented at all the coinage towns, Chagford, Ashburton, Plympton, and Tavistock, taken together, 426 pieces, or ingots, of tin, weighing in all 75,091 lb. This gives an average weight of 176 lb. per ingot.

Chagford took pride of place at this coinage; not only was a greater weight of tin coined at Chagford than at any of the other three towns, but also the weight per ingot was greater. The total weight coined at Chagford was 33,348 lb., in 169 pieces: an average of 197 lb. per ingot.

At Ashburton, 5,037 lb. were coined, in 30 pieces, an average of 168 lb. per ingot.

These figures, recording actual practice, accord well with the size of the moulds which yet survive. They also indicate that there was a wide divergence in the methods of the counties of Devon and Cornwall; a difference which has not hitherto been recorded.

Writing of Cornwall, in 1602, Carew states that the tin was "cast into pieces of a long and thick squareness, from three to four hundred pound waight". This was but seven years later than the coinage above referred to. We can test this by reference to the account book of Robert Trencreek, Councillor at Law, Justice of the Peace, Tinner, and Farmer, who resided at Treworgan, St. Erme, Cornwall. The book is in my hands, and I find that he entered his stock of tin at ten coinages in the years 1580-5 inclusive. He coined fifty-two and a half pieces, of a total weight of 18,094 lb., an average of 345 lb. per ingot. He gives his pieces in pairs, for the more part, hence the individual weights are not available; but one piece must have weighed 408 lb. or over; and one piece cannot have been more than 270 lb. in weight; while he specifies three single ingots of 374, 302 and 302 lb. respectively.

We may take the Michaelmas coinage, 1595, for Cornwall, when the total weight coined in Cornwall was 290,260 lb., in 842 pieces, giving an average ingot weight of 345 lb. At Truro, where Trencreek probably presented his ingots, the average weight was 351 lb. It follows that in Cornwall the moulds were very considerably larger than in Devon, with few exceptions.

Only one Dartmoor ingot is known to survive, and that was found in the year 1879, when a field was being drained in the valley of the Piall Brook, near Slade, Cornwood. It was given by the late Mr. J. D. Pode, the owner of the land, to the Plymouth Institution. If it were not cast in one of the moulds at the Lower Blowing-House on the Yealm (22), then there must have been, somewhere, a precise duplicate of that mould. Fig. 95 in the text shows the ingot fitted into the mould, and also indicates how the stick was set to form the hole. Pl. 67A gives a photograph of the ingot, which weighs 52 lb. It will be noticed that the ingot by no means fills the mould, which was not quite level when the casting was made. There must at times have been these relatively small surpluses after the normal ingots had been cast.

MORTAR-STONES (Pl. 64, 65B, 69B, 70B, 71B)

The material for the mortar-stones was always either hard, fine-grained felsite, or, rarely, quartz-schorl rock. The number of mortars in a stone may vary from one, as on the Erme (15) to five, as at Little Horrabridge (39). They are frequently arranged in line, from two to four, of the latter only one instance is known, at Little Horrabridge (39) (Fig. 98).

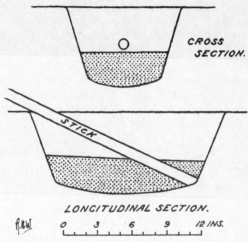

FIG. 95. Slade ingot and Yealm mould.

In size the mortars vary from 12 in. to 6 in. in diameter, and from 9 in. to 2 in. in depth, according to the amount of use which they have received. Those of greater diameter are usually the deeper, but there is no fixed ratio; much depended on the nature of the stone. They are approximately hemispherical, but in some the depth is greater than half the diameter, in some it is less. The extremes are: an example 10 in. in diameter by 9 in. in depth, and another 9 in. in diameter by 3 in. in depth.

That they were used as mortars, in which to pound ore, and possibly slag, is certain. But the nature of the pestle can only be guessed. It may have been wood bound with iron. Or stone balls, such as that found at Black Tor (35), may have been used where finer grinding was desired. Near St. Columb in Cornwall small ingots of tin were found which had been cast in mortars as moulds; this is believed to be unique.

It should be remembered that the ore, whether stream or mine, was allowed to accumulate and to remain undressed until a convenient amount had accumulated, or until the nearing 'coinage' demanded its dressing and smelting if it were to be coined and freed for sale without further delay. These 'coinages' were normally half-yearly so that six months' produce would usually be dressed at one time; but in later years intermediate coinages were introduced and known as post-coinages, whereby more frequent sales became possible.

The occasion of the dressing and purifying the ore was known as the 'wash', from the nature of the final process, which was one of levigation by water. Until this wash the amount of black tin which had resulted from recent operations was unknown, and in consequence no one of the partners in a work knew what would be the amount of his share. So that all might be open and above board it was enacted that "all comparteners and owners of Tynworkes when they goe about to make theire wash ought to give lawfull warneing to theire Comparteners which have borne the charges with them in workeing of theire Tynne". (Bailiff of Blackmore.)

The wash over, the black tin was divided among the adventurers according to their several holdings. References to expenditure at the 'wash' occur in Trencreek's accounts, thus, 1586: "Too hem (George Coyt) ye wasshe daye at hoome . . . xij d.; costs at ye wasshe in ye onne work . . . ij s.j, d, in ye other work . . . xix d. ob."

Since all ore, whether stream or mine, contains quartz and other vein minerals intimately mingled with the black tin, the first necessary process was to reduce the ore to such size particles as to admit the separation of the vein-stuff from the true ore, although this separation is never absolute. The ore had to be crushed.

There is ample evidence that, on Dartmoor, this crushing was often, probably in most instances, carried out at the blowing-house. Hence the considerable deposits of crushed sand found, for instance, at the house opposite Thornworthy (2) at Gobbet (10), Colleytown (36) and Outcombe (38). And the mortars found at the blowing-houses were for this purpose.

Since the slag often contained a considerable percentage of metallic tin in pearls or 'prills', this also was broken small and examined, and the richer parts treated either by further crushing, and washing or possibly sieving, or by resmelting. But neither the nature of the slag, nor the quantity would account for the number of the mortars or their size and form.

CRAZING MILLS

The crazing mill was another device for reducing the ore to a fine sand. It consisted of two granite mill-stones, the lower of which was fixed, while the upper revolved. The ore, already reduced to a fine gravel, was fed between the two and ground to a fine sand. Except in detail it was strictly comparable to the mills for stone-ground flour.

Only three blowing-houses on Dartmoor are known to have had crazing mills, but it is not safe to assume that these were all.

At Gobbet (10) both the lower and the upper stones are still to be seen. The working faces have a diameter of 3 ft. Although a sufficiency of water would here be available to drive the mill off a water-wheel, the upper stone would not appear to be adapted to that method of drive. The four holes on its upper surface may have provided the grip by which it was turned, and this may have been by man power, but more probably by a horse moving in a circle round the mill. See Fig. 96 for details of the stones.

CRAZING MILL, COBBET.

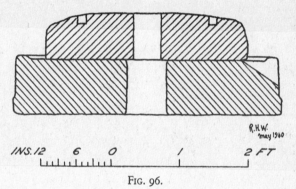

R.H.W.
may 1960

INS. 12   6   0   1   2 FT

FIG. 96.

At Yellowmead (37) only one of the millstones remains, and that has been built into a hedge, so that only one face can be seen. It is smaller than the Gobbet stones, being 28 in. in diameter, and the mill was probably driven by the water-wheel.

At Outcombe (38) only one of the millstones is to be seen but the other may be merged in the ruins. The stone which is visible is the upper, and was certainly driven off the water-wheel; it is 1 ft 11 in. in diameter. It may be noted that the wheel-pits indicate that the water-wheels at both Yellowmead and Outcombe were larger than the average, possibly to supply the extra power which the crazing mills demanded.

Pl. 67B is from a photograph of the millstone at Outcombe, and Fig. 97 gives a drawing.

The following extract from Trencreek's accounts may be of interest as an example of the phraseology of the year 1584, "lx hoggeshedde of Crasyns gryndid". It would appear that the product of the crazing mill was known as *crasyns*.

KNACKING MILLS OR STAMPS

Knacking mills or stamps were of later date than crazing mills, which, however, persisted after the introduction of stamps, for some time at least. Carew writes (1602): "The stone . . . is first broken in peeces with hammers; and then carryed, either in waynes, or on horses

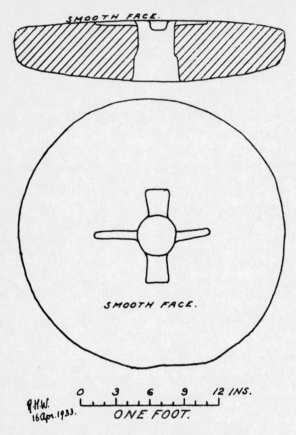

FIG. 97. Crazing-Mill Stone, Deancombe.

backs, to a stamping mill, where three, and in some places sixe great logges of timber, bound at the ends with yron, and lifted vp and downe by a wheele, driuen with the water, doe breake it smaller. If the stones be ouer-moyst, they are dried by the fire in an yron cradle or grate. From the stamping mill, it passeth to the crazing mil, which betweene two grinding stones, turned also with a water-wheele, bruseth the same to a fine sand: howbeit, of late times they mostly use wet stampers, & so haue no need of the crazing mils for their best stuffe, but only for the crust of their tayles." This passage at once shows the date of the transition from dry to wet stamping, and indicates that even so the crazing mill had not wholly lost its use. With improved stamps it later perished.

Stamps do not need to be housed in a masonry building; at the most an open shed to keep the ore dry might be needed in the days of dry stamping. The wheel, its axle and the supports would all be in wood, with only some iron fittings; and are thus shewn by Borlase (*Natural History of Cornwall*, Pl. XIX) as late as 1758. There was nothing enduring to mark the site, saving the leat, and possibly a stone-faced bank from which the ore was fed into the 'pass'.

A name may outlast timber; there is, for instance, a *Knacking Mill Gulf* on the Erme (19), but we do not know at what date it acquired that designation. Documentary evidence does, however, show when some knacking mills were on Dartmoor. Thus the Forester's account for Dartmoor contains an entry of 3d. rent "for a mill called Kakking Mill, and a mill called Blowing Mill, two acres of land in the Forest in the west part of the water of Tawe let to Thomas Takfield, as appears by the Court Roll of 11 May 27 Henry VIII." A.D., 1535. Earlier than this, in 1504, in the Minister's accounts, under the heading of Farm of Mills, we find entry at Ashburton of a Tynmill and a Knackyngmyll. And, later, in 1603, the Corporation of Plymouth compromised with William Crymes as to a supply from the Plymouth Leat on Roborough Down to two tin mills, knocking mills or Classe mills, which sounds as though blowing-houses, crazing mills and knocking [or knacking] mills were there combined; although we may merely be meeting a specimen of legal redundancy.

As to the technique of preparing the ore for separation it is necessary to discriminate between stream tin and lode tin.

Stream tin was for the main part rich in ore and small in size; an occasional stone might need breaking by the hammer, but the ultimate reduction to the necessary fineness could readily have been accomplished in the mortars. Lode tin, whether derived from the mine or, as was far more usual on Dartmoor, from open cuttings, is not only in larger masses, but contains much more veinstone and the total quantity to be treated per unit of ore is much greater. It was probably to handle this lower grade ore that the knacking mill came into use. As long as the dry stamping process prevailed, the ore as it left the stamps was still unfitted for dressing, and it had to be reduced to finer stuff. This could certainly have been accomplished in the mortars; none the less the crazing mill was employed, at times at least, and it accomplished by horse or water-power that which involved the labour of men with the mortars.

The wet stamps, which came into use toward the end of the sixteenth century, could bring the stuff as it came from the hammers into condition in one process, and the crazing mill was retained only for that part which required exceptionally fine subdivision.

The point to be observed is that for stream tin the Dartmoor tinners could, and probably often did, dispense with all but the mortar-stones. And mortars could have been made to suffice for much of their lode tin.

THE DATE OF THE BLOWING-HOUSES

It is to be expected that there would have been blowing-houses on Dartmoor in the middle of the fourteenth century, but not that recognizable remains would have survived. The habit of pulling down and rebuilding seems to have been very firmly established, although when Carew speaks of the owners burning the houses once in every seven or eight years to recover the light tin driven up from the furnace by the blast, the context suggests that it was the thatched roof which was so sacrificed.

The probability of the same site having been adopted for successive houses has already been indicated; and the return of the tinners to a neighbourhood already exhausted for stream tin must have been of constant occurrence when lode tin became the main object of search. This in itself would lead to the reconstruction of the blowing-house which served the earlier tinners.

On the whole, it is probable that no remains are earlier than the fifteenth century, or later than the first half of the seventeenth. But there are no sufficient criteria for dating.

There should, however, be ample documentary evidence. The blowing-houses had to be registered; the makers of white tin were to attend the Stannary courts at every court to take oath that they would not assent to the making of any corrupt metal. Hence the rolls of the Stannary court should present constant references of value.

As to the rental of such houses as were within the Forest of Dartmoor, these should find entry in the rolls of the Duchy courts. And those houses which were on the Commons of Devon and within the adjacent manors would be traceable in the court rolls of the several manors, where these have been preserved. But the times are out of joint for record searching, and but a few instances can be given of the class of information which should be available.

1532. *Forest of Dartmoor Court Rolls.* Richard Cole, Richard Hele, and William Hele the son of Nicholas Hele pay 3d. the rent of a Mill called *Well Lake Mill.*

1538-9. Richard Coole and Thomas Hele pay 3d., the rent of mill called *Wallack Mill.*

Well Lake Mill and Wallack Mill were the same, and can be clearly identified as the building herein described as Blacklane Brook (22), so that building is satisfactorily dated.

1535. *Forest of Dartmoor Court Rolls.* Thomas Takfield pays 3d. the rent of a mill called *Blowing Mill*, in the west part of the water of the Taw.

This building has not yet been identified, but will be the subject of search.

1603. *Plymouth Municipal Records.* Agreement between the Corporation and William Crymes for a supply of water from the Plymouth leat to two tin mills, knocking mills or classe mills on Roborough Down.

No remains of these buildings have as yet been identified.

1654. *Lease of Tin Bounds.* Sir Richard Strode, Charles Arrundle, John Bunshole, William May, John Baylaie, lease to Matthew Yandall and Roger Williams the younger, of Walkhampton, a certain tin work known as *Blacktor*. Bounds given and the fact that the work was a lode work stated.

This may give a hint as to the date of one of the blowing-houses herein described as Black Tor Falls (34), (35).

1480–1597. *The parish accounts of Chagford.* Ormerod (*T.D.A.* i, 5, p. 110) deals with the interest taken in tin works by the various wardens of the parish.

He mentions no blowing-houses; these were not his subject. But it is possible that here may be another and rather surprising source of information.

*   *   *

I must make it clear that the term 'blowing-houses' has been used to describe buildings in which, in some instances, there is no proof that smelting was ever carried on. In theory at least there may have been buildings exclusively devoted to either of three purposes of the tinners; (a) the *blowing-house* proper, where the ore was smelted, (b) the *knocking mill*, where the ore was reduced to powder by a primitive form of stamps, driven by water-power, an alternative name being clash or classe mill, (c) the *crazing mill*, where the ore, after being stamped in the knocking mill, was ground to a finer powder between granite millstones. That one building sometimes served all three purposes may be seen at Gobbet (10), where there are mould-stones, mortar-stones and crazing mill stones. That many buildings served as both blowing-houses and knocking mills is certain; there are at least eight known buildings in which both mould- and mortar-stones have been found. On negative evidence, i.e. the apparent absence of any mould-stone where mortar-stones have been found, or of any mortar-stones where a mould-stone has been found, there are many buildings which may possibly have been restricted to a single purpose, either stamping or smelting. Hence the title of this section had better been 'The Tinners' Mills on Dartmoor', since all buildings provided with water-wheels were described as 'mills' by the tinners.

There is another point on which I feel that what is written above may be misleading. I have spoken of the mortar-stones in a manner which involved that they were used for the crushing of tin-ore and slags by hand. This has been the general assumption. But many years ago my father suggested that these mortar-stones may have been the dies or anvils between which and the stamps the ore was crushed. At the time at which he wrote we had little knowledge of the knocking mills, and were not in a position either to question or confirm the suggestion. I now realize that there are available criteria by which the matter might be determined.

In the first place, with very few exceptions, these mortars are arranged in groups of two or three. Two mortars, if in the same plane, must of necessity have a common axis, but it is also found that where three occur their centres lie in a straight line. This linear arrangement is consistent with their use in connexion with stamps lifted by cams or pegs set in a horizontal cylinder or axle.

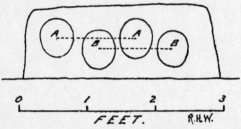

FIG. 98. Blowing-house, Little Horrabridge, plan of mortars.

Further, the more part of the groups of either two or three mortars will be found on stones which are roughly rectangular, and allow no more than a reasonable margin outside the mortars. Two examples may be cited from Nosworthy (32). Of these one stone has mortars on one face only, which are spaced 9½ in. apart, centre to centre; their average diameter is 9 in., the stone is 1 ft 2 in. in length by 1 ft 4½ in. in width. The other stone has a pair of mortars on each of two adjacent faces; on one face the mortars lie 9½ in. apart, centre to centre, are 7½ in. in diameter, and the face of the stone measures 3 ft by 1½ ft. On the adjacent face the mortars are set at 9¾ in. centres and are 6¼ in. in diameter; the face of the stone is 3 ft in length by 1 ft 2 in. in width. The spacing, centre to centre, thus varies between the extremes of 9½ to 9¾ in., a divergence fully consistent with the use of the stones under one and the same pair of roughly framed stamps, in fact negligible.

At Black Tor Falls (35) a pair of mortars on one stone are 10¼ in. centres, and a pair on another stone at 10 in. centres. At Deancombe, Outcombe (38), three pairs are respectively at 10¾, 10 and 10 in. centres.

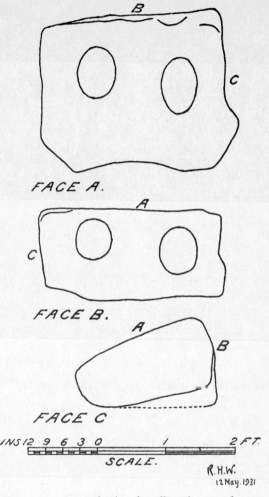

FACE A.

FACE B.

FACE C

INS 12 9 6 3 0   1   2 FT.

SCALE.

R.H.W.
12 May. 1931

FIG. 99. Mortar-stone from Glazebrook Mill, with pairs of mortars on adjacent faces.

A stone at Glaze Meet (14) has a pair on each of two faces, the centres of each pair some 14 in. apart (Fig. 99).

The stone at Little Horrabridge (39) which presents four mortars in approximate line on one face is unique as far as at present known, but it is no exception to the rule that three truly associated mortars are the limit; the four really form two pairs, and the pairs have no common axis. Centre to centre the one pair is spaced at $13\frac{1}{2}$, and the other at $12\frac{1}{2}$ in., see Fig. 98. Two other stones on this same site, each with a pair of mortars, yield central distances of $13\frac{1}{2}$ and 12 in. respectively.

Often, on a stone of which the length and breadth are approximately equal there will be found four mortars set quadrilateral-wise, and not infrequently another four mortars will be found on the reverse of the stone. In every such instance the mortars resolve into pairs.

The least spacing of centres which I have measured has been 9 in., and the greatest has been 14 in. Ten inches is, perhaps, the most frequent dimension.

I cannot see how these conditions should arise, or would serve any useful purpose were the mortars used with pestles worked by hand. But there are such as would be essential with batteries of mechanically operated stamps; and the dimensions cited accord well with the spacing of the bearings where there is good reason to believe that such stamps were once in operation. It is notable that the mortar-stones, being of carefully selected fine-grained granite, were not infrequently diverted from their original purpose, to which by continued use and wear they had become unfitted, and converted into bearings for the axles driving the stamps.

I conclude that Carew's statement (see p. 320 above) as to procedure in Cornwall might be applied to Dartmoor; with this amendment, that for "three and in some places six great logges of timber" there should be substituted *two and in some places three*. His reference to drying the ore before stamping it suggests that in some buildings where open fireplaces are found, but no mould-stones, the fireplace might have been used for drying the ore prior to stamping, if overmoist, "by the fire in an yron cradle or grate".

Further Documentary Evidence. I have on my shelves a large paper copy of Risdon's *Devon*, which bears the armorial bookplate of Henry Woollcombe, Recorder of Plymouth, 1833–7, and the later bookplate of Dr. William Woollcombe. The book is interleaved and extra-illustrated, in part with engravings, in part with sepia drawings by Henry Woollcombe, who has also made manuscript notes on the margins and the interleaves, and has affixed press cuttings to the margins. Most of these cuttings are from archaeological notes contributed to the local press, some apparently by Woollcombe himself. Among these excerpts is one from the *Western Times*, December 1830, which runs as follows: "Buckland Abbey, 10. Thomas Whyte was the next Abbot and was still living in 1530. Among other leases I find one dated 1 November, 1511, granting to William and Jane Dunster the reversion of an estate, 'apud Lader Torre, cum uno molendino pulsatili ad stannum pulsandum infra Manerium nostrum de Walkhampton'." Term 70 years. Rent fixed at 9s. 8d. A mill for beating tin would be a 'knocking mill'. In the present instance the building referred to was almost certainly that near Nosworthy (32), but there is another possible identification,

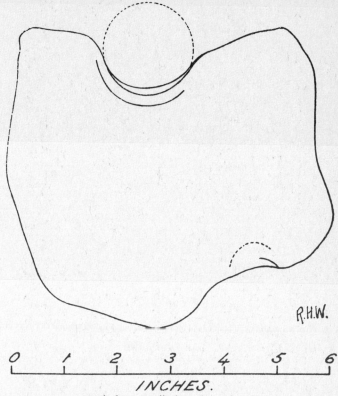

Fig. 100. Black Tor Falls (No. 34). Stone bearing.

Riddipit (33). Mortar-stones are found on both sites, and, up to the present, moulds have not been seen at either. Lader Torre is an earlier form of Leather Tor.

There is one other matter which I might well add as confirmatory of the above statement that peat charcoal was early used for smelting tin. On the 31st July, 18 John, 1216, John granted to William Briwere the custody of the Castle of Lydford with all its appurtenances. Pursuant to this we find that on the 3rd May 3 Henry III, 1219, the king directs a writ to William Briwere, commanding him to permit the men of

Joan, Queen of England, to dig, burn and lead away from the turbary of Dartmoor to her Stannary as they used and ought.

It is impossible to attribute to the word 'burn' any meaning other than 'convert into charcoal', since none would desire to literally *burn* peat, and lead away the ashes.

A list of articles by the author on Dartmoor tin-works is appended below. These should be consulted for further details and for various additional photographic illustrations of tinners' relics.

1892　The Erme, Yealm, and Torry. *P.I.*, 11, pp. 174–83.

1914　Stray notes on Dartmoor tin-working. *T.D.A.*, 46, pp. 284–9

1927　A blowing-house in the parish of Chagford. *T.D.A.*, 59, pp. 343–5

1929　Stray notes on Dartmoor blowing-houses, II. *T.D.A.*, 61, pp. 401–3

1931　Blowing-houses in the valley of the Walkham (moorland). *T.D.A.*, 63, pp. 361–7

1932　Blowing-houses in the valleys of the Sheepstor Brook and the Glazebrook. *T.D.A.*, 64, pp. 273–8

1933　Blowing-houses in the valleys of the Sheepstor Brook, the Meavy, the Erme, and the Avon. *T.D.A.*, 65, pp. 307–21

1938　Dartmoor blowing-houses. Stray Notes, III. *T.D.A.*, 70, pp. 451–4

1940　Notes on some Dartmoor blowing-houses. *T.D.A.*, 72, pp. 201–7

(ED.)

THE TENANTS AND COMMONERS
OF DARTMOOR

NOTE. *Numerals in brackets throughout this chapter are page references to the first volume of the* Publications of the Dartmoor Preservation Association (1890).

PRIOR to the year 1204, for a period the precise commencement of which is unknown, the whole of Devon, with possible slight exception, was royal forest and subject to the Forest Laws. In that year, and as we may believe under pressure, King John, on the 18th day of May, granted a charter which was ostensibly to disafforest all Devon up to the metes and bounds of Dartmoor and Exmoor. It has been doubted whether the formalities necessary to give effect to this charter were ever observed. Be that as it may, the Great Charter of John removed some at least of the oppressive features of the Forest Laws, and especially revoked the eleventh article of the second Henry's Assize of the Forest, 1184, which called upon all men to attend the forest courts on the summons of the master forester; while article 47 of the Great Charter provided that all forests afforested in the reign of John should at once be disafforested.

That these measures were by no means fully observed may be judged by the terms of the first Charter of the Forest which had general application throughout England, that of Henry III, 1217.

This, by clause 2, enacts that all lands afforested by Henry II should be viewed, and if any land had been afforested other than land in royal demesne, to the loss of the owner, it should be disafforested, but if it were the king's land it should remain a forest, saving to those who had previously enjoyed the same all common of herbage and other matters, while, by clause 3, without inquiry, all lands afforested by Richard I and John, except lands in royal demesne, should be disafforested forthwith. By clause 10 the severity of the Forest Laws was mitigated, in terms which sufficiently indicate what that severity had been; it was conceded that no man should lose life or limb for breach of forest. None the less, if any were taken and convicted of such breach he should be heavily fined, if he had the wherewithal to pay such fine; and if he had not the wherewithal he should be thrown in prison for a year and a day; and if after such year and a day he could find pledges for his conduct he might leave prison, if not he was to abjure the realm of England. Inasmuch as Henry was not of age in 1217 this charter was issued in his name by William Marshall, Earl of Pembroke.

Even so matters do not appear to have advanced greatly, and it was not until the statute of 9 Henry III, 1224, that there was general and satisfactory action. Since Dartmoor Forest was presumedly perambulated in 1224 it may be that the present status of that area was not fully defined before that date. But one important fact remains, both the charter of John and the Charter of the Forest contained clauses saving the rights of common then enjoyed.

It may be asked why, when John disafforested Devon, it was held reasonable that he should retain Dartmoor and Exmoor as royal forest. The answer is that both were royal demesne. Domesday does not mention the Forest of Dartmoor, but the entry as to Lydford runs: "The King has a Borough, Lideford. King Edward held it in demesne . . ."; and Lydford was in the hands of the King in 1 Richard I, 1189–90. The evidence is that at all significant dates Dartmoor was appurtenant to Lydford.

The county of Devon appears to have been afforested before 1199, since John, Earl of Mortain (afterwards King John) granted a charter to the men of Devon in respect of the Forest of that county (2). How burdensome the royal forests had been to the community may be judged from the fact that the king claimed jurisdiction over all woods and forests whether in royal demesne or in the hands of subjects, and under the heading of 'forests' fell large areas of common land, while the tenacity with which the crown clung to these oppressive rights is shown by the tenth clause of the Charter of Liberties of Henry I, 1101. This charter was expressly for the relief of the realm from unjust exactions; nevertheless clause 10 enacts: "The forests, by the common consent of my barons, I retain in my hands, as my father held them."

But even the forests had their mitigations and were subject to public rights, as may be judged from the charter clauses saving such. The rights were and are those which consist with the original status of common land, varied later by the reserve of certain areas as royal hunting grounds, with the consequent restrictions on common rights, but not with their complete denial. One such restriction was the closure of the forests by night. In days when so much of the land remained unenclosed, rights of common were a first necessity of agriculture and even royal prerogative would have suffered from the impoverishment which would have followed their denial; in this danger lay the salvation of the commonalty.

It is not to be thought that royal forests had their origin in Norman times. Canute in his day enacted "I will that every man be worthy of his hunting in wood and field on his own estate. And let every man abstain from my hunting." It was the abrogation of the first clause of this, and the denial of the right of every man to the hunting on his own estate, which led to the gross evils of the later forests.

Birkett writes (*xvi–xvii*):

1. "Every inhabitant in a Forest—meaning every owner or occupier of land within a Forest—may by prescription have Common of pasture in respect of his holding; and though his lands may be put out of the Forest by Perambulation he may still, by special reservation, enjoy such right.

2. "There may also be a usage for all owners and occupiers of land in a vill or town adjacent to a Forest to have Common of pasture for their commonable beasts levant and couchant in the vill or town.

3. "A man must only take Common with his own beasts, unless there is a special custom to the contrary providing for the payment of fees, known as agistment fees.

4. "'All manner of beasts' (says Manwood) 'are commonable in a Forest, except goats, geese, sheep and hogs'; but Common may be had for all these by license.

5. "The classes of persons to whom I have referred as legally entitled to Common of pasture may also take turf for fuel, and sand and stone for use upon their buildings, from the waste of a Royal Forest."

The numbering of the above paragraphs is not in the original.

Dartmoor has long since ceased to be a forest. On the 10th October 1239, Henry III granted to his brother Richard, Earl of Poitou and Cornwall, "our Manor of Lydford, with the castle of the same place, and all its appurtenances, together with the Forest of Dartmoor" (5). By this grant the Forest became a Chase, and that not necessarily because it passed to a subject who in himself had no power to hold a forest court, but because the King did not further grant that the Earl and his heirs might upon request made in Chancery have Justices of the Forest; which, had it been granted, would have constituted Dartmoor a Forest at Law. Lydford and Dartmoor reverted to the Crown in 1300, on the death of Edmund Earl of Cornwall; and in 1337 Edward III granted "the castle and Manor of Lydford with appurtenances, and with the Chase of Dartmoor with appurtenances" to Edward the Black Prince, Duke of Cornwall; since which date Dartmoor has been appurtenant to the Duchy of Cornwall.

The grant to Richard, Earl of Poitou, in 1239, is of interest because it was in consequence thereof that the perambulation of 1240 was made, the return of which is the earliest record of the boundaries, there being no extant return of the perambulation of 1224, if indeed, any was made.

It may be useful to refer at this stage to a diagram which is drawn at the foot of a document entitled "*Instructions for my Lorde Prynce to the Kyngs most Honorable Counsell concerning my said Lord Princs Forrest of*

Dartmore in the Countye of Devonshire and in the moores and wasts of the same belongyn." The period is the reign of Henry VIII (*48* and *168*). The diagram was evidently intended to enable the "Kyngs most Honorable Counsell" to form a mental picture of the relationship of Dartmoor Forest to those areas associated with it, or claiming rights within its borders, and it may serve our purpose to the same end. With great simplicity it consists of four concentric circles. The area within the central circle is described as follows (modernizing the spelling somewhat) "*This little compass betokenith the Forest".* Of the space between the central and the second circle it is written: "*The seconde compass betokenith the Waste which Lieth from the Forest to the Cornditches, and it is called the Commons of Devonshire."*

We know from the document itself that the first circle is merely marked by metes and bounds "by cause there is no warde between the Forrest and the Wast aforesaid".

The second circle, the cornditches, is a true physical boundary between the enclosed lands and the waste, and there were in it, and still are, gates known as Leapgates, giving access to the Commons of Devon, and across the Commons to the Forest. The reference to these is: "*The little strikes about the Cornditches is called the leapgates for to go into the Waste Moors and Forest."*

Between the second and third circles are the lands in venville: "*The third compass betokenith the Vyndefeilde men the which be the King's and my Lord Prince his tenants."*

Finally the fourth circle "*betokenith the whole shire of Devonshire".*

Formal as it may be this is a very good picture of the county of Devon as seen by the true Dartmoor man. First, at the centre of all things, the Forest with its ancient tenements and their owners and occupiers; then a belt of common land, in many parishes, but unified by the common rights exercised over all but minor areas; this belt often regarded as the purlieus of the Forest. Thirdly, another belt, of parishes and vills in venville, where lived the venville tenants whose rights were second only to those of the ancient tenements. Fourthly, the rest of Devon, the land of the 'strange men' and 'foreigners or wreytors (writers)', who, none the less had their own rights on the Commons of Devon and in the Forest, excepting the inhabitants of Totnes and Barnstaple, who having no rights must have been something less than foreigners, and for whom no nomenclature appears to have been devised.

THE FOREST OR CHASE

In 1627 William French and others filed a bill in the Exchequer against William Barber the parson of Lydford, respecting tithes of Dartmoor (*62 et seq.*). Depositions were taken in this suit, in the course of which depositions William Torre, of Widdicombe, says: "A great part of the Forest of Dartmoor is a barren, hilly place, and dangerous to be passed through in winter by reason of mires, waters and rocks, and that the parish church of Lydford lieth on one side of the Forest of Dartmoor. He saith that there are divers valleys enclosed in part of the said Forest, and many inhabitants do dwell in the wild Forest so enclosed." Robert Hannaford of Widdicombe says there are about thirty-five ancient tenements in the Forest besides newtakes. William Pellow, of Lydford, deposes that the farthest parts of the parish of Lydford, near the wild wastes, are good land, and inhabited by rich inhabitants, and tilled with oats and rye, and with manurance tilled with barley. This optimistic view was not shared by the defendants in another suit in which, in 1702, Thomas Bernaford, rector of Lydford, sought to recover tithes in the waste of Dartmoor (83). They say that the thirty-five ancient tenements, they believe, were not worth the charges of building and enclosing thereof, being mostly barren ground, but have been improved by the owners. And, as to newtakes, they affirm that the enclosing of such newtake doth generally cost such taker £20, and doth not yield 20s. per annum when so enclosed. Perhaps we may accept a middle view if we accept also the evidence of Edward Hunt of Chagford, in 1627, "that the free tenants within the Forest do account their privileges of the Forest as good as their enclosed tenements, and that the common of pasture of most of the free tenants in the Forest is worth more than the services which they do to the Duchy of Cornwall for the same." It is true that Hunt was the son of a former parson of Lydford, who had, in 1610, sought to recover tithes on the herbage of Dartmoor, and this may have, perhaps, made him quite unconsciously, somewhat of a partisan.

There is general agreement that the ancient tenements were thirty-five in number, but a list given by Anthony Torr, of Bishops Tawton, in 1702 (88–90), accounts for only thirty-four, namely:

Rennidge and Warner, three tenements Pizwell, one tenement Hastiland (Hartiland), one tenement Riddam, three tenements Barbary (Babeny), three tenements called Brimpston, four tenements called Huccaby or lying in Huccaby, one tenement called Dury or lying in Dury, three tenements Hexworthy, three tenements called Sherborne or lying in Sherborne, five tenements called Dunabridge or lying in Dunabridge, one tenement Brownberry, one. tenement called Princehall, one tenement Bellaford, two tenements called Bellaford, one lying in Bellaford, and the other called Lake.

Merripit, where, however, there were two tenements, Higher and Lower, seems to be an obvious omission.

All the ancient tenements were held as copyhold or customary freehold, and were wholly within the Forest. In a copyhold the tenant has nothing to show as evidence of right but a copy of an entry in the roll of the manor court. All changes of ownership are made by surrender to

the lord to declared uses, in the case of a sale to the uses of the purchaser;
the lord accepts the surrender and admits as tenant the person to whose
use the surrender has been made. Thus at each surrender the tenement
is for a time, however brief, in the hands of the lord, yet not at his dis-
posal; for, as Coke writes, "in Admittances upon surrender, the Lord
to no intent is reputed as owner, but wholly as an instrument, and the
party admitted shall be subject to no other charges or incombrances of
the Lord, for he claims his estate under the party that made the surrender". The sole interest which the lord has in any surrender is the
relief or payment made according to the custom of the manor for admission. On the other hand a copyhold tenant cannot deal with his
tenement by deed, or execute a lease for a longer term than one year.
In all dealings he must invoke the form of surrender and admission, and
the evidence of title is ever the entry in the manor court roll. Indeed,
in general, although he can select and determine his heirs, he cannot
devise his tenement by will, but must surrender to the use of his last
will and testament, and in his will declare his intent. In this the Court of
Chancery had some discretion which could be exercised in favour of the
eldest son, or for the benefit of creditors where the will charged the
copyhold land for their payment.

Copyhold could only exist in manors where, time out of mind, it
had been the custom. Thus the ancient tenements are very properly
so called, and are evidence of very early enclosure within the Forest. "A
Copyhold Estate cannot be made at this day, for the Pillars of it are, that
it hath been demised Time out of mind by Copy of Court Roll."
(Jacob.)

But it behoved a copyholder to do all his services and break no custom of the manor, under penalty of becoming subject to the lord's
will. Observing these restrictions he was correctly described as a customary freeholder.

The holders of the ancient tenements within the Forest owed service
to the lord of the manor, services fixed by custom and the burden of
which could not be increased at the will of the lord. They were to
attend the three weeks' court at the Castle of Lydford; they were to
attend three times a year at Lydford Castle Court to present all matters
and misdemeanours and things presentable within the Forest. They were
to present all estrays at the next law court. They collected and gathered
the rent and paid it at Exeter. They had to assist at three drifts yearly for
cattle and one for horses depasturing upon the Forest, to Dunnabridge
Pound, or in the North Quarter to Creber Pound, and to attend there
two or three days and nights for the watering and depasturing of the
said cattle near the said pound, and to drive such as were not owned to
Lydford for estrays. And every of the said tenants was to have upon
bringing the said cattle and horses to Dunnabridge Pound a halfpenny
loaf (another witness says one halfpennyworth of bread for each day's

service, and yet another has heard that for their pains they had in ancient times a noble, but now only a halfpenny loaf). All are agreed that in default of his service at the drift the tenant forfeits a noble (6s. 8d.) (*64–65*).

One cannot imagine the tenants becoming unduly lively or restive on either one halfpenny loaf for two or three days, or even one loaf a day. But it was thought expedient to provide and maintain stocks at Dunnabridge Pound, and in 1620 it was found necessary to repair these stocks (*60*). (Burnard has thought that the so-called Judge's Chair at Dunnabridge Pound is no more than the seat of the stocks, and I entirely agree, especially as I find stones so worked as to suit perfectly for the under part of the actual stocks.) It may, of course, have been the owners of cattle agisted on the Moor who became restive and needed restraint.

Notwithstanding the statement that tenants failing to attend the drifts forfeit a noble, the jury of the court appears to have exercised its right of making the punishment fit the crime, since no amercement can be fixed in amount beforehand; thus, in 1583, at the court of Lydford East, it was presented that John Ellett and Robert French had not made 'les drifts' as was their duty, and they were each amerced sixpence (*126*).

The holders of the Ancient Tenements, as they had their services and rents to render, had also their rights to enjoy. In an action for the recovery of tithes, 1699 (*80 et seq.*), the defendants say that the Forest men who are such as have their tenements enclosed from the common Forest, pay nothing for depasturing their sheep and other cattle on the said Forest. And in a similar action, in 1702 (*91*), Richard Bold, of Tamerton Foliot, gentleman, aged 56, deposes that the Forest men have the privilege of turf-paring, of cutting of fuel, and of taking stones, paying nothing for the same.

The tenants of the Ancient Tenements had also the right to enclose newtakes, a right strictly limited and which can in no way be held to justify the enclosures which were made in the eighteenth and nineteenth centuries. In the action of 1702 (*83*), above referred to, the defendants say: "The heir to each and every of the said tenants, on the death of each of the said tenants, and also every purchaser that shall purchase the inheritance of any such ancient tenements, have by the custom aforesaid liberty to enclose eight acres of the said waste or forest ground, as of right belonging to each of the said tenements so descended or purchased, paying one shilling yearly for the same to Her Majesty's use, her heirs and successors, according to the said ancient custom time out of mind used; which said eight acres is commonly called a newtake, and is usually confirmed to such heir or purchaser, their respective heirs and assigns, for ever, by copy of the Court Roll of Her Majesty's Castle Court of Lydford, under the seal of the said Court, by the Steward there for the time being; the same being first viewed, meted out, and presented by four of the ancient tenants of the said thirty-five tenements who are in no way concerned in such newtake otherwise than viewing and presenting the same."

John Gaskyne of Withicombe, yeoman, aged 73, deposes (*85*) to a knowledge of eleven parcels of land commonly called newtakes, lying in the said Forest, Chase or Moor; and doth know divers other parcels of lands also called newtakes, lately taken in and enclosed from the said moor. This is a significant division, between the newtakes and the divers other parcels of ground 'also called newtakes'. Another witness, Anthony Torr, of Bishops Tawton, gives a list of seventeen newtakes with their tenants (*90*), from which it is apparent that these divers other parcels of ground were enclosed with no regard as to the limitation to eight acres. Already, in 1702, there had commenced the application of a policy which, in the eighteenth and nineteenth centuries, was to rob the commoners of most of the best grazing.

We may illustrate this point by three examples; the first two so-called newtakes on Anthony Torr's list are 'two called Bradrings' in the tenancy of Sir Thomas Leare. These are probably the smallest mentioned in the list, yet the lesser is 17½ acres in area, and the larger measures 24 acres. A more representative example is Laughterhole, which has an area of 75 acres. I take the measurements from a plan of the Forest, prepared in or shortly after the year 1800. At one time an attempt was made to justify such areas by reference to the fact that, as Torr puts it, the Reeve and three other owners of ancient tenements measured out for a newtake 'eight acres of clear ground'. It was suggested that all bogs, mires and rocks were mere surplus, and the only area to be considered was to be suitable rough pasture. So that a newtake might greatly exceed eight acres, and yet have no more than eight acres of 'clear ground'. It must be doubtful whether this form of special pleading ever deceived anyone. No man would be likely to enclose 75 acres, at the cost of a stone fence 2,354 yards in length, to secure an acreage of eight acres which would need no more than 800 yards of fence. Nor in truth is there any one of the large enclosures, and 75 acres came to be relatively small, of which it can be said that any but a very small part is either bog, mire or rock.

The idea of enclosing Dartmoor, which was thus improperly put in action, with the connivance of a new class of holders of the ancient tenements, was nothing new. In the days of Charles II, 1666, the King contracted with Sir Gervase Lucas and certain partners of Sir Gervase for a partition of Dartmoor between the King and the commoners having rights upon the Moor (*77-78*); Sir Gervase and his partners to treat with the owners and tenants for the setting out and enclosing of a considerable part or proportion to His Majesty's use, and the division of the residue among the owners and commoners in such manner as should be agreed between them. Sir Gervase and his associates to hold the lands apportioned to the King for fifty years at one fourth the clear yearly value, and the King to grant to the owners and commoners or their appointees the rest of the land to be set out and allotted to them to be held in free socage without rent.

Sir Gervase was given three years in which to treat with the owners and commoners, and, apparently, that period did not suffice for the persuasion of such interested persons to sell their birthright. Indeed, considering the rights of all Devon on the Commons and in the Forest an agreement was hardly probable. From the time when the Forest ceased to interest its owners as a hunting ground there was usually someone to suggest its plunder to the advantage of the Duchy, an advantage in which that someone was to have a part or share. Thus, in the reign of James I we find a person unknown writing to the Earl of Salisbury suggesting that the King should take tithe of the 100,000 horse-loads annually taken of Dartmoor peat, certain profits being allowed out of such tithe to the ingenious fellow who conceived the idea and to Sir Walter Monson (58). The deviser of this source of revenue says that he was an old servant of the late Queen, and has never received the reward meant for him. The idea was not adopted. It is not known where the mover in this matter obtained his statistics, but 100,000 horse-loads would be little less than 15,000 tons, certainly more than 10,000, and it cannot be accepted that such quantity of peat was ever cut in any one year. All the attempts at 'improving' Dartmoor have been founded on similar cupidity and equally gross error. There may, it is true, have been an occasional adventurer, such as Buller, who worked, equally in error, but with the full assurance that he was serving his country.

There were other dwellers within the Forest besides those who occupied the ancient tenements. In 1354, the Black Prince made an order that the Foresters in calving-time should make lodges in their Bailiwicks, and live continually in the Moor so long as the calves were tender, to save them from the herdsmen who have to be upon the Moor to take charge of the cattle; the 'calves' in question being the young of the deer (22). In 1360, the Prince ordered the receiver of the Duchy to build a suitable lodge in his Chase of Dartmoor for the use of the chief Forester and the other Foresters (24). But these officials were not the only inhabitants other than customary tenants. We find a class known as 'censarii', evidently landless men, since the Bailiff of Dartmoor, in 1350–1, accounts for 2s. 2d. from the censarii, and not more, because some of the censarii took lands, 'and are therefore quit of their censum' (21). The censum was a species of poll tax, levied at the rate of 2d. yearly on every man, and on every woman 1d. The total varied considerably; in 1342–3 it was 5s. 6d. (16); in 1344–5 it amounted to 4s. according to a survey, but in actual receipts that year no more than 8d. (17); in 1350 it reached 2s. 2d. (21).

In some instances the bailiff gives names, but I have no transcripts of those lists, nor any means of knowing the proportion of men to women; one may say that the numbers probably varied at the dates above given from not less than 40 persons to not less than 3.

Some of those who paid this rent or tax were doubtless herdsmen in charge of flocks and herds for which 'night rest' within the Forest had been paid; others may have been tinners, for, although the ordinary working tinner raising the ore appears to have worked in the Forest by day only, those in charge of blowing-houses and knacking mills may well have found it impossible to confine their work to daylight only, since there were processes which could not be interrupted short of completion. Some of these tinners may have been exempt as holders of land, since the tin mills within the Forest were on land leased from the Duchy, and there are entries of odd acres taken here and there, some of which we know to have been occupied in connexion with the working of tin.

THE COMMONS OF DEVON

At a court of survey held at Okehampton in the year 1608, before Sir William Strode, Knight, and other commissioners (52), the jury found that the soil of divers moors, commons and wastes, lying for the most part about the forest of Dartmoor, and usually called the common of Devonshire, was parcel of the Duchy of Cornwall, and that the foresters and other officers of His Majesty and his predecessors had always been accustomed to drive the said commons and waste grounds, and all the commons, moors and wastes of other men (lying in like manner about the said Forest) home to the corne hedges and leape gates round aboute the same common and forest, some few places only exempted, and that the said foresters and officers have taken and gathered to his majesty's use at the times of drift within the same commons such profits and other duties as they have and ought to do within the said Forest; " how be it they intend not herebye to prejudice the particular rights which any other persons claim for themselves or their tenants in any commons or several grounds in or adjoining to the said common or Forest, but do leave the same to judgement of law and to the justness of their titles which they can make to the same."

One of the few places exempted by the jurors may have been the Chase of Okehampton, which has for a short distance a common boundary with the Forest; but of this I know no proof.

The jury's finding very fairly presents the custom which had prevailed from before legal memory; their delicacy in handling the claims of other than the Duchy reflects the fact that at times and in places the rights of the Duchy had been challenged, and in some few instances contested by force. The court rolls show that the court of the manor of Lydford exercised effective control over the Commons of Devon, extending to and including the cornditches which bounded the enclosed lands, and the leap gates, or lid gates, which gave access from the in-country to the Commons of Devon. (As a proper name the word *Lidgate* is still in use, being applied to the gate which gives access to Buckfastleigh Moor, at the end of the lane leading from Buckfastleigh to Hayford.)

There are ample references in the rolls of the manor court of Lydford to show the effective exercise of this control. Thus in the court of Lydford West, 21st September 1688 (*113*), the jury presented the inhabitants of Wapsworthy in that they permitted a fence called Wapsworthy Hedge to be ruinous and decayed, therefore let them be distrained. At the next court, held on the 12th October of the same year (*113*), it was certified that Wapsworthy Hedge had been repaired by the inhabitants, therefore let the amerciaments be withdrawn. The hedge is described as being "iuxta Forest de Dartmore".

At the court of Lydford North, on the 21st day of September 1579 (*121*), the jury presented that a certain wall, between the lands of Richard Ellacott called Sowtherly and the Forest of the Lady the Queen, and a gate called Sowtherly gate were ruinous and fallen; and Ellacott may have a day to repair the wall and gate before the next court under penalty of ten shillings. At the next court, held on the 15th October of the same year (*121*), it was certified that Richard Ellacott, Roger Knight, Henry Walter, Anthony Rondell and others had repaired all the walls and gates (one other gate and two other walls had been presented as ruinous) "therefore withdraw the process".

But the court at times failed to enforce its orders. There was a bad instance of west country obstinacy at Brisworthy, where, by the jury on the 21st September 1582 (*127*), it was presented that the gate known as Harte Gate,[1] and the hedge adjoining were permitted by the inhabitants to be ruinous. This presentment appears to have been futile, since, on the 5th May 1586 (*132*), the Forester declared, on his oath, that Hart gate, which the inhabitants of Brisworthy ought to repair, was in ruin. On the 4th May 1587 (*138*), the jury presented that Harte gate was still in ruin, and it was ordered that the inhabitants of the vill of Brisworthy be summoned to the next court. Nothing appears to have happened, for, on the 8th May 1589 (*143*), it was again ordered that the inhabitants of Brisworthy should be summoned to the next court, in the matter of Hart gate. At that next court, 29th May of the same year (*143*), the inhabitants failed to attend, and were amerced in the sum of sixpence. Beyond the fact that this entry was repeated in later courts nothing happened until 5th May 1608 (*111*), when the transgressors were named, being John Bowden, Barnard Torre, Thomas Bowden, Richard Harrys, William Dunridge, and Walter Steart; it

[1] In the index to the work cited Hart Gate and Hartford Gate are referenced as identical in error; Hartford Gate is Harford gate in the parish of Harford.

appears that Hart gate was still ruinous, and it was ordered that the persons named be distrained. Then, 21st September of the same year (*113*), these same people were found to have offended in the matter of pasturing sheep on the Forest, and they were amerced in eighteen pence for not attending to answer in that matter. It was found necessary to repeat the entry of this last amercement in several later courts; but there, as far as I know, the matter ended. I can only say that my early recollection is that Hart gate was still ruinous, and now there is no gate.

The fact was, as will be seen later, that mere amercements were of little use where the persons amerced were outside the jurisdiction of the court in the matter of distraint; and I fancy that the charge in respect of pasturing sheep on the Forest was the Duchy's effort to visit a sense of crime upon the vill of Brisworthy. On the whole, it would not have paid the vills to neglect their duties, and a reminder usually sufficed to secure reparation of gates and hedges.

The fact that the Commons of Devon spread over so many parishes and make contact with so many manors and other territorial interests has inevitably led to dispute; and since the decay of the efficiency of the Duchy courts, which accompanied the loss of interest in Dartmoor as a hunting ground, the private challenge to public rights has grown. It has been seen that the jury of 1608 made cautious reference to this difficulty. The idea of dogging other people's cattle off a certain area of common and reserving it for your own cattle was quite early developed, and, in 1468–9, John Foger was presented and amerced for daily driving away with his dogs the cattle of divers people agisted in the King's Moor, and making that part of the Moor his own proper common (*96*). This unneighbourly habit is by no means unknown to-day. Other persons claimed exclusive right of common and in pursuance of such claim drove off cattle agisted on such common, as estrays. Thus, in 1478–9, John Hawston, of Elberton, was attached to answer to the Lord for yearly driving the Forest of the Prince and the cattle there agisted, from Yealm Head through all the land of Stealdon (Stalldon) and thence to a place called Quykbeme, and thence to Redlake Head, and thence to Fishlake, and from Fishlake to Hurtlake, and thence to Erme Head, and impounding them at Torrycomb, in the pinfold there, to the damage of the Prince yearly 40s. (*97*). The lands within these bounds were in part Commons of Devon, in part Forest.

Yet others evaded the Duchy drift by driving their cattle off the commons before the day of the drift; thus in 1586 the jury presented that William Chubb had driven the Common called Stayldon (Stalldon) before the drift of the Lady the Queen (*136*).

The counterpart of this last proceeding was pound breach, the taking from the pound of cattle rounded up by the Duchy officers as estrays. In 1512, John Coole of Slade, Thomas Coole, Anthony Stodeford Thomas Hakker, Thomas Cade, Robert Dunning, Henry Fleisslemond

Robert Stephyn, John Whyte snr., John Whyte jnr., John Lowde, John Dean, Hugh Hele, Robert Brokyng and Nicholas Hele riotously took and drove away 16 steers of the estrays of the lord the King, and at the next manor court were fined accordingly, but did not pay. More than this, on the 22nd July 1512, they repeated the offence on a larger scale, unlawfully and riotously taking and driving away out of the liberty of the Manor of Lydford, into which they had broken, 40 oxen and steers, and 10 geldings of the goods and chattels of the said John Coole, taken by the Bailiff of the Lord the King of his Manor afore-said, and imparked at Brattor within the liberty of the Forest of Dart-moor, by virtue of a certain precept of *fieri facias* to the same Bailiff directed, in contempt of the aforesaid King. And this they had done by command of the said John Coole (*41–2*). The offenders were again fined, and again they did not pay.

The entry continues: "And the amount can not be levied because the parties do not dwell within the liberty, and have no goods or chattels there by which they can be distrained." In the result the fine was never levied.

Summarized, the Foresters impounded certain cattle, the property of John Cole as estrays. John Cole presumedly held that he had rights of common, not appurtenant to the Manor of Lydford, and he and his associates broke into the pound and drove away the cattle. Being fined for the offence, they neglected to pay. Thereupon a writ of *fieri facias* was directed to the Bailiff of the manor, calling upon him to levy a distress, in pursuit of which writ the Bailiff seized yet other and more cattle, the property of Cole, and impounded them. Presumedly he seized these within the liberty of the Forest. Thereupon Cole and his associates committed pound breach and recovered the cattle. After which we must assume that Cole kept his cattle out of the liberty of the Forest. As to the writ of *fieri facias*, this was using in a lower court the forms appropriate to a higher. From a higher court the writ would have been directed to the Sheriff, who could have followed the dis-traint and retaken it wherever it might have been, but the Bailiff, out-side his manor, was nobody. It will be seen that the threat of distraint could not always have been a very effective deterrent.

Enclosure has been the worst enemy of Dartmoor. In the Forest the Duchy has qualified as the worst despoiler by encouraging and permit-ting newtakes vastly larger than the area fixed by custom. On the Com-mons of Devon the Duchy stood to lose rather than to gain by en-closure. It has been the private individual who has there been the offender. The habit of land-grabbing is of ancient origin, much earlier than the first available instance from Dartmoor, which dates 1441–2, when John Jeffery was summoned to answer the King for entering the King's Moor between Badeworth (Batworthy) and Mangersford, and appropriating 40 acres of land to his own use (*96*). This would be in the valley of the North Teign, and the land may have been in part in the Commons of Devon, in part in the Forest. The next similar entry is in 1468–9, when Reginal Cole and others are summoned to answer for enclosing, imparking and detaining 200 acres of common pasture of Devon, between the Erme and the Arm (Yealm) (*96*). This was on the Commons of Devon, and we see the early stages of the dispute which led to the insurrection headed by John Cole in 1512. There are other entries in the rolls, alleging similar offences.

Another matter of fairly common complaint was the closing or obstruction of roads and lanes leading to the Moor, to the hindrance of those driving cattle on to the Moor and Forest, or bringing cattle away therefrom. The Abbot of Buckland was one such offender. In the year 1478 the Abbot was presented for preventing by threats and force the herds of the Lord the King and other men, as well of Devon as of Cornwall, to the number of 200 and more from putting their cattle on the Forest (*97*). This may have been armed opposition rather than physical closure of roads. The Abbot also claimed 10,000 acres of the Forest and Commons (*37*). A commission was issued to inquire into the matter and the jury found for the King and the Commons of Devon (*165*). It is to be feared that neither the Abbot of Buckland nor his brother Abbot of Buckfast were at all times good neighbours of Dartmoor.

VENVILLE

On the 1st September 1377, Richard II granted to Richard de Abberbury the custody of the Forest of Dartmoor, to hold for the term of his life with all things to the said custody belonging, and also with the profits of the herbage of the said Forest, without paying any rent (*26*).

This led to an authoritative statement as to the nature of the *Fines Villarum*, Abberbury claiming that the receipts therefrom, together with other profits of the Forest, were rightly his; and, the auditors of the Duchy retaining such receipts as falling without the terms of the grant, Abberbury petitioned the king for an Inquisition to determine the point in dispute (*27*).

An Inquisition was granted and was taken on the 19th June 1382, at Lydford. The jurors found that "the *fines villarum* ought to be paid by the tenants of divers vills next to the Forest of Dartmoor, from the time whereof memory is not, to the Lord the King, and his progenitors, having profits within the Forest of Dartmoor, to wit that the tenants of the said fined vills, with their beasts, may have agistments from the rising of the sun to the setting thereof, and not by night. And the aforesaid tenants of the venvills shall have coals, turf, heath, furze and stones for their own use for the aforesaid fine; and as to coals and turf as well, the aforesaid tenants, as strangers of the whole county of Devon, may hire one pit yearly for making coals there, and digging turfs for fivepence. They have so used the premises from time whereof memory is not. And whether the premises belong to the King, or to the custody of the Forest, they know not" (27). A finding of little avail to Abberbury, but informative as to the nature of venville rents.

At a date not precisely known, but about 170 years later than that of the last cited document there was prepared another entitled "Instructions for my Lord Prince to the King's most honorable council concerning my Lord Prince's Forest of Dartmoor, and in the moors and wastes to the same belonging" (164).

This sets out, *inter alia*: "Every man of the vyndefelde be the Kyng's Tenantes and beryth there Rente as more playnely apperyth in the Kyngs Bockes, and shall with there catell as they may wynter upon there holdynges come to the Kyngs Forrest by Sonne, and goo home by Sonne; and if he be attayched by the Foster after sonne, he shall be amercyd iij d every night in the yere if he be attayched. And the said tenantes shall have in the Forrest of Dartmore all that maye doo hym good excepte grene ocke and venyson, and if any of the said tenants shall have more catell than they maye wynter apon his teneure, For to paye then as a strange man; That ys for every oxe, cowe, and heaffer j d. ob. And for every mare, horse, and geldyng ij d" (164).

Although the venville tenants might only depasture the Forest by day, yet that inconvenience could be avoided, since, on the payment of an additional threepence a year they may depasture by night also. See *Survey of Duchy*, 1608 (54).

The Forester's account for 20–21 Henry VII, 1505–6, gives the following list of the vills paying venville rents (39 et seq.):

EAST BAILIWICK
    villat de Chagford xijd
    hamelett de Tenkenhmhome infra parochia de Chagford iiijs
    villat de Hareston xxd
    villat de Litterford in parochia de North Bovye iiijd
    hamelett de Hokyn in eadem parochia iiijd
    hamelett de Kyndon jd
    hamelett de North Worthied in parochia de Whitecombe (Wide-
        combe) iiijd ob.
    villat de (blank) in eadem parochia iijs
    villat de Shirwell in eadem parochia iijs
    hamelett de North Catrowe in eadem parochia xviijd
    villat de Higher Catrowe in dicta parochia iijs vijd
    villat de Grendon in eadem parochia xijd
    villat de Fenne in parochia de Chagford iiijd ob.
    villat de Jurston in eadem parochia viijd
    villat de Willuhed in eadem parochia vd
    villat de Esworthie vjd
    villat de Higher Jurston iijd

villat de Chalnecombe in parochia de Manoton vjd

WEST BAILIWICK

villat de Shawe vijd
villat de Brightesworth in parochia de mewe ijs
hamelett de Louyngton in eadem parochia ijd
villat de Gadmewe in eadem parochia ijd
villat de Mewey ijd
parochia de Shidford (Sheepstor) iijs
villat de Dencombe in parochia de Walcamton xviijd
parochia de Sampfnd Spauley xijd
parochia de Whitechurche xijd
parochia de Peturspavy vd
villat de Chodlype vd
Twyste in parochia de Tavestoke ijd ob.
Raddyche et Pytchclyff iijd
Margaretlond in eadem parochia ijd

SOUTH BAILIWICK

villat de Helle xviijs
hamelett de Stourton in parochia de Bulkefastlegh xvijs
villat de Shiridon in parochia de Dene (Dean Prior) vijd
villat de Vgbirough vd

NORTH BAILIWICK

villat de Trulegh (Throwleigh) ijs vjd
villat de Collerowe in parochia de Chagford vijd ob.
parochia de Southtawton vijs iiijd ob.
villat de Sele vjd ob.
parochia de Kelston iijs (Belston)
villat de Hellestoke ijs vjd
parochia de Stourton (Sourton) iiijd ob.
parochia de Bridestowe ijs
villat de Willesworthe ijs

In 1624 we find the list for the North Quarter to be (60):

Item for the venvell of Throwlye	2—6
(no entry for Collerowe)	
Item for the venvell Rente of South Tauton	8—0
(no entry for Sele)	
Item for the venvell Rente of Bellsoun	4—4
Item for the venvell of Holstocke	2—6
Item for the venvell of Sorton	0—4½
Item for the venvell of Briddestowe	2—0
Item for the venvell Rent of the Hamlet of Wolsworthie	2—0

In 1505–6 the totals are: East Quarter £0 18s. 9d., West Quarter
£0 11s. 0½d., South Quarter £1 16s. 0d., North Quarter £1 0s. 11d.;

total for the four quarters £4 6s. 8d. (*39*). This may be compared with the figure given in an 'extent' of Dartmoor, dated 1344–5, where the total of the venville rents is entered as £4 0s. 0d. (*19*).

As to the north quarter where we have details in 1505–6 (*39*) and 1624 (*60*), the earlier total is £1 0s. 11d. and the later, although there are fewer entries or items, is £1 1s. 8½d. But it does not follow that, although fewer items are stated, any rent has been omitted; thus the South Tawton item of the later list may well include both South Tawton and Sele of the earlier.

We also know the account of venville rents collected in the south quarter in the year 1584; it runs (*149*):

Parochia de Holl (Holne)	xviijs
Buckfastleigh	xvijs
Skyrdon (Skorriton)	vijd
Vgborough	vd

making a total of thirty-six shillings, the same amount as was collected in 1505–6.

In 1342–3 we have the accounts of John Dabernan, receiver (*16*); at that time the Moor was divided into three 'quarters', east, west and south, and he accounts for a total of £4 12s. 7d. in respect of venville rents. It is obvious that, subject to incidents of collection, the rents in venville were a constant sum. Mr. Percival Birkett (*Dartmoor Preservation Association*, I, page *xxv*) concludes: "I understand the Venville tenants to be the owners and occupiers of all land in respect of which Venville rents are now, or formerly were, paid to the Duchy. In some cases these rents are paid by the Overseers of the poor in respect of the whole of the land in the parish; in other cases by the tenants of specific farms, manors or vills."

There can be no doubt these payments were true rents, and in no way fines in the modern acceptance of the word, that is to say penalties for trespass. *Fine* and *redditus* were synonymous, and the wording of the findings by the various juries engaged on inquisitions is in itself fully sufficient to establish this. As to the word *venville*, the men of Dartmoor have recast the phrase *fines villarum* in this more "suent" and acceptable form.

The venville tenants had responsibilities as well as rights; the *Instructions for my Lord Prince* make it clear that the vyndefyld Tenants owed suit to the manor court of Dartmoor, they were to come to his Grace's Court holden at his Manor and Castle of Lydford as often as they were summoned for the King and my Lord Prince, there to present all faults belonging or appertaining to the Forest of Dartmoor and the Commons of Devon (*161*). It would appear that the courts, at which all matters and misdemeanours within the Forest were presentable, were held three times a year at Lydford; the tenants of the thirty-five ancient tenements within the Forest also owed suit. There was some irregu-

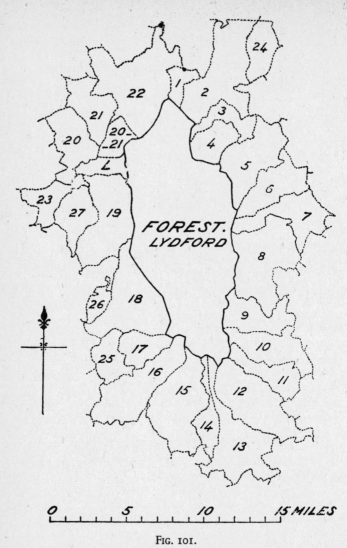

FIG. 101.

DESCRIPTION: The Forest or Chase of Dartmoor, boundary shown in full line, lies wholly within the parish of Lydford; its area is 76·6 square miles. The boundaries of the border parishes are drawn in dotted lines. Of these parishes Nos. 1 to 22, inclusive, extend to and touch the Forest. That part of the parish of Lydford which lies without the Forest has an area of 3·4 square miles; thus the whole extent of Lydford parish is 80 square miles. It makes contact with the border parishes numbered 1 to 23 inclusive.

The reference numbers are as follows: 1, Belstone. 2, South Tawton. 3, larity in the dates of these courts, but they were more usually held early in May, in July, and on or about the 21st September. At times there would appear to have been no more than two courts in the year, but rarely there were four.

The inquisition of 1382 speaks of the venville vills as "next to the Forest of Dartmoor" (27). John Gaskyne of Withicombe, in his deposition made in the matter of a suit concerning tythes, in 1702, speaks of the venville men (86) "who live in the parishes adjoining the purlieus of the said Forest, Moor or Waste". Similar phrasing may be met elsewhere, but the words *next to* or *adjoining* must not be interpreted too strictly, there were and are lands in venville in parishes no parts of the boundaries of which touch the Forest; such parishes, for instance, as Tavistock and Meavy, while Whitchurch, Sampford Spiney and Meavy extend to the Commons of Devon, which may be regarded as purlieus of the Forest, but do not make contact with the Forest. None the less the parishes must have had a very real urge to have some common boundary with, and to extend to, the Forest, as a reference to the map of Devon will clearly show. No less than twenty-two parishes so extend (twenty-three if we include what I might call 'Lydford without'). In many instances the connexion is effected by means of a mere corridor. Harford and Ugborough afford extreme examples. In Ugborough, from Spurrels Cross to the Forest Boundary is a distance of nearly four miles; the width of this northward extension of the parish nowhere exceeds three-quarters of a mile, and is at places less than one-quarter. Parallel with this runs a strip of similar length belonging to Harford, and this strip nowhere exceeds one mile in width, while in places it is reduced to a little over a quarter of a mile. See Fig. 101.

Since the Forest is wholly within the parish of Lydford and 'Lydford without' is touched by a parish which does not reach to Dartmoor, it follows that the parish of Lydford has, at one place and another, contact with twenty-three other parishes; a condition probably unique, but which hardly justifies the pleading of John Leere, John Brounston and Thomas Fleshman, all of the parish of Tavistock, who say, in 1665, that the parishes bordering the Forest are at least forty in number (76).

It should be noted that the lists of vills in venville which have been given above are certainly not complete. They are conclusive only as to rents received at their several dates.

Throwleigh. 4, Gidleigh. 5, Chagford. 6, North Bovey. 7, Manaton. 8, Widecombe. 9, Holne. 10 ,Buckfastleigh. 11, Dean Prior. 12, South Brent. 13, Ugborough. 14, Harford. 15, Cornwood. 16, Shaugh Prior. 17, Sheepstor. 18, Walkhampton. 19, Petertavy. 20, Bridestowe. 21, Sourton. 20–21, lands common to Bridestowe and Sourton. 22, Okehampton. 23, Brentor. 24, Spreyton. 25, Meavy. 26, Sampford Spiney. 27, Marytavy. L, that part of Lydford which lies without the Forest.

FOREIGNORS AND WREYTORS

We owe the phrase 'foreignors and wreytors' to Daniel Honnawill, yeoman, in his deposition of 1702 (*88*). At an earlier date, 1381–2, in the matter of an inquisition respecting Richard Abberbury's grant of the custody of the Forest, the word is '*extranei*' (*27*) which may be translated 'strangers' (literally 'outsiders'). These people are defined as being all the inhabitants of Devon, except those of Barnstaple and Totnes, and excepting also the Forest men and the Venville men. Why Barnstaple and Totnes should be something less than foreignors is not known. As boroughs they may have been outside the Forest of Devon when that had its greatest extent, but so must Exeter almost certainly have been, and the exclusion from privilege of common does not extend to Exeter.

With the exception mentioned, all the inhabitants of Devon had a right of common in the Commons of Devon, without any payment, provided "the said commoners will be deposed upon a book unto the King's officers that their cattle did not come and pasture within the bounds of the Forest" (*48*). But if their animals pastured within the Forest, then the commoners aforesaid must pay for every ox, cow or heifer 1½d. and for every mare, horse and gelding 2d.

The *Instructions for my Lord Prince* (*c.* 1542), before referred to, make the further statement that if cattle come out of Cornwall into the Commons of Devon, or apparently into the Forest, the same payments as last named should be made (*164*). Notwithstanding which statement it is doubtful whether the Cornishmen had any rights of common on either the Forest or the Commons of Devon; their user was probably at the will of the Lord.

For sheep the men of Devon paid nothing either in the Forest or in the Commons of Devon. As to coals and turf as well, the strangers of the whole county of Devon might hire one pit yearly for making coals and digging turfs, for fivepence (Abberbury Inq. 1381–2) (*27*).

The use of the term *wreytors* as an alternative for *foreignors* or *extranei* presents no real difficulty if we transcribe it to its modern spelling, when it appears as *Writers*. Whatever cattle were the subject of grazing charges were of necessity entered on the agistment roll, and were thus *scripti*. The Forest tenants depastured their sheep and other cattle in the Forest, without payment. The venville men so depastured their animals, but subject to the limitation that they must not exceed the number that they could winter at home; if they exceeded this number of beasts they must pay for the excess, and so, in respect of the excess there must be entries in the agistment roll, and in that respect the venville men might at times be described as *writers*. The foreigners, of the rest of Devon, could depasture cattle on the Commons of Devon free of charge, but only if they deposed on oath that the cattle did not stray off the commons into the Forest. For all pasturing in the Forest they paid per

head of beasts, and entries were necessary on the roll. These foreigners
were accordingly pre-eminently the men whose business it was to see
that their beasts grazing on the commons or in the Forest were written
in the agistment roll, and hence they were called *writers*.

The phrasing of the court rolls bears out this explanation; we find:

1382–3. Robert Stoke presented as having cattle agisted in the Forest
non scripti (*95*).

1443–4. Robert Breston, a venville man, attached to answer for having
15 cattle wintering out of venville (that is to say more than he
could winter at home) agisted in the Forest, and *non scripti* (*96*).

Those who dug peat within the Forest, excepting the holders of the
ancient tenements, were subject each to an annual charge of 5d., and
their names were also entered on record; the same phrase was used in
respect of them in the manor court roll, thus: 1410–11. John Jose summoned to answer that he, being *non scriptus*, dug coals *in vasto domini* (*95*).

FOLDAGE

No unlicensed person might be in Forest or Chase by night. The
Forest men, who held the ancient tenements, and whose houses were
within the Forest, necessarily were privileged. The *censarii*, not being
occupiers of ancient tenements, but resident in the Forest, paid a poll
tax. The venville men could compound for the privilege by paying
night rest of 3d. the year.

It appears from the Inquisition of 1388 (*28*), made at the petition of
Abberbury, that the 'foreigners' had devised a convenient method of
avoiding the prohibition of staying in the Forest with their herds by
night, or rather a workable scheme for avoiding the necessity of so
staying. They constructed folds near the Forest, presumedly on the
Commons of Devon; the animals passed the night in these folds and
depastured the Forest by day. And, as Abberbury asserts by the connivance of the foresters, they derived the further advantage that in
place of a payment of 1½d. per head for their cattle they each paid but
2d. for 'foldage' which covered the charge for all the animals. To this
the foresters added another penny, making threepence in all, whereof
the Duke received twopence and the foresters took the third penny.
This was an extremely bad bargain for the Duke, and it is not surprising that John Dabernon, Constable of Lydford Castle and Receiver of
the monies arising out of Dartmoor, at that time Steward of Edward
Prince of Wales, ordered that the men having animals and folds should
pay 1½d. yearly for every animal, like the rest of the foreigners, should
be discharged of the payment of the 2d. for foldage, and incidentally
discharged also of the payment of the penny which the foresters had
kept. With that order 'foldage' died; but the auditors of the Duchy
accounts, finding it entered in previous years, desired that Abberbury
should still account for it; hence Abberbury's petition, and the inquisi-

tion which freed him from the demand. A good instance of interested persons attempting, and for a time successfully, to vary an ancient custom.

THE MANOR COURTS

While still a royal Forest, Dartmoor must have had a court of swainmote, the holding of which was, by the Charta Forestae, 1217, restricted to thrice in the year, namely in the beginning of fifteen days before Michaelmas, about the feast of St. Martin, and in the beginning of fifteen days before the feast of St. John the Baptist. No records of the swainmote courts appear to have survived, and in 1239 Dartmoor ceased to be a forest and became a chase. The first courts of which we have knowledge were the three weeks' courts at Lydford (73) (84), and the courts held three times a year at the same place (73). The forest men were to come to both these courts; the venville men appear to have been summoned to the court held thrice yearly, and not to the three weeks' court, but some witnesses state that venville men might be called, individually, to the three weeks' court (87) (88). What were these respective courts? They are variously described in the rolls as of 'the manor of Dartmoor', of 'the manor and forest of Dartmoor' and of 'the manor of Lydford'. Evidently manor courts, although there are instances of the heading of the roll being 'Dartmoor, *curia legalis Foreste de Dartmoor tenta apud* Lydford'.

In general there were two classes of manor court, the one a necessary incident of every manor, and known as the court baron, strictly requiring that there should be freeholders of the manor, but still held by use and custom where there were no freeholders, but only copyholders. This was, as its name implies, the lord's court and had jurisdiction in matters affecting the lord and his tenants. The second, the court leet, could only be held by Charter, and in some manors. It was a court of record for the punishment of all offences against the Crown, under high treason, but not empowered to award punishment involving life and limb.

In early days at least the court baron was often held every three weeks, while courts leet were held three times a year. From the fact that the forest men, who were the customary tenants of manor, were required to attend the three-weekly courts, while others such as the venville men as a body owed no such suit, it appears that these courts, although at times spoken of as 'the Forest Courts', were courts customary, the equivalent of courts baron. But one cannot readily believe that attendance was very regular; there must have been many essoigns, or excuses. The inhabitants of Babeny and Pizwell had long been excused attendance at the parish church at Lydford, and permitted to attend for worship at Widecombe, Bishop Bronescombe having determined, on the evidence of credible witnesses, that it was eight miles from Babeny and Pizwell to Lydford in fine weather, and fifteen miles in time of storm, when tempest and overflows of water prevailed. It was certainly no less distance to the castle. It is true that they were only to attend in turn, three at a time (*88*). The venville men were to attend only when summoned, which was two, three or four times a year, but one witness says they were to take their rota of three-week courts; these courts to which the venville man came we know, from the rolls, to have been combined courts baron and leet. There were presentments of the deaths of customary tenants, naming the next heir (*147*); and surrenders of tenements, followed by the admission of new tenants (*123*). Decay of hedges and gates was reported; and there were presentments relating to the Forest, such as mastiffs remaining unclawed (*109, 110*), that is to say without three claws of the forefoot cut off by the skin, or in the alternative the ball of forefoot cut out. And persons were presented for poaching (*114*).

On the other hand there were entries of misdemeanours which were not directed against the lord, but were presentable at the leet. For example, on the 21st September 1586 (*137*), Humfrey Pitford sought remedy against John Thorn and Maria his wife in the matter of "quinque les Callacowe et hulland bands tres les handkerchiefs et unum les wollen wastecoatt", and the aforesaid John and Maria did not come to answer the aforesaid Humfrey in the matter of the plaint. Wherefore it was ordered that the Forester appoint two honest and lawful men to value the aforesaid goods, and he appointed accordingly William Gill and Thomas Batten, who being sworn, upon their oaths assessed the value at 6s. 8d. This was an ordinary civil case, in which the lord cannot be supposed to have had any personal interest. It affords an excellent example of the strain put upon the latinity of the Steward, or the Bailiff, and the consequent use of mixed tongues, low Latin, English and a sprinkling of Norman French articles.

The courts were not without their touch of pomp and circumstance. The Officials seem to have anticipated the British Broadcasting Corporation, by many years, in their taste for incidental music. At the Court held at Lydford on the 22nd September, 5 James I (*109*), the jury presented Abell Whitechurch, the Forester of the West part of Dartmoor, in that he neither had nor sounded his horn at that Law Court, and he was amerced two shillings, for according to custom he had ought.

TITHES, AND OTHER PAROCHIAL MATTERS

The Forest appears at all times to have been regarded as within the parish of Lydford, probably as a matter of convenience in secular affairs. In such matters the Forest was a place to itself, the *Instructions for my Lord Prince* clearly stating that "if a man die by misfortune, or be slain within the said Forest, mores and waste, the Crowner of Lydford shall crown and sit upon him, for the said Forest, moors and waste is out of every tithing" (*164*). It may be added that, if out of every tything, then also out of every hundred. The Forest did not fit in with the normal units of local government.

The same was to some extent true in matters ecclesiastical. Dartmoor as a royal forest was not tithable, but Henry III in 1236–7 granted to God and the Church of St. Petrock at Lydford, and the chaplain ministering in the same church, whosoever for the time being shall be chaplain there, for his maintenance, the tithe of the herbage of the Moor of Dartmoor (*5*). Two years later Henry granted the Forest of Dartmoor to his brother Richard, Earl of Cornwall (*5*). The Chase, as it now became, would have remained tithe-free, but for the grant voluntarily made by Henry. We have the accounts of Edward, Earl of Cornwall, for 1296–7. From this it appears that sixty shillings were paid to the parson of Lydford, as and for the tithe (*9*). Seeing that the receipts from the herbage of the Forest did not amount to thirty pounds (*10*) this may be taken to have been an equitable composition.

If sixty shillings is regarded as insignificant toward the living expenses of the parson we may compare it with the wages paid to the foresters and other officers. There were six foresters in the year 1301–2, who received 62s. between them (*11*), or at the rate of 10s. 4d. apiece; while the stipends and food of twelve herdsmen, from May to August, cost in all 66s. 6d. (*11*) or at the rate of 5s. 6½d. a head. In 1316–17, the stipend and keep of six foresters cost 42s., at the rate of 7s. a head (*13*). So that, on comparison, the parson's 60s., which was a part only of his revenues, would not appear entirely inadequate.

This composition of sixty shillings became customary.

It is to be noted that when Bronescombe, in 1260 (Rowe, 1896, p. 267), attached the ancient tenements to the parish of Widecombe, for certain religious observances, he determined that Lydford should still be their mother church, but that the vicar of Widecombe should receive the tithe lambs. It nowhere appears that either the Crown or any other having interest in the Forest confirmed this decision.

As the years passed the parsons of Lydford became dissatisfied with the 60s. composition, and sought to increase their revenues by actions for tithes directed against individuals. It is noteworthy that in their pleas they do not mention the composition. The trouble began in 1610, when William Hunt, the rector of Lydford, filed a bill against parishioners of Sampford Courtenay, Whitchurch and Tavistock for the tithe of the agistment of sheep on Dartmoor and the Commons of Devon (*56–7*); the men were not his parishioners, nor were the Commons of Devon any part of his parish. Next year he followed this with another bill (*57*), against Gregory Newman the vicar of Walkhampton, and parishioners of Petertavy, Tavistock, Bickleigh, Bridestowe and Spreyton. Apparently Newman of Walkhampton was getting tithes which Hunt of Lydford considered should be his. Incidentally Hunt, in his replication, gives the information that the vicar of Widecombe had in fact received and still did receive the tithe lambs and the offerings of the dwellers in the Forest tenements, as determined by Bronescombe. Mr. Stuart Moore did not search for the verdict in these cases; but we learn from the pleadings in a later case that, in or about the year 1622, one Richard Harbin, a layman, having obtained a lease of the tithes of Lydford, brought a similar suit, which was either stayed by order or withdrawn (*80*).

Again, in 1625–6, a rector of Lydford, William Barber, was seeking to recover tithes, but this time in the Court Christian. William Northcote of Sampford Spiney brought a suit for the prohibition of Barber's suit in the Court Christian (*61*), and the Exchequer of Pleas granted the prohibition. Subsequently Northcote appears to have satisfied the law barons, by sufficient witnesses, that no tithe was due. The judgement was not entered up, but the tithes were not paid. Barber was persistent, and brought another suit in the Ecclesiastical Court, whereupon William French and others filed, in 1627, a bill in the Exchequer (*62*). In 1630, an order was made to stay the proceedings in the Ecclesiastical Court, and that this cause should be tried at the assizes (*67*). The result has not been seen, but the pleadings in the later suit above referred to state that Barber's claim was dropped.

These various suits resulted, in one instance, in testimony by a witness as to the character of his rector. William Pellow, of Lydford, says of Barber that he keepeth a good house for the entertainment of his neighbours and the poor, that the poor were much relieved by him, and that he is a man of honest conversation, duly dischargeth his cure in preaching, and demeaneth himself well, and hath a great charge of children (*65*).

Parsons came and went, but the dispute as to the tithes remained. In 1682–3 we find Michel Man, John Hext and William French seeking to have Richard Pote, the rector of Lydford, restrained from bringing suits of law for tithes in the Forest (*76*). Their statement is that Pote well knew in his own conscience and by long observation that tithes in kind were not due, nevertheless out of a surly and greedy mind and humour and covetous desire to wrest and extort from them tithes which he well knew did not belong to him, he brings suit at law. Pote replies that he ought to have tithes from the plaintiffs, but that there has been a collection to prosecute him, and that he is thereby reduced to extreme poverty. The result is not known, but it does not appear that the tithes were ever paid.

The conflict was not ended, for, in 1689, David Birchincha, rector of Lydford, brought an action against certain parishioners of Lydford for tithes (*78*). In this action he was successful; and thereupon, in 1692–3 he brought a further action, this time against tenants in other parishes (*79*); there was no answer, so presumedly he succeeded. But two at least of the defendants would appear to have still refused to pay, and, in 1699 he filed another bill against these two, and other defendants (*80*), with what success I do not know, but the claim against other than his parishioners may well have failed.

Still the matter was not effectively decided. Thomas Bernaford, rector of Lydford, found it necessary, in 1702, to bring an action against John Hext and others (*83*), claiming tithes in the tithable places in the Parish of Lydford, in the waste of Dartmoor, from thirty-five ancient tenements, and the newtakes thereto belonging. This action was vigorously contested, but ended in a finding for the rector, on the 10th June 1706. I do not know what happened thereafter.

It is not for me to revise the decisions of the courts, but it is significant that the rectors met no success until the case came before tribunals which were far removed in date, and very possibly in knowledge, from the origin thereof.

The one happy feature of the whole dispute is the contribution to the history of Dartmoor, its tenants and its customs which can be derived from the voluminous depositions in the successive suits. That consolation is ours alone; it never softened the acerbity of the disputants.

LAW REFERENCES

1607 Le Court Leete et Court Baron, *John Kitchen*
1650 The Compleat Copy-Holder, *Sir Edward Coke*,
         with which is bound:
         Relation between the Lord of the Manor and the Copyholder, *Charles Calthrop*
1671 Les Termes de la Ley
1672 *Manley's* Interpreter of Words and Terms used in the Law
1743 The New Law-Dictionary, carefully abridged, *Giles Jacob*
1756 Statutes at Large, made for the Preservation of the Game
1876 Select Charters and other Illustrations of English Constitutional History, *William Stubbs*

THE MOORSTONE AGE

QUARRYING for granite was almost unknown on Dartmoor earlier than the opening years of the nineteenth century; then, at Heytor in Ilsington, and Foggintor in Walkhampton, quarries were opened from which large quantities of stone were ultimately taken. But surface granite, undressed, was already in use during the Early Bronze Age. And stone cut and dressed from surface blocks was in use before the Norman Conquest.

It must not be thought that these surface blocks necessarily yielded stone of poor quality; the larger masses are but superficially affected by weathering, and in some localities, such as Foggintor and Hentor, the stone is so far unaffected by exposure that the edges of the blocks are still sharply angular.

There were two excuses for the use of surface stone; the right to take stone did not extend to a right to quarry, also, the cost of quarrying was avoided. There was another good reason for its use—in the main it proved a durable material.

There were, however, rare instances of bad selection; for example there is in Harford Churchyard an altar tomb bearing the date April 1633. The inscription is in raised letters, and is now almost illegible. Three hundred and seven years after the erection of the tomb it was with great difficulty, and only under the most favourable conditions of lighting, that I was able to decipher the inscription.[1] By way of contrast the inscription, also in relief, from the Old Town Conduit in Plymouth, erected in 1598, is still perfectly clear; so much depends on selection.

Surface stone is still used for local purposes, and even at times in the making of granite setts for carriageways in towns. An interesting note on its use is to be found in the *Gentleman's Magazine* (1849, Part II,

---

[1] It may be well to preserve the matter of this inscription:

HERE LY(ETH)	AND THOMAS
IOAN THE WIFE	THERE SONNE
OF RICHARD	WHO DIED THE
PREDIOX WHO	XIX OF APRILL
DIED THE XI OF	1633
APRILL 1633	

p. 494) where, writing of the danger to the *Men Skrifa* (Madron, Cornwall) which had fallen, a writer says that it had been re-erected some twenty years earlier, but had again fallen, adding: "At that period (the period of its re-erection) the act of raising it was simply one of laudable reverence, for, whether standing or prostrate, its situation in an out-of-the-way croft seemed to promise it a sufficient security from injury. The case is, however, widely different now, when there is such a demand for our granite; and as the surface blocks are specially coveted, not only because they are more durable than the quarried material, but also because they are cheaper—leave being readily obtained for their removal, which renders the land available for tillage—it is much to be feared that the inscribed stone, no longer distinguished by its upright position, will be treated with as little ceremony as the nameless ones amongst which it lies."

Such were the conditions in west Cornwall a hundred years ago, and on Dartmoor matters were certainly no better; indeed they are still very unsatisfactory.

So far as they gave it any thought it must have comforted the conscience of the stone-mason, and reassured his customers, to believe in the superiority of surface stone. At least it usually proved a sufficient and satisfactory material.

For this rock the constant name was *moorstone*; the word *granite* was foreign to the western vocabulary prior to the advent of the systematic geologist. A kindred material, the felsite which occurs as a dyke on Roborough Down (South Devon) was known as *Roborough Stone*. The quarries on the course of this dyke could not have yielded as much of this rock as is known to have been used, largely in ecclesiastical buildings; and much must have been derived from surface blocks. Roborough Stone was favoured by the church-builders of the Perpendicular Period. It was also in use for domestic utensils, such as mortars and troughs. Richard Strode, in his will, 12th October 1464, directs that a new window of "Rowburgh-stone" shall be placed in the chapel of the Guild of St. Catherine in the church of Plympton St. Mary and that, in an arch under this window, his tomb shall be constructed, "fact' de petra vocat' vulgariter Bere Stone vel alias de petra vulgariter vocat' Rowburgh Stone". In the event Roborough Stone was used for the window, and Bere Stone for the tomb.

In the following notes I give some account of the many uses to which Moorstone and Roborough Stone were applied.

GATE AND DOOR HANGERS

Certain holed stones, often found in use as gate-posts, have puzzled western antiquaries. One such stone, from the head of Portland Lane, Sheepstor, now serves as a gate-post of an adjacent field (Fig. 102, 1; Pl. 72B). Alike in Devon, where the holes more usually extend but

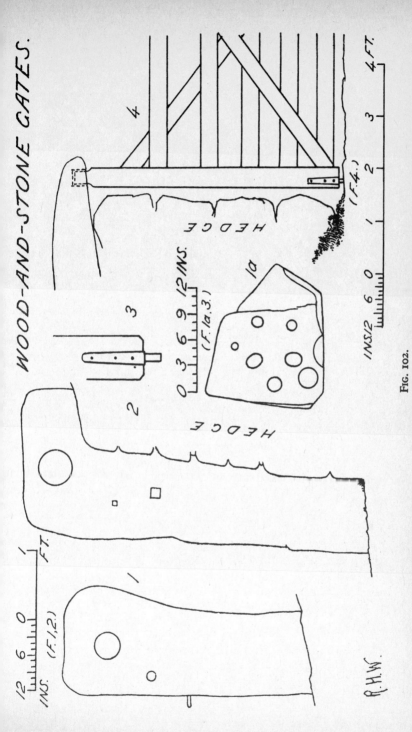

WOOD-AND-STONE GATES.

HEDGE

HEDGE

R.H.W.

Fig. 102.

1, 1a. Near Portland Lane, Sheepstor.   2. Longstone.   3. Wormhill, pin.   4. Wormhill, complete gate-hanger.

partly through the stone, and in Cornwall, where they more usually pierce the stone, they have been regarded as of prehistoric origin. In the Isles of Scilly where, on Tresco, there is a stone pierced with two such holes, the idea is accepted that lovers, standing one on either side, passed their hands through the holes, and, clasping hands, plighted their troth. The impossibility of their clasping hands under such conditions is not regarded as relevant evidence to the contrary.

There is no call for ingenious speculation. The Rev. S. Rowe, writing from personal observation (1848, p. 89), says: "The primitive contrivance for hanging gates of the moorland crofts and commons, may be seen employed in this neighbourhood (Chagford). No iron hinge of any kind, nor gate-post, is employed. An oblong moorstone block, in which a socket is drilled, is built into the wall, from which it projects sufficiently to receive the back stancheon of the gate, while a corresponding socket is sunk in a similar stone fixed in the ground below, unless a natural rock should be found *in situ*, which is frequently the case. The gate, thus secured, swings freely, swivel-like, in these sockets; and thus, from materials on the spot, without the assistance of iron, a simple, durable and efficient hinge is formed by the rural engineer."

I doubt the strict accuracy of a part of this description. A wooden stanchion turning in a hole in granite, set at ground-level, and often filled with water mingled with sand from the adjacent track, would be fretted away and worn out in short time.

With one possible exception, near Lydgate, Buckfastleigh, I have found no trace of lower sockets in any way comparable to the upper. The bottom of the stanchion has always been armed with an iron pin, fitting into a small hole in a stone at or slightly above ground-level. The bed-stone of the gate-hanging at Portland Lane (Fig. 102, 1*a*) was not in granite, but in altered slate, and had been used for a sufficiently long time for the pin on the gate to wear a number of successive sockets until each in turn became too deep for convenience. There is one other correction to be made: the holed-stone, the upper socket, was rarely built into the hedge but more usually laid upon the top of it.

The holed-stones, a term which I confine to the upper hangers, varied in size. They had to be sufficiently heavy to resist the pull of the gate, and sufficiently long to balance securely on the top of the hedge. It must be remembered that, when they were in general use, few gates much exceeded five and a half feet in length, yet some of the stones were sufficient and adequate to be retained in use in days when eight-, or even nine-feet gates had come into favour. Many of the holed-stones were fitted by size and shape for use as gate-posts of the modern type, and many were ultimately so used, remaining thus on their original sites.

The combined gate and hanger were usually called a 'wood-and-stone' gate, a term frequently corrupted to 'wooden stone'.

There is a wood-and-stone gate on Peck Farm, in the parish of Lust-leigh (Pl. 72A), at the point where the track from South Harton to Peck enters the enclosures of the latter farm (6 inch O.S., sheet c, NE., lon. 3°-44'-58", lat. 50°-37'-47½"); and another gate at Wormhill (Fig. 102, 3 & 4; Pl. 73A) in the parish of North Bovey, 350 ft east of the entrance to Wormhill, and on the north side of the Tavistock—More-tonhampstead road (6 in. O.S., sheet xc, sw., lon. 3°-48'-54", lat. 50°-38'-53"). Originally this was a six-foot gate, but at the time the photo-graph was taken it had been enlarged to ten feet, an alteration which overtaxed the capacity of the holed-stone, and eventually led to the use of the modern type of gate-hanging. Here, as is frequent, the pin on the bottom of the hanging style of the gate had occupied a succession of sockets in the foot-stone, a new socket being formed when its pre-decessor became unduly worn.

There is a wood-and-stone gate at Cockstor in the parish of Peter-tavy, at the east end of the Cockstor moor-lane (6 in. O.S., sheet cvi, NW., lon. 4°-5'-15", lat. 50°-33'-46½").

Of the three gates mentioned above, that at Peck Farm was in decay when last I saw it; I do not know whether it has been restored, nor whether the restoration has been on the old lines. The gate at Wormhill was a ten-foot gate hung on a holed-stone originally intended to take a six-foot gate; when last I saw it the attempt to hang the longer gate in this manner had been abandoned, and a gate-post of modern type has been substituted: this example was thus lost. As to the gate at Cockstor, Mr. Bellamy tells me that, as long as he occupies the farm, no change will be made, beyond necessary repair and renewal; for that deter-mination we are grateful to him. Cockstor affords one of the few Devonshire examples of a holed-stone in which the hole completely pierces the stone. I know of but one other instance, and that disused, built into the western hedge of the track leading from Merrivale to Davytown, at a point 450 ft north of the Davytown court-gate: Walk-hampton parish (6 in. O.S., sheet cvi, SE., lon. 4°-2'-51", lat. 50°-32'-29½"). On this same track there is, near Little Wonder Bridge, over the Pila Brook, a holed-stone of ordinary type, which has been broken and built into a wall; and at Hucken Tor, worked in rock *in situ*, at road level, are the marks left by the iron pin which shod the hanging style of a former gate.

Although usually lying free on the hedge-top, holed-stones were at times built into masonry. Thus, at Forder in the parish of Gidleigh (6 in. O.S., sheet lxxxix, NE., lon. 3°-52'-53", lat. 50°-41'-24") one side of the entrance to the yard is formed by the quoin of a building, and built into that quoin is a holed-stone, at 7 ft above ground level, which once formed the upper socket in which turned the yard gate or door (Fig. 103).

Holed-stones were also used as hangers for barn doors. Examples can be seen at Foxworthy in the parish of Lustleigh (6 in. O.S., sheet c, NE., lon. 3°-45′-21″, lat. 50°-37′-28½″), and at Peck, in the same parish (6 in. O.S., sheet c, SE., lon. 3°-45′-14″, lat. 50°-37′-52″).

In the old house at Yardworthy, in the parish of Chagford (6 in. O.S., sheet lxxxix, SE., lon. 3°-52′-9½″, lat. 50°-39′-2″) there are two interesting examples of this type of hanging. In the stone which forms the roof of the porch is a hole 2¾ in. deep and 2¾ in. in diameter which formed the upper hanging of the entrance door; the sill has been lost, and with

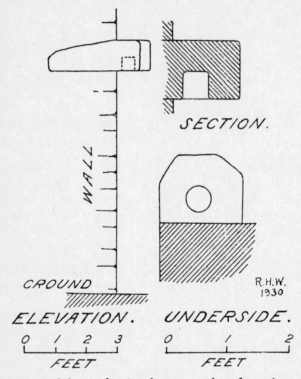

SECTION.

WALL

GROUND

R.H.W.
1930

ELEVATION.   *UNDERSIDE.*

0   1   2   3   0   1   2

FEET   *FEET*

FIG. 103. Holed stone forming the upper socket of a yard gate, Forder (Gidleigh).

it the bearing of the lower hanging. There is, however, a window opening, which was never glazed but was closed with a shutter, the upper hinge of which was formed by a hole in the lintel, 2 in. in diameter and 2 in. in depth. The lower hinge was formed by a slight hole in the sill; the dimensions of this hole are sufficiently small to indicate that an iron spill must have been used at this bearing. I regard the building as being fourteenth-century work (see p. 403).

As to dimensions I have taken the figures for the first twenty-two holed-stones which I have listed. I find the mean diameter of the holes to be 4·92 in., and the mean depth 4·24 in.; with the following extremes: diameters, greatest 7½ in., least 2½ in.: depths, greatest 6 in., least 2¼ in.. But, if we omit the two least diameters and the two least depths, we get ranges of: diameters, 7½ in. to 4 in.; depths: 6 in. to 3 in.; and these are more representative figures.

In general the holed-stones have much the same size and proportions as modern gate-posts, except that their width is somewhat greater as compared with their thickness. It is, however, true that some few are irregular in form, subject always to there being at least one flat face to rest on the hedge.

At Longstone, by Burrator Reservoir, Sheepstor, a holed-stone re-used as a gate-post stands 5 ft 5 in. out of the ground, and measures 2 ft 1 in. in width at the top (Fig. 102, 2). At Fernworthy, in Lydford parish, there were three holed-stones, two of which were used as gate-posts. One, at the court gate, stood 3 ft 5 in., was 27 in. at its greatest width, and 13 in. thick. Another, at the moor gate, still stands 5 ft 5½ in. high; and the third, built into a wall, is 5 ft 6 in. in length, 23 in. in width at one end, and 18 in. at the other. There is built into the boundary wall of Natsworthy Manor, Widecombe-in-the-Moor, a holed-stone, 6 ft 9 in. in length, 13 in. wide at one end, 2 ft 3 in. at the other, and with a least thickness of 9 in.; longer stones are known.

The general principle of the wood-and-stone gate was probably in early use; it has certainly not been confined either to Dartmoor or the British Isles, and it is known in China. In our local form it may be primitive, but it is not the simplest device which has been used. It has disadvantages; it needs a real gate, a piece of carpentry; the head of the hanging style must of necessity become worn by the friction of the stone in which the hole is formed; the iron pintle at the foot of the hanging style is probably but slowly affected, but it wears the socket in the foot-stone, and a new socket is then necessary. Against these disadvantages it has one quality which specially suited it for certain positions; it can be easily and quickly opened and closed. A man on horseback can open the gate, ride through, and then close the gate behind him without dismounting. The slip-bar gate, described below, involved that the rider should dismount, tether his horse, take down the bars, lead his horse through, replace the bars, and remount. Hence it came that the wood-and-stone gate was rarely used except at the entrances to courts or yards, or across accommodation roads, or public roads where these needed to be closed, as at moor gates; while slip-bar gates were never used in such places, but were essentially field-gates.

SLIP-BAR GATES

Slip-bar gates are found in four variants.

(a) *Double Slot gates.* Two granite posts are each vertically slotted at intervals, the spaces between the slots being the same in both. The slots in one post are made twice the depth of those in the other. These posts are set vertical. Then, if a clear opening of, say, 6 ft is required, the posts are set at that distance apart; in one the slots will be 2 in. in depth, in the other 4 in.

Bars or poles of 6 ft 4 in. in length are then inserted in the deeper slots, and pushed well home; the free end of the bar is brought opposite the shallower slot in the other post, and again pushed well home, being thus partly withdrawn from the deeper slot. There is left a bar 6 ft 4 in. in length, spanning the 6 ft space between the posts, and resting 2 in. at either end in the slots. A peg put through the bar against the post with the deeper slots fastens it securely.

There is a pair of posts of type (a), now diverted to use as ordinary gate-posts at Cudliptown, in the parish of Petertavy (6 in. O.S., sheet xcviii, sw., lon. 4°-5′-11″, lat. 50°-35′-40½″). Some work was added on conversion to present use. The slots in the right-hand post are 4 in. deep, those in the left-hand post are 2 in. deep (Fig. 104, 1, 2).

(b) *Slot-and-L gates.* In this type one post is slotted precisely like the posts with the shallower slots in type (a). On the other post, in position corresponding to these slots, a series of grooves is cut, in the form of inverted L's. The horizontal arm of the L forms a notch in one face of the post. In general the slots in the one post, and the grooves in the other, are about 1¾ in. in depth. In these gates the length of the bar should be equal to the distance between the posts, plus the depth of the slot and the groove; the bar cannot be removed by endwise movement. But, at the groove end, with vertical posts, it would be in no wise fixed. It is possible to devise methods of fixing this end, but they would not be simple, and would be tiresome to apply.

Short of absolute security, relative security might serve all practical purposes; and this was accomplished by setting the posts leaning somewhat away each from each. The ends of the bars can then be pressed down in the vertical leg of the L, and thus jammed into position. This was apparently sufficient to meet the difficulty.

At North Creber, in the parish of Gidleigh (6 in. O.S., sheet lxxxix, NE., lon. 3°-53′-47″, lat. 50°-40′-33″) there still stands a gate of this type, complete in all respects, and preserving its original dimensions. Two other posts, one from South Creber and one from Lakeland, both in the parish of Chagford, have been noticed. The stone from South Creber has been shaped by the old method of cleavage, as to which see later. The stone from Lakeland has L-shaped grooves on two adjacent sides, having served two adjoining gateways (Fig. 104, 3; Pl. 73B).

Type (b) was the most popular of all, and among the many posts which yet remain some few show divergencies from the type, as, for example, the post from North Creber.

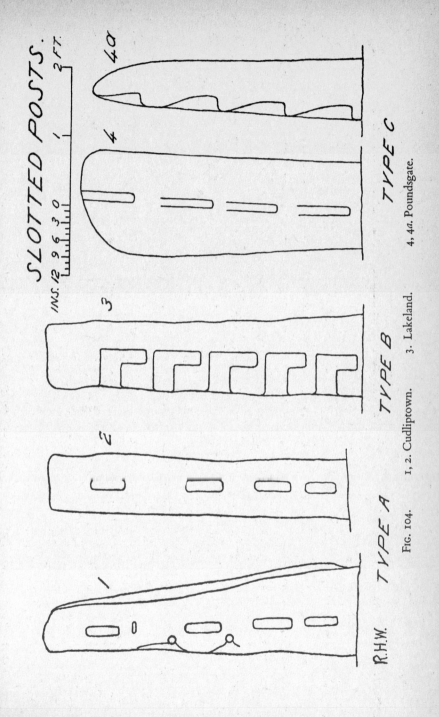

SLOTTED POSTS.

INS. 12 9 6 3 0 — 1 — 2 FT.

TYPE A   TYPE B   TYPE C

R.H.W.

Fig. 104.

1, 2. Cudliptown.   3. Lakeland.   4, 4a. Poundsgate.

(c) *Slot-and-Arc gates.* This type is rare. One post is of the common slotted type. In the other, in place of slots of even depth throughout, the upper end of the slot starts flush with the surface of the post and then proceeds in a curve, deeper and deeper into the post, reaching at the bottom of the slot the same depth as in the ordinary type. The posts were set slightly farther apart at the top than at the base. The wooden bars were first inserted in the slots of the post with normal slots, and were then dropped vertically into the curved slots of the other, and pressed down. They were thus jammed between the two posts, and held relatively firm.

An example is to be found by the roadside opposite Northaway, in the parish of Widecombe-in-the-Moor (6 in. O.S., sheet c, sw., lon. 3°-48′-12″, lat. 50°-34′-34″). A similar stone is to be found at Poundsgate, in the parish of Widecombe (Fig. 104, 4, 4a).

(d) *Locked-bar gates.* This is not a common type, but it is less rare than type (c). As in all the types, one post is an ordinary slotted stone; the other post has no slots, but cut out from one face of the stone at a corner are rectangular depressions, corresponding in number and in height above the ground to the slots in the former. These depressions are deep enough to take the whole thickness of the bars.

The gate is mounted by placing one end of each bar in a slot of the slotted post, and then bringing the other end, keeping the bar level, to and into a depression in the other post. When all the bars have been so placed the gate has been closed; but the arrangement is unstable; a moderate breeze, or the slightest pressure, displaces the bars. The difficulty is met by placing a slip of wood, set vertical, over the ends of the bars as they lie in the recesses, and securing the wood to the post by an iron eye, set in the moorstone and passing through a slot in the wood, through which eye a wooden wedge is passed. A similar device is that used for simultaneously locking a set of drawers in a cabinet. Thus types (a) and (d) are the two in which positive locks hold the bars.

There is a recessed post which stands at Cudliptown in the parish of Petertavy (6 in. O.S., sheet xxxviii, SE., lon. 4°-5′-49½″, lat. 50°-35′-11″) (Fig. 105, 1). A similar gate is still in use at the entrance to the field in which lies Puggiestone, in the parish of Chagford (6 in. O.S., sheet lxxxix, NE., lon. 3°-51′-32½″, lat. 50°-40′-21½″).

The distribution of these gate-hangers and posts is interesting. I have specifically mentioned but few of many. They are most frequent on the east of Dartmoor, and especially around Chagford, in an area extending west of the town to the unenclosed moorland. There are three holed-stones at Fernworthy, and several slotted posts. In Widecombe, Manaton, North Bovey and Moretonhampstead parishes, to the west and south, holed-stones and slotted posts are common. In the Ancient Tenements of the Dart Valley these relics are less frequent, but far from rare; while, to the south-west, there are two holed-stones

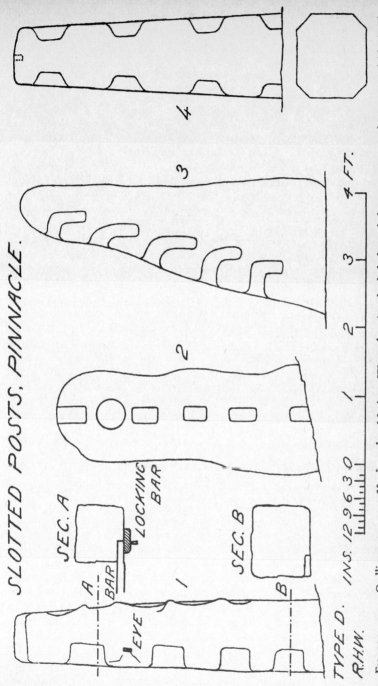

SLOTTED POSTS, PINNACLE.

TYPE D. INS. 12 9 6 3 0

R.H.W.

Fig. 105. 1. Cudliptown. 2. Yardworthy, Mariners Way, showing both hole and slots. 3. Particulars not available (Ed.). 4. Gidleigh, a deposed pinnacle.

and several slotted posts in Sheepstor parish; at least three holed-stones, and several slotted posts in Walkhampton parish; and, farther west, a number of slotted posts in Marytavy and in Meavy; to the south there are occasional slotted posts in Plympton St. Mary and South Brent parishes. As far south as Prawle I have found a slate post in which the slots were carried right through the stone, Cornish fashion. Lastly, there are wooden posts, a few on Dartmoor, and a few in the South Hams, which in form and purpose simulate the granite posts which I have described. It would appear that these gates attach to the earlier agricultural enclosures, but not to the earliest. I doubt that any, except those with wooden posts, have been constructed since wheeled agricultural vehicles came into use, although many remained in use after alteration to suit the new conditions. This consideration does not carry us to any really early date. The grandfather of the brothers Fabyan and John Amery was the first in the parish of Lustleigh to employ a wheeled cart in agriculture, and his neighbours held him to be foolish, in that such employment brought the need for altering the width of all his gateways. With greater precision as to date I may quote Fraser, who, writing in the year 1794, says of the South Hams: "Carts are little used for the purposes of agriculture, but when they are, they are of the common kind, and drawn both by oxen and horses." Marshall, 1796, with even greater particularity, writes: "Formerly, CARRIAGE of every kind was done entirely on the BACKS OF HORSES, except in harvest, when sledges, drawn by oxen, were sometimes used; also heaps of manure, in the field, were dragged abroad in small cart sledges, either by oxen or horses. Twenty years ago, there was not a 'pair of wheels' in the country, at least not upon a farm; and nearly the same may be said at present." The change from pack-horse to horse-and-cart was far from complete in the early years of the nineteenth century.

One other attempt may be made to establish some form of chronology in the matter. All the holed-stones and slotted posts which I have seen, so far as they have been shaped by cleavage, show the use of the earlier method of splitting the stone. I except two examples to which I will later refer. The earliest date for the use of the later method of splitting, the use of the drill, which I can establish on Dartmoor, is 1803. But no industrial technique is ever abruptly abandoned; it lingered on here and there.

There are two slotted stones which have been split from their parent masses by the use of the drill. Neither of these presents good workmanship; the slots are no more than roughly shaped depressions, which serve their purpose, but mark the stones as makeshift replacements. The more presentable of these two stones is to be found at the south end of Blackslade Drive, in the parish of Widecombe (6 in. O.S., sheet cviii, NW., lon. 3°-48'-2", lat. 50°-33'-51"). Its companion in the gateway is a normal L stone.

PLATE 65

A. Furnace. Black Tor.

B. Mortars, Black Tor.

PLATE 66

A. Mould. Colleytown, Sheepstor.

B. View of stone shown in Fig. 89. Hook Lal e, Erme.

PLATE 67

A. Ingot from Piall Valley.

B. Crazing Mill Stone. Outcombe (Deancombe).

PLATE 68

A. General view of blowing-house near Henglake, Avon.

B. Lower blowing-house, Walkham. View including float and mould-stone.

PLATE 69

A. Mould-stone, in garden of 'Outer Down', Chagford.

B. Mortar-stone, in garden of 'Outer Down', Chagford.

PLATE 70

A. Float from furnace, Yellowmead.

B. Mortar-stone with four mortars and three bearings. Nosworthy.

PLATE 71

A. Mould-stones. Longstone, Sheepstor.

B. Mortar-stone in wall between Soussons Common and
Runnage. (The staff is 3 ft 6 in. long.)

PLATE 72

A. Wood-and-stone gate, Peck Farm, Lustleigh.

B. Holed gate-hanger now used as gate-post,
near Portland Lane, Sheepstor.

PLATE 73

B. Slotted gate-post, Lakeland, Chagford.

A. Gate-hanger, Wormhill.

PLATE 74

A. Quern, Ditsworthy Warren, Sheepstor.

B. Cheese press, set in cobbled paving. Gratton farm, Meavy.

PLATE 75

A. A cider mill.

B. Abandoned apple-crusher, Merrivale.

PLATE 76

A

B

Cider mill, Longstone, Sheepstor. (A) Before restoration, the edge runner
lying on its side. (B) The pound stone during restoration.

PLATE 77

A. The Lichway by Whittaburrow.

B. Stepping stones on the Lichway, Willsworthy Ford.

PLATE 78

The Clapper Bridge on the Lichway, Baggator Brook.

PLATE 79

B. Guide-stone removed from the track to
Lowery Farm.

A. Guide-stone between Tavistock and Ashburton,
446 yd NW of Yellowmead Farm, Walkhampton.

PLATE 80

B. Broad-and-narrow work in old building at Challacombe.

A. South gable, Old Yardworthy, showing broad-and-narrow work.

PLATE 81

Old Yardworthy building, porch

Plate 82

Higher Godsworthy, Peter Tavy.

PLATE 83

1. Nuns Cross Farm.   2. John Bishop's house, Swincombe.

PLATE 84

A. Shilston, Throwleigh.

B. Lower Tar, Widecombe-in-the-Moor.

PLATE 85

Ash-house, Shapley, (1) view with door, (2) view with hatch.

PLATE 86

Ash-house, West Combe, North Bovey.

PLATE 87

Potato cave, Huntingdon Warren, (1) interior, (2) entrance.

PLATE 88

A. Delta of a tributary of the Radaven, formed by flood of
17 August, 1917.

B. Gully opposite South Down, Meldon, eroded in storm of
17 August, 1917.

PLATE 89

A. Boulder moved by the Cowsic in flood.

B. Parted block of granite, Huntingdon Warren.

PLATE 90

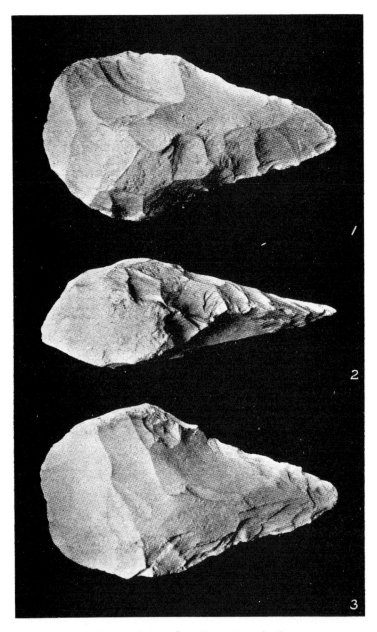

Flint implement from Brent Moor (x ¾).

PLATE 91

Stone implement, Marytavy.

PLATE 92

Chair at Dunnabridge Pound, with Miss Dinah Tuckett, the pound-keeper.

PLATE 93

A.   'Parliament Rock', Crockern Tor.

B.   Hobajons Cross.

Richard Hansford Worth

I think that none of the holed-stones or slotted-stones, with the possible exception of two last mentioned, have been made since the year 1800, and that most are much older.

There is one stone which is both slotted and holed. It stands beside the Mariners Way, at Yardworthy, in the parish of Chagford. Since it stands erect, its last use was as a slotted stone. (6 in. O.S., sheet lxxxix, SE., lon. 3°-52'-6", lat. 50°-39'-11".) (Fig. 105, 2.)

PINNACLE TO GATE-POST

In the village of Gidleigh, at the south end of a footpath which leads to Moortown, stands a gate-post, the form of which I was long unable to explain. It is a dressed stone, square in section, with an interrupted chamfer at each angle. At the top is a drilled hole, indicating that there was a spill for the attachment of a finial[1] (Fig. 105, 4).

During the Chagford meeting of the Devonshire Association, 1947, we visited Throwleigh, and there, in the churchyard, found a short length of similarly dressed stone forming part of the base of a memorial cross. Inquiry revealed no more than that this stone had been found in the hedge of the churchyard. A later visit disclosed a further fragment lying in the yard. This seemed to connect it with the church, and, in fact the pinnacles of the tower were found to consist of four similar stones, each standing on a plate on a short square base.

At Gidleigh church the bases still stand, but the pinnacles are missing. It is evident that the gate-post is a deposed pinnacle. At Chagford similar pinnacles have recently been taken down, presumably as needing re-setting, but have not been replaced; because, it is said, they are unorthodox and cannot be true pinnacles. They should certainly be restored to their position on the tower, as evidence of a local contribution to architectural design. The evident intent of the builders was to obtain, in a manner suited to the moorstone's intractibility, something of the effect of crocketting.

The location of the Gidleigh gate-post is 6 in. O.S., sheet lxxxix, NE., lon. 3°-52'-54½", lat. 50°-40'-50".

STILES

An occasional stile will be found consisting of two slotted moorstone posts set in the ground, with wooden bars set in the slots. I have seen such a stile near Bowden, in the parish of Hennock. The bars are not removable, except by taking down one of the posts.

A more interesting type of stile consists wholly of moorstone; the design is such as might have been originated by a carpenter, involving mortices, tenons and rebates. I give details of the posts of a stile, now

---

[1] Ornamentation, such as bunches of foliage, given to the peaks of Gothic pinnacles, etc. (ED.)

dismantled, at Sortridge, in the parish of Whitchurch; it has the advantage of being dated. (6 in. O.S., sheet cvi, sw., lon. 4°-6'-27", lat. 50°-31'-9".) (Fig. 106, 1, 1*a*, 1*b*.)

The posts are squared and wrought; one face of each bears a mortice and a rebate, one face of each has an inscription, the remaining two faces are plain. The mortice is vertical, 13 in. in length, 3 in. in width, and 1½ in. deep. The rebate is horizontal, extends across the full width of the stone, is 4½ in. wide, and 1¼ in. deep. A vertical slab of stone, which formed the riser or bar of the stile, was formerly supported in the mortices, and a horizontal slab, forming a step, rested in the rebates. These two slabs have been removed, and the posts are used as gate-posts. I am indebted to Col. Marwood Tucker for permission to measure and photograph these stones. The initials on the stone are those of John (or Julius?) and Elizabeth Glanvill, and the date is 1666. A few years later, in 1681, the southern approach to Walkhampton church was improved, and a stone stile erected; of this the two posts and the step remain (Fig. 106, 2). There is an inscription on the adjoining wall: "T B 1681", the initials being those of the vicar.

Two stiles in Meavy Lane, in the parish of Meavy, are undated, but valuable as being complete. The first of these stiles is on the left-hand side of the road from Meavy to Yelverton, at the entrance to a field-path leading to Gratton and at a distance of 1,660 ft from the Great House, Meavy; the other is on the right-hand side, 500 ft nearer Yelverton, at the entrance to a footpath leading to Lower Lake. I call these the Eastern Stile and the Western Stile respectively. (Eastern: 6 in. O.S., sheet cxii, NW., lon. 4°-3'-53½", lat. 50°-29'-17". Western: same sheet, lon. 4°-3'-58½", lat. 50°-29'-20".) (Fig. 106, 3, 3*a*.)

There is a slight difference in the design, the Western Stile being on steeply sloping ground; a strut has been placed between the feet of the posts. Both these stiles would appear to be on church paths.

A similar stile once stood at the entrance to Sheepstor churchyard from the east. Of this the posts remain; a complete example is to be found at Moretonhampstead.

CLAPPER BRIDGES

In any country where the native rock yields large slabs of sound stone, it is to be expected that streams should be crossed by bridges in which the roadway is formed with such slabs as imposts; especially where the bridges are for the use of foot-passengers, or pack-horse traffic. And on Dartmoor, clapper bridges, some very small, others as large as those at Postbridge and Belliver, are numerous. It is probably misleading to term the larger of these structures 'cyclopean', and thus suggest by one phrase, not only an exaggerated magnitude, but also an antiquity which cannot be proven. Fords and stepping-stones preceded bridges; and it seems certain that bridges were not early features on Dartmoor tracks,

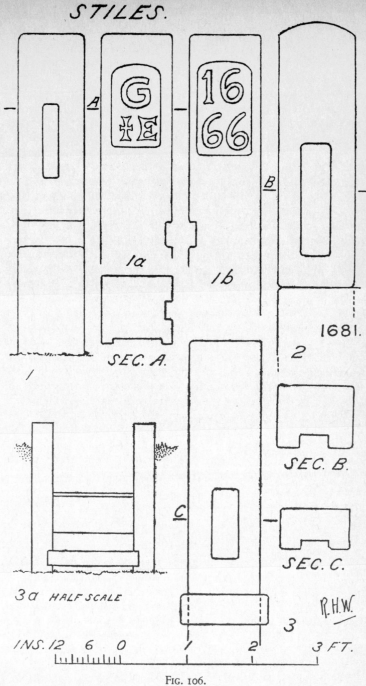

STILES.

FIG. 106.

1, 1a, 1b. Sortridge.   2. Walkhampton.   3, 3a. Meavy Lane.

since, in 1260, Bishop Bronescombe could determine, on the evidence
of credible witnesses, that it was eight miles from Babeny and Pizwell
to Lydford in fine weather, and fifteen miles in time of storm, when
tempest and overflows of water prevailed. At such times fords and
stepping-stones are of little avail.

There yet remain some of the fords and stepping-stones which preceded the bridges. On the East Dart at Postbridge the stepping-stones
still remain at a point a little less than 150 yards above the clapper
bridge. The stones are exceptionally large, and have been so little disturbed by floods that passage is still practicable for the active and sure-
footed. (6 in. O.S., sheet xcix, SE., lon. 3°-54'-42", lat. 50°-35'-38".)

At Marchants Bridge, in the parish of Meavy, on the direct line of
the road there are stepping-stones and a ford, both still in use. But for
greater convenience the road has at some time been diverted along the
right bank of the river to a point 250 ft above the ford, and an arched
bridge of the old pack-horse type has been constructed. This involved
some very awkward angles, not too troublesome to the traffic of the
day; but difficult during the late war to the mechanized army of the
U.S.A., which, after breaking down the parapet and part of the arch
of the bridge, took perforce to the ford.

At Gratton, also in Meavy parish, and a little over a mile below
Marchants Bridge, a ford for cattle and vehicles and a 'clam' for foot-
passengers afforded the only crossing until, in 1887, a substantial arched
bridge was constructed. The difficulties for armed forces were here
more tragic; a quartermaster and his horse were drowned during
the autumn manœuvres of 1873, when attempting the ford during a
flood.

But clapper bridges, when with growing traffic necessities they were
constructed, did not prove an answer to the threat of the floods. Of the
four largest, at Dartmeet, Postbridge, Belliver and Cadworthy (on the
Plym), Dartmeet has been twice damaged by flood within memory,
and Belliver also stands incomplete. Postbridge, as far as is known, has
only been damaged by human action[1]; and there is no record that Cadworthy bridge was other than perfect up to the time of its replacement
by the modern structure.

A clapper which apparently spanned the West Dart at Twobridges
as late as 1765, was probably removed when the new road was constructed shortly after the year 1772, and diverted to cross the West Dart
below its junction with the Cowsic. Donne, in his map published 1765,
shows the track crossing both streams above their point of junction;
and shows, in place of the present Plymouth Road, a moorland track,
marked out by guide-stones at frequent intervals. It was from the
presence of *two bridges*, the one over the West Dart, and the other over

---

[1] See Crossing, 1909, p. 467. (ED.)

the Cowsic, that the locality took its name,[1] with the alternative of *Potato Market*, the spot to which potatoes from the Moretonhampstead district were brought for sale to buyers from Plymouth and Tavistock. The clapper across the Cowsic still stands. It is a structure little above the water level, and was washed away by the great flood of 17th July 1890, a flood which at Postbridge just overtopped the lowest of the imposts. Postbridge stood unharmed; and the Cowsic bridge was later restored by the Dartmoor Preservation Association.

On lesser tracks, such as the *Lichway* and the *Mariners Way*, which have never been formalized into roads, there are still many clappers of relatively small size, two of which I have illustrated (see frontispiece and Pl. 78).

I doubt that any of the larger structures is other than post-medieval, say, not earlier than 1400. The latest, which already might, at sight, be judged the contemporary of its fellows, was erected at Teignhead in or about the year 1780, to give access to some new enclosures. Crossing gives its length as *c*. 28 ft with a width of 6 ft 9 in. The same author gives the dimensions of Postbridge as 42 ft 8 in. in length, and from 6 ft 9 in. to 6 ft 5 in. in width. The width in each instance affords sufficient proof that the bridges were not intended for wheeled vehicles; and so we find that at Teignhead there is a ford beside the bridge, and that at Postbridge the river-bed is well adapted for fording. Both bridges are of three spans, and both are in the parish of Lydford, and the Forest of Dartmoor.

Miss Ernestine Symes Saunders, has kindly sent me a drawing of Postbridge, made by her great-grandfather, Emmanuel Jeffery of Exeter; this is the earliest view of the bridge of which I have knowledge.

There is an example of a small clapper in private lands, at Rowbrook, in the parish of Widecombe-in-the-Moor (6 in. O.S., sheet cvii, SE., lon. 3°-51'-32", lat. 50°-32'-9½").

QUERNS

I myself have stayed in a cottage where the bread supply was all baked on the hearth; and the flour was from corn grown in the parish, and ground at the local mill. But I have not been able to trace, within living memory, the use in Devon of the hand-mill or quern. Yet at one time they must have been common objects of domestic economy; and their remains are to be found, from Axmouth in the east to Bere Ferrers in the west, and from Tiverton in the north to Ivybridge in the south. Only the under-stone is usually found; that was a substantial

[1] This derivation is not adopted by the authors of the *Place Names of Devon* (p. 197) in view of its earliest form, *Tobrygge* (meaning evidently "at the Bridge"). This reference incidentally shows that there was a bridge here in the reign of Henry VI. (ED.)

object, and had the further advantage that, divorced from its original purpose, it remained of use as a small, shallow trough. The upper-stone was a mere disc, rarely exceeding 2½ in. in thickness, and when it lost its job it was not worth preserving.

It has been said that the upper-stones are rare because the lords of the manors regarded querns as illicit competitors with their manor mills, in the interest of the franchise of which they seized the upper-stones and destroyed them. The output of a quern was so small, and the labour involved so considerable, that its competition with the mill can hardly have roused the most rapacious miller to such action. The querns were standbys to meet occasional need; at all times at least after the manorial system was fully established. It would be strange had the destruction been confined to the upper-stones, were such destruction purposeful; strange also if all the under-stones which remain had been in use in households which owed suit to the manor mill. Notwithstanding which the Abbot of St. Albans sought, in the fourteenth century, to prevent the use of querns by the townsfolk, and claimed the monopoly of grinding his tenants' grain. Thirteen of the tenants, however, maintained their right to use hand-mills, as having been enjoyed of old, and some claims were raised to the privilege of grinding oatmeal only, by means of a hand-mill (Evans, *Ancient Stone Implements of Britain*, 2nd ed., p. 258).

The manorial lords had no statutory right to the assize of mills, which could only arise by custom; thus the tenants on their part could also plead custom, and sometimes, as in this case, they succeeded in the plea.

The complete quern, omitting from consideration prehistoric examples, was constant in its essentials. A good specimen, of which nothing but a part of the ironwork is missing, is preserved at Sortridge House in the parish of Whitchurch. The under-stone is approximately circular, its mean diameter is 16 in., and its thickness is 5 in. In this stone a shallow, circular trough is cut, 8½ in. in diameter, and 1½ in. in depth. Radially from the circumference of this trough a channel has been cut, through which the ground material escapes and is collected. At the centre of the trough in the under-stone there has been set a vertical spill of iron; of this little is now left above the level of the stone. The upper-stone is 8½ in. in diameter at the top and 8 in. in diameter at the bottom being tapered somewhat, which involves that the sides of the trough in the under-stone are also tapered, though this is not a constant feature. The stone is pierced with a central hole, 1½ in. in diameter; it is 2½ in. thick at the centre, and 1½ in. thick at the circumference. On the upper surface are four small holes or depressions, set symmetrically; and on the lower face there is a slot 4½ in. in length by ⅞ in. in width, and about ¼ in. in depth. In this slot once fitted an iron strip, passing across, but not completely blocking, the central hole in the stone; and itself drilled at the centre to permit the spill in the under-stone to pass through. The spill and plate together held the upper-stone approximately centred. In all its working parts this example is typical. In its external form and the manner in which the flour is delivered it corresponds with most of the querns of the Isles of Scilly, where there are many, but with few Devonshire querns. We may safely apply what we know of the manner of working the querns in the Isles to meet the absence of any Devon record.

In the few upper-stones which have so far been found in Devon there is no adequate provision for setting a handle or handles. The four shallow holes which are found are neither sufficiently large nor deep enough for this purpose. The same is true in the Isles of Scilly.

But Borlase (*Observations on the Ancient and Present state of the Islands of Scilly*, 1756, p. 69) gives an account of the manner of use of the querns; and Troutbeck (*A survey of the Ancient and Present State of the Scilly Islands*, ? 1793) copies this and makes some slight additions.

Borlase writes: "Every house is furnished with a Handmill. This Mill consists of two small stones of about two feet in diameter, and four inches thick, in the shape of common Mill-stones, which may be set closer to one another or wider (as they chuse to have coarser or finer Meal) by raising or depressing the upper stone; the Mill is placed at such a height from the ground [Troutbeck says in a square frame of wood] as a man may stand and easily turn the upper stone by means of a stick five feet long, and one inch and a half in diameter, one end of which rests in a socket made for it in the middle of the *Radius* of the upper stone, and the upper end is inserted in a hole in a beam of the chamber above; in these two holes, the long stick standing obliquely, turns easily with the hand, but the stones being of small *Area*, and little weight, the Corn is a long while a grinding."

Borlase is mistaken as to the size of the stones; very few ever attained a diameter of two feet; a more usual diameter for the upper-stone was one foot or less. The hole for the driving-stick was not set at half the radius of the upper-stone, but was distinctly nearer the circumference. There was not one hole only, but for the more part there were four holes; and, by shifting from one to the other the wear of the stone was kept more uniform. He does not say how the stones were spaced nearer or farther each from each, but this was readily done by varying the thickness of the strips of iron let into the underside of the upper-stone.

The following notes may give some idea of the varied detail to be found in the querns.

1. *Axmouth*, from *Oxdown Farm*, but now forming a cap on the gate-pier of a house on the south side of the Seaton Road, near the river (Fig. 107, 1). Perhaps the most elaborately decorated of any that I have seen in Devonshire: ten-sided, with panel ornament; and, on

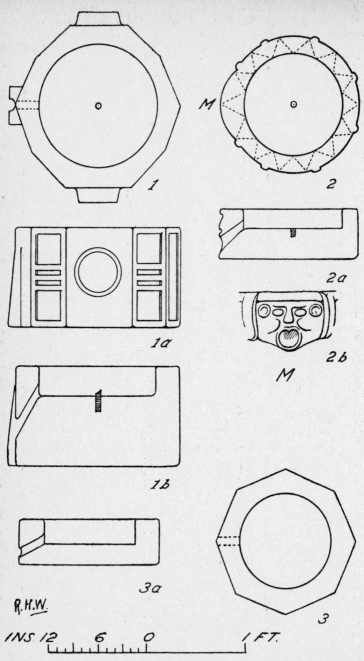

R.H.W.

FIG. 107.

1. Axmouth, plan: (*a*) side view; (*b*) section.
2. Ivybridge, plan: (*a*) side view; (*b*) section.
3. Bere Ferrers, section and (*a*) plan.

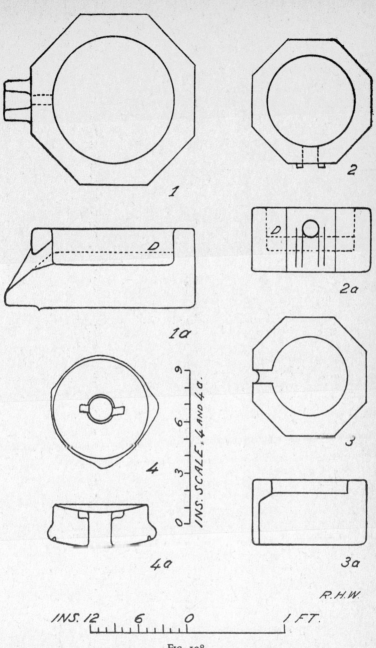

QUERNS.

FIG. 108.

1. Goodameavy House, plan: (a) section.
2. Ditsworthy, plan: (a) section.
3. Barnecourt, plan: (a) section.
4. Tavistock Church, plan of under side: (a) section of upper stone.

two opposite sides, are projections much like trunnions, for which there would be no purpose. Probably these fitted into sockets in the wooden frame which held the quern. The diameter of the trough is 14½ in. and its depth 3½ in. The stone is unusually thick and heavy, being 12 in. in depth. The aperture for the escape of the flour is placed at an angle and not on the centre of a face.

2. *Barnecourt*, Lustleigh parish (Fig. 108, 3; Pl. 74A). A small and plain example. Octagonal. Trough 9 in. in diameter and 1½ in. deep. Total thickness of stone 7½ in. Channel for flour in centre of one side of octagon, an open channel, extending the whole depth of one side.

3. *Bere Ferrers*, in church (Fig. 107, 3). A small octagonal stone, diameter of trough 11 in., depth 3 in., total depth of stone 5¼ in. Flour aperture at one of the angles of the octagon, a plain hole, with no external groove or lips.

4. *Buckland Abbey*, Buckland Monachorum (Fig. 109, 1). Now set on a lawn, forming with the annular trough of an apple mill the stone-work of a fountain. This stone is Roborough Elvan. The quern is octagonal, diameter of trough 17¼ in., depth 4 in., total depth of stone 13 in. One side of the octagon is occupied by a mask, gargoyle fashion. Through the widely opened mouth of the mask, stretched the wider by the first fingers of two sculptured hands, the flour was delivered.

5. *Cockstor Farm*, Petertavy. Octagonal, now set in the paving of the yard as a small trough.

6. *Corntown*, Cornwood (Fig. 109, 3). Octagonal. Diameter of trough 11¼ in. at top, 10 in. at bottom, the sides being tapered; depth of trough 2½ in.; total depth of stone 7½ in. Two sides of the octagon are produced to form a spout for the delivery of the corn.

7. *Ditsworthy Warren*, formerly at Longstone, Sheepstor. Material, Roborough Elvan (Fig. 108, 2). Octagonal. Diameter of trough 10⅞ in., original depth 3 in., has been deepened to 5 in. to adapt the quern to use as an ordinary trough. Total depth of stone 7½ in. Outlet for flour in middle of one side, and on either side of the hole a fillet ¾ in. wide, raised approximately three-sixteenths of an inch. One of the many devices used to prevent the flour from 'straying'. This is the quern which, from lack of experience, I falsely identified as a form of cheese-press base. The owner, Mrs. E. Ware, had no knowledge of its former use.

8. *Goodameavy House*, Meavy (Fig. 108, 1). Material, Roborough Elvan. Octagonal; diameter of trough 15 in., original depth 2½ in., has been deepened to 4 in. (as at Ditsworthy). Total depth of stone 9 in. Flour discharged at centre of one side, projecting from which is a spout.

9. *Harford Bridge Farm*, formerly at *Harrogrove*, Marytavy. Octagonal. Diameter of trough 9¼ in.

10. *Ivybridge*, Western Road (Fig. 107, 2). In the garden of Mr. J. T.

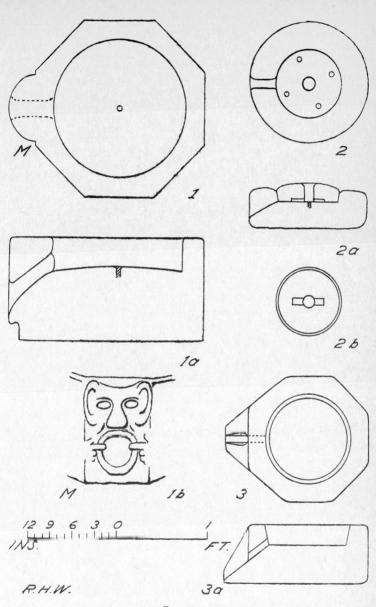

FIG. 109.

1. Buckland Abbey, plan: (*a*) section; (*b*) mask.
2. Sortridge, plan: (*a*) section; (*b*) under side of upper stone.
3. Corntown, plan: (*a*) section.

Yabsley's house; original location unknown. Material, Roborough
Elvan. Circular, but divided by fillets into eight panels, one of which,
larger than the others, bears a mask, the mouth of which forms the
outlet for the flour. Diameter of trough 11¾ in., depth 2¼ in. The rim
of the stone ornamented with a lightly incised chevron.

11. *Sortridge House*, Whitchurch (Fig. 109, 2). Approximately circular. Diameter of trough 8½ in., depth 1¼ in. Total depth of stone 5 in.

12. *Tiverton*. Octagonal, dimensions not taken.

Collecting the dimensions, given in inches, we get:

	(1)	(2)	(3)	(4)	(5)	(6)	(7)	(8)	(9)	(10)	(11)
Diam. of Trough	14½	9	11	17¼	—	11¼	10⅞	15	9¼	11¾ '	8½
Depth of Trough	3½	1½	3	4	—	2½	3	2½	—	2¼	1½
Depth of Stone	12	7½	5¼	13	—	7½	7½	9	—	5¾	5

Mean diam., 11·81 in.; greatest, 17·25 in.; least, 8·5 in.

I believe the above figures to be representative, and I doubt if there
are many true querns in Devonshire in which the troughs are more
than eighteen inches in diameter, or less than eight inches; although one,
at least, cannot have exceeded six inches.

QUERNS, UPPER-STONES

Upper-stones are rare. One is to be found at *Sortridge*, still associated
with the under-stone (Fig. 109, 2). Two others have come to rest in
ecclesiastical surroundings, to which they were admitted probably by
reason of the raised crosses carved upon their upper faces.

Tavistock, in the Church of St. Eustachius (Figs. 108, 4; 110). Diameter
of working part 5¾ in. Greatest thickness of stone 2⅜ in. Under surface
is not plane, but concave to the extent of ⅜ in. Feed hole 1¼ in. in diameter. The underside is recessed for an iron plate, such as I have described in the general description. Since, however, in this instance the
recess is ⅜ in. in depth, either the plate must have been unusually thick,
or oak may have been used in place of iron, but the width of the recess
does not seem sufficient for the use of wood. The trough in the under-
stone cannot have been of greater diameter than 6 in., nor of greater
depth than 1 in. The possible output in flour from such a quern must
have been small, but other things than grain may have been ground.

Fillham, Ugborough. At Lower Fillham House, in the ruined chapel
in the grounds, there lies an upper-stone.

Nosworthy, Walkhampton parish. Mr. G. W. Copeland found, in the
ruins of Nosworthy farm, a broken upper-stone, of which he has kindly
given me details. The break coincides with a diameter, so that one-half
of the stone is all that remains. The diameter is 10 in., and the greatest
thickness of the stone is 3⅝ in. The central aperture is *c*. 1¾ in. in diameter. On the upper side is a hole or depression near the margin; this
is 1 in. in diameter, tapering somewhat downward, and is ⅞ in. deep.

No handle could have been set in it, but it would serve well to take the end of the sloping stick with which Borlase says the stone was turned in the Isles of Scilly. It is usual to find four such holes, but in this instance there can, at the most, have been but two. The under face is slotted for the usual iron plate.

Millbay, East Portlemouth. I have seen a stone from Millbay, 17½ in. in diameter, which was said to have been the upper-stone of a quern. I cannot accept the identification, some of our smaller water-mills had some pairs, at least, of quite small stones. I take this to be a stone from the mill which gave its name to the bay.

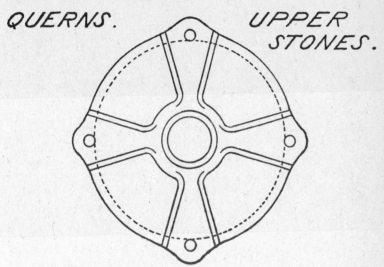

QUERNS.   *UPPER STONES.*

FIG. 110. Tavistock Church, upper surface.

BASES OF CHEESE-PRESSES

In general the stone base of a cheese-press was a flat stone of a few inches in thickness, more usually circular in outline, but always with a prolonged projection, or 'snout', extending from the circle. Concentric with the outline of the circular part of the stone a shallow channel was cut, making a complete circle. Within this circle, diametrically, two other channels were formed at right angles, the one extending to the circumference of the circular channel, but no farther, the other produced at one end to the extremity of the 'snout', which was throated.

Upon this stone, within the circular channel, was placed the curd, with a layer of straw, and possibly of cheese-cloth, between it and the stone. The curd was confined by a hollow cylinder of wood, also lined with cheese-cloth. A circular board was placed on the top of the curd, and upon this a heavy stone weight.

The whey, expressed from the curd, found its exit by the cross diameters or direct to the circular channel; thence the extension of one of the cross channels conducted it to the end of the 'snout', which, being throated, did not permit the liquid to run back along the underside of the stone, but confined the drip to one point, where it was readily caught in a bucket or other vessel.

There were, of course, modifications, but the principle remained the same; and such variations as were made will be sufficiently illustrated in the examples given.

1. *Brisworthy Farm*, parish of Meavy. Stone circular. Diameter of circular channel 18 in., thickness of stone 5¼ in. Two diametrical channels. 'Snout' throated. (Fig. 111, 1).

2. *Gidleigh Park*, Gidleigh. Stone octagonal. Diameter of circular channel 14½ in., thickness of stone 9 in. Two diametrical channels. 'Snout' lost by breakage.

3. *Gratton*, Meavy. Stone circular. Diameter of circular channel 16 in., thickness of stone 6½ in. 'Snout' rather unusually prolonged. (Pl. 74B.)

4. *Longstone*, Sheepstor. Stone circular. Diameter of circular channel 15 in., thickness of stone 6½ in. 'Snout' broken, but has been rather unusually prolonged. One diametrical groove extending from the 'snout' to near the farther circumference of the circular groove (Fig. 111, 5).

5. *Greencliff*, Milton Combe, parish Buckland Monachorum. Stone pear-shaped. Mean diameter of the misshapen circular groove 19 in.; one diametrical channel, extending from the 'snout' to join the farther circumference of the circular groove. 'Snout' but slightly protuberant. Thickness of stone not known (Fig. 111, 4).

6. *Sheepstor Churchyard*. Stone circular. Diameter of circular groove 12½ in. Two diametrical grooves. The throating of the 'snout' is well marked. (Fig. 111, 2.)

Presumedly because this stone bears a cross within a circle, it has been placed in the churchyard; where one hopes it may long be preserved. For a similar reason Crossing has stated that there is the head of a wheel-cross in the farmyard at Gratton (3).

STONE BASES OF CIDER PRESSES

The cider press base is but an enlarged edition of the cheese press, without the diametrical channels. These are not needed, since the apple juice can escape freely from all faces of the pile of alternating layers of straw and crushed apple pulp. One example will suffice.

Longstone, Sheepstor. Stone circular, with moderate extension of 'snout'. Diameter of stone 5 ft 10 in., thickness 9 in. Internal diameter of circular channel 4 ft 6 in., width of channel 3½ in. at top and 2½ in. at bottom, 1 in. deep at the shallowest, deepening to 1¾ in. at the outlet.

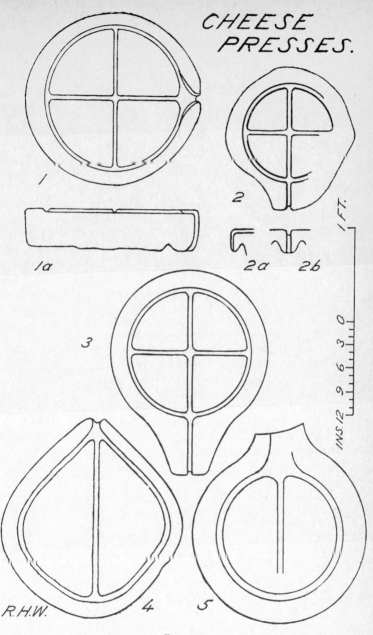

CHEESE PRESSES.

R.H.W.

FIG. III.

1, 1a. Brisworthy (plan and section).
2, 2a, 2b. Sheepstor. 3. Gratton. 4. Milton Coombe. 5. Longstone.

There are many such cider press bases, which are to be found through-out Devon and Cornwall. The smallest example which I have seen is at St. Michael's Mount, Cornwall. The width of the stone is 3 ft and the length 3 ft 7 in.

The olive presses in Tripoli, in the days when climate and soil were alike consistent with the extensive cultivation of the olive, were pro-vided with very similar stone bases. I take a description from Cowper's *Hill of the Graces*, p. 149.

"These . . . are large slabs of stone lying generally flush with the earth, and, when *in situ*, directly in front of the senam itself. Their surface measurement is generally 6 feet to 8 feet square, but with a pro-jection at one side. On the surface is cut a square or round groove or channel, 4 to 5 inches wide, and from this run two branch channels, one to one end of the projection, and the other to a side or corner. In all cases, the spout-like projection is turned away from the senam towards the enclosure."

It should be explained that the 'senam' is a stone structure consisting of two pillars, usually monoliths, resting on the tops of which is a stone lintel or transom. Worked in the pillars are slots and recesses, in which it seems fairly certain that wooden beams were fixed. The correspond-ing structure in the Devon press is wholly of wood, and serves to adjust the lever by which pressure is applied to the crushed apples.

It is not impossible, but I think improbable, that our Devonshire press should be a copy of the Tripolitan device. It is more likely that similar needs were independently met by similar inventions.

POUND-STONES, OR CIDER MILLS

Crushing the apples preparatory to the extraction of the juice was accomplished in at least three different ways. For small quantities of apples, and for all soft fruit from which wine was to be made, the larger of the domestic stone-mortars were used, and at times one meets with press bases, little larger than the bases of the cheese presses, on which the juice was extracted. Such bases have deeper grooves than the cheese-press form.

For a long period of years, and, indeed, up to the present time, mills were in use, consisting of an annular trough in which runs a millstone, on its edge; much like a type of mortar-mill which can still be seen in action. In the apple-mill a horse was harnessed to the end of the axle of the millstone, and, walking in a circular track, kept the edge millstone constantly rolling in the trough (Fig. 112, 1; Pl. 75A). This type of mill had many uses. Those mills used for apple crushing were reserved to that purpose; but others served to grind bark for tanneries, to reduce rag to pulp for paper making, to grind paint, to crush grain to meal, an even to prepare coarse flour.

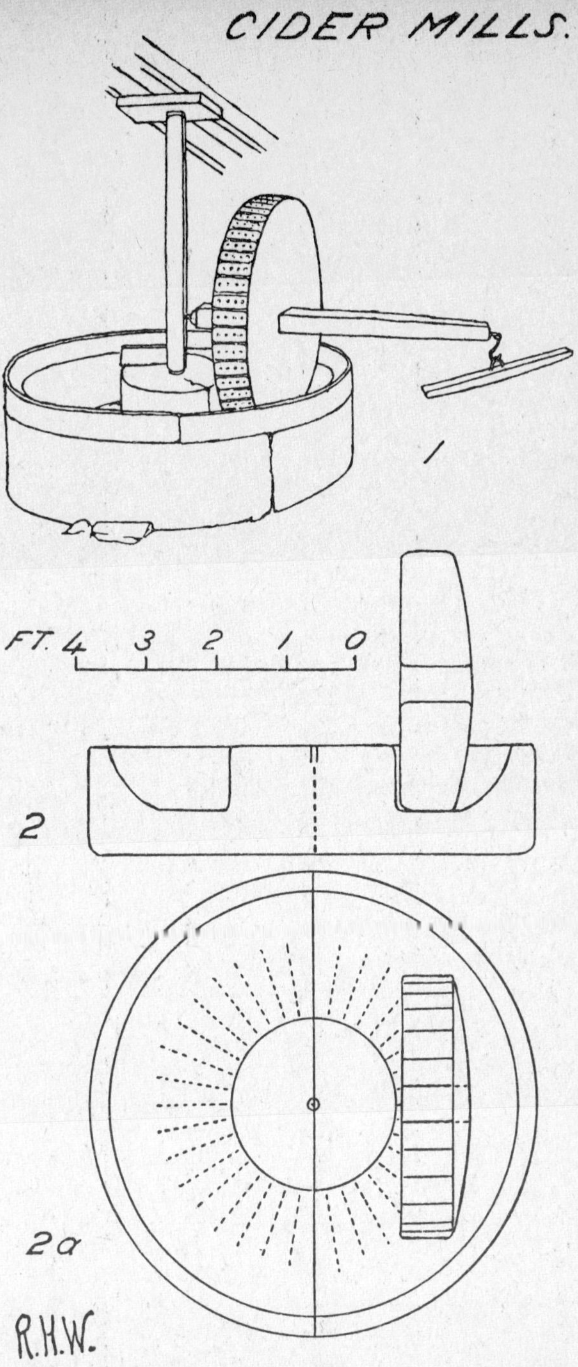

CIDER MILLS.

FT. 4 3 2 1 0

FIG. 112.

1. A cider mill in working order.   2. Remains at Longstone.

The apple-mills were not fitted to produce a smoothly ground pulp, but a pulp in which the cellular structure of the fruit was thoroughly broken up. The features of design were arrived at as the result of experience, and not with a knowledge of the cellular structure of the fruit. The floor of the annular trough was corrugated radially, even at times armed with radial iron bars, and the tread of the wheel was also corrugated. It resulted that the wheel did not move forward smoothly, but was continually lifted and dropped through a small height, and thus the pulp was at once ground and pounded. The operation of 'pounding' was not regarded as having been completed until the pips of the apples were found to have been crushed. It is significant that the whole process was known as 'pounding' and not as grinding.

All those pound-stones which I have seen are circular in plan, as is indeed necessary to the convenience of the track for the horse. A few of the larger are monoliths, but for the more part the stones are formed in two semicircles, clamped together at the diameter. The stones varied considerably in size; in my experience the largest have been found on the sites of monastic establishments.

1. There was formerly a pound-stone at Buckfast Abbey, which was reputed to be the largest in Devon; it is now lost. In the year 1788, Andrews of Modbury, in his manuscript *Journal of an Excursion on Dartmoor*, describes this stone as being 11 ft in diameter and 6 ft high from the bottom, about half of it being underground. In the year 1792, *Antiquarius Secundus*, writing in *The Gentleman's Magazine*, gave the dimensions as 9 ft diameter, 18 in. underground and 18 in. above ground. Laskey, who contributed a revised and enlarged version of Andrews's journal to *The Gentleman's Magazine*, in 1796, cites a "learned gentleman" as giving the diameter of the stone at 9 ft 4 in., and the depth 3 ft 6 in., whereof one-half was above and one-half below ground. Andrews was a careful man, but it is to be feared that he fell in error, or was misinformed, on this matter. I conclude that the diameter of the stone was at most 9 ft 4 in., and I doubt the alleged depth of 3 ft 6 in.; few such stones are more than 2 ft deep at the circumference.

2. Though there was undoubted rivalry between the monastic establishments in south-west Devon, it is unlikely that it extended to the provision made for the manufacture of cider; but in that matter Buckland Abbey excelled Buckfast. There is still preserved at Buckland a pound-stone, now forming part of a fountain, which stone is 10 ft 2 in. in diameter, and 20 in. in depth at the margin. It is a monolith.

3. I have been unable to find at Tavistock any pound-stone which could be identified as having one time been the property of the Abbey; but the Priory of the Isles of Scilly, the buildings of which were on Tresco, was a daughter house of Tavistock, and on the summit of Dolphin Hill in that island there is a pound-stone; the workmanship is less regular than that shown by the Devon examples. The diameter is

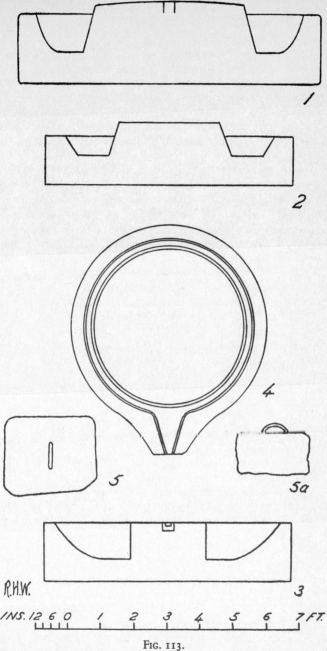

R.H.W.

INS. 12 6 0   1   2   3   4   5   6   7 FT.

FIG. 113.

1. Shilston, section.   2. Sourton, section.   3. Lower Collard, section.
4. Longstone, plan   5. Longstone, stone weight.

8 ft 4 in.; the depth of the stone cannot be ascertained except by excavation. This stone is a monolith.

4. At Shilston in the parish of Modbury is a fine example of the monolithic pound-stone. Its diameter is 9 ft 2 in.; the depth at the margin is 2 ft, and 2 ft 4 in. at the centre, where, as in some other instances, the central boss stands higher than the margin (Fig. 113, 1). This stone is no longer in use, having been replaced by the later device of a pair of granite rollers.

5. At Lower Collard, in the parish of Shaugh Prior, is one-half of a two-piece stone; the diameter is 7 ft 6 in., and the depth at margin is 1 ft 8 in (Fig. 113, 3).

6. At the old home of the Elfords, Longstone, in Sheepstor parish, the remains of a cider mill are complete, the pound-stone, edge runner, and granite vat to receive the juice. These have been re-erected by the Plymouth Corporation, but not for use (Fig. 112, 2; Pl. 76).

The pound-stone is in two parts; its diameter is 6 ft 6 in., and the thickness at the rim is 1 ft 7 in.

7. A stone at Torquay was at one time a part of the collections of the Torquay Natural History Society. It was too large to be displayed and passed to the possession and care of Mr. L. E. Currey, to whom I am indebted for measurements which I neglected to take when I had the opportunity. It is a one-piece stone; its diameter being 8 ft 3 in., the depth at the margin 18 in., and the same at the centre. The channel is armed with 1 in. diameter bars of iron, set radially. The stone came from Ilsham Manor. Approximate weight 4½ tons.

8. Eight hundred yards to the east of the westernmost rocks of Sourton Tors, a few yards south of a track which at that point forms the boundary of Bridestowe parish (Devon, 6 in. O.S., sheet lxxxviii, NW., lon. 4°-3′-29″, lat. 50°-41′-14″), lying on the open moor will be found the half of a two-piece pound-stone, from the margin of which a fairly large piece has been broken (Fig. 113, 2). Not far to the west of this point can be found the spot where the stone was worked. It was abandoned in consequence of an injury which it received in transport. The diameter of this stone is 7 ft 6 in. Its thickness at the margin is 1 ft 5 in., and at its centre 1 ft 10 in. The effective depth of the annular trough is 7 in., but the width of the margin is also 7 in., and it is fairly obvious that the rim was intended to be heightened in wood, as was not unusual.

It would be easy to supply details of many more pound-stones but the above eight are fully representative.

EDGE RUNNERS

The granite wheels which are the actual crushing implements are never more than one in any cider mill, although in some other uses of the same type of mill two wheels will be found. In the cider mill the wheel is plane on the side toward the centre of the pound-stone, and convex on the side toward the circumference. It is usually about 9 in. thick at the rim, and a foot thick at the centre, where it is pierced by a hole about 7 in. square. The tread of the wheel is slightly rounded, and is fluted parallel to the axle. It generally weighs about thirteen hundred-weight. The following examples are representative.

	Diameter	Thickness		Hole	Flutes width
		Margin	Centre		
1. Lower Collard	4′ 0″	9″	12″	7″ × 7″	2⅝″
2. Longstone	3′ 7″	9″	12″	6″ × 6″	5″
3. Notter, Cornwall	3′ 7″	8″	10½″		
4. Doe Tor Farm, Lydford	3′ 5″	7½″		6½″ × 6″	
5. Ilsham Manor	3′ 11″	11″	12½″	7″ × 7″	6″

Approximate weight fifteen hundredweight.

The stone at Doe Tor is unfinished; it is set in the outer fence of the enclosures (Devon, 6 in. O.S., sheet lxxxviii, sw., lon. 4°-4′-19″, lat. 50°-38′-48″). The perforation to take the axle is incomplete, extending less than halfway through the stone.

As the stone now stands one cannot see the failure or imperfection which probably accounts for its abandonment.

See Figs. 112 and 113.

ROLLER MILLS FOR APPLES

Later in date than the pound-stones, and often replacing them, were the roller mills; in which the apples were passed between two, often slightly grooved, cylinders of granite. The axles of these cylinders were placed horizontally, and over them was built an open bin with sloping sides. Apples placed in the bin were perforce conducted to the rollers, gripped and crushed. This type of crusher is still in use, neither it nor the pound-stone being wholly obsolete.

1. In the year 1931 one of these rollers was still to be seen in the village of Holne, lying in a heap of miscellaneous objects and materials just off the roadside; it was probably thought that it might be of some further use. The roller was of normal dimensions, although larger are to be found. Its length was 15½ in., and its diameter 13½ in.

2. In the hamlet of Michelcombe, in the parish of Holne, there was, in 1931, a pair of closely similar cylinders, which also lay very near the roadside.

3. At Coldstone, in the parish of Shaugh Prior, is a similar cylinder taken from a dismantled cider mill; its length is 17 in. and its diameter 16 in.

4. When the pound-stone (4) at Shilston was disused, it was replaced by a pair of cylinders or rollers, which, in the year 1934, were in use, and are, I believe, still used.

I am much indebted to Captain A. Rodd of Yelverton for supplying certain measurements of the pound-stone at Buckland Abbey; and to Mr. L. E. Currey of Torquay for measurements of the Ilsham Manor stone, now in his garden. Mrs. M. M. Currey, in view of my interest in the matter, kindly sent me a sketch by the late Louis Upcott, a Devonshire man, of a woodcut by E. Calvert (d. 1883) which is reproduced in Laurence Binyon's *Landscape in English Art and Poetry* Calvert also was of Devon birth.

The title of this cut is the *Cider Feast.* I agree with Upcott's comments: "This is a mixture of classical fancy and rustic reality. No doubt the Devon girls danced with the men, but no Devon farm-girl dressed like that. The figures and draperies have been copied from Greek vases. . . . The cider-making process is shown. In the centre is a stone trough with a stone wheel drawn round by a yoke of oxen. . . . A girl is pouring apples into the trough from a bucket: another comes balancing the basket on her head. The cider press is shown behind, under a thatch-roof. . . . The apple juice is shown flowing into a shallow vat. . . . In all the pounds I knew the apples were not pulped, as here, but sliced by revolving knives like the common turnip-cutter or hay-chopper."

For myself I would add that the mechanical details in the cut appear to me to present difficulties at least as great as the costumes and attitudes of the figures. The interest lies in the yoke of oxen. I do not think that the artist, although his imagination could introduce the classic dance in our county's orchards, would in the interest of art have supplanted the horse by oxen, had the horse supplied the normal motive power in his experience.

The bruised and crushed apple pulp was built up on the stone base of the cider press in alternate layers of straw and pulp, the whole covered with a board to which pressure was applied by means of a lever of the second order, the length of the lever being not infrequently 30 ft. At the end of the lever a weight was hung. By this means an approximately constant pressure was maintained; the more constant in that the height of the fulcrum could be adjusted from time to time as the height of the column of straw and pulp became less from the loss of apple juice.

The weight used was a block of granite of convenient size, usually but roughly wrought. The block carried an iron eye by which it could be slung. These weights were sufficiently heavy to be inconvenient to handle, and tripods and blocks were often used to lift them when the lever was being set.

The weight at Longstone is 2 ft 9 in. in length and 2 ft 3 in. in breadth, approximately rectangular with a depth or thickness of 14 in., and its weight approximately 1,200 lb (Fig. 113, 5).

In the Dartmoor area the apple juice was received in a granite vat. The use of granite extended some distance from the moorland; for

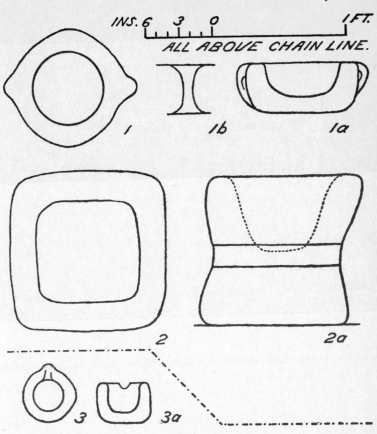

Fig. 114.

1. North Bovey Church, plan: (*a*) section; (*b*) handle.
2. North Bovey Church, plan and (*a*) section.
3. Churston Ferrers, plan and (*a*) section.

example a stone vat was in use at Shilston, Modbury. The charge that
cider was responsible for *Devonshire colic* could hardly be maintained
in such instances, however true it may have been where lead-lined con-
tainers were employed.

The vat at Shilston, now used as a trough for the pump and rain-
water, is approximately circular, the stone being 42 in. in diameter and
16 in. in depth; the inside measurements are 35 in. in diameter and 9 in. in
depth; thus the capacity of the vat is 31 gallons when filled to the brim.

DOMESTIC MORTARS

There is a small type of domestic mortar which I have never known
to be made in either moorstone or Roborough stone; the material used,
in my experience, being either Cataclews stone, or one of the kindred
rocks of Devon or Cornwall. Even as the bases of cheese-presses, and
both the upper and lower stones of querns, have been accepted as
ecclesiastical antiques, so to a greater extent have these small mortars,
while a larger type is not infrequently claimed as an early font. There
are five or six small mortars in the parish church of Dittisham, and one
at North Bovey. I have heard varied explanations of their use. It is
claimed that they were holy-water stoups; alternately they are identified as the begging bowls of mendicant friars; and yet, again, it is said
that the grain for the eucharistic wafer was ground in these mortars.

1. In North Bovey Church is a good example of the small type of
mortar, approximately circular, with projecting lobes as handles. The
overall width at the handles is 1 ft, and at right angles to this it is 10 in.
The depth of the stone is 4½ in. The basin is 6½ in. in diameter, and 3 in.
in depth; the bottom is rounded, the section approximating to a semi-
ellipse (Fig. 114, 1).

There are varied forms which defy classification. Many were cup-
shaped with a slight lip; some of these may possibly have been lamps.

2. At Churston Ferrers, built into the wall of an old cottage, was
found an object now in the Royal Albert Memorial Museum, Exeter.
The material is not granite, but sandstone. The greatest diameter of the
stone is 9¾ in., and the least is one inch less; the height is 7 in. The outline is not truly circular, but one deviation from the circle is obviously
intentional, since it provides a lip. The cavity or cup is 5 in. in mean
diameter, and 4½ in. deep at the centre. The bottom is relatively flat,
rounding into the sides. This may be called a cup-shaped object, although it has no handle. (See Fig. 114, 3.)

My attention was kindly called to it by Dr. Blackie, curator of the
Royal Albert Memorial Museum.

3. From the bottom of a well at Turnchapel, in the parish of Plym-
stock, was obtained a shallow bowl with a lip, made of Roborough
stone. This was shown to me by Mr. J. J. Judge, to whom I am much
indebted.

The outside diameter of the bowl is 10 in.; its circular outline is fairly regular, but broken by a half-inch projection at the lip. The top edge is fully rounded in section and the curve of the inner surface merges in the curve of the outer. The height of the stone is 4 in., and the cavity of the bowl is 2¼ in. in depth. The bowl has a flat circular base 3¾ in. in diameter. The size is too great to allow one to be tempted to identify this bowl as a lamp; the base too small to admit any but light grinding or crushing.

4. In North Bovey Church is a mortar the shape of which is, in my experience, unusual. In plan it is square with slightly curved sides, and fully rounded angles; 14 in. by 14 in. at top and base; height 13 in. At the centre of its height the stone is constricted to 11¼ in. The cavity is also square on plan, with rounded angles, and measures at the top 9 in. by 9 in.; it is 4½ in. square at the bottom, which is slightly rounded; and 6½ in. deep. The material is granite.

5. The larger mortars usually show better workmanship and finish, and are sometimes claimed as fonts. Because it is under present conditions the easiest of access for me I have selected as an example the mortar in the church of SS. Nicholas and Faith, Saltash, Cornwall.

* * *

[This article unfortunately remains unfinished. It was the last the author wrote.—ED.]

ON DARTMOOR TRACKS AND
GUIDE-STONES

THE simplest, and probably the only useful, classification of tracks on an open moorland is into the discontinuous and the continuous.

It will be found that on Dartmoor the discontinuous tracks serve always to avoid or circumvent some natural obstacle, a mire, a tract of 'vaen', a clitter of rocks or the passage of a stream. With slight exception, wherever such obstacles exist, those who are moor-wise will have no difficulty in finding the safe and convenient way ready defined to their use.

Some few of these passes are the work of man, especially at fording places, but the great majority have been formed by successive generations of grazing animals. The cattle, sheep and ponies range widely; even sheep which have adopted a lair are constantly on the move within their accepted limits. In passing from place to place the animals meet the patches of unfavourable ground and seek the nearest safe going; thus their traffic marks out tracks, and as such tracks become marked they are consistently followed. Even in the bracken, which can be a sufficient obstacle, once the ponies have forced their way through they tend to follow the same course again and again; labour-saving is not a merely human habit.

Once past the obstacles such tracks may quickly be lost, but from favourite pasture to favourite pasture they may be defined over considerable distances, and on steep hillsides there are also continuous tracks; sidelong ground is yet another form of obstacle. The hillside tracks are usually multiple, one above the other on the slope, in approximately parallel lines.

The feature of all these cattle tracks, except river crossings, is that they contour the ground, and it is extremely rare to find a track which breasts a hill.

Of continuous tracks there are two classes, those which, starting from the margin of the moor, reach a defined point within its area, and there cease; and those which traverse the moor from enclosed land to enclosed land.

The first class may have one of three intents: access to turbaries for fuel, with which may be joined access to the banks of streams for the purpose of gathering rushes; access to mining works, quarries or clay pits; and roads for the driving of cattle to the pastures.

There are two ways known as 'Blacklane' and one as 'Blackwood Path', all three of which, whatever their other uses, appear to have been for the conveyance of turf or peat. The Blacklane which has given its name to Blacklane Brook which joins the Erme near the head of that river is also used for cattle driving, but, indeed, there are none of these ways but are used for all purposes to which they may be convenient.

A well-marked track passes over the western flank of Piles Hill and Three Barrows in the Erme Valley, and at Three Barrows it has been described as being paved. It leads to turf ties near the Redlake, and there is no evidence of purposeful paving. The ground at Three Barrows is a mass of loose stone, a clitter of very small blocks, with practically no soil. Indeed, stone for the Redlake railway was derived by direct excavation from this area and it was quite unnecessary to screen the material before it was sent to the breaker. In such ground constant traffic beats down the surface to the semblance of a pavement.

The mine tracks are all relatively late in their present form; there is no evidence of any defined way to the old stream-works. Some of the roads to Eylesboro Mine are probably formed on old tracks, but of this there is no certainty. The roads to Knack Mine on the Taw and to Forest Mine on the West Ockment may also be in part coincident with old tracks. .

Dartmoor in the old days had advantages, relative only, as a means of passage between the enclosed lands by which it is surrounded. The open moor, notwithstanding its exposure, and despite its mires and bogs, was more suitable for pack-horse traffic than the deep and miry lanes of the in-country. One could circumvent a Dartmoor bog, but to the unfathomable mud of the Devonshire lane of the day one was confined by the hedges. Even in the days of the waywardens, who had power to enter lands and take stone and sand for the roads, and who could call upon the parishioners, according to their ability, to provide labour, carts, waines, tumbrells, dung pots or Courts, sleads, carres or drags for transport, there were but six days in each year appointed, on which there was a levy of labour and transport throughout each parish, men, horses and oxen, drays, dung pots, etc. Six days of energy, three hundred and fifty nine days neglect, and one can imagine the result. Little wonder that the way from Plymouth to Exeter lay across the open moor, rather than by the roads of the South Hams. Matters were much as in Hayti, where the Negro Republic formerly held that "the good Lord destroyed the roads by his storms, and in His good time would repair them". In 1411, Bishop Stafford sanctioned the description of a road from Plymouth as "deep and full of mire, exceeding perilous and harmful to travellers and toilers thereby". Risdon bears testimony to the condition of such Devon roads as existed in his time, writing: "This country, as it is spacious, so it is populous, and very laborious, rough and unpleasant to strangers travelling those ways, which are cumbersome and uneven, amongst stones and rocks, painful for man and horse: as they can bear witness who have made trial thereof. For be they never so well mounted on horses out of other countries, when they have travelled one journey in these parts, they can, in respect of ease of travel, forbear a second." He adds, as a silver lining to the cloud: "and therefore so much the less passable for the enemy with his troops of war." In which respect it has to be remarked that the disability cut both ways, and Raleigh was driven to report that ordnance could not be brought to Plymouth by land, by reason of the badness of the roads.

There is no room for wonder that, even as late as 1699–1700, the Corporation of Plymouth paid two pounds "towards defraying the charges of 'putting vpp Moorestones on Dartmoor in the way leading from Plymouth towards Exon for guidence of Travellers passing that way' ". (See p. 397.)

Writing in 1800, Martin Dunsford of Tiverton, said:[1] "The tracks over the Moor before the new roads were made, were marked by high stones, placed about a mile asunder, but just discernible in good weather from one another." The present existing stones and the evidence of the map lead one to believe that he greatly over-estimated the distance. He added: "Tho' a company of five or six of us, at mid-day, in the midst of summer, we missed at one time, the next stone mark, and wandered an hour in different parties, in search of the road, making signals to each other; and we should perhaps have wandered 'till night, if a cutter of turf we met, had not led us to the right path." One is not so impressed with the difficulties the party encountered after reading, a few pages later, that one of his party, on mounting his horse found himself with his head toward the tail of the steed, and that several successive essays produced a similar effect.

The train-bands on their way from Exeter to Plymouth passed through Ashburton and Buckfastleigh, by Yalland Farm to Shipley, crossed the Avon, and proceeded by way of Diamond Lane, across the moor by Ball Gate to the ford at Glasscombe Corner, thence by Spurrells Cross to Harford Moor Gate where they returned to the enclosed lands.

Such late uses of moorland tracks, and the undoubted needs of far earlier years, make it unnecessary to invoke the priors or the monks as the great track-makers. It is more probable that long before the monasteries existed the principal tracks were already well defined. The hands of the monks may well be traceable in the more numerous crosses

[1] M. Dunsford, *Miscellaneous Observations in the course of five Tours*, Tiverton, 1800.

which mark the southern tracks of Dartmoor.[1] Wayside crosses are not unknown elsewhere, but are much more closely set in the south. None the less, it would be of interest to know when the 'traditional' 'Abbot's Way' first received that name; and why its alleged course from Buckfast to Nuns Cross is unmarked by crosses, if we except Huntingdon Cross, by Wallabrook foot. It is not the best route from Buckfast to Nuns Cross, involving as it does the crossing of the Avon, at times a very inconvenient river. If the Abbot of Buckfast did sponsor a way, it was by Holne across Holne Ridge to Horns Cross, thence over Horse Ford on the O Brook to the two crosses on Down Ridge, and so to the cross on Ter Hill, continuing by way of Mount Misery where there is still one cross, and formerly there were two; passing on to Childes Tomb, also formerly marked by a cross, then to a cross set on a boulder to the west of Fox Tor Mire, and so to Nuns or Siwards Cross.

From this last point the only course effectively marked by crosses runs westward. There is the socket of a cross in a boulder near the footbridge over the Devonport Leat about five hundred yards from Nuns Cross; there are then two more crosses, the western of which is very near Classenwell Pool. The track appears to have passed down Raddick Lane to a bridge or ford at Leather Tor Bridge, thence along the course of the present road to Cross Gate, where there is another cross. Until recent years a cross base was to be found set on the north side of the road opposite Lower Lowery; this has now been broken up and removed by quarrymen. Near Dousland, at the entrance to Burham, is a cross base, which has very probably been removed from near Yennadon cross roads; and, following the narrow lane from Yennadon Cross to Walkhampton Church, another cross base will be found close to the church house. Hence there is a track past Dittisham to Huckworthy Bridge. A cross above Huckworthy Bridge, and two on Whitchurch Down complete the route to Tavistock. There is also a cross at Moorshop, but that lies off the route, still, and since it was functioning as the threshold of a pigsty, it may have been brought some little distance from its proper site.

But after all, it is not certain that the monks erected or procured to be erected these crosses. Siwards, or Nuns, Cross was in existence before Amicia, Countess of Devon, granted to Buckland Abbey the lands of Walkhampton, 1280, and at the same date another wayside cross, known as Smalacumba, probably sited near Ringmoor Cot,[2] was also in being. Since these were named as boundary marks it may be argued that such was their sole intent, but there was also a 'Yanedonecrosse'

---

[1] Dartmoor crosses and their remains are already well described and illustrated, thanks to the efforts of William Crossing (1887, 1892, 1909) and E. Masson Phillips (1937–43). (ED.)

[2] See *T.D.A.* Vol. lxxiv, p. 203. (ED.)

which must have stood very near the point now known by the same name in respect of cross roads. It remains that Sywards Cross now stands by an ancient track, and that Yanedonecrosse, now possibly represented by the base near Dousland, stood also where there is now a road.

There is but space to write of one other ancient track, and that briefly. The Lichway along which the dead were borne to the church at Lydford for burial, but which there is no reason to believe was exclusively appropriated to that end. Indeed, although none now traverse the whole length of this track, it is still in use as regards parts of its length for local purposes (Pl. 77A).

The vills of Babeny and Pizwell and their neighbours, ancient tenements on the eastern extreme of the Forest, lie eleven and a half miles from Lydford Church, in a direct line; while the Merripits and other ancient tenements by Postbridge are approximately two miles nearer. No direct course is possible, certainly not to bearers of a corpse. The consequent inconvenience for all church purposes was recognized as early as 1260, when Bishop Bronescombe ordered that, as regards 'Balbenye' and 'Pushyll', the inhabitants "omnia in vita et morte ecclesiastica percipiant sacramenta in ecclesia de Wydecombe".

For purposes of burial, therefore, the eastern end of the track has not been used since the thirteenth century. It was not necessarily abandoned for all purposes, since the dwellers in the eastern quarter would have other need to visit Lydford. But with the vast enclosures made at the beginning of the nineteenth century any track then existing would have been severed. There were certainly alternative routes: the Bishop found that the way to Lydford which had to be taken in bad weather was seven miles longer than that which served when the weather was good. Both the shorter and the longer course may well have been by way of a ford or bridge at Belliver, and thence over Lakehead Hill; the shorter path continuing to Longaford Tor, in an approximately direct line, thence across the neck between Beardown Tors and Lydford Tor, and so to a ford over the Cowsic under Conies Down Tor. The longer road, to account for its additional length must have kept to the south, crossed the Walkham at Merrivale and approached Lydford through Petertavy; but all this is speculative.

From the ford over the Cowsic, however, to a ford over the Walkham under Whittaburrow, past the menhir on Launceston Moor, keeping a little north of Whittor, and so down to Brousentor, there is still a well-defined track, which continues to an old clapper bridge across the Baggator Brook (a bridge which at one time also gave access to Standon, but has now been rendered obsolete by a later structure higher up the stream) (Pl. 78). At the clapper bridge two courses were open, either to follow the brook down to its junction with the Tavy—a little above the junction there is a ford over the Tavy—and from this to follow a track, largely between hedges, to Willsworthy; or, keeping north, to strike the Tavy at a point five hundred yards higher up that stream, where there is a ford with stepping-stones of a very unusual type, the stones being selected for their length, and that length ranging up and down stream, an arrangement said to have been made to enable the bearers to pass with the body between them (Pl. 77B). This ford again leads to a track to Willsworthy. From Willsworthy the road to the old pound at Willsworthy Bridge was followed, and thence the course of Willsworthy Brook, along Snap Lane (see Frontispiece), and so by a field-path past Yellowmead Farm, and across Black Down to Beardon Gate.

This western part of the track, from the Cowsic, is still called the Lichway, and when the little clapper bridge in Snap Lane was washed away, a few years since, it was spoken of as the bridge over which the dead had always been carried in former times. The impost of the bridge has not been lost, and the abutments still stand; it will shortly be restored.

*   *   *

The use of guide-stones, in post-medieval times, may be illustrated by reference to the old track between Tavistock and Ashburton.[1]

Dr. David C. Prowse writes: "In 1911, or perhaps earlier, my father, the late Col. A. B. Prowse, noted on the slopes of North Hessary Tor a standing stone, not marked on the 6-inch Ordance Survey of 1904. This is the stone which is now the easternmost of those known to exist on this tor. He also found another post of this series (all of which are inscribed 'T' on the one side, and 'A' on the other side) acting as a gatepost in the Swincombe Farm enclosures.

In August 1913, my father, my brother, Dr. A. S. Prowse, and myself were associated in the discovery of four more such stones on the slopes of North Hessary Tor.

In October 1925 I noticed a gate-post in the Yellowmead enclosures, near Foggintor Quarries, which bore the letters 'T-A', and the farmer, Mr. Edward Cole, told my wife and myself that there was another nearer the farmhouse. This my wife, Dr. Dorothy E. Prowse, located. Yellowmead Farm was enclosed by Mr. George Cole, the father of our informant. In October 1925 I found a second stone in the enclosures of Swincombe Farm, also serving as a gate-post. In August 1924 the late Mr. George French, of Postbridge, told my father that he remembered a stone with T and A on opposite sides being found when the old farmhouse at Tor Royal was taken down; it had been serving as a lintel."

[1] The following paragraphs were originally published as a joint article with Dr. David C. Prowse (*T.D.A.* Vol. lxvi, p. 317). (ED.)

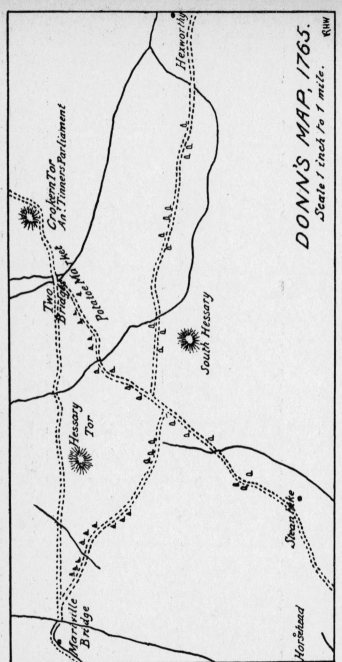

FIG. 115.

Map labels: DONN'S MAP, 1765. Scale 1 inch to 1 mile. RHW; Hexworthy; Croken Tor An Tinners Parliament; Two Bridges; Potatoe Market; South Hessary; Hessary Tor; Merrivale Bridge; Siwan Lake; Horsehead

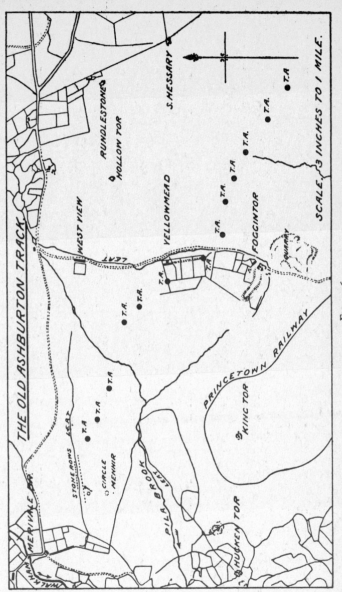

FIG. 116.

Mrs. Eckett Fielden, having been informed by Mr. Samuel Pearse
that one of these guide-stones had been taken, many years ago, for use
as a gate-post at Lowery Farm, near Dousland, kindly passed the information to me. Mr. Pearse has since kindly answered my inquiries
as to this matter. A view of this stone in its present site is given in
Pl. 79B.

Prior to 1911 six guide-stones were known, marking out a way from
near the east end of the Merrivale stone rows to a point approximately
1,600 ft south-east from Yellowmead Farm. These stones stand some
5 to 7 ft in height, and are, for the more part, some 15 in. by 10 in. at
the base. All these six are shown on the Ordnance Survey. One of them
is shown in Pl. 79A.

A characteristic common to all the stones is an incised letter 'T' on
the side towards Tavistock, and a letter 'A' on the side towards Ashburton. It is certain that they marked a track. As to their date, they can
hardly have been erected since the present main roads across Dartmoor
have existed. All the stones, both those formerly known and those discovered in 1924 and since, have been split from parent blocks, and the
splitting has been accomplished in the old style by means of slots, and
not by the present method of drilled holes. The method of splitting
dates the stones as not later than 1820, probably not later than 1810; at
some time between these dates the stonemasons' methods changed.

Reference to Donne's map of Devon, published in 1765, carries us
back another fifty years. On that map there is shown a track starting a
little to the east of Merrivale Bridge, and passing along the line still
marked out by the stones, extending beyond that line to cross the
present Plymouth-Princetown road some distance north of Devil's
Bridge, thence passing to the north of South Hessary Tor, crossing the
Swincombe, passing to the north of Fox Tor Mire, and so by Hexworthy and Cumsdon Rock to Holne and Ashburton.

For its whole length as far as Hexworthy this track is shown as
marked out by guide-stones; and these are more especially formally
indicated at the end near Merrivale. From this map it appears that the
road from Dousland past Stanlake to the site which Princetown now
occupies was also provided with guide-stones, as also its extension to
Two Bridges. Fig. 115 is a reproduction of a part of Donne's map.

It is evident that, prior to 1765, the principal tracks in this neighbourhood, including both the Tavistock-Ashburton and the Plymouth-
Ashburton ways, had been marked with guide-stones.

When this marking was done we cannot determine, but it would
appear probable that it was in 1699–1700. In that year the Receiver's
Book of the Plymouth Corporation contains the following entry:
"Item paid towards defraying the charges of putting vpp Moorestones
on Dartmoor in the way leading from Plymouth towards Exon for
guidence of Travellers passing that way the sume of £2-0-0."

As we have said, six of the guide-stones have been known as still in being. We now fill an apparent gap by identifying the two stones used as gate-posts at Yellowmead; and we add five other stones, carrying the line about one thousand yards ESE. from its former apparent terminus. Of these five stones all but the easternmost have fallen. That stands 5 ft 6 in. above ground, and measures 15 in. by 11 in. at the base. The plan inserted (Fig. 116) gives the positions of all that can certainly be identified. There is one fallen stone about 200 yds eastward of the last shown, which is in doubt, but excavation will determine the question as to whether it is a member of the series. The stone which was removed to Lowery can still be seen functioning as a gate-post hard by Lowery Crossing; it stands immediately inside the north hedge of the road, and fifty yards east from the crossing-keeper's cottage. Mr. Samuel Pearse, of Broomhill, Harford, tells us that this stone was, he understands, brought back to Lowery by his great-uncle, on his return with an empty cart from Princetown, where he had been delivering farm-produce to the Prison, then occupied by French and American prisoners of war. As Mr. Pearse believes, it was taken from some point between the end of the range of stones as we have now planned it, and the present site of the Princetown Railway.

We think it probable that here and there there yet remain some of these guide-stones which are as yet unknown to us; some, perhaps fallen and thus hidden, others pressed into service as gate-posts, or otherwise used on farms and in buildings.

The idea of such posts was an elaboration of the earlier use of crosses as marking tracks. This very track from Merrivale would lead, not only to the way north of Fox Tor Mire, but also to another route south of the Mire. A route which starts at that Clapham Junction of our moorland tracks—Siwards or Nuns Cross—and is marked out by a cross on the southern verge of the mire, within the present newtake, by Childes Tomb, another cross at Mount Misery in the angle of the abandoned Fox Tor Farm, crosses on Ter Hill and Down Ridge, and Horns Cross on Holne Moor, and so on to Holne. The guide-stones were, however, set at much closer intervals than the crosses, on the average, perhaps, at every two hundred yards.

The stones found acting as gate-posts at Swincombe, and the stone which was used as a lintel at Tor Royal, are the only known survivors of those which marked the eastern part of the track. If Donne's map is reliable in detail, there were far fewer stones to the mile at this part.

The idea of indicating direction by initial letters cut in guide-stones is by no means confined to the series which we have described. On the road from Holne to Ashburton, at a junction near Gallantry Bower, there is a much more formally shapen stone with the letter 'A' to indicate the direction to be followed for Ashburton; and, on the road from Moretonhampstead to North Bovey, at a crossing about half a mile north of North Bovey, an old cross has been similarly inscribed on its faces, and this serves as a guide-post. These are by no means exceptional.[1]

[1] These old guide-posts have been described and illustrated in *Notes on some old roadside stones in south-west Devon* by E. Masson Phillips (*T.D.A.*, Vol. 75, 1943, pp. 141–65).

THE DARTMOOR HOUSE

AFTER the period of the hut-circles, the remains of which are so numerous on Dartmoor, there is a long gap in the record of the habitations of man on the moor. It is true that certain camps on the moorland borders date, probably, from the Early Iron Age, as, for example, Cranbrook with its stone-faced ramparts. But nothing is known of the dwellings which must, presumedly, have been within the ramparts.

The first evidence of residential occupation during the historic period lies in the place-name *worthy*. This, as a suffix to personal names, is common in the area surrounding the Forest, and is found also within the Forest bounds; it cannot well be later in origin than Saxon time. But at none of the many *worthys* are there any buildings, erect or ruined, which can be assigned to so early a period.

What is probably the oldest building of a domestic character still standing is at Yardworthy (I) in the parish of Chagford. This may have been erected early in the fourteenth century. It is now roofless, and one end wall has been removed; the quoins have not, however, been disturbed. We are thus able to say that the internal length of the building was 32 ft (or two 'bays' of 16 ft) and the width 14 ft 6 in. Its principal architectural feature is the porch, a massive granite structure, a view of which, showing also the window, is given on Pl. 81. A full description of the building will be found in Vol 67 of the *Transactions of the Devonshire Association*, pp. 127–30.

In considering the age of buildings, seemingly early, and certainly primitive in the inconveniences which they present as dwellings, there is one criterion which in itself will serve to dismiss all claims to real antiquity. If the stones have been split by means of drilled holes, then the building can be but few years earlier in date than 1803, in which year the earliest known local use of this method was made.

Before the use of the drill the custom was to employ a pointed hammer, known as a 'pick', with which to form a series of grooves along the line of the intended parting, and into these grooves wedges were driven. With the coming of the drill, round holes took the place of the grooves, and a tapered iron or steel cylinder replaced the wedge, a few strips of steel being placed to line the hole before the tapered cylinder was inserted, to reduce friction. Certain guide-stones, placed on the moor in 1699–1700 (pp. 397–400), were cut by the groove-wedge method, which certainly remained in exclusive use for many years after that date. Indeed, the Rev. Edward Atkyns Bray, an observant man, and a native of Tavistock, saw the drill in use for the first time within his experience on 17th May 1831, when he visited the quarries at and near Swell Tor (Mrs. Bray, *Borders of the Tamar and the Tavy*, 1st ed., Vol. 1, p. 280). The quarries had then been some years in existence, and no trace can be found among their waste of the use of the older method of working. Doubtless the local men retained their accustomed habit and method for a not inconsiderable time after the introduction of the drill, and there is evidence that the new way of working was not generally established until several years after its introduction. The one safe conclusion is that where it occurs it marks a date not earlier than 1800.

On the other hand, there are two features which, if found, are both jointly and severally presumptive evidence for a date not later than 1600, and are both consistent with a possibly much earlier date. These are, the 'broad-and-narrow' quoins, and the stone sockets in which doors have turned in place of hinges.

Broad-and-narrow quoins are not to be confused with the better-known form often called *long-and-short*, which is by some assumed to mark Saxon work, but is certainly in places of much later date. The two structural methods have this much in common, both are in theory unsound, but both afford examples which have stood the test of centuries. An apparently unsound design may often prove satisfactory if the workmanship is adequate.

In broad-and-narrow work the quoin stones are mere 'shiners', showing a considerable area on the face of the wall, but presenting a trivial depth in its thickness. A stone may show a face of 20 superficial feet on one face of the quoin, and but 3 sq. feet on the other face; five feet in length and four feet in height on the one face, and nine inches in length and four feet in height on the other. That is to say that the bed on which it sets may extend no more than nine inches into the wall. The photo (Pl. 80B) of an old building at Challacombe in the parish of Manaton will serve better than an extended verbal description.

The south gable of the old Yardworthy building (Pl. 80A) provides another example. See also Fig. 117, drawn from a different building in the same parish (Yardworthy II): here it will be seen that an internal quoin at a door opening has been similarly treated.

Holed-stone hangers for doors and shutters in domestic buildings are rarely found. Examples are described in the Twelfth Report of the Dartmoor Exploration Committee, *T.D.A.*, Vol. 67, p. 127. Inside the porch of the first Yardworthy cottage the door had no frame, nor hinges in the ordinary sense (p. 360). Two projections from the back style of the door engaged, the one in a hole in the slab which forms

the roof, and the other in a hole in the stone sill, and on these two pivots
the door turned. A window shutter was similarly hung (there is no
evidence of glazing).

Much more common are similar, but larger, hangers for barn doors,
yard gates, and field gates. Within the past few years one such gate
hanging·has been in use in Wormhill, in the parish of North Bovey,

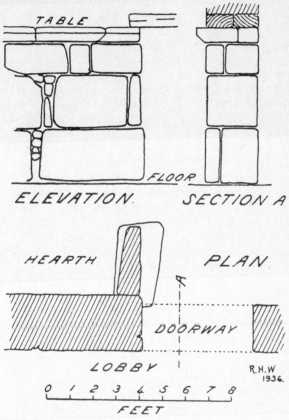

FIG. 117. Broad-and-narrow work, Yardworthy II.

and another at Peck Farm in the parish of Lustleigh; while at Cox Tor
Farm, in Petertavy parish, a gate so hung may still be seen (see p. 356
and Pl. 72, 73). As to yard gates, a good specimen of such a hanging
may be seen at Forder, near Throwleigh (see Fig. 103, p. 360). This
hanger, although still in place, is not in use. Stone hangers for barn
doors, not now in use, may be seen at Foxworthy and Peck Farm, both
in the parish of Lustleigh.

I doubt whether any of these hangings for house doors have been made since the middle of the fifteenth century; or for barn doors at a later date than 1600; while the gate-hangings are probably all datable before 1700. But these figures are admittedly of somewhat uncertain validity, as clear evidence is wanting.

This much can be said: during the last years of the sixteenth century, the whole of the seventeenth and the early years of the eighteenth, there was a fairly general habit of dating new buildings; in addition to which stray evidence is at times available, as when Robert Furse of Mores-head writes for the information of his heirs that he "made the porch and entereye and seled the hall and glaste all the wyndoes". He must have written this not earlier than the year 1573, nor later than 1593. He inherited the house in 1573, which dates the building as earlier than that year; and it can still be seen that Furse had some little difficulty in fitting the new work to the old. In none of these dated buildings is there any broad-and-narrow quoin work, or any holed-stone hanger for a door.

The most primitive in appearance of all the houses or ruined houses on Dartmoor are the small cottages which were erected for their own use by workmen and smallholders in the nineteenth century, mainly between the years 1800 and 1871. Apparently the rage for making the desert blossom as the rose spread from the large-scale 'improvers' to a class which had but its labour to expend to waste, and no capital to endanger. But in some instances these buildings were undoubtedly erected by workmen attracted to the moor by the newly opened quarries, and by the opportunities of employment afforded by the larger enclosures then made or making.

One of the earliest of these cottages of which we have knowledge stood to the north of the Tavistock-Moretonhampstead road near Over Tor. Bray records that, in 1802, at this spot he found a man engaged in building a hut; on inquiry he was informed that the man had a grant, from Mr. Lopez, of several acres around, and intended to reside there with his family. The foundations yet remain, but no enclosure except a small garden plot. Since, however, the house and garden adjoin a prehistoric pound, it is very possible that the intention was to restore the walls of the pound (p. 139; Fig. 35), and make this the first of the intended enclosures.

Other huts, equally primitive, were later erected near Rundlestone, and were occupied within my memory. Further afield the house at Nuns Cross was built in or about 1871 by Richard Hooper, who also enclosed the land of Nuns Cross Farm. This house still stands, but is now used as a cattle-shed. I remember Richard Hooper when he still occupied the house; and shortly after its abandonment as a dwelling I took a photograph (Pl. 83, 1). If it be questioned how men and their families could live in such structures, I can only say that they still do so live in Ireland, and tell you a tale of Dartmoor. When a cottage at Fox Tor, a structure of no great age, was falling into grievous disrepair, it was occupied by Eden the moor-man, and its roof was patched in any and all ways, including turves. A visitor to the moor took shelter there during a thunderstorm, and found the roof leaky, and the shelter but partial. He asked Eden why he did not thatch the roof. Said Eden: "Who's going thatching in this weather?" Eden was told he could thatch when it was fine; but replied: "Who's to waste fine weather filling holes that ain't hurting?" On Dartmoor the more part of us have a share of that logic which has raised some to eminence in the law.

Some of the settlers' houses were of a better type. There was John Bishop, a strong man, proud of his strength and gladly spending it in labour. You may be fortunate enough to hear tales of him, always told with pride. He lived at Swincombe, and a view of his house, now no longer a dwelling, will serve as an example of the more comfortable sort (Pl. 83, 2.).

Between the end of the twelfth and the beginning of the nineteenth centuries all the houses within the Forest of Dartmoor would appear to have been either cottages or farmhouses, if one excepts a possible inn. In the border parishes the same was in effect true. Even the manor houses had either developed from farms, or were occupied by lords of the manor, who were themselves farmers; of many it might be said that they belonged to both classes. When the class of yeoman farmers came into being it will be found that they followed two pursuits, that of agriculture, and that of judicious matrimony. It was by the latter industry that estates were aggregated, and the yeomen transformed into minor landed magnates. Once established in the marriage market, a run of male heirs secured the fortunes of a family. Failure of heirs male meant heiresses or co-heiresses, and, in the game of 'beggar my neighbour', heiress and land alike went to enhance the importance of another name.

Few of the families neglected agriculture. I have elsewhere referred to such combinations as landowner-councillor-at-law-farmer-and-tinner; that was in Cornwall. In Devon, Robert Furse rightly sets marriage as the chief foundation of his family fortunes, but he does not neglect agriculture. He writes of his ancestors John and Mary Furse: "God did so prosper thym that before she dyed they hadde cccc bullocks and grate store of monye and other quyche stuff" (see Carpenter, 1894). It is not surprising that the needs of the farm left their mark on the structure of the house. Little by little, it is true, a certain aloofness arose between the parlour and the cowshed; but it never became very pronounced. It was fortunate that the cowshed odour was held to be healthy, for of a certainty it was never absent.

In the 'black house' of Lewis, within living memory, the humans and the kine dwelt under one roof, in the several undivided moieties of one apartment, and having one common means of access. During the winter the manure accumulated, so that one went up a step at the entrance. In the spring, when the dung was carried to the field, one went down two steps on entering. Nothing as primitive can now be found on Dartmoor, but the house-and-shippen under one roof is still common in various forms. These may best be illustrated by means of diagrams, no one of which will be the plan of a building actually in existence, but none of which will contain any detail which cannot be found in some one or more of the existing houses. The following types may be recognized (see Fig. 118 *A*, *B*, *C* and *D*: it may be noted that in all types the houses are, with few exceptions, one room deep):

(*A*) Dwelling-house and shippen form together a single rectangle, of the same depth throughout its length. The house-part is enclosed by four masonry walls, and hence a complete structure were the shippen removed. It is convenient to consider the shippen as built up against the end of the house. The means of entrance, to shippen and house alike, is a doorway opening into the shippen hard by the house. Often, in the back wall of the shippen, another doorway was formed immediately opposite the front door; traces of this will always be found unless the structure is built against high ground at the back; but sometimes, in the course of alterations, the back door has been built up.

Men and animals[1] both use the front door, the men more usually turning to the right after entry, and obtaining access to the house by a door in its side wall. Thus the way to the house is through the shippen. Two practical advantages are secured by this arrangement, on the one hand access can be had to the animals in their stalls without leaving the shelter of a roof; and, on the other, the house has no door leading directly into the open, a matter making for the comfort of those who occupy a living-room with an open-hearth fire.

For the further avoidance of draughts the fireplace is constructed in the wall between house and shippen, and there also will be found the brick or stone oven.

The open hearth as a focus of domestic and social life is a favourite subject with writers on country matters. Sentiment aside, it is the meeting place of all the winds of heaven in conspiracy to waft the domestic circle up the chimney. It is not surprising that a wooden screen was constructed at right angles to the wall, between the door and the hearth; usually with a seat on the fireward side. This may have been the precursor of the 'settle', which was by no means a mere article of furniture, but often a fixture.

The room entered from the shippen is the living-room; beyond this lies the dairy on the far side of a front-to-back partition, which in

[1] It may be well to remember that draught oxen, as well as milch cows, horses, and, at times, sheep needed housing and care.

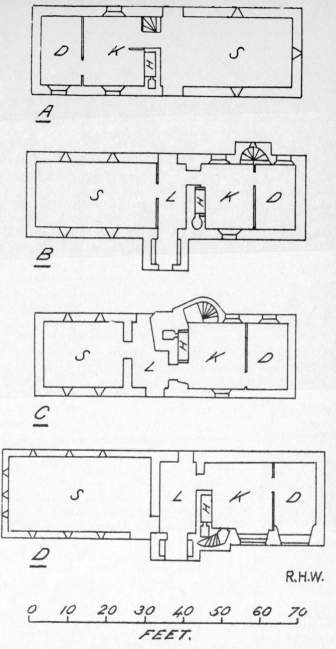

R.H.W.

FIG. 118. Diagrams of early types of house.

earlier work is a panelled oak screen extending from floor to ceiling; in later years many of these dairies were diverted from their purpose and became parlours; a new dairy being built, usually in the form of a lean-to. From the living-room a spiral stairway, in the thickness of the wall, there thickened for the purpose, leads to the upper floor. The stairs are in granite, or, comparatively rarely, in solid oak. A feature in all original work is the entire absence on both floors of any passages or corridors; the rooms open out, each from each.

The plan of such a house is shown in diagram *A*. Certain qualifications are necessary: the house does not always lie to the right of the building; sometimes the house is to the left and the shippen to the right. The door from the shippen to the house may be, and usually is, immediately within the entrance, but it may be on the other side of the hearth, between the hearth and the back wall. The stairway may be in either the back or the front wall, more frequently in the back wall.

An example is provided by Colliehole Cottage, Chagford. The shippen is not now used for animals, but the stalls are still in place, in every way a perfect example.

Another, at Higher Godsworthy, Petertavy, is interesting as showing the changes which were at times made as social requirements became more exacting (Pl. 82). A good porch, with seats, leads into the shippen or barn. Originally, on passing through the porch into the barn one turned sharply to the right to enter the house through a door in the party wall between house and barn. At some later, but not recent date, this door to the house was built up in thin masonry, a new door to the house made in the front wall immediately adjacent to the porch, and a small pent roof projected to make a shallow porch to this new entrance. We thus get one of the features of type *D*, the separate entrances, but no lobby, nor any direct access, nor access through the lobby from house to shippen or barn.

(*B*) The first modification of the scheme outlined under *A* was the construction of a wooden partition, parting off some six feet from the floor space of the shippen at the end next to the house, and thus forming a lobby between shippen and house. A neutral space, if you will, but still used by both men and animals. In the same way in which an inner door from the shippen gave access to the house, in this type another internal door or opening, through the wood partition, gave access for the stock from the lobby to the shippen. It is very possible that this alteration was intended solely to shelter the stock from the draughts of the front and back doors, which now opened into a lobby. Certain it is that the improvement in the access to the house can have been but slight, with the animals still coming in at the front of the lobby, and the manure still, presumedly, taken out at the back.

(*C*) The next change was merely in material as far as the ground floor was concerned. A masonry wall was substituted for the wooden partition dividing the lobby from the shippen. But this made possible an alteration on the first floor; by supplying support for a partition over; whereby a space equal to that covered by the lobby was taken from the loft over the shippen, and converted into a room. Coincident with this change the lobby was usually made wider, eight feet or more in width. This type is represented at Old Belliver. Here what was once the shippen became a parlour with a room over, to serve which an additional stairway had to be constructed.

FIG. 119. The lobby, Shilston, Throwleigh, looking to main entrance.

Types B and C are represented by Warne's Kitchen, Eastontown, Sampford Spiney, a building at the back of Eastontown house; and by Higher Shapley, Chagford, in its original condition, before the addition of the rather elaborate porch in 1776, a structure now in precarious condition. With that addition and other alterations it passed over to type *D*. It would appear that the partition between the shippen and the lobby has always been in masonry; and there is a table or course on the house wall to carry the joists of the floor above, which are notched down upon it.

(*D*) Finally the animals were excluded from the lobby, and given a separate entrance to the shippen from the outside. This entrance was by a door alongside what had now become the house door; an entrance

from the lobby to the shippen was still retained, but solely for the purpose of access to the cattle without necessity for leaving shelter. With
this change the lobby, at last, becomes a part of the house.

Perhaps the finest example of Type *D* is Shilston, Throwleigh. The
house is dated 1656. In this building the house part lies to the left.
(See Pl. 84A and Fig. 119.)

Hole, Chagford, is little if any less in standing than Shilstone, from
which it differs by the presence of a porch, and the fact that the house-
part is to the right, while there are no outside steps to the loft. The main
staircase has solid oak stairs. Slight alterations in the interior have been
made comparatively recently, and the back door of the lobby has been
built up. Lightly incised upon the porch is the date, 1668.

All these types have been liable to subsequent alteration, and it is
common to find houses where the shippen has been converted into an
extension of the house room.

It is not surprising to find the house-entrance of type *D* provided
with a porch, but there are instances of the single entrances of types *A*,
B and *C* having porches; it is possible that in some of these examples the
building was a barn and not a shippen.

It would seem that the shippen almost always had a loft over, although that loft might be a mere space in the roof. When, in consequence of the provision of a room over the lobby, or a more com-
modious loft, it became necessary to support the upper floor joists on
the wall at the back of the main fireplace of the house, our ancestors
were wise in their precautions against fire, and the joists did not enter
the wall, which might have brought them dangerously near the flue;
but a dressed stone table projecting on the lobby side of the wall served
as a support (see Fig. 117, on page 405). I, who remember when an oak
beam in Foulston's 'Freemasons' Hall', in Cornwall Street, Plymouth,
was found burnt nearly through at a hearth, can appreciate that good
building construction is not peculiar to more recent years. I remember
also the builder's apprentice who was asked:"What would you do if a
joist were so placed that if it bore on the wall it would enter a flue?" and
who replied:"Well, Mr. X (his employer) nails a slate on the end of en."

The desire to reach the animals without leaving the cover of a roof
was met in more ways than one. Thus at Cholwich Town, in the
parish of Cornwood, the door to the shippen does not connect with
the passage entered from the main door of the house, but with another
passage entered by the door leading to the yard. The shippen is still
used as a cowshed, but the door has been built up.

The changes made at Higher Godsworthy have already been described. At Morshead, in Dean Prior, the plan may formerly have
closely resembled that of Shilston, but changes were long ago made.
There, however, subsequently to these changes, a door was formed
between an inner apartment and a stable, now a cowshed, that too has

since been built up. The house, once the home of Robert Furse, has now been partly demolished.[1]

Examples might be cited from every moorland parish, but the above can be accepted as characteristic. Changed ideas and altered manners have brought new needs; in most instances the shippen will now be found to have been converted to form part of the dwelling. But the typical Dartmoor house is no more than one room in depth. It can be conveniently enlarged by the conversion of the shippen, to which there is access from the passage, it cannot be enlarged otherwise by extension of length, except the new rooms are approached through the older rooms. In this dilemma a frequent expedient is to build on 'outshots' with pent roofs as extensions of the ground floor. These outshots can rarely be added at the back of the house, without considerable excavation. Old Belliver affords instances of such outshots, they are certainly later than the main building, against which they may be seen to have been built; and one, the dairy, has necessitated the closing of a former window. Good instances of similar outshots were formerly to be seen at Headland Warren, now spoilt by recent alteration, and may still be found elsewhere.

The space between two such outshots, one on either side of the door, if roofed over makes an effective porch, and this is often found. It might be thought that on the moors a porch was almost an essential; indeed some of the hut-circles even are supplied with flanking walls to the entrances. But where a large passage or lobby lies between the entrance and the living-room the need for a porch is scarcely felt. It is quite true that, notwithstanding settles and other devices for shelter, the neighbourhood of a wide hearth with its great chimney appears to be the home of the winds, but no porch cures or can cure that defect.

None the less, porches are frequent, are roomy, and are often distinct embellishments of the house. From the ample seats which are usually found it would appear that they largely served as summer-houses or garden rooms.

The second half of the seventeenth century was a great period of house building on Dartmoor, in which many, if not all, the houses were dated and signed by their owners. Around Chagford and Wide-combe the hallmark of houses of this period is the semicircular granite arch of the entrance door; on the western side of the moor the four-centred arch held its own. The older form, the segmental arch, was not entirely abandoned in either area, but was rarely used.

Although a little earlier than the period, the old house at Longstone,

---

[1] For further information on the Furses see Carpenter (1894), who gives an account of the manuscript history of the family left us by Robert Furse. It will be noted that when he came into the Morshead property, in 1573, some at least of the windows were not glazed.

Sheepstor, was a fine example of the free use of the four-centred arch. Built in 1633 by Walter Elford and Barbara his wife, it was unfortunately modernized in Georgian days, and has since, in consequence of the construction of the Burrator Reservoir, become a ruin. The very pig's-houses had good granite dressings. Some of the old doorways from Longstone have been removed to the grounds of Burrator Lodge, the residence of the foreman of the waterworks, and with them the date stones of the house and of the windstrew, as well as the cider mill (Pl. 76) and cheese press.

On the other hand, Lower Tar, Widecombe, is the latest of the round-arched type of house, it is dated 1707 (Pl. 84B). It has the characteristic porch with a room over, and a dressed granite doorway, the head semicircular with the letters 'I.T.', and the date '1707' in the spandrils, on shields flanked with oakleaves. The porch is central to the building, but, as we face it, the house-part lies wholly to the left and to the right are farm buildings.

There is an outshot, but it is built on to the farm buildings, and not to the house.

The water supply was twofold, by means of a pump from a well, the pump in a pump-house which will be seen in the view, and by means of a potwater leat conducted from a moorland stream, and running in a gutter which passes under the pump-house and across the court. This gutter is also shown.

The use of potwater leats was general; many served more than one house, and many still in use are some miles in length. Sometimes, as at Ditsworthy Warren, the waters of the leat are conducted into the house and there is a chute in a room or chamber adjoining the living-room. The distribution of the water with due regard to the rights of the several users has always been a matter of import. A frequent arrangement was to insert a 'bull's-eye' in the side of the leat where a branch left it for a farm near its course. One such bull's-eye may be seen near Meavy village, where it is inserted in the bank of a mill leat. It consists of a round hole, about one and a half inches in diameter, drilled in a granite slab, eight inches in thickness. Another may be seen on the Sortridge leat, near Windy Post; here the hole is a little over an inch in diameter, a more usual dimension. Warleigh, in Tamerton, was formerly supplied through a bull's-eye inserted in the bank of the Plymouth leat at Roborough. The aperture at Windy Post is more scientifically arranged than is usual, being provided with a weir on the leat, whereby the head over the aperture is rendered more constant. But it must be admitted that no such device wholly removes the risk of neighbourly unpleasantness: it is on the one hand so easy to persuade floating obstacles to enter the aperture and cause a partial blockage, and on the other hand so tempting to pond up the leat by the aid of a few turves and so get a greater head and consequent discharge. At times both parties to the use of the water resort to these devices, while still maintaining absolute good humour, each to each.

Masonry is the material of the Dartmoor house as we know it, and it is probable that it has ever been so. There is an ample supply of rock, while timber would need to be fetched from a distance. Cob, so freely used elsewhere in Devon, is practically unknown within the granite area, where the soil and subsoil are alike unsuited to that form of construction. It is found on the borders, and there only.

Our ancestors, with open hearths, wide chimneys, wood and peat fires, and some at least with thatched roofs, had learned a wholesome fear of fire. The precaution which that fear induced, already indicated, is further evidenced by a number of small buildings still standing near moorland farms—the ash-houses. The ash-house was a small building,

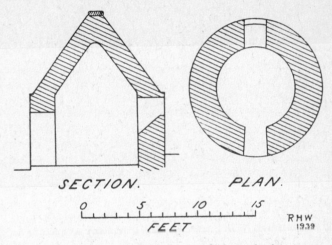

SECTION.   PLAN.

0   5   10   15
└┴┴┴┴┴┴┴┴┴┴┴┴┴┴┴┘
            FEET   RHW
                                    1939

FIG. 120. Ash-house, Lower Hisley, Lustleigh.

with an earth or lime-ash floor, the walls of masonry; the roof in the round type a hollow cone of masonry, in the square type covered with cleft granite posts. Those circular in plan had on one side a door, and opposite the door a small opening at a few feet above ground level and also provided with a door or hatch. The ashes and embers were taken every night from the hearth and placed in the ash-house, into which they were emptied through the hatch, which was placed on the side nearest the homestead. In some of the few square ash-houses the ashes were placed in the house at the same door by which they were subsequently removed.

These little buildings were always at a distance from the main house, often, where the farm was by the roadside, on the far side of the road. (There is one notable and extreme departure from this rule; at Wrangaton Manor, in Ugborough parish, the ash-house is placed at the back of the hearth, and from the hearth the embers were thrown directly into the ash-house. Although under the general roof, it has its own arched masonry ceiling, and is thus completely fireproof.)

Mr. Wills of Rudge, Lustleigh, has told me that he, as a boy, lived at the adjacent farm of Lower Hisley, and it was part of his work to carry out the ashes every night. The system thus extends to within living memory; and yet there are many countrymen and women to whom the uses of these buildings are unknown. Naturally the insatiable curiosity of the children has to be met; for them has been devised the explanation that these are pixy houses, and the doors are placed away from the farm because the little folk do not like being overlooked.

I give a plan and section of the ash-house at Lower Hisley (Fig. 120), and views of the ash-house at Shapley, North Bovey (Pl. 85 A and B); and at West Combe in the same parish (Pl. 86).

I wonder whether these little round buildings were the basis of the guide-book assertion that, on Dartmoor, there were many round towers, like those of Ireland? It is possible.

There is one other appurtenance of many Dartmoor houses, now fallen into disuse, which has proved puzzling to strangers: and that is the potato cave.

It was not every house which could have its cave. The possibility depended on the geology of the neighbourhood. They are found only in granite areas, and then only where the granite has been weathered to some little depth and converted into 'growan'. In growan the granite has been changed, by the break-up of its felspar, into a soft, sandy rock (see p. 7). It is easily excavated but still sufficiently coherent to be self-supporting, so that a heading driven into it will need no timber to sustain its roof. In this material short tunnels were driven in from the hillsides, in length from twenty to forty feet, in height from six to seven feet, and in width from three to six feet. At places more extensive chambers were excavated. Granite jambs and lintel at the entrance, and a wooden door completed the cave. Their general condition was damp, but not wet; if water was struck the cave was a failure. These caves were usually near the house, opening sometimes into the courtyard.

The knowledge of the use of these structures is by no means lost, but it is on the way to oblivion. The forgetfulness which shrouds so many simple things is too marked to leave any ground for faith in the reliability of alleged tradition. When we started the first serious archaeological work on Dartmoor, the best of us, of whom Mr. Robert Burnard was assuredly one, were without sufficient evidence or experience, we were pioneers opening new ground. It followed that we made mistakes, not in record but in interpretation. I have no regret that we published, we at least preserved the facts.

In the *Transactions of the Plymouth Institution* (Vol. 10, p. 232) Burnard figured two of these caves, at Deancombe, as tinner's caches. He learnt the error later, and himself constructed a small cave at Huccaby, the last of its race.

To mention a few only, such caves can be found near Colley Town, at Yellowmead, Leather Tor, Deancombe and Riddypit in the valley of the Meavy; at Routrundle in the Walkham Valley; and at Huntingdon Warren in the valley of the Western Wallabrook. At Yellowmead the chamber was branched and rather wider than usual. Since it is necessary to keep above the saturation level, the cover here as elsewhere was rather shallow. Someone planted beeches over the cave, these grew to be large trees, their weight broke the roof, and the trees falling into the cavity ended the career of that cave. At Huntingdon Warren the captain of the Huntingdon tin mine saw in the cave the beginning of a possible exploratory driveage, and obtained consent from the tenant of the Warren to the continuation of the excavation into the hill. This carried the work deeper, to below saturation level, the cave was flooded, and so remains, thus its useful life was ended. Pl. 87A shows the flooded cave at Huntingdon, and Pl. 87B gives a view of the entrance. I do not know any potato cave of the type described which is still in use.

On the whole the houses of the moor bear evidence of considerable prosperity cn the part of their builders. They are sound, and for their date roomy. The granite dressings are at times simple, but are substantial and sightly. Quite unexpectedly one finds, here and there, moulded oak beams and joists, even in small buildings. That the cots of the labourers may have been small and inconvenient may well be admitted, but neither as small nor as inconvenient as in the in-country; the very plenty of building material, and the practice of the labourers themselves in the construction of stone fences ensured the contrary. One need only look at the little colony of Peat Cot, formed by men who worked by day and fenced their land and built their house in the few hours of daylight left by that work, to realize that (with the exception of Nuns Cross Farm) there is no evidence that any capable man need be other than reasonably housed. It is to be doubted whether there were any labourers without independent holdings on Dartmoor, except the tinners; and the latter lived in the villages on the border and walked to their work.

From the Dartmoor house has come many a family which has played a great part in its time: one has only to instance the Heles of Cornwood. The recruitment of the active life of the nation from the countryside, and from yeoman families, has been a great feature in past history;[1] while the traditional dullness of the rustic-bred would seem

[1] Hoskins & Finberg (1952) show how a large class of landed gentry arose from twelfth and thirteenth-century pioneer freeholders. The history of the Cholwich family, who originally farmed a small outlying part of Cornwood, on the edge of Dartmoor, is a revealing example. (ED.)

to be, as are most traditions, a very modern error, in view of the many men learned in the law with whom the hills of Dartmoor have endowed, or afflicted, the community.

REFERENCES

CARPENTER, R. J., 1894. Furse of Moreshead. *T.D.A.*, Vol. 26, pp. 168–83.

HOSKINS, W. G., & FINBERG, H. P. R., 1952. *Devonshire Studies*. London. Jonathan Cape.

ON DARTMOOR PLACE-NAMES[1]

THE study of place-names has been at one time enthusiastically pursued, at another almost wholly neglected; a science thus interrupted in its growth is dwarfed in its accomplishment. Chief among the losses suffered, is an absence of restraint. Sciences, like men, have their wild oats to sow in youth; and the study of place-names has had its youth renewed so often that its harvest of indiscretion is prodigious. This makes it advisable, in considering the place-names of any district, to adopt strict criteria of interpretation, and to rigidly exclude, as valueless, all interpretations not conforming to such criteria. If a reasonable degree of certainty is to be attained, it would appear that the following requirements are none too exacting:

1. The name should never be divorced from the place. None but those perfectly familiar with the geography of a place are qualified to attempt the problem of its name.

2. Of all possible interpretations, that which makes the name descriptive of the place as it still exists, or as it is known to have existed within historic time, is the most probable, and should be preferred.

3. No violence should be done to the forms of the language in which the name is assumed to have been framed. As an example: it is not permissible to derive 'Bowerman' from *Vawr maen*, the Great Stone, since the Celtic form would be *maen vawr*, as in the 'Man of War' rock off the Cornish coast.

4. No mutation or change of form should be accepted for which there exists no known precedent, supported by documentary evidence; and, on the other hand, no change of form should be rejected as impossible, on the authority of a textbook.

5. Since the history of a place, if known, may be a valuable aid in

---

[1] This article was written before the publication of *The Place-Names of Devon* (*P.N.D.*), but is by no means superseded by that work. Not only are there here various additional data and suggestions based on local knowledge, but also, where opinions diverge, it should not be assumed that those of the authors of the *P.N.D.* are necessarily the more correct. What is perhaps the more remarkable, in a subject so fraught with uncertainty, is the large measure of common ground between different modern authorities. (ED.)

the interpretation of its name, the student should be well informed in local history; on the other hand, none but the most restrained use should be made of the presumed meaning of a name, as an aid to the reconstruction of a forgotten past.

6. It may be granted that some names are capable of direct translation, to modern English. For example, 'stickle-path' equals *the steep path*.

It may be that there is interest in devising elaborate and imaginative interpretations of place-names; it may be that some students regard a confessed ignorance of the origin of a name as a confession of incapacity; for such the modern crossword puzzle may provide congenial occupation.

In the following notes I have endeavoured to exclude all but the simplest interpretations; it is quite possible that at times I have been too ingenious, and have failed to fully observe my own criteria.

Many, in fact most, place-names are constructed from a noun and a qualifying adjective, which latter may be the possessive of a personal name. It is convenient to give some general consideration to these separately, taking first the nouns. The nouns, many of them, present modern English forms; others are to-day either obsolete or obsolescent; others yet have suffered strange change in their centuries of being. It is regarding these last that the following notes will be most detailed.

NOUNS

Ball, 'a hill of rounded outline'. A specialized use of the common English word. As examples, Hemerdon Ball, Corringdon Ball, Cuckoo Ball are all rounded hills.

Beam, I agree with Crossing[1] that this has a mining signification. It may refer to the 'rocking beam' of a pump used for mining purposes. Examples are: 'Caters Beam', 'Omen Beam', etc.

Beare, beer, or *bere. A.-S.* Bearu, bearo, 'a grove, a wood'. 'Black Tor Beare', as which Black Tor Copse was described, in 1588 and again in 1608, is a clear instance of the use of the word with this meaning; it is probably used in the same sense in 'Bair Down' opposite Wistman's Wood, and derives from the proximity of that wood. 'Beara', in South Brent, seems to be another clear example. But 'bere', meaning 'barley', is an alternative which introduces an uncertainty in many instances.

Combe, 'a valley'. Besides the very obvious change to *cum* or *cam*, there exists a form *am* or *ham* (the 'h' very lightly stressed), and this latter version is at times interchangeable with *ken* or *chen*.

An interesting example is 'Birkham Gate', which is on the road to Eyelesboro, at the eastern fence of Ringmoor and hard by Sheepstor Brook. More formally this is still called 'Burracombe Gate'. The

---

[1] W. Crossing, in his *Guide to Dartmoor*, pp. 9–40, gave the most complete glossary of Dartmoor terms hitherto published. (ED.)

name does not appear on any map, and hence, without a personal knowledge of the neighbourhood, it would give no clue to the identification of the 'Biricombaforda' of the charter granted by Isabella de Fortibus, in 1291. In view of the existence of Burracombe Gate near the head of the Sheepstor Brook, and of Burra Tor near the outfall of that stream into the Meavy, it appears at least probable that the whole valley was formerly known as Biracombe, Bearacombe, or Burracombe, 'the wooded valley'; it still shows more timber than the average of Dartmoor combes.

At Deancombe, in the parish of Sheepstor, is an old tenement, the buildings long in ruins, which is variously called 'Outam', 'Outham', or 'Outcombe'; and the last of these names very accurately describes it, since it is, indeed, 'out the combe'.

'Bycacumbayoneda', a name which occurs in the charter of Isabella de Fortibus, previously referred to, is now known as 'Bickham'. Without multiplying examples, it will be evident that many (perhaps all) of the 'hams' of Dartmoor have no connexion with the A.-S. *ham*, a homestead.

Walkhampton appears in the *Inquisitio Geldi* as 'Walchentone', in 1505–6 it is 'Walcamton'; in the days of Henry VIII it appears on a map as 'Walkynton'; and, within my recollection, it has been called 'Wackenton' by the older moormen. The original form was probably 'Wallacombe-ton',[1] in which the apparent redundancy of either the *ham* or the *ton* no longer appears.

In the days of Henry VIII, Okehampton appears as 'Okenton',[2] and so I have heard it called by the older men. Perhaps the origin may be found in 'Oak-combe-ton'?

Cleave, A.-S. cleof, 'a cliff'. Appears in 'Lustleigh Cleave', 'Tavy Cleave', etc. At first sight it may seem unimportant that the word denotes the cliff bounding the valley, and not the cleft or valley itself. But the fact has significance, and is emphasized by the occurrence of the name 'Shilly Cleaves', near Plymouth, at a place where the name can only refer to an old sea cliff of slate, bounding land now reclaimed.

Cut, 'a track or way, formed by removing the soft surface soil, and leaving exposed the harder, and often stony, subsoil; a way artificially formed through a mire'. The best known example is 'Cut Lane', from which 'Cut Hill' is named.

Down, needs no definition, commonly appears as 'don', as in 'Butterdon'. But a further change has, in some instances, occurred: thus, 'Sciredon', as it was written in A.D. 1275, has now become 'Skeriton', and the 'Leweneston' of 1275 is probably identical with the modern 'Leusdon', while 'Steapedon' (1346–7) has become 'Steeperton'. In

---

[1] See discussion in *P.N.D.*, p. 243, where this plausible suggestion is not considered. (ED.)

[2] 'Okement-tun' preferred as origin by *P.N.D.* (ED.)

modern pronunciation the use of *don* or *ton*, indifferently, is frequent.

Ford, 'a way, not necessarily restricted to the passage or crossing-place at a stream'. In Petertavy parish, that portion of the Lichway which lies between Lanson Moor Reeve and White Barrow is known as 'Sandy Ford'; and the south-east angle of the newtake, which it skirts, is called 'Sandy Ford Corner'. This Sandy Ford is a trackway devoid of any stream crossings. The name does not appear on the Ordnance map.

It is important to note that, on Dartmoor, *ford* is often but a variant of *worthy*, *q.v.*

Girt or *gert*, 'a valley with steep sides; a mine gully' (*A.-S.* grút, 'a gulph an abyss'?). The tor at the entrance to the valley of Tavy Cleave is known as 'Gert Tor', a name sometimes assumed to be derivable from 'Great Tor',[1] a suggestion supposed to be supportable by Blackmore's 'girt Jan Ridd'. But whereas he was an outstanding person, there is nothing exceptional about the tor to justify the adjective. Its situation at the entrance to the valley or 'gert' would, however, make it reasonable to call it the 'valley tor'. And this would accord with the fact that the tors which crown the cliff or cleave are known as 'Tavy Cleave Tors'.

Hole, *A.-S.* hole, 'a valley'. This term is usually applied to a restricted area, and not to a complete valley. 'Laughter or Larter Hole', and 'Horse Hole', both in the Dart watershed, are examples. Even this simple word presents its difficulties as a component in place-names, thus: Larter Hole is sometimes changed to 'Larter Hall', and the parish of Holne is constantly spoken of as 'Hole', and frequently appears as such in documents.

Lake, 'a brook, a tributary stream'. This word is never used on Dartmoor with its present literary significance; a sheet of standing water, of whatever size, is invariably called a 'pool'.

It would hardly appear necessary to refer to so well-known a word, were it not for the fact that an antiquarian so well qualified as Davidson has mistaken its meaning.

Man, 'a standing stone, a menhir'. As in 'Beardown Man'. It has been stated that this word derives from the Celtic 'maen', a stone. If that were true one would expect to find other Celtic forms associated with it, a line of evidence which is entirely wanting. I prefer to believe that the stones are so called by reason only that, seen against the skyline, they do indeed present some resemblance to a human figure.

Tor, 'a hill, more usually a hill crowned with rock, and recently used for the crowning mass itself'. The difficulty presented by this word is its constant duplication by the moormen. Thus, 'Hen Tor' becomes 'Hentor Tor', and 'Harter Tor' may equally well be 'Har', 'Hare', 'Hart', or 'Harter' Tor. Of tors devoid of rocky crowns, I may name 'Clay Tor', a hill in the Walkham Valley, and bearing the name since

---

[1] But this was written 'Gordetorre' in 1306 (*P.N.D.*, p. 233). (ED.)

1665, at the latest; while 'Udal Tor', now Roborough Rock, is an early example of the name attaching to a rock mass only.

Well, 'a well or spring, running water'. This word has been mentioned to direct attention to the frequent confusion of *well* and *hill*; a confusion so complete that it is at times impossible to determine which is intended. Both degenerate into a terminal *el*, which later scribes restore as fancy prompts. Thus, at varying dates, we read: Pusshill, 1260; Pishull, 1300, 1304, 1354; Pushull, 1316; Pulleshull, 1380; but—Peasewell *alias* Pusswell, 1628; and Piswell, in 1704; while to-day the name has settled down to Pizwell. In 1539 the adjacent ford was called 'Peselford'. Here the concordance of the earlier forms points to *hill* as the true interpretation. But what certainty have we that the process of change may not have occurred more than once?

An additional difficulty arises from the occasional change of *hill* to *hall* and *hel*, or, as seen above, to *hull*.

Worthy, A.-S., 'an enclosed homestead'. Of all the varied components of Dartmoor place-names this has acquired the greatest number of variants; it has changed to *ary* or *ery*, to *ford*, with or without the prefix *a*, to *over*, *ever*, *iver*, and also to *eny*.

There is ample evidence of these changes; Hisworthy Tor is constantly referred to as 'Hessary otherwise Hisworthy'. On Exmoor, Pinkworthy is alternatively called 'Pinkery'. On Dartmoor, Brisworthy is sometimes called 'Brisery' and sometimes 'Briseny'.

All these forms can be seen to follow the rapid pronunciation of the name; the 'ford' form is less obvious. We may start with a simple example: Blachford, in Cornwood, is in the Exeter Domesday '*Blacheorda*', where 'eorda' is the Norman scribe's attempt at 'worthy'. In the Exchequer Domesday, it is 'Blacheurde', the final *e* of which would be pronounced. Omit the final *a* from *eorda*, or the final *e* from *eurde*, and there is left, in either instance, a form from which the 'ford' variant is directly derivable. Since the manor is now invariably called 'Blachford', it may be objected that such, possibly, it always has been; but we have documentary evidence to the contrary, for in the Tax Roll of Devon (1302–3) the manor appears as 'Nitherblacchesworthy', and, in the seventeenth century it appears in a deed as 'Blachford otherwise Blachworthy'.

Now Blachford is a collection of syllables which the Devonshire ear accepts, but if you similarly alter 'Cadworthy' to 'Cadford', you arrive at a certain harshness of sound which no Dartmoor man will leave unmodified; accordingly Cadworthy, on the Plym, has become 'Cadaford' and 'Cadever', and while the bridge is sometimes rightly called 'Cadaford Bridge' (in 1407 it was 'ponte de Cadeworthi'), wiseacres of the past have turned 'Cadever' into 'Cadover', and thence postulated the existence of a river, which the poet of Dartmoor, with finely unconscious humour, has described as the 'ever brawling Cad'.

The change from 'aford' to 'ever' needs no prolonged discussion, resulting naturally from rapid pronunciation. It should be noted that all three forms, Cadworthy, Cadaford, and Cadever, are in present use.

The distribution of the 'worthys' in Devonshire affords some evidence that the name intended, not merely an enclosed homestead, but, more frequently, one of recent origin, a 'newtake' from the moors. The *worthys* cluster around, and some occur within, Dartmoor, Exmoor, and the moorlands, formerly unenclosed, of north and north-west Devon. They were the homes of the pioneers who went out into the waste places. And it is noteworthy that, in the majority of instances, the distinctive prefix is a personal name: thus, Brisworthy—Brictric's worthy, Cadworthy or Cade's worthy, Trowle's worthy, Hexworthy or Hick's worthy, Eggworthy—another Hick's worthy, the change being identical with that in 'Egg Buckland'. There are examples of other classes of prefix, but rare; one such is 'Middleworth', in Sheepstor.

Here, then, is a place-name which is dim history, the evidence of days when the Saxons were advancing the bounds of agriculture at the expense of the wastes. A similar use of personal as place-names occurred much later, when the old manorial system was breaking up and giving place to fixity of tenure.[1] Tenements took the name of their occupiers, for example, at Compton Gifford, we find: 'Dunn's Fields', 'Yonge's', 'Kitt's', etc.

Both were times of new things, and for those novelties no pre-existent names were available, the personal name came most readily to hand to supply the need.

It is highly probable that many of the 'fords' on Dartmoor, perhaps all which are attached to enclosed lands, were in their origin 'worthys'. The same may be said of the 'ivers', 'evers', and the further variant 'ifer'. Thus 'Belliver', on the East Dart, and 'Vitifer', on the West Webburn, would be Bellworthy and Vitworthy respectively. It should be noted that, in 1702, Bellever appears as 'Bellaford'; and, in 1609, it was written in a single entry in the manor court rolls of Lidford: 'Beltabur, Anglice Bellavur', and 'Bellabour'.[2]

Yeo, A.-S., eá, 'running water'. A specialized use of this word arose in connexion with the mining industry, and extended even to Cornwall. The Bailiff of Blackmore wrote, in 1586, 'and every (tin) work may lawfully fetch their water from their river, which the Tinners commonly call the Yeo, without denial or contradiction'. In this manner the word 'yeo' came to be more particularly applied to such streams as were the sources from which those artificial water-courses, called 'leats', were drawn. It was thus that the River Ashburn, at Ashburton, the

---

[1] See Hoskins & Finberg (1952). (ED.)

[2] However, all renderings prior to 1600 point to 'ford' compounded with wielle (spring, running water) as the original form (*P.N.D.*, p. 192). (ED.)

source and 'yeo' from which the leat of such importance to the industries of that town was drawn, came to be called, and is still called, the Yeo, to the exclusion of its true name. It was the 'yeo' in distinction from the mill-leat.

ADJECTIVES AND OTHER PREFIXES

Black, this may derive from two very different sources, either 'bleak' or 'black', both of which, however, come from the *A.-S. blaec,* meaning pale or colourless. Hence, if we regard the first meaning, the limit of paleness is white, places bleak and exposed are apt to be covered with snow, and hence to be white at times. The other extreme of colourlessness, is black. I am well aware that this is a restatement of common knowledge, but I have made it as an admission that there may be truth in elaborate derivations, little as they are to be encouraged. The task of determining which meaning of 'black' is intended in any Dartmoor place-name is wellnigh hopeless; so many places are both black and bleak. *Erica cinerea* is not inaptly named, and it is by no means the only moorland plant which is dark in shade when dry, and practically black when wet. *Calluna vulgaris* has a very similar effect as a ground covering. On the other hand, places where these plants grow are often exposed and bleak.

Who shall say which of the alternatives was in the mind of the man who first gave name to 'Black Down', Mary Tavy?

Brent, a word barely obsolescent, 'steep, lofty, prominent'. Occurs in Brent Hill, in the parish of South Brent, and in Brent Tor, in the parish of the same name. The most familiar present use of the word is in the phrase, 'brent brow', descriptive of a lofty forehead. Both Brent Hill and Brent Tor are border heights of exceptionally bold outline, and from their abruptness and their height form landmarks visible over wide stretches of country.

The attempt has been repeatedly made to derive the *brent* element in these names from 'brennen', to burn. It has been variously argued that both hills are formed of igneous rocks, a fact of which our forebears were certainly in total ignorance, and that both hills may have been used as beacons; but, if so, why was the ordinary habit of calling them 'beacons' departed from? We have plenty of examples, such as 'Ugborough Beacon', 'Cosdon Beacon', and others.

Butter or *Buttern,* utter, 'outer'? Occurs in 'Butterdon', 'Buttern Hill', etc. In every instance the situation of the place conforms to the suggested derivation of the name, and 'Outer Down', 'Outer Hill', etc., would be accepted as good nomenclature. A marsh near Plymouth was known as 'the Utter Marisch' in the sixteenth century.

Chaw, a 'jackdaw'. I am indebted to Mr. Hannaford, lately the tenant of Headland Warren, for directing my attention to the use of this word in the place-name 'Chaw Gully', applied to one of the old mining excavations at Birch Tor (Pl. 7A). As Mr. Hannaford put it, 'Chaw Gully is called after the jackdaws that used to build there; and a proper lot there were before I got tired of them and shot them out of it.' The modern pronunciation of 'Chough', still used for the Cornish Chough, is 'chuff', but in the old days it was sometimes spelt, and I suspect more frequently pronounced, 'cow', 'chow', or 'chaw'. The name covered, not only the jackdaws, but also other members of the corvine race. It should be noted that Crossing has anticipated me as to this.

Corn, in 'Corndon', etc. A.-S. corone, 'a crown', or coronian, 'to crown'. The hills and ridges to which the name of 'Corn' has been applied are all the crowning heights of their respective groups of hills.[1] It is interesting to find that 'Corndon Tor', over Dartmeet, is called by Rowe (1856), 'Quarnian Down'.

Dewer, in 'Dewerstone'. I, myself, have joined in the attempt to derive this from the Celtic, and to translate the name as 'stone by the water'. I admit the position to be untenable, and I withdraw. As an alternative the A.-S. duua, 'a dove or pigeon', may be suggested. The 'Rock of the Pigeons' is a very appropriate name; although, of late years, 'Jackdaw Castle' would be even more fitting.

Hell, A.-S. helle, 'clear, eminent'. The word occurs in Hel Tor, near Moretonhampstead, and that height is indeed singularly prominent as a feature of the landscape.

Homer, 'nearer home', the antithesis of 'outer'. A frequent element in Dartmoor place-names. It is of constant occurrence in field names, such as 'Homer New Park'. A good example of its use is 'Homer Redlake', a tributary of the Tavy; there is also a companion, the 'Outer Redlake'. As another example we may take 'Homerton' or homer down, on the West Ockment.

Lynch, *Lynx*, etc. A.-S. hlinc, the nearest synonym of which is 'ridge'. Such ridge may also be a boundary, artificial or natural; or the word may denote a path on the crest of a ridge.

Lynch Common, in the Meavy Valley, Lynch Tor, in the Tavy Valley, Lynx Tor, by the Lyd, and Lints Tor, on the West Ockment, are all in the nature of forelands.

Leather, in 'Leather Tor'. A.-S. hlead, 'a steep, a cliff'. The name has been variously spelt: 'Laddre-torre', 1362; 'Ladderrtor', 1417; and 'Leddertor', 1477. If any tor on the moor deserves to be described as a cliff, it is Leather Tor.

Newley, in 'Newley Combe', a valley joining the Meavy Valley above Sheepstor. A.-S. neowel, 'profound, deep, a deep gulph'. An essentially accurate description of the combe. In 1443, the name is spelt 'Newelcombe'.

Riddy, in 'Riddy Pit', in the Meavy Valley. A.-S. riðe, 'a well'. A spring still rises in this hollow.

[1] But see discussion in *D.P.N.* (p. 268). (ED.)

Red, in the many 'Redlakes'. This presents a possible ambiguity, the syllable is always pronounced 'rid'. The reference may in some instances be to the colour of the bed of the stream, in summer; when, the water being low, the limonite, formed by the oxidation of ferrous carbonate, derived from the bogs, colours the stones. But this feature is by no means markedly developed in many of the streams called by this name. It is to be noted that many of the 'Redlake' valleys are places to which the moormen still resort to cut reeds for thatching, and 'reed lake' is probably the correct interpretation.[1]

Rough, or *Row*, in the name of many tors. The local pronunciation always makes this rhyme with 'cow'. *A.-S.* rúh, 'rough'. From varied reasons the tors so named deserve the adjective.

Rundle, in 'Rundlestone', one of the Forest bounds, near Princetown. It has been suggested that the original Rundlestone was a stone post, bearing the letter 'R', formerly standing at a point near the Tavistock-Princetown road, below Rundlestone Tor. Admittedly it would be the one artificial bond mark, where all the rest (excepting Syward's Cross) were natural objects, since the 'furnum regis', although a building, was not erected as a boundary mark. Admittedly this post did not lie on the boundary of the forest, as set forth in the earlier perambulations, or as now recognized; which is a straight line joining North Hessary Tor and Mis Tor Pan. And, further, it offered no feature corresponding to its name. But, if we abandon this identification, and give to 'Rundle' the meaning of 'roundel', we have, in Rundlestone Tor, a natural object which fulfils all the conditions; it lies on the precise line of the boundary, and presents good reason for its name. A 'roundel', in common parlance, as in heraldry, was a small circular object. The principal feature of Rundlestone Tor, which I take to be the original Rundlestone, is a great, sloping mass of granite; it has in it one rock-basin, 28 in. in diameter by 5 in. in depth, which must have been formed before the present slope was assumed (Fig. 8, p. 33); and, at the summit, a later basin, also 28 in. in diameter, and, on the average, perhaps 7 in. in depth. The Rundlestone now measures 23 ft by 23 ft, but many feet have been cleaved by the quarrymen from the north end.

Rock-basins are only formed on approximately horizontal surfaces, and the accident of this slab having fallen out of level, after the first basin had formed, and yet in such manner as to permit the formation of a second basin near the summit, makes it unique in my experience; and certainly makes the rock-basins, or 'roundels', very exceptionally prominent.

This rock, with its considerable area, its thickness of 4 ft 6 in., and the circles of its rock-basins, certainly agrees with the description given, in 1736: 'a Great Stone call'd Roundle'.

[1] *D.P.N.* prefers the former on etymological grounds. (ED.)

Rules, or *Roos*, a tor so called, and sometimes known as 'Rolls Tor', one mile north by west from Merrivale Bridge. In 1665, written 'Rulestorre'. *A.-S.* hruse, 'a rock, a hill'.

Sharp, all the many tors known as 'Sharpitor', and 'Sharp Tor', are distinguished by their acute outlines, at least as seen from certain view-points. But, in some instances, 'scarp' would be equally applicable.

Smear, in 'Smear Ridge', Petertavy. *A.-S.* smea, 'fine, narrow, acute'. An appropriate description of this particular ridge.

Staple, in 'Staple Tor'. *A.-S.* steopl, 'a tower'. The rock masses of Great Staple Tor include some, as prominent features, which are certainly reminiscent of the flanking towers of a great gateway.

Stannon, Standon Hill, etc. *A.-S.* stennen, 'stony'.

Stinka or *Stenga*, a word not yet obsolete, meaning 'a pool, or standing water'. In the north, a moorhen is still spoken of as a 'stank-hen'. The word occurs on Dartmoor in 'Stinka Tor' and 'Stingers Hill'. The first-named place is written 'Steinigtor' in 1608, and 'Stinkatorr' in 1702. Some years ago, when walking to the tor with Mr. J. S. Amery, a casual remark of his gave the clue to the meaning of the name. He remarked that the tor was unique on Dartmoor, in that the rocks rose, practically, from a pool of water. In fact, no more apt description could be given than 'the tor in the pool or marsh'. This tor, which has no hill of its own, is one of those in which the word 'tor' attaches to a mass of rock alone. (Stingers Hill is also a very marshy spot.)

Wella, or *Walla*, in 'Wallabrook'. There are so many Walla Brooks on the moor that some reference must be made to this word, although no really satisfactory and complete explanation can be given. The Western Wallabrook is very frequently mentioned in documents relating to the Forest. The name occurs in the following forms: 1300, Walebrook; 1344, Wallabrook, Wellabrook, Willabrook; 1358, Wallbrook; 1476, Walbrook; 1491-2, Walbrook, Waterwald brook, this possibly an error for Wester Wald brook; 1557, Welbrook; 1608, Wallebrook; 1689, Walter Brook; 1699, Wellow Brook; 1702, Walla-brook, Welbrook. Here the earlier forms all correspond to the present version. Many, varied, derivations have been suggested.

At one time the favourite suggestion was a derivation from the *A.-S.* 'Wealhas', meaning—strangers, foreigners, and hence the Welsh. This involves the idea that on the banks of all these little streams there dwelt, in Saxon times, small colonies of Celts; in Celtic 'reserves', as it were. Or, in the alternative, that such brooks were temporary boundaries, at which the Saxon wave checked. There is no surviving evidence of any kind in support of either alternative.

A more hopeful idea is that involved in the possible connexion of 'walla' with the Cornish 'heul', a mine working. And, as if to support this, there is a tributary of the Avon called the 'Bala Brook', while 'bal' is a well-known variant of 'huel'. But this admits of critical test:

mine workings are not lost by lapse of time, leaving no surviving traces. And the valleys of the Wallabrooks are by no means places where, taking them as a whole, the remains of ancient workings are prominent.

The *A.-S.* Waella, or wille, 'a well', is yet another possibility, phonetically at least; but the attempt to explain its use, by saying that these streams were called 'Wallabrook', which had their source in definite springs, or wells, in distinction to those which grew to be brooks by mere seepage from the bogs, is unsustainable. In the first place, it involves a system of fine geographical classification, inappropriate to the date of origin of the names; and, in the second place, the streams in question do not, to-day, present the peculiarity in question. On the other hand, 'waella' sometimes has the meaning—'running water'; but I hesitate to say that this more general meaning, as opposed to the particular meaning attached to our present use of the word, was ever really well established.

There remain two other possible sources for the name. It may be a corruption of 'walter brook', the 'tumbling or rolling brook', in which connexion it is well to remember the shortening of the Christian name Walter to Waller. It would then derive from the *A.-S.* waeltan.

Ot it may represent 'willow brook'; the *A.-S.* wileg—'a willow', being its source. Here we have a physical characteristic which cannot be affirmed or denied, as the result of inspection. Time brings its changes to the brook-side vegetation, and the hand of man has not been idle.

I have purposely dealt fully with this last example[1]; it is useful to present the uncertainty and difficulty of the study of place-names. Only a small percentage will ever admit of reasonable certainty of interpretation; the place-names of Dartmoor are like its hut-circles, they yield evidence but sparingly, here and there a flint chip, a potsherd, or a spot of charcoal; here and there a recognizable syllable, but no more.

One conclusion, and one only, I draw from such study as I have given to the subject—if you except the principal rivers, whose names would follow their course upward, there are no traces of Celtic influence, or of any but Saxon occupation, in the Dartmoor place-names. It may be objected that 'combe' is the Welsh 'cwm', and 'tor' is the Welsh 'twr'. I care not from whom the Saxons learnt these words, so only that they learnt them not on Dartmoor. Except where other Saxon forms are in evidence, both 'combe' and 'tor' are almost absent from Cornwall. On the other hand, these words are frequently met with in West Saxon charters. As frequent constituents of the place-names of Devon, they were brought here by the Saxons.

[1] If, indeed, the earliest known forms are considered, it would appear that there have been at least three separate origins. Thus the Dart Wallabrook seems to be *Wēala brōc* (stream of the Britons), the Avon Wallabrook *Wielle-brōc* (brook fed by a spring), while the Teign Wallabrook, if originally *Wotesbroke*, may incorporate a personal name. See *P.N.D.*, p. 16. (ED.)

There is no novelty in this conclusion. Nearly fifty years ago my father wrote: "The singular paucity of Keltic names on Dartmoor proves two things. First, that during British times Dartmoor was practically unknown to the Saxons. Second, that the Britons of Dartmoor were included in the general expulsion."[1] For myself I am prepared to state the case in another, and simpler form, without traversing these conclusions.

I would merely say that, on Dartmoor, there was no simultaneous occupation by Celt and Saxon; and, further, there was an interval between the Celtic and the Saxon occupation.

[1] "Notes on the Historical Connections of Devonshire Place-names", *T.D.A.*, 1878, Vol. 10, pp. 276–308.

APPENDIX I

THE FLOW OF DARTMOOR RIVERS

RIVER FLOODS

THE highest rate of flow attained in a flooded river may be expressed as a function of the intensity and duration of the rainfall. In a river, the watershed of which is practically impervious, the upward limit is not reached until the flow of the stream discharges in each unit of time the full amount of rain falling upon the watershed in a similar period, less some slight reduction by unavoidable evaporation. In practice no watershed of more than a trifling area may be regarded as practically impervious, and there is some loss by percolation, as well as by evaporation.

The simplest case to consider involves the following conditions: rainfall starting simultaneously over the whole area of the watershed, continuing at a uniform rate for an appreciable time, and ceasing suddenly. Such conditions are never absolutely fulfilled, but approximations thereto are of frequent occurrence. It is, therefore, of interest to trace the growth of a flood so caused.

The first of the rain is expended in wetting the herbage, the grass, bracken and heather. This once thoroughly wetted, the whole of the remaining fall reaches the ground, the surface of which is rarely thoroughly saturated except during a storm; hence a further expenditure of rainfall goes to completely saturate the ground. Then, subject to small loss by evaporation and percolation, the remaining rainfall flows off the ground and ultimately reaches the river.

Assuming a gauge to be fixed in the river at any point, whereby the rate of flow of the stream may be observed, the flow from that part of the watershed immediately adjacent will first reach the gauge; and with the continuance of the rain this flow will be maintained. It will be joined by the yield of more and more distant parts of the watershed as time passes, until, should the rain so long continue, the yield from all points on the watershed will be flowing over the gauge. With this the extreme of the particular flood will be reached, and the magnitude of that extreme will then depend solely on the intensity of the rainfall. But, should the rain cease before the flow from the most distant gathering ground has reached the gauge, then the magnitude of the flood will be less and will be a function of the duration as well as of the intensity of the rainfall.

If the rain continues for a period sufficient to establish the greatest rate of flow corresponding to the intensity of the rainfall, then should the rain maintain the same intensity for a further period there will be a maintained flood at the maximum rate. It is notable that, except in very small watersheds, there is very rarely any such maintained flood; and it is extremely rare to find the maximum of any flood equal to the maximum that the intensity of the rainfall could create, given a sufficient duration.

The smaller the watershed, the more frequently will floods approximate to the possible maximum, and similarly the steeper the slopes of the gathering ground and the steeper the gradient of the river channel, since all these conditions render it more probable that the yield from the greater part of the gathering ground will have reached the gauge before the storm has ceased.

A curve showing the variation in the flow of a flooded river plotted against time elapsed from the commencement of the storm will have characteristics varying with the nature of the gathering ground. The normal Dartmoor watershed is relatively impervious, is steep, and has a river of rapid fall. The flood curves show a first rise of no great rapidity, followed as the ground gets saturated and the surface flow becomes well established, by a very rapid rise due to the increasing area of watershed which contributes to the flow, the curve becomes a straight line of steep inclination. With floods of great magnitude, the peak, once reached, is rarely maintained for more than about fifteen minutes; then, with the cessation of the storm, the flood rapidly lessens, at first in a straight line curve, and subsequently more and more slowly. It is notable that the die-away curve for any one stream has always the same form, a small flood diminishes at the same rate as does the residuum of a great flood when it has fallen to the magnitude of peak of the smaller.

Fig. 121 gives the standard flood curve of a watershed of 800 acres at the head of the Yealm. It is derived from the records of four separate floods, each of which was superimposed on an initial flow of about five and a half million gallons a day. The rising curve is that of the greatest flood alone, the three other, lesser floods, rose slightly less rapidly. The die-away curve is shared by each flood as far as its height extends. The peak of the curve represents a flow at the rate of 134,380,000 gallons a day, or 128,700,000 gallons per day superimposed on the initial flow of 5,680,000 gallons a day; the rate of flow so superimposed is the true measure of the flood. Stating the rate of flow as gallons per day the growth of the flood was as follows. In the first half-hour the increase was such as, if continued for an hour, would have added 1,200,000 gallons per day to the initial rate of flow, in other words the increase was at the rate of 1,200,000 gallons per day, per hour, in the second half-hour it was at the rate of 6,000,000 g.p.d., per hour, in the third half-hour 48,400,000 g.p.d., per hour, in the fourth and fifth half-hours 101,000,000 g.p.d., per hour. The rate of fall is such that a flood which increases the rate of flow of the river by 128,700,000 gallons per day, when the initial flow is about 5,000,000, is reduced in the first ten minutes after the peak has been passed to about 128,300,000 gallons a day, from which it falls to half this value in 78 minutes, to one quarter value in 158 minutes, to one eighth value in 255 minutes, to one sixteenth in 405 minutes, to one thirty-second in 585 minutes, to one sixty-fourth in 16 hours, and to one eighty-eighth in 26 hours.

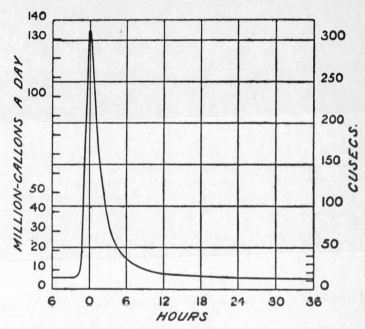

FIG. 121. Standard flood curve of 800-acre watershed of Upper Yealm.

Another and better method of units is to state the flow in cubic feet per second, per thousand acres. The records of different watersheds are then directly comparable. The Yealm watershed is 800 acres, and a flow at the rate of one cubic foot per second, per thousand acres, is accordingly the equivalent of 432,000 gallons a day.

One hundred and twenty-eight million, three hundred thousand gallons a day would thus be expressed as 297 cusecs, approximately.

Table I gives the hourly decay of the rate of flow of flood waters on the 800 acres watershed of the Yealm, starting with an addition of 128,300,000 gallons a day, or 297 cusecs to the initial flow of 5,680,000 gallons a day, or 13·15 cusecs.

In this computation account has been taken of the fact that, in the absence of rain, the flow of the river would fall in 24 hours, from 5,682,000 gallons a day to 4,299,100 gallons a day.

TABLE I. THE DECAY OF A FLOOD FLOWING FROM THE
YEALM WATERSHED OF 800 ACRES

Hour	Rate of flow in 1,000 gallons per 24 hours	Rate of flow in cubic feet per second per 1,000 acres (cusecs)	Rate of flow at the commencement of each hour, expressed as a percentage of the rate of flow at the commencement of the previous hour
0	128,300	297·0	
1	75,100	173·8	56·53
2	46,300	107·2	61·65
3	26,900	62·3	58·10
4	17,900	41·4	66·54
5	12,900	29·9	72·07
6	9,560	22·3	74·81
7	7,400	17·1	76·68
8	5,850	13·5	79·05
9	4,700	10·9	80·34
10	3,800	8·8	80·85
11	3,200	7·4	84·21
12	2,800	6·5	87·50
13	2,500	5·79	89·29
14	2,250	5·21	90·00
15	2,100	4·86	93·33
16	2,000	4·63	95·24
17	1,920	4·44	96·00
18	1,850	4·28	96·35
19	1,760	4·07	95·14
20	1,700	3·94	96·59
21	1,650	3·82	97·06
22	1,600	3·70	96·97
23	1,550	3·59	96·88
24	1,500	3·47	96·77
25	1,460	3·38	97·33
26	1,460	3·38	100·00

It will be seen that there are slight irregularities in the progression of the figures in the above table. These are due to the difficulty of sufficiently refined measurement, no attempt having been made to fair the curve. And, although the table shows the increase of flow left at the end of the 25th hour to be the same as at the beginning, this is not strictly accurate, as there is a continued slow decrease, lasting some days.

A comparison of the flood characteristics of some typical Dartmoor watersheds can be made. There was a large, but not extreme, flood, the

peak of which was reached near midnight on the 24 November 1929.
The record of this on the Yealm watershed is available, and Mr. S. C.
Chapman, M.Inst.C.E., has kindly supplied the records of the same
flood on the South Teign and the Trenchford watersheds, while Mr.
F. Howarth, M.Inst.C.E., has been equally kind in affording informa-
tion as to the Meavy watershed.

The comparative data are given in Table II.

TABLE II

Watershed	Area (acres)	Rainfall (in.) 23 Nov.	24 Nov.	Greatest Rate of Flow Galls. per day	Cusecs
Yealm	800	0·45	2·39	134,380,000	311
Meavy	4,660	0·79	2·02	504,000,000	200[1]
S. Teign	2,400	0·79	2·60	238,750,000	184
Trenchford	805	0·28	2·68	55,000,000	127

The gross rates of discharge are here given, without deduction of the
initial flow on which the flood was imposed. To complete the information it is necessary to add the actual yield of the rivers in the 24 hours
commencing 6 hours before the peak of the flood, and ending 18 hours
after the peak (Table III).

TABLE III

Watershed	Flow off in 24 hours: gallons	Gallons yield per 1000 acres in 24 hours
Yealm	36,662,500	45,828,120
Meavy	184,140,000	39,515,020
S. Teign	105,025,000	43,760,420
Trenchford	31,025,000	38,540,370

It must not be supposed that the influence of this flood was exhausted
in the given 24 hours.

Unfortunately there is no self-recording rain-gauge on either of the
above-named catchments, and we do not know whether the intensity
of the rain was quite the same on each, so that, as regards the yield of
the river at the peak of the flood, no strict comparisons are possible,
but the influence of the size of the watershed is apparent. From the
curve of flow it may reasonably be concluded that the storm did not
continue, even on the 800 acres of the Yealm, a sufficient time to cause
a maximum which fully represented the intensity of the rainfall; on the
Meavy, with 4,660 acres of watershed, the duration of the storm would
be far less adequate. The explanation of the relatively low peak attained
by the S. Teign is probably to be found in the fact that on that river
there were two peaks of almost equal intensity of flood, whereas on
the Yealm and the Meavy the second peak was distinctly subordinate.

[1] In 1899 a flood on the Meavy reached a flow of 530 cusecs.

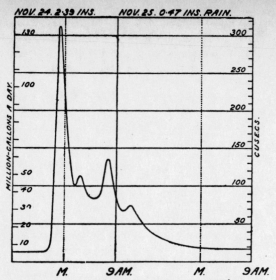

FIG. 122. Flood of 24 November 1929, Yealm.

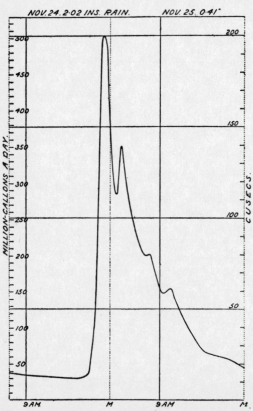

FIG. 123. Flood of 24 November 1929, Meavy.

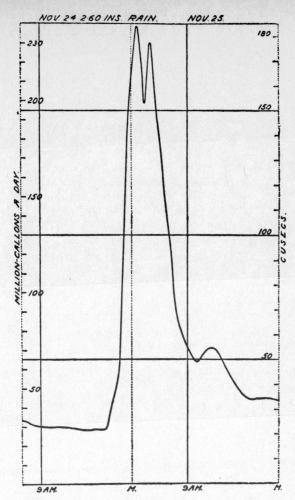

FIG. 124. Flood of 24 November 1929, South Teign.

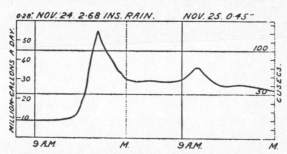

FIG. 125. Flood of 24 November 1929, Trenchford Brook.

But Trenchford obviously stands outside the group formed by the other three streams, and the results confirm what has been said as to the differences between the eastern area and the rest of Dartmoor.

When we come to the yield per 1,000 acres in 24 hrs we find that, as regards the Yealm, the S. Teign and the Meavy, the yields are inverse to the size of the catchments; but here again the Trenchford Stream, although less markedly, is in a separate class.

Figures 122 to 125, respectively, give the curves of the flow of the Yealm, the Meavy, the S. Teign at Fernworthy, and the Trenchford Stream in the flood of 24 November 1929. With the exception of the Meavy diagram, all are to the same scale. The scale of the Meavy is the same as for the others as regards time, but in the matter of flow each unit of length represents 2·4 times the value that it has on the other diagrams, a necessity arising from considerations of space. Lastly, it may be noted that the greatest rate of flow on the Yealm in this flood was equivalent to rainfall at the rate of 7·42 in. per day.

THE FLOOD OF 17 AUGUST 1917, ON THE REDAVEN AND THE WEST OCKMENT

The above details apply to a great flood of common order; there is another order of flood, which might be described as either 'extreme' or 'catastrophic'. Such occur but rarely. Three have been known in my lifetime, but I doubt if these floods occur, on the average, more than once in a century.

As regards one such, that of the 17 August 1917, I had the good fortune to be exposed to the full force of the storm which caused it, in the area in which it attained its greatest intensity. Mr. J. S. Amery and my wife shared the experience. It was a thunderstorm, remarkable for the extreme intensity of the rainfall. The slopes of the ground at the point from which we observed it are as steep as 1 in 4, but the whole area of grass was constantly under a thin layer of water, from which the raindrops splashed as they would from a pool. The slopes of South Down, Meldon, were visible after the storm, and it was seen that the fields were filled to the level of the tops of their lower hedges. (Fields were reported as having been similarly filled near Tavistock in a previous storm, I think in 1891.) The front of the storm was narrow, its belt of greatest intensity was of still less width. It crossed a belt of the valley of the West Ockment, but it occupied practically the whole area of the watershed of the Redaven. The effect was, therefore, less in proportion on the Ockment.

On the Redaven, which has a watershed of 990 acres (say 1,000), the highest rate of flow was 3,900 cu. ft of water per second, which is, with 1,000 acres watershed, 3,900 cusecs. The West Ockment, being only subject to the storm over a part of its much larger watershed of

10,810 acres, showed no similar intensity of flood, the flow being no more than 2,600 cu. ft per second, equivalent to 240 cusecs, well within the limit of common floods.

Reverting to the Redaven, the maximum rate of flow was the equivalent of 3·9 in. of rainfall per hour; and, all things considered, it is probable that for at least half an hour the rain was falling at the rate of 6 in. per hour.

The flow of the Redaven falls every year to about one cusec so that the flood reached 3,900 times the normal dry weather flow.

Such a storm performs wonders in the matter of denudation. On the slope of Longstone Hill there was a shallow channel, carrying the drainage of the old road to the Forest Mine, and pointing to the West Ockment some hundred yards below the stepping stones under South Down. Before the storm this may have been 4 ft wide, and perhaps 3 ft deep at its greatest section; after the storm it was found to have been excavated to a depth of from 15 ft to 17 ft 9 in. and a length of 206 ft (Pl. 88B). At the foot of the Redaven, there had been an alluvial flat between this stream and the West Ockment, grass-grown, level, and at one time a garden. The Redaven carried down boulders and and stone and blocked its former channel, cutting a new channel across this flat; it covered a space of 300 ft by 250 ft with rocks and boulders, obliterating the grass which it did not tear away, and stranding boulders of over a ton weight on ground 8 ft above its original channel. [Pl. 88A shows a similar effect in a tributary stream.]

OTHER CATASTROPHIC FLOODS

Catastrophic floods are very rare and very local. It is doubtful whether they occur at an average of one a century, and it seems certain that there are many Dartmoor watersheds which have not received such a visitation within the period of history.

It may be of interest to consider the possible intensity of a catastrophic flood. We may start with the assurance that a rainfall of three inches in half an hour is a possibility. It is also certain that some small watersheds on Dartmoor are practically impervious, and are more than sufficiently steep to ensure that in less than half an hour they could yield a peak flow practically equivalent to the rate of rainfall over the whole area. It follows that on small watersheds a flood peak might reach the rate of 6,000 cusecs per thousand acres. Probably no Dartmoor watershed of over 300 acres in extent has ever approached this extreme.

Records are of necessity very meagre. The mere fact of a very great flood lives in the minds of the people for a few generations, but only as a record of destruction. Data of rainfall and flow-off are not matters which have found preservation, or which could have been ascertained.

Occasionally someone was impressed and made a diary entry, or else placed an inscription in the valley. On the 3 August 1628, John

Rattenbury, of Okehampton, was moved to enter in his diary the following words: "About four o'clocke in the afternoon, immediately after evening prayer ended att the Church of Okehampton, there being noe raine perceived to fall within or neare this towne, and the streets being verye drye, the water now called Lede, or East water was suddenly risen about some v, foote at the Easte bridge running more violent than had usually been knowne, and twas conceived the water did savour and smell of some brimstone."

This, however, was not an instance of a really great flood. On the Cowsic, a little below the aqueduct of the Devonport water supply, there lies on the bank a boulder bearing the inscription:

THIS STONE WAS
REMOVED BY A FLOOD
17

Unfortunately the date was never completed, but the inscription was almost certainly cut at the instance of the Rev. E. A. Bráy, whose father enclosed Beardown, a work which he commenced in or about 1780. It would appear that the incomplete date lay somewhere between this date and 1800. The stone weighs five tons and is well above the ordinary level of the stream. We certainly have the record of a great flood (Pl. 89A).

About an hundred years later this same Cowsic, in 1890, broke into a very great flood, which did not, however, again move the inscribed boulder, but did wash away Beardown Bridge. The same storm affected the River Walkham, where Eggworthy Bridge was destroyed; while on the Tavy the Abbey Bridge Weir at Tavistock was washed away. Thus three watersheds were affected, and the storm must have been relatively extensive with a heavy intensity, but found no record except possibly at some monthly rainfall stations. The date was 17 July 1890.

THE RELATION BETWEEN RAINFALL AND THE
YIELD OF STREAMS

In times of drought every river is sustained by the deferred flow from previous rainfall. At any except the longest continued droughts, the flow of a river after 24 hours without rain will be appreciably reduced. The extent of the reduction is strictly governed by the initial flow, provided that is not much above the mean daily yield of the river. There exists for every river a fixed régime, from which it is possible to foretell the flow at the end of any period of drought, if the flow at the commencement of the period and also the number of days of continuous drought are known. For every river this régime must be ascertained by observation. On the 800 acres at the head of the Yealm watershed it is such that, starting from a yield of 4,000,000 gallons a day, this will be reduced by six days of continuous drought, to 2,000,000, by eighteen days of continuous drought to 1,000,000, and by forty days of continuous drought to 500,000. Another six days will bring the flow down to 415,000 gallons a day, after which the fall is very slow, to a minimum which has not been ascertained by observation. It follows that, if the initial flow is known, it is possible to predict the total flow of the river over any period of successive rainless days.

Fig. 126 gives graphically the régime ascertained for the Yealm watershed of 800 acres.

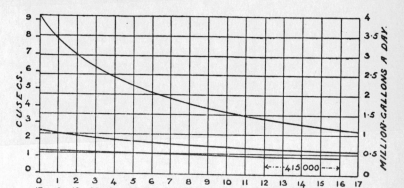

FIG. 126. Drought regime of 800-acre watershed on Upper Yealm.

In a year of mean rainfall 92 per cent of the rain finds its way into, and flows off in the stream of, the upper Yealm. Since the dry days and periods are sustained at the expense of the rainfall days, it is obvious that the immediate run off of rain on wet days or in wet months must bear a less proportion to the rainfall than 92%. To ascertain what proportion of the rain falling in any month actually flows off in the stream during the month it is necessary to know: (a) the rainfall; (b) its equivalent in gallons of water, having regard to the area of the catchment; (c) the actual total flow of the river during the month; (d) the total flow which would have passed down the river had there been no rain during the month.

Then $c-d$ = the yield during the month due to the rainfall a. Table IV gives some selected months from the records of the Yealm watershed.

TABLE IV

Month	(a) inches	(b) gallons	(c) gallons	(d) gallons	(c–d) gallons	(c–d) as a percentage of (b)
November 1929	21·06	381,354,448	325,570,960	26,874,000	298,696,960	78·33
December 1926	1·22	22,019,328	50,995,891	39,830,000	11,165,891	50·71
May, 1927	1·20	21,693,384	22,278,937	18,254,000	4,024,937	18·55
April 1929	1·13	20,462,040	17,268,581	15,506,000	1,762,581	8·62
29 August to 26 September 1928 }	0·80	14,486,400	17,750,406	16,932,000	818,406	5·65

The flow of the river at the commencement of the several periods was as follows: Nov. 1929, 1,642,743 gallons a day; Dec. 1926, 3,019,329; May 1927, 906,669; April 1929, 701,442; 29 Aug. 1928, 852,391.

It remains to express the total yield during each of the above periods as a percentage of the equivalent of the rainfall during the period; the results are as follows: Nov. 1929, 85·37%; Dec. 1926, 231·59%; May 1927, 102·70%; April 1929, 84·39%; 29 Aug. to 26 Sept. 1928, inclusive, 122·53%.

To collect the information given above: November 1929 was an extraordinarily wet month, at many stations the wettest ever recorded. In that month 78·33 % of the rain which fell flowed off as it fell; the total yield of the river, including the yield of previous storage, amounted to no more than 85·37 per cent of the equivalent of the rain falling in the month. But we know that, on the twelve months, at least 92% of the rain found its way to the river; and it may be asked how this is possible if in the wettest month the figures were so much less. The answer is to be found in the comparison of the flow of the river on the first and last days of the month, the initial flow was 1,642,743 gallons a day, the flow on the last day of the month was 4,763,799 gallons a day, so that there was a large carry forward.

The effect of a similar carry forward can be seen in the next two sets of figures. The rainfall in December 1926 was practically identical with that of May 1927, yet the yield of the river in the first-named month was 50,995,891 gallons, as against 22,278,937 gallons for May 1927. But December 1926 followed a month with 14·30 in. of rainfall; while May 1927 followed a month with 4·03 in. of rainfall. And, further, December 1926, opening with the ground saturated by the previous rain, its own rainfall found its way to the stream in a much larger degree than did the rainfall of May 1927.

If occurring after a spell of dry weather, summer showers contribute but little to the river, as will be seen from the data given above; less than 5% of the fall may be effective.

Records of exceptional circumstances are always of interest, I have accordingly prepared a chart of the flow of the Yealm in November 1929 (Fig. 127). It well illustrates the evanescent nature of floods, and the uniformity of their die-away curves.

The close relation between the yield of a river and the rainfall is axiomatic, but even axioms are none the worse for clear statement. I have prepared Fig. 128, which correlates the rainfall and the yield of the Yealm watershed for the year December 1926 to November 1927, inclusive. This shows the cumulative rainfall and the cumulative yield of the stream, the record for each month being successively added. The The scales for rainfall and for yield have been selected to bring the total rainfall for the year and the total yield into coincidence. This must

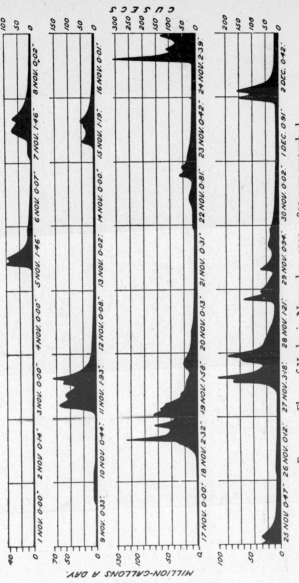

FIG. 127. Flow of Yealm in November, 1929. 800-acre watershed.

not be taken as indicating equality, since the total rainfall was 77·483 in., of which no more than 71·32 in. found their way to the stream. While the coincidence between the curves is marked, it will yet be seen that at times of low rainfall the stream yields more and at times of high rainfall less than the mean annual percentage of the immediate rain. This, as I have said, must follow from the fact that although no rain may be falling, the river still flows.

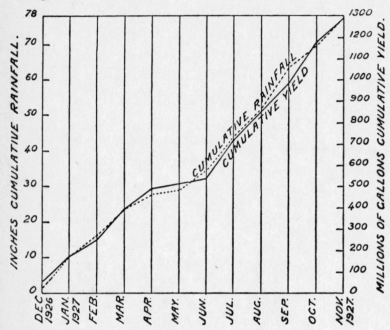

FIG. 128. Rainfall on and yield of 800-acre watershed of
the Upper Yealm; Dec. 1926 – Nov. 1927.

SOME DRY WEATHER YIELDS OF DARTMOOR WATERSHEDS

The first nine months of the year 1929 was very nearly the driest successive nine months recorded on Dartmoor. At South Brent the rainfall of these nine months was 29·86 in., while for the corresponding months in 1921 it was 29·53.

On the Torquay watershed, Trenchford, the first nine months of 1929 were the driest on record.

But the distribution of the rain was such that there were no very prolonged periods of absolute drought, and hence few streams fell to their true minima yields. None the less, the flows recorded in 1929 are good measures of dry weather yields, short, in most instances, of the extreme.

TABLE V. LOWEST YIELDS IN 1929

Stream	Date	Area of watershed acres	Flow in gallons per 24 hours	Flow in cusecs
Yealm	29 Sept.	800	415,260	0·961
Bala Brook	29 Sept.	1,380	590,300	0·792
Meavy	26 July	4,660	3,814,000	1·265
S. Teign	25 Sept.	2,400	1,256,000[1]	0·969
Trenchford	15–28 Sept.	805	71·324	0·164
Blackingstone	13–29 Sept.	445	38,066	0·158

The high figures for dry weather flow and minima for the Meavy are not really comparable with the other returns, the Devonport leat traverses the watershed, which it undoubtedly feeds in dry weather. In some years the Meavy shows a greater yield than the whole rainfall which its catchment receives.

The ascertained minima for several streams at periods of extreme drought are given in Table VI.

TABLE VI. MINIMA FOR PERIODS OF EXTREME DROUGHT

Stream	Area of watershed acres	Cusecs
Meavy	4,660	1·111
West Dart	1,728	0·697
Cowsic	1,334	0·796
Blackabrook	1,600	0·607
Swincombe	3,622	0·809
Trenchford	805	0·146
Blackingstone	445	0·158

Among these figures it may be remarked that there is some doubt whether the minimum for the Meavy should not be set at 1·09 cusecs; and in any event see the above note as to the Meavy.

The minima which have been recorded from watersheds where only short-term records are available have been collected in Table VII. Some of these are probably very near to being true minima.

TABLE VII. MINIMA FROM WATERSHEDS OF SHORT RECORD

Stream	Area of Watershed acres	Yield as cusecs per 1000 acres
Swincombe	3,620	0·809
S. Teign	2,400	0·740
Bala Brook (Avon)	1,380	0·664
Yealm	800	0·753
Butterbrook (Erme)	480	0·600
Harbourne	400	0·700

[1] Possibly to some extent increased by leakage from Vitifer Leat.

The figure for Harbourne, however, is for one year's observation only: the true minimum is probably near 0·60. It is also very doubtful whether the yield of the Swincombe in extreme drought exceeds the yield of the Cowsic. But the Devonport leat traverses the watershed of the Swincombe as well as that of the Meavy, and the rather high figure may well be due to leakage from that leat.

My sincerest thanks are due to Mr. S. C. Chapman and Mr. F. Howarth, and my respect to the memory of the late Mr. Harry Francis for information freely given, which has enabled me to check my personal observations, and to fill gaps in my statement; the figures for watersheds under their control have mostly been supplied, always checked, from data which they have given.

Note. Wherever the word '*cusecs*' occurs in a table or diagram, it is to be read as '*cusecs per thousand acres*'.

Note. It will be found that above I have frequently stated quantities of the order of many millions with the apparently minute accuracy involved in using single units. It should be understood that no pretence is made to the high degree of accuracy which this might be supposed to suggest. It is my habit, where figures are the result of direct observation, to give them as observed, without substituting the nearest 'round numbers': they are quite as easily handled, and the personal equation is eliminated.

APPENDIX II

NOTES ON GRANITE

WEATHERING

THERE is no evidence either documentary or physical that quarries were worked in the Dartmoor granite prior to the early days of the nineteenth century. Shallow working on the Roborough Down elvan was certainly earlier, but even as to this Marshall, writing in 1796, speaks of "Rooborough stone" as then being found scattered in detached blocks. He refers also to "Moorstone or Quartzose Granite" as being found plentifully.

This old name 'moorstone' was applied to the surface blocks and boulders which were the sole source of granite for building purposes. All such blocks must have been exposed to weathering through long ages, and yet many of them were found to yield building material of good quality. Even in these days of quarries the surface stone is still resorted to, and much of it is excellent.

It is obvious that the Dartmoor granite does not yield readily to the weather. The hut-circles, stone rows, kistvaens and other works of the early bronze age were constructed with unwrought surface blocks; and in the three to four thousand years which have elapsed since they were erected there is no evidence that any appreciable deterioration has been caused by the weather.

Siwards Cross is referred to in a document of the thirteenth century, and, beyond its wanton breakage in the nineteenth, it stands to-day much as it must have left the mason's hands.

Fice's Well by the Blackabrook near Princetown bears on its lintel the inscription, in raised letters, "I F 1568", and the conduit which stood outside Old Town Gate in Plymouth, and which is now incorporated in part in a drinking fountain at Drake's Place, is dated 1598, also in raised letters. In each instance the inscription is still clear, so that over three centuries on the moorland heights or in a town atmosphere have had little effect upon the granite surface. It is true that the Plymouth City Council has caused the letters at Drake's Place to be chased around their outline with a point, and has thus exercised its best endeavours to shorten their being.

On the other hand some of the inscriptions on old altar tombs in moorland churchyards are badly worn, as far as the raised letters on the flat slab are concerned. The majority of these date from the seventeenth century. Since the water lodges between the letters on the horizontal slab, the conditions are not favourable to the preservation of the inscriptions. Even so, many are in good condition, as for example the grave of John Gray, who died at North Bovey on the 21 December 1643.

Incised inscriptions, still quite legible, may be found on memorials which date from the seventh century or thereabout, as in the Vicarage Garden at Tavistock.

With these evidences of the enduring quality of Dartmoor granite we may contrast the certainty of its ultimate yield to the elements. On many a Dartmoor Tor it is quite possible in the darkest of foggy nights to determine the points of the compass; and this by noting the face on which the rock has been most deeply incised by the weather, That face will be approximately towards the S.S.W., the direction of the prevailing and wettest wind. The joints which mark out the pseudo-bedding and the more or less vertical joints which cross these give access to the drifting rain, and thus form planes of weakness. On the whole the coarse-grained granites, with the larger felspar crystals, yield more readily; the finer grained rocks are less affected.

At solid angles between two planes the moisture can penetrate from two directions simultaneously. Thus all edges are liable to more intense attack than are plane surfaces. At solid angles formed by three planes the moisture can penetrate from three directions simultaneously, and thus corners are liable to even more intense weathering. From the suppression of angles by weathering rounded forms arise. The extent of such rounding depends on the nature of the rock. It may be very marked, as at Higher Whiten Tor on the West Dart, or a mere dulling of the angles, as at Hen Tor in the Plym Valley. At times this action results in the formation of a poised block, a good example of which is to be seen on Great Mis Tor, near the rock basin (Pl. 11A). And the poised block may be so balanced as to be capable of movement, when it is known as a 'logan'.

This suppression of angular form is not confined to sub-aerial rocks; it occurs also below ground level. Here, too, the primary agent is moisture. At the shallower depths it may in the past have been aided by frost; but, since the action has been traced at depths greater than 100 feet, frost can hardly have been an essential auxiliary, even during the Ice Age. Large areas of Dartmoor are underlain, not by solid granite, but by a decomposed granite, locally known as growan. In this growan will be found boulder-shaped cores of undecomposed granite, material better calculated to resist decomposition, either from difference in composition or mineral form, or because originally a large mass marked out by pseudo-bedding and joints, alongside smaller masses so marked out. The disease known as growanization spreads along the joints, whether horizontal or vertical, and if it proceeds inward from every joint with equal speed, will obviously have affected all parts of a small block long before the heart of a large block has been attacked. Like subaerial weathering it tends to suppress edges and angles, and thus the cores of the larger blocks may be left in boulder form as hard masses in the body of the growan. The roadside near Sheepstor Dam at Burrator shows some such boulders; others may be seen at Inga Tor, in the quarry, and yet others near Lustleigh Station, in the railway cutting.

It is not every fine-grained granitic rock that can resist either weathering or growanization. By the same roadside near Sheepstor Dam may be seen a vein of pink felsite in the granite, as thoroughly reduced to growan as the granite itself. And at Riders Rings, in the Avon Valley, a similar felsite has been in part weathered to a material so soft that it has been denuded, leaving in the surface soil very numerous spheres of quartz-and-schorl, which were formerly distributed through the felsite like figs in a pudding.

Sometimes the chief effect of weathering is to open up the joints of the granite, and reduce it to a collection of scattered blocks. From these the 'clitters' of the tors are derived. Such clitters are well developed at Hen Tor, and on Mis

HEN TOR.

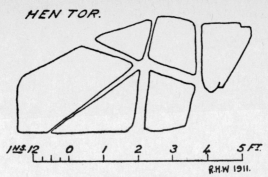

R.H.W 1911.

FIG. 129. Parted block of granite, Hen Tor.

Tor. Wistmans Wood owes its existence to three such clitters, and so deep is the mass of rocks that all the time which has elapsed since its formation has not sufficed for the infilling of the cavities between the blocks by vegetable soil.

Even after a block has been removed from its parent living rock it is still liable to subdivision by the weather. There lies near the summit of Hen Tor a slab of which a measured sketch is given in Fig. 129. It is now in six parts, but if any reader has a mind to treat the drawing as a jig-saw puzzle it will be found easy to restore the original form. A view of a less elaborate parting, from Huntingdon Warren, is given in Pl. 89B.

Rock basins are another effect of weather action (see pp. 28–32).

GEOLOGY

The following references should be added to the list at the end of the chapter on Dartmoor granite (p. 63) (ED.).

Brammall, A., 1926a. The Dartmoor Granite. *Proc. Geol. Assn.:* Vol. 37, pp. 251–77.

Brammall, A., 1926b. Excursion to Dartmoor. *Proc. Geol. Assn.*, Vol. 37, pp. 278 82.

Brammall, A. & Harwood, H. F., 1932. The Dartmoor granites: their genetic relationships. *Quart. Journ. Geol. Soc.:* Vol. 88, pp. 171–237.

Fitch, A. A., 1932. Contact metamorphism in South-Eastern Dartmoor. *Quart. Journ. Geol. Soc.*, Vol. 88, pp. 576–606.

APPENDIX III

ON TWO STONE IMPLEMENTS

A FLINT IMPLEMENT OF PALAEOLITHIC TYPE FROM DARTMOOR

IN May 1931, during a walk on the Moor, I obtained a flint implement which presents features of interest and a problem. It belongs to the type which Evans has called *"tongue shaped"*, and which more recently has mainly been described as *Coup de poing* or *Hand-Axe*. The implement is 108 millimetres in length, its greatest width is 60 millimetres, and its greatest thickness (at the bulbous end) is 37 millimetres, the weight being 6·44 ounces. The material is grey flint, more fully whitened by soil agencies and with a more completely matt surface than I can match among the items of my Dartmoor collection. Only where a slight tint of grey yet remains is there any trace of the natural lustre of flint. It is true that flints from Dartmoor vary much in externals, some are as fresh as when struck from the core, and others are much patinated. But, for the more part, those most bleached show signs of having been fired, and have probably been at or very near the surface when heather fires have raged. Fire does not appear to have touched this implement. Its appearance is consistent with, but does not fully imply, a great age.

Had I seen it in a general collection, without indication of locality, I would have unhesitatingly identified it as a palaeolith of comparatively early type, both from the form and workmanship. Among other resemblances to the early type, this implement has a considerable patch of the original outer skin of the flint nodule left, at the bulbous end. Form and condition are thus consistent with palaeolithic origin.

On the other hand, it is not fully agreed that these tongue-shaped forms are wholly confined to times earlier than the neolithic. Evans himself writes that he has found them associated with polished tools on the shores of Lough Neagh, but he claims that these later examples, though analogous in form, differ in character of workmanship; and, while a single specimen may be doubtful, groups can be discriminated. Since this example is, as far as I know, unique in being of Dartmoor origin, group comparison is impossible. It lies before me, beside a palaeolith from Kent. I can only say that it is more typical than the type.

The one certainty is that it adds to the published record of Dartmoor a new form of implement; which *may* be a relic of palaeolithic man; or *may* be evidence that this form of tool was not unknown to the builders of the hut-circles.

The locality of the find was on the water-parting between the Avon and the Erme, near Western Whitaburrow, at an elevation of approximately 1,450 feet O.D.

Plate 90, figs. 1, 2 and 3 supply photographs of this implement. If any similar finds on Dartmoor are known, it would be of great interest to have details.

A STONE IMPLEMENT FOUND NEAR WHEAL JEWELL, MARYTAVY

At one of the winter meetings of the Plymouth Branch of the Devonshire Association Mrs. Terrell showed a stone implement which had been found at Wheal Jewell, near Willsworthy, in the parish of Marytavy. This has some unusual features, and by the kindness of Mrs. Terrell I have been permitted to photograph and describe it.

The implement is made from the local 'epidiorite', it is in part rough-hewn; in part has been ground and polished. The stone where polished is nearly black.

The length of the implement is $7\frac{3}{8}$ in., its greatest width at the cutting edge is $3\frac{1}{16}$ in., and its greatest thickness is $1\frac{3}{8}$ in. The three photographs on Plate 91 show either face and a side view. It will be seen that the tool has a general resemblance to a celt, but is very unusual in that the grinding is asymmetrical, the upper face in the photograph being strongly curved, and the under face nearly straight. At about two-thirds of the length from the cutting edge the stone has been reduced by two large flakes having been struck off, as shewn in the upper figure. Between these the surface is that of a natural joint in the rock, and will be seen to have weathered a much lighter colour. The end farthest from the cutting edge is partly shaped by nature and gives no evidence of any intent to create a pointed tool.

The reduction of the section to which I have referred has the effect of giving a very comfortable grip when held in the hand with the curved face of the edge downward, and I attribute some importance to this fact, since that is precisely the position in which the implement would be held were it a flenching tool used for removing hides from carcases.

I have in my collection a flenching tool in stone, used within a generation by Canadian Indians; the curves at the edge are precisely similar to those of the implement under consideration, the curve on the one side being marked, with a practically plane face on the other side. The Indian tool is smaller, but the grip is identical.

I believe this implement from Marytavy to have been a flenching tool, and I am not prepared to assert that it belongs to the days of pre-history, nor am I prepared to deny.

Evans, 1890 (p. 139, fig. 85), figures a somewhat similar stone, but with the convexity of one face at the edge even more marked. This implement was found in the Shetlands, and is said to appear to be made of a hard clay slate. He figures yet another (p. 122, fig. 66) from Yorkshire, and that has been formed from hard shelly limestone. In each case which he quotes the choice of material makes it more likely that the stones had some such use as the removal of hides, rather than that they were axes, adzes or other cutting tools. The Indian tool to which I have referred is formed in schistose rock.

APPENDIX IV

STONE ROWS AND ASTRONOMICAL THEORY

(Extract from the *President's Address*, Plymouth Institution, 1906, dealing with start-ling claims by Sir Norman Lockyer in a work entitled *Stonehenge and other British Stone Monuments astronomically considered*.)

NO stone row on Dartmoor that attains any length is absolutely straight, and no circle of any dimensions is truly circular. Regarding orientation, there are two definite facts observable: the direction of length of the Dartmoor kistvaen points, with scarcely a single exception, somewhere within the NW. and SE. quadrants; the Dartmoor stone rows point, with slight exception, somewhere within the NE. and SW. quadrants,[1] but in either case there is a range of over one hundred degrees; and individual kistvaens and rows are fairly uniformly distributed throughout that range.

It is notorious that where a row descending a hill reaches a position out of sight of its point of origin, there it will deviate, sometimes wildly, from its course; if, climbing up the far slope of the valley, it once again gets within sight of its commencement, the alignment is again directed toward it, but exactitude is neither accomplished nor apparently desired.

Now, in this apparent indifference to mathematical accuracy, there is a diffi-culty for those who desire to make of the stone rows and circles early astro-nomical instruments of precision. A little ingenuity reduces the difficulty. The nutation of the earth's axis and precession of the equinoxes cause the apparent position of any star in the heavens to shift slightly as the years pass by. Take, then, a stone row which has one slight change in direction, you may say that one part was constructed at a given date, and the remainder added years later when the star had varied in declination. Since you may call either end of the row the earliest, this meets all possible cases of slight distortion, where only two directions are involved. Or, again, in travelling over ground of varying in-clination, no stone row could be straight were it kept constantly directed on the rising or setting place of a star, for the height of the horizon would vary, and with it the star's amplitude. Hence it might be expected that alignments on un-even ground would curve. But this last solution of one of the difficulties con-fronting certain astronomical theories is also one of the most critical tests of the accuracy of such theory. Truly, the stone row on the Erme (see p. 204, fig. 72, Pl. 43), the longest known in the world, does pursue a serpentine course over the hills, but that course is entirely inconsistent with the suggested explanation. It turns too much, or it turns too little; it refuses to faithfully and consistently deviate in even the right direction. This is awkward, but not to be permitted to negative a promising hypothesis while human ingenuity yet exists. I proposed

[1] This generalization has been modified (see p. 242). (ED.)

the matter for Sir Norman Lockyer's consideration, and he replies in *Nature* of 13th July 1905. First by pointing out that a stone row may not always be what it seems—it might be a hedge or a road, for instance—secondly, in the following words:

"I think it possible that in the Staldon Moor Row we have a mixture of religious and practical intention, at which I have before hinted. Both Mr. Lukis and Mr. Hansford Worth have studied this monument, which is two miles and a quarter long. There is a circle at the south end about sixty feet in diameter, while at its northern end there is a cairn. Where the line starts from the circle the direction of the row is parallel to many sight-lines in Cornwall, and Arcturus would rise in the azimuth indicated. But this direction is afterwards given up for one which leads towards an important collection of circles, and it crosses the Erme, no doubt at the most convenient spot. More to the north it crosses another stream and the bog of Red Lake. All this is surely practical enough, although the way indicated might have been followed by the priests of the hut circles to the stone circle, to prepare the morning sacrifice, and go through the ritual."

Thus Sir Norman, and so we come back to the white-robed priest, this time engaged in producing a combination of cathedral and signpost which must probably stand unique. I fear this ill-conditioned row had to be disposed of to clear the ground for further advance.

I am content to test the point of mixed uses for stone rows by Sir Norman Lockyer's own selected instance. Here is an alignment beginning with a circle and barrow, and ending in a barrow. It has associated with it at least one cairn. In this and its construction it is the counterpart of other rows, only its length is exceptional.

Wherever it curves it does so for the obvious reason that the point of origin is lost to view, and I may add that its departures from the right line cannot be accounted for by variations in the height of the horizon coupled with constancy to one bright particular star.

The important group of hut-circles to which it is said to directly lead is, I presume, at Erme Pound. It does not lead to this enclosure, but passes by on the other side of the river. And it takes about the worst possible ground of approach. The modern track (indicated on the Ordnance map) shows how it should have proceeded, had that been its objective. It continues northward, it is suggested, in order to point the proper crossing of Redlake and the adjacent miry ground. A quite unnecessary act on its part, as many other crossings are better and there is no serious difficulty anywhere. But why does it go further north still? It leads nowhere but to a barrow.

Beginning nowhere, topographically speaking, it ends nowhere, and as a directing mark is valueless. Now if there were priests, and they did indeed visit the circle of a morning, they would soon have beaten a track of quite sufficient distinctness for their feet to feel, even were their eyes elsewhere. You know the ordinary Dartmoor track, worn by casual and infrequent use; it is easily followed, and here I dare assert the priests must have made a comparative turnpike had they assiduously followed their duties.

And why, I ask, should the priests from Erme Pound and the adjacent enclosure have required to frequent Staldon Circle in bad and misty weather when in fact they had an excellent stone row of their own actually touching one of

their enclosures on Brown Heath? Whatever the value of the suggestion that
the southern end of the long alignment in Erme Valley was constructed to point
to Arcturus, the statement that the remainder of the row was a track line to
guide priests or wayfarers to and from Erme Pound or across Redlake seems to
me to do violence to every feature of the case. It could hardly have been made
by anyone really familiar with the neighbourhood, which by the way I believe
the author of the latest astronomical theory has never visited.

Let us clearly understand Sir Norman Lockyer's views on the astronomical
uses of Dartmoor stone rows and circles. He began his labours with Egyptian
temples, next attacked Stonehenge, then the Cornish remains, and, I believe,
Maes Howe in the Orkneys, and has ended for the time on Dartmoor. His
astronomy is of course beyond criticism, and, indeed, all that is required is a
good star map, a knowledge of the precession of the equinoxes and a table of
declinations and amplitudes.

He assumes priest astronomers, and that they were interested in the May
and solstitial year, and above all in sunrise on May Day and at the solstices.
This being so, he assumes that they used certain morning stars as heralds of the
sun's advent on these especial days, and pointed stone rows and other monuments to the place of rising of these stars. The Pleiades were to his mind the
favourite constellation, but Arcturus, Betelgeuse, Sirius, Antares, and the sun
itself, are also involved.

In all, six stars and the sun are utilized for this theory, and the other variants
are: dates from 2170 B.C. to 700 B.C.; seasons, May morning, November,
February, December, and August; pointers, stone rows, the undefined centres
of circles, modern stone directing-posts (selected), selected barrows out of
many, medieval crosses, menhirs, 'priests' houses', by which title cromlechs
are, it appears, to be known in future, earth banks, and natural hills. The construction of a single monument is, if necessary, assumed to have been spread
over 400 or 500 years or more.

Granted the same wide range, you can obtain coincidences anywhere. I am
prepared to prove that the rope-walks of Devon and Cornwall all have
astronomical significance if you will accept as proof the results of such method
as I have described.

Coincidences, I have said, must arise; I will emphasize this from our theorist's
own work. At the Hurlers, in Cornwall, he found that a line from the southern
circle to a medieval cross pointed to November sunset; he promptly annexed
the cross, saying that it replaced an ancient menhir. Around the Hurlers are
many barrows; out of these four were selected. One gives a line to Arcturus,
1900 B.C.; another to Sirius, 1690 B.C.; a third to November sunrise; and a
fourth to Antares, 1720 B.C. But all these bearings are not from the same circle,
nor are all the barrows utilized: the selection is that of such as serve the theory,
and no other principle is involved.

We then come to Merivale (see p. 215, fig. 74). There we are told that the
avenues were directed on the Pleiades in 1580 B.C. and 1420 B.C. respectively,
and the Pleiades are selected because it is on equally good authority asserted that
the Hecatompedon at Athens was aligned on that constellation in 1495 B.C.
There are cairns and a kistvaen handy, but these return no favourable result.
There is, however, a circle, which in fact is a misshapen ellipse, and there are
five or six modern or comparatively recent stone directing-posts, marking out

a line toward Foggintor. Two of these separately aligned with the assumed centre of the circle are also brought into use.

The reason assigned is that they give astronomical bearings and are larger than boundary stones should be. The first is true, the second founded on ignorance. Six-feet bound stones are not uncommon and can be purchased at half a crown apiece.

More startling still, a small branch row, which would ordinarily be judged an afterthought to the southern avenue, is alleged to have been directed to Arcturus in 1860 B.C., or 280 years before the erection of any part of the remainder of the monument. The South Avenue itself must, according to the hypothesis adopted, have been under construction for a period of at least 160 years.

In considering the Merivale avenues, Sir Norman provides for us a criterion which may be applied to his other selected instances with a view to estimating his consistency. He determines that the 'blocking-stone' was really a sighting stone erected at that end of the row toward which the priestly observer looked, and hence at the end over which the particular star to be observed would rise or set.

Challacombe stone rows, not far from Grimspound, lie on the north slope of a hill and point 23° 37′ NW. or SE. (see p. 226). Southward they terminate in a fine blocking-stone, which, viewed from the north end, breaks the southern horizon (Pl. 47, 2). Northward one row appears to have a small blocking stone, which, viewed from the south end, is lost under the mass of Birch Tor (Pl. 47, 1). Observe that if you or I wished to point a stone row to the north horizon we should select a southern slope, and so let it be directed to the sky, and a north slope if we desired to point to the south horizon. In no case should we direct it to the base of a hill and have to transfer the alignment by estimation up the whole slope before we reached the sky line. The hill above the north end has an elevation of 4° 50′. Again the theory clashes with the plain probabilities of the case: the southern blocking-stone has to become a 'terminal menhir', the difficulty of the northern hill is ignored, and the row claimed as pointing to setting Arcturus in the northern sky as warning the sunrise of the summer solstice 1860 B.C. If this be so, one must despise the judgment of the primitive astronomer. His obvious advantage lay in constructing this row on the south slope, letting it break the sky line, and obtaining a greater angular elevation of the horizon, thus making the direction "useful for a longer period of time"; and he would have placed his blocking-stone at the north and not at the south end, if it was to act as a sighting point for a northerly direction.

But Trowlesworthy (see p. 209) presents an even better instance of haphazard coincidences utilized to support preconceived theories. I premise that Sir Norman has never visited the stone row of this hill, and that six-inch Ordnance maps are not a very closely contoured.

The double row is curved. This is shown, but none too accurately, on the Ordnance: there the curvature is five degrees, in fact it is 7° 30′ 0″. Five degrees, according to the theorist, means that this row was fifty years under construction; correct this, and we shall not be far wrong in substituting seventy-five years. It pointed to Arcturus in, say, 2100 B.C., we are told. If so, why is there a circle at the north (or Arcturus) end? Elsewhere we are led to believe that the circle was the place occupied by the observer; it should therefore be at the south end. But in any case the matter is unimportant, for it is the fact that each end of the avenue is invisible from the other, a rather startling circumstance in any monument used as a pointer.

The single row is supposed to have been dedicated to the Pleiades, its date 1680 B.C. It too is kinked, in this case to the extent of 6° 30'. A blocking-stone at the eastern end and a comparatively high stone at the west conform to the criterion before given and accord to the proposed assignment of the monument. But the east end is provided with a circle, which is contrary in its suggestion, as indicating that the observer stood here and looked west. Emmett's Post, a somewhat doubtful tumulus, is worked in and aligned with the circle of the avenue on the solstitial sunset in December. We may let that pass, with the sole remark that there is also a stone cross not very far from Emmett's Post, and if the cross at the Hurlers is adopted for a sight line, why not this mediæval monument also? But the Ordnance shows another tumulus or barrow lying temptingly in Azimuth s. 64° E. of the same circle. This, we are told, gives the May year sunrises in November and February. It calls from the astronomer the remark, "The remains here are most interesting. This is the only monument on Dartmoor in which I have so far traced any attempt to locate the sun's place at rising either for the May or solstitial year." It is rather hard to have to destroy this assertion, but in truth the barrow is behind a hill and cannot be seen from the circle; which goes to show that mere inspection of Ordnance maps does not suffice for archæological investigations, and that so inclusive are the conditions which Sir Norman Lockyer allows himself that our rude forefathers could not avoid having their works swept up into his all-capturing net, even when they took the precaution to negative the idea of sight-lines by placing each of two objects on alternate sides of an obscurant rise in the ground which must convince everyone that here at least astronomical significance is absolutely inconceivable.

When a scientist, eminent in his own particular branch, attacks problems of a baffling nature, armed with a few Ordnance sheets, and prepared by visits to occasional localities of interest, his lightest word, on the faith of his well-earned reputation, is apt to be treasured by the general public. I wish to enter a caveat. I assert not, I deny not. Stone rows may have been astronomical observatories, or very probably they were not. In any case, one can devise a much simpler, but equally fanciful, explanation, which inclusively embraces all stone rows and all kistvaens, and requires the sun alone, out of the whole host of the heavens. Given a little time, yet other schemes could be brought into existence, consistent with the facts. Such artificial products prove nothing, except the ingenuity of their inventor. But they should avoid utilizing directing-posts, crosses, and tumuli on the far side of intervening hills, and should not claim such precise knowledge of the supposed cult of the May and solstitial years. One could prefer not to call cromlechs 'priests' houses', or to assert that barrows, cairns, and graves found associated with stone rows were later additions. And when a stone row fails to conform to a theory it is not well to dub it a footpath. These appear to me to be blemishes. Of Sir Norman Lockyer's absolute desire to aid in the solution of what has long been, and must, I fear, remain, a mystery, I have no lingering doubt. His work is one of all honesty of purpose, and the defects are due to insufficient acquaintance with the whole of the circumstances. None the less, it is a duty which is owing to the public that his great authority in matters astronomical should not be allowed to bias our minds or divert our criticism when he wanders in archæological paths. And if occasionally the one available argument is the *reductio ad absurdum*, believe me, it is adopted in no unkindly spirit.

He is not the first to bring astronomy forward to explain our megalithic monuments. In 1750 Chapple had constructed out of Drewsteignton Cromlech (Fig. 60) a complete observatory. A few years later Polwhele cited his discoveries, and added, after setting them forth minutely, "All this is wonderful indeed."

APPENDIX V

INDEX TO DARTMOOR LOCALITIES FOR BARROWS, CAIRNS, AND KISTVAENS

MENTIONED IN THE TRANSACTIONS OF THE DEVONSHIRE ASSOCIATION

O = Actual results of opening or reopening Barrows, by accredited observers. *Localities entered in italic.*
Rep. = Reported on completely, usually with some detail.
L = Quotation, or reference.
R = Passage reference only, without detail.
B = BARROW COMMITTEE'S REPORT.
E = DARTMOOR EXPLORATION COMMITTEE'S REPORT.

Locality	Nature of Data	Vol. of T.D.A.	Report	Page
Amicombe Hill	L	14	B4	158
Archerton	L	14	B4	158
Archerton Tennis Ground	Rep.	22	—	207
„ „	Rep.	23	—	314
„ „	Rep.	70	B57	60
Archerton Newtake	O	33	E7	135
Archerton Newtake, between Row Tor Marsh Brook and Cherrybrook	O	33	E7	136
Auswell (Ausewell, Awsewell, Hazwell)	R	6	—	263
„ „	L	11	B1	147
„ „	Rep.	54	B41	69

Avon Valley (see Black Tor, Brent Fore Hill, Brent Moor House, Brockhill Ford, Buckland Ford, Huntingdon Warren Ho.)
Aylesbarrow (see Eylesbarrow)

Locality	Nature of Data	Vol. of T.D.A.	Report	Page
Barn Hill, Whitchurch	Rep.	52	B39	79
Bear Down House, near	L	22	—	201
Bellaford (Bellever, Belliver) and Lakehead Newtakes (see Lakehead and Bellaford Newtakes)				
Bellaford Newtake	Rep.	22	—	206
	Rep.	67	B54	78
Bellaford Tor, western slope	O	33	E7	136
„ „ south west slope	Rep.	22	—	203
Belstone Tor	R	20	B10	46
Blackabrook, nr. Princetown	Rep.	44	B31	83
„ „	Rep.	57	B44	71
„ „	Rep.	60	B47	77
„ nr. Ockery Br.	Rep.	33	—	496
„ and W. Dart, between	Rep.	44	B31	84
„ Blakey Tor	Rep.	44	B31	84
„ S. of Round Hill	Rep.	22	—	203
„ (see also Round Hill; Royal Hill)				
Black Down, Lydford	L	11	B1	148
„ „	R	20	B10	47
„ (see also Black Hill, White Hill)				
Black Hill (Gibbet Hill) Lydford	Rep.	23	B13	118
Black Newtake, nr. Cherrybrook	Rep.	22	—	204
„ „	Rep.	70	B57	62
„ (see also Dunnabridge Common)				
Blackslade Down	Rep.	66	B53	41
„ (see also Tunhill Rocks)				
Black Tor, Avon Valley	Rep.	78	B65	49
Black Tor, Meavy Valley	L	14	B4	157
Blackey Tor (see Blackabrook)				
Brent Fore Hill, Avon Valley	Rep.	41	B28	93
Brent Moor House, Avon Valley	Rep.	78	B65	49
„ „	Rep.	79	B66	31
Bridestowe, Crossheath Burrow	Rep.	30	B17	79
Bridestowe, Leawood Plantation	Rep.	84	—	242
Bridford	L	11	B1	148
„	Rep.	73	B60	56–9
Brisworthy, Ring Moor Down	O	42	B29	62
„	O	48	B35	99
Broad Down (Broadun), Postbridge	L	14	B4	158
„ „ „ „	O	26	—	192
Brockhill Ford, Avon Valley	Rep.	81	B68	53
Brownheath, Erme Valley	Rep.	4	—	502
„ „	Rep.	51	B38	79
Buckland Ford, Avon Valley	Rep.	78	B65	49
Burford Down, Erme Valley	Rep.	53	B40	84
„ „	Rep.	37	—	460
Butterdon Hill (Butterton)	Rep.	37	—	460

Locality	Nature of Data	Vol. of T.D.A.	Report	Page
Redlake Foot, Erme Valley (see Erme Pound)				
Renny (Ranny) Brook, Yealm Valley	Rep.	71	B58	70
,, ,,	Rep.	77	B64	55
,, ,,	Rep.	81	B68	53
,, ,,	Rep.	82	B69	45
Riddon Ridge	O	46	B33	94
Ring Hill: Postbridge	O	35	B22	141
Ringmoor Down	Rep.	42	B29	62
,,	Rep.	73	—	234
,,	Rep.	76	B63	39
,, (see also Brisworthy, Guttor, Legis Lake and Tor)				
Roborough Down	L	11	B1	158
,,	Rep.	81	B69	54
Round Hill, Princetown	Rep.	33	—	496–8
,, ,,	Rep.	44	B31	84
,, ,,	Rep.	57	B44	71
,, (see also Blackabrook)				
Roundy Park, Postbridge	Rep.	34	B21	113
Router (Row Tor) Brook	Rep.	23	—	313
,, (see also Archerton Newtake)				
Royal Hill, Princetown	Rep.	22	—	205
,, ,,	Rep.	33	—	499
,, ,,	Rep.	40	B27	84
,, ,,	Rep.	60	B47	77
Saddleborough, Shaugh	Rep.	17	B7	130
Seven Lords Land, Hemsworthy Gate	Rep.	66	B53	41
Sharpitor (Sharp Tor), Ugborough	L	11	B1	15
,, ,,	L	14	B4	156
,, ,,	R	20	B10	47
,, ,,	Rep.	79	B66	33
Sharpitor (Sharp Tor), Meavy Valley	Rep.	55	B42	50
Shaugh Common (see Hawk's Tor, Saddleborough, Shaugh Moor)				
Shaugh Lake	O	28	B15	84
Shaugh Moor	Rep.	50	—	403
Shavercombe: Plym Valley	Rep.	4	—	513
,, ,,	Rep.	22	B12	50
,, ,,	O	33	B20	119
,, ,,	Rep.	65	B52	83–4
Shell Top	O, Rep.	4	—	507, 509
,,	R	20	B10	47
,,	Rep.	24	B14	47
Shelstone (Shilstone) and En(d)sworthy	L	14	B4	153
,, (see also Drewsteignton)				

Locality	Nature of Data	Vol. of T.D.A.	Report	Page
Shuggledown (Shuffledown, Shoveldown)	Rep.	4	—	509
,,	Rep.	64	—	284–5
,,	Rep.	69	B56	97
Single Barrow (see Hamel Down)				
Skir Hill (see Hensroost)				
Snowdon	Rep.	37	—	459
Sousson's Common	Rep.	30	E5	2
,, ,,	Rep.	22	—	206
,, ,,	O	35	B22	142
,, ,,	O	36	B23	101
,, ,,	Rep.	58	B45	117
,, Red Barrows	O	35	E9	144
Spurrell's Cross, Erme Valley	Rep.	40	—	282
Stall Down, Stalldon, Stall Moor	Rep.	24	B14	48
,, ,,	Rep.	29	E4	146
,, ,,	Rep.	37	—	461
,, ,,	Rep.	38	—	536
,, ,,	Rep.	50	B37	186
,, ,,	Rep.	73	—	227, 235
,, ,,	Rep.	75	B62	55
Stanlake, Meavy Valley	Rep.	79	B66	31
Stannon Bottom	O	28	B15	84
Stannon Hill	L	22	—	201
Stannon Hill, Little Newlake	Rep.	70	B57	59
Stannon Newtake	Rep.	37	—	459
Steeperton Tor Ridge	Rep.	22	—	189
Stennen Hill, nr. Powder Mills	Rep.	70	B57	61
Swincombe (see Childes Tomb, Fox Tor Mire and Newtake, Joan Ford's New-take, O Brook, Princetown)				
Tavy Valley (see Hare Tor, Homer Redlake)				
Teign Head	R	20	B10	46
Thornworthy: Chagford	O	12	—	365
,, ,,	R	20	B10	46
,, ,,	Rep.	29	B16	70
,, ,,	L	22	—	202
,, ,,	Rep.	69	B56	75
,, ,,	Rep.	64	—	287
Three Barrow Tor (Three Barrows)	O	5	—	553
,, ,,	L	11	B1	159
,, ,,	L	14	B4	155
,, ,,	R	20	B10	47
,, ,,	Rep.	69	B56	81
,, ,,	L	76	B63	40
Tor Royal (see Crock of Gold)				
Top Tor, Widecombe	R	66	B53	41

Locality	Nature of Data	Vol. of T.D.A.	Report	Page
Yealm Valley (see Harrowthorn Plantation, Renny Brook)				
Yellow Mead, Lydford	Rep.	23	B13	118
Yellowmead Down, Sheepstor	Rep.	54	B41	70
„ „	Rep.	69	B56	99
Yellowmead Farm, Walkhampton	Rep.	80	B67	37
Yes Tor	R	20	B10	46

Note. For barrows associated with stone rows, see also Vol. 78 : 285–315, and Vol. 79 : 175–86. A revised list of kistvaens is given by C. E. Birkett Dixon in Vol. 84 (BR70) : 249–53.

APPENDIX VI

STRAY NOTES ON THE TEIGN VALLEY

SPINSTERS ROCK

LIKE many dolmens, or as we more usually call them, cromlechs, the Spinsters Rock consists of a cap-stone supported by uprights, the spaces between which admit ready access to the area covered by the cap-stone (p. 180). But the evidence seems conclusive that in their original form the dolmens constituted completely enclosed chambers, in which four stones at times sufficed to form the sides and ends, while in other and larger of these structures it took a greater number to close the space.

At Chun dolmen near St. Just, there are but two side and two end stones, and it is at once apparent that a dolmen is but a larger form of the kistvaen; at Trethevy, St. Cleer, a single stone at either end suffices, but for the sides two stones on either side are required.

Now, as a general rule under such circumstances, three points of support, and three only, will be found to be effective; hence any of the enclosing stones can be removed, provided that three are left so placed that the centre of gravity of the cap-stone falls within the triangle formed by their points of contact with it.

Here at Spinsters Rock three supporters and three only now hold up the cap; at Lanyon Quoit, in Madron, four supporters have been left, but in effect only three function. The robbery which took from both these dolmens the greater number of their enclosing stones led, in each case, to ultimate disaster. Lanyon Quoit fell in the year 1815, and was re-erected in 1854, with no respect to its original form. The Spinsters Rock fell in the year 1862, on Friday the 22nd January. Happily Mr. G. W. Ormerod had made camera lucida sketches of it on the 9th September 1858 (see Fig. 60). The dolmen was restored in November of 1862, but here too the restoration does not fully reproduce the original form; the eastern stone has been placed almost at right angles to its original position, and the cap-stone, instead of resting on the top of the northern support, rests in a notch cut in its bevelled slope.

The same form of theft has been practised on a smaller scale upon the kistvæn at Meacombe, in Chagford parish, where the end stones of the kist have been removed and the side stones, with the cover-stone, left standing as a trilithon. And the same reason has in each case induced the thieves to stay their hands at partial wreckage, which reason is fear of the consequence of inducing the fall of the impost, much smaller at Meacombe, but still weighing more than two tons..

The cap-stone or quoit is irregular in form, a feature which has no doubt contributed to the confusion that attaches to its alleged dimensions. In 1789 the Rev. John Swete states the length "from N. to S. edge to be 14½ ft", and also "a similar length from E. to W.", but adds that it was "in width 10 ft". These statements present difficulties. They may mean that the diagonals were each 14½ ft in length, and the width 10 ft.

In the same year John Andrews of Traine, Modbury, gives the measurement of the longest side as 11 ft 9½ in., the breadth at the widest end as 9 ft 2 in., and at the narrowest end 6 ft 2 in. And he alone of all who took measurements supplies a sketch plan.

In 1796, Polwhele and N.E.,[1] who are supposed to have derived their information from Swete, says, "from N. to S. 14½ ft and from E. to W. 10 ft." Lysons affirms that the measurements are; length about 12 ft and breadth 9 ft. this in 1807.

According to Ormerod the greatest length parallel to the sides is about 14 ft, and the mean length 13 ft 6 in, the greatest breadth 10 ft and the mean breadth 9 ft 10 in. He wrote in 1872.

Rowe, 1830, evaded the difficulty by giving the circumference, which he says is 41 ft, which would accord fairly well with Lysons. From all which we may learn the desirability of preparing a measured drawing when describing objects of irregular outline. Admittedly a foot more or less in either or any dimension, except the thickness, would be of no archæological importance; what is important is the reliance which we place or may hold ourselves entitled to place on the observers.

There are but two other graves on Dartmoor which may fairly be described as dolmens, one on Brent Fore Hill near Corringdon Ball Gate, and the other on Cuckoo Ball, near West Peek, in the parish of Ugborough. Both are much ruined. (See p. 180).

In 1838 the Rev. William Grey conceived that he had discovered a group of double stone rows associated with stone circles to the west of the dolmen, and

---

[1] Miss Cecily Radford has kindly helped me in the matter of 'N.E.' She has in her possession a copy of *Essays by a Society of Gentlemen of Exeter*, in which has been inserted a copy of a letter which, on the authority of the late Mr. Winslow Jones, identifies 'N.E.' a contributor of several essays, as the Rev. John Swete, who used the finals of his name instead of the initials, thus 'johN swetE'. This fully accounts for the constant agreement of N.E. with John Swete. It also, thanks to Miss Radford, solves a problem which I had abandoned as unsolvable.

in the same year, in company with his brother, he made a plan on the spot, which was completed at the hotel at Okehampton the same evening. The plan was made by pacing only, and the north point was only approximate.

Mr. Ormerod prepared a plan from Mr. Grey's data, which plan received Mr. Grey's approval, and was published by Ormerod. It must be said that if any such discovery could have been proved it would have established the former existence of a group of circles and rows which for complication and incomprehensibility would be unique.

There have been and still are some few standing stones, but none of these, scattered as they are, can be made to do duty for any part of Grey's supposed discovery.

Swete, in 1779, "in the adjoining field to the West" (of the dolmen) "remarked several conical pillars about 4 ft high. On the Southern side there are three standing in a direct line from East to West, the distance from the most Western one to the middle one was 212 paces, from the middle to the one on the East 106, just one half of the former, by which it would seem that an intermediate one at least had been removed. In a parallel line to the north are two other remaining erect, the one from the other distant about 52 paces, nearly one fourth of the greatest space on the opposite line, the area between is 93 paces, in the midway of which at the Eastern extremity stands the Cromlech."

It will be seen that this description involves five stones in all, three in a line which is at least 795 ft in length, and in a parallel line, 232 ft away, two other stones 130 ft apart, a most exiguous *via sacra*, for such Swete held it might have been. Grey attempts to account for 105 stones. Andrews in 1789 makes no mention of any standing stones. Polwhele at first contents himself with a verbatim copy of Swete, and later adds to the "two rows of pillars," "several columnar circles", but condescends to no detail. N.E. in or before 1796, Lysons in 1807 and Rowe in 1828 are all silent, but, in 1848, Rowe writes that Polwhele's "two rows of pillars marking out the processional road of the Druids, and several columnar circles will now be sought in vain, even if they existed, to the extent described by the author".

It has long seemed to me that the time was overdue for someone, in the interests of archæology, to deal in an even more summary manner with the Rev. W. Grey's 'discovery'. There is no evidence that prior to 9.30 a.m. on Wednesday, 4th July 1838, any person other than Grey or his brother ever saw, or imagined that he saw, the remains which the pair conceived that they then surveyed. And it is certain that no independent observer has since reported having seen those remains; while it is, or should be, common knowledge that uninformed enthusiasm can gravely over-stimulate the imagination.

BRADMERE POOL

While here we may well take the opportunity of visiting Bradford, or Bradmere Pool, as to which I may quote Swete (September 1789): "The little eminence chosen for our repast overhung what a year or two since was called Bradford Pool, a vast hollow excavated through a succession of ages by miners. The tin works, however, had been given over for a considerable period owing to a vast quantity of water which had overwhelm'd the bottom. It had been drained lately by some enterprising persons by means of adits drove under the hill on which the Cromlech stands."

At some time prior to 1848, the adit to which Swete refers had collapsed and become choked, thus allowing the water to accumulate once more in Bradford, and Rowe found it a pool again. Rowe was a sound observer, but had two weaknesses, the one for the Druids, whose hand he saw everywhere, the other for the scholarship of Col. Hamilton Smith, to whose views he deferred always.

Rowe writes: "Bradford, or Bradmere Pool, is popularly reported to occupy the site of an ancient tin mine. . . . On the south side, the bank rises steeply from the brink of the pool, and forms, apparently, the slope of an earthwork, where the vestiges of a ditch or moat can be traced, surrounding a mound of elliptical form, measuring, on the top, one hundred feet by one hundred and thirty. There seems to have been a provision for draining this piece of water, should occasion require. There are too many indications of regularity and design to admit the supposition that this mound is nothing more than the upcast of an abandoned mine." He then proceeds to state that if the evidence of entrenchment be thought too slight, there is yet another hypothesis, which connects this pool with the legendary erection of the cromlech. That legend is a variation of the three spinsters' tale, and attributes the erection of the cromlech to an old man and his three sons. Obviously, says Rowe, Noah and his sons; this leads to the Deluge, and the Deluge leads to Mt. Ararat; thus we come to Arkite Worship; and on Arkite Worship Col. Smith was an authority. It appears that the pool is intended to be reminiscent of the waters which covered the earth, and the waste heap of the mine to be a miniature Mt. Ararat. "As for the sloping ditch forming a road," says Smith, "it may have served for the covered coracle, containing the novice in his mystic regeneration, and second birth, to be drawn up from the waters to the mimic Ararat of Gwidd-mau."

Rowe admits that the evidence for a sacred mound and lake may be questioned as insufficiently conclusive. But, says he, "it can scarcely be imagined that the memory of the flood should not have reached our Celtic ancestors two or three thousand years ago," and proceeds: "The tradition of the deluge, being thus manifestly familiar to the primitive inhabitants of our island, it is far from improbable, that indications of its existence would be found in their religious rites and monumental relics. And, if, as some antiquaries contend, cromlechs are Arkite cells, not only is plausibility added to the conjecture, which interprets the legend of the erection of the Drewsteignton cromlech, by three young men and their father, who came down from the heights of Dartmoor, as originating in an obscure and perverted tradition of Noah and his three sons— but the probability of an Arkite character pervading the accompanying archæological relics, is increased in proportion."

Which shows how very tidy our early antiquaries were in their methods, and how fully aware they were that, taking a number of convergent assumptions it would be found that they gave mutual support, but how sadly they failed to realize that no truth could be demonstrated by the concurrence of an assembly of guesses.

THE HILL CAMPS[1]

Prestonbury is one of a group of three camps, Cranbrook, Prestonbury and

[1] These and others around the fringes of Dartmoor, are attributed to Iron Age A. (ED.)

Wooston. Their sites are at different elevations; Cranbrook, the highest, touches and just exceeds 1,100 ft above Ordnance Datum, Prestonbury rises to a trifle above 800 ft, and Wooston attains 650 ft. But, different as are their levels, one feature is common; each occupies the extreme of a hill spur, planted on the summit with precipitous slopes on three sides, and a relatively level approach on the fourth. At Prestonbury there are gradients of 1 in 1·5 on the south of the camp; 1 in 2 on the west; 1 in 5 on the north, but to the east there is an approach on practically level ground.

At Cranbrook the northern slope varies from 1 in 5 to 1 in 1·5, the western slope is comparatively gentle being no more than 1 in 12; to the east it is in places 1 in 6, while southward there is an approach on level ground. Wooston stands on ground which north, east and west falls at gradients between 1 in 1·3 and 1 in 2·4; to the south-west it can be approached over ground falling toward the camp 1 in 15.

At Prestonbury and at Cranbrook the contours have led to a marked strengthening of the defences on the side of easiest approach. Three ramparts defend the camp of Prestonbury on the eastern flank, whereas one rampart suffices for the other flanks. Cranbrook presents a much more formidable defence to the south, where the approach is over practically level ground, than on the north where the gorge of the Teign presents natural defence. The graduation is unusually marked; to the south there is a length of 220 ft where the defence is an outer ditch and rampart, followed by an inner, deeper ditch and higher rampart. To the east the camp presents 160 ft of the inner ditch and rampart, with no outer works; to the west 190 ft, with outer rampart, but no outer ditch, and an inner ditch and rampart.

East and west the earthworks cease abruptly, and the cincture is closed by a rubble mound, the ruin of a stone wall, originally 6 ft 9 in. in thickness, and of unascertainable height, the wall as well as the high stone face of the inner rampart, elsewhere, having formed for many years a convenient quarry for road metal.

At Wooston the bank is continuous around the camp, although now less marked on the eastern side, but there are detached outworks to the south which are a little difficult to understand in the absence of a precise survey, which I have never prepared.

Excavations were made at Cranbrook, with slight result. Some pottery, however, was found. A feature sometimes found in camps attributed to the Neolithic Age is well marked, the presence of causeways of approach, formed by strips of the natural ground, left at its original level, traversing the ditches and giving access to the camp through openings in the ramparts. It is not certain that this form of approach was limited to works of the Neolithic Age.

It has been fashionable to describe this group of camps as so sited that they commanded the valley of the Teign, which by their aid could be closed to invaders. This application of the principles of modern strategy to prehistoric camps has two defects. In the first place, these hill-top sites had not the course of the river, except in the distance, within visual observation, and sallies from the camps would be made down declivities of such gradient that the danger to life and limb would be as great as any danger from the enemy.

Secondly, no sane commander would lead his forces up the banks of the Teign, with no room for deployment, and no chance to manoeuvre on either side of the line of advance except upon ground of precipitous slope. The approach to the high lands could readily be made along the ridge of the hills and by side valleys, on good ground by-passing the hillcrest camps at a convenient distance.

It would appear that the camps were places of refuge in times of stress and disturbance, unlike the Dartmoor pounds, which were in daily occupation and use. In construction and in location they are wholly unlike the pounds.

OAK COPSE AND CHARCOAL

In the days when oak copse was grown largely for the production of bark for the tanyards, when in fact leather was a reliable product, some part of the poles was usually converted by the charcaol burners after the bark had been stripped. The method followed was to heap the poles around a small central core of brushwood, inclining them toward the centre, and thus building a truncated cone, with an opening or chimney left at the top, the remainder of the surface covered closely with turf, except for a few small openings left for draught during the first ignition of the wood. The centre being set alight, and the fire well distributed through the mass by the careful manipulation of the draught, the chimney and all other openings were closed, and combustion allowed to proceed in the presence of as little air as sufficed to keep the fire alight.

The more volatile components of the wood were thus either driven off or consumed, and the fixed carbon remained as charcoal. Under favourable conditions the charcoal obtained was about 16 % of the weight of the wood used.

It has long been known that the more complex devices for the control of the draught would yield in use a higher percentage of charcoal, and in modern practice retort-fired wood may give 27 %. It was held, however, that the product of the simple pile was harder and thus more desirable than charcoal made by most of the more elaborate processes. But much depended upon the skill of the men in charge, and charcoal burning was a skilled trade, its secrets of manipulation somewhat jealously guarded.

In combination with other elements carbon forms 51 % of the weight of wood, on the mean of five species of trees; while the fixed carbon recoverable as charcoal ranges, according to the process adopted, between 16 and 27 %, at the best little more than one half the total carbon.

In the early years of the nineteenth century, according to Vancouver, oak coppice in Devonshire was cut every sixteen years or from that upward to twenty; it fetched, standing, from £15 to £20 an acre; near Torrington, where it was allowed to stand for thirty years's growth, its value was £35 per acre.

The usual appropriation of the oak wood, after peeling every branch of an inch or more in diameter, was to select all the best poles for building, fencing, paling and making hurdles, to tie the brushwood in faggots and convert the remainder into charcoal; the charcoal fetching about four shillings a hundredweight on the spot, and being sold to wool-combers and other customers, chiefly from the manufacturing towns.

Charcoal was largely used for scalding milk (it is stated by Fraser) the pans being made of either tinned copper or brass; and the little stoves being nothing more than deep, cup-shaped hollows sunk in a granite stone, as we know from examples still remaining, but disused. Earthenware pans were also in use, but brass was supposed to raise more cream.

Writing in 1796, Marshall records the fuel of farmers and cottagers in the enclosed country to be invariably wood; on the skirts of the mountains peat, while Plymouth had a supply of Newcastle coals. He says that Spray Faggots (4 ft long and 3 ft girth) were sold at 16d. a dozen to the King's bakehouses, presumably at the Victualling Yard at Plymouth.

In 1788, John Andrews of Modbury, noted that: "The scarcity of fuel begins to be a serious inconvenience in most parts of the County: the farmers find it very difficult (notwithstanding the severity of the laws) to prevent their hedges etc. being plundered by the poorer sort of people, who cannot afford to buy: and the evil seems to be increasing."

It will be seen that oak coppice and its products bulked far larger in those days in the national and local economy. With the introduction first of tan extracts from the wood rather than the bark, then of chrome tanned leather, and with the increasing use of mine coal, the coppice rapidly declined in value. But yet it is within my recollection that the coppice was regularly cut, rinded for bark, and the poles converted into charcoal, the faggots sold as firewood. And until but a few years ago I knew a dairy in which the milk was scalded in a brass pan.

Here, in the valley of the Teign, the collier lingered still, when the younger generation in my western quarter held him not in memory even. It has taken a world war to bring him back to both quarters; but he is no longer the skilled builder of a pile, he is the operator of an oven.

On the 20th September 1892, at a meeting of the Teign Naturalists Field Club, Dr. Pearson, Rector of Whitestone, read a short paper on the accounts of one of his predecessors in that living, with special reference to the proceeds of about 25 acres of oak coppice in the years from 1817 to 1843. The Rector of that period was evidently a man of business habit; he gave details of the yield in bark, poles and faggot wood produced, the cost of labour, cartage, etc., and the price of bark per cwt. To the year 1837 a note is added, stating that the gross value of the proceeds of the coppice during twenty-one years up to that date had been £788; the expenses £225 and net profit £563 or about £26 10s. per annum. The highest value received for bark had been 10s. 7d. per cwt. in 1818, and the price had scarcely ever fallen below 7s. It will be seen that the figures confirm Vancouver's statement as to the value of coppice, being somewhat over £1 per acre per annum. This, compared with agricultural values of the day, was a favourable return from the steep hillsides, unsuited to any other form of cultivation, at a time when the average rent of tillage and grass land was 41s. 6d. per acre in the South Hams, and no more than 14s. 6d. an acre around Holsworthy. But, according to Marshall, writing in 1796, there had at that time been a marked rise in the price of coppice, between the years 1783 and 1794 it had advanced from £10 to £15 per acre, and within memory the price had been as low as £5. He attributes the rise to an increase of demand from Ireland for the bark, and the effect of the war on the price of wood.

MILLS

The river which runs at the foot of Prestonbury has also in the past played a part in the life of the district, a part which has taken on a changed character. In Elizabethan days and earlier it was the source of water and power for the tinner. There yet remain two leats, or rather in one case the channel only, now dry. Of these leats one provided power for a tin mill opposite Thornworthy; its channel is now dry. The other served a tin mill near Outer Down, and this leat is still in use, having been extended to Combe Farm and the Sanatorium. At both mills tin was crushed, washed and smelted. (See p. 292).

Other leats there were which supplied power to various mills, flour, woollen and edge-tool. Some few of these mills are now idle, even ruined, for instance the mill at Fingle Bridge.

Omitting the tin mills there were fourteen in all, with powers varying from 4 to 19 horse-power. Two of these mills are derelict, four have been wholly or partly diverted from their original use to domestic purposes of light and power. The flour mills are now gristing and agricultural mills. Two new power stations have been formed, the one to supply electricity to Outer Down, the other to Castle Drogo; and one new station is for the purposes of the clay works.

The iron or edge-tool mills still work, and still supply hooks, bills, etc., to the neighbourhood; they hold their own against Sheffield, because their quality of work is at least as good, in most instances better; their choice of patterns is far larger, and there are parochial fashions of traditional forms and balance even in such things as hedging hooks.

Of all the mills it may be said that they were constructed to come near to fully utilizing the mean flow of the river, and at the same time to be workable in dry times, but not in excessive drought. As a help toward this possible adjustment some have two, or even three wheels. Both overshot and breast wheels are to be found, according to the available fall.

But the day of small sources of power is, I fear, passing; and until the oil resources of the world fail the internal combustion engine will be the enemy of small water-powers. The Teign as a source of water grows in importance, as a source of power it unfortunately decays; and the two uses are not, under present Parliamentary practice, compatible.

APPENDIX VII

ON DUNNABRIDGE POUND AND CROCKERN TOR

DUNNABRIDGE POUND is not isolated from cultivated land and as nearly as the year 1305 there is an entry in the Minister's accounts of new rent for 96 acres of land at "Donebrugge, in the waste of the King". While an extent of the Prince's Manors, made March 1345, gives William Dunnybrigge as one of the Dartmoor tenants.

The Pound may be said to be as old as the Forest, perhaps older, but its first mention appears to be in 1342, when the Bailiff takes credit for 3d expended on a new lock for the gate; later, in 1660, the Reeve of the Manor of Lydford laid out 3s. 4d. for repairing the Pound walls, gate and stocks at Dunnabridge. In 1627, in the course of a suit respecting tithes on Dartmoor, Robert Hannaford, of Widdicombe, deposes that the tenants of the Ancient Tenements "have been accustomed time out of mind to make three several drifts yearly for cattle and one for horses depasturing upon the Forest to Dynabridge Pound, and are to attend there two or three days and nights for the watering and depasturing of the said cattle near the said Pound, and to drive such as are not owned to Lydford for estrays, and every of the said tenants is to have upon bringing of the said cattle and horses to Dynabridge Pound a halfpenny loaf, and that such as do make default of such service do forfeit 6s. 8d."

In 1625, in a bill in the Exchequer, filed by Sir Thomas Reynell, it is stated that it has been customary to make four drifts for cattle in the Forest of Dartmoor, in four several parts of the Forest, at any time after 23rd June and before 6th August. The cattle are to be driven to a Pound called Donnabridge Pound if they are found in the east, west, and south quarters of the Forest, and if found in the north quarter of the Forest, to a Pound called Crebar Pound. If cattle are not claimed within three days they are driven to the Castle of Lydford, and remain as goods estrayed until the 16th August, and if not claimed within eight days from that, are forfeited.

At the Manor Court of Lydford East, in 1586, the jury presented that the Pondefald de Dunnabridge and the Pondefald Castr de Lidford and the Castr de Lydford were out of repair to the extent of twenty pounds value.

There is a mention of Erme Pound in the Court Rolls of 1532-3, but only as identifying the position of certain land lying near by. There is no known entry having reference to Halstock Pound in the Minister's accounts.

Erme Pound is in plan an irregular ellipse, with a major axis of approximately 340 ft and a minor axis of 200 ft; its area is about 1·23 acres. There are a number of hut-circles within the Pound and it may well be an early Bronze Age structure, restored and adapted. There are no houses near the Pound, except the ruins of a small building which has a stone seat carried completely round its walls on the inside. This may have been a shelter for those attending the drift.

Dunnabridge Pound is also an irregular oval, but with much less divergence in its diameters, which are 375 ft and 340 ft respectively (approximately). Its area is about 2·3 acres. There are no hut-circles. It has been suggested that this also is founded on a prehistoric enclosure, but this is by no means certain; there are other similar Pounds in the neighbourhood, which are also without hut-circles, and all may well be early intakes of the historic period. For long years there have been farms in the immediate neighbourhood of Dunnabridge, and the need for shelter can never have been so marked as at Erme Pound. Accordingly the only protection from the weather is that afforded by a hooded seat immediately within the gate; as to which, more later.

Creber Pound, in Gidleigh Parish, is merely a space left between the enclosures of the farms which lie next the open moor; the roads to the moor, and the roads to the in-country, being alike closed by gates; there is left an irregular enclosure which has been brought into use as a drift pound.

Halstock Pound is but a small matter, a quadrilateral measuring about 90 ft by 60 ft; once situated on the border of the open common, but, as it now stands, taken out of enclosed lands. Its antiquity may well be doubted.

As to the Pound at Lydford Castle, that never appears to have had status as a drift pound. It was, however, the Manor Pound in the strictest sense of the word, to which the others were subservient.

The Chair at Dunnabridge (Pl. 92) lies immediately to the west of the entrance to the Pound; it is constructed in the thickness of the wall, and consists of a low stone bench; at the back is a single slab, and above the slab a little walling, to make good to the hood, which consists of a large flat stone of granite. This is supported by two slab-like posts, one at either end. The whole is such a rudely formed seat and shelter as might well be provided for the bailiff, or other officer of the Forest, who presided at the claiming of the cattle and colts. It is no ruder than many a moorland structure, and the covering slab is quite in accord with Dartmoor usage. Such slabs may be found over porches, as at Old Yardworthy, and a barn at Sherril; over shutes and water troughs, as at Old Belliver and Dunnabridge Farms, and even over shelters for bee-butts, as at Brownberry, hard by the Pound.

But Bray (1831) has "not the slightest doubt of the high antiquity of this massive Chair. . . . I am fully convinced that it was originally designed for . . . no less perhaps than an Arch-Druid, or the President of some Court of Judicature." "Had I any doubt before that the Pound was erected on the base of an ancient British, or rather Celtic circle, I could not entertain it now."

Others have seen in it the 'Judge's Chair', brought from the meeting place of the Stannary Parliament on Crocken Tor; and yet others, notably Crossing, have identified it as a dolmen, or cromlech. Miss Dinah Tuckett, the pound-keeper, is convinced that the actual seat is the Judge's Chair from Crockern, and the hood-stone the old table around which the stannators gathered, while a stone on the ground at the east end is one of the legs of the table, the other leg having been broken and lost.

In fact nothing could be less likely to be identified as a dolmen at the instance of a trained archæologist; and if the hood were once the stannary table, then the congestion around it must have seriously inconvenienced the four times twenty-four jurates which attended from the stannaries of Chagford, Tavistock, Ashburton and Plympton.

But there remains one suggestion that has not heretofore been made; it involves a sad fall from the seat of the Judges to the penitential stool of the unruly. Crossing notes that quite near the chair are the remains of a stone with several circular holes, the stone broken across the holes. This means that on the edge of the stone are several semicircular notches. Provide a falling bar in wood, with corresponding notches, place the whole in front of the chair, and you have all the essentials of stocks; and we know that there were stocks at Dunnabridge. Now although Crossing regarded this as a purely humorous suggestion, it may be the truth.

*   *   *

Near Dunnabridge Pound are the ruins of Drownberry Farm, where there survives an old shelter for bee-butts, used within living memory. Here again a flat granite slab was the roof, the slab measuring 5 ft 6 in. by 3 ft and 4 in. in thickness. The chamber for the hives is 4 ft 4 in. long by 2 ft 6 in. deep, and 1 ft 9 in. high. A wooden door, hinged at the bottom, formerly existed, and when this was lifted and secured it sheltered the hives completely.

At Dunnabridge Farm, within the entrance to the courtyard of the old farm, are a shute and a trough. Here again is a structure roofed with a granite slab, the dimensions of which are 6 ft 4 in. by 7 ft 9 in. by 5 in. to 7 in. thick. Bray identifies this slab as the Stannary Table brought from Crockern Tor. Miss Dinah Tuckett repudiates the suggestion, and says that it was erected by members of her family when the Tucketts occupied Dunnabridge. She says that she has good reason to know "as there were seventeen to family".

It has been said that Judge Buller brought the stannary table from Crockern and erected it either at Dunnabridge Pound or Farm, but this can hardly be true since the Pound has always been in Duchy hands, and Buller never had any interest in Dunnabridge Farm. Burt, in his notes to Carrington's *Dartmoor*, rejects this allegation as a calumny on yet other evidence.

Bray gathered the information that the shelter over the shute was erected in 1751, or thereabouts (eighty years before 1831). He gives a drawing showing the slab supported over the trough and shute by three rude stone walls. Now although there was a Tuckett the tenant of Dunnabridge in 1831, the family had not been there eighty years. Yet Miss Tuckett may be right in that her family erected the stone, but on new walls built in masonry, the old dry walling having probably failed. As to its being the Stannary Table, Bray is satisfied, although his informant denied the fact and gave good grounds for the denial. Yet he was elsewhere informed that Mr. Leaman (?), who owned Dunnabridge Farm, had drawn the stone from Crockern, and that it took twelve yoke of oxen to draw it. This seems improbable since it would weigh less than two tons.

On Crockern Tor, where the Stannary Parliament used to meet, there was said to be "a table and seats of moorstone, hewn out of the rocks". Risdon first made this statement in 1630 (?). Polwhele, in 1793, adds details: "On this Torr, not long since, was a warden's or president's chair, seats for the Jurors, a high corner stone for the cryer of the court, and a table, all rudely hewn out of the rough moorstone of the Torr, together with a cavern, which for the convenience of our modern courts, was used in these later days as a repository for wine."

It will be noted that Polwhele adopts Risdon's phrase "hewn out", which certainly does not suggest such an object as a thin slab set upon legs in imitation of a domestic table. Polwhele speaks of the rocky furniture in the past tense, while John Laskey, writing in 1796, probably strikes the truth in saying: "We now proceeded to investigate the Torr and searched for the table, seats, etc., said to have been used in the Stannary Parliaments held here, but we could not discover them, and we were led to imagine the rocks and detached smaller masses were used for that purpose; and for this, in the rude age of simplicity, the Torr seems well adapted, consisting, not like most of the other Torrs we visited, of high and steep piles of rocks, but of a great number of separate ones scattered on the ground to a considerable extent, some in single masses, others double and triple in such manner as may tolerably well serve for tables and seats, and be fancied as such by a fertile imagination; as to anything regular or artificial, there did not appear to us the smallest trace."

In 1802, Bray visited Crockern Tor, and he, having fertile imagination, saw in the scattered masses of rock some semblance of arrangement, but his description is honest, and need not mislead our generation. One rock he figured, and that still stands (Pl. 93A). He says that he does not know whether it was shaped by Nature or by Art. In 1831 he again visited the Tor, this time in the company of

Hannaford, his tenant at Beardown, who identified the particular rock as the Judge's Chair. On this occasion Bray concluded that the 'Chair' was little, if at all, assisted Art. He says that it was also known by the name of the 'Parliament Rock'.

Certainly the Tor has been visited in search of stone from time to time up to recent years, but it would appear that little had been lost, the eye of imagination can still discover as much or as little as Bray ever saw. It is, perhaps, fortunate that it was not until long after Bray's time that a workman found, under a flat stone upon the hillside, a most excellent ground stone hammer, or Polwhele's cave for cellarage of wine might have been given as companion a cupboard for the safe keeping of the Warden of the Stannaries' gavel.

APPENDIX VIII

DARTMOOR RAILROADS

IN Devon and Cornwall, as elsewhere throughout the country, most of the earlier rail- and tramways were subsidiary to canals. The first form of tramway of which we have record in the north of England was employed for the carriage of coal from the pit mouth to the canal, and in the west the earlier ways were auxiliaries either to canals or harbours.

THE HEYTOR RAILWAY[1]

The Heytor railway was three years later in date than the Morwellham incline, but of a more primitive character, resembling, in fact, an Egyptian quarry-road almost as much as a modern tram-line.

In 1792 Mr. James Templar obtained an Act for the construction of a canal from Bovey Tracey to Newton to communicate with the river Teign, and made it at his own expense, completing it in 1794 to Stover. This canal, known as the Stover Canal, is six and a half miles long.

The same Mr. Templar also completed, and likewise at his own expense, a tramroad from Heytor to Stover to communicate with the canal. This tramway, opened in 1820, was made with the intention of developing the Heytor granite quarries; and at the same time workmen's dwellings were erected in a sheltered position on the flank of the tor. These dwellings are now known as 'The Buildings'.

The way itself consists of two parallel lines of granite blocks, each line having a rebate worked along its outer half. The gauge, or distance between the rebates, is exactly 4 ft. The depth of the rebate varies in places from 3 to 6 in., and the

[1] For further details and illustrations, see Amery Adams' article (*T.D.A.*, Vol. 78, 1946, pp. 153–60). See also *The Haytor Granite Tramway and Stover Canal* by M. C. Ewans (1966).

action is precisely similar to that of the Coalbrookdale cast-iron rails, and very like that of the check or guard rail now fitted to lines on sharp curves or at crossings. The horizontal portion of the rebate carried the weight, while the vertical portion bore against the inner circumference of the wheel, and kept it in its place.

At one place at Bovey rails of iron almost precisely similar to the Coalbrookdale pattern have been used, where the line crosses a stream by means of a wooden bridge. At curves the stones do not seem to have been dressed to form, but short, straight stones were worked in, which by the constant friction of the wheels soon wore down to a sufficiently accurate shape. The stones vary much in all dimensions, but perhaps an average block would be 4 ft long and 1 ft 6 in. square; many of them are as long as 7 ft. Points and crossings were formed in large blocks by working grooves 6 in. wide and 2 or 3 in. deep. At no place was any serious cutting or embankment attempted, for the greater part both being only such as were necessary to carry the road along the inclined face of a hill. No attempt was anywhere made to bond together or connect the stones.

The reason for the substitution of granite for iron in this tramway is of course evident. Where granite was to be had for the cost of production, it is not surprising that as a material it should have been adopted. And it does not follow that because the material was cheaper it was necessarily inferior. The cast-iron rails at that time in vogue were a constant source of annoyance and expense, invariably giving way at the wrong moment, and being very uncertain in their general behaviour when heavily laden. Now the Heytor granite is an exceptionally good material, and the granite-way as laid was far superior in many respects to the cast-iron rail. This tramway was thoroughly efficient, and quite up to its work; for the two large blocks of granite having the city arms upon them, at either end of London Bridge, came from the Heytor quarries over this line to Stover, and were thence shipped to London. The Waithman monument, in Ludgate Circus, was also quarried at Heytor, and brought down over this tram-line.

I have already alluded to the Heytor granite as an exceptionally good stone. It is a fine-grained porphyritic rock which can be obtained in blocks of almost any desired size; but owing to the lie of the jointing it involves a large expenditure of labour to quarry out, and from this reason has now ceased to be extensively worked. The quarry has not, however, been altogether deserted, as a few men were employed there when last I visited it, on which occasion Mr. Barry, C.E., of Newton (to whom I must express my indebtedness), very kindly walked over the railway with me. Besides the principal quarry at Heytor, branch lines were also run to neighbouring quarries, but the whole tramway has now fallen into disuse. As to the trucks, they were merely modified road waggons. The wheels, as in all the earlier rolling stock, ran free on the axles, and I am informed by Mr. Barry that the leading truck of a train usually had shafts.

PLYMOUTH AND DARTMOOR RAILWAY

We now come to the Plymouth and Dartmoor Railway, the first idea of which originated with Sir Thomas Tyrwhitt. This gentleman's statement, made at Plymouth to the Chamber of Commerce, is of considerable interest. Briefly stated, the following prospects were held forth.

The barren slopes of Dartmoor were to be reclaimed, to which end lime and sea-sand were to be imported as manures. Pauperism was to be decreased, and a flourishing colony of agriculturists was to be planted on the moor. By this means Plymouth would acquire a valuable back-country, which would materially increase her prosperity as a port. It was in fact to be an undertaking profitable alike both to the nation and to the shareholders, the latter apparently expecting an 18 % return on their capital. As the subject is of such local interest, I think it may be well to give an abstract of Sir Thomas Tyrwhitt's statement, which is also a good example of the early railway prospectus. Sir Thomas said: "To reclaim, and clothe with grain and grasses a spacious tract of land now lying barren, desolate, and neglected; to fill this unoccupied region with an industrious and hardy population; to create a profitable interchange of useful commodities between an improvable and extensive line of back-country, and a commercial seaport of the first capabilities, both natural and artificial; to provide employment for the poor of several parishes; and to alleviate the pressure of parochial burdens by a method, at once simply ingenious, and comparatively inexpensive, form altogether such a stimulus to adventure, and such a scope for exertion, especially to a wealthy company, as must dilate the benevolent heart of the patriot, whilst it emboldens the capitalist gladly to lend his assistance in carrying the plan into execution."

The last sentence evidently implies a doubt that the "benevolent heart of the patriot" counted for much unless the security was good. Continuing his statement, Sir Thomas Tyrwhitt divides his subject into five heads; viz., I. Plan; II. Expense; III. Funds; IV. Income; V. Benefits.

I. *Plan*. The road will commence at Dartmoor Prison, which lies about twelve hundred and fifty feet above the sea, and thence traverse the Moor and Roborough Down in a south-westerly direction, to the Laira at Crabtree, by a gradual fall of half an inch in three feet. The distance between the two places will not, in all probability, exceed twenty miles, according to the line marked out in the plan; and the road ought to be an ascending and descending one, or what is technically called a "double road".

In a footnote to this last clause, it is explained that a double road occupies 18 ft of land in width.

II. *Expense*. It is calculated that the present road may cost £2000 per mile.

III. *Funds*. To meet the charges, both direct and contingent, it will be necessary perhaps to raise £45,000 by subscription, in shares of £25 each.

A somewhat encouraging footnote is here appended, with a view probably to future financing operations. "Experience has proved in Scotland that not less than 18 % may be derived from railroads."

IV. *Income*. The principal part of this, at first, will arise from the tonnage of importable and exportable commodities.

Importable Commodities

Lime. In cultivating the moor and other unimproved parts on both sides of the road, this must be esteemed an indispensable article, not merely in the onset but during the long course of successive years.

Sea Sand. Many assigning much importance to this article prefer it to lime as a manure.

Timber. In proportion as buildings accumulate around the road, as population increases, and as the wants of culture diffuse themselves, will be the want of this valuable article, to which in fact hardly any limit can be placed in a region so denuded of wood as Dartmoor.

Coal. Next to timber justly ranks this essential of domestic life.

Culm.

Groceries. *Tea* and *sugar* are become absolute necessaries in the present day, and these, added to *wine, spirits, beer, porter,* and other *household requisites,* would be sure to give birth to a productive tonnage.

Furniture. The *colonisation* of Dartmoor will carry in its train a necessity not only for the importable commodities before spoken of, but for many others, which, though of comparatively inferior consequence, will be more or less wanted by the colonists. Amongst them is furniture.

The use of this term [colonisation] the author hopes will not be objected to; it being equally applicable, in his opinion, to the improvements contemplated on Dartmoor as to like designs in Canada.

Planting. In the progress of colonisation the formation of plantations will become essentially requisite, as much for the sake of rural embellishment as to protect the newly-enclosed grounds and buildings.

Exportable Commodities

Granite. Beside the weightier stone for government or private uses, the Company would be enabled to supply, with the same ease and profusion, curbs and paving stones, gate-posts, highway stones, and gravel, at a rate which, it is presumed, would undersell those procurable in any other quarter.

Peat. It is impossible to view the face of Dartmoor without feeling sensible of the numerous uses to which the superabundance of peat in this district may be applied. Amongst others, the heat given by a combination of peat with coal is allowed to be exceedingly powerful; and the author has reason to believe that iron, fused with this admixture, is less liable to crack than when coal alone is employed in the process.

Mining Products. Mr. Mawes, the celebrated mineralogist, who has investigated the forest of Dartmoor with much attention, is of the opinion that the latter contains the mineralogical productions of almost every clime, with but few exceptions. If iron, copper, and tin could be raised and smelted on the spot, without the necessity of resorting elsewhere, the saving of expense, both to Government and the public, might be decidedly pronounced incalculable.

Flax. This next article, unlike the preceding ones, is not indigenous; but experiments have proved that it may be naturalized on the soil of Dartmoor, and perhaps to an extent which will ultimately render unnecessary all foreign importations of it—for the port of Plymouth, at least, and its neighbourhood.

Hemp. If hemp can be reared on the bogs of Russia, it is without doubt equally capable of cultivation on Dartmoor and Roborough Down.

Travelling Vehicles and Parcels are also included among the sources of income, as also is the *Transfer of Convicts to Dartmoor Prison.*

Such being the benefits which, in all good faith, were stated to be derivable from the construction of this line, it is not surprising that the matter should have been taken up by a company, and accordingly we find a Plymouth paper indulging in the following somewhat high-flown language:

"The time is at length arrived so long, and yet whether in good report or evil report, so invariably anticipated by us, when the benefits of this measure are to be thrown open to the public. To Sir Thomas Tyrwhitt, as the original projector of this railway, and his able coadjutors in this port and other places, who have advanced cautiously but steadily to their object, may be assigned a praise which future generations will gratefully rejoice to perpetuate. It is not simply for themselves, but for posterity that they have devoted their time, their talent, and their capitals to the realization of a plan which not only reflects the greatest honour on the county of Devon, but will prove on the whole of this neighbourhood an inexhaustible source of advantage. Whether nationally or locally considered, it is a theme of proud congratulation. Whilst the region around, once apparently condemned to sterility, by the use of proper manures, will take its merited rank in British agriculture."

Sir Thomas Tyrwhitt was an eminently practical and thorough-going man, but events have shown that his estimate of the agricultural value of Dartmoor was fortunately wrong. Although Plymouth has lost the valuable back-country promised her, and Dartmoor is still apparently condemned to what is called sterility, it must not be lost sight of that its value as an unenclosed space, where the public may trespass off the roads without being taken for amateur poachers, and where they can wander unfettered by hedges, or fear of damaging crops— its value, in fact, as a public park, similar to though smaller than the great American national parks, will grow and increase year by year; while it is probable that as a sheep run and cattle pasture of the first order it is of much greater value than it ever could be as very inferior arable land.

A tender for the ironwork of the line was accepted on terms much below the estimate, and two hundred men were set to work quarrying and dressing granite on the moor, a lease of stone on Walkhampton Common having been granted by Sir M. M. Lopes.

The road as constructed consists of a single line only, and this doubtless accounts for the capital raised under the first Act, passed 2nd July 1819, amounting only to £27,783, instead of £45,000, as estimated by Sir Thomas in his statement. On 20th September 1819, the first general meeting of the proprietors took place, when a managing committee was elected: Mr. William Stuart, superintendent of the Plymouth Breakwater works, being engineer; Mr. Hugh Mackintosh of London, contractor for forming the road; and Messrs. Bailey and Co., also of London, contractors for the ironwork. It being found necessary to continue the line from Crabtree to Sutton Pool, so as to obtain better shipping facilities, an Act was passed (8th July 1820) authorizing this extension, the estimate for which amounted to £7,200. A further Act was obtained (2nd July 1821) authorizing certain deviations, including a tunnel at Leigham, the estimated expenditure for the tunnel and other extra works being £5,000. The total estimate was by these means brought up to £39,983.

The total length of line from Princetown to Sutton Pool is 25 m. 2 qr. 6 ch., of which in 1826 over 23 miles had been completed. In this year the contractors, both for road and ironwork, were Messrs. Johnson and Brice of London, and Mr. Roger Hopkins had succeeded Mr. Stuart as engineer.[1]

[1] On the 13th of October of this same year an advertisement appeared in the *Plymouth Telegraph and Chronicle*, asking tenders for the excavating and completing of the tunnel at Leigham, and also the making of certain cuttings and

The tunnel at Leigham, in the twentieth mile from Princetown, is 620 yards long, 9ft 6 in. high, 8 ft 6 in. broad, and its greatest depth below ground is 109 ft. It has no lining, but is left as cut through the rock.

The completed portion of the line was opened for public use on 26th September 1823. I take the following description of the proceedings on that occasion from *The Telegraph and Chronicle*, under date Plymouth, Saturday, 27th September 1823:

"*Plymouth and Dartmoor Railway*. Our various readers, both local and distant, will learn with the sincerest pleasure that this great work, so long the object of our hopes and fears, and well designated by a worthy nobleman as the glory of the county, is now happily open for general trade. Yesterday was devoted to the celebration of the joyous event, and its festivities commenced with a public breakfast, liberally given by Sir Thomas Tyrwhitt, the original projector of the undertaking, at his Wharf on Roborough Down, where three marquees were erected, and every elegant species of viand provided for the reception and gratification of the company, which comprised much of the respectability and worth of the port and its neighbourhood.

"The South Devon Band enlivened the scene with its choicest airs; but unhappily the weather was unfavourable, which drove many away ere the departure of the procession through the tunnel could be arranged. A long file of cars partly laden with granite, and partly with stewards and other individuals, accompanied by the band, and ornamented with flags, after the breakfast set off for Plymouth. on their arrival at which place they were heartily greeted by the huzzas of a large concourse of people, anxiously waiting their arrival, being saluted on their way by some petards at Hoo Meavy, and attended throughout the progress by a numerous cavalcade on horse and foot.

"About fifty gentlemen then sat down to a handsome dinner at the Royal Hotel, who did not separate until a late hour."

In the same paper are also notices of a last and final call of 10 % per share, signed by William Burt, clerk to the Company, and also a notice of a general meeting of proprietors of the Plymouth and Dartmoor Company, signed: Morley, Masseh Lopes, Edmund Lockyer, William Elford, and John Pridham.

The line, as originally laid, consisted of parabolic edge-rails[1] set in cast-iron chairs, and these fastened down to stones averaging 2 ft 6 in. long by 1 ft 6 in. wide, and of varying depths. Some of these rails had lap-joints, and others butt-joints; two different forms of chairs being used to suit the different joints. The gauge of the line was 4 ft 6 in.

Short sidings, and other portions not subjected to much wear, were laid in

---

embankments from thence to Crabtree and Sutton Harbour. Application to be made to Mr. Roger Hopkins, engineer and mineral surveyor, 6 Tavistock Street, Plymouth.

[1] With reference to these cast-iron edge-rails, I may mention, as a curious fact, that in excavating in the fourth cylinder for the new Laira Bridge, on the Plymouth and Dartmoor Extension Railway, one of these rails was brought up from the bed of the Laira. The depth to which it had sunk below the surface of the mud could not be ascertained; but owing to the hard layer of clay and stones which Mr. Rendel placed over that portion of the river, it was probably lying very near the surface.

granite stones, averaging 4 ft long by 1 ft broad. These stones were arranged differently to those used at Heytor. The wheels ran on them precisely as on the iron rails, the inner edges of the granite being dressed to take them, and the outer portion of the stone being rough-picked to below the level of the dressed portion, forming in fact a granite in place of an iron rail.

The points and crossings were made in cast-iron, and the one feature noticeable is that the crossings had a movable tongue 1 ft 5 in. long, similar to the points.

As the old rails wore out, and when the manufacture and use of rolled-iron rails became more general, these took the place of the old cast-iron edge-rail. They were used in lengths of from 10 to 18 ft, and being all flat-footed, were not secured to the stones by chairs, but were spiked down. The joints between two rails were made with a clasp, which gripped the flanges of both, the whole being usually secured to a stone. The rails were spiked to the same stones to which the original chairs had been fastened. Besides these, other stones were packed under the rails so as to, as far as possible, ensure a continuous solid bed. The rolled-rails were of various patterns; the four more especially used being: (1) an ordinary bridge rail weighing 45 lb. per yard; (2) a solid rail of similar form weighing 60 lb. per yard; (3) a Vignoles flange rail weighing 53¼ lb. per yard; (4) a similar but smaller rail weighing 38¾ lb. per yard.

The traffic over this line gradually decreased until 1880, when the portion between Princetown and the 'Rock' was reconstructed for locomotive purposes, and a connection effected with the Great Western Railway at Yelverton.

The alterations were completed, and the railway opened, in August 1883, the permanent way being the standard Great Western (narrow-gauge).

APPENDIX IX

DARTMOOR AND THE SERVICES

PUBLIC INQUIRY, 16TH JULY, 1947

Evidence presented by Richard Hansford Worth, M.I.C.E., F.G.S., on behalf of the Devonshire Association for the Advancement of Science, Literature and Art (founded 1862), and the Dartmoor Preservation Association (founded 1887)

I AM a chartered civil engineer, I was admitted an associate member of the Institution of Civil Engineers in 1893, and some years later transferred to the class of member. I am a fellow of the Geological Society of London and a member of the Mineralogical Society.

During the past sixty years I have used every opportunity to study Dartmoor, and my professional work has given me special occasions to that end. I published my first paper on a Dartmoor subject in 1889.

I have examined the map deposited with the Devon County Council at Exeter, for the purposes of this inquiry, which I hereafter will refer to as the "deposited map". Upon this map five adjacent areas are indicated as sought for occupation by the Forces on Dartmoor for training purposes.

These areas are as follows. (1) Coloured blue on the map, described as "War Department owned land". (2) Coloured red on the map, described as "Artillery Range Area, Annual Agreement with the Duchy of Cornwall". (3) Coloured green on the map, described as "Extensions to Artillery Range". (4) Coloured yellow on map and striped red, described as "R.M. and Army user with live ammunition". (5) Coloured yellow on map, described as "Army user with no live ammunition (No Exclusion of Public from this Area)". It is added that (3), (4) and (5) with the NW. and SE. gun sites are proposed new acquisitions. The areas of the land are: (1) Blue, 5·5 sq. miles; (2) red, 23·7 sq. miles; (3) green, 6·5 sq. miles; (4) yellow, striped red, 18·6 sq. miles; (5) yellow, 9·2 sq. miles; making a total of 63·5 sq. miles.

I have omitted certain gun sites or parts of gun sites which lie outside the coloured areas.

By implication the whole of the blue and red areas are to be regarded as previously occupied for military purposes, but this needs qualification, the red area certainly was not wholly in occupation as an artillery range, nor even as part of the danger zone to the south of the former range. We are not told strictly what manner of use is intended within this red area, nor whether the public is to be admitted as heretofore when actual firing is not in progress.

The blue area is unaltered in boundary, but we are not told whether its past user is to be continued without alteration, nor whether the public is to be admitted when operations are not in progress. If there is to be a change to a more burdensome user of these lands, that, as against the commoners and the general public alike, is a new acquisition; and full information upon this question should we submit, be before this inquiry.

The two green areas, both numbered 3, are described as extensions of the Artillery Range, but here again no discrimination is made between the actual range and the danger area attached thereto, and the same questions fall to be answered as in respect of the red area.

The yellow area, striped red, No. 4, is stated as intended to be devoted to user with live ammunition by the R. Marines and the Army. On the south this area is for a length of two miles bounded by an unfenced main road, for a further length of half a mile either by a rough stone fence adjoining the road or by a leat or water course running parallel to the road and but some 50 ft away from the same. It is obvious that for safety there must be a neutral zone between the actual exercise ground and the road, but no indication of this is afforded. I have been told that the Devon County Council has been assured that no live ammunition will be used within 500 ft, or 500 yds, it seems uncertain which, from the road, but that is no part of the scheme as presented on the deposited map, which is the sole basis of this inquiry. I say that, from my personal knowledge of the exercises which were carried out on Dartmoor during the past war, 500 yds would not be sufficient safety zone on these boulder-strewn hillsides; and that, for this and other reasons, which I will later present, no live ammunition should be used south of a line drawn from a little north of Great Mistor to a little north of Great Staple Tor.

And I further say the loss of this grazing ground, over the whole area of the land coloured yellow and striped red, is a loss to which the commoners should not and need not be subjected, nor should or need the public unrestricted access to the same area be denied.

The statement appeared in the public press that the exercises with live ammunition were to be carried out over the same land (coloured red) which is proposed to be used as an artillery range; and there is certainly sufficient suitable ground within that area. The statement was officially corrected on the 2nd January 1947; but it had received support from a map issued by the Devon County Council to those attending a conference at Exeter on the 11th April 1947.

The first opportunity of obtaining knowledge of the actual detail and extent of the present suggestions came with the advertisement in the public press of 27th June 1947, when it was made known that a plan had been deposited at the offices of the Devon County Council at Exeter, which might be inspected by those interested. It may not have been appreciated that among those interested as commoners were all the men of Devon, saving only the inhabitants of Totnes and Barnstaple. The time allowed for the preparation of any evidence in opposition to the scheme, as then, for the first time, declared, has thus been no more than nineteen days, and we submit that the task of preparing such detailed evidence as should be presented at this inquiry has been rendered unduly difficult. I ask indulgence if my evidence is not presented in due logical order.

This proposed area for practice with live ammunition (yellow striped red) includes 6·6 sq. miles of the watersheds of the West Dart, the Cowsic and the Blackabrook, within the watershed of the former Devonport water-supply, now, by the extension of the Borough of Plymouth transferred to that authority. As a water engineer I cannot think that battle practice by bodies of troops over and within the watershed utilized for a public domestic supply can be other than a grave potential danger. We have no knowledge what precautions, if any effective precautions are indeed possible, are intended to be taken. Or in what way the intakes and leats are to be protected from physical damage; or safe access to the works by the officials and workmen of the water-supply undertaking assured.

I leave the question of threatened antiquities and of Wistman's Wood to later evidence on the general matter of antiquities and objects of scientific interest.

The yellow area, numbered (5), is stated to be for Army occupation with no live ammunition, the public is to have access. There are within this area important antiquities, and I will later suggest modification in the boundary of the area, and the addition to it of a small part of the red and eastern green areas, with a view to bringing within it yet other antiquities. But I realize, from previous experience, that, while such modification will preserve the public access to the antiquities, it will not and cannot ensure the preservation of the antiquities. Here again a part of the red could be attributed, in substitution, to these military purposes, and the north part is clearly indicated.

As to the gun areas, for their size and number they either involve the certain destruction or the greatest danger to the greatest possible number of antiquities. I will revert to this under the heading of *Antiquities*.

COMMONERS' RIGHTS

Rights of common on the Forest of Dartmoor and the Commons of Devon are held by so many classes, and people so many in number, that Mr. Stuart Moore advised that the question of sufficiency of common could hardly be raised by would-be enclosers. The evidence upon which this dictum was found set out in the first publication of the Dartmoor Preservation Association, *Short History of the Rights of Common upon the Forest of Dartmoor and the Commons of Devon, by Mr. Stuart A. Moore, with an introduction by Sir Frederick Pollock, Bart., and a contribution by Mr. Percival Birkett*, Plymouth 1890.

For present purposes I put in, as a part of my evidence, a reprint of a paper from Vol. 76 of the *Transactions of the Devonshire Association*, which was written as a key to the documentary evidence collected by Mr. Stuart Moore.

Summarized, the following have rights of common within the Forest and on the Commons of Devon, which lie without but contiguous with the Forest (but not all lands contiguous with the Forest are necessarily Commons of Devon).

(1) The holders of the Ancient Tenements enclosed from the Forest, who pay nothing for depasturing their sheep and other cattle, and who have the privilege of turf-paring, of cutting of fuel, and for taking stones, paying nothing for the same. This class has been materially reduced by the purchase by the Duchy of Cornwall of ancient copy-hold tenements.

(2) The Venville tenants, living in vills next to the Forest of Dartmoor, and paying for their privileges certain fixed rents, either singly or collectively. These have the right to agistments for their beasts from the rising of the sun to the setting thereof, but not by night; none the less they might depasture by night also on payment of a fixed additional sum. And they may take coals, turf, furze and stones for their own use.

(3) The "Foreigners", being all the other inhabitants of Devon, except those of Barnstaple and Totnes. These had free pasturage in the Commons of Devon, so only that they would depose that their cattle came not into the Forest, but they might depasture the Forest on making certain fixed payments; they might also, for a fixed payment have pits for the digging of turfs.

Naturally, the nearer the commoners were to Dartmoor, the greater the advantage they might derive from their rights therein, but cattle have been brought in the past for considerable distances to the rough hill pasture, which is still an important feature in the agricultural economy of Devon. There are also parochial and manorial common lands, to some extent formerly part of the Commons of Devon, which also play their part in Devon agriculture.

All the encroachments now proposed by the forces are to the reduction in area of these various rights of common, and the diminution of the enjoyment of such areas as are still to be permitted to be depastured, whatever arrangements may be made for driving the commons to remove cattle from danger when the Services' operations are in progress, and permitting them to return when such operations are discontinued for the time.

During the past war, in connection with the battle-training on Dartmoor very considerable lengths of barbed-wire entanglements were erected on Dartmoor, to the destruction of many sheep which perished miserably involved in the wire. Much of this wire still remains. Shelter trenches were also dug on many commons, in numbers; some of these have been refilled, but very many remain open and dangerous. There is no assurance that such dangers will not be brought into existence on the battle-training areas now proposed; nor, indeed, any statement as to the manner of user which will be made of the lands, except that, for its safety, the public will be excluded from the areas where live ammunition will be used.

The Dartmoor farmer is a hardy, industrious man, to whom his common rights are often the essential of success; and he stands to lose heavily, often irretrievably by the loss of limitation of those rights. The nation, also, will lose, especially when we are, as now, driven to the utmost of our capacity in the task of lessening the burden of importing food. For this reason we urge this further necessity of locating the battle-practice areas within the area which is assigned to artillery purposes. To do otherwise is to squander national resources.

ANTIQUITIES

Dartmoor has the greatest collection of antiquities of the Early Bronze Age which is to be found in the British Isles. No mere museum collection, but the homes, the graves and the monuments of men who, at the dawn of the age of metals in our country, lived and worked among its hills in surroundings little altered since their day. It may be described as an irreplaceable document, happily preserved to our times. It has not been reserved to the present threat to bring to our minds its value, and its value to future years. The Archæological literature of Dartmoor had its origin in the last decade of the eighteenth century, in the days of Polwhele, Bray, Sweete and their associates. It was a humble beginning, clouded and overshadowed by mythical scholarship and Druidical nonsense. But it marked the origin of an intelligent interest in the past; an interest which has lived to outgrow its youthful error, and to make the archæology of Dartmoor an essential contribution to the study of human origins.

In the summers of 1827 and 1828, four members of the Plymouth Institution explored Dartmoor; they were Henry Woollcombe, Hamilton Smith, John Prideaux and Samuel Rowe. Their observations were sound, their interpretations certainly mistaken, and they incumbered themselves with Arkite Worship, additional to the Druids.

In 1848, the Rev. Samuel Rowe published his work entitled *A Perambulation of Dartmoor*.

With the formation, in 1862, of the Devonshire Association, the opportunity came for a more organized exploration of the Moor, and a more regular publication of results. In 1877 the Association appointed a Dartmoor Committee, which published three reports. In 1878 it appointed a Barrow Committee, which has not confined its operations solely to Dartmoor, but which has published sixty-four reports, and has at the present two in the press. One hundred and thirty-five Dartmoor graves have been described, planned and illustrated.

The Dartmoor Exploration Committee, appointed in 1893, has, at intervals, published thirteen reports, and still continues. A part of its work has been the thorough excavation of one hundred and twenty hut-circles, and the somewhat less thorough examination of eighty more. In addition to the work of the Committees and Recorders, other members of the Association have written many papers on the pre-history of Dartmoor. I myself have issued full descriptions of the sixty-one stone rows, a class of monument in which Dartmoor is peculiarly rich; and, coming to a later age, I have prepared and issued detailed descriptions of the tin mills (most of which now remaining are of Elizabethan age) the known number being forty-three. The stone cricles, retaining circles and menhirs have all received attention and record, but the work is not as yet finished. Thus I hope to have shewn that others as well as myself have valued the archæological record of Dartmoor sufficiently to give their time and labour to the attempt at complete record. It is not we local workers who alone value the treasure-house of Dartmoor and recognize its importance to the science of Archæology.

GEOLOGY

Not only local workers, but also geologists and mineralogists from other counties than Devon and other lands than Britain, have studied the granite of the Dartmoor highland, and its associated rocks. Its geology, like its archæology, is part of the essential evidence in a far wider story than that of Devon. It is probably true that in geology that tale has been less completely told than in archæology; but in neither study has the evidence been exhausted.

BOTANY

In botany Dartmoor presents an especial feature, its ancient oak woods, of which Wistman's Wood, on the banks of the West Dart is the best known, and on the whole the most important. Black Tor Beare, on the West Okement, differs in that the more part of its trees were cut in or about the year 1620, so that few of the present trees are probably more than three hundred and twenty years old; but one at least is a specimen as striking as any in Wistman's Wood. Piles Copse, on the Erme has probably been cut at an even later date, but that also gives valuable evidence of the effect of the Dartmoor climate on the growth of the oak. Wistman's Wood is commonly accepted as unique.

WILD LIFE

The effect of a prolonged and large-scale invasion of a land which hitherto except for the artillery range, has enjoyed for centuries that peace which follows the exclusion of agriculture and husbandry, must be marked. There will probably be other witnesses who are better qualified by detailed and specialist knowledge to speak on this matter.

I have thus sketched the value of Dartmoor to students of various sciences with a view to avoiding repetition in the further evidence which I offer.

GUN AREAS

The gun areas have unfortunately been so placed that in many instances their use must cause irreparable damage.

It is understood that from each and every gun area the direction of fire will be toward the red area, and that it is intended the projectiles shall always fall within that area. This matter has never been made quite clear.

(a) The northernmost gun area, in the valley of the Lyd, is situate at a level of 1,000 ft above O.D. and would presumably be used for eastward and north-eastward fire, in which event the range would be over a hill or hills from 700 to 900 ft above the guns and an error in elevation might easily lead to the shell falling on those hillsides. I do not decry the ability of the gunners when I suggest the possibility of error, since it must be remembered that this is to be used as a training ground, and error is natural to beginners. This particular gun area is shewn as occupying a space of half a mile long by quarter of a mile wide of the valley of the Lyd, at a point which is the most frequented by the inhabitants of Lydford and the visitors to that resort; and the firing will be across the tors, "Great Links", "Arms", and "Brae", and over the valley of the Doe Tor Brook, which some years ago was specifically excluded from the area now coloured blue. This spells ruin to Lydford.

(b) A gun area at the western extreme of the blue area, partly within and partly without that area. This might well be set further east so as not to interfere with the ancient track from Lydford to Willsworthy. There is no reason why it should not be set wholly within the blue area, thus avoiding any fresh take from what is now free land. This area measures one half mile by a little under a half mile.

(c) A gun area east of Cudliptown, Marytavy, on Whit Tor and Lanson [Langstone] Moor. This is most unfortunately placed. It covers the whole site of White Tor Camp, a prehistoric camp of great interest, and of a type unique on Dartmoor. The existence of the camp and of the gun area are not compatible. It also covers the site of a prehistoric pound and hut-circles. Further it includes the longstone or menhir, from which the adjacent Moor takes its name, also a kistvaen, and part of a stone row associated with the menhir. This has already been an unfortunate neighbourhood; during the late war the forces sprayed the face of the menhir with machine-gun fire, and wrecked a fine stone circle lying a little to the east on the same moor, reducing some of the stones to fragments, breaking and uprooting others. It was, before this destruction, the most finely sited circle on Dartmoor.

The only remedy for the wholesale destruction which the construction and use of this gun area involves is to shift the whole area to the north until it lies clear of the camp, the menhir and stone row alike; and to prohibit the use of mechanical traction in a manner which might interfere with either of the objects of antiquity. We know what the services can do with early camps; they used a camp on Roborough Down and an outwork connected with it as ready-made banks and obstacles for the purpose of tank practice over banks.

The Whit Tor Camp and the pound will be found figured and described in detail in the sixth Report of the Dartmoor Exploration Committee, *T.D.A.*, vol. 31, pp. 146-55. In which is a map showing that there are numerous minor remains in addition to those mentioned. The menhir to which I have referred will be found, described and illustrated in the *T.D.A.*, vol. 72, p. 197 and Pl. ix [p. 270 and Pl. 60A of this book]. While the kistvaen is described, planned and illustrated in the fifty-fifth Report on Barrows, *T.D.A.*, vol. 68, p. 49, and Pl. ii.

(d) Gun area on Roose Tor and Great Staple Tor. Extreme length north to south rather over three-quarters of a mile, extreme width east to west rather less than three-quarters of a mile.

This, again, is an unfortunate selection, some attempt seems to have been made to avoid the summit rocks of Roose Tor and Great Staple Tor, but the attempt is far from sufficient, and both rock masses are involved, while the guns are set south of the tors, which, with a northward direction of fire involves the rocks being subject to the blast. A number of hut-circles are also involved in the area. The only possible method of avoiding damage is to shift the gun area to the north-east, clear of both tors. Also this gun area is within the limits of the battle practice with live ammunition; and we know the manner in which such rocks have been regarded by the services as targets made and appointed for their purposes, witness the summit rocks of Ugborough Beacon, and also Little Mis Tor.

Great Staple Tor is one of the most noteworthy rock masses on Dartmoor. It will be found illustrated on Pl. x, fig. 22, of my Presidential Address to the Devonshire Association, vol. 62. A copy of this address I hand in, to which I will hereafter refer as "Presidential Address". [Reprinted above as the first chapter of this book.]

About the middle of the illustration last mentioned will be seen a curious arrangement of rock, consisting of a flat slab, looking rather like a hand or paw, resting on a round stone which is precisely over the edge of another rock. This natural grouping is instructive to the geologist, and was early, and incorrectly identified, as a 'tolmen', the supposed handiwork of the Druids. This false identification we owe to the Rev. E. Bray, who entered it in his notebook in 1802–3.

(e) Gun area on Mis Tor and Little Mis Tor. Greatest length, north to south, one mile, greatest width five-eights of a mile. Here an attempt has been made to exclude the summit rocks of Great Mis Tor, but they are by no means effectively cleared, and Little Mis Tor is disregarded. The guns will mainly be south of Great Mis Tor, which will be subject to the blast. The one possible remedy is to move the gun area to the north and east. It is to be noted that this area is also within the limits devoted to battle practice with live ammunition, so that the mere shifting of the guns is a quite inadequate provision for the safety of the summit rocks.

There are special reasons why the summit rocks of Great Mis Tor should be guarded from harm, apart from the general principle that such summit rocks are a chief characteristic of Dartmoor scenery.

There is on the summit of the Tor a rock basin, known as Mis Tor Pan, which is on the boundary of the Forest, and also on the boundary of the adjacent Common of Walkhampton. This rock-basin is, first of all, in the nature of an historic document, it is mentioned in a Charter of Isabella de Fortibus, Countess of Albemarle and Devon, and Lady of the Isle, whereby, in 1290, she confirmed the charter of her mother Amicia, Countess of Devon and Lady of the Isle, granting certain lands to the Abbey of Buckland, Mistorpanna being one of the bounds of such lands.

In 1608, in a survey of the Forest, "*a rocke called mistorrpan*" is given as one of the bounds; and Mistorpan is mentioned in 1702. From my earliest recollection the same name attached to this rock-basin. This certainly places the basin in the category of ancient monuments, and as such it should be scheduled, but it lies in Duchy lands.

The basin is also an interesting geological exhibit; it has a long history of record. Bray, in 1802, gives its dimensions, he is followed by Rowe, in 1828; Ormerod, in 1858; Sophia Dixon, in 1875; and myself, in 1929. No other rock-basin has so full or so long a record. Mis Tor Pan will be found described and illustrated in the Presidential Address, pp. 78, 79; and pl. xv, figs. 33 [pp. 29–30, Fig. 5, and Pl. 15A of this book].

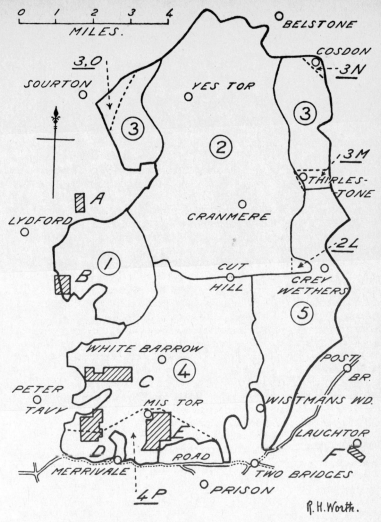

FIG. 130

Whole area sought to be acquired by Services is bounded by Strong full line.

Sections appropriated to various specific purposes are bounded by lighter full line.

Numerals within circles are the official numbers attributed to the sections on the Deposited Plan.

Suggested Amendments (other than the drastic reduction of the whole area) are shewn in dotted line, and each identified by a numeral accompanied by a letter, thus: 2, L, Sittaford Tor; 3, M, Thirlestone; 3, N, Cosdon; 3, O, Sourton Tors; 4, P, Mis Tor and Staple Tor (as to these see text).

Gun-sites, hatched and lettered A, B, C, E, F. (These letters do not appear on the Deposited Plan.)

There is another interesting geological feature at Mis Tor, the weathered, rounded block, left precariously poised on its native mass, and standing near the rock-basin. A description will be found in the Presidential Address, pp. 74-5, and an illustration, pl. xi, fig. 23 [Pl. 11A above].

For the safety of the public, and the preservation of Mis Tor and Staple Tor, I suggest that the southern boundary of the land coloured yellow and striped red should be removed to pass 100 yards to the north of the rocks of each tor, and should lie in a straight line between those points, passing thereafter west-ward through a point lying 100 yards north of the summit of Cocks Tor, and eastward to the south end of Holming Beam Plantation. All the land cut off from the land striped red to the south of this new boundary might be coloured yellow, and be available for exercises without live ammunition, the public having access thereto.

(f) Gun area on Laughter Tor. The selection of this site would appear to have been singularly unfortunate. There is certainly no reason why it should take into its area a menhir and part of a stone-row, or why it should break across the road from Dunnabridge to Postbridge, yet it does all three. The remedy would be to move the area a little west and a little north; and this remedy should certainly be applied. The menhir is described and illustrated in *T.D.A.*, vol. 72, p. 197, and pl. iv, fig. 2 [p. 270 and Pl. 56B above].

While we certainly wish to press that the matter of placing the battle practice areas, with and without live ammunition, in the artillery ground, coloured red on plan, should be more fully inquired into, I have already suggested a variation of the boundary of the practice area with live ammunition, as a mitigation of the evils which would follow the present scheme; and there are modifications of the boundaries between the red, green and yellow areas on the eastern side, which we believe could be made without real disturbance of the scheme, and which would lessen the loss of amenities.

There is no apparent reason why the south-east angle of the red area at Sittaford Tor should jut out abruptly for half a mile, except that this follows the boundary of the land held under an annual agreement from the Duchy of Cornwall. If the boundary between red and yellow were here altered to pass due south from Little Varracombe, thus throwing into the yellow area the tongue which now juts out to Sittaford Tor, it would give the public access to that tor, which affords a good landmark and an excellent outlook. There is a logan stone among its rocks, and the Grey Wethers circles are near, so that it is not infrequently visited. The transfer of this area from red to yellow would be a gain to the public and could be no loss to the forces.

Farther north, where the boundary between the yellow and green runs east and west above Hew Down, it would be an advantage were that boundary set half a mile farther north, and the boundary between green and red straigh-tened, so as to give access to The Thirlestone and Watern Tor.

The Thirlestone is our most marked example of lamellar pseudo-bedding in granite, and of importance as a geological feature, it is figured in the President's Address, pl. iv, fig. 11, and described on p. 67 [pp. 18, 28, and Pl. 3B above]. The total area of land used by the services would not be affected by these changes.

At the south end of the yellow land, where an embayment free from service use runs up from Two Bridges to the weir across the West Dart, an attempt is apparently made to exclude Wistman's Wood from the service area, but the clearance provided is doubtfully sufficient. This might be enquired into, the necessary deviation of the boundary would be slight. As to the ancient oak-woods see the President's Address, pp. 58, 59, and pl. i, figs. 4 and 5; as also *T.D.A.*, vol. 54, pp. 291–342 [pp. 9–10, 74–98, and Pl. 21–3 above].

There are certain monuments of importance for which it is difficult, if not impossible, to make due provision, except by the abandonment of battle practice areas outside the lands coloured red.

One of these, in the area coloured yellow and striped red, is Bear Down Man. It should be possible to prevent the spraying of this menhir with machine-gun bullets, but I doubt this would be accomplished over any lengthy period. The forces insist on using menhirs as targets. Bear Down Man is strikingly placed, and its loss would give rise to justifiable bitterness. It is described and illustrated in *T.D.A.*, vol. 72, p. 191 and pl. ii and iii [p. 265 and Pl. 54 above]. White Moor Stone, and White Moor Stone Circle are two other monuments which this scheme will bring into danger. They are situate in the eastern green area.

White Moor Stone is described and illustrated in *T.D.A.*, vol. 72, p. 192, and pl. iv, fig. 1 [p. 266 and Pl. 56A above]. The Circle is described and planned in the fourth Report of the Dartmoor Exploration Committee, *T.D.A.*, vol. 29, pp. 147–8, and inset plan.

The Grey Wethers, already mentioned, are two stone circles closely associ-ated, and situate in the area coloured yellow. They have been described and planned more than once; the last detailed reference will be found in *T.D.A.*, vol. 71, pp. 326–7 [pp. 258–60 above]. They will not be in danger from artillery or rifle fire, but the difficulty which attends the protection of ancient monu-ments in areas used by the services is that a mechanized army in passing leaves a trail of destruction in its wake.

It should be possible to give some protection by declaring and marking safety zones around stone monuments, and excluding mechanized vehicles from those zones. But even this will hardly serve to save stone rows and circles, or kist-vaens; perhaps, defined tracks might be delimited for the passage across or around these, even as fords are the crossing places of rivers.

There are two other important antiquities which would be in grave danger were the present plan of the scheme strictly adhered to, two Tinners Mills in the Walkham valley. These are especially interesting. One is, in fact, the only blowing house which still has sufficient of the furnace left to clearly indicate its structure. The suggested alteration of the south boundary of the area coloured yellow and striped red would preserve these mills from injury. In the alterna-tive, moving the boundary of this area to a 100 yards east of the river bank should be effective. But in this valley there are many hut-circles for which no effective protection can be given. Full illustrated descriptions of these tin mills will be found in *T.D.A.*, vol. 63, pp. 361–7, pl. xx, xxi, xxii [pp. 300–10, Fig 99, Pl. 69 above].

It has been impossible to prepare a complete list of the antiquities which are threatened by this scheme. For every antiquity mentioned I have given a reference to literature concerning it. Nothing has been cited which has not been thought worthy of past description and record. All are objects which we have valued long before the present threat arose, the loss of which will be a real loss to the science of archæology, and a loss not merely local.

ADDENDUM

Further regarding the two areas coloured green on the Deposited Plan. The eastern area extends north to include the summit of Cosdon. This appears to be with a view to adjusting the area to boundaries founded merely on ownership. It is obvious that there is no valid reason for disturbing public rights and amenities, except that of necessity; and the extension of the eastern green area to the summit of Cosdon is certainly not founded on any necessity connected with the use of the red area for artillery purposes. Without any disadvantage to service user the boundary might be drawn a quarter of a mile further to the south-west in the manner which I have indicated by a dotted line; thus leaving free access for the public to the summit of this noted hill, with its prospect across north Devon.

Similarly as regarding the western green area, there is no advantage to the services in absorbing the summit of Sourton Tors—nor in closing the ancient track known as the Kings Way, which I have indicated by a dotted line. This Hill, also, gives a fine prospect across north Devon, it is easy of access from the road, the rock masses which crown it are at once fine, and unusual in that they are not granite; and I suggest that it would be right, and obviously right, to place the boundary of the forces user to the east of the Kings Way, and parallel to that track, at a distance of 150 yards.

Of particular interest is the geology of Sourton Tors, which has been the subject of several workers' investigation, myself among others; and in the interest of amenities and science the hill summit should remain open to the public.

GENERAL REFERENCES

BARING-GOULD, REV. SABINE, 1900. *A Book of Dartmoor*. London. 4th ed., 1923

BARROW COMMITTEE [of the Devonshire Association], 1879–1950. First to sixty-ninth Reports. *T.D.A.*, Vols. 11–82 (exc. 25–7)

BIRKETT, PERCIVAL (see Dartmoor Preservation Association)

BRAILSFORD, J. W., 1938. Bronze Age stone monuments of Dartmoor. *Antiquity*, Vol. 12, pp. 444–63

BRAY, MRS. A. E., 1838. *Traditions, Legends, Superstitions, and Sketches of Devonshire on the Borders of the Tamar and the Tavy, illustrative of its Manners, Customs, History, Antiquities, Scenery, and Natural History, in a series of letters to Robert Southey, Esq.* 3 vols. London. New ed., 1879

BURNARD, ROBERT, 1888 & 1889. On the track of the Old Men, Dartmoor. *P.I.*, Vol. 10

1890–4. *Dartmoor Pictorial Records*, 1 to 4

BURT, W. (see Carrington)

CAMDEN, W., 1586. *Britannia*. 1695, ed. Gibson. 1789–1806, ed. Gough

CARRINGTON, N. T., 1826. *Dartmoor: A Descriptive Poem*. (With preface by W. Burt). 2nd ed. London

CHUDLEIGH, JOHN, 1893. *Devon Antiquities*. 2nd. ed.

CROSSING, WILLIAM, 1887. *The Ancient Crosses of Dartmoor*. Enlarged edition. Exeter and London. New ed., 1902

1892. *The Old Stone Crosses of the Dartmoor Borders*

1905. *Gems in a Granite Setting*. Plymouth

1909. *Guide to Dartmoor*. Plymouth. 2nd ed., 1912

DARTMOOR EXPLORATION COMMITTEE [of the Devonshire Association], 1894–1906, 1935, 1937. First to thirteenth Reports. *T.D.A.*, Vols. 26–38 (exc. 22 & 26), 67, 69

DARTMOOR PRESERVATION ASSOCIATION, 1890. A short history of the Rights of Common upon the Forest of Dartmoor and the Commons of Devon. (By Stuart A. Moore, with Introduction by Sir Frederick Pollock, Bart., and a contribution by Percival Birkett.) *Dartmoor Preservation Association Publications No. 1*. Plymouth

DE LA BECHE, H. T., 1839. *Report on the Geology of Cornwall, Devon and West Somerset*. London

DEVONSHIRE ASSOCIATION FOR THE ADVANCEMENT OF SCIENCE, LITERATURE AND ART: Reports and Transactions. 1863 onwards, in progress (*T.D.A.*). [Numerous articles on, and references to, Dartmoor. Dartmoor literature indexed by Prowse, 1905; see also the Key to the Transactions issued in 1929.] (See also Barrow Committee; Dartmoor Exploration Committee)

DONNE, T., 1765. *Map of Devonshire*

EVANS, JOHN, 1897. *The Ancient Stone Implements, Weapons, and Ornaments of Great Britain*. 2nd. ed.

Flora of Devon (see Martin, Rev. W. Keble)

GEOLOGICAL SURVEY OF GREAT BRITAIN, 1912. *The Geology of Dartmoor*. London

GOVER, J. E. B., MAWER, A., & STENTON, F. M., 1931–2. The Place-Names of Devon. *English Place-Name Society*. Vols. viii & ix. Cambridge. [P.N.D.]

HARRIS, G. T., 1938. Address of the President: an ecological reconnaissance of Dartmoor. *T.D.A.*, Vol. 70, pp. 37–55

KING, R. J., 1856. *The Forest of Dartmoor and its Borders*

LYSONS, D. & S., 1822. *Magna Britannia, Devonshire*

MARTIN, REV. W. KEBLE, & FRASER, GORDON T. (edit.), 1939. *Flora of Devon*. Arbroath. [Some corrections and additions in *T.D.A.*, Vol. 73, pp. 239–74 (1941); and additions in subsequent Reports of the Botanical Section of the Devonshire Association]

MOORE, STUART A. (see Dartmoor Preservation Association)

ORMEROD, G. WARING, 1858. Account of certain supposed British and druidical remains in the parishes of Chagford and Gidleigh, and the adjoining part of the Forest of Dartmoor. *P.I.*, Vol. 1, 1858, pp. 20–4
1873. *Notes on Rude Stone Remains situate on the easterly side of Dartmoor*. Privately printed

PAGE, J. L. WARDEN, 1889. *An Exploration of Dartmoor and its Antiquities with some account of its borders*. London

PHILLIPS, E. N. MASSON, 1937–43. The Ancient Stone Crosses of Devon. *T.D.A.*, Vol. 69 (1937), pp. 289–342; Vol. 70 (1938), pp. 299–340; Vol. 71 (1939), pp. 231–41; Vol. 72 (1940), pp. 265–72; Vol. 75 (1943), pp. 259–66

PLACE-NAME SOCIETY, ENGLISH (see Gover, Mawer, & Stenton)

PLYMOUTH INSTITUTION AND DEVON & CORNWALL NATURAL HISTORY SOCIETY: Annual Reports and Transactions. 1827 onwards, in progress (*P.I.*)

POLWHELE, REV. RICHARD, 1793. *Historical Views of Devonshire*, Vol. 1 1797. *History of Devonshire*. 3 vols. Exeter

PROWSE, ARTHUR B., 1905. An index of references to Dartmoor and its borders contained in the 'Transactions', Vols. 1 to 30. *T.D.A.*, Vol. 37, pp. 482–567

RISDON, TRISTRAM, 1620 (*c.*). *The Chorographical Description or Survey of the County of Devon*. (MSS. only) First printed ed., 1714. New ed., with additions, 1810

ROWE, J. BROOKING (see Rowe, Samuel)

ROSE-TROUP, FRANCES, 1929. *The New Edgar Charter and the South Hams*. *T.D.A.*, Vol. 61, pp. 249–80

ROWE, REV. SAMUEL, 1848. *A Perambulation of the Antient and Royal Forest of Dartmoor*. 2nd ed., 1856. Plymouth
  1896, revised edition by J. Brooking Rowe (Exeter and London) [including useful bibliography of literature on Dartmoor up to that year]

SPENCE BATE, C., 1869. On the prehistoric antiquities of Dartmoor. *T.D.A.*, Vol. 4, pp. 491–516
  1872. On the original map of the Royal Forest of Dartmoor, illustrating the perambulation of Henry III, 1240. *T.D.A.*, Vol. 4, pp. 510–48

TANSLEY, A. G., 1939. *The British Isles and their Vegetation*. 2nd (corrected) ed., 1949, in 2 vols.

Victoria County History of Devon, The, ed. by W. Page. Vol. 1, 1906, London

WESTCOTE, THOMAS. *View of Devonshire in MDCXXX with a pedigree of most of its gentry*. 1845, edited by Rev. G. Oliver & Pitman Jones. Exeter

WORTH, R. N., 1886. *A History of Devonshire*. London

LOCALITY INDEX

SUBJECT INDEX

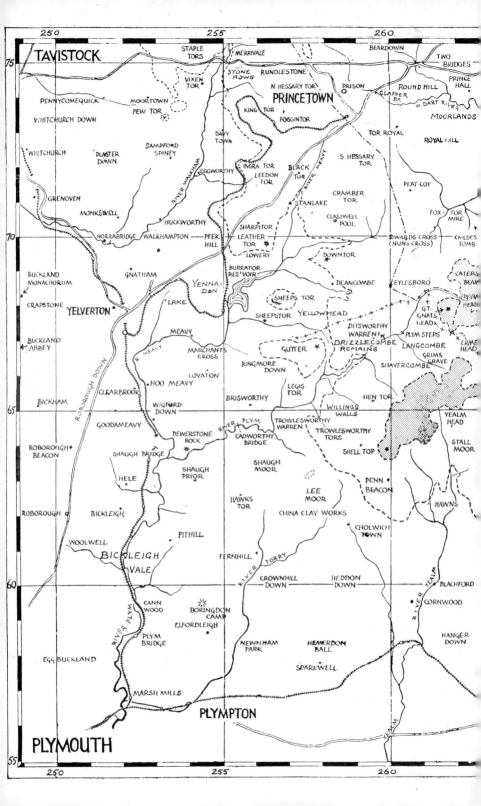